بسم الله الرحمن الرحيم

Principles of Islamic Law
The Methods of Interpretation of the Texts
(*Uṣūl al-Fiqh*)

Principles of Islamic Law

The Methods of Interpretation of the Texts

(*Uṣūl al-Fiqh*)

Saim Kayadibi

IBT

Islamic Book Trust
Kuala Lumpur

First published 2017
This revised edition 2018
Islamic Book Trust
607 Mutiara Majestic
Jalan Othman
46000 Petaling Jaya
Selangor, Malaysia
www.ibtbooks.com

Islamic Book Trust is affiliated with The Other Press Sdn Bhd.

Perpustakaan Negara Malaysia Cataloguing-in-Publication Data

Saim Kayadibi
Principles of Islamic Law : The Methods of Interpretation of the Texts (Usul al-Fiqh) / Saim Kayadibi.
Includes index
Bibliography: p. 493
ISBN 978-967-0526-33-1
1. Islamic law--Methodology.
2. Islamic law--Interpretation and construction.
I. Title
340.59

Printed by
SS Graphic Printers (M) Sdn Bhd
Lot 7 & 8, Jalan TIB 3, Taman Industri Bolton,
68100 Batu Caves, Selangor Darul Ehsan.

For my beloved Wife

Contents

Preface

In the past couple decades, interest in learning and teaching Islamic law has increased in both the Muslim and non-Muslim world. The popularity of Islamic banking and finance has especially triggered scholarly studies in this field, since the study of *uṣūl al-fiqh* is the essence of comprehending the law revealed by the Lawgiver. In order to fully implement the intention of the Lawgiver in the field of *tashrīʿ*, as well as in Islamic banking and finance, properly learning the components of *uṣūl al-fiqh* is highly essential for those who are both theorists and practitioners. A better understanding of the principles of Islamic law and the methods of interpretation of the texts is necessary to appropriately convey the message of the eternal sources to the experts, just as a driver's licence is necessary to drive a car and a medical certificate is necessary to practice medicine – without these certificates, one may cause a serious accident or death. Such an understanding will protect students, especially those of the younger, technologically advanced generation, from reckless approaches towards *aḥkām* of the *Qur'ān* and the *Sunnah*. Studying the principles of Islamic law, *uṣūl al-fiqh*, is as essential as studying other sciences to be qualified in Islamic sciences, since they are a manifestation of divine law, which reflects the rules (*aḥkām*) derived from the main sources, the *Qur'ān* and the *Sunnah*, which are simply called the *Sharīʿah*.

It is a blessing from Allah that a considerable number of studies have appeared on principles of Islamic law and interpretation of the texts especially during the last decades. Despite the number of studies done on Islamic law, the works dealing with *uṣūl al-fiqh*, which specifically focuses on the interpretation of the texts and the methods used by the jurists, are reasonably limited in providing such knowledge to students in a holistic manner, especially in the English language.

Nevertheless, there have been some significant contributions to the field of principles of Islamic law in the English language, such as Abdur Rahim, *The Principles of Muhammadan Jurisprudence*, published in 1905; Subhi Mahmassānī, *Falsafat al-Tashrīʿ fī al-Islam*, translated into English in 1961; Ahmad Hasan, *Principles of Islamic Jurisprudence, The Command of the Sharīʿah and Juridical Norm*, published in 1993; *Doctrine of Ijmāʿ in Islam*, 1978; *Analogical Reasoning in Islamic Jurisprudence*, 1986; Muhammad Hashim Kamali, *The Principles of Islamic Jurisprudence*, 1989; Imran Ahsan Khan Nyazee, *Islamic Jurisprudence*, 2000; *Theories of Islamic Law, the Methodology of Ijtihād*, 2002; and Sukrija Husejn Ramic, *Language and the Interpretation of Islamic Law*, 2003, from which I have benefited much while constructing this work. The classical works, written in Arabic and some of which have been translated into English and Turkish, are many and have benefited multilingually; all of these are listed in the bibliography.

It would obviously be unbelievable for students, theorists and practitioners of the present Muslim generation to turn a blind eye to the great intellectual heritage of legal doctrines inherited from the classical Muslim jurists and scholars. In order to find solutions to the current issues, we must take into consideration the classical as well as modern works in this field, of which this study is an abridged version, to make it comprehensible for all. It is obviously known that Allah created everything in an appropriated measure; nothing is left on its own. Rather, everything is structured by principles and values.

The book in your hand, *Principles of Islamic Law– The Methods of*

Interpretation of the Texts (Uṣūl al-Fiqh), is aimed to help students, lawyers and people interested in the study of Islamic law to understand the field comprehensively. This work is, indeed, a comprehensive study in its field, authored in a clear and simple manner that meets the requirements of a needed textbook on principles of Islamic jurisprudence (*uṣūl al-fiqh*), and consisting of six chapters, including an introductory chapter.

Chapter one, the introductory chapter, highlights the development of the principles of Islamic law and the three distinct approaches of the formulation of *uṣūl al-fiqh*. It also gives the definitions of *uṣūl al-fiqh*, explains the *ḥukm sharʿī* with its essential terms related to *uṣūl al-fiqh*, the *Sharīʿah* and its components dealing with *al-aḥkām al-iʿtiqādiyyah* (rulings related to beliefs), *al-aḥkām al-khuluqiyyah* (rulings related to moral and ethics) and *al-aḥkām al-ʿamaliyyah* (rulings related to the sayings and doings of the individuals and their relationships with others). The chapter also deals with the characteristics of the *Sharīʿah*; differences between *mujtahid* and *faqīh*, *ijtihād* and *taqlīd*, *muqallid* and *faqīh*, *qawāʿid al-fiqhiyyah and uṣūl al-fiqh*; and the meaning of *adillah*.

Chapter two is devoted to the sources of Islamic law, classifying them into two types, as unanimously accepted sources (the primary sources), such as the *Qur'ān*, the *Sunnah*, *ijmāʿ*, (consensus) and *qiyās* (analogy); the controversial sources (the secondary sources), such as *istiḥsān* (juristic preference), *maṣlaḥah mursalah* (public interest) or *al-istiṣlāḥ*, *istiṣḥāb* (presumption of continuity), *qawl al-ṣaḥābī* (the sayings of a Companion of the Prophet (ṣ)), *ʿurf* (custom), *sadd al-dharāʾiʿ* (blocking the means), *sharʿ man qablanā* (revealed laws preceding the *sharīʿah* of Islam) and *istiqrāʾ* (induction).

Chapter three deals with the *ḥukm sharʿī* (*aḥkām*) in detail; the problem of good and evil; the *maḥkūm ʿalayh* (the subject) for whose conduct the *ḥukm* is stipulated (i.e. the *mukallaf*); the different types of *ahliyyah* (capacity), such as *ahliyyah al-wujūb* (the capacity for acquisition of rights and obligation) and *ahliyyah al-adāʾ* (the capacity for execution or performance of duties); *'awāriḍ al-ahliyyah* (circumstances affecting legal capacity); the *maḥkūm fīh* (the act) along with its conditions; and the types of rights, such as the rights of Allah (*ḥuqūq Allah*) and the rights of man (*ḥuqūq al-'abd*). The fourth element of the *ḥukm shar'ī* is also dealt with in this chapter, as are its types, such as *al-ḥukm al-taklīfī* (defining law) and *al-ḥukm al-waḍ'ī* (declaratory law).

Chapter four investigates the methods of deducing the rules (*aḥkām*) from the sources, considering their four divisions in detail. The first division is based on the formation of words (*alfāẓ*) and consists of *'āmm* (general), *khāṣṣ* (specific), *mu'awwal* (interpreted) and *mushtarak* (equivocal, the common word). The *khāṣṣ* is subdivided into *muṭlaq* (absolute), *muqayyad* (limited), *amr* (command) and *nahy* (prohibition). The second division is based on the usage of the words and consists of *ḥaqīqah* (literal), *majāz* (metaphorical), *ṣarīḥ* (clear) and *kināyah* (allusive). The third division is based on the degree of the word's clarity (*wuḍūḥ*) or obscurity. From this viewpoint, words are divided into the two main categories: clear (*wāḍiḥ*) and unclear (*ghayr wāḍiḥ*). The clear words consist of *ẓāhir* (manifest), *naṣṣ* (explicit), *mufassar* (unequivocal) and *muḥkam* (perspicuous). The unclear words consist of *khafī* (obscure), *mushkil* (difficult), *mujmal* (ambivalent) and *mutashābih* (intricate). The fourth division is based on the rules of indications (textual indication, *dalālāt*) and consists of *'ibārah al-naṣṣ* (explicit meaning), *ishārah al-naṣṣ* (alluded meaning), *dalālah al-naṣṣ* (the inferred meaning), *iqtiḍā' al-naṣṣ* (the required meaning) and *mafhūm al-mukhālafah* (divergent meaning). The concept of conflict (تعارض) between these methods are taken into consideration from the viewpoint of *Ḥanafī* and *Shāfi'ī* approaches.

Chapter five focuses on the concept of *ijtihād*, its validity, its types, its conditions, areas where *ijtihād* is applicable, its value (*ḥukm*), its relationship with *ra'y* and *istiḥsān and ijtihād* by *ra'y* at the time of the Prophet (ṣ) and the Companions. It also covers the concept of *taqlīd* (imitation), its definition, its ruling (*ḥukm*), *talfīq*, *takhayyur*, *tarjīḥ*, legal loopholes (*ḥīlah shar'īyyah*) and *maqāṣid al-Sharī'ah* (the higher objectives of Islamic law).

Chapter six discusses the concept of abrogation (*naskh*), its definition, its types, its conditions, the historical approaches to it, the differences between *naskh* and *takhṣīṣ*, the subject matter of *naskh* and the time of *naskh*. The chapter also deals with *ta'āruḍ al-adillah* (conflict of evidences), the place of the conflict of evidences, the method to be followed in resolving conflicts, resolving conflicts among the *nuṣūṣ* (texts), resolving conflicts through recourse to the Companions and *ijmā'* and resolving conflicts of *qiyās* (analogy).

This work, therefore, contributes to the heritage of the principles of Islamic law and the methods of interpretation of the texts (*uṣūl al-fiqh*), inshallah.

With that I would like to thank everyone who has assisted me directly or indirectly in the production of this work, which has taken six years to complete. In fact, the work would have been completed much earlier if I had not assumed an administrative responsibility in the Rectory Office of International Islamic University Malaysia (IIUM), which, along with some other obstacles I had to tackle, made me extremely busy. Nevertheless, with the constant help and the grace of Allah, the work has come to completion and therefore I am very grateful to Allah. I hope that this work will be accepted as *ṣadaqah jāriyah* by Allah. May Allah bless all the scholars from whom I have benefited while writing this book and grant them Paradise.

I am also indebted to the staff of Islamic Book Trust and its respected director, Hj. Koya, for his fatherly cooperation, as well as brother Yusoff Sultan, in publishing this manuscript.

Saim Kayadibi
International Islamic University Malaysia (IIUM)
Gombak, Kuala Lumpur, November 2016

CHAPTER ONE

Introductory Chapter
Parameters of *Uṣūl al-Fiqh*

Introduction to Uṣūl al-Fiqh

Islamic law has been developed over the centuries using a variety of methods of *ra'y* and *ijtihād*. In the very early stage of legislation of Islamic law, the growth of the Muslim world presented people with new challenges. These included rapid urbanization, multicultural relationships and new responses that required the Muslim jurists to provide vigorous efforts to resolve the problems and issues of the Muslim community using their personal discretion and *ijtihād* based on the texts (*al-nuṣūṣ*). The process of systematic reasoning, analogy (*qiyās*), began as a methodological solution to operate with the appearance of the legal schools of thought (*madhāhib*), in which the process of legal reasoning is in fact technically called a model of legal reasoning (*ijtihād*).[1]

Since *ijtihād* is defined as "the expenditure of efforts to arrive at righteous judgement," relying on the *Qur'ān* and the *Sunnah* of the Prophet (ṣ) is necessary to judge accordingly. From this reality, whoever does not judge based on the divine law (*Sharī'ah*) is considered a disbeliever ("*Whoever did not judge by what Allah revealed – those are the unbelievers*"),[2] wrongdoer ("*Whoever did not judge by what Allah revealed – those are the wrongdoers*")[3] and transgressor ("*Whoever did not judge by what Allah revealed – those are the transgressors*").[4] Divine law is not confined to the *Qur'ān* alone, but rather consists of the *Sunnah* as well as the derivatives of the main sources, such as *ijmā'* (consensus) and *qiyās* (analogy).

The fact that the tradition of *fiqh* existed earlier than the formulation of its principles does not mean that the principles had never been used prior to *fiqh*. Although *fiqh* appeared much earlier than its principles, it coexisted with *uṣūl al-fiqh*. It is logical that certain principles must be used to derive rulings from the *Qur'ān* and the *Sunnah* by exercising *ijtihād*. Nevertheless, the revelation was alive in case any problems were solved by what was revealed to the Prophet (ṣ) by his actions, sayings and tacitly approved *Sunnah*, which were considered part of the *Sharī'ah*, as confirmed by the Lawgiver when He says, "*Nor does he speak out of desire. It is naught but revelation that is revealed*".[5] Since the source of *Sharī'ah* is alive, there was no need for relying on certain principles besides the *Qur'ān* and the *Sunnah* of the Prophet (ṣ), nor was *ijtihād* exercised by the Companions during his lifetime. The problems faced by the Muslim community during the period of the Prophet (ṣ) were easily and effectively solved, as he was the supreme authority to comment on the verses and explain them to the people. When the Companions were dispersed to different parts of the world, their connections among them were lost. The understanding of the textual sources were diversified. Following the demise of the Prophet (ṣ), the problems increased and were of a more complex nature. The Companions had the *Qur'ān* and the *Sunnah* to decide on the new obstacles stemming from social life.[6] They also needed to use their own opinion to decide which verse or *ḥadīth* could be applied to a case. Thus, the Companions employed their own opinions not only to understand the verses correctly and apply them to new problems, but also to achieve a solution for more problematic cases on which no verses were directly available.[7] Yet after the demise of the Prophet (ṣ) no principles were formulated by the Companions for solving new problems that occurred. They simply were to recourse to the *Qur'ān* and the *Sunnah*, and if they failed to find answers to their new problems, they would look for solutions in light of the main objectives of the *Sharī'ah*, or by recourse to analogical reasoning (*qiyās*). The Successors of the Companions also followed the same method and did not formulate principles; they simply acquired knowledge directly from the Companions.

Although the source of law in the first and second period was confined to the *Qur'ān* and the *Sunnah*, it was expanded in the third period, as the growth of the Muslim society engendered different social issues and problems, which created possible confusion and mistakes in the understanding of the textual sources. Accordingly, Muslim jurists began to exercise *ijtihād* in a variety of fields because of the wide range of inquiries, which brought different opinions and disputed issues from the territorial sphere of Islam. The diversity of juristic opinions and confusion in different territories accentuated the need for clear regulations. Among these were the disputes between the *Ahl al-Ḥadīth* and *Ahl al-Ra'y*, respectively known as the jurists of Madinah and Iraq. Therefore, the jurists realized the necessity of formulating certain principles and setting up certain criteria to remove disagreements on the disputed matters and prevent misuse of the concept of *ijtihād* from inappropriated people. Also, the need for a methodology to regulate *ijtihād* became increasingly obvious when the scholars became confident about the subject matter of the *Sunnah* in collecting and documenting the *ḥadīth* heritage, which encouraged them to elaborate on the law. The compilation of the vast *ḥadīth* heritage logically brought the consolidation of *uṣūl al-fiqh*, and the formulated principles and set of criteria established the principles of Islamic law (*uṣūl al-fiqh*) as a *Sharī'ah* discipline after a long run of exclusive scholarly works.[8]

Jurists used different types of methods and approaches in the discussion of the problems and principles of Islamic law. It has been identified that the jurists applied three distinct approaches in their analysis and formulation of the *uṣūl al-fiqh*.

The first approach is a theoretical approach that was called the method of the theologians (*ṭarīqat al-mutakallimīn*), known as *uṣūl al-Shāfi'iyyah*, which was adopted by the *Mu'tazilah*, *Shāfi'īs* and *Mālikīs* in their compilation of this discipline. Basically, the jurists articulated principles of *fiqh* that were substantiated by proofs, irrespective of their agreement or disagreement on the positive law or subsidiary legal rules (*furū'*) as brought down from the early jurists.[9] This approach is mainly concerned with the exposition of theory rather than practical aspects of the relavant issues. The followers of this method mostly were concerned with expressing the theoretical principles of *uṣūl al-fiqh* without necessarily endeavouring to relate these to the *fiqh* itself. Their theoretical explanation of *uṣūl al-fiqh* did not take into consideration their practical application in the area of the *furū'*. They did not contribute to the development of the practical rules of *fiqh* due to the inclination of them in complex issues of philosophy, such as *'iṣmah* of the prophets prior to their prophetic mission and matters concerning the status of the individual or his responsibilities prior to the revelation of the *Sharī'ah.*[10] The following works are some of the products of this method: *al-Burhān fī Uṣūl al-Fiqh* by Imām al-Ḥaramayn 'Abd al-Malik al-Juwaynī (d. 413 AH), *Kitāb al-'Umad* by al-Qāḍī 'Abd al-Jabbār (d. 415 AH), *Kitāb al-Mu'tamad* by Abū al-Ḥusayn Muḥammad b. 'Alī al-Baṣrī (d. 436 AH), *Al-Mustaṣfā min 'Ilm al-Uṣūl* by al-Ghazālī (d. 505 AH), *al-Maḥṣūl* by Fakhr al-Dīn al-Rāzī (d. 606 AH) and *al-Iḥkām fī Uṣūl al-Aḥkām* by Sayf al-Dīn al-Āmidī (d. 631 AH).

The second approach is distinguished by its practical character, aimed at confirming the juristic principles reported to have been applied by the early jurists in their actual reasoning. It is an applied and pragmatic study of the points of detail of *fiqh* as brought down from the early *Ḥanafī* jurists. This method establishes the principles which are subservient to the derivative laws of legal school and therefore focuses on the juristic principles, rules and regulations that were applied by the master jurists in their arguments in deriving the rules of law. The principles were inferred from the points of detail of *fiqh* articulated by these master jurists. Mostly *Ḥanafī* jurists followed this approach. Therefore, it is called the method of the *Ḥanafīs* (*uṣūl al-Ḥanafiyyah* or *ṭarīqat al-fuqahā'*).[11] Also it's known as deductive approach which resembles pracmatic aspects of the relevant issues in which the detailed of the *fiqh* (*furū' al-fiqh*) is concerned. Although the theoretical approach tends to envisage *uṣūl al-fiqh* as an independent discipline to which the *fiqh* must conform. The practical approach, on the other hand, attempts to relate the *uṣūl al-fiqh* more closely to the detailed issues of the *furū' al-fiqh*. Therefore, the *Ḥanafīs* have endeavoured to explain the principles of *uṣūl al-fiqh* in combining them with the *fiqh* itself and tend to be more practical in their approach to the issue. For example, the *Ḥanafīs* attempt to make a necessary exception in order to reach a conciliation, or they try to adjust the theory to the extent that the conflict in question is removed when they find a principle of *uṣūl* to be in conflict with an established principle of *fiqh*.[12] Some important works of this method are listed below: *al-Fuṣūl fī al-Uṣūl* by Abū Bakr Aḥmad b. 'Alī al-Jaṣṣāṣ (d. 370 AH), *Taqwīm al-Adillah* and *Ta'sīs al-Naẓar* by 'Ubaydullah b. 'Umar al-Dabbūsī (d. 430 AH), *Kanz al-Wuṣūl ilā Ma'rifat al-Uṣūl* by Fakhr al-Islam al-Bazdawī (d. 482 AH), *Uṣūl al-Sarakhsī* by Shams al-A'immah al-Sarakhsī (d. 490 AH), and *Kashf al-Asrār* by 'Abd al-'Azīz b. Aḥmad al-Bukhārī (d. 730 AH).

The third approach is aimed at establishing the original principles as well as confirming the questions of detail of *fiqh* as brought down from the early jurists by means of these principles. Thus, this approach is a combination of the previous two methods, combining both the original and confirmatory principles. This method is also adopted by numerous schools of thought. The following works are some of the products of the combined method: *Badī' al-Niẓām al-Jāmi' bayna Kitābay al-Bazdawī wa al-Iḥkām* by Aḥmad b. 'Alī al-Sā'ātī (d. 694 AH); *al-Tanqīḥ* and its commentaries *al-Tawḍīḥ* by Ṣadr al-Sharī'ah 'Ubayd Allah b. Mas'ūd (d. 747 AH) and *al-Talwīḥ* by Sa'd al-Dīn Mas'ūd b. 'Umar al-Taftāzānī (d. 792 AH); *Jam' al-Jawāmi'* by Tāj al-Dīn 'Abd al-Wahhāb b. 'Alī al-Subkī (d. 771 AH); *al-Taḥrīr* by Ibn al-Humām (d. 861 AH), and its commentary *al-Taqrīr wa al-Taḥbīr* by Muḥammad b. Muḥammad Amīr al-Ḥajj (d. 879 AH); and *Musallam al-Thubūt* by Muḥibb Allah b. 'Abd al-Shakūr al-Bihārī (d. 1119 AH), and its commentary *Fawātiḥ al-Raḥamūt* by 'Abd al-'Alī Muḥammad b. Niẓām al-Dīn al-Anṣārī (d. 1235 AH). A large number of works were produced on *uṣūl al-fiqh* during the classical period. Nevertheless, only some of them have been listed here.[13] It is worth mentioning here a work which is comprehensive and unique in its field related to the philosophy (*ḥikmah*) of *tashrī'* and the objectives of the *Sharī'ah*, *al-Muwāfaqāt fī Uṣūl al-Fiqh* of Abū Isḥāq Ibrāhīm al-Shāṭibī,[14] who is called the father of *maqāṣid*.

The principles of Islamic law, *uṣūl al-fiqh*, are the mother of whole Islamic sciences. I call it the mother because of its role in the interpretation and comprehension of the laws of the Lawgiver to reflect the objectives of humanity's creation. Just as the Lawgiver emphasises it in the *Qur'ān* ("*And I have not created the jinn and the men except that they should serve Me*")[15] the main purpose of the creation of man is to be a worshipper, and thus without knowing the objectives of the Lawgiver, the purpose will not be achieved unless His sources, the *Qur'ān* and the *Sunnah*, are interpreted appropriately.

In the face of diverse opinions, according to some sources, the first work that reportedly came into being on this field was *Kitāb al-Ra'y* by Abū Ḥanīfah (d. 150 AH). It was followed by works by Abū Ḥanīfah's disciples, namely *Kitāb al-Uṣūl* by Abū Yūsuf (d. 182 AH) and *Kitāb Uṣūl al-Fiqh* by Muḥammad b. al-Ḥasan al-Shaybānī (d. 189). However, these works were reportedly lost before the work of al-Shāfi'ī (d. 204 AH) known as *al-Risālah*. It is a well-known treatise on *uṣūl al-fiqh* and is the first comprehensive work in the field. In the centuries that followed, more works were produced on the subject by significant scholars. From the *Ḥanafīs*, there are *Ma'ākhidh al-Sharā'ī'* by Abū Manṣūr al-Māturīdī (d. 333 AH) and *Uṣūl al-Karkhī* by Abū al-Ḥasan al-Karkhī (d. 340 AH). From the Shāfiʿīs, there are *al-Burhān fī Uṣūl al-Fiqh* by Imām al-Ḥaramayn ʿAbd al-Malik al-Juwaynī (d. 413 AH), *Kitāb al-ʿUmad* by al-Qāḍī ʿAbd al-Jabbār (d. 415 AH), *Kitāb al-Muʿtamad* by Abū al-Ḥusayn Muḥammad b. ʿAlī al-Baṣrī (d. 436 AH), *al-Mustaṣfā min ʿIlm al-Uṣūl* by al-Ghazālī (d. 505 AH), *al-Maḥṣūl* by Fakhr al-Dīn al-Rāzī (d. 606 AH) and *al-Iḥkām fī Uṣūl al-Aḥkām* by Sayf al-Dīn al-Āmidī (d. 631 AH).

To commence with the study of the main sources of Islamic law, the composition of the principles of Islamic law should be elaborated briefly to help students and researchers better understand the field. As we know, Islamic law, particularly Islamic jurisprudence, is a religious law and is based on the texts of the *Qur'ān* and the *Sunnah* of the Prophet (ṣ). Although the science of Islamic law is used simultaneously with principles of Islamic jurisprudence, the author is willing to use it differently since Islamic law is a term which indicates a kind of law that is Islamic, is derived from Islamic values and uses specific methods and principles which indicate the whole Islamic legal system. The details of Islamic law are elaborated within the concept of *aḥkām* (rulings). Nevertheless, it may be said that Islamic law is a more general term than Islamic jurisprudence since jurisprudence is the result of the law and details of it. Hence, even if these two terms have slight differences in the technical sense, Islamic law and Islamic jurisprudence are simultaneously used by the scholars, and the principles of Islamic law or the principles of Islamic jurisprudence are used as *uṣūl al-fiqh*.

This part of the study clarifies the source of the principles of Islamic jurisprudence (*uṣūl al-fiqh*), how it is derived from the sources and how it is classified, comprehended as well as applied. Firstly, the concept of this study, *uṣūl al-fiqh*, should be clearly defined with its two components separately as *uṣūl* and *fiqh*. Following the clarification of these two components, the combination of that is defined and consequently the concept of the principles of Islamic jurisprudence (*uṣūl al-fiqh*) will be comprehended fully *inshallah*.

The definitions of the two mechanisms will help us to understand the nature of the *aḥkām* of the principles of Islamic jurisprudence and the nature of the sources from which the *aḥkām* (rulings) or the laws are derived.

We shall now firstly explain the definitions of the two mechanisms since these terms that are crucial in understanding the discipline of *uṣūl al-fiqh* (the principles of Islamic jurisprudence).

Definition of Uṣūl

In certain cases, this is defined as something upon which another thing is constructed, be it material or spiritual: *mā yustanad wujūdu al-shay'i ilayhi.*

Here it has the meaning of foundation (*asās*).[16] The term *aṣl* is used in the sense of the Arabic word "*maṣdar*" (source). The term *uṣūl* is the plural of *aṣl*, and it is "*something from which another thing originates or is sourced.*" Thus, the origin of a thing is its *aṣl*; that is the reason for translating the word *aṣl* as "root" *(judhr)*. It also means *nasab* (lineage or stock), *'illah* (cause or reason). Another meaning is *ḥaqīqī*, which means true, genuine, authentic or real.[17]

Technical applications of the word (*aṣl*) in Islamic law are as follows: One of the uses of *aṣl* is the meaning of *dalīl*. The word *dalīl* was applied to mean a guide leading a caravan, or a scout finding the trail. In this sense, a directory, like a telephone directory, may be called a *dalīl*, because it leads us to a number or an address.

In Islamic law, the word *dalīl* is used in two ways. *Dalīl tafṣīlī* is like an individual verse of the *Qur'ān* or an individual *Sunnah* in *aḥādīth*. We may refer to it as "specific evidence," though it is sometimes translated as "detailed proof." For example, Allah says,

> "*Forbidden to you (for marriage) are your mothers, your daughters, your sisters...*"[18]

It indicates a *ḥukm* (rule), which is obvious: marriage to mothers, daughters and sisters is forbidden.

> "*And come not near to unlawful sexual intercourse...*"[19]

This verse indicates *a ḥukm* (rule), which is also obvious: do not commit adultery.

As compared to *dalīl tafṣīlī* (specific evidence), the *dalīl ijmālī* or *kullī* is general evidence, because it contains within it a large amount of specific evidence. The *dalīl ijmālī* has nothing to do with direct, absolute order and prohibition. However, it produces general rulings as *wujūb* (necessity) and *taḥrīm* (prohibition). The *Qur'ān* is general evidence: it contains a large number of specific evidences[20]:

> "*And perform al-ṣalāh*"[21]

is the *aṣl* which makes prayer obligatory in the *Qur'ān*.

The word (*a-ṣ-l*) is also used to indicate the foundation upon which analogy is constructed. An example in the *Qur'ān*:

> "*O you who believe! Intoxicants (all kinds of alcoholic drinks)...are an abomination of Satan's handiwork. So avoid (strictly all).*"[22]

This is the general prohibition of drinks which contain intoxicants.

As a *ḥadīth* confirms, "Every drink which contains intoxicant is *khamr* (wine) and every *khamr* is forbidden."[23]

Therefore, *khamr* is an original case (*a-ṣ-l*) or basis for the prohibition of *nabīdh* (fermented dates); the *'illah* of intoxication is found in both, but is extrapolated from *khamr*, which is the *aṣl*.[24]

In addition, *aṣl* is sometimes applied in the sense of the original rule. Hence, the maxim says:

> "*Al-aṣl fī al-ashyā' al-ibāḥah.*"

This means the original rule for all things is permissibility. Another use of *aṣl* is that the meaning of general principles of jurisprudence (*al-qawā'id al-fiqhiyyah*) governs the law and its interpretation.

An example is "*lā ḍarar wa lā ḍirār fī al-Islam*", which means "*Harm is neither inflicted nor reciprocated in Islam*"[25]; it is an *aṣl* in the principle of Islamic law. It also means *al-rujḥān* (preference, preferability), and as jurists say, "*al-aṣl fī al-kalām al-ḥaqīqah,*" which means that literal meaning rather than metaphor is to be understood.[26]

Dalīl (proof) is distinguished from *amārah* (indication), which literally means sign or allusion. A sign indicates the existence of a thing without the need for rational proofs like the *minārah* of a mosque, and a milestone of the road.[27] *Dalīl* could only relate to evidence which leads to a definitive ruling or to positive knowledge (*'ilm*). *Amārah* on the other hand is reserved for evidence or indication that only leads to a *ẓannī* (speculative) ruling.[28] In this way, the term *dalīl* could only be concerned with the definitive proofs, namely the *Qur'ān*, the *Sunnah* and *ijmā'*, while the remaining proof which contains a measure of speculation, such as *qiyās, istiḥsān, istiṣḥāb, maṣālih mursalah*, could fall under the category of *amārah* (signs or allusions, probable evidence). However, most jurists consider both *dalīl* and *amārah,* whether *qaṭ'ī* (definitive) or *ẓannī* (speculative), to be a *dalīl* (proof). *Amārah* becomes a *dalīl* if the *ḥukm shar'ī* is deduced from it.[29]

After all these explanations on the concept of the term *aṣl*, we can say that *aṣl* is actually *dalīl,* which is a proof or an evidence of Islamic law.[30]

The jurist seeks the *dalīl ijmālī* or *kullī* (general evidence), yet the *adillah al-tafṣīliyyah* (specific evidence) is the subject field of the mufti. Therefore, *uṣūl al-fiqh* (the principles of Islamic jurisprudence) is called *adillah al-fiqh al-kulliyyah* (proofs or evidences of general *fiqh*).

The juristic scholars (*uṣūlī*) define the term *uṣūl al-fiqh* in two separated parts: *uṣūl* and *fiqh.* As I have covered the term *uṣūl* (plural of *aṣl*) above, the term *fiqh* now will be elaborated.

Definitions of Fiqh

In the linguistic sense, the term *fiqh* is synonymous with *al-fahm* (understanding).[31] The *Qur'ān* has used the word *fiqh* in its general sense of "understanding" in several places:

> "*O Shu'ayb! We do not understand much of what you say.*"[32]
> "*So what is wrong with these people that they fail to understand a single fact.*"[33]
> "*They have hearts wherewith they understand not.*"[34]

These derivatives of the word *fiqh* imply an understanding of Islam and consideration of religion. The same meaning is also revealed in a *ḥadīth* of the Prophet (ṣ):

> "He for whom Allah wills His blessings is granted an understanding of *dīn*."[35]

In addition, the term *'ilm* (knowledge) was used for the same literal meaning of *fiqh* (understanding) in the early period of Islam, as the Prophet (ṣ) blessed Ibn 'Abbās (d. 68) saying:

> "*Allāhumma faqqihhu fī al-dīn*" (O Allah, give him understanding in religion).[36]

The Prophet (ṣ) could not have meant absolute knowledge of the law. However, it is clear that the Prophet (ṣ) meant a deeper understanding of Islam in general.

The term *fiqh* also means *kalām*, which Abū Ḥanīfah (d. 150) defines as:

> "*Ma'rifat al-nafsi mā lahā wamā 'alayhā,*" which means "a person's knowledge of his rights and obligations."[37]

Al-Fiqh al-Akbar which is attributed to Abū Ḥanīfah (d. 150) and against the beliefs of *ahl al-qadar* deals with the basic tenets of Islam like faith, unity of Allah, His attributes, the life hereafter, prophecy etc. These are problems which are dealt with in *kalām* and not in the discipline of law.[38]

Fiqh is used to mean the exercise of intelligence, as the Successors of the Companions of the Prophet (ṣ) at most were *fuqahā'* (jurists) who gave legal judgments using their own intelligence and reason in solving legal problems. In that respect the term *fiqh* is also used for the knowledge of the law. It is used here in the famous tradition of Mu'ādh ibn Jabal (d. 18/640). When the Prophet (ṣ) intended to send him to Yemen, he was encouraged to exercise his intelligence to find a solution.[39]

Technically, the definition of *fiqh* is confined to Islamic law alone. Among the scholars, Shāfi'ī's (d. 204/819) definition is widely known: "The knowledge of the legal rules (*aḥkām al-shar'iyyah*) pertaining to conduct, derived from their specific evidences."

(*al-'ilmu bil-aḥkām al-shar'iyyah al-'amaliyyah al-muktasab min adillatuhā al-tafṣīliyyah*).

On the other hand, "It is a compilation of the legal rules pertaining to conduct that have been derived from their specific evidences."[40] The definition of *fiqh* can be understood in stages. Then the meaning of *fiqh* will be the knowledge of the *aḥkām al-shar'iyyah.* Therefore, *fiqh* is not the law itself; in other words, it is a knowledge or understanding of Islamic law.

Nyazee clarifies that the definition was structured based on the *Shāfi'ī* methodology of interpretation and does not adapt completely with the methodology of the other schools. It is centred on the specific evidences (*adillah tafṣīliyyah*) and, therefore, it prevents the use of the purposes of Islamic law (*maqāṣid al-Sharī'ah*), which are general evidences (*kulliyyah*). If the Shāfi'ī definition is used to conclude the meaning of *fiqh*, the principle of *maṣlaḥah* (reasoning through general evidences or the purpose of law) cannot be used to derive the rules (*aḥkām*). It confines the activity of the jurists to a very limited method of interpretation. The definition also excludes the use of the *qawā'id al-fiqhiyyah*, unless these principles are explicitly mentioned in the texts of the *Qur'ān* and the *Sunnah.* As the *Shāfi'ī* scholars reject the concept of *istiḥsān*, the definition excludes naturally the use of *istiḥsān* which in many cases is based on the preference of a wider form of *qiyās* (analogy).[41]

In addition to the above definition, a famous Shāfi'ī scholar, al-Ghazālī, defines *fiqh* as:

> "An expression for the knowledge of legal rules established specifically for human conduct."[42]

Imām al-Rāzī provides a more precise definition:

> "The knowledge of the legal rules pertaining to conduct with reference to their sources, when this knowledge is not obtained by way of necessity."[43]

Finally it can be simplified as "*fiqh* is the knowledge of the *shar'ī aḥkām* derived directly from the specific evidences in the texts or extended through reasoning from general propositions of the *Sharī'ah* in the light of its *maqāṣid*."[44] He explains that what it is meant by "general propositions" which means all those general principles that are laid down or supported by the *Sharī'ah* whether directly or indirectly.[45]

Sharī'ah and fiqh

Although these two terms are used interchangeable, there are some differences between them. The term *sharī'ah* has a wider meaning than *fiqh*. The definition, however, indicates that *fiqh* is a knowledge of that law, its jurisprudence, while the *sharī'ah* is the law itself. Nevertheless, the term *sharī'ah* includes both law and the tenets of faith, that is, the *'aqā'id*.

The religion of Islam with its law, *sharī'ah*, consists of a complete system of life that is compatible with the need of human being of all times. As a religion, Islam was chosen for the whole mankind and it is confirmed by the *Qur'ān* that the perfection of the religion is completed: "*This day have I perfected for you your religion and completed My favour on you and chosen for you Islam as a religion*".[46]

The Lawgiver left nothing neglected in the Book relating to human beings. It is mentioned in the *Qur'ān*, "*We have not neglected anything in the Book*".[47]

Literally the word *sharī'ah* is derived from the root "sh-r-'a" (شرع) which means the road to water, the straight path to be followed. The *Qur'ān* indicates the same meaning: "*Then We have made you follow a course in the affair, therefore follow it, and do not follow the low desires of those who do not know*".[48]

Technically the *Sharī'ah* is defined by al-Qurṭubī as the canon of Islam, all the different commandments of Allah to mankind.[49] It is also defined by some scholars as the injunctions revealed to the Prophet (ṣ) of Allah related to law or belief.[50]

The *Sharī'ah*, the complete law of Allah, consists of a variety of commandments related to mankind which can be mainly divided into three types. The first is ***al-Aḥkām al-I'tiqādiyyah*** (rulings related to beliefs) such as the belief in Allah and the Day of Judgement. The second is ***al-Aḥkām al-Khuluqiyyah*** (rulings related to moral and ethics) such as honesty, sincerity, truthfulness etc. The third is ***al-Aḥkām al-'Amaliyyah*** (rulings related to the sayings and doings of the individuals and his relationships with others) which is also called *fiqh*.[51] Therefore, the *Sharī'ah* is the wider circle which includes all human activities, while fiqh is confined to human acts. *Sharī'ah* is the body of revealed injunctions found both in the *Qur'ān* and the *Sunnah*, while *fiqh* is one of the components of the *Sharī'ah*. It is definite that the *Sharī'ah* is unchangeable, whereas some rulings of *fiqh* would be changed according to the changes of the time and circumstances. *Sharī'ah* is based on revelations in which knowledge is obtained solely from the *Qur'ān* and the *Sunnah*, while *fiqh* is based on knowledge of reasoning and deductions.[52] Despite the fact and the distinctions between *Sharī'ah* and *fiqh* are clearly made, many scholars interchangeably use these terms.

The Characteristics of the Sharīʿah

The Lawgiver has revealed His laws to mankind through prophets in order to guide them to the right path, lead them out of the depths of darkness into light. The *Qur'ān* indicates this reality:

> "*Alif Lam Ra. (This is) a Book which We have revealed to you that you may bring forth men, by their Lord's permission from utter darkness into light – to the way of the Mighty, the Praised One*".[53]

With this, the following points may be considered to be some of the characteristics of the *Sharīʿah*:

1. The completed and perfected religion of Allah

According to the *Qur'ān*, Allah revealed that the religion had been completed and was perfect: "*This day I have perfected your religion for you, completed My favour upon you, and have chosen for you Islam as your religion*".[54]

In the context of religion, the purpose of establishing the *Sharīʿah* is to inculcate in man those fundamental principles which represent the unalterable character of religion, and which cannot be changed.[55] Therefore, the meaning of the religion should be taken in terms of general principles, faith (*iʿtiqād*), ethics (*akhlāq*) and acts of worship (*ʿibādāt*). Thus, the *Sharīʿah* encompasses all areas, including *al-aḥkām al-iʿtiqādiyyah, al-aḥkām al-akhlāqiyyah,* and *al-aḥkām al-ʿamaliyyah* related to all of creation.

Shāṭibī (d. 790/1388) emphasizes on this matter saying that the purpose of perfection in the religion is about general principles but not a particular principle. The concepts of *ḍarūriyyāt*, *ḥājiyyāt* and their *taḥsīniyyāt* are well explained. Sometimes, it is based on the *ijtihād* principle, it might be essential to deal in some particular matters by implementing general principles. Performing *ijtihād* is verified in the *Qur'ān* and the *Sunnah* and so *ijtihād* must be performed in order to render Islam beneficial and precise. Therefore, there is a role retained for *ijtihād* in the *Sharī'ah* and *ijtihād* is only possible for the issues that have no references in the text. It is an impossible task to locate all particular issues in the verses, since particular issues are endless and cannot be listed or numbered. The meaning of perfected religion in the verse can be identified as; all the general principles which might be needed for any particular issues are available in the *Qur'ān*.[56]

2. Eternal validity of the Sharī'ah

According to the *Qur'ān*, Allah guaranteed that the *Qur'ān* is preserved forever: "*We have, without doubt, sent down the Message; and We will assuredly guard it (from corruption)*".[57]

It is confirmed that the *Qur'ān* is the last sacred book and Muḥammad (ṣ) is the seal of the Prophets, there will be no more books and messengers. There must be a mechanism would adjust the legal system to ever evolving social cultural circumstances. The mechanism is the principles of Islamic law (*uṣūl al-fiqh*). The *Sharī'ah* maintains its eternal validity through this mechanism by competent scholars. As the Prophet (ṣ) said "*On the eve of every century, Allah will send to my community a man who will renew it dīn (religion)*"[58]

3. The Universality of the Sharī'ah

The *Sharī'ah* was revealed as a system of life for all humanity not for a certain period of time or people. The *Qur'ān* indicates this purpose: "*We have not sent you (O Muḥammad) but as a universal (Messenger) to men, giving them glad tidings, and warning them (against sin), but most men understand not.*[59]

Since the Prophet (ṣ) was sent for all humanity, the *Sharī'ah* then must be a legal system for all of mankind. Qaradāwī says that the purpose of sending the *Sharī'ah* for all mankind is because the *Qur'ān* has righteous and convenient codes for all societies, all territories and all circumstances.[60]

"And We have sent you (O Muḥammad) not but as a mercy for the 'Ālamīn (mankind, jinns and all that exists)".[61]

Ibn 'Āshūr emphasises that Islam offers the same values for people in no matter which era they live and they had lived and Islam has great capability of integrating it into different societies without bringing them difficulties by implementing the *Sharī'ah.*[62]

4. The Fundamental human rights and equality character of the Sharī'ah:

In terms of creation, all humans are created equal and free that is one of the fundamentals of Islam which considers all peoples are equal and free. The freedom is one of the natural (*fiṭrī*) rights of people and it cannot be transferred to anyone as 'Umar (*ra*) said, "How dare you enslave people while their mothers gave birth to them freely."[63] The Prophet (ṣ) united all people referring to Ādam as saying "You are all from Adam."[64]

The equality character of the *Sharī'ah* provides *musāwāt* (equality) to people that all human beings are equal in terms of creation, as the *Qur'ān* indicates this sense: "*O mankind! We created you from a single (pair) of a male and a female, and made you into nations and tribes, that ye may know each other (not that ye may despise (each other). Verily the most honoured of you in the sight of Allah is (he who is) the most righteous of you.*"[65]

This character is also emphasised by a *ḥadīth* of the Prophet (ṣ) as saying "O mankind, your Lord is one and your father is one. There is no virtue of an Arab over a foreigner nor a foreigner over an Arab, and neither white skin over black skin nor black skin over white skin, except by righteousness (taqwā). Have I not delivered the message?"[66]

One step further, Islam considers all Muslims are brothers "The believers are nothing else than brethren, therefore make peace between your brethren and be careful of (your duty to) Allah that mercy may be had on you".[67]

5. The flexibility nature of the Sharīʿah

The principle of flexibility is one of the most crucial concepts of the *Sharīʿah* as this principle allows changes and thinking through different dimensions in order to reach a solution for newly emerging challenges.

The meaning of flexibility must be clarified that the concept of flexibility does not mean a loss of dignity and decency of the inalterable essence of the *Sharīʿah*. The implementation of rules is not confined to a single method as the need of the people is constantly developing, the *Sharīʿah* has the capability to address and respond to the new and unknown issues of all eras.[68] In that respect, fully comprehending the objectives of the *Sharīʿah* will help solving problems with the flexibility nature of the *Sharīʿah*.

It is very important to analyse the causes behind the text in order to understand what it really means and refers to, thus rendering the text applicable to later eras. It is obvious that the text has never been changed or transformed; however, the understanding and interpretation of the *naṣṣ* has been subject to transformation, so that they could become rulings for what was new and unknown. Accurate understanding and interpretation of *naṣṣ* requires serious work and certain conditions. Knowledge of linguistics, history, sociology, and awareness of the *Shārīʿs* purposes are essential elements when interpreting *naṣṣ* into a situation other than what is literally indicated.[69]

6. The divine nature of the Sharīʿah:

The *Sharīʿah* is mainly a divine in origin based on sources originated directly or indirectly from divine revelation, therefore, it is incomparable to works of any man-made law. The *Qur'ān* was sent by Allah Who knows needs of His subjects well. He does not discriminate one race over another, one territory over another, as the Creator of all, His subjects are equal in their nature regardless of who they are, what they look like, where they live. He, therefore, sent laws, which either can be derived from the main sources, the *Qur'ān* and the *Sunnah*, or from all the secondary sources, to choose the real followers of Him and to determine who is best in deeds. The *Qur'ān* emphasizes the authenticity of the saying of the Prophet (ṣ) that the *Sunnah* is also based on revelation: "*Nor does he speak out of desire. It is naught but revelation that is revealed.*"[70]

It is necessary to all Muslims, who believe in Allah and the Messenger (ṣ), must maintain and implement the laws of Allah as indicated in the *Qur'ān*: "*It is not fitting for a Believer, man or woman, when a matter has been decided by Allah and His Messenger to have any option about their decision: if any one disobeys Allah and His Messenger, he is indeed on a clearly wrong Path.*"[71]

The character of a faithful Mu'min is emphasized by the following verse: "The response of the believers, when they are invited to Allah and His Messenger that he may judge between them, is only to say: We hear and we obey; and these it is that are the successful."[72]

However, there is a misconception, encouraged to an extent by decades of Western Orientalism, that the *Sharī'ah* is not compatible with changing nature of the time and circumstances because of its divine origins. Due to this misconception they assume that it has a static character which cannot be developed. In fact, it is completely vice-versa.

7. The Unified character of the Sharī'ah:

According to the *Qur'ān* the *Sharī'ah* has a unified character which requires holistic approach as it is indicated here "*Do you then believe in a part of the Book and disbelieve in the other? What then is the reward of such among you as do this but disgrace in the life of this world, and on the day of resurrection they shall be sent back to the most grievous chastisement, and Allah is not at all heedless of what you do*".[73]

The *Sharī'ah* may be resembled to a human body that is one unit rather than being divided into parts of body, soul emotions and so on, so does the *Sharīʻah*.[74] In connection with this ʻUmar b. ʻAbd al-ʻAzīz, emphasised on the issues of *aḥkām* saying "Execution of penalties is not any different from practising *ʻibādāt* such as prayers and religious tax."[75]

Differences between mujtahid and faqīh

The *mujtahid*, one who determines the particular value of such injunctions in the light of both the language of the text as well as the general objectives and principles of the *sharīʻah*.[76] It implies that there should be someone who is deriving the law from the texts by using some effort. This person was termed a *faqīh* in earlier times. However, a distinction was drawn between the terms *mujtahid* and *faqīh* in later times. The term began to indicate or applied to the jurist who derives his knowledge from the collection of *fiqh* and these collections contain the options of the *mujtahids*. Nevertheless, the laws derived from the collections by the *mujtahid* become a source of law for the *faqīh*. He is still considered as a *muqallid* (imitator/follower) because he is using the laws that were derived from the specific evidences by other *mujtahids*. Consequently, it can be simplified that the *mujtahid* derives the law for the first time using the sources of Islamic law, while the *faqīh* uses this already derived laws by other jurists.

Differences between ijtihād and taqlīd

Ijtihād, at first hand, is a concept for the activity of the *mujtahid* that makes use of all the source of Islamic law to derive a new *ḥukm* (ruling). The substantive knowledge that is derived by the effort of the *mujtahid* is called *fiqh*. It should be noted that the absolute *mujtahid*, who is founder of a specific schools of thought, relies on the principles of interpretation, as well as the general principles of the substantive, procedural law and the jurisprudence.[77]

Taqlīd, on the other hand, is the activity of the *faqīh* who has not yet reached to the level of *ijtihād* and he is using the laws that were derived from the specific evidences by other *mujtahids.* In the linguistic sense, *taqlīd* means following the opinion of another. It is allowed when its legal justification is found. Although there are disagreement among the scholars, it is a permissible act and the details of it will be discussed later *inshaAllah.*[78]

Differences between muqallid and faqīh

In general *muqallid* is a person who is following the opinion of the *mujtahid.* As it was defined earlier, *faqīh* is also a person who is not able to undertake independent *ijtihād* since he lacked the requisite qualifications or skills. At the same time, an ordinary person who does not have any knowledge of *fiqh,* follows the opinion of the *mujtahid* in the daily performance of his duties or in other matters of the law, is also called *muqallid.* Then, a question arise. Thus, what is the difference between an ordinary *muqallid* and a professional *muqallid* who is *faqīh*?

The difference can be explored as that of it is based on the understanding of the texts in which the opinion of the *mujtahids* are recorded and the sources from which these opinions have been derived. If a *faqīh* reads the sources, besides having a knowledge of Islamic law, is able to extend the law through reasoning from principles, on the basis of a methodology called *takhrīj.* However, if an ordinary person reads these sources he may find a number of opinions on a single issue and he cannot determine what the law is on the issue. Thus he must go to the *faqīh,* who will be able to state which opinion is upheld by the specific schools of thought at a certain time or which one is preferred.[79]

Following the explanation of the components of *uṣūl al-fiqh* individually as *uṣūl* and *fiqh,* it is worthy to explain the definition of *fiqh* according to Shāfi'ī's definition. Remember that *fiqh* was defined as the knowledge of the *shar'ī aḥkām* which means a ruling of Islamic law.

The *ḥukm sharʿī* is therefore defined as: "A communication from Allah, the Exalted, related to the acts of the subjects through a demand or option, or through a declaration." *(Huwa khiṭābullahi taʿālā al-mutaʿalliq bi-afʿāl al-mukallafīn bil-Iqtiḍāʾ aw al-takhyīyr aw al-waḍʿ.)*[80]

The above definition of *al-ḥukm* is found only amongst the *uṣūlī* (juristic scholars). The first point of the definition is that any communication must be from Allah otherwise it is not accepted and cannot be considered as *a ḥukm*. This communication is related to the actions of the subject (*mukallaf*).

The communication related to the act of the subject (*mukallaf*) from Allah can either be in the form of a demand (*iqtiḍāʾ*) or a choice (*takhyīr*) or a declaration (*waḍʿī*).

The relationship also enables the *mujtahid* (jurist) to evaluate the requirements, and to judge whether it is for the command for the act or the prohibition. Allah says "*O you who believe! Observe ṣawm (fasting).*"[81]

This contains *a ḥukm* which demands obedience.

> "*And come not near to the unlawful sexual intercourse.*"[82]

This verse contains *a ḥukm* which requires prohibition.

The *ḥukm* (rule) is clarified through a request (*ṭalab* or *iqtiḍāʾ*). The request in this case is communicated in the form of a command of an act or its prohibition. The request may or may not be binding. When the request is binding, it creates *wujūb* (an obligation) or *taḥrīm* (prohibition), which are established by *dalīl qaṭʿī* (definite proof). When the request is not binding, then the ruling creates *nadb* (recommendation) or *makrūh* (discouraged), which are established without definitive proof.

Allah says "*O you who believe! Fulfil (your) obligations.*"[83]

This verse is addressed to the *mukallaf* (subject), and consists of a particular demand. And "*O you who believe! Let not a group scoff at another group, it may be that the latter are better than the former....*"[84]

This *Qur'anic* text conveys a prohibition to the *mukallaf.* The freedom of choice is given to the *mukallaf* (subject) a choice to commit the act or avoid it.

On the other hand if the subject is free to perform the act it is known as mubaḥ (permissible). For example "*But when you finish the iḥrām pilgrimage (of ḥajj or 'umrah), you may hunt...*"[85]

This *ḥukm* conveys an option for the *mukallaf* (subject) and he has the freedom to act or not to.

As a final point of the definition, the communication may be clarified through an enactment or declaration; this is neither a demand nor an option. However, it is in relation to an act which is connected to another act by reason of *sabab* (cause), *sharṭ* (condition) or *māni'* (impediment).

For example, "*...and ḥajj to the House is a duty that mankind owe to Allah for those who can afford the expenses...*"[86]

Financial ability is the condition for the application of the rule.[87]

The identification of *ḥukm shar'ī* is perceived differently between the *uṣūlī* (juristic scholars) and the *fuqahā.*

For instance Allah says "*And perform al-ṣalāt*"[88] which is a *ḥukm shar'ī* itself according to the *uṣūlī.* However, according to the *fuqahā',* it is the effect or the result of the demand in this verse, namely the *wujūb* (obligation), which represents the *ḥukm shar'ī.*[89]

Simply, the *ḥukm shar'ī* consists of four fundamental elements. These elements are: the *Ḥākim* (Lawgiver), the *maḥkūm 'alayh* (the subject), the *maḥkūm fīh* (the act of the *mukallaf*), and the *ḥukm* (ruling).

The *Ḥākim* (Lawgiver): The first element of the *ḥukm shar'ī* is the *Ḥākim* (Lawgiver) who is the true source from which the *ḥukm* originates. Allah Almighty is the original source for Islamic law that is the absolute *Ḥākim* (Lawgiver).

The *maḥkūm 'alayh* (the subject): The second element of the *ḥukm shar'ī* is the *maḥkūm 'alayh* (the subject) for whose conduct the *ḥukm* is stipulated, that is *mukallaf.* Then what/who is the *mukallaf*? Simply the *maḥkūm 'alayh* (the subject) or the *mukallaf* (subject) is the person whose act appeals a *ḥukm*, or a *ḥukm* requires him/her to act in a prescribed manner. In legal a phrase, he is known as the *mukallaf.* A *mukallaf* is a person who retains legal capacity, whether he acts directly or through given authority.

The maḥkūm fīh (the act): The third element of the *ḥukm shar'ī* is the *maḥkūm fīh* (the act).

The *ḥukm* (ruling): The fourth element of the *ḥukm shar'ī* is the *ḥukm* (ruling). Thus, basically, the *ḥukm* (rule) is divided into two main categories: the first is *al-ḥukm al-taklīfī* (the obligation, creating rule, defining law) and the other is *al-ḥukm al-waḍ'ī* (declaratory law). In contemporary common law, Hart has divided it into primary and secondary rules. The only difference is that the rules of Islamic law are based on religious law. The Muslim jurists designate the category of primary rules as *al-ḥukm al-taklīfī* (defining law). The category of secondary rules is designated as the *al-ḥukm al-waḍ'ī.*[90] *Al-ḥukm al-taklīfī* (defining law) is a communication from Allah, the exalted, related to the acts of the *mukallaf* (subjects), which consists of a demand or an option; it arises in the five categories of *wājīb* or *farḍ* (obligatory), *mandūb* (recommended), *makrūh* (adversity), *ḥarām* (prohibited) and *mubāḥ* (permissible). In addition, the *Ḥanafī* School deduces seven varieties from the same definition: 1. *farḍ* (obligatory) 2. *wājīb* (obligatory) 3. *mandūb* (recommended) 4. *makrūh karāhat al-taḥrīm* (strongly disapproved) 5. *makrūh karāhat al-tanzīh* (disapproval) 6. *ḥarām* (prohibited) 7. *mubāḥ* (permissible).

Al-ḥukm al-waḍ'ī is a communication from Allah which is related to the acts of the *mukallaf* (subject) in a manner that is declaratory, in another word it is explanatory component for *al-ḥukm al-taklīfiyyah* through its fundamental tools which consist of 1. *Al-sabab* (the cause) 2. *Al-Rukn* (the element), 3. *Al-sharṭ* (the condition) 4. *Al-māni'* (the impediment), 5. *Al-Ṣiḥḥah, al-Fasād, al-Buṭlān* (the Validity, the

Nullity, the Vitiation).[91]

Individually these classifications are accepted by all the majority of the *Sunnī* schools. As we mentioned that the *Ḥanafīs* deduces seven categories from the same definition. The first one is *farḍ* (obligatory): This *al-ḥukm al-taklīfī* (defining law) arises from an evidence or source that is definitive with respect to its implication. The second one is *wājīb* (obligatory): This *al-ḥukm al-taklīfī* (defining law) is slightly weaker than the first in its demand for commission. It arises from a source that is probable with respect to its implication and authenticity. The demand, however, has been expressed in binding terms. The third one is *mandūb* (recommended): This *al-ḥukm al-taklīfī* (defining law) is a difference *ḥukm* between recommendation and the two kinds of obligation. The difference that is based on the binding nature of the command. The source is probable, but the demand is expressed in non-binding terms. The forth one is *makrūh karāhat al-taḥrīm* (strongly disapproved): This *al-ḥukm al-taklīfī* (defining law) arises from a probable evidence expressed in binding terms which is closes to prohibition. The fifth one is *makrūh karāhat al-tanzīh* (disapproval): This *al-ḥukm al-taklīfī* (defining law) is an act whose omission is demanded by the Lawgiver through a probable evidence expressed in non-binding terms. The sixth one is *ḥarām* (prohibited): This *al-ḥukm al-taklīfī* (defining law) arises from a definitive evidence. The seventh one is *mubāḥ* (permissible): This *al-ḥukm al-taklīfī* (defining law) is not a duty that is created and the subject is given a choice to perform the act or not to perform it. However it may sometimes create obligations and duties with respect to other individuals. For example, it may be said that it happens in the case of a person appointing another his agent or concluding a contract with him.

On the other hand, *al-ḥukm al-waḍʿī* can be classified and simply covered by the following concepts: as it was classified, in general, by Nyazee into three types: The first classification of *al-ḥukm al-waḍʿī* is the classification of secondary rules into *sabab* (the cause), *sharṭ* (condition), and *mānī'*(the impediment), which are considered more with this classification by the *uṣūlī* scholars. The second classification of *al-ḥukm al-waḍ'ī* is the classification that the *faqīh* scholars give emphasis more since it concerns to the performance of acts. These are *al-ṣiḥḥah* (validity), *fasād* (nullity), and *buṭlān* (vitiation). The third classification of *al-ḥukm al-waḍ'ī* is the classification that it helps to jurists identify the general principles of the law and the exceptions to these general principles and which ae used as a tool for achieving analytical consistency. These are *'azīmah* (a comprehensive general rules) and *rukhṣah* (exemptions).

The details of *al-ḥukm al-taklīfī* (defining law) and *al-ḥukm al-waḍ'ī* (declaratory law) will be elaborated afterwards.

The meaning of Shar'īyyah

According to the Shāfi'ī's (d. 204/819) definition of *fiqh* which is "The knowledge of the legal rules (*aḥkām al-shar'īyyah*), pertaining to conduct, have been derived from their specific evidences." (*al-'ilmu bil-aḥkām al-shar'iyyah al-'amaliyyah al-muktasab min adillatuhā al-tafṣīliyyah*).

To remember that it was defined as "It is a compilation of the legal rules pertaining to conduct that have been derived from their specific evidences."[92]

It may also be understood that the knowledge which is pertaining to the legal rules must be a knowledge of legal rulings that is *shar'īy*, otherwise it will not be considered as *fiqh*. Thus the term *Shar'īyyah* was included within the definition and therefore, it is a legal word which is derived from "*sh-r-'a* (legal); *ta-sh rr-'a*" (legislation), it excludes *al-aḥkām al-ḥissiyyah* (law of sense perception: for instance fire burns, wood floats on water, the sun shines), *al-aḥkām al-'aqliyyah* (rational rules, for instance one is half of two, etc.), *al-aḥkām al-lughawiyyah* (linguistic rules, like the doer of an act is called the subject) and *al-aḥkām al-waḍ'īyyah* (declaratory rules).[93]

The meaning of 'Amaliyyah

It is not enough to be a knowledge of legal rulings that is *shar'īy,* so long as it is not a practical knowledge. Thus this term was included within the definition. Therefore, the rulings (*aḥkām*) that are must be practical *aḥkām.*

The term *al-aḥkām al-'amaliyyah* are divided into three types: *fi'lī* (physically), *qalbī* (which takes place in the heart) and *qawlī* (relating to speech). The physical acts as the acts of prayer, murder, homicide; the *qalbī* acts as intention, love, hate, etc.; and *qawlī* acts as recitation during prayers, offer and acceptance in a contract, etc.

According to Imām al-Rāzī (d. 606) the meaning of the term *al-'amaliyyah* does not contain all of *al-aḥkām al-fiqhiyyah*, since *al-aḥkām al-fiqhiyyah* contains also *naẓarī* (theoretical) rules.[94] Some sources of law such as *ijmā'* (consensus), *qiyās* (analogy) are considered to be *naẓarī* (theoretical). *Al-aḥkām al-'amaliyyah* excludes *al-aḥkām al-ī'tiqādiyyah,* which is belief in the existence of Allah, His oneness, His qualities, the truth of the mission of the Prophet (ṣ), belief in the Day of Judgment etc.

The meaning of Muktasabah

It means that which is obtained. Thus, any type of knowledge which are not obtained are not considered as *fiqh.*[95] The obtained knowledge is the knowledge of the jurist (*faqīh)* and the follower (*muqallid*). The term al-*muktasabah* excludes the knowledge of the *shar'ī aḥkām* (legal rules) which pertains to man's knowledge of Allah. This knowledge is not granted by the way of performing *ijtihād* but only by way of divine revelations concerning Allah's angels and prophets etc.[96]

The meaning of Adillah

It is also to be considered as *fiqh*, the derived rulings must be obtained through *adillah* (evidences).

The term *adillah* is a plural of *dalīl*, which contains the meanings of *ishārah* (indication, sign, token, and symptom), *murshid* (guide, conductor), *burhān* (proof, evidence), and *shāhid* (witness). It also means "*kitābun yustarshad bihī*" (guide book, itinerary), or *fihrist* (index).[97]

Linguistically *dalīl* means that which leads or guides to anything sensible or moral. The term means in a literal sense a proof, evidence, indication or guide.

Technically *al-dalīl* means a proof or evidence of a practical *ḥukm* (rule) of the *Sharī'ah* which is inferred. It is also defined as something which guides one to the practical rule of the *Sharī'ah* by the correct understanding.[98]

One of the main features of the Islamic *sharī'ah* is that it is based on evidence or proof deduced from the *Qur'ān* or the *Sunnah* through *ijtihād* which conforms to these two sources of Islamic law. Consequently, it can be stated that the sources of Islamic law are mainly either revelation or non-revelation[99]:

Revelation is considered to be of two types:

1. *Al-waḥy al-matlū* or *waḥy ẓāhir* (recited or manifest revelation), which is defined as communication from Allah to the Prophet Muḥammad (ṣ), conveyed by the angel Gabriel, i.e. the *Qur'ān*.
2. *Al-waḥy ghair al-matlū* or *waḥy bāṭin* (un-recited or internal revelation). This consists of the inspiration (*ilhām*) of concepts only: Allah inspired the Prophet (ṣ) and the latter conveyed the concepts in his own words, i.e. the *Sunnah*, which comprises the sayings *aḥādīth* of the Prophet (ṣ).[100]

Non-revelation refers to *ijmā'* (consensus of *mujtahidīn* of the Muslim community), *qiyās* (analogy) or *istidlāl* (inference). In addition, Imām al-Shāṭibī (d. 790/1388) divided the sources of the *sharī'ah* into two types: either pure transmitted (*al-naql al-maḥḍ*) or pure opinion (*al-ra'y al-maḥḍ*). Opinion (*ra'y*) is not considered as a source of *sharī'ah* unless it is based on transmitted proof.[101]

Another classification of *adillah sharīʿah* is the *qaṭʿī* (definitive) and the *ẓannī* (speculative).[102]

The *adillah sharīʿah* have also been categorized into transmitted (*naqlī*) and rational (*aqlī*). The transmitted proofs, *adillah naqliyyah*, are the *Qur'ān*, the *Sunnah*, and *ijmāʿ*. Two other transmitted proofs are the rulings of the Companions and the laws revealed prior to the advent of Islam (*sharʿ man qablanā*). Rational proofs are *adillah ʿaqliyyah* namely *qiyās*, *istiṣḥāb*, etc.[103] *Adillah* is further classified by al-Āmidī (d. 631/1233) into *mustaqil* (independent) – such as the first three sources of the *sharīʿah* and *muqayyad* (dependent).[104]

In general, and more practical sense, the sources of the *sharīʿah* (*al-maṣādir al-sharīʿah*) are further divided into two types:

A. Unanimously accepted sources: 1. The *Qur'ān*, 2. The *Sunnah*, 3. *Ijmāʿ*, (consensus), 4. *Qiyās* (analogy).

B. Controversial sources: 1. *Istiḥsān* (juristic preference), 2. *Maṣlaḥah mursalah* (consideration of public interest), 3. *Istiṣḥāb* (presumption of continuity), 4. *Qawl al-Ṣaḥābī* (the sayings of a companion of the Prophet), 5. *ʿUrf* (custom), 6. *Sadd al-dharāʾiʿ* (blocking the means), 7. *Sharʿ man qablanā* (revealed laws preceding to the *sharīʿah* of Islam) and 8. *Istiqrāʾ* (induction).[105]

The sources of *sharīʿah* are identified in the *Qur'ān* as follows: "*O you who believe! Obey Allah and obey the Messenger (Muḥammad) and those of you (Muslims) who are in authority. (And) if you differ in anything amongst yourselves refer it to Allah and His Messenger.*"[106] The reference to *Qur'ān* is pointed out in the verse as "*Obey Allah*" and the reference to the *Sunnah* as "*Obey the Messenger.*" *Ijmāʿ* is also referred to in the idea of obedience to "*Those of you who are in authority*" and the last part of the verse "*If you differ in anything amongst yourselves refer it to Allah and His Messenger*" which requires the referral of disagreement to Allah and His Messenger, is in effect a clear authorisation for the principle of *qiyās*.[107]

Finally, *adillah tafṣīliyyah* (specific evidences) which is excluded from the definition of *fiqh*. Thus the knowledge of the *muqallid* (one who follows the opinion of another) is different from the knowledge of jurists and the knowledge of the leaders of the schools of thought.[108] It is not permitted for the *muqallid* to obtain his knowledge of *fiqh* directly from the *Qur'ān* and the *Sunnah*. However, a *faqīh* can obtain his knowledge from the *Qur'ān* and the *Sunnah* directly.

Definition of Uṣūl al-fiqh

After defining all of the components of *uṣūl al-fiqh* individually as *uṣūl* and *fiqh* as well their elements, now, it is worthy to explain the definition of *uṣūl al-fiqh*.

The meaning of *uṣūl al-fiqh* (the principle of Islamic jurisprudence) is combined by the understanding of the meaning of *uṣūl* and *fiqh* individually. The term *uṣūl al-fiqh* now can be defined as:

> "The principles by the use of which the mujtahid arrives at legal rules through the specific evidences." (*Heya al-qawā'id allatī yutawaṣṣal bihā al-mujtahid ilā istinbāṭ al-aḥkām al-shar'iyyah al-'amaliyyah min adillatihā al-tafṣīliyyah.*)[109]

The above definition indicates that the *uṣūl al-fiqh* are a structure of principles of interpretation by the effort given by the *mujtahid* who is able to derive new rulings from the detailed evidences in the *Qur'ān*, the *Sunnah*, *ijmā'*, *qiyās* or in the controversial sources of Islamic law.

In its wider sense, it is defined by al-Rāzī as it follows: "It is an expression that includes all the paths (evidences) leading to *fiqh* when these are considered in a broad sense, and for the legal reasoning proceeding from these paths, as well as the status (skill) of the person undertaking such reasoning."[110]

The word paths (*ṭuruq*) is consisted of all kind of evidences (*adillah*) and including signs (*amārah*), and the legal validity and strength of the general evidences such as the legal validity of *ijmā'* as a source of Islamic law, as well as legal reasoning which includes general principles such as *istiḥsān* and *maṣlaḥah.*

Al-Ghazālī also defines it as follows: "*uṣūl al-fiqh* is an expression employed for the evidences of these legal rules and for a knowledge of the broad ways in which they reveal such rules, and not by way of a specific indication."[111]

According to the above definition, since the *uṣūl al-fiqh* is described as also *qawā'id* (principles), the definition of the *qawā'id* and the *qawā'id al-fiqhiyyah* should be elaborated here.

Qawā'id al-Fiqhiyyah and Uṣūl al-Fiqh

Simply *qawā'id* (plural of *qā'idah*) means principles and therefore *qawā'id al-fiqhiyyah* means the principles and the maxims of *fiqh,* that is, the principles of Islamic law. For linguistic meaning the following verse is evidenced "*And when Ibrahim and Ismail raised the foundations of the House: Our Lord! Accept from us; surely Thou art the Hearing, the Knowing:*"[112]

Technically it is defined by al-Zarqā' "It is the general *fiqh* principles which are presented in a simple format consisting of the general rules of *Sharī'ah* in a particular field related to it."[113] Since the *qawā'id al-fiqhiyyah* also means general principles, they can be applied to various issues related to *fiqh.* For example the following maxim "matters are determined according to intention" (*al-umūr bi-maqāṣidihā*) which indicates that all issues pertaining to intention are covered such as the intention in prayers, in doings, in transactions, in sayings, etc. Although the *qawā'id al-fiqhiyyah* is defined as general principles, these may not cover all of the *fiqh* issues deducing the *aḥkām.* Yet these maxims played a great deal of role in the formation of Islamic law since they are used as principles for deducing rules in various *fiqh* issues.[114]

Due to the role played by the two concepts of that *uṣūl al-fiqh* and *qawā'id al-fiqhiyyah,* sometimes these are confused with one another.

As it is known that *uṣūl al-fiqh* is the general sources and principles of Islamic law while the *qawā'id al-fiqhiyyah* is a body of abstract rules which are derived from the detailed study of the *fiqh* itself, which consists of theoretical guidelines in the different areas of *fiqh* issues such as transactions, matrimonial law, evidences, etc. and therefore, these are an integral part of *fiqh*. Despite the close similarities of *qawā'id al-fiqhiyyah* with the *uṣūl al-fiqh* and the former being an integral part of the *aḥkām*, *uṣūl al-fiqh* is totally a separate concept. The former may resemble the expression *uṣūl al-fiqh*, however not a part of it and therefore, these two concepts are totally different from one another. This is why the maxims are not lasting proofs of divine law, yet they can never be treated as sources of Islamic law. In regards to *qawā'id al-fiqhiyyah*, mainly over 200 legal maxims have been collected and compiled in works known as *al-Ashbāh wa al-Naẓā'ir* authored by Jalāl al-Dīn al-Suyūṭī and Ibn Nujāym al-Ḥanafī. One hundred of these maxims have been adopted in the introductory section of the *Ottoman Majallah*.[115]

The *Ottoman Majallah* that is *Majallah al-Aḥkām al-'Adliyyah*, consisted of 1851 articles, introduced in 1869 by the Ottoman State. This was the first codification of Islamic law. For the codification and the preparation of the *Majallah*, the Ottoman State established an association called *Majallah Jam'iyyeti* (Association of *Majallah*) under the chairmanship of Ahmed Jawdat Pasha, Minister of *Dīwān-i Aḥkām-i 'Adliyyah* (civil court). It was adopted and applied in many countries such as Turkey, Egypt, Hijaz, Iraq, Syria, Jordan, Lebanon, Cyprus, Palestine and Israel and yet it remained in force until 1928 in Albania, Bosnia and Herzegovina, until 1984 in Kuwait. Even today, it is still in force some decrees of *Majallah* in Israel,[116] and in *Sharī'ah* Courts in Malaysia.

Nevertheless, not all of the *qawā'id* (maxims) of the *qawā'id al-fiqhiyyah* was formulated or codified all at once by a particular jurist or at a particular time. Yet it was formulated and developed during the time of the revival of *fiqh* activities. Most of the maxims of *fiqh* were developed by early *Ḥanafī* jurists, but still authors of many maxims are not known except for those maxims originally derived from the *ḥadīth* of the Prophet (ṣ) or may be attributed to particular scholars such as "*no harm shall be inflicted nor reciprocated in Islam*" (*lā ḍarara wa lā ḍirār fī al-Islam*)[117] is a maxim which was derived from the *ḥadīth* of the Prophet (ṣ) and "A ruler is not permitted to take anything that belongs to a person except through a proper way which has already been established" (*laysa li-al-imām an-yukhrija shay'an min yadi aḥad illā bi-ḥaqqin thābit ma'rūf*) is a maxim which was attributed to Abū Yūsuf (d. 181 AH) which is quoted in his well-known book "*Kitāb al-Kharāj*."[118]

The early works on the formulation of the maxims of *fiqh* have been traced back to as early as the third century *hijrī*. Therefore, the history of the maxims in a general sense is parallel with that of the *fiqh* itself however, mainly the maxims were developed during the era of imitation (*taqlīd*), while the *fiqh* was developed and naturally contributed during the first three centuries of Muslim scholarship, which is known as the era of *ijtihād*. The maxims of *fiqh* may also be known by the following terms *Al-Qawā'id*, *Al-Ashbāh*, *Al-Furūq*, *An-Naẓariyyah al-Fiqhiyyah*.

Among them, not all but a few, Abū Ṭāhir al-Dabbās who formulated seventeen maxims from the *Ḥanafī* sources and al-Karkhī increased this maxims to thirty-nine. However, it is recorded that the earliest compilation in the form of a note of such maxims was manuscripted by Abū al-Ḥasan al-Karkhī (d. 334 AH) which was exemplified later by Najm al-Dīn Naṣafī s 710 AH). Yet another *Ḥanafī* jurist Abū Zayd al-Dabbūsī (d. 430 AH) elaborated some of the significant maxims in his book *Ta'sīs al-Naẓar*. Later on many books authored on this field and finally these maxims were incorporated into the famous Ottoman work of *Majallah al-Aḥkām al-'Adliyyah* which consisted of 1851 articles.

The four school of thoughts contributed to the literature on legal maxims, among the well-known literatures on this field include the following manuscripts: *Takhrīj al-Furū' 'alā al-Uṣūl* by Imām Abī Manāqib Shihāb al-Dīn al-Zanjānī **al-Shāfi'ī** (d. 656 AH); *Anwār al-Burūq fī Anwā'al-Furūq* known al *Kitāb al-Furūq* by Imām Shihāb al-Dīn al-Qarāfī **al-Mālikī** (d. 684 AH); Al Qawā'id by 'Abd ar-Raḥmān Ibn Rajab **al-Ḥanbalī** (d. 795); *Al-Ashbāh wa al-Naẓā'ir* by Ibn Nujaym **al-Ḥanafī** (d. 970 AH); *Al-Ashbāh wa al-Naẓā'ir* by Jalāl al-Dīn al-Suyūṭī al-Shāfi'ī (d. 1201 AH); *Durar al-Ḥukkām* by Ali Haydar Efendi (d. 1918 CE) and *Sharḥ al-Majallah* by the former Mufti of Homs Sheikh Muḥammad Khālid al-Attasī and its competition by his son al-Sheikh Ṭāhir al-Attasī were works of the interpretation of *Majallah al-Aḥkām al-'Adliyyah.* In addition to these classical works, there are also contemporary works, among the famous include the followings: *Al-Madkhal al-Fiqhī al-'Āmm*, by Muṣṭafā Aḥmad Al-Zarqā'; *Al-Qawā'id al-Fiqhiyyah Nash'atuhā wa Taṭāwuruhā Dirāsat Muallifātihā* by Sheikh 'Ali bin Aḥmad al-Nadawi; *Al-Naẓariyyah al-Fiqhiyyah* by Muḥammad bin Wahbah al-Zuḥailī etc.[119]

The early juristic scholars have chosen the following five essential maxims called "*al-qawā'id al-fiqhiyyah al-aṣliyyah*," or the normative legal maxims which represent the essence of the *Sharī'ah* as a whole and simply the rest are considered an elaboration of these five: "*Harm must be eliminated.*" (*ad-ḍarar yuzāl*); "*Acts are judged by the intention behind them*" (*al-umūr bi-maqāṣidihā*); "*Certainty is not overruled by doubt*" (*al-yaqīn lā yazūl bi-shshak*); "*Hardship begets facility*" (*al-mashaqqah tajlib al-taysīr*); "*Custom is the basis of judgment*" (*al-'ādah muḥakkamah*).

Consequently, the *uṣūl al-fiqh* is a discipline of law, a kind of methodology for *tashrī' al-Islāmī* (legislation of Islamic law) which uses principles and methods for deriving aḥkām (rulings) which are taken from general evidences, the rules of interpretation, deduction and the sources of Islamic law. *Uṣūl al-fiqh* also includes the kind of general evidences that are indicative to the *aḥkām* of Allah and the sources of Islamic law, as well as proofs or evidences on how to arrive at the *aḥkām* (rulings).

Notes

[1] Saim Kayadibi, *Istiḥsān the Doctrine of Juristic Preference in Islamic Law* (Selangor: IBT, 2010), p. xxviii.

[2] *Qur'ān* 5:44.

[3] *Qur'ān* 5:45.

[4] *Qur'ān* 5:47.

[5] *Qur'ān* 53:3-4.

[6] Ahmad Hasan, "*The Early Development of Islamic Jurisprudence*" (Islamabad: Islamic Research Institute, 1994), p. 117.

[7] Kayadibi, *Istiḥsān*, p. 100.

[8] Ahmad Hasan, *Principles of Islamic Jurisprudence, The Command of the Sharī'ah and Juridical Norm* (Islamabad: Islamic Research Institute, 1993), p. 16-17; Abū al-'Aynāyn Badrān, "*Uṣūl al-Fiqh al-Islāmī*" (Alexandria: Muassasah Shabāb al-Jāmi'ah, 1404/1984), p. 12; Muhammad Hashim Kamali, "*Principles of Islamic Jurisprudence*" (Cambridge: Islamic Text Society, 1997), p. 4.

[9] Ahmad Hasan, *Principles*, p. 18.

[10] Kamali, *Principles*, p. 8.

[11] Ahmad Hasan, *Principles*, p. 19.

[12] Kamali, *Principles*, p. 8.

[13] Ahmad Hasan, *Principles*, p. 18-20.

[14] Kamali, *Principles*, p. 9.

[15] *Qur'ān* 51:56.

[16] Mollah Husraw, Muḥammad bin Firāmūz (885/1480), "*Mir'āt al-Uṣūl Sharḥ Mirkāt al-Wusūl*" (Istanbul: Matba'ah al-Amīrah, 1309), v. 1 p. 56 ; Laknawī, 'Abd al-'Ali Muḥammad bin Nizām al-Dīn Anṣārī, Baḥr al-'Ulūm, Abū al-'Abbās, Ḥanafī (d. 1180/1767), "*Fawātiḥ al-Raḥamūt sharḥ Musallam al-Subūt fī Uṣūl al-Fiqh*" (Cairo: Matba'ah al-Amīriyyah Bulāq, 1906), v. 1, p. 8; Anṣārī, Abū Zakarīyyah Shaikh al-Islam "*Ghāyāt al-Wuṣūl sharḥ lub al-Uṣūl*" (Cairo: Muṣṭafā bāb al-Ḥalabī wa awlāduh, 1360/1941), v. 1, p. 18.

[17] See Elias A. Elias, "*Elias Modern Dictionary*," 5th edition (Cairo: 1950); Joseph Catafago, "*English and Arabic Dictionary*" (London, 1958); Hans Wehr, "*A*

Dictionary of Modern Written Arabic," edited by J. Milton Cowan, 4th edition (Germany: 1979); Imran Ahsan Khan Nyazee, "*Islamic Jurisprudence*," (Kuala Lumpur: The Other Press, 2003), p. 26-27.

[18] *Qur'ān* 4:23.

[19] *Qur'ān* 17:32.

[20] Ibn Amīr al-Ḥajj Muḥammad bin Muḥammad Shams al-Dīn (d. 879) "*Al-Taqrīr wa al-Takhbīr 'alā Taḥrīr al-Kamāl ibn al-Humām fī 'Ilm al-Uṣūl*" (Cairo: Maṭba'ah al-Amīriyyah Bulāq, 1316), v. 1 p. 17; See Nyazee: *ibid*, p. 27-28.

[21] *Qur'ān* 2:43.

[22] *Qur'ān* 5:90.

[23] Abū Dāwūd Sulaymān bin al-Ash'ās (d. 275/888) "*Sunnan*" iii, 1043, *ḥadīth* no: 3672, tr. Ahmad Hasan, Lahore: Muḥammad Ashraf 1984.

[24] See Nyazee, p. 27.

[25] Ibn Mājah Abū 'Abd Allah Muḥammad (d. 273/886), "*Sunan*," ii, 784, *ḥadīth* no: 2340, Istanbul, 1981.

[26] See Laknawī, 'Abd al-'Ali Muḥammad bin Nizām al-Dīn Ansārī, Baḥr al-'Ulūm, Abū al-'Abbās, Ḥanafī (d. 1180/1767), "*Fawātiḥ al-Raḥamūt Sharḥ Musallam al-Subūt fī Uṣūl al-Fiqh*" (Cairo: Matba'ah al-Amīriyyah, Bulāq, 1906), v. 1, p. 8; Jamāl al-Dīn 'Abd al-Raḥīm al-Ḥusayn Isnawī Shāfi'ī (d. 772/1370), "*Nihāyāt al-Sūl fī Sharḥ al-Minhāj al-Uṣūl*," (Beirut: 1982), 1, p. 18.

[27] 'Abd al-'Azīz bin Aḥmad bin Muḥammed, 'Alā al-Dīn al-Bukhārī. (d. 730/1329), "*Sharḥ Kashf al-Asrār 'alā Uṣūl al-Bazdawī*" (Beirut: Dār al Kutūb al-'Arabi, 1394), p. 1086.

[28] Āmidī, Sayf al-Dīn al-Āmidī (d. 631/1233), "*al-Iḥkām fī Uṣūl al-Aḥkām*," ed. 'Abd al-Razzāq 'Afīfī, 2nd ed. (Beirut: Maktabah al-Islāmi, 1402/1982), v. 1, p. 9.

[29] Taqīy al-Dīn Abū al-'Abbās Aḥmad b. 'Abd al-Ḥalīm Ibn Taymiyyah (d. 728/1328), "*Al-Musawwadah fī Uṣūl al-Fiqh*" (Cairo: Al-Maṭba'ah al-Madani, 1964), p. 573.

[30] Abū 'Alī Badr al-Dīn Muḥammad bin 'Alī Shawkānī (d. 1250/1834), "*Irshād al-Fuḥūl ilā Taḥqīq al-Ḥaq min 'Ilm al-Uṣūl*" (Cairo: 1937), p. 3; Ibn Amīr al-Ḥajj Muḥammad bin Muḥammad Shams ad-Dīn (d. 879), "*Al-Taqrīr wa al-Takhbīr 'alā Taḥrīr al-Kamāl ibn al-Humām fī 'Ilm al-Uṣūl*" (Cairo: Matbaah al-Amīriyyah Bulāq, 1316), v. 1, p. 17.

[31] For the transformation of the Muslim understanding of the concept of *fiqh* in the last two centuries, see: Murteza Bedir, "Fikih to Law: Secularization Through

Curriculum," in *Islamic Law and Society* 11, 3, Leiden, 2004, p. 378-401.

[32] *Qur'ān* 11:91.

[33] *Qur'ān* 4:78.

[34] *Qur'ān* 7:179.

[35] Muslim, *Kitāb al-Amārah.*

[36] Muḥammad Ibn Sa'd (d. 230/844), "*Al-Ṭabaqāt al-Kubrā*" (Beirut: 1957), v. 2, p. 363.

[37] 'Ubayd Allah Ibn Mas'ūd bin Tāj al-Sharī'ah al-Ḥanafī, Ṣadr al-Sharī'ah (d. 747/1346), "*Al-Tawdīḥ fī Ḥall Jawāmid al-Tanqīḥ*" (Karachi: 1979), p. 22-25. Explaining the definition given by Abū Ḥanīfah, he says that it includes three things: 1-knowledge of the teneth of faith, 2-knowledge of ethics and mysticism (Sufism), 3-knowledge pertaining to acts. The first is covered by "*'ilm kalām*," the second by ethics and mysticism and the third by *fiqh*. Therefore, he says if you wish to confine the definition to *fiqh* alone, that is, "*Al-fiqh al-Aṣghar*," you must add at the end of the definition the word "*'amalan*" (with respect to acts).

[38] Ahmad Hasan, "*The Early*," p. 3.

[39] See Abū Dāwud, "*Sunan*," tr. Ahmad Hasan, Lahore, 1984 iii. 1019 *ḥadīth* no: 3585.

[40] 'Abd al-Raḥmān bin Jād Allah al-Bannānī, al-Maghribī (d. 1198/1784), "*Ḥāshiyah 'alā Sharḥ Jalāl al-Dīn al-Maḥallī 'alā Jam' al-Jawāmī' li Ibn Subkī*" (Cairo: 1937), v. 1 p. 32; Molla Husraw, "*Mir'at al-Uṣūl*," v. 1 p. 50; Ṣadr al-Sharī'ah, "*Al-Tawdīḥ*," v.1, p.26. He did not use the word "*al-muktasabah.*"

[41] Imran Ahsan Khan Nyazee, "*Islamic Jurisprudence*," (Kuala Lumpur: The Other Press, 2003), 30.

[42] Al-Ghazālī, *Al-Mustaṣfā' min 'Ilm al-Uṣūl*, vol. 1, p.3-4.

[43] Al-Rāzī, *al-Mahṣūl fī 'Ilm Uṣūl al-Fiqh*, vol. 1, p. 78.

[44] Nyazee, *ibid.*

[45] Nyazee, *ibid.*, 31-32.

[46] *Qur'ān* 5:3.

[47] *Qur'ān* 6:38.

[48] *Qur'ān* 45:18.

[49] Al-Qurṭubī, *Al-Jāmī' li Aḥkām al-Qur'ān* (Cairo: Dār al-Kutub al-Maṣriyyah, 1939), vol. 16, p. 10; 'Abdul Karīm Al-Zaydān, *Al-Madkhal li Dirāsat al-Sharī'ah al-Islāmiyyah* (Baghdād: Mu'assasah al-Risālah and Maktabah al-Quds, 1976), p. 38.

[50] Muḥammad 'Ali bin 'Ali al-Taḥwānī, *Kashf 'Iṣṭilāḥāt al-Funūn* (Beirut: Dār Ṣadr, 1961), v.3, p. 759.

[51] Al-Zaydān, *ibid.*, p.67.

[52] Mohamad Akram Laldin, "*Islamic Law an Introduction*," (Kuala Lumpur: Research Centre of iium, 2006), p. 7-8.

[53] *Qur'ān* 14:1

[54] *Qur'ān* 5:3.

[55] Nasafī,'Abd Allah bin Aḥmad bin Maḥmùd Ḥafiz al-Din Ab Al-Baraqât Al-Ḥanafi (d. 710/1310) "*Madārik al-Tanzīl wa Haqāik al-Ta'wīl*" (Beirut: nd.), 5, 401.

[56] Shāṭibī, "*Al-I'tiṣām*," v.1, p.305; "*Muwāfaqāt*," v. 1, p. 32, 77.

[57] *Qur'ān* 15:9

[58] Abū Dāwūd, "*Sunnah*," ii, 518.

[59] *Qu'ān* 34:28

[60] Qaradāwī, "*İslam Hukuku Evrensellik Süreklilik*," tr. By Yusuf Işıcık and Ahmet Yaman (Istanbul: Marifet Yayınları, 1999), p. 26.

[61] *Qur'ān* 21:107

[62] Ibn 'Āshūr, "*Maqāṣid*," p. 98.

[63] Ibn 'Āshūr "*Maqāṣid*," p. 107-108.

[64] *Khutbah al-Wadā* (last ceremony): see in Muḥammad Ḥamidullah, "*İslam Peygamberi*" (Istanbul: 1980).

[65] *Qur'ān* 49:13

[66] *Musnad Aḥmad, ḥadīth* no: 22978

[67] *Qur'ān* 49:10

[68] Qaradāwī, "*İslam Hukuku evrensellik süreklilik*," p. 40; Zarkā, "*Madkhal*," v.1, p.149; Sawa Pasha, "*İslam Hukuku Nazariyatı Hakkında bir Etüt*," v.2, p.358.

[69] For this, see: Shalabī, "*Ta'līl*"; Shāṭibī, "*Muwāfaqāt*"; Būtī, "*Ḍawābiṭ al-Maṣlaḥah*"; Abū Sunnah, "*Al-'Urf*."

[70] *Qur'ān* 53:3-4

[71] *Qur'ān* 33:36

[72] *Qur'ān* 24:51

[73] *Qur'ān* 2:85 see also: 4:150-151

[74] Qaradāwī, "*Khaṣā'is*," 108.

[75] Ibn Sa'd , "*Al-Tabaqāt*," v. 378.

76 Zakī al-Dīn Sha'ban, "Manhaj al-Qur'ān fī Bayān al-Aḥkām," in ed., Muḥammad Tawfiq 'Uwayḍah, *Al-Fiqh al-Islamī Asās al-Tashrī'* (Cairo: Maṭābi' al-Ahrām, 1971), p. 22-23.

77 Nyazee, *ibid.*, p. 25.

78 *Ibid.*

79 Nyazee, *ibid.*, p. 25-26.

80 Ṣadr al-Sharī'ah, *ibid.*, v. 1, p. 13; Bannānī, "*Ḥāshiah*, v. 1 p. 32; Nyazee: *ibid.*, p. 64.

81 *Qur'ān* 2:183

82 *Qur'ān* 17:32

83 *Qur'ān* 5:1

84 *Qur'ān* 49:11

85 *Qur'ān* 5:2

86 *Qur'ān* 3:97

87 Abū Ḥāmid Muḥammad ibn Muḥammad Ghazālī (d. 505/1111), "*Al-Mustaṣfā' min 'Ilm al-Uṣūl*" (Cairo: al-Maktabah al-Tijāriyyah, 1356/1937), v. 1 p. 42; Shawkānī, "*Irshād*" p. 6; Zuhaylī, "*Uṣūl*" p. 37-43.

88 *Qur'ān* 2:43

89 Ṣadr al-Sharī'ah, "*Al-Tawdīḥ*" v.1, p. 13; Isnawī, "*Sallam al-Wuṣūl*" v. 1, p. 24.

90 Herbert Lionel Adolphus Hart, "*The Concept of Law*" p. 77-96 quoted from Nyazee. *Ibid.*, p. 57-58.

91 Zuhaylī, *ibid.*, v. 1, p. 37; Khallāf, 'Abd al-Wahhāb (d. 1376/1956), "*'Ilm Uṣūl al-Fiqh*," 12th edn. (Kuwait: Dār al-Qalām, 1398/1978). See for the use of English terminology: Nyazee, *ibid.*; Kamali, "*Principles*," p. 321-353.

92 'Abd al-Raḥmān bin Jād Allah al-Bannānī, al-Maghribī (d. 1198/1784), "*Ḥāshiah 'alā Sharḥ Jalāl al-Dīn al-Maḥallī 'alā Jam' al-Jawāmī' li Ibn Subkī*" (Cairo: 1937), v. 1 p. 32; Molla Husraw, "*Mir'at al-Uṣūl*," v. 1 p. 50; Ṣadr al-Sharī'ah, "*Al-Tawdīḥ*," v. 1, p. 26. He did not use the word "*al-muktasabah*."

93 Bannānī, 'Abd al-Raḥmān bin Jād Allah al-Bannānī, al-Maghribī (d. 1198/1784), "*Ḥāshiah 'alā Sharḥ Jalāl al-Dīn al-Maḥallī 'alā Jam' al-Jawāmī' li Ibn Subkī*" (Cairo: Muṣṭafa Bābī al-Ḥalabī, 1937), v. 1 p. 33, Isnawī, "*Sallam al-Wuṣūl*," v. 1, p. 25. For more about *Sharī'ah* see: 'Abd al-Raḥmān I. Doi, "*Sharī'ah the Islamic Law*" (London: Ta Ha Publishers, 1997).

93 *Qur'ān* 2:43

94 Isnawī, "*Sallam al-Wuṣul*," v. 1, p. 26; Molla Husraw, "*Mar'at al-Uṣūl*," v. 1, p.

48-54.

[95] Ṣadr al-Sharī'ah, "*Al-Tawdīḥ*," v. 1 p. 26.

[96] Ibn al-Ḥājīb, "*Mukhtaṣar*," v. 1, p. 25; Ibn Amīr al-Ḥajj," *Al-Taqrīr wa al-Takhbīr*," v. 1 p. 20.

[97] Elias A. Elias,"*Elias Modern Dictionary*," 5th edition (Cairo: 1950); Joseph Catafago "*English* and *Arabic Dictionary*" (London: 1958); Hans Wehr "*A Dictionary of Modern Written Arabic*," edited by J. Milton Cowan, 4th edition (Germany: 1979).

[98] Zuhaylī, *ibid*., v. 1, p. 417.

[99] Isma'īl Sha'bān Muḥammad, "*Uṣūl al-Fiqh al-Muyassar*" (Cairo: Kitāb al-Jāmī' Tawfiqiyyah, 1994), v. 1, p. 47.

[100] Zuhaylī, *ibid*, v. 1, p. 417.

[101] Abū Isḥāq Ibrāhīm bin Mūsa al-Ghirnāṭī Shāṭibī (d. 790/1388), "*Al Muwāfaqāt fi-Uṣūl al-Sharī'ah*," ed. 'Abd-Allah Diraz. (Beirut: Dār al-Ma'rifah), v. 3 p. 36.

[102] Abū 'Ali Badr al-Dīn Muḥammad bin 'Ali Shawkānī (d. 1250/1834), "*Irshād al-Fuḥul ilā Taḥqīq al-Ḥaq min 'Ilm al-Uṣūl*" (Cairo: 1937), p. 47; Abū al-'Aynayn Badrān, "*Uṣūl al-Fiqh al-Islāmi*" (Alexandria: Muassasah Shabāb al-Jāmi'ah, 1404/1984), p. 53.

[103] Badrān, "*Uṣūl al-Fiqh al-Islāmi*," p. 54-55.

[104] 'Ali bin Abī 'Ali Muḥammad bin Sālim Al-Tha'labī, Sayf al-Dīn Al-Āmidī (d. 631/1233), "*Al-Ihkām fi Uṣūl al-Ahkām*," ed. 'Abd al-Razzāq 'Afifi, 2nd ed. (Beirut: Maktabah al-Islāmi, 1402/1982), v. 1, p. 260.

[105] Controversial sources number as many as 45. (See Ṭūfi, "*Risalah al-Maṣlaḥah*") 19 of them, as Qāsimi indicated, were *dalāil* quoted from Qarafi (d. 684/1285); Qāsimī then discovered 26 more by the way of induction (*istiqrā*). See: Kaşif Hamdi Okur "*Maqāṣid ve Ictihād*," in *Islamic Legal Philosophy Researches* (Konya: Yediveren, 2002), p. 275.

[106] *Qur'ān* 4:59

[107] Kamali, "*Principles*," p. 10.

[108] Mollah Husraw, "*Mir'āt al-Uṣūl*," v. 1 p. 56; Isnawī, "*Sallam al-Wuṣūl*," v. 1, p. 27.

[109] 'Uthmān b. 'Amr b. Abū-Bakr b. Yūnus Abū 'Amr Jamāl al-Dīn Ibn Ḥājib (d. 646/1249), "*Mukhtaṣar Muntahā' al-Sūl wa al-'Āmal* " (Constantinople: al-Maktabah al-Islāmiyyah, 1310), v. 1 p. 4.

[110] Al-Razi, *al-Mahsul fil 'ilm Usul al-Fiqh*, v. 1, p. 80.

[111] Al-Ghazālī, *al-Muṣṭaṣfā min 'ilm al-Usul*, vol. 1, p. 3-4.

[112] *Qur'an* 2:127.

[113] Muṣṭafā Aḥmad Al-Zarqā' *Al-Madkhal al-Fiqhī al-'Āmm*, 9th ed. (Damascus: Dār al-Fikr, 1968), v. 2, p. 924.

[114] Mohamad Akram Laldin, "*Islamic Law an Introduction*," (Kuala Lumpur: Research Centre of IIUM, 2006), p. 128-129.

[115] Kamali, *Principles*, p. 5-6.

[116] Ahmed Akgündüz, "*Introduction to Islamic Law*," (Istanbul: Pasifik Ofset, 2010), p. 249.

[117] Ibn Mājah Abū 'Abd Allah Muḥammad (d. 273/886), "*Sunan*," ii, 784, *ḥadīth* no: 2340, Istanbul, 1981.

[118] Al-Zarqā', *ibid*., v. 2, p. 969; Laldin, *ibid*., p. 131.

[119] Al-Zarqā', *ibid*., v. 2, p. 969; Laldin, *ibid*., p. 131-134.

CHAPTER TWO

The Sources of Islamic Law

Introduction

As it has been discussed some definitions of the composition of the principles of Islamic jurisprudence (*uṣūl al-fiqh*) in the introductory chapter, the fundamental source of Islamic law will be discussed here in details for certain extend.

Basically, all rulings of Islamic law are based ultimately on the *Qur'ān* and the *Sunnah*. In other words, the *aḥkām shar'īyyah* (legal rules) are produced using particular methods and mechanisms which are applied to the general rules given originally by Allah Himself.

Islamic legal theory is, in general, based on four sources[1] – the *Qur'ān*, the *Sunnah*, *ijmā'* (consensus), and *qiyās* (analogy) – which are unanimously accepted by all the *Sunnī* schools of law. *Shī'ī* and *Ẓāhirī* legal theory is different.[2]

The *Qur'ān* is the first source of law for Muslims who seek guidance. If one finds the answer within the *Qur'ān* there is no need to resort to other sources. However, if one does not find his answers within the *Qur'ān*, one should seek enlightenment from the *Sunnah*. Nevertheless, the exact indication of the rulings of the *Qur'ān* can only be understood by the explanation of the *Sunnah*. Without recourse to the *Sunnah* the *ḥukm* remain unexplained. The *Sunnah* also prevents the *Qur'ān* from being misunderstood and protect it from making misleading interpretations. If the required knowledge is not obtained from these two sources, one should look to *ijmā'* (consensus) for an answer; if the desired information is still not forthcoming, one must finally turn to *qiyās* (analogy).

The *ḥadīth* below, narrated from Mu'ādh ibn Jabal (d. 18/640), shows the sequence in which rulings are to be sought from the sources. Explaining the methodology of the jurists in discovering and applying the law, scholars usually quote this Tradition. When the Prophet (ṣ) intended to send Mu'ādh ibn Jabal to Yemen, the Prophet (ṣ) asked him: "How will you judge when the occasion of deciding a case arises?" He replied: "I shall judge in accordance with Allah's book." The Prophet (ṣ) asked: "What will you do if you do not find guidance in Allah's book?" He replied: "I will act in accordance with the *Sunnah* of the Messenger of Allah." The Prophet (ṣ) asked: "What will you do if you do not find guidance in the *Sunnah* of the Apostle of Allah and in Allah's Book?" He replied: "I shall do my best to form an opinion and spare no pains in my search for truth." The apostle of Allah then patted him on the chest and said: "Praise be to Allah who helped the messenger of the Apostle of Allah to find an answer which pleases the Apostle of Allah."[3]

Also, the same method of discovering and applying the law was used by the Companions of the Prophet (ṣ).[4] Mihrān bin Maymūn reports that Abū Bakr (d. 13 AH) referred to the *Qur'ān* whenever a claimant-defendant asked him for guidance. If he was unable to find the result in the *Qur'ān,* he would then seek a judgment in the *Sunnah.* Failing to discover the answer within these sources, he would then consult the righteous men of the community who would convene to discuss the matter and arrive at a solution. If they arrived at an opinion which was unanimously accepted, the consensus was that he should judge accordingly. 'Umar and other companions of the Prophet (ṣ) applied these methods of judgment and consequently the Muslim community also accepted this procedure.[5]

This shows that Islamic law is able to find answers for human problems and develops itself naturally. Based on Mu'ādh's answer, "*I shall do my best to form an opinion and spare no pains*" can we say that human opinion influences Islamic law? Is this a proof that Islamic law can deal with any issues relating to human life? And, is Islamic law itself developing further and evolving over time?

It was mentioned that Islamic law has specific sources or evidences to rely upon for deducing rules. Therefore briefly it was elaborated that one of the main features of the Islamic *sharīʻah* is that it is based on evidence or proof deduced from the *Qur'ān* or the *Sunnah* through *ijtihād* which conforms to these two sources of Islamic law. Consequently, it can be stated that the sources of Islamic law are mainly either revelation or non-revelation[6]:

Revelation is considered to be of two types:

1. *Al-waḥy al-matlū* or *waḥy ẓāhir* (recited or manifest revelation), which is defined as communication from Allah to the Prophet Muḥammad (ṣ), conveyed by the angel Gabriel, i.e. the *Qur'ān.*
2. *Al-waḥy ghair al-matlū* or *waḥy bāṭin* (un-recited or internal revelation). This consists of the inspiration (*ilhām*) of concepts only: Allah inspired the Prophet (ṣ) and the latter conveyed the concepts in his own words, i.e. the *Sunnah,* which comprises the sayings *aḥādīth* of the Prophet (ṣ).[7]

Non-revelation refers to *ijmāʻ* (consensus of *mujtahidīn* of the Muslim community), *qiyās* (analogy) or *istidlāl* (inference). In addition, Imām al-Shāṭibī (d. 790/1388) divided the sources of the *sharīʻah* into two types: either pure transmitted (*al-naql al-maḥḍ*) or pure opinion (*al-ra'y al-maḥḍ*). Opinion (*ra'y*) is not considered a source of *sharīʻah* unless it is based on transmitted proof[8].

Another classification of *adillah sharīʻah* is the *qaṭʻī* (definitive) and the *ẓannī* (speculative).[9]

The *adillah sharīʻah* have also been categorized into transmitted (*naqlī*) and rational (*aqlī*). The transmitted proofs, *adillah naqliyyah,* are the *Qur'ān,* the *Sunnah,* and *ijmāʻ*. Two other transmitted proofs are the rulings of the Companions and the laws revealed prior to the advent of Islam (*shar' man qablanā*). Rational proofs are *adillah 'aqliyyah* namely *qiyās*, *istiṣḥāb*, etc.[10] *Adillah* is further classified by al-Āmidī (d. 631/1233) into *mustaqil* (independent) – such as the first three sources of the *sharī'ah* and *muqayyad* (dependent).[11]

In general, and more practical sense, the sources of the *sharī'ah* (*al-maṣādir al-sharī'ah*) are further divided into two types:

A. Unanimously accepted sources (The Primary sources): 1. the *Qur'ān*, 2. the *Sunnah*, 3. *ijmā'*, (consensus), 4. *qiyās* (analogy).

B. Controversial sources (The Secondary sources): 1. *Istiḥsān* 2. *Maṣlaḥah mursalah* (consideration of public interest), 3. *Istiṣḥāb* (presumption of continuity), 4. *qawl al-ṣaḥābī* (the sayings of a companion of the Prophet), 5. *'urf* (custom), 6. *sadd al-dharā'i'* (blocking the means), 7. *shar' man qablanā* (revealed laws preceding to the *sharī'ah* of Islam) and 8. *istiqrā'* (induction).

The sources of *sharī'ah* are identified in the *Qur'ān* as follows: "O you who believe! Obey Allah and obey the Messenger (Muḥammad) and those of you (Muslims) who are in authority. (And) if you differ in anything amongst yourselves refer it to Allah and His Messenger."[12] The reference to *Qur'ān* is pointed out in the verse as "*Obey Allah*" and the reference to the *Sunnah* as "*Obey the Messenger.*" *Ijmā'* is also referred to in the idea of obedience to "*Those of you who are in authority*" and the last part of the verse "*If you differ in anything amongst yourselves refer it to Allah and His Messenger*" which requires the referral of disagreement to Allah and His Messenger, is in effect a clear authorisation for the principle of *qiyās*.[13]

The Qur'ān

The first unanimously accepted source of Islamic law is the *Qur'ān* which is not only the first source of Islamic law but also, as far as it is concerned, is the only source and all other sources are explanatory to the *Qur'ān*. Alternatively, all other sources are dependent on the

Qur'ān in respect of the focal principle of Islamic law. However, in terms of interpretation of the *Qur'ān*, and to know its indicaations the *Sunnah* is essential and unavoidable.

Definition of the Qur'ān: The Qur'ān in 'ilm al-uṣūl al-fiqh:

The theologians when discussing the attributes of Allah, define *Qur'ān* as the meaning of the essence of Allah expressed in utterances or words, yet the *'ulamā' al-uṣūl* treat the *Qur'ān* as a connection of utterances from which *aḥkām* (practical rules) may be derived. Here the utterances are Arabic words. The scholars defined the *Qur'ān* follows:

It is Arabic utterance or words indicating or explaining the meaning of the speech of Allah sent down to the Prophet (ṣ), conveyed by the Angel Gabriel and written in the book, transmitted to us by *tawātur* (continuous testimony) starts with the *sūrah al-fātiḥah* and concludes with *sūrah an-nās*.

It is a proof of the prophecy of Muḥammad (ṣ), the most authoritative guide for Muslims and the first source of the *sharī'ah.*[14] It should be noted that some words of non-Arabic origin occur in the *Qur'ān* but this usage is confined to odd words. A phrase or a sentence of non-Arabic origin does not occur in the *Qur'ān.*[15]

Characteristics of the Qur'ān

The definition of the *Qur'ān* reveals the following obvious characteristics:

a. Any speech other than that of Allah is excluded.
b. Any non-Arabic speech of the previously revealed books is excluded.
c. Any Arabic non-revealed speech including the *Sunnah* and *ḥadīth qudsī*[16] is excluded.
d. Any part that is not established by continuous testimony, such as variant readings, is excluded.

e. Any revelation sent down without the challenge of *i'jāz* (inimitability) such as previous revelations and the *Sunnah* is excluded.[17]

Aḥkām (ordinances) of the Qur'ān

The *Qur'ān* ordinance /legislation cover several aspects of the life of the *mukallaf* (the subject). The *aḥkām* include the following types:

1. *Aḥkām i'tiqādīyyah* (creed/ convictional).
2. *Aḥkām khuluqīyyah* (ethical and moral).
3. *Aḥkām 'amalīyyah* (practical)

The third type of *aḥkām* (*aḥkām 'amalīyyah*) is related to sayings, actions, contracts and behaviour of the *mukallaf* (the subject). Thus *aḥkām 'amalīyyah* is the *fiqh* of the *Qur'ān* and is the aim of *'ilm uṣūl al-fiqh* (principles of jurisprudence). They are classified into two types:

a. *Aḥkām al-'ibādāt* (worship or devotional matters) which regulate the relationship between the *mukallaf* and his Allah such as prayers, fasting, *zakāt* (alms), *ḥajj* (pilgrimage).
   The *aḥkām* in the *Qur'ān* about *'ibādāt* (worshipping) consists of approximately 90 verses.[18]
b. *Aḥkām al-mu'āmalāt* (transactions) which regulate the dealings of the *mukallaf* with others as individuals or groups, such as commercial, civil, criminal, constitutional, international, economical and financial legislations.[19] Of these, family matrimonial law accounts for 70 verses; law of contracts and torts accounts for 70 verses; judiciary 13 verses; criminal law 30 verses; administrative law 10 verses; international law 25 verses and fiscal law about public revenues, public expenditures altogether are 317 verses.[20]

The Sunnah

The concept of the *Sunnah* is also unanimously accepted as the second source of Islamic law (*sharī'ah*). The *Sunnah* of the Prophet (ṣ) is a proof of Islamic law, and attests to the *Qur'ān's* authority. As the *Qur'ān* indicates the Prophet's teachings are also divinely inspired. "*Nor does he speak of (his own) desire. It is only a revelation revealed.*"[21]

Therefore, the Prophet's words are *ḥujjah* (*dalīl*, evidence, proof) for Muslims; and may have power like that of the *Qur'ān*. The *Qur'ān* commands submission to the Prophet (ṣ) and makes it a sense of duty for Muslims to bow to its judgment and its authority without question. As is indicated in the *Qur'ān*: "*And whatever the Messenger (Muḥammad) gives you, take it and whatsoever he forbids you, abstain*"[22] "*He who obeys the Messenger (Muḥammad), has indeed obeyed Allah*"[23].

The word *Sunnah* is derived from the root verb *s-n-n*, which the 'Arabs used to describe the continuous and gentle flow of water; the water flows so gently it appears as one cohesive body.[24] The literal meaning was used by 'Arabs to describe a clear path or to imply a customary practice, or an established route of conduct whether good or bad; this conduct was set by an individual or a community. It refers to way, custom and habit of life, whether it be good or bad. The *ḥadīth* of the Prophet (ṣ) indicates this meaning as he said: "Whosoever does a good *Sunnah* in Islam, he will get the reward for it and the reward from other people doing the same thing until the Day of Judgment. And whosoever does a bad *Sunnah* in Islam, he will have the punishment from doing it and the punishment of others who practice it"[25]

The opposite of the *Sunnah* is *bid'ah* (innovation), which is characterised by lack of precedent or continuity with the past. Azharī (d. 370/980) maintains that *Sunnah* is the good path only, hence the term *ahl al-Sunnah* which means those who follow the *Sunnah* correctly.[26] It also means "The trodden path and was used by the pre-Islamic 'Arabs to denote the model behaviour established by the forefathers of a tribe."[27]

As a general legislative term, the *Sunnah* is used to imply the practical reality of Islamic *sharī'ah* and its concepts, whether it came from the *Qur'ān*, *ḥadīth* or was deduced from these two sources. In this manner, the *Sunnah* includes *khabar* (news or report) and *athar* about the Prophet (ṣ) and the precedent of the Companions.

The *Muḥaddithīn* (narrators) refer to the *Sunnah* as all that is narrated from the Prophet (ṣ), his acts, his sayings and whatever he has tacitly approved, in addition, all of the reports describing his physical attributes and characters before and after the revelation.[28]

Suyūṭī (d. 911/1505) reports Ibn Ḥanbal (d. 241/855) as saying "For us the *Sunnah* refers to *athar* (impressions, impacts) of the Prophet (ṣ), the *Sunnah* is the *tafsīr* (interpretation) of the *Qur'ān* and it is the *dalā'il* (indications or proofs) of the *Qur'ān*."[29]

'Ulamā' of fiqh: the main concern for these scholars is to search for the *ḥukm* (ruling) of *sharī'ah* with regard to the acts of an individual or group. For these *'ulamā'*, the *Sunnah* primarily refers to "*Al-Ṭarīqah al-muttaba'ah* (the path followed or the way shown) in the religion, excluding *farḍ* / *wājib* (obligatory)." Laknawī (d.

1304/1886) defines the *Sunnah* as an act which, when it is performed results in *thawāb* (reward) and when it is not performed, results in *'itāb* (blame) but not in *'iqāb* (punishment).[30] According to Baiḍāwī (d. 685/1286), the *Sunnah* refers to the *mandūb* (commendable), which he defines as any act that will gain praise for the dutiful person and will not lay blame on the one who abandons the duty; such an act is called both *Sunnah* and *nāfilah.*[31]

'Ulamā' of uṣūl al-fiqh: the main concern for the *'ulamā'* of *uṣūl al-fiqh* is to search for a *dalīl shar'ī* (legal proof) with regards to the *aḥkām al-shar'īyyah* (juristic rulings). Their search into the life of the Prophet (ṣ) is based on his position as messenger of Allah conveying the laws that govern the lives of people. The Prophet (ṣ) set the principles for *mujtahidīn* (competent jurists) after him.

Consequently their interest in the life of the Prophet (ṣ) is in his *aqwāl* (sayings), *af'āl* (acts) and tacit *taqrīr* (approval) of the acts or sayings of the Companions. They believe that the *aḥkām* legislate them as the second source of *sharī'ah* next to the *Qur'ān.* For the *'ulamā' of uṣūl al-fiqh*, the *Sunnah* refers to whatever came from the Prophet (ṣ) in the form of a saying, act or tacit approval, other than the *Qur'ān*[32].

The juristic usage of the *Sunnah* has two different meanings. According to the *'ulamā' of uṣūl al-fiqh*, *Sunnah* refers to a source of the *sharī'ah* (Islamic law) where legal proofs accompany the *Qur'ān.* According to the *'ulamā' of fiqh* (juristic scholars), the *Sunnah* primarily refers to a legal value, which falls under the category of *mandūb.*

Types of the Sunnah

The *Sunnah* is mainly classified in two types: the *Sunnah* which the *aḥkām* are derived is also called the classification of the *Sunnah* based on its nature. The *Sunnah* which is transmitted to us. This type is called the classification of the *Sunnah* based on its written record that is the classification of *ḥadīth.* The word *Sunnah* is more comprehensive than *ḥadīth.* Thus, the word *ḥadīth* has a meaning narrower than that of *Sunnah.* Some traditional scholars use the term *ḥadīth* synonyms with *ḥadīth* that is reported from the Prophet (ṣ) in terms of words, acts and approvals.[33] Accordingly, the scholars of *ḥadīth* (*muḥaddithūn*) consider the division of *ḥadīth* based on the quantity of narrators who transmitted the *ḥadīth* of the Prophet (ṣ) and based on the quality of the narrators who narrated the *ḥadīth.*

Types of the *Sunnah*

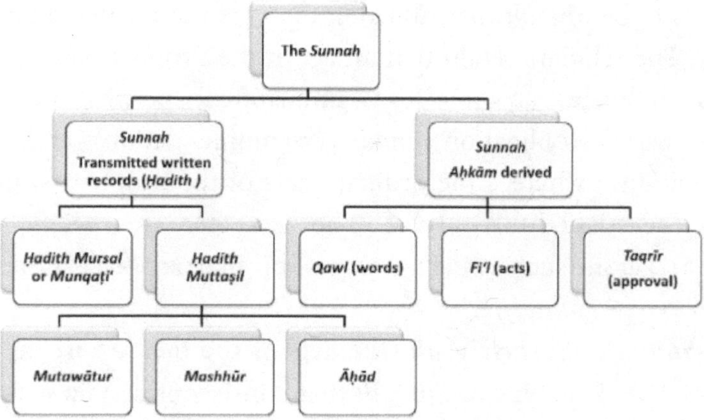

The *Sunnah* which the *aḥkām* are derived: It is the *Sunnah* that the *aḥkām* are derived is also called the classification of the *Sunnah* based on its nature. This type of *Sunnah* is of three types. These are *Sunnah qawliyyah* (sayings of the Prophet (ṣ)), *Sunnah fi'liyyah* (acts of the Prophet (ṣ)) and the *Sunnah taqrīriyyah* (the tacit approval given by the Prophet (ṣ)).

***Al-Sunnah al-Qawliyyah* (the saying of the Prophet** (ṣ)): This type of *Sunnah* is consisting of the sayings of the Prophet (ṣ) which the law or the explanation of the *aḥkām* are derived. Thus not every saying of the Prophet (ṣ) is a source of law. In order to be a source of law, the intention of the saying should be the placing of the law or its explanation. For example, "Entitlement to revenue depends on a corresponding liability for loss" (*al-kharāj bi-ḍḍimān*); "The (reward of) acts, depend upon the intentions" (*innamā al-a'māl bi-nniyāt*); "no harm shall be inflicted nor reciprocated in Islam" (*lā ḍarara walā ḍirār*) are considered *sunnah qawliyyah.*

***Al-Sunnah al-fi'liyyah* (the acts of the Prophet** (ṣ)**)**: This type of *Sunnah* contains the acts of the Prophet (ṣ) that regards to a legal content, such as his fasting, his prayer and his performance of *ḥajj*. The act of the Prophet (ṣ) is considered in the following types: 1. The ordinary physical acts that can be performed by every human being such as drinking, walking, sitting etc. Although some jurists consider such acts to be *mubaḥ* (permissible), they are not meant to place any rulings. The scholars retain that an act of the Prophet (ṣ) concerning rulings indicate absolute or unqualified permission, which include *wujūb* (obligation), *nadb* (recommendation) and *ibāḥah* (permissibility) whereas the ordinary acts of the Prophet (ṣ) indicate *ibāḥah* (permissibility) only. 2. The acts that are specific to the Prophet (ṣ) alone such as the number of his marriages. 3. The acts that regards to new rulings.

***Al-Sunnah al-taqrīriyyah* (the acts of the tacit approval of the Prophet** (ṣ)**)**: This type of *Sunnah* that consists of certain acts of the Companions and the maintenance of silence by the Prophet (ṣ) without expressing disapproval. His silence is called *taqrīr* (tacit approval) which is considered a *sunnah* that becomes a source for the permissibility of an act or a statement. The Companions often referred their case through statements such as "we used to do such-and-such while the Prophet (ṣ) was alive".[34]

The *Sunnah* which is written records (*Ḥadīth*): This type is called the classification of the *Sunnah* based on its written records with respect to its modes of transmission which is considered with mainly two types: *ḥadīth muttaṣil* (continuous) and *ḥadīth mursal* or *munqaṭi'* (discontinued). As it is mentioned above, the scholars of *ḥadīth* (*muḥaddithūn*) consider the division of *ḥadīth* based on the quantity of narrators who transmitted the *ḥadīth* of the Prophet (ṣ) and based on the quality of the narrators who narrated the *ḥadīth*. In terms of quality it is classified into two types namely *maqbūl* and *mardūd ḥadīth*. The *maqbūl ḥadīth* consists of *ṣaḥīḥ* (authentic), *ḥasan* (good) while the *mardūd ḥadīth* consists of *ḍaīf* (weak). Additionally, *ḥadīth* that is based on the origin of narrators is considered three types, *marfūʿ*, *mawqūf* and *maqtūʿ*. This category specifies whether a narration is attributed to the Prophet (ṣ), the Companions, and the Successors or a latter comer in sequence.

In addition to that, in terms of compilation of *ḥadīth* (*tadwīn al-aḥādīth*), in *ḥadīth* literature it's found that there are two types of compilations, namely *musnad* and *muṣannaf*. In *musnad* collections, the collected *aḥadīth* are arranged alphabetically under the names of the Companions on whose authority these *aḥadīth* were reported such as the *Musnad* of Ibn Ḥanbal (d. AH 241/855 CE), while in *muṣannaf* collections, *aḥadīth* are recorded under various headings dealing with juridical subjects such as *al-Ṣiḥaḥ al-Sittah* (The Six Authentic Books of *Ḥadīth*), namely the compilations of Al-Bukhārī (d. AH 256/870 CE), al-Muslim (d. AH 261/874 CE), Ibn Mājah (d. AH 273/886 CE), Abū Dāwūd (d. AH 275/889 CE), Al-Tirmīdhī (d. AH 279/892 CE), and An-Nasāʾī (d. AH 303/916 CE). However, it's known that Imām Mālik (d. AH 179/795 CE) was the first to undertake the comprehensive and systematic compilation of *aḥādīth*. His work is known as *Al-Muwaṭṭā*ʾ (The Trodden Path) and later on the other compilations followed to came into existence.

It's very important to note that the Companions played an important role in learning and teaching the *aḥādīth* of the Prophet (ṣ) and they used all the methods applied by the Prophet (ṣ) himself to teach the *Sunnah*, and they committed *aḥadīth* of the Prophet (ṣ) to memorize. At the early state of the revelation the Companions paid all their attention to preserve the *Qur'ān*. Despite of the prohibition of writing down of the *aḥādīth* of the Prophet (ṣ) at the early stage, the Companions later on began to write down the *aḥādīth* of the Prophet (ṣ) when there was no anymore fear of abandoning the *Qur'ān* and yet the Prophet (ṣ) approved of writing down his *aḥādīth*. Accordingly, there were many Companions recorded *aḥādīth* of the Prophet (ṣ) and later on especially during the reign of 'Umar ibn 'Abdul 'Azīz (AH 97-101/715-19 CE), in the beginning of the second century of the *Hijrah*, *aḥadīth* were collected and written down by significant scholars from different part of the Muslim territories.

The *ḥadīth muttaṣil* (continuous) whose chain of narration (*isnād*) is complete. This type of *ḥadīth* has a complete chain of transmission in which the narrators are mentioned from the last narrator all the way back to the Prophet (ṣ) and no narrator is missing. The majority of scholars have divided the continuous *ḥadīth* into the three categories of *mutawātir* (continuously recurrent), *mashhūr* (well-known) and *āḥād* (solitary).

Ḥadīth Mutawātir: *Mutawātir* literally means continuously recurrent. Technically it means a report by an indefinite number of people related in such a way as to preclude the possibility of their agreement to maintain a lie. This possibility is inconceivable owing to their large number, diversity of residence, and reliability.[35] This type of *ḥadīth* applies to the complete chain of transmission in which the narrators are mentioned from the last narrator all the way back to the Prophet (ṣ), for example: "acts are determined by intention, and to each person belongs what he intends". Including the reports about the rates of *zakāt* and the number of the daily prayers.

The *tawātur* is considered in two types, *tawātur* in words or verbal *mutawātir* (*tawātur bil lafẓ*) and *tawātur* in meaning or conceptual *mutawātur* (*tawātur bil ma'na*). If however, all the narrators are in agreement about the two types of *tawātur*, in words and meaning, the *ḥadīth* indicates *tawātur* by its very words.

***Tawātur* in words or verbal *mutawātir* (*tawātur bil lafẓ*)**: All the reports must be identical on the exact wording of the *ḥadīth* as they were uttered by the Prophet (ṣ) himself. For example the *ḥadīth* which is reported Abū Hurairah as the Prophet (ṣ) said: "Whoever deliberately lies about me must prepare himself for a place in Hell-fire."[36] This type of *mutawātir* is very rare occurrence compared to the other type of *mutawātir*. The exact number of the verbal *mutawātir* is a subject of disagreement, despite the fact that it does not exceed ten *aḥadīth*.[37]

***Tawātur* in meaning or conceptual *mutawātir* (*tawātur bil ma'na*)**: This is when the reports of a large number of the transmitters of *ḥadīth* agree in their meaning but differ in wording or in form, only their common meaning is considered *mutawātir*. This kind of *mutawātir* is numerous in the *ḥadīth*. The acts and sayings of the Prophet (ṣ) were witnessed by a large number of the Companions and their reports have been transmitted by multitudes of people throughout the ages related to the manner of performing the obligatory prayers, the rituals of *ḥajj*, fasting, the quantities of *zakāt*, the implementation of *ḥudūd* and rules relating to retaliation (*qiyās*), etc. Therefore, the verbal and actual *Sunnah* explain the essence of the live of the Prophet (ṣ).[38]

When the issue comes to the value (*ḥukm*) of the *mutawātir*, it is indicated by the majority of scholars that the authority of a *mutawātir ḥadīth* is equivalent to that of the *Qur'ān*. The universal continuous testimony (*tawātur*) creates certainty (*yaqīn*) and the knowledge that generates is equivalent to knowledge that is attained through sense-perception.[39]

There are certain conditions in order a report to be classified as *mutawātir* only when it fulfils the following conditions of which firstly must be met from the origin of the report to the very end:[40]

1. The report that was narrated by reporters must be based on knowledge that is attained through sense-perception, if otherwise, is not considered *mutawātir*.[41]
2. The chain of transmitters is sufficiently long and in every period or generation must be large enough to preclude their

conclusion in propagating falsehood. Thus the number of transmitters is satisfactory.[42] Some scholars have attempted to specify a minimum number varying from as low as four to as many as twenty, forty and seventy up into the hundreds. All these specification are based on analogical deduction such as the requirement of four is based on the similar number of witnesses which constitute legal proof; twenty is an analogy to the verse from the *Qur'ān* in *sūrah al-Anfāl* which is "*If there are twenty steadfast men among you, they will overcome two hundred [fighters]*"[43], etc. however, the majority opinion, which is represented by al-Ghazālī, reveals that all the analogies are arbitrary and have no bearing on the point. The knowledge, confirmatory evidence and trust-worthiness of reporters that must be credited even in cases where the actual number of reporters is not very large. Thus, certainty is not necessarily a question of numbers.[44]

3. The transmitters are not biased in their cause and are not associated with one another through a political or sectarian movement.
4. The transmitters are identifiable and are known to possess the qualities of good Muslims, must be upright person, pious, trustworthy, and they must neither be infidels nor profligates (*kuffār wal-fussāq*).

The *mutawātir ḥadīth* conveys definitive knowledge (*'ilm qaṭ'ī*) and is also definitive with respect to its authenticity. The *mutawātir ḥadīth* is therefore, *qaṭ'ī* with respect to knowledge as well as *thubūt*. With that respect, *qaṭ'ī al-thubūt* means that we are certain about its narration from the Prophet (ṣ).[45]

Ḥadīth Mashhūr: It is the type of *ḥadīth* which is one the number whose reporters do not reach the level of *tawātur* in the first generation. Despite the fact that a *ḥadīth* which is originally reported by one, two or more Companions from the Prophet (ṣ) or from another Companion but has later become well-known (*mashhūr*) as later as the second or even the third century of *Hijrah* and narrated by an indefinite number of people from the next generation, Successors (*Tābi'ūn*). It is necessary that the transmission of the report should have taken place during the first or the second generation following the demise of the Prophet (ṣ).[46] This type of *ḥadīth* was added by the *Ḥanafīs* who consider it lesser in strength than the *mutawātir ḥadīth* but stronger than the *khabar wāḥid*. The *ḥadīth* about the prohibition of marrying the maternal or paternal aunt of an existing wife belongs to this type of *ḥadīth*.[47] "No woman shall be married simultaneously with her paternal or maternal aunt"[48] which has qualified the general provisions of the *Qur'ān* on marriage in *sūrah al-Nisā'*[49]. Also the following *ḥadīth* is considered within this category. "The killer shall not inherit" (*lā yarithu al-qātil*) which qualifies the general conditions of the *Qur'ān* on inheritance in *sūrah al-Nisā'*.[50]

***Ḥadīth Āḥād* (Solitary *ḥadīth*)**: Linguistic and technical sense of this type of *ḥadīth* is confusing since *āḥād* refers to a meaning of "one" in the language, but technically it is a *ḥadīth* which has not met the requirements *mutawātir*. Therefore, the *ḥadīth āḥād* or the *khabar wāḥid* is reported by one or two narrators from the beginning of its chain up to the end of the compilation of the traditions. Therefore, the narrators do not reach the level of *tawātur* in either of the first three periods that of the Companions (*Ṣaḥabah*), the Successors (*Tābi'ūn*) and the Successors of the Successors (*Tab'Tābi'ūn*). Since all the traditions were compiled and all became well-known, no reference is given afterwards.

Imām Shāfi'ī refers to it as *khabar al-khāṣṣah*, which applies to every report narrated by one, two or more persons from the Prophet (ṣ) but which fails to fulfil the requirements of either the *mutawātir* or the *mashhūr*.[51] According to Imām Aḥmad Ibn Ḥanbal and some others, the *ḥadīth āḥād* can engender positive knowledge but it does not impart positive knowledge on its own unless it is supported by extraneous or circumstantial evidence. This is the view of the majority.[52] Although the majority of jurists agree that *āḥād* may establish a rule of law provided that it is related by a reliable narrator and the contents of the report are not offensive to reason, the *Ẓahirī* school unquestioningly accept the authority of the *ḥadīth āḥād.*[53]

In general, the jurists do not rely on the *ḥadīth āḥād* in matters of faith (*aqā'id*), but in matters of conduct which is covered by the *mu'āmalāt* that is the matter of *fiqh*. According to the majority of the scholars of the four *Sunnī* schools, acting upon the *ḥadīth āḥād* is obligatory even if the *ḥadīth āḥād* fails to engender positive knowledge since *ẓann* is sufficient as a basis of obligation in practical legal matters.[54] However, for a matters of belief must be founded in certainty since Allah indicates in *sūrah al-Najm* "*and verily conjecture does not avail against the truth at all*"[55]. Therefore, being conjectural, the *āḥād* does not establish the truth in matters of belief.

As we mentioned above, in terms of quality it is classified into two types namely *maqbūl* and *mardūd ḥadīth*. The *maqbūl ḥadīth* consists of *ṣaḥīḥ* (authentic), *ḥasan* (good) while the *mardūd ḥadīth* consists of *ḍaīf* (weak). This classification of the *āḥād ḥadīth* is based on the reliability and memory of the reporters. Thus these three types are considered part of the classification of the *āḥād ḥadīth.*

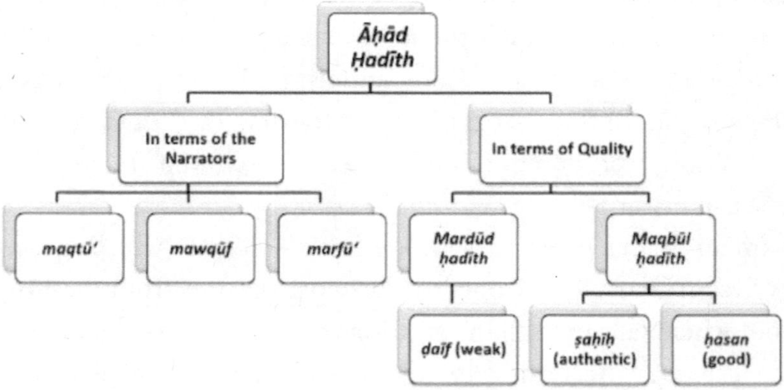

The *ṣaḥīḥ ḥadīth* (authentic): It is defined as a *ḥadīth* with a continuous chain (*isnād*) all the way back to the Prophet (ṣ) consisting of trustworthy (*amīn*), reliable (*'adl*) and upright persons who also possess strong memories and whose narration is free of irregular (*shādh*), defective (*mu'allal*) both obvious and of indirect faults.[56] The *mursal*, *munqaṭī'* and *mu'dhil aḥadīth* are excluded from the category of *ṣaḥīḥ ḥadīth* (authentic) due to the discontinued nature. The *mursal* is what the Successors (*Tābi'ūn*) have narrated from the Prophet (ṣ) without mentioning the Companions, while the *munqaṭī'* is when a single narrator is absent in one or more places in the chain (*isnād*) in one hand and the *mu'ḍal* is a *ḥadīth* where two or more narrators missing from one or more places in the chain (*isnād*) in the other hand.

The *ḥasan ḥadīth* (good): It is a *ḥadīth* that falls between *ṣaḥīḥ* (authentic) and *ḍa'īf* (weak), and despite its narrators are known for truthfulness, they have not attained the highest degree of reliability and prominence. They are among the truthful (*ṣadūq*) that is one who is not known to have committed a forgery or serious faults and they are accepted (*maqbūl*) which implies that there is no proof to the effect that his report is unreliable. Thus, *ḥasan ḥadīth* (good) is different from the *ṣaḥīḥ*.[57]

The *ḍa'īf ḥadīth* (weak): It is a *ḥadīth* whose narrators do not possess the qualifications required in *ṣaḥīḥ* (authentic) and *ḥasan* (good). It is weak because of a weakness that exists in its chain of narrators or in its textual contents, as well as its narrator is known to have not possess strong memories (*dhābit*), or his integrity and piety has been subjected to serious doubt. The *ḍa'īf ḥadīth* (weak) has variety of types such as *mursal* (whose chain of narration is incomplete), *shādh* (a *ḥadīth* with a poor *isnād*), *munkar* (a *ḥadīth* whose narrator cannot be classified to be upright and possess strong memories) and *muḍḍarib* (a *ḥadīth* whose contents are inconsistent with a number of other reports and none of which can be preferred over the others).[58]

The *ḥadīth mursal* or *munqaṭi'* (discontinued) whose chain of narration is incomplete and broken. Remember that the *Sunnah*, written records (*ḥadth*), has been considered mainly two types with respect to its modes of transmission: *ḥadīth muttaṣil* (continuous) and *ḥadīth mursal* or *munqaṭi'* (discontinued). The *ḥadīth* from which a narrator is missing is called *mursal* by the *Ḥanafīs* while a narrators among the Companions is missing is called *munqaṭi'* by the Traditionists (*Muḥāddithūn*). The *ḥadīth mursal,* is a *ḥadīth* whose chain of transmitters does not extend all the way back to the Prophet (ṣ), which consists of *mursal, munqaṭī'* and *mu'ḍal.*

The *mursal* is what the Successors (*Tābi'ūn*) have narrated from the Prophet (ṣ) directly without mentioning the Companions. According to al-Shawkānī, "The majority of scholars of *uṣūl* have defined *mursal* as a *ḥadīth* transmitted by one who has not met with the Prophet (ṣ) and yet quotes the Prophet (ṣ) directly. The transmitter may be a Successor or a follower or anyone after that."[59] However, the *munqaṭī'* is when a single narrator is absent in one or more places in the chain (*isnād*), while the *mu'ḍal* is a *ḥadīth* where two or more narrators missing from one or more places in the chain (*isnād*). The scholars agreed that these are not acceptable.[60]

The *ḥadīth qudsī*: It is what has been transmitted to us as isolated reports from the Prophet (ṣ) with its chain (*isnād*) going back to his Lord. Nevertheless, *ḥadīth* in all of its varieties consists of divine inspiration which is communicated in the words of the Prophet (ṣ) as it is indicated in the *Qur'ān* "*Nor does he speak out of desire. It is naught but revelation that is revealed*".[61] Not all the *ḥadīth* may be ranked on equal basis with the *Qur'ān* such as the prayer cannot be performed by reciting the *ḥadīth,* nor the recitation of *ḥadīth* is considered part of the *Qur'ān*. The *ḥadīth qudsī* is different from the other varieties of *ḥadīth* in form only. Despite the Prophet (ṣ) himself did not distinguish *ḥadīth qudsī* from other *aḥadīth*, the scholars introduced it as a separate category at around the fifth century of *Hijrah*. It is necessary to highlight here that, the *Qur'ān* which consists of manifest revelation (*waḥy ẓāhir*) and internal revelation (*waḥy bāṭin*). The manifest revelation (*waḥy ẓāhir*) is a communication from Allah to the Prophet Muḥammad (ṣ), conveyed by the angel Gabriel in the very words of Allah, while the internal revelation (*waḥy bāṭin*) is the inspiration (*ilhām*) that is inspired by Allah to the Prophet (ṣ) which conveys the concepts in his own words.[62]

Ijmā' (consensus)

The *Qur'ān* and the *Sunnah* are the main sources of Islamic law as mentioned above. *Ijmā'* is, in reality, subsidiary to them and applied when the original sources are silent on a certain problem. *Ijmā'* plays a very important role and undertakes the most essential role in the development of Islamic law in the history. *Ijmā'* is the third source of the *sharī'ah* as the following verses and *ḥadīth* indicate.

> The *Qur'ān*: "*O who believe! Obey Allah and obey the Messenger (Muḥammad) and those of you (Muslims) who are in authority. If you differ in anything amongst yourselves refer it to Allah and His Messenger, if you believe in Allah and in the Last Day. That is better and more suitable for final determination.*"[63]

There are different interpretations of *'ulūl amr* (those in authority). They can be leaders, commanders of an expedition, scholars, jurists, the Companions of the Prophet (ṣ), Abū Bakr and 'Umar, and the *Sulṭān*[64]. *'Ulūl amr*, according to Fakhr al-Dīn al-Rāzī (d. 606/1210), means the scholars.[65]

Shāfi'ī quotes the following *āyah* (verse) to support the authority for *ijmā'*.[66] "And hold fast all of you together the Rope of Allah (*Qur'ān*), and be not divided amongst yourselves"[67], In addition, here are some *aḥadīth*:

> "My community shall never agree on an error."[68]

> "Allah will not let my community agree upon an error."

"I beseeched Almighty Allah not to bring my community to the point of agreeing on *khaṭa'* (error) and He granted me this."

"The hand of Allah is with the community and (its safety) is not endangered by isolated oppositions."

"Whoever leaves the community or separates himself from it by the length of a span is breaking his bond with Islam."

"Whatever the Muslims deem to be good is good in the eyes of Allah."[69]

Definition of ijmā'

Ijmā' is the verbal noun of the Arabic word *ajma'a* (أجمع), which is derived from *(j-m-a',(*جمع*) ajma'a* (أجمع), *ijmā'* (إجماع). The root meaning of *ijmā'* (إجماع) is "to collect, to gather up, assemble, and congregate,"[70] as Allah indicates in the *Qur'ān* "*then resolve upon your affair and (gather) your associates*".[71]

Ijmā' has another meaning "composing and settling a thing that has been unsettled, as an opinion which one determines, resolves or decides upon." Therefore, it stands for determining, resolving or deciding an affair so as to make it firmly settled (after it had been unsettled in the mind). Alternatively after considering what might be its issues or result, and saying at one time 'I shall do this', and at another time, 'I shall do that'. Hence the phrase, (*ajma'tu 'alā al-amr* or *ajma'tu al-amr*) which means I determined, resolved and decided whom the affair.[72] The word *ajma'a* has another meaning, which is, to reach unanimous agreement. As an example: "*ajma'a al-qawm 'alā kadhā*" which means the people reached a unanimous agreement on such and such.[73]

Technical Definition: *ijmā'* is a unanimous agreement of the jurists of the Community of a particular era on a certain issue.[74]

The consensus of *mujtahids* (competent scholars) from the *ummah* of Muḥammad (ṣ), after the demise of him, in a determined period upon a rule of Islamic law (*ḥukm shar'ī*).

Āmidī (d. 631/1233) defines it as: the unanimous agreement of the *mujtahidīn* (competent scholars) of the Muslim community of any period following the demise of the Prophet Muḥammad (ṣ) on any matter.[75] Ghazālī's view on *ijmā'* is an agreement of the community of Muḥammad (ṣ) on a religious point.[76] Briefly *ijmā'* is defined as the "agreement of the scholars."[77] *Ijmā'* applies to all the religious legal questions and agreements on any point whatsoever (*amr* or *amrun mā*).[78] All problems relating to the *sharī'ah* are covered by *ijmā'*.

Types of ijmā'

Based on the way it is formed, *ijmā'* may be divided into two types: a) *ijmā' ṣarīḥ*, b) *ijmā' sukūtī.*[79]

a. *al-ijmā' al-ṣarīḥ* (explicit *ijmā' 'aẓīmah*): occurs when all *mujtahīds* (jurists) are united on a specific issue and express opinions which are unanimous. *'Aẓīmah* in the context of *ijmā'* means the agreement of Muslims on the essentials of Islam. It contains the fundamentals of religion over which there is no dispute, such as the necessity of prayer, fasting during *Ramaḍān*, the *ḥajj* (pilgrimage), prohibition of adultery, of usury, and of marrying one's own mother or sister, etc.

b. *al-ijmā' al-sukūtī* (tacit *ijmā' rukhṣah*): This occurs when some of the *mujtahidīn* (jurists) of the community express an opinion on disputed issue and others, after examining the expressed opinion remain silent. The silence is a sign of acceptance.[80] This kind of *ijmā'* is a presumptive *ijmā'*, which only creates a probability (*ẓann*).

Sarakhsī (d. 483/1090) states that Allah has not put the community in hardship, therefore the silence of scholars over an opinion will be considered sufficient for the validity of *ijmā'*.[81] Bazdawī (482/1089) indicates that *ijmā'* by silence is valid on two conditions: the opinion of a single scholar or a group of scholars should reach all the remaining scholars; and that the time of consideration of the disputed problem should lapse.[82] Ghazālī (d. 505/1111) rejected the validity of *ijmā' sukūtī* saying that tacit agreement was neither an *ijmā'* nor an authority.[83]

Ijmā' is also sub-divided into the following categories: 1. religious-legal (*shar'ī*), 2. worldly (*dunyawī or ghayr shar'ī*), 3. intellectual (*'aqlī*), 4. sensory (*ḥissī)* 5. customary (*'urfī*), 6. etymological (*lughawī*)[84].

Arkān (essential requirements) of ijmā'

It is obvious from the definition of *ijmā'* that the pillar or prerequisite of *ijmā'* is the consensus of the competent scholars (*ittifāq al-mujtahidīn*) and without a unanimous agreement no *ijmā'* will materialise. Similarly, the condition that all *mujtahidīn* should be from the Muslim community is in fact a condition that the *mujtahidīn* themselves have to fulfil and does not constitute an independent *rukn* of the agreement. Also, where there is only one *mujtahid* in the Muslim community or *mujtahidīn* of a certain locality, race, colour, school or following, no *ijmā'* is expected to materialise; nor does it constitute an essential requirement (*rukn*) of the agreement in question. They are merely conditions and controlling factors to achieve the agreement which is the pillar of *ijmā'*.[85] Ghazālī [86] maintained that the layman's opinion should be taken into account because of the *ḥadīth* "My community does not agree on error", which includes both laymen and *mujtahid*. *'Ismah* (infallibility, immunity from making errors) is a grace of Allah bestowed on the whole community and is the doctrinal basis of *ijmā'*.[87] Bazdawī (482/1089)[88] suggested that no discrimination should be made between the laymen and the jurists regarding the essentials of the faith; *ijmā'* is confined to the *mujtahidīn* only with regard to matters which require expert knowledge.

Qiyās (analogical deduction)

The fourth unanimous principle of Islamic law is analogy (*qiyās*) which is the developed version of opinion (*ra'y*). The tradition of Mu'ādh Ibn Jabal (d. 18/640),[89] which indicated earlier, is that the jurist was permitted to give his own opinion, and act upon it as a source of law for a solution.

Definition of qiyās

Qiyās (قياس) and *qā'is* are verbal nouns, which have the same meaning; measuring or ascertaining the amount, value or quality of something. It is derived from root *q-y-s* and that is why the scales are called *miqyās*. An Arabic idiom "*qāsat al-thawba bi al-dhirā'*" means the cloth was measured by the yardstick.[90]

Qiyās also means similarity, with a view to suggesting equality or similarity between two things whether sensible or moral. For example "I have compared this book with this book," "Zayd compares with Khālid in intelligence and descent," "this person is not evaluated with that person" which means they are not the same value. As the term *qiyās* is used for measuring and comparing, disagreement among *'ulamā'* emerged as to whether *qiyās* in both of the meanings are real or whether one is real and the other is metaphorical.[91]

In the *uṣūlī* (juristic) definition, technically, the *qiyās* is the extension or application of *sharī'ah* value from an original case (*aṣl*), to a new case (*far'*), where the latter has the same effective cause (*'illah*) as the former. The original case is regulated by a given text (the *Qur'ān* and the *Sunnah*), and *qiyās* seeks to extend the same textual ruling to a new case.[92]

In technical sense, more clearly it is defined as "the assignment of the *ḥukm* of an existing case found in the texts of the *Qur'ān*, the *Sunnah*, or *ijmā'* to a new case whose *ḥukm* is not found in these sources on the basis of a common underlying attribute called the *'illah* of the *ḥukm*".[93]

It is also defined as "the equality of a case, whose *ḥukm* is not mentioned explicitly in the texts, with a case whose *ḥukm* is mentioned, on the basis of the equality between the underlying causes found in the two cases".[94]

To explore the definition, the mujtahid renders two cases in terms of the *ḥukm*, when he sees a new case which has no *ḥukm* for it at the first stage. But he realizes the *'illah* of the new case matches with the *'illah* of the already existing case which the text of the *Qur'ān* or the *Sunnah*, or the *ijmā'* contain a case whose *'illah* is known to the *mujtahid*. Since the *ḥukm* of the original case has already been laid down, the *mujtahid* will assign the *ḥukm* of the existing case to the new case due to the common *'illah* (cause). The rendering equal or assignment is called *qiyās* in the methodology of the jurists.

Āmidī (d. 631/1233) gives some definitions of *qiyās* as follows: **a.** *qiyās* means attaining the truth, **b.** *qiyās* is the use of effort to derive the truth, **c.** *qiyās* stands for similitude, **d.** *qiyās* is an indication leading to the truth, **e.** *qiyās* is a knowledge acquired through reflection on a known case.[95]

Baqillānī (d. 403/1013) defines *qiyās* as: "To arrive at a judgement on *(ḥaml)* a known, using a precedent set with a previous, by establishing or rejecting a law on the basis of a connecting link (*amr jām'*)."[96] The *Ḥanafī* jurist, Ṣadr al-Sharī'ah ('Ubayd Allah bin Mas'ūd d.747/1346) defines *qiyās* as "extending the *sharī'ah* value from the original case (*aṣl*) over to the subsidiary (*far'*) by reason of an effective cause (*'illah*) which is common to both cases and which cannot be understood from the expression (concerning the original case) alone."[97]

Abū Bakr al-Jaṣṣāṣ (370/955) gave his own definition, stating "*Qiyās* is nothing but the return of the parallel case (*far'*) to the original (*aṣl*) on the bases of the idea or reason (*ma'nā'*) which combines both cases and necessitates equality between the rules of law about them."[98]

The main sphere for the operation of human judgement in *qiyās* is identification of a common *'illah* between the original and the new case. Once *'illah* is identified the rules of analogy necessitate the ruling of the text be followed without any interference or change.

Arkān of qiyās

The essential requirements (*arkān*) of *qiyās* as indicated in the above definitions are summarized with the following explanation.

The main requirement is the original case *(aṣl)*, namely a ruling given in the text, and which the analogy seeks to extend to a new case. The second requirement is the new case (*far'*) where a ruling is needed. The new case must not be covered by the text or *ijmā'* and must not result in altering the law of the text; this would mean over-ruling the text by *qiyās*. The third essential is the effective cause (*'illah*), which is an attribute (*waṣf*) of the *aṣl* and is found to be in common between the original and the new case. The final element is the rule (*ḥukm*) governing the original case, which is extended to the new case.

An example of *qiyās* is as follows:

> *"O you who believe! Intoxicants (all kinds of alcoholic drinks), and gambling, and al-ansāb, and azlām (arrows for seeking luck or decision) are an abomination of Satan's handiwork. So avoid (strictly all) that (abomination) in order that you may be successful."*[99]

In this verse, the drinking of wine is clearly forbidden. If this prohibition is extended by analogy to *nabīdh*, the original case (*aṣl*) would be wine that is forbidden by the *Qur'ān;* the parallel case (*far'*) is *nabīdh;* the cause (*'illah*) is intoxication, which is common to both cases, and the rule of law of the original case (*ḥukm*) is prohibition. *Nabīdh* is also forbidden because of the same cause (*'illah*), which is intoxication, according to the *naṣṣ* (text) "Every intoxicant is *khamr* and every *khamr* is forbidden."[100]

The *Ḥanafī* jurist Bazdawī (d. 482/1088) confined the essential requirements of *qiyās* to the common effective cause (*'illah*) alone. Both Bazdawī and Āmidī (d. 631/1233) are of the view that the result of *qiyās*, namely the *ḥukm al-far'* (ruling extended to the new case), should not be included in the essential requirements (*arkān*) of *qiyās*. Isnawī has, on the other hand, included the *ḥukm al-far'* in the essential requirements of *qiyās*.[101]

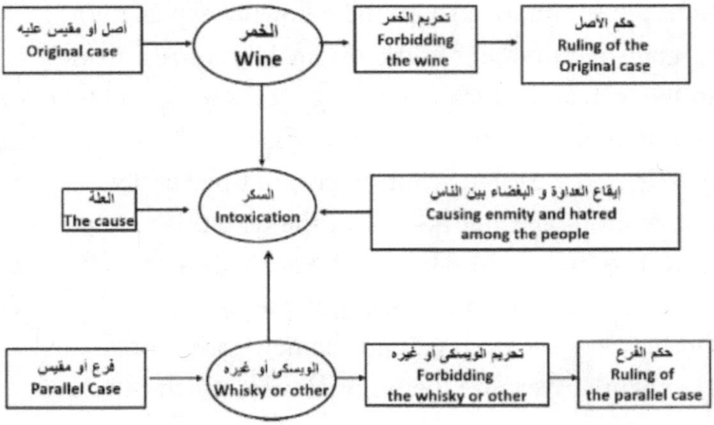

Variety of qiyās

Qiyās is divided into three categories based on the strength or weakness of *'illah* (cause).[102] Its types will be briefly illustrated.

1. ***Qiyās al-awlā* (analogy of the superior):** This is when the effective cause is more evident in the parallel case than the original case; it is then called *qiyās al-awlā*. Giving an example we can illustrate the *Qur'ān* text in respect of parents "*Say not to them (parents) a word of disrespect, nor shout at them but address them in terms of honour.*"[103] From this one may understand that rebuking or beating them is prohibited too, and in fact is even more obvious than verbal abuse – a deduction made based on analogy.

2. ***Qiyās al-musāwāt* (analogy of equals)**: This is when the *'illah*

is common to both the parallel case and the original case, as deduced by analogy. An example is: "*If they commit illegal sexual intercourse, their punishment is half that of free women*".[104] The text of the *Qur'ān* prescribes half the punishment for the bondswoman (slave women) if they are guilty of adultery. This rule will also apply to a male slave by analogy if they commit illegal sexual intercourse (*zinā'*); the punishment is fifty lashes. Making analogy over the bondman (slave) is the same punishment as that of bondswomen.

3. ***Qiyās al-adnā* (analogy of the inferior)**: This is when the effective cause is less evident in the parallel case than in the original case. The prohibition of *nabīdh* on the analogy of prohibition of wine and inflicting the same punishment for the drinking of *nabīdh* fall under the category of *qiyās*. In this example the intoxication of *nabīdh* is less in severity than that of wine.

Qiyās has been divided into a further two categories:[105]

a. ***Qiyās jalīy* (obvious analogy)**: This type of *qiyās* is one where the inability to differentiate (*nafy al-fāriq*) between the original case and the parallel case is certain, or one where the possibility of differentiation is weak. It has been illustrated in the tradition of the Prophet (ṣ) by the analogy of a female slave with a male slave therefore the equation between the *aṣl* (original case) and *far'* (parallel case) is obvious and the disagreement between them is removed by clear evidence.
b. ***Qiyās khafī* (latent, hidden analogy)** is one where the possibility of differentiating between the original and the parallel case is strong, or uncertain. Shawkānī illustrates this with a reference to the two types of wine, namely *nabīdh*, and *khamr*. *Nabīdh* is obtained from dates and *khamr* is obtained from grapes. The rule of prohibition is analogically extended

to *nabīdh* despite some difference that might exist between the two.[106] In other words, the removal of uncertainty in the *qiyās khafī*, between the *aṣl* (original case) and *far'* (parallel case) is by means of presumption (*ẓann*). *Qiyās khafī* and *qiyās al-adnā* are significantly parallel. Consequently, according to *Ḥanafī* jurists, *qiyās khafī* is actually considered to be *istiḥsān*.[107]

Various views over qiyās

The *'ulamā' al-uṣūl* (juristic scholars) are in agreement on the necessity of *qiyās* in affairs of life (*al-'umūr al-dunyawīyyah*) such as medicine and food. The *'ulamā'* are also in agreement on *qiyās* which came from the Prophet (ṣ). However, regarding *shar'ī* affairs (legal matters), the *'ulamā'* are not united. Is *qiyās* approved by *sharī'ah*? There are five views:[108]

1. The majority of jurists believe that *qiyās* is a source of legislation in *sharī'ah* and practical *aḥkām*. According to Subkī (771/1369)[109] *qiyās* suits the religious communal requirement, and accords with the *Qur'ānic* verse: "*Consider, O you possessors of eyes!*"[110] Consideration in this context means attention to similitude and comparison between similar things.
2. Both reason (*'aql*) and transmitted evidence (*dalīl naqlī*) indicate that acting according to *qiyās* is *wājib* (obligatory). This is the view of Qaffāl (d. 365) and Ḥasan al-Baṣrī (d. 436/1044).
3. *Qiyās* is *wājib* for only two situations otherwise it is prohibited to act according to *qiyās*, this is the view of Qāshānī (d. 427), Nahrawānī (d. 390/999) and Dāwūd al-Isfaḥānī (d. 270/884):

   a. The *'illah* (cause) of the *aṣl* (original cause) should either be clearly stated or hinted at.

b. The *'illah* (cause) of the *far'* (parallel case) is more evident than in the original case.

Their view is that *'aql* has nothing to do with these two forms, neither with *wājib* nor with *taḥrīm* of *qiyās,* because the *'illah* is evidently clear (*thābitah bi yaqīn*).

4. *Ẓāhirī* School and Shawkānī (d. 1250/1834) held the view that *qiyās* is rationally permitted. However, they do not consider that it works in *sharī'ah*. Ibn Ḥazm's claim is based mainly on two points: first one is that the *naṣṣ* (texts, verses) of the *Qur'ān* and the *Sunnah* accommodate all incidents. The second one is that *qiyās* is an unnecessary addition to the *naṣṣ*, therefore the *qiyās* abuses the integrity of the text.[111]
5. *Shī'ah Imāmīyah* and Naẓẓām (d. 221/836) from among the Mu'tazilah hold the view that to perform *qiyās* through reasoning in *sharī'ah* is impossible.[112] They concluded that the two different *qiyās* will lead to contradictions for one *ḥukm*. These *'ulamā'* do not consider *qiyās* as a proof of *sharī'ah*.

Dihlawī (d. 1762) expresses the following statement stating the necessity of taking into consideration *maṣlaḥah* while performing *qiyās*:

> "When Allah had revealed to His Prophet a statute of the *sharī'ah* and had demonstrated the wisdom and good reason for it, the latter was then qualified to operate with the consideration of expediency (*maṣlaḥah*) set out to him, and to take the *maṣlaḥah* as the effective cause (*'illah*) and pivot of the stature. This was the *qiyās* practiced by the Prophet (ṣ). The *qiyās* left to the community (*ummah)* is to find out the effective cause underlying a stature and to take that as its pivot".[113]

Given Dihlawī's acceptance of *qiyās*, his rejection of the use of *ra'y* and *istiḥsān* comes as a surprise, "For *ra'y* in connection with the *sharī'ah* leads to *taḥrif* (distortion).[114] Hence the Prophetic tradition: "He who inserts into our religion something that is foreign is to be repulsed." This also has a bearing on anybody who makes use of *istiḥsān* advancing a discretionary opinion contrary to strict analogy for reasons of public convenience."[115]

It is obvious that *istiḥsān* does nothing more than prefer the principle of *maṣlaḥah* to *qiyās*.[116] In reality the principle of *istiḥsān* is not a judgment that is merely based on *ra'y* and personal *maṣlaḥah* (benefit) but in contrast it is a method of activating the application of *sharī'ah* and the general purposes (*maqāṣid al-'āmmah*), because one who performs *istiḥsān* must consider the *sharī'ah's* purpose in any matter. For example performing *qiyās* in a case would cause one to avoid *maṣlaḥah* and bring about *mafsadah* (harm) from a different angle.[117] In unexpected situations eventually *istiḥsān* replaces *qiyās*.[118]

Controversial sources of Islamic law

In addition to the unanimous sources mentioned above, the *Sunnī* schools consider other sources for Islamic law. These sources are somewhat controversial and not universally accepted by all Islamic schools of thought (*madhāhib*).

The main controversial sources of Islamic law are as follows

1. *Istiḥsān* (juristic preference), 2. *Maṣlaḥah mursalah* (consideration of public interest), 3. *Istiṣḥāb* (presumption of continuity), 4. *Qawl al-Ṣaḥābī* (the saying of the Companion of the Prophet), 5. *'Urf* (customary law), 6. *Sadd al-Dharā'i'* (blocking the means), 7. *Shar' man Qablanā* (revealed laws preceding to the *sharī'ah* of Islam) and 8. *Istiqrā'* (induction).

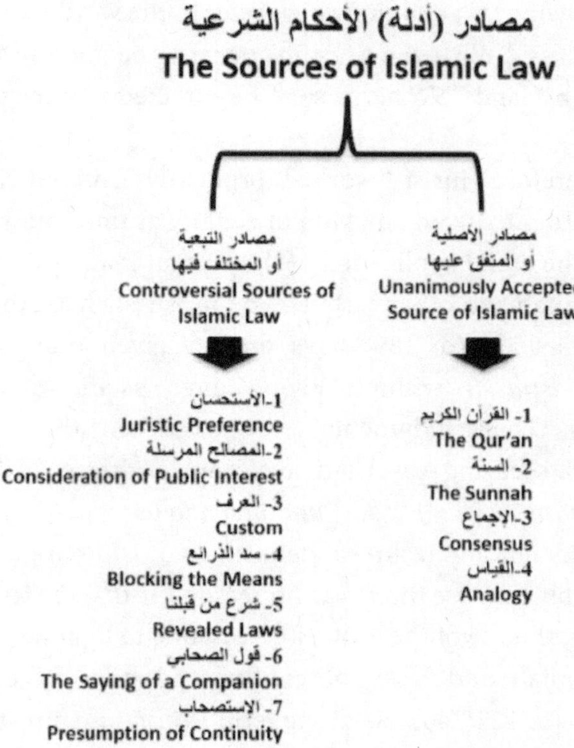

Istiḥsān (juristic preference)

The concept of *istiḥsān* is an essential source of Islamic law which provides significant ways to solve current problems occurred due to the changing needs of the society.

Linguistically, the word *istiḥsān* means to consider something good which is derived from the word "*ḥasuna*" (حسن) which means being good or beautiful. It also means to approve, or to consider something preferable. The *Ḥanafī* jurists have mainly quoted two verses from the *Qur'ān*, and *aḥādīth* which reflect the root of the word *ḥa-su-na* (حسن). Allah says: "*who listen to the word and follow the best of it* [*aḥsanahu*]. *Those are the ones Allah has guided and endowed with understanding*",[119] and "*And follow the best [aḥsan] of what has been sent down to you from your Lord*".[120]

The following two *aḥādīth* which refer to the word *ḥa-su-na* as the Prophet (ṣ) says: "What the Muslims deem to be good is good in the sight of Allah " and "No harm shall be inflicted nor reciprocated in Islam".[121]

It is therefore, jurists worked prudently using their personal opinion in order to avoid any kind of rigidity or unfairness that might result from the literal application of the present law.

Abū Ḥanīfah and other early *Ḥanafī* jurists such as Abū Yūsuf (d. 182) and Shaybānī (d. 189) have directly given rulings using the concept of *istiḥsān* without giving any specific definitions or explanations. Their judgments were based on the fundamental principles of securing ease and avoiding hardship: "*Allah intends facility and ease for you, He does not intend to put you to hardship.*[122]

There was not any technical definitions of *istiḥsān* given by early scholars simply because there was no reason for *istiḥsān* to be defined. Nevertheless, the use of the term *istiḥsān* came to light before the time of Abū Ḥanīfah and was not confined to him. When Iyas bin Mu'āwiyah's (d. 122/740) use of the term *istiḥsān* is compared to Abū Ḥanīfah's, much similarity can be seen. For them, the main purpose of applying *istiḥsān* was to avoid the possibility of causing harm to the public interest. The reason for their emphasis on *istiḥsān* was their desire to avoid the negative results that often occurred when *qiyās* was applied incorrectly. Although the meaning of it was used with different terms such as "discretion" (*istiṣwāb*), a research finds that as a technical sense the term *istiḥsān* was not used before Iyas bin Mu'āwiyah.[123]

In technical sense, among the jurists there was no consensus as to the precise meaning and definition of *istiḥsān*. Yet in spite of all the different definitions, the meanings are very close. In fact all the definitions may be derived from that of Karkhī which is arguably more comprehensive than the others.

Abū al-Ḥasan al-Karkhī (d. 340/952) defines *istiḥsān* as follows: "*istiḥsān* is when one takes a decision on a certain case different from that on which similar cases have been decided on the basis of its precedents, for a reason which is stronger than the one found in similar cases and which requires departure from those cases".[124] According to al-Jaṣṣāṣ (d. 370/981) it is the "Departure from a ruling of *qiyās* (analogy) in favour of another ruling which is considered preferable."[125] Bazdawī (d. 482/1089) defines it as, "It is one of the two *qiyās*".[126] 'Abd al-'Azīz al-Bukhārī, who interprets *Uṣūl al-Bazdawī*, points out that, "it is a particularisation of *qiyās* (analogy) due to stronger evidence."[127] Sarakhsī (d. 483/1090) who defines it as "abandonment of an opinion to which *qiyās* would lead in favour of a different opinion when supported by stronger evidence and adapted to what is acceptable to the public," looks at *istiḥsān* from a different perspective and categorises it in two types: the first one is called: "*ijtihād al-taqdīrī*," which allows jurists all to give rulings and on which there is no cause for disagreement amongst the scholars. The second one is the evidence (*dalīl*), which is in the mind and is set against the explicit analogy. According to Sarakhsī, evidence which opposes the established ruling appears stronger after considering evidence concerning similar cases; therefore ruling with evidence at hand is called *istiḥsān*.[128]

On the contrary, Imām Shāfi'ī[129] (d. 204) wrote a book titled "*Ibṭāl al-Istiḥsān*" (Invalidating Juristic Preference) and declared famously: "Whoever approves of juristic preference is making himself the lawmaker."[130] The fact that the *Ḥanafīs* were attacked by the *Shāfi'ī* jurists, and especially by Shāfi'ī himself, shows that the *Shāfi'ī* schools did not recognize *istiḥsān* as a basis of Islamic law and considering it "Arbitrary law-making in religion" is because, indeed, *Shāfi'ī* jurists did not understand what the *Ḥanafīs* meant by *istiḥsān*. Therefore, *Ḥanafī* jurists spent much time defending their position and trying to show that *istiḥsān* is a valid source of law, and not merely an ad hoc method.[131] Despite Shāfi'ī's rejection, Imām Mālik (d. 179 AH) give high credit on it and strongly support the use of it as he said, "*Istiḥsān* represents nine-tenths of human knowledge".[132]

Al-Shāṭibī, (d. 790/1388) who is one of the prominent scholars dealing with the concept of *maqāṣid* (objective of the *sharī'ah*) considers *istiḥsān* a source of Islamic law. He emphasises that the interpretation should not be based on desire, and that the jurists must have a full understanding of the intention of the Lawgiver. When presented with a new problem the jurists will resort to *istiḥsān* if the use of the strict application of analogy will lead to loss of *maṣlaḥah* or the possibility of evil. He, therefore, defines *istiḥsān* as "An evidence embedded (*yanqadiḥu*) in the mind of the jurist but which words will not allow him to express."[133]

Ḥanafī scholars see *istiḥsān* as a valid source of *sharī'ah* and a basis for the formulation of legal rulings. They also see most criticism of *istiḥsān* as the product of misunderstanding, and the imputation to Abū Ḥanīfah this is because of ulterior motives. However, it is difficult to believe that he would have abandoned a ruling that had been established on true *sharī'* foundations for his personal preference.[134]

The definition of al-Karkhī (d. 340/952) has been espoused and accepted by many jurists such as Ṭūfī (d. 716/1317), Shīrāzī (d. 476/1083), Ghazālī (d. 505/1111), and the contemporary jurist Abū Zahrah (d. 1974), indicating that it contains all types of *istiḥsān* in general.[135] Consequently, it may be highlighted that the concept of *istiḥsān* is an evidence which is preferred over an accepted established ruling after ensuring that this evidence does not contravene the Islamic legal ruling.

The application of *istiḥsān* appears originally as a reaction to the concept of *qiyās*, and mainly when a jurist is faced with a problem for which he cannot arrive at a ruling from the definitive sources of law, within the *Qur'ān* and the *Sunnah*, he then searches for precedent and tries to find a solution by making a comparison with a previous case. As Sarakhsī says that *qiyās* is of two types, the investigation may reveal two different solutions: one of which is based on an explicit (*jalī*) analogy and the other on an implicit (*khafī*) analogy. If they contradict each other, then the jurist may reject the former in the favour of latter. The implicit analogy is considered to be more effective and therefore is preferred over the explicit. Departure from one type of *qiyās*, i.e. *jalī*, to another type of *qiyās*, i.e. *khafī*, is simply called *istiḥsān*. For example: According to *Ḥanafī* rulings, when transferring the ownership of agricultural land, all of the ancillary rights (*ḥaqq al-irtifāq*) attached to the property, such as the right of water (*ḥaqq al-shurb*), the right of passage (*ḥaqq al-murūr*) and the right of flow (*ḥaqq al-masīl*), are also transferred. This is indisputable, even if it is not stipulated explicitly in the document. Besides this, in the contract of lease (*ijārah*), even if the ancillary rights are also not explicitly mentioned in the document, the usufruct (*intifā'*) is considered part of the contract. So, the leaseholder is able to benefit from these rights.

Another transaction, which resembles both contract sales and leases, is called *waqf* (charitable endowment). If it is considered from the point of view of the donor, *waqf* resembles a contract of sale, because the ownership changes hands. Considering it from the side of the donee, *waqf* resembles a contract of lease (*ijārah*), because both involve a transfer of usufruct (*intifā'*). However, the ownership is not transferred to the other party.

According to these explanations, the contract faces two different *qiyās* (analogy) rulings when the property is donated as *waqf* (charitable endowment): if it is compared to a contract of sale, what is not included in the contract and is not specified in it, such as the ancillary rights (*haqq al-irtifāq*) will not be included. If it is compared to a contract of lease, the ancillary rights will be included in the scope of *waqf*, even if these are not explicitly mentioned and specified by the donee. Here, the first instinct is to compare *waqf* with a contract of sale; comparing it to a contract of lease comes to mind only after investigation. Therefore, comparing *waqf* to a sale is called an explicit analogy (*qiyās jalī*), while comparing it to a lease is called implicit analogy (*qiyās khafī*).

Consequently, including the ancillary rights in the transaction of the *waqf* without requiring any statement or permission from the donee is a ruling of *istiḥsān.* If, however the ancillary rights are not included it is a ruling of *qiyās* (analogy).[136] The main reason for the preference of *istiḥsān* over analogy is that such analogy would lead to unfair results: the *waqf* of cultivated land without its ancillary rights would frustrate the basic purpose of *waqf*, which is to facilitate the use of the property for charitable purposes. Usufruct is the essential purpose of *ijārah*, and this would enable us to say that *waqf* can be deemed valid even if it does not specify the ancillary rights to the property in detail. Therefore, it is compared to a lease in order to avoid hardship for the people.[137]

As we see, the effective cause of the implicit analogy, which is not contrary to the *Shārīʿs* (Lawmaker) purposes, is stronger than the explicit analogy, and therefore it is preferred over explicit analogy so that the benefits of the people will be secured.

Types of Istiḥsān

Despite the controversy over the division of *istiḥsān*, it is divided mainly into two types:

a. Analogical *istiḥsān*, which consists of a departure from *qiyās jalī* to *qiyās khafī*.
b. Exceptional *istiḥsān* (*istiḥsān istithnāī*) which consists of making an exception to a general rule of the existing law; it is approved when the jurist is convinced that by making such an exception, justice might be better served.[138] After confirming the division of *qiyās* into two types – the explicit and the implicit – Ṣadr al-Sharīʿah (d. 747/1346) calls the implicit (*khafī*) analogy *istiḥsān*. However, *istiḥsān* is more comprehensive than implicit analogy: while every implicit analogy can be called *istiḥsān*, not every case of *istiḥsān* can be called implicit (*khafī*) analogy. *Istiḥsān* is an evidence (*dalīl*)

which is established against explicit analogy. Ṣadr al-Sharīʻah then says that it is divided into several types such as *ijmāʻ*, *ḍarūrah* (necessity), *athar* etc.[139] Another jurist Bazdawī (d. 482/1089) also indicates that *istiḥsān* is an implicit analogy, and says that its other types consist of *athar*, *ijmāʻ* (consensus) and *ḍarūrah* (necessity).[140]

The contemporary scholar Khallāf (d. 1376/1956) divides *istiḥsān* into two main types[141]:

1. *Istiḥsān* which is departure from one ruling to another. It includes: **a.** the requirement that the departure be from *qiyās jalī* to *qiyās khafī*, **b.** the requirement that the departure be general text (*naṣṣ ʻām*) to a specific ruling (*ḥukm khāṣṣ*), and **c.** that the departure be from the general rule of the existing law to an exceptional law.
2. *Istiḥsān* based on *sanad* (evidence), which the departure requires. This type of *istiḥsān* is considered by the schools of thought (*madhhabs*) along the following lines. The *Ḥanafīs* divide *istiḥsān* in general sense into four types:

a. *istiḥsān* based on *athar*, which is the textual evidences in the *Qur'ān* and *Sunnah*, **b.** *istiḥsān* based on *ijmāʻ* (consensus), **c.** *istiḥsān* based on *ḍarūrah* (necessity), **d.** *istiḥsān* based on *qiyās khafī* (implicit analogy). Ibn Nujāym (d. 970/1562) has summarised the divisions recognized by the *Ḥanafīs* as follows: *istiḥsān* is based on *naṣṣ* (*athar*), *ijmāʻ* (consensus), *ḍarūrah* (necessity) and *qiyās khafī* (implicit analogy).[142]

The *Ḥanbalī* School has not pronounced officially on the divisions within *istiḥsān*. However, particularly, their *istiḥsān* can be divided into three types:

a. departure from a ruling in favour of *naṣṣ*, **b.** departure from *qiyās* in favour of the saying of the Companions, **c.** departure from *qiyās* in favour of a stronger one. They have also pointed out that the departure from *qiyās* may be in respect of *naṣṣ* of which *khabar al-wāḥid* (isolated tradition), *ḥadīth mashhūr* (well known tradition), *ḥadīth mutawātir* (widely spread tradition) and textual evidences from the *Qur'ān* are some examples. Sometimes, the departure occurs in favour of the saying of the Companions, even if it is against *istiḥsān*. These types are agreed upon among the scholars. In spite of this, if the departure applies to another analogy, the scholars on this issue are in disagreement. In addition, departure in favour of a stronger analogy is recognized.

The *Mālikīs* divide *istiḥsān* into four types: **a.** *istiḥsān* based on *'urf* so long as it does not contradict textual evidence, **b.** *istiḥsān* based on *maṣlaḥah* (benefit), **c.** *istiḥsān* based on *ijmā'* (consensus), **d.** departure from *qiyās* in order to avoid hardship and secure benefit for man.[143]

Analogical istiḥsān (Departure from qiyās jalī to qiyās khafī)

Ḥanafīs consider *qiyās* into the *jalī* (explicit) and the *khafī* (implicit). *Jalī* is an analogy where the *'illah* (effective cause) appears at first glance, without careful consideration needing to be given to it. For example, the prohibition of *nabīdh* appears to follow on by analogy from the prohibition of wine. However, *qiyās khafī* is one where the effective cause (*'illah*) is understood after careful consideration and reflection.[144] In other words, *qiyās khafī* is preferred over *qiyās jalī* if they are opposed to each other, on account of the effective cause (*'illah*) which is stronger in *khafī*. Therefore, it is called the *qiyās* of juristic preference (*istiḥsān al-qiyās*).[145]

Ḥanafī jurists point out that the *qiyās khafī*, which they called *istiḥsān* is in reality a kind of *qiyās* and therefore, its ruling can be moved referred (*ta'diyah*) to other cases.[146] In order to refer a ruling of *qiyās*, it must be related to an effective cause (*'illah*) that is based on another cause (*'illah*). Every ruling which is based on *'illah* would be referred to other cases (*furū'*) which have a similar *'illah*. This is the ruling of the validated *qiyās*. *Ta'diyah* (referring a ruling to another case) is an indispensable factor of an effective cause (*'illah*) according to the *Ḥanafīs*.[147]

For example: If a group of people gain unlawful entry into a house, steal collected commodities and load them on one person's back and that person carries the commodities outside while the others are not carrying anything, according to *qiyās*, the punishment is only applied to the person who carried the commodities. However, according to *istiḥsān* the punishment is applied to all of those who were involved in the robbery.[148]

In this case, there are two contradictory *aṣl* (original cases): the first involves a group of people who encourage one of their number to rape a woman. In this case, there is no conflict among the jurists and the penalty is applied only to the rapist. This is a ruling of *qiyās* as opposed to *istiḥsān*. The second case is that of a group of people who congregate with the intention to attack, kill and rob people of their commodities; in this case, the penalty of highway robbery is applied to all. This case is not disputed by jurists because they agree that the punishment must be applied to all who are involved in the highway robbery. According to the *Qur'ān*:

> "*The recompense of those who wage war against Allah and His Messenger and do mischief in the land is only that they shall be killed or crucified or their hands and their feet be cut off from opposite sides, or be exiled from the land. That is their disgrace in this world, and a great torment is theirs in the Hereafter. Except for those who (having fled away and then) came back (as Muslims) with repentance before they fall into your power; in that case, know that Allah is Oft-Forgiving, Most Merciful.*"[149]

After investigating carefully, it becomes clear that comparing the house robbery to a highway robbery offers a clearer solution than comparing it to rape.[150] The departure from one original case (*aṣl*) to another because of the stronger reason is a solution sought by *istiḥsān* in order to better protect society.

Exceptional *istiḥsān* (*istiḥsān istithnāī*): Departure from the general rule of the existing law to an exceptional law. The exceptional *istiḥsān* is represented here by the example of charitable endowment (*waqf*) made by someone mentally defective (*safīh*) who is under the protection of a guardian. This is based on the *istiḥsān* ruling which permits the mentally defective to make such endowments regardless of whether or not they are under someone's guardianship. It is based on the benefits of the people because permitting it by way of *istiḥsān* may encourage people to do charitable and good works. According to *qiyās,* however, a mentally defective person cannot make a charitable endowment (*waqf*) under protection of a guardian. The charitable endowment is a kind of donation (*tabarru'*) and a person under guardianship is not eligible to give donations.[151] *Istiḥsān* departs from the established ruling and thus validates the donation.

However, if the one under guardianship does make a charitable endowment, what is the position? According to the general rule, which is *qiyās*, this donation is not valid if the mentally defective (*safīh*) makes a donation. Al-Khussāf, a *Ḥanafī* jurist, observes that this donation may cause harm to him self, and therefore is not valid. However, Abū Yūsuf is of the opinion that it is valid. However, all *Ḥanafī* scholars agreed that if he donates something after he leaves the guardianship, it is valid.[152]

Istiṣḥāb (presumption of continuity)

Like the other controversial sources, it is secondary to the *Qur'ān*, the *Sunnah*, *ijmā'* and *qiyās*. *Istiṣḥāb* is validated by the *Shāfi'īs*, the *Ḥanbalis*, the *Ẓahirīs*, and the *Shī'ah* schools, but the *Ḥanafīs*, the *Mālikīs* and the *Mutakallimūn*, including Abū al-Ḥasan al-Baṣrī, do not consider it a source of *sharī'ah*.[153]

Definition of istiṣḥāb

Literally, the word *istiṣḥāb* comes from the root (*ṣ-ḥ-b*), from which verbs such as to accompany, to remain along with as opposed to separating or departing from, for example, the action of taking a book or a friend along whilst travelling is called *istiṣḥāb*.[154]

Technically, the jurists define *istiṣḥāb* as "a ruling presuming that the present or future status of an issue continues to remain invariably the same as it was in the past, owing to the unavailability of a reason (evidence) to warrant the establishment of any changes of that status".[155] A similar definition considers *istiṣḥāb* to be "believing that the existence of something in the past or present renders it obligatory to presume the variability of that existence in the present and future".[156] A third definition given by the jurists is as follows: *istiṣḥāb* means to adhere to a well-established ruling due to the unavailability of any evidence to warrant any change".[157] When a doubt is raised in regard to any issue in existence, the ruling of *istiṣḥāb* states that the issue can continue to exist as before. The same ruling of *istiṣḥāb* is also applied to non-existent issues. For example, when a property is transferred from one owner to another, the ownership of the property continues to remain the right of the first owner until it is transferred to the second owner and the transfer is confirmed by evidence.

Status of istiṣḥāb as a source of Islamic law

The status of *istiṣḥāb* among other sources of *sharī'ah* is well explained in the statement of al-Khawārizmī (d. 665/1267) as quoted by Shawkānī, namely that *istiṣḥāb* is the last resort of *muftī* (judge). If the *muftī* is asked about an issue he should pursue the ruling first from the Book, then the *Sunnah*, then *ijmā'*, then *qiyās*. If he fails to find the ruling in these sources, he takes the ruling on that issue from *istiṣḥāb* whether the status is positive or negative. If the jurist has any hesitation regarding a ruling then the ruling continues as it was originally established. If, however, the hesitation was in order to prove the ruling, and no proof is established, then the principle to follow is that there is no evidence to prove the ruling and the status should be changed."[158]

Types of istiṣḥāb (presumption of continuity)

With regard to the existence of a ruling, *istiṣḥāb* is divided into the following types:

1. ***Istiṣḥāb al-ibāḥah al-aṣlīyyah lil ashyā'*** **(presumption of original permissibility for objects)**: This means that one is to presume the continuation of its permissibility until the contrary is proven. When there is no ruling, then it is presumed to be permissible. All objects, contracts, and services which are beneficial to man are lawful on the grounds of original permissibility. In the case of legal prohibition, *istiṣḥāb* presumes the continuity of this prohibition until evidence is established to suggest that it is no longer prohibited. The principle of permissibility (*ibāḥah*) begins in the *Qur'ān*: "*It is He who has created for you all that is on the earth*"[159] and "*Allah has subjugated to you all that is in the heavens and on the earth.*"[160] These verses indicate that man should be able to use the resources of the world around him for his benefit unless he has been clearly prohibited.[161]
2. ***Istiṣḥāb al-barā'ah al-aṣlīyyah*** **(presumption of original freedom from responsibility):** It is a fundamental principle, according to Islamic law, that a person is free from obligations unless there is evidence to the contrary. For example, no one is required to perform a sixth *ṣalāt* (prayer) in one day.[162] According to *al-Majallah* "If one person destroys the property of another and a dispute ensues as to the amount thereof the statement of the person causing such destruction shall be heard, and the requirement of the proof as to any amount in excess thereof is upon the owner of such property."[163]
3. ***Istiṣḥāb al-waṣf*** **(presumption of attributes)**: This means that everything remains as it was until evidence warranting

any changes are established. This was formulated in *al-Majallah* as "It is a fundamental principle that a thing shall remain as it was originally".[164] For example, the "*mafqūd*" (missing person) is assumed to be alive until evidence is established to prove his death. The Jurists agreed by consensus that his heirs cannot inherit his property until his death has been established. According to most jurists, no one can benefit from any property bequeathed to the missing person until his status is established; the condition of inheritance is fulfilled by proving that the heir (missing person) is alive at the time of the deceased's death. As opposed to other schools of thought, the *Ḥanafī* School maintains that a missing person cannot inherit from anyone.[165]

Maṣlaḥah Mursalah (public interest) or al-istiṣlāḥ

Another controversial source of Islamic law is *maṣlaḥah* which is based on benefit and avoiding harm. After the unanimous sources, *istiṣlāḥ* is a legitimate basis for legislation. When the *maṣlaḥah* is identified and the *mujtahid* does not find an explicit ruling in the main four sources, the jurist can resort to further steps to protect social benefit and to prevent corruption in the earth.[166] However, *maṣlaḥah* should not contradict the *sharī'ah* and its general objectives.

In this context, Shāṭibī (d. 790/1388) indicates[167] that the purpose of the *sharī'ah* is to promote people's welfare and to prevent corruption and hardship; it is clearly explained in the *Qur'ān* "*We have not sent you but as a mercy for all creatures*"[168], and "*He (Allah) has not laid upon you an hardship in religion*".[169]

Definitions of maṣlaḥah

Linguistically, *maṣlaḥah* means: benefit / beneficial, appropriate/ suitable, convenient and so on. Literally, *maṣlaḥah* is the opposite of *fasād* (evil) according to *Lisān al-'Arab*. In *al-Mu'jam al-Wasīṭ*, *maṣlaḥah* is the removal of evil. The word *maṣlaḥah* is derived from the root (*ṣ-l-ḥ*). Its plural form is *maṣāliḥ* and it is synonymous with *istiṣlāḥ*. *Mafsadah* is its precise antonym. The verb "*ṣaluḥa*" means something which has become beneficial or suitable. When someone "*aṣlaḥa*," he removes the evil. *Mursalah* means unrestricted. According to *Lisān al-'Arab*, the verb "*arsala*" means to remove the restriction or to ignore it.[170]

Technically, *maṣlaḥah mursalah* is defined by Shāṭibī as that which concerns the subsistence of human life, the completion of man's livelihood, and the acquisition of what his emotional and intellectual qualities require of him, in an absolute sense.[171] It is more technically defined as a consideration which is proper and harmonious (*waṣf munāsib mulā'im*) with the objectives of the Lawgiver; it secures a benefit or prevents a harm, when the *Qur'ān* or the *Sunnah* provides no indication as to its validity or otherwise.[172]

It is obvious that the concept of *maṣlaḥah* has a very close relationship with *maqāṣid al-sharī'ah* (objectives of the *sharī'ah*), as *maqāṣid* are defined briefly as obtaining *maṣlaḥah* (benefit) and preventing *mafsadah* (evil). These two concepts (*maṣlaḥah* and *maqāṣid*) may sometimes be used interchangeably. The first significant work in this was done by Ghazālī (d. 505/1111) who wrote: "In a real sense *maṣlaḥah* consists of obtaining *manfa'ah* (benefit) and preventing *maḍarrāt* (evils). However, we do not use that meaning… for the term *maṣlaḥah*, we mean, to protect the objectives of the *sharī'ah* (*maṣlaḥah al-sharī'ah* or *maqāṣid al-sharī'ah*) which consist of five essential values, namely religion, life, intellect, lineage and property."[173] Imām al-Qarāfī (d.685/1286) adds sixth one as honour (*sharaf*) to these values,[174] and the seventh one is considered as the value of state.[175]

Types of maṣlaḥah

Ibn 'Āshūr (d. 1973) divides *maṣlaḥah* into two types: **a.** *al-maṣlaḥah* *al-'āmmah* (public benefit), which is a benefit that is useful to all, or to the majority of the community; and **b.** *al-maṣlaḥah al-khāṣṣah* (specific benefit), which is individual consideration of the benefits for people.[176]

With regard to the social order, it is divided into three categories: **a.** *ḍarūriyyāt* (essentials), **b.** *ḥājiyyāt* (complement-aries), **c.** *taḥsīniyyāt* (embellishments).

Regarding the whole community, its groups and individuals *maṣlaḥah* is either **a.** *kullī* (whole) or **b.** *juz'ī* (partial). There are also three types of *maṣlaḥah* in respect of the people's situations: **a.** *qaṭ'ī* (definite), **b.** *ẓannī* (speculative), **c.** *wahmī* (imaginary).[177]

Briefly the main divisions of *maṣlaḥah* are as follows:

***Ḍarūriyyāt* (essentials):** These are things on which the lives of people depend, and the neglect of which causes total disruption and anarchy. Ibn al-Ḥājib, al-Ghazālī and Shāṭibī consider these to be the five essential values, namely religion, life, intellect, lineage and property. Qarāfi adds a sixth essential, protecting honour (*sharaf*) which guarantees the other five because they will indirectly fall into danger if it is missing; this is attributed to Ṭūfī.[178] It is highly desirable to mention the value of "state" as the seventh value, for it indirectly guarantees the others in the same way as does the value of honour. The first five essentials must not only be upheld but also protected against any real or unexpected threat to their safety. Destroying one of the five essential values is *ḥarām* according to Ghazālī.[179] The five values would be protected in two ways: **a.** maintaining the subsistence, **b**-removing the disruptions.[180]

Nevertheless, in my perception, the *darūriyyāt* are now seven in number: religion, life, intellect, lineage, wealth, honour and state. They are considered essential because neglecting them would cause total social disruption and anarchy.

***Ḥājiyyāt*:** These are those things which, if neglected, many cause hardship to the community, but not its collapse. Shāṭibī (d. 790/1388) says that *ḥājiyyāt* are those things which are needed to enhance comfort and avoid hardship. If they are not taken into consideration, people would face harm and difficulties. However, those difficulties are not as dangerous as neglect of the essentials."[181] In the field of *'ibādāt* (worship), *ḥājiyyāt* includes the concessions (*rukhaṣ*) that the *sharī'ah* grants to the sick and to travellers, permitting them to forego the fast and to shorten the prayers (*ṣalāt*) in order to avoid hardship.

Taḥsīniyyāt*:** These are also known as ***kamāliyyāt (embellishments) and are supplementary to the previous types. This category represents the interest and awareness of the *mukallaf*. Shāṭibī says that it may be summarized as part of social and moral etiquette in the field of *'ibādāt*, such as eliminating dirt, considering all types of cleanness; or in the field of customary matters, such as good conduct in eating, avoiding wastefulness in consumption; in the field of transactions, such as not selling something which is impure; and in the field of *jināyat* (criminal offence), such as the prohibition on the killing of women, children and scholars whilst on *jihād*.[182] Therefore *sadd al-dharāi'* (blocking the means) is considered as a kind of *taḥsīniyyāt*.

Shurūṭ (conditions) of *maṣlaḥah mursalah*:

Some strict and indisputable conditions have been set in order that *maṣlaḥah* be considered a valid source.

A vital condition of *maṣlaḥah* is that it must be appropriate to the objectives of the *Shār'* (Lawgiver). Ghazālī says that "Interpreting the *maṣlaḥah* as protecting the *maqāṣid al-sharī'ah* (objectives of the lawgiver), nobody would oppose obeying the *maṣlaḥah* unless they could produce positive evidence".[183] He adds "We occasionally consider *maṣlaḥah* and rulings when indications interchangeably reflected one another."[184]

The following conditions are intended to ensure that the concept of *maṣlaḥah* is not established arbitrarily or by individual whim.

1. *Maṣlaḥah* must not be in conflict with a principle or value

which is sustained by a *naṣṣ* (text) or *ijmāʿ*.[185]

2. *Maṣlaḥah* must be genuine (*ḥaqīqīyyah*) as opposed to imaginary (*wahmīyyah*), which is an improper ground for legislation. For example the recording of marriages in the court and the issue of marriage certificates or the recording of contracts in the registry department prevents *shahādāt al-zur* (false testimony) and stabilizes the *muʿāmalāt* (contracts)[186].
3. *Maṣlaḥah* must be *kullīyyah* (general) so as to secure its benefits and prevent harm as a whole, not to a particular person or group of people.[187]

   Besides these conditions, Imām Mālik (d. 179/795) considers further two other conditions:

4. The *maṣlaḥah* must be *maʿqūlah* (rational) and acceptable.
5. *Maṣlaḥah* must prevent or eradicate hardship, which the *Qur'ān* expresses in the *sūrah al-mā'idah* (5:6) "*Allah never intends to impose hardship upon people*",[188] yet Ghazālī (d. 505/1111) maintained that *maṣlaḥah* must involve *ḍarūriyyāt* (essentials) for its validation.[189]

Consequently, the main purpose of the law is to obtain benefit (*jalb al-ṣalāḥ*) and avoid evil (*dafʿ al-fasād*). *Maṣlaḥah* would be obtained by improving man's situation and removing evil, because man is the vicegerent on earth and holder of His truth; therefore making him peaceful would reflect in world peace too.[190] If the evaluation of the *maṣlaḥah* and *mafsadah* were the responsibility of mankind, the Lawgiver's objectives would be in jeopardy.

In this context, Shāṭibī says "In the religious context the aim of obtaining benefit (*jalb al-ṣalāḥ*) and avoiding evil (*dafʿ al-fasād*) is to provide the needs of this world for the sake of the hereafter, and not to provide personal desires or avoid personal hatreds. Religion prevents people from following their desires and guides them to be a servant of Allah."[191] Allah clearly indicates this in the *Qur'ān*: "*And if the truth had been in accordance with their desires, verily, the heavens and the earth, and whosever therein would have been corrupted.*"[192]

'Urf (customary law)

The concept of *'urf* is also considered to be one of the controversial sources of Islamic law amongst the jurists.

Definition of *'urf*: *'Urf* as a noun derived from its Arabic root "*'a-r-f*" (عرف) to know. According to *Lisān al-'Arab*, *'urf*, *'irfān* and *'ārifah* all have the same meaning, i.e. anything that the people know as good (*khayr*) as opposed to *munkar* (evil), or any effort you make by speech or action to help others.

Recognizing someone's service or help offered to another to enable them to achieve an ambition is also covered by this concept. Generally, the word is mostly used for a higher level of feelings and a good and dignified expression.[193]

'Urf (custom) and its derivative *ma'rūf* appears in the *Qur'ān* in *sūrah al-Ā'rāf* (7:199) "Keep to forgiveness, enjoin *'urf* (*wa'mur bil 'urf*) and turn away from the ignorant".

Zamakhsharī (d. 538/1144) in his commentary on this verse states that: "*'Urf* is known as a beautiful (nice or good) deed."[194] Another word largely synonymous with *'urf* is *'ādah* (habit – plural *'ādāt* or *'awāi'd*) which means repetition or recurrent practice of an individual or a group.[195]

Technically, *'urf* is defined as "Habitual practices which are acceptable to people of sound nature".[196] *'Ādah* is defined as "habitual practices without a rational relationship."[197]

Types of 'urf

'Urf is primarily divided into two types: *qawlī* (verbal) and *fi'lī* or *'amalī* (actual or practical). An example of verbal *'urf* is the word *walad* which means the offspring, whether a son or a daughter, although in its common usage *walad* is used to denote a son only. It

occurs in the *Qur'ān*: "*Allah commands you as regards your children's (inheritance): to the male, a portion equal to that of two females...*".[198] An example of actual *'urf* is the *bay' al-ṭa'āṭī* (give-and-take sale) which is normally concluded without utterance of offer and acceptance.[199] These *'urf*, either *qawlī* or *'amalī*, eventually are divided into two types: *al-'urf al-'āmm* general custom and *al-'urf al-khāṣṣ*" (special custom).[200]

Conditions of the validity of 'urf

a. *'Urf* must not contradict a *naṣṣ*, or definitive principles of the Islamic law.[201]
b. *'Urf* must be continual or prevalent in most cases. The practice of that *'urf* by a few individuals or of a limited number of people among a large community will not be authoritative.[202]
c. The existence of *'urf* (custom) must be established at the time of the transaction.[203]
d. *'Urf* (custom) must not contravene the clear requirements of an agreement.[204]

Consequently, the following principles, mentioned in *al-majallah*, point out the prevalence of *'urf* in legislation:

- Custom is an arbitrator; that is to say, custom, whether public or private, may be invoked to justify the giving of judgment.[205]
- In the presence of custom, no regard is paid to the literal meaning of a thing.[206]
- Effect is only given to custom where it is of regular occurrence or when universally prevailing.[207]
- A matter recognized by custom is regarded as though it was a contractual obligation.[208]
- A matter established by *'urf* (custom) is like a matter established by law.[209]

To change *'urf* without consideration for the harm that this may cause is clearly unacceptable.[210]

Sadd al-Dharā'i' (blocking the means)

The validity of this concept amongst the jurists is considered controversial; the *Ḥanafī, Shāfi'ī* and *Ẓāhirī* jurists do not recognize it as a source of Islamic jurisprudence, yet *Mālikī* and *Ḥanbalī* jurists have validated it as a principle of *sharī'ah*.[211]

Definition of sadd al-dharā'i'

Sadd al-dharā'i' (blocking the means) consists of two terms; first, *sadd* (blocking) and second, *dharī'a'*, plural *dharā'i'* (means). Blocking the means implies blocking the means of evil but not blocking the means of good. In juridical application, the concept of *sadd al-dharā'i'* also extends to "Opening the means to beneficence." For this reason some jurists use the term *dharā'i'* (means) alone as a title for the doctrine. The literal meaning of each term will clear this point. According to *Mu'jam Maqāyīs al-Lughah* and *Mukhtār al-Siḥāḥ*,[212] the term *sadd* literally means a barrier between two things, for example a mountain. It also means blocking a gap with landfill to level it; *dharī'a'h* are the means or the causes used to achieve or obtain a certain thing or end.[213]

Shāṭibī (d. 790/1388) defines *dharī'a'h* as "That means by which a prohibited end or thing (containing evil) is obtained."[214] It is obvious that this definition refers exclusively to meaning evil, evil that must be blocked. Other jurists such as Ibn al-Qayyīm (d. 751/1350) define *dharī'a'h* as that which is a means or a way to something.[215] Here (something) implies juridical obedience or disobedience to Allah. Qarāfī (d. 684/1285) considers *dharī'a'h* to be the means to beneficence or evil: the former must be embraced whilst the latter must be blocked. He states that "As the means to evil is prohibited (and must be blocked), the means to *wājib* (obligatory action) is obligatory. The bases regulating the rulings on affairs are two parts. The first part is *maqāṣid* (objectives), which contains the beneficence and evil each in itself. Second, *wasā'il* (means) which are the ways leading to them. The ruling on the ways to obtain the objective or end is the same as the ruling on the objective itself."[216]

Types of dharā'ī' (means)

Its types are considered from two perspectives: the result discovered by Ibn al-Qayyīm in *"I'lām al-Muwaqqi'īn"*[217]; and the degree of probability, or otherwise, of leading to an evil as discussed by Shāṭibī in *"Al-Muwāfaqāt."*[218]

First: An example of means which leads to evil or harm is the digging of a deep pit next to the entrance to a public place which is not lit at night; thus anyone who enters the door is very likely to fall into it. That action is completely forbidden as it might cause harm to someone.[219]

Second: Means which are rarely expected to lead to evil and are likely to lead to a benefit. An example is digging a water hole situated in a place which is unlikely to harm anyone.[220]

Third: Means which are most likely (*al-ẓann al-ghālib*) to lead to evil. For example selling weapons during warfare or selling grapes to a wine maker. However, Shāṭibī says that these transactions are invalid according to the consensus of the *'ulamā'*. Briefly, when there is a strong likelihood that they would lead to evil, the means may be declared forbidden.[221]

Fourth: Means which frequently lead to evil. An example is deferred sales (*buyū' al-ajal*), which mostly leads to usury (*ribā'*).[222]

Consequently, the main understanding of the whole concept of *sadd al-dharā'i'* was founded on the idea of preventing evil before it happens. When the result is expected to be good or commendable, then the means will be acceptable. However when the result is expected to be blameworthy then the means will be considered blocked, regardless of the intention of the perpetrator, or the actual recognition of the result itself.

Additionally, if the act performed leads to the situation where the evil is either equal to or bigger than the benefit, then the means must be blocked too, according to the general principle "repelling an evil is preferable to securing a benefit."[223]

Qawl al-Ṣaḥābī (Saying of the Companion of the Prophet (ṣ))

Many disputes have occurred over the validity of *qawl al-ṣaḥabī*, but briefly the *Ḥanafī Mālikī*, *Ḥanbalī* and *Shāfi'ī* Schools in general have validated the concept as a source of the *Sharī'ah*.[224]

Definition of the Term

The word *ṣaḥābī* is derived from the root "*ṣ-ḥ-b*" and the verb *ṣaḥibah* or *ṣaḥabah* (to accompany) and *ṣuḥbah* (companionship), which imply continuity of contact and narration of *ḥadīth* from the Prophet (*ṣ*). *Qawl al-Ṣaḥābī* consists of two words; "*qawl*" (saying) and "*ṣaḥābī* – plural – *ṣaḥabah*" the Companions. According to most jurists[225] anyone who met the Prophet (*ṣ*), while believing in him, even for a moment, and died as a believer, is considered "*ṣaḥābī*" (Companion) regardless of whether he or she narrated any *ḥadīth* from the Prophet (*ṣ*) or not.

Jurists agree that the *ijmā'* (consensus) of the Companions of the Prophet (*ṣ*) is a binding proof, and represents the most authoritative form of *ijmā'*. The question arises, however, as to whether the saying or *fatwā* of a single Companion should also be recognized as a source of law and should take precedence over other sources such as *qiyās* or the *fatwā* of other *mujtahidūn*.[226]

There is no disagreement among the jurists that the saying of a Companion is a proof, which commands obedience if it is not opposed by other Companions. Rulings on which the Companions were known to be in agreement are binding. The jurists are however in disagreement with regard to rulings which were based on opinion (*ra'y*) and *ijtihād*, and also in those matters where the Companions differed among themselves.

There is a general agreement among jurists that the ruling of one Companion is not a binding proof over another Companion, regardless of whether the ruling in question was issued by one of the Caliphs, a Judge or a leading *mujtahid* among their number. The jurists did differ as to whether the rulings of a Companion are binding on Successors (*Tābiʿūn*) and the succeeding generations of *mujtahidīn*. There are four views on this[227], which are briefly summarized as follows:

1. The *ijtihād* of the Companions is not a proof and is not binding on the succeeding generations of *mujtahidūn* or anyone else. This view is held by the *Ashʿarīs, Muʿtazilīs*, Imām Aḥmad, and al-Karkhī.[228]

2. The *fatwā'* of the Companions takes priority over *qiyās*, regardless of whether it was in agreement with *qiyās* or not. This was the view of Imām Mālik, Imām Shāfiʿī, Imām Aḥmad, and some of the *Ḥanafī* jurists.[229]

3. It is acceptable when it is in agreement with *qiyās*. In such a case, *qiyās* comes before the ruling of the Companion. This is a later view of Imām Shāfiʿī.[230]

4. It is acceptable when it is in a conflict with *qiyās* but not when it agrees with *qiyās*. This is the view of Imām Abū Ḥanīfah.[231]

Despite of some disagreement among the scholars of the leading *madhhab* regarding the *fatwā* of Companions, all the *Imāms* of the four *madhhab* considered it to be an authoritative source.

Sharʿ man qablanā (revealed laws preceding to the sharīʿah)

This subject represents the extent to which the *sharīʿah* of Islam is related to the laws of previous revelations. The *Qur'ān* and the *Sunnah* have chronicled the lives of previous Prophets and some of the rulings of the revelations they received.[232] The *Qur'ān* confirms the essence of believing in the oneness of Allah and the need for divine authority and guidance to maintain good conduct and the principles of morality and justice that represent ordinary reason and the matter of all divine religions.[233] The same religion has been ordained from the previous prophets and nations, as is indicated in the *Qur'ān*: "*He (Allah) has ordained for you the same religion (Islamic Monotheism) which He ordained for Nuḥ (Noah), and that which We have revealed to you (O Muḥammad), and that which We ordained for Ibrāhīm (Abraham), Mūsā (Moses) and 'Īsā (Jesus) saying you should establish religion (i.e. to do what it orders you to do practically), and make no divisions.*"[234]

For example, several rulings (*aḥkām*) such as fasting and law of retaliation have been ordained before in previous revelations, "*O believers, fasting is prescribed for you as it was prescribed for those who came before you*".[235] Similarly, the matter has to be hightlighted that each one of the previous religions was sent to different nations who have distinctive features which cause the *aḥkām* of Allah, *ḥalāl* or *ḥarām* to be different in nature. Despite of the fact that the *Sharī'ah* may upheld some of the *aḥkām* of the previous religions such as the law of retaliation (*qiṣāṣ*) and some of the *ḥadd* penalties which were commanded in the Torah have also been commanded in the *Qur'ān*,[236] as Allah states in the *Qur'ān*: "*And we ordained therein for them life for life, eye for eye, nose for nose, ear for ear, tooth for tooth and wounds equal for equal.*"[237]

It must be explicitly stated here that matters concerning faith, which relates to the existence of God, is forever applicable and everlasting reality. The issue of *tawḥīd* (oneness of God) must be the most essential purpose of all the *Samawī* religions to proclaim.

Besides, Muslim jurists may have different opinions pertaining to the enforceability and applicability of the practical laws of the previous revealed laws. Nevertheless, it has to be accepted that the laws that were revealed before the advent of Islam which are not mentioned neither in the *Qur'ān* nor in the *Sunnah*, are not the issue of the Islamic law which means that these laws are not applicable at all. If, however, a ruling which may be prohibited in the previous law and permitted in the *Sharī'ah*, for example eating fat of the ox and the sheep. In regards to such cases the ruling of the *Sharī'ah* must be followed. It's illustrated in the *Qur'ān* as Allah says "*For those who followed the Jewish Law, We forbade every (animal) with undivided hoof, and We forbade them that fat of the ox and the sheep, except what adheres to their backs or their entrails, or is mixed up with a bone: this in recompense for their wilful disobedience: for We are true (in Our ordinances).*"[238] The permissibiliy of such items come with the following verse: "*Say: "I find not in the message received by me by inspiration any (meat) forbidden to be eaten by one who wishes to eat it, unless it be dead meat, or blood poured forth, or the flesh of swine,- for it is an abomination – or, what is impious, (meat) on which a name has been invoked, other than Allah's. But (even so), if a person is forced by necessity, without wilful disobedience, nor transgressing due limits,– thy Lord is Oft-forgiving, Most Merciful.*" Similarly, the legality of spoils of war which was prohibited before advent of Islam and it has declared by the Prophet (ṣ) that it is permissible: ""Taking booty has been made lawful to me, but it was not lawful to anyone before me."[239]

Nevertheless, the matters related to the *Shar' man qablanā* (revealed laws preceding to the *sharī'ah*) depends on the approval of the last revealed laws of Allah that is the *Qur'ān*.

Istiqrā' (Induction)

Istiqrā' is a *ḥujjah* (proof) according to the *Shāfi'ī, Mālikī* and *Ḥanbalī* Schools, however, the *Ḥanafī* School does not accept *istiqrā'* as an independent *dalīl* (proof) in proving a *ḥukm shar'ī*.[240]

Istiqrā' (induction) is a process of reasoning by which a general ruling for a certain issue is drawn from a set of principles constituting that issue, based on the fact that the ruling applied to the premise must apply to the whole issue or some of the issues. The general ruling goes beyond the information contained in the principles and does not necessarily follow from them. *Istiqrā'* is divided into two types:

a. *Istiqrā' tāmm* (complete induction) is arrived at by exploring the entire premise with the exception of the premise of disagreement. These results give a definitive (*qaṭ'ī*) ruling.

b. *Istiqrā' nāqiṣ* (incomplete induction) is achieved by following the point of disagreement comparing it with other point. The ruling in this case is mostly probable (*ẓannī ghālib*). Jurists of *uṣūl* use complete *istiqrā'*.[241]

Conclusion

A brief introduction to the legal theory (*uṣūl al-fiqh*) behind the general principles of Islamic law is now concluded. The majority of jurists agree that the four fundamental principles are unanimously accepted. There are also other principles that are activated when fundamental principles are silent and unable to help the law for its continuity. However, while there is unanimity on the four main sources of law, there are considerable differences of opinion on the validity and application of the controversial sources.

Notes

[1] The *Qur'ān* and the *Sunnah* are the two main sources of Islamic Legal Theory. However, the majority of jurists are of the view that Islamic law is based on four sources. It took the jurists considerable time to prove through the texts of the *Qur'ān* and the *Sunnah* that *ijmā'* is a valid source of law, and any that *ḥukm* (ruling) based on it should be accorded the status of the *ḥukm* of Allah. And *qiyās* was also successfully used to deduce the law from the *Qur'ān* and the *Sunnah*. The law deduced by *Qiyās* and *ijmā'* are actually dependent on evidence from the two main sources.

[2] Imran Ahsan Khan Nyazee, "*Theories of Islamic Law*" (Delhi: 1996), p. 131.

[3] See Abū Dāwud, "*Sunan*," tr. Ahmad Hasan (Lahore: sh. Muḥammad Ashraf,

1984), iii. 1019 *ḥadīth* no: 3585.

[4] Ibn al-Qayyīm Muḥammad b. Abū Bakr b. Ayūb b. Sa'd Shams al-Dīn Dimishqī (d. 751/1350), "*I'lām al-Muwaqqi'īn min Rabb al-'Ālamīn,*" edt. 'Abd al-Raḥmān al-Wakīl, Cairo v. 1 p. 51; Zaydān 'Abd al-Karīm, *ibid.*, p. 143.

[5] Wahbah Zuhaylī, "*Uṣul al-Fiqh al-Islāmi*" (Beirut: Dār al-Fikr al-Mu'āsir, 1406/1986), v.1 p. 418.

[6] Isma'īl Sha'bān Muḥammad, "*Uṣūl al-Fiqh al-Muyassar*" (Cairo: Kitāb al-Jāmī' Tawfīqiyyah, 1994), v. 1, p. 47.

[7] Zuhaylī, *ibid.*, v. 1, p. 417.

[8] Abū Isḥāq Ibrāhīm bin Mūsa al-Ghirnāṭī Shāṭibī (d. 790/1388), "*Al Muwāfaqāt fī-Uṣūl al-Sharī'ah,*" edt. 'Abd-Allah Diraz (Beirut: Dār al-Ma'rifah), v. 3 p. 36.

[9] Abū 'Ali Badr al-Dīn Muḥammad bin 'Ali Shawkānī (d. 1250/1834), "*Irshād al-Fuḥul ilā Taḥqīq al-Ḥaq min 'Ilm al-Uṣūl*" (Cairo: 1937), p. 47; Badrān, "*Uṣūl,*" p. 53.

[10] Badrān, "*Uṣūl,*" p. 54-55.

[11] Al-Āmidī, "*Al-Ihkām,*" v. 1, p. 260.

[12] *Qur'ān* 4:59

[13] Kamali, "*Principles,*" p. 10.

[14] Bannānī, "*Ḥāshiah,*" part 1, p. 223.

[15] Maḥmūt Shaltūt, "*Al-Islam 'Aqīdah wa Sharī'ah*" (Kuwait: Maktabi Dār al-Qalam, 1966), p. 23.

[16] *Ḥadīth Qudsī* or holy *ḥadīth* is a sub-category of *ḥadīth* which is saying of the Prophet (ṣ). It is considered to be the word of Allah, repeated by the Prophet (ṣ) and recorded on the condition of an *isnād* (chain of verification by authorities who heard from the Prophet) but this report is not part of the *Qur'ān.*

[17] Ghazālī, "*Al-Mustaṣfā',*" part 1, p. 68; Abū Muḥammad Muwaffiq al-Dīn, 'Abd Allah bin Aḥmad bin Muḥammad bin Qudāmah, Al-Maqdisī (d. 620/1223): "*Rawḍah al-Nāẓir wa Jannat al-Manāẓir*" (Cairo: Matba'ah al-Salafiyyah, 1342), part 1, p. 184; Imām Abī 'Abd Allah Muḥammad bin Idrīs Shafi'ī (d. 204/819), "*Al-Risālah,*" edt. Muḥammad Sayyīd Kīlāni, 2nd ed. (Cairo: Muṣṭafā al-Bābi al-Ḥalabī, 1983), p. 41.

[18] M. Mustafa Azami, "*Al-Mustashriq Schacht wa al-Sunnah al-Nabawīyyah*" (Riyad: 1985), p. 77.

[19] Khallāf, "*'Ilm,*" p. 33; Zuhailī, *ibid.*, part 1, p. 438; Zakīy al-Dīn Sha'bān, "*Uṣūl,*" p. 42.

[20] Khallāf, *ibid.*, p. 32-33; Zaydān, "*Al-Wajiz fī Uṣūl al-Fiqh,*" p. 126-127; Fahrettin Atar, "*Fıkıh Uṣulü*" (İstanbul: MŰİFY, 1996), p. 33-34; See: M. Mustafa Azami, "*Al Mustashriq,*" p. 74-77. According to him *aḥkām* verses reaches up to 393.

[21] *Qur'ān* 53:3-4.

[22] *Qur'ān* 59:7

[23] *Qur'ān* 4:80

[24] Ibn Manẓūr, *ibid.*, part 17, p. 92.

[25] Muslim, *Ṣaḥīḥ*, 2:704-705

[26] Abū Manṣūr Muḥammad b. Aḥmad Al-Azharī (d. 370/980), "*Tahdhib Al-Lughah*" (Cairo: al-Dār al-Misriyyah, 1966), part 4, p. 298.

[27] Fazlur Rahman "*Islam*" (London: 1966), p. 44.

[28] Shawkānī, "*Irshād,*" p. 33.

[29] Jalāl al-Dīn 'Abd al-Raḥmān bin abī Bakr bin Muḥammad bin Sābiq al-Din al-Khudayrī al-Suyūtī (d. 911/1505), "*Muftāh al-Jannah fī al-Ihtijāj bi al-Sunnah*" (Beirut: 1987), p. 46.

[30] See in M. Ismā'īl Sha'bān, "*Uṣūl al-Fiqh al-Muyassar,*" v.1 p.176.

[31] Naṣr al-Dīn 'Abd Allah bin 'Umar bin Muḥammed bin 'Ali Al-Shīyrazī Bayḍāwī (d. 685/1286), "*Al-Ibhāj fī Sharh Al-Minhāj 'alā' Minhāj al-Wuṣūl ilā 'Ilm al-Uṣūl,*" Beirut, part 1, p. 56.

[32] Āmidī, "*Al-Iḥkām,*" part 1, p. 169; Bayḍāwī, *ibid.*, part 2, p. 170; Shawkānī, "*Irshād,*" p. 33.

[33] Nyazee, *Islamic Jurisprudence*, p. 165.

[34] Abdur Rahim, *Jurisprudence*, p. 137; Mahmassānī, *Falsafah*, p. 132.

[35] Kamali, *Principles*, p. 68; Shawkānī, *Irshad*, p. 46; Abū Zahrah, *Uṣūl*, p. 84

[36] Abū Dāwud, *Sunan* (Hasan's trans.), III, 1036, *ḥadīth* no. 3643

[37] Badrān, *Uṣūl*, p. 78

[38] Isnawī, *Nihāyah*, II, 185; Abū Zahrah, *Uṣūl*, p. 84; Khallāf, *'Ilm*, p. 41

[39] Kamali, *Principles*, p. 70.

[40] Ghazālī, *Mustaṣfā*, v. 1, p. 86; Shawkānī, *Irshād*, p. 48

[41] Ghazālī, *Mustaṣfā*, v. 1, p. 86; Khudarī, *Uṣūl*, p. 214

[42] Shawkānī, *Irshād*, p. 47; Hitu, *Wajīz*, p. 294

[43] *Qur'ān* 8:65

[44] Ghazālī, *Mustaṣfā*, v. 1, p. 88; Shawkānī, *Irshād*, p. 47; Hitu, *Wajīz*, p. 295

[45] Nyazee, *Islamic Jurisprudence*, p. 170.

[46] Abū Zahrah, *Uṣūl*, p. 84; Shawkānī, *Irshād*, p. 49

[47] Al-Sarakhsī, *Uṣūl al-Sarakhsī*, v. 1, p. 321.

[48] Ibn Mājah, *Sunan*, II, 913, *ḥadīth* no. 2735; Muslim, *Ṣaḥīḥ*, p. 212; *ḥadīth* no. 817; Badrān, *Uṣūl*, p. 85

[49] *Qur'ān* 4:24.

[50] *Qur'ān* 4:11

[51] Shāfi'ī, *Risālah*, p. 159; Abū Zahrah, *Uṣūl*, p. 84; Maḥmasānī, *Falsafah*, p.74

[52] Shawkānī, *Irshād*, p. 48-49

[53] Āmidī, *Iḥkām*, v. 1, p. 161; Maḥmasānī, *Falsafah*, p. 74.

[54] Kamali, *Principles*, p. 72; Badrān, *Uṣūl*, p. 91; Khudarī, *Uṣūl*, p. 227

[55] *Qur'ān* 53:28

[56] Shawkānī, *Irshād*; p. 64; Hitu, *Wajīz*, p. 321

[57] Muhammad Mustafa Azami, *Studies in Ḥadīth Methodology and Literature* (Indianapolis: American Trust Publication, 1977), p. 62; Muṣṭafa Ḥusnī Sibā'ī, *Al-Sunnah wa Makānatuhā fil-Tashrī' al-Islāmī*, 3rd ed. (Beirut, np, 1982), p. 95.

[58] Sibā'ī, *Al-Sunnah*, p. 96.

[59] Shawkānī, *Irshād*, p. 64.

[60] Hitu, *Wajīz*, p. 316; Kamali, *Principles*, p. 80.

[61] *Qur'ān* 53:3-4

[62] Abū Zahrah, *Uṣūl*, p. 59; Khallāf, *'Ilm*, p. 23; 'Abdur Raḥīm, *Jurisprudence*, p. 69

[63] *Qur'ān* 4:59

[64] Abū Ja'far Muḥammad b. Jarīr Tabarī (d. 310/922), "*Jāmi' al-Bayān Ta'wīl al-Qur'ān*" (Bulāq: 1329), v. 8, p. 486-490.

[65] Muḥammad b. 'Umar b. al-Ḥusayn Abū 'Abd Allah Fakhr al-Dīn Rāzī (d. 606/1210), "*Mafātīḥ al-Ghayb: Al-mushtahar bi-al-Tafsīr al-Kabīr*" (Cairo: al-Matba'ah al-Āmirah al-Sharafīyah, 1324-1327), v. 3, p. 242-43.

[66] Ghazālī, "*Al-Mustaṣfā'*," v. 1, p. 111.

[67] *Qur'ān* 3:113

[68] Abū 'Abd Allah Muḥammad Ibn Mājah (d. 273/886), "*Sunan*," II, 1303, *ḥadīth* no: 3950, Istanbul, 1981.

[69] Ghazālī, "*Al-Mustaṣfā'*," v. 1, p. 111; Āmidī "*Iḥkām*," v. 1, p. 220-221.

[70] E.W. Lane, *ibid.*; Ibn Manẓūr, *ibid.*

[71] *Qur'ān* 10:71

[72] E.W. Lane, *ibid.*; Ahmad Hasan, "*The Doctrine of Ijmā' in Islam*" (Islamabad: Islamic Research Institute, 1992), p. 15.

[73] Āmidī, "*Al-Iḥkām*" part 1, p. 101; Mas'ūd bin 'Umar bin 'Abd Allah Sa'd al-Dīn Taftazānī (d. 793/1390), " *Al-Talwīḥ 'alā Al-Tawḍīḥ*" on the margin of 'Ubayd Allah bin Mas'ūd Ṣadr al-Sharī'ah" (Cairo: 'Īsā al-Bābi al-Ḥalabī 1327/1957), part 2, p. 41; Bukhārī, "*Kashf,*" part 1, p. 946; Shawkānī, "*Irshād,*" p. 63; Ibn 'Abd al-Shakūr,Muḥib Allah al-Baḥarī al-Hindīy (d. 1119/1707) "*Musallam al-Thubūt ma'a Fawātiḥ al-Raḥamūt fī Uṣūl al-Fiqh*" (Cairo: 1906), part 2, p. 166.

[74] Bukhārī, "*Kashf,*" v. 3, p. 227.

[75] Āmidī, "*Iḥkām,*" v. 1, p. 196.

[76] Ghazālī, "*Mustaṣfā',*" v. 1, p. 110.

[77] Aḥmad bin Idrīs bin 'Abd al-Raḥmān, Abū 'Abbās Sha'b al-Dīn al-Sanhājī al-Mālikī Qarafī (d. 684/1285), "*Sharḥ Tanqīḥ al-Fuṣūl fī Ikhtisār al-Mahṣūl fī al-Uṣūl,*" edt. Tāhā 'Abd al-Raūf Sa'd, (Cairo: Maktabah al-Azharīyyah, nd.), p. 141.

[78] 'Ubayd Allah Ibn Mas'ūd bin Tāj al-Sharī'ah al-Ḥanafī Ṣadr al-Sharī'ah (d. 747/1346), "*Al-Tawdīḥ fī Ḥall Jawāmid al-Tanqīḥ*" (Cairo: Maṭba'ah Muḥammad 'Alī Ṣabīh, nd.), v. 2, p. 41.

[79] Sha'bān, "*Uṣūl,*" p. 45.

[80] Ghazālī, "*Al-Mustaṣfā',*" v.1, p. 121; Āmidī, "*Al-Iḥkām,*" v. 1, p. 129; Shawkānī, "*Irshād,*" p. 74; Molla Husraw, "*Mar'āt al-Uṣūl,*" v. 2 p. 259; Laknawī, "*Fawātiḥ al-Raḥamūt,*" v. 2, p. 232; Ibn Amīr al-Ḥajj, "*al-Taqrīr,*" v. 3, p. 101; Bukhārī, "*Kashf,*" v.2 p. 948; Isnawī, "*Sallam al-Wuṣūl,*" v. 2, p. 375; Bannānī "*Ḥāshiah,*" v. 2 p. 163.

[81] Muḥammad bin Aḥmad bin Sahl Abū Bakr Shams al-Aimmah al-Ḥanafī Sarakhsī (d. 483/1090), "*Al-Uṣūl,*" edt. Abū al-Wafā' al-Afghānī, (Beirut: Dār al-Fikr, 1991), v. 1, p. 305-306.

[82] 'Ali bin Muḥammed bin 'Abd al-Karīm Abū al-Ḥasan Fakhr al-Islam al-Bazdawī al-Ḥanafī (482/1089), "*Uṣūl Al-Bazdawī on the margin of 'Abd al-'Azīz al-Bukhārī Khashf al-Asrār*" (Istanbul: 1308), p. 339, reprint, Beirut Dār al-Kitāb al-Arabi 1394/1974.

[83] Ghazālī, "*Al-Mustaṣfā',*" v. 1, p. 121-122.

[84] Ahmad Hasan, "*The Doctrine of Ijmā' in Islam,*" p. 104.

[85] Zuhaylī, "*Uṣūl,*" part 1, p. 536-537.

[86] Ghazālī, "*Al-Mustaṣfā*," v. 1 p. 101.

[87] Āmidī, "*Al-Ihkām*," v. 1, p. 226.

[88] Bazdawī, *ibid.*, v. 3, p. 239.

[89] See Abū Dāwud, "*Sunan*," tr. Ahmad Hasan (Lahore: sh. Muḥammad Ashraf, 1984 iii. 1019 *ḥadīth* no: 3585.

[90] Āmidī, "*Ihkām*," v. 3, p. 183

[91] Āmidī, "*Al-Iḥkām*," v. 3, p. 183; Ibn 'Abd al-Shakūr, "*Musallam al-Thubūt*," part 2, p. 246.

[92] Āmidī, "*Al-Iḥkām*," v. 3, p. 186; Shawkānī, "*Irshād*," p. 198; Kamali "*Principles*," p. 198.

[93] Nyazee, *Islamic Jurisprudence*, p. 214

[94] Nyazee, *ibid.*

[95] Āmidī, *ibid.*, v. 3, p. 262-65.

[96] Āmidī, *ibid.*, v. 3, p. 273. See in Ahmad Hasan, "*Analogical Reasoning in Islamic Jurisprudence*" (Islamabad: Islamic research Institute, 1986), p. 101.

[97] Kamali "*Principles*," p. 200.

[98] Abū Bakr Aḥmad b. 'Alī al-Rāzī Jaṣṣāṣ (d. 370/981), "*Al-Fuṣūl fī al-Uṣūl*," edt. Ājil Jasīm al-Nashmī, (Kuwait: Wazārāh al-Awkāf wa al-Shu'ūn al-Islāmiyyah, 1988, qf. from Ahmad Hasan "*Analogical reasoning*," p. 100.

[99] *Qur'ān* 5:90

[100] Sulaymān bin al-Ash'ās Abū Dāwūd (d. 275/888), "*Sunnan*," iii, 1043, *ḥadīth* no: 3672.

[101] Āmidī, "*Al-Iḥkām*," v. 3, p. 193; Bukhārī, "*Uṣūl*," v. 3, p. 344; Isnawī, "*Nihāyāt*," v. 4, p. 53; Kamali, "*Principles*," p. 200-216.

[102] Isnawī, "*Nihāyāt*," v. 3, p. 33; Āmidī, "*Al-Iḥkām*,"v. 3, p. 22; Ibn Abd al-Shakūr, "*Musallam*," part 2, p. 320; Ibn 'Amīr al-Ḥajj, "*Al-Taqrīr*," v. 3, p. 221; Baidhawī, "*Al-Ibḥāj*," v. 3, p. 18.

[103] *Qur'ān* 17:23.

[104] *Qur'ān* 4:25.

[105] Āmidī, "*Al-Iḥkām*," v. 3, p. 63; Taftazānī, "*Ḥāshiyah*," part 2, p. 247; Ibn 'Abd al Shakūr, "*Musallam*," part 2, p. 320; Molla Ḥusraw, "*Mir'āt al-Uṣūl*," v. 2 p. 336; Ṣadr al-Sharī'ah, "*Al-Tawdīḥ*," v. 2, p. 82; Ibn 'Amīyr al-Ḥajj, "*Al-Taqrīr*," v. 2, p. 222; Ahmad Hasan, "*Analogical Reasoning*," p. 83.

[106] Shawkānī, "*Irshād*," p. 222; Ibn Qayyīm, "*I'lām*," v. 1, p. 178. See in Kamali

"*Principles*," p. 215, and Ahmad Hasan, *ibid.*, p. 83.

107 Bukhārī, "*Kashf*," part 2, p. 1122; Taftazānī, "*Talwīḥ*," v. 2, p. 81; Ibn 'Abd al-Shakūr, "*Musallam*," part 2, p. 320.

108 Ghazālī, "*Al-Mustaṣfā*," part 2, p. 56,59,70; Āmidī, "*Al-Iḥkām*," part 3, p. 64; Shāshī Isḥāq bin Ibrāhīm Abū Ya'qūp al-Khorasānī al-Shāshī (d. 325/937), "*Uṣūl al-Shāshī with 'Umdah al-Ḥawāshī*" (Delhi: 1303), p. 91; Taftazānī, "*Talwīḥ*," part 2 p. 53; Bukhārī, "*Uṣūl*," part 2, p. 990.

109 Subkī, 'Abd al-Wahhāb bin 'Alī bin 'Abd al-Kāfī Tājj al-Dīn al-Subkī (d. 771/1370), "*Jam' al-Sharḥ al-Jalāl al-Maḥallī 'Alā' Jam' al-Jawāmī'*" (Cairo: Maktabah al-Tijārīyyah, nd.), part 2, p. 177.

110 *Qur'ān* 59:2

111 Abū Zahrah, Muḥammad (d. 1395/1974), "*Uṣūl al-Fiqh*" (Cairo: Dār al-Fikr al-'Arabi, 1958), p. 179-180. See in Kamali "*Principles*" p. 220.

112 'Alī Taqīy Ḥaydarī, "*Uṣūl al-Istinbāt*" (Baghdat: Matba'ah al-Rābitah, 1959), p. 259-73; Hāshim Maghrūf Ḥusaynī, "*Mabadi' al-'Āmmah li al-Fiqh al-Jaghfarī*" (Baghdat: Dār al-Nashr li al-Jam'īyyīyn Maktabah al-Naḥḍah, nd.), p. 290.

113 Shaḥ Walī Allah Dihlawī (d. 1176/1776), "*Ḥujjah Allah al-Bālighah*," 1954/5, I, 130, Delhi, qf. J M S Baljon, "*Religion and thought of Shah Wali Allah Dihlawi*," Leiden: E. J. Brill, Netherlands, 1986, p. 169.

114 Dihlawī, "*Tafhīmati Ilāhiyyah*," Dabhel 1936, I, 40; II, 133, qf. Baljon *ibid.*, p. 170.

115 *Ibid.*

116 Shāṭibī, "*Al-Muwāfaqāt*," v. 1, p. 40.

117 *Ibid.*, v. 2, p. 233.

118 *Ibid.*, v. 4, p. 206.

119 *Qur'ān* 39:18

120 *Qur'ān* 39:55

121 Ibn Mājah, "*Sunan*," ii, 784, *ḥadīth* no: 2340; Shāṭibī, "*Muwāfaqāt*," v. 3, p. 17; Khudarī, "*Tārīkh*," p. 199.

122 *Qur'ān* 2:185

123 See more about *istiḥsān*: Saim Kayadibi, *Istiḥsān the Doctrine of Juristic Preference in Islamic Law* (Selangor: IBT, 2010).

124 Bukhārī, "*Kashf*," part 4, p. 3.

125 Kamali, "*Istiḥsān*," p. 24; Al-Jaṣṣāṣ, "*Al-Fusūl*," v. 4, p. 234.

[126] Bazdawī, "*Usūl,*" v. 4, p. 3.

[127] Bukhārī, "*Kashf,*" v. 4, p. 3; Taftazānī, "*Talwīḥ,*" v. 2, p. 163; Ibn al-Ḥājib, "*Muntahā,*" p. 207

[128] Sarakhsī, "*Uṣūl,*" v. 2, p. 200.

[129] For more about Imām al-Shāfi'ī see: Abū 'Iyd Ḥasan Muḥammad Salīm, "*Al-Imām al-Shāfi'ī wa Atharuhu fī Uṣūl al-Fiqh,*" unpublished PhD dissertation at Faculty of *Sharī'ah* and Qānūn Al-Azhar University, Egypt,1976.

[130] Anṣārī, "*Ghāyat al-Wuṣūl,*" p. 139; 'Alwānī, "*The Ethics,*" p. 75; Ghazālī, "*Mustaṣfā,*" v. 1, p. 274, *ibid*, "*Mankhūl,*" p. 374; Isnawī, "*Nihāyat al-Sūl,*" v. 4, p. 399.

[131] Kayadibi, *Istiḥsān*, p. 115.

[132] Abū Zahrah, "*Uṣūl,*" p. 207; Shāṭibī, "*Al-I'tiṣām,*" v. 2, p. 137.

[133] Shāṭibī, "*I'tiṣām,*" v. 2, p. 137.

[134] Bukhārī, "*Kashf,*" v. 4, p. 3.

[135] Ghazālī, "*Mustaṣfā,*" v. 1, p. 283; Juwaynī, "*Talkhīṣ,*" v. 3, p. 311,313.

[136] Sha'bān, "*Islam Hukuk Ilminin Esaslari,*" p. 168; Khallāf, "*Masāder,*" p. 72.

[137] Ibn al-Humām, "*Fatḥ al-Qadīr,*" v. 6, p. 215; Khallāf, "*Masāder,*" p. 72-73; Sha'bān "*İslam Hukuk Ilminin Esaslari*" p. 168.

[138] Ibn al-Humām, "*Taḥrīr,*" v. 4, p. 78; Bazdawī, "*Kashf*" v. 4, p. 3, 5-6; Jaṣṣāṣ, "*Al-Fuṣūl*" v. 4, p. 234, 243; Ṣadr al-Sharī'ah, "*Tawḍīḥ,*" v. 2, p. 162-163.

[139] *Ibid.*, v. 2, p. 161-163.

[140] Bazdawī, "*Uṣūl,*" v. 4, p. 3, 5-6. See: Anṣārī, "*Fawātiḥ*" v. 2, p. 320-321; Sarakhsī, "*Uṣūl,*" v. 2, p. 200, 202-203.

[141] Khallaf, "*Maṣāder,*" p. 72,

[142] Ibn Nujaym, "*Fatḥ al-Ghaffār*" v. 3, p. 30.

[143] Shāṭibī, "*Al-Muwāfaqāt,*" v. 4, p. 208.

[144] Ḥasan, "*Analogical reasoning,*" p. 92.

[145] Bazdawī, "*Uṣūl,*" v. 4, p. 6; Sarakhsī, "*Uṣūl,*" v. 2, p. 203

[146] Sarakhsī, "*Uṣūl,*" v. 2, p. 202, 203, 206; Bazdawī, "*Uṣūl,*" v. 4, p. 3, 6, 10; Nasafī, "*Kashf,*" v. 2, p. 296; Ṣadr al-Sharī'ah, "*Tawḍīḥ,*" v. 2, p. 162, 169.

[147] Karamastī, "*Al-Wajīz*" p. 185; Bazdawī, "*Uṣūl,*" v. 3, p. 389; Sarakhsī, "*Uṣūl,*" v. 2, p. 192, 206; Bukhārī, "*Kashf,*" v. 3, p. 389; v. 2, p. 11.

[148] Sarakhsī, "*Uṣūl,*" v. 2, p. 201; Jaṣṣāṣ, "*Fuṣūl,*" v. 4, p. 238.

[149] *Qur'ān* 5:33-34

[150] Jaṣṣāṣ, "*Fuṣūl*" v. 4, p. 239.

[151] Zaydān, "*Al-Wajīz*" p. 232.

[152] Ibn Humām, "*Fatḥ al-Qadīr,*" v. 6, p. 201.

[153] Abū Muḥammad 'Alī al-Andalūsī al-Ẓāhirī Ibn Ḥazm (d. 456/1064), "*Al-Iḥkām fī Uṣūl al-Aḥkām*" (Beirut: Dār al-Kutup al-'Ilmīyyahm nd.), v. 5, p. 590; Ibn al-Ḥājib (d. 646/1249), "*Mukhtaṣar al-Muntaha' al-Sūl wa al-'Amal* " (Constantinople: al-Maktabah al-Islāmiyyah, 1310), p. 217; Baiḍāwī, "*Al-Ibhāj,*" part 3, p. 111; Bukhārī, "*Kashf,*" v. 2, p. 1098; Molla Ḥusraw "*Mar'āt al-Uṣūl,*" v. 2 p. 367; Sarakhsī, "*Uṣūl,*" v. 2, p. 225; Bannānī, "*Ḥāshiah,*" part 2, p. 285; Abū Zahrah, "*Uṣūl,*" p. 286.

[154] Al-'Ālim Aḥmad b. Muḥammad b. 'Alī al-Fayyūmī Muqrī, (d. 770), "*Misbāḥ al-Munīr fī Gharīb al-Sharkh al-Kabīr li al-Rāfī',*" edt. Abd al-'Aẓīm al-Shannāwī, (Cairo: Dār al-Ma'ārif, nd.)

[155] Isnawī "*Nihāyat,*" part 3, p. 131.

[156] Qarafī, "*Tanqīḥ,*" p. 199.

[157] Bazdawī, "*Kashf,*" part 3, p. 377.

[158] Shawkānī, "*Irshād*" p. 237.

[159] *Qur'ān* 2:29.

[160] *Qur'ān* 45:13.

[161] Sha'bān Zakīy al-Dīn "*Islam hukuk ilminin Esaslari,*" tr. Ibrāhīm Kāfi Dönmez, Ankara 1990, p. 189; Abu Zahrah, "*Uṣūl,*" p. 236; Khudari, "*Uṣūl,*" p. 354-355.

[162] Shawkānī, "*Irshād,*" p. 238.

[163] Al-Majallah, clause: 8

[164] Suyūṭī, "*Al-Ashbāh,*" p. 47; Majallah al-Aḥkām al-'Adlīyyah, clause: 5.

[165] Abū Zahrah, "*Uṣūl,*" p. 236; Shawkānī, "*Irshād,*" p. 238; Kamali, "*Principle,*" p. 301-302.

[166] Kamali, "*Principle,*" p. 268.

[167] Al-Shāṭibī, "*Al-Muwāfaqāt,*" v. 2, p. 3.

[168] *Qur'ān* 21:107.

[169] *Qur'ān* 22:78.

[170] Ibn Manẓūr, *Lisān al-'Arab.*

[171] Al-Shāṭibī, "*Al-Muwāfaqāt,*" v. 2, p. 25.

[172] Badrān, *ibid.*, p. 210.

[173] See: Ghazālī, "*Al-Mustaṣfā*," p. 174-179.

[174] Ibn 'Āshūr, "*Maqāsid el-Sharī'ah al-Islāmīyyah*," p. 123.

[175] The details of the seven essential values will be elaborated under the topic of *maqāṣid al-sharī'ah* in chapter five.

[176] Ibn 'Āshūr, "*Maqāsid al-Sharī'ah al-Islāmīyyah*," p. 123.

[177] Ibn 'Āshūr, *ibid.*, p. 138.

[178] Ibn 'Āshūr, *ibid.*, p. 139.

[179] Ghazālī, "*Al-Mustaṣfā*," v. 1, p. 288.

[180] Shāṭibī, "*Al-Muwāfaqāt*," v. 2, p. 8.

[181] *Ibid.*, v. 2, p. 10-11.

[182] Shāṭibī, "*Al-Muwāfaqāt*," v. 2, p. 327.

[183] Ghazālī, *ibid.*, v. 1, p. 311.

[184] Ghazālī, "*Al-Mankhūl min Ta'līqāt al-Uṣūl*," Al-Ṭab'ah al-Thāniyah, Dār al-Fikr al-Arabi, Damascus, p: 355.

[185] Ḥasan bin Muḥammad bin Maḥmūd Aṭṭār (d. 1250/1835), "*Ḥāshiyah 'Alā Sharḥ Jalāl al-Maḥallī 'Alā Jam' al-Jawāmi*" (Egypt: Maṭba'ah 'Ilmīyyah, 1316 AH), part 2, p. 339.

[186] Zuhaylī, "*Uṣūl*," part 2, p. 799.

[187] Khallāf, "*'Ilm*," p. 87; Badrān, "*Uṣūl*," p. 214.

[188] Shāṭibī, "*Al-I'tisām*," v. 2, p. 307-314.

[189] Ghazālī, "*Al-Mustaṣfā'*," v. 1, p. 141.

[190] Ibn 'Āshur, "*Maqāṣid*," p. 121.

[191] Shāṭibī, "*Al-Muwāfaqāt*," v. 2, p. 29-30.

[192] *Qur'ān* 23:71

[193] Ibn Manẓūr, "*Lisān*," part 11, p. 144.

[194] Zamakhsharī, jār Allah Maḥmūd bin 'Umar (d. 538/1144), "*Al-Kashshāf al-Ḥaqā'iq Ghawāmiḍ al-Tanẓī wa 'Uyūn al-Aqāwīl fī Wujūh al-Ta'wīl*" (Beirut: Dār al-Kitāb al-'Arabi, 1366), part 2, p. 138.

[195] Ibn Manẓūr, "*Lisān*," part 4, p. 311.

[196] Zuhaylī, "*Uṣūl*," part 2, p. 828.

[197]Kamal Muḥammad bin 'Abd al-Waḥīd bin 'Abd al-Ḥamīd bin Mas'ūd al-Ḥanafī Ibn al-Humām (d. 861/1457), "*Al-Taysīr Sharḥ al-Tahrīr fī Uṣūl al-Fiqh*" (Cairo: al-Amīyrīyyah Bulāq, 1317), part 1, p. 317.

[198] *Qur'ān* 4:11

[199] Sha'bān, "*Islam Hukuku*," p. 175.

[200] Abū Zahrah, "*Uṣūl*," p. 217; Sha'bān, *ibid*., p. 176; Fahreddīn Atar, *ibid*., p. 88. Zuhaylī, "*Uṣūl*" v. 2, p. 829; Ismā'īl, Muḥammad Sha'bān,"*Uṣūl al-Fiqh al-Muyassar*," *ibid*., v. 2, p. 285.

[201] Kamali, "*Principles*," p. 286; Ismā'īl, "*Uṣul*" v. 2, p. 289; Atar, "*Fıkıh Usulü*," p. 89.

[202] Ismā'īl, "*Uṣūl*," v. 2, p. 289; Kamali, "*Principles*," p. 286; Atar, *ibid*.

[203] Ismā'īl, *ibid*.; Kamali, *ibid*.

[204] *Ibid*.

[205] Al-Majallah: clause: 36.

[206] *Ibid*., p. 40.

[207] *Ibid*., p. 41.

[208] *Ibid*., p. 43.

[209] *Ibid*., p. 45.

[210] See: *Majmā' al-Fiqh al-Islāmī*, "*Karārāt wa al-Tawsīyyāt*," Kuwait, 1988.

[211] Ismā'īl Hakkı Izmirlī (d. 1946), "'*Ilm al-Khilāf*" (Istanbul: 1330), p. 130; Shāfi'ī, "*Al-Ūmm*" (Beirut: 1983), v. 3, p. 272; Muḥammad Muṣṭafā Shalabī, "*Uṣūl al-Fiqh al-Islāmī*" (Beirut: 1986), p. 304.

[212] Ibn Fares, Aḥmad (d. 395/1004), "*Mu'ājam Maqāyīs al-Lughah*" (Beirut: Dār Iḥyā' al-Turāth al-'Arabi), part 3, p. 66; Al-Rāzī, Muḥammad b. Abī Bakr (d. 660), "*Mukhtār al-Ṣiḥaḥ*" (Beirut: Dār al-Ma'rifah, nd.), p. 113.

[213] Ibn Manẓūr, "*Lisān*," part 8, p. 96; Anees Ibrahīm, "*Al-Mu'jam al-Wasīṭ*" (Cairo: Dār al-Ma'ārif, 1973), part 1, p. 310.

[214] Shāṭibī, "*Al-Muwāfaqāt*," part 4, p. 198.

[215] Ibn al-Qayyīm, "*I'lām al-Muwaqqi'īn*," part 3, p. 147.

[216] Qarāfī, "*Kitāb Anwār*," v. 2, p. 33.

[217] Ibn al-Qayyīm, "*I'lam*," v. 3, p. 147.

[218] Shaṭibi "*Al-Muwāfaqāt*," v. 2, p. 358-361.

[219] *Ibid*., v. 2, p. 358.

[220] *Ibid*., v. 2, p. 359.

[221] Abū Zahrah, "*Uṣūl*," p. 231; Shāṭibī, *ibid*., v. 2, p. 361.

[222] Ibid; see them in detail in Kamali, "*Principles*," p. 310-320.

[223] Al-Majallah: clause: 30.

[224] Shawkānī, "*Irshād*," p. 213; Ghazāli, "*Al-Mustaṣfā*," v. 1, p. 135; Āmidī, "*Al-*

Iḥkām," v. 3, p. 133; Shīrāzī, "*Sharḥ al-Luma,*" p. 50; Molla Husrāw, "*Mar'āt al-Uṣūl,*" v. 2 p. 250; Bannānī, "*Ḥāshīah,*" part 2, p. 288.

[225] Ibn 'Abd al-Shakūr, "*Musallam,*" part 2, p. 120; Bannānī, "*Ḥāshiah,*" v. 2, p. 146.

[226] Kamali, *Principles*, p. 210.

[227] Shawkānī, "*Irshād,*" p. 213; Isnawī, "*Nihāyat,*" part 3, p. 173; Ghazālī, "*Al-Mustaṣfā',*" part 1, p. 135; Āmidī, "*Al-Iḥkām,*" part 3, p. 133; Banānī, "*Ḥāshiah,*" part 2, p. 288; Maḥmūd bin Aḥmad bin Maḥmūd Abū al-Manāqib Sha'b al-Dīn, Zanjānī min al-Shāfi'ī (d. 656/1258), "*Takhrīj al-Furū' 'Alā al-Uṣūl,*" edt. Muḥammad Adīb Ṣālīḥ (Dimishq: Muassasah al-Risālah, 1962), p. 82.

[228] Muḥammad bin Aḥmad bin 'Alī al-Idrīsi, al-Sharīf Tilmisānī al-Mālikī (d. 771/1370), "*Muftāḥ al-Wuṣūl Ilā Binā' al-Furū' 'alā al-Uṣūl,*" Jāmi'ah al-Azhar, Kullīyah al-Sharī'ah reg.no: 72 Cairo, p. 120.

[229] Bukhāri, "*Kashf,*" part 2, p. 937; Ibn al-Qayyīm, "*I'lām,*" part 1, p. 30 and part 4, p. 156.

[230] Banānī, "*Ḥāshiah,*" part 2, p. 289.

[231] Bukhārī, "*Kashf,*" part 2, p. 938.

[232] Zuhaylī, "*Uṣūl,*" part 2, p. 838.

[233] Kamali, "*Principles,*" p. 229.

[234] *Qur'ān* 42:13

[235] *Qur'ān* 2:183

[236] Abū Zahrah, *Uṣūl*, p. 242.

[237] *Qur'ān* 5:45.

[238] *Qur'ān* 6:146

[239] Muslim, *Ṣaḥīḥ*, p.301, *ḥadīth* no. 1137.

[240] Ghazālī, "*Al-Mustaṣfā',*" v. 1, p. 33; Shāṭibī, "*Al-Muwāfaqāt,*" v. 3, p. 298-304.

[241] *Ibid.*

CHAPTER THREE

The *Ḥukm Shar'ī* (*Aḥkām*)

The *ḥukm shar'ī* in its literal sense carries the meaning of a rule of Islamic law. Thus *aḥkām* (rules) is the plural form of *ḥukm* (rule), which means rule, command, the absolute, order, judgment, injunction, prescription, and decree.[1] This rule could be a rule of any kind; it is to command one to delegate an order to another whether approval or disapproval. You could say that the moon is rising or the moon is not rising,[2] or that fire burns.

Technically, it is considered a rule of Islamic law. Āmidī (d. 631/1234)[3] defines *adillah* as the science of the proofs of *fiqh* and the indications that they provide with regard to the *aḥkām* of the *sharī'ah*.

The *ḥukm shar'ī* consists of four fundamental elements. These elements are: the *Ḥākim* (Lawgiver), the *maḥkūm alayh* (the subject), the *maḥkūm fīh* (the act of the *mukallaf*), and the *ḥukm* (ruling).

The first element of the *ḥukm shar'ī* is the *Ḥākim* (Lawgiver) who is the true source from which the *ḥukm* originates. Allah Almighty is the original source for Islamic law that is the absolute *Ḥākim* (Lawgiver) of everthing in this world and the Hereafter.

The second element of the *ḥukm shar'ī* is the *maḥkūm alayh* (the subject) for whose conduct the *ḥukm* is stipulated, that is *mukallaf*.

The third element of the *ḥukm shar'ī* is the *maḥkūm fīh* (the act).

The fourth element of the *ḥukm shar'ī* is the *ḥukm* (ruling). It is an Arabic word *ḥukm* (pl. *aḥkām*) in its literal sense means a command as mentioned above. It is also considered Islamic law.

The *ḥukm sharʿī* is therefore defined as: "A communication from Allah, the Exalted, related to the acts of the subjects through a demand or option, or through a declaration." (*Huwa khiṭābullahi taʿālā al-mutaʿalliq bi-afʿāl al-mukallafīn bil-iqtiḍāʾ aw at-takhyīyr aw al-waḍʿī.)*[4].

The above definition of *al-ḥukm* is found only amongst the *uṣūlī* (juristic scholars). The first point of the definition is that any communication must be from Allah otherwise it is not accepted and cannot be considered *a ḥukm*. This communication is related to the actions of the subject (*mukallaf*).

The communication related to the act of the subject (*mukallaf*) from Allah can either be in the form of a demand (*iqtiḍāʾ*) or a choice (*takhyīyr*) or a declaration (*waḍʿī*).

The relationship also enables the *mujtahid* (jurist) to evaluate the requirements, and to judge whether it is for the command for the act or the prohibition. Allah says;

> "*O you who believe! Observe ṣawm (fasting).*"[5]

This verse contains *a ḥukm* which demands obedience.

> "*And come not near to the unlawful sexual intercourse.*"[6]

This verse contains *a ḥukm* which requires prohibition.

The *ḥukm* (rule) is clarified through a request (*ṭalab* or *iqtiḍāʾ*). The request in this case is communicated in the form of a command of an act or its prohibition. The request may or may not be binding. When the request is binding, it creates *wujūb* (an obligation) or *taḥrīm* (prohibition), which are established by *dalīl qaṭʿī* (definite proof). When the request is not binding, then the ruling creates *nadb* (recommendation) or *makrūh* (discouraged), which are established without definitive proof.

Allah says "*O you who believe! Fulfil (your) obligations.*"[7]

This verse is addressed to the *mukallaf* (subject), and consists of a particular demand. And "*O you who believe! Let not a group scoff at another group, it may be that the latter are better than the former....*"[8]

This *Qur'anic* text conveys a prohibition to the *mukallaf.* The freedom of choice is given to the *mukallaf* (subject) a choice to commit the act or avoid it.

On the other hand if the subject is free to perform the act it is known as *mubaḥ* (permissible). For example "*But when you finish the iḥrām pilgrimage (of ḥajj or 'umrah), you may hunt...*"[9]

This *ḥukm* conveys an option for the *mukallaf* (subject) and he has the freedom to act or not to.

As a final point of the definition, the communication may be clarified through an enactment or declaration; this is neither a demand nor an option. However, it is in relation to an act which is connected to another act by reason of *sabab* (cause), *rukn* (element), *sharṭ* (condition), *māni'*(impediment), *ṣiḥḥah, fasād, buṭlān* (validity, nullity, vitiation).

For example, "*...and ḥajj to the House is a duty that mankind owe to Allah for those who can afford the expenses...*"[10]

Financial ability is the condition for the application of the rule.[11]

The identification of *ḥukm shar'ī* is perceived differently between the *uṣūlīs* (juristic scholars) and the *fuqahā.*

For instance Allah says "*And perform al-ṣalāt*"[12] which is a *ḥukm shar'ī* itself according to the *uṣūlīs*. However, according to the *fuqahā'*, it is the effect or the result of the demand in this verse, namely the *wujūb* (obligation), which represents the *ḥukm shar'ī.*[13]

Basically, *ḥukm shar'ī* (legal rule) is divided into two main categories: the first is *al-ḥukm al-taklīfi* (defining law) and the other is *al-ḥukm al-waḍ'ī* (declaratory law). In contemporary common law, Hart has divided it into primary and secondary rules. The only difference is that the rules of Islamic law are based on religious law. The Muslim jurists designate the category of primary rules as *al-ḥukm al-taklīfi* (defining law). The category of secondary rules is designated as the *al-ḥukm al-waḍ'ī.*[14] *Al-ḥukm al-taklīfi* (defining law) is a communication from Allah, the exalted, related to the acts of the *mukallaf* (subjects), which consists of a demand or an option; it arises in the five categories of *wājīb* or *farḍ* (obligatory), *mandūb* (recommended), *makrūh* (adversity), *ḥarām* (prohibited) and *mubāḥ* (permissible). In addition, the *Ḥanafī* School deduces seven varieties from the same definition: 1. *Farḍ* (obligatory) 2. *Wājīb* (obligatory) 3. *Mandūb* (recommended) 4. *Makrūh karāḥat al-taḥrīm* (strongly disapproved) 5. *Makrūh karāḥat al-tanzīh* (disapproval) 6. *Ḥarām* (prohibited) 7. *Mubāḥ* (permissible).

The *ḥukm al-waḍ'ī* is a communication from Allah, the exalted, related to the acts of the *mukallaf* (subject) in a manner that is declaratory (*waḍ'ī*), in another word it is explanatory component for *al-ḥukm al-taklīfiyyah* through its fundamental tools which consist of 1. *Al-sabab* (the cause) 2. *Al-rukn* (the element), 3. *Al-sharṭ* (the condition) 4. *Al-māni'*(the impediment), 5. *Al-ṣiḥḥah* (the validity), 6. *Al-fasād* (the nullity), 7. *Al-buṭlān* (the vitiation), 8. *Al-'azīmah* (strict rul es), and 9. *Al-rukhṣah* (concessionary rules).[15]

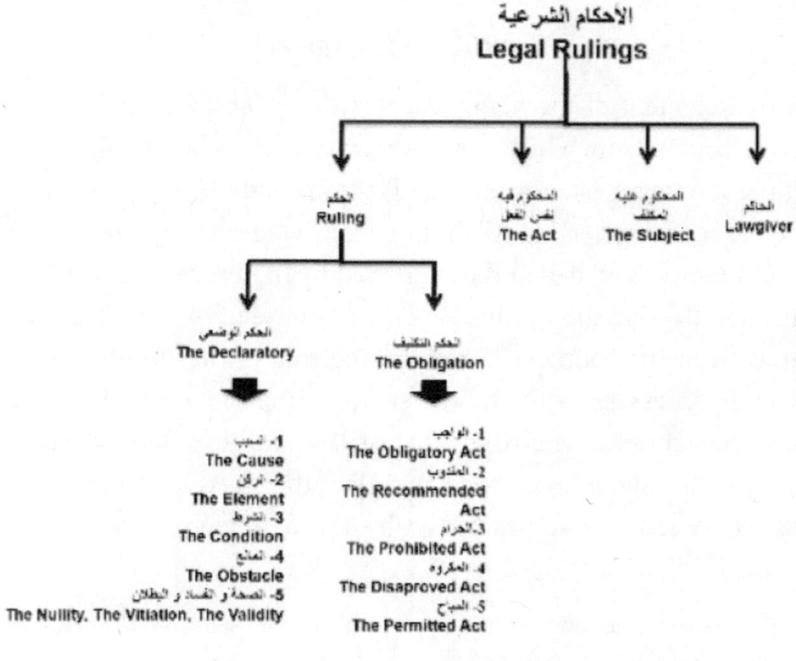

On the other hand, the *al-ḥukm al-waḍ'ī* can be classified and simply covered by the following concepts: as it was classified, in general, by Nyazee into three types:

The first classification of *al-ḥukm al-waḍʿī* is the classification of secondary rules into *sabab* (cause), *sharṭ* (condition), and *mānīʿ* (impediment), which are considered more with this classification by the *uṣūlī* scholars.

The second classification of *al-ḥukm al-waḍʿī* is the classification that the *faqīh* scholars give emphasis more since it concerns to the performance of acts. These are *al-ṣiḥḥah* (validity), *al-fasād* (nullity), and *al-buṭlān* (vitiation).

The third classification of *al-ḥukm al-waḍʿī* is the classification that it helps to jurists identify the general principles of the law and the exceptions to these general principles and which are used as tools for achieving analytical consistency. These are *al-ʿazīmah* (a comprehensive general rules) and *al-rukhṣah* (exemptions).

The Ḥākim (Lawgiver)

The first element of the *ḥukm sharʿī* is the *Ḥākim* (Lawgiver) who is the true source from which the *ḥukm* originates. Allah Almighty is the original source for Islamic law that is the absolute *Ḥākim* (Lawgiver).

Ḥākim (Lawgiver), is Allah, one from whom the communication (*khiṭāb*) issues is related and is conveyed by the Prophet (ṣ) explaining it through the *Sunnah* of him. After the demise of him, jurists derived rulings from the sources. Therefore, the role of the Prophet (ṣ) is to convey the message of the Lawgiver, while the role of the jurists is to derive new rulings. The originator of law and giver of command is evidenced by the sources of Islamic law that *ḥākim* in this sense is Allah. This sense is substantiated by the following verses from the *Qur'ān*:

> "*The command rests with none but Allah: He declares the truth, and He is the best of judges*".[16]

> *"Surely, His is the command and He is swiftest in taking account".*[17]
>
> *"And it behoves not a believing man and a believing woman that they should have any choice in their matter when Allah and His Messenger have decided a matter; and whoever disobeys Allah and His Messenger, he surely strays off a manifest straying".*[18]
>
> *"and whoever did not judge by what Allah revealed, those are they that are the unbelievers".*[19]

The above verses indicate that Allah is alone the Lawgiver. There is no dispute between the *ahl al-Sunnah* and the *Muʿtazilah* that Allah alone is *Ḥākim*. In spite of the fact that the dispute between these two groups is centred on the question whether intellect can perceive the divine law without the *Sharīʿah* or not. Nevertheless, both agree that human intellect has no role to play in respect of giving command and dictating the law to mankind. The *ahl al-Sunnah* hold the view that intellect cannot perceive the divine law by itself and it can only be known through the prophets and scriptures sent by the Lawgiver, while the *Muʿtazilah*, on the other hand, holds the view that intellect can perceive the divine law without recourse to the *Sharīʿah*. They think that the goodness and badness of human acts are their essential qualities which can be known through intellect. Thus, there is no need for the *Sharīʿah* to know them.[20] However, *Imām* Ghazālī emphasises that human intellect (*ʿaql*) alone is not a source of law in its own right.[21]

The problem of Good and Evil

Despite the concept of good and evil of acts relate to the theology, the jurists have discussed it in the field of *uṣūl al-fiqh* under the sub-theme *ḥākim*. The problem may occur due to the meaning of *ḥākim* which conveys two meanings, namely the creator, originator or provider of law, the original source of law (*muthbit al-aḥkām*), while other meaning is the perceiver, revealer, discoverer or signifier of law (*mudrik, muẓhir al-aḥkām*).

For the first meaning, the *ahl al-Sunnah* and *Mu'tazilah* are agreed that Allah alone is the *ḥākim* that is the originator and provider of law. However, the dispute occurs between them in the second meaning. The *ahl al-Sunnah* believe *ḥākim*, in the sense of discoverer or perceiver, is the *Sharī'ah* not intellect, while the *Mu'tazilah* think that in the same sense, the *ḥākim* is the intellect.[22]

The *ahl al-Sunnah* declares their theological believes with the following statement: "The Lawgiver is Allah, the Exalted, and the revealer is the *Sharī'ah.*"[23]

For them the reaching of the call (*bulūgh al-da'wah*) is an essential condition to invite unbelievers to account, while for the *Mu'tazilah* this condition is not essential for inviting a man to account because he is logically required to believe in Allah on account of possessing the intellect.[24]

The dispute among the both groups occurs from their disagreement regarding the question whether the goodness and evil of acts are rational or legal. Therefore, the meanings of goodness (*ḥusn*) and badness or evil (*qubḥ*) is defined as follows:

Abū al-Ḥasan al-Baṣrī (d. 436 AH), *Mu'tazilī* jurist, defines both *ḥasan* and *qabīḥ*.

"*Ḥasan* (good) is one which a person who is able to perform it freely and has the knowledge of its goodness performs it."

"*Qabīḥ* (evil) is one which a person who is able to perform it freely and has the knowledge of its evil does not perform it."[25]

There are agreed meanings of goodness (*ḥusn*) and evil (*qubḥ*) among the both groups and the agreed meanings of these terms are rational which human reason can realize them without recourse to the *Sharī'ah*, on one hand. These are as follow:[26]

1. Anything, which is in harmony with nature, is called *ḥasan* (good) such as being grateful to someone who has done something good, helping someone who is in need of something, etc. while the *qabīḥ* (evil) is vice-versa that means,

anything, which is not harmony with nature, such as being ungrateful to someone who has done something good, taking someone's property illegally, etc.

2. The term *ḥusn* carries the sense of perfection (*kamāl*), such as truth, generosity, and knowledge, while the term *qubḥ* carries the sense of imperfection of deficiency (*naqṣ*), such as ignorance, stinginess, lie, etc.

On the other hand, these two groups have different opinions on the following meanings of the terms which create dispute among them. For example, *ḥasan* means an act whose performance is praised in this world and the results will be given as reward in the hereafter. However, *qabīḥ* is an act whose commission is condemned in this world and the results will be given as punishment in the hereafter. According to this interpretation, the *ahl al-Sunnah* and the *Muʿtazilah* have been disputed and there will be three viewpoints about it as follows:

1. Viewpoint of al-Ashʿarīs

The goodness and evil of acts are known through the *Sharīʿah*, and therefore, whatever the lawgiver commands is good, such as faith, prayer, etc. and whatever He forbids is evil, such as infidelity, all kind of *ḥarām* acts, etc.[27] Thus, Abū al-Ḥasan al-Ashʿarī (d. 936) maintain that good and evil are not determined by reference to our perception or the nature of things, but are determined by the Lawgiver. Whatever, the Lawgiver deems to be good, it must be good and whatever is deemed to be evil then it will be evil. Therefore, the criterion of the good and evil is the *sharīʿah*, not human intellect (*ʿaql*). According to this view, if a person happens to be living totally in an isolated environment and has never received and message of the Lawgiver, he is not considered a *mukallaf* and he will not be punished as it is indicated in the *Qur'ān*: " *and We never punish until We had sent messenger (to give warning)*".[28]

Another verse confirms such meaning "*Messengers who gave good news as well as warning, that mankind, after (the coming) of the messengers, should have no plea against Allah: For Allah is Exalted in Power, Wise*".[29]

In yet another verse affirms that punishment is only imposed after the people are properly warned by Messengers "*And if We had inflicted on them a penalty before this (revelation), they would have said: 'Our Lord! If only you had sent us a messenger, we should certainly have followed Your Signs before we were humbled and put to shame'.*"[30]

The *Ash'arī*, therefore, uphold the view that the *mukallaf* who has not received the command of the Lawgiver is not responsible, unless the message reached to him. The advent of the Islam is the basis for obligation.[31]

2. Viewpoint of Mu'tazilah

The goodness and evil of acts can be known through human reason and therefore, it does not necessarily depend on the *Sharī'ah*. The followers of Ibrāhīm al-Naẓẓām (d. 845), the *Mu'tazilah*, have held the view that the law of Allah regarding the conduct of the *mukallaf* even without the mediation of scriptures and messengers can be identified by human intellect (*'aql*). The followers of this view have considered the goodness and evil of acts to be three types[32]:

a. That which can be comprehended by the intellect of necessity (*ḍarūrī*), such as the evil of the harmful lie and the goodness of the beneficial truth.

b. It is difficult to distinguish in some situation the benefit of truth and harm of lie except by the guidance of the human intellect to a right path.

c. Things that which can be known only through the *Sharī'ah*, such as the goodness of fasting on the day of *Ramaḍān*, and the evil of fasting on the first day of *Shawwāl*, the number of daily prayers and their *rakaʿāt*. These kind of acts cannot be determined by simply recourse to the human intellect.

3. Viewpoint of Māturīdīs

The followers of Abū Manṣūr al-Māturīdī (d. 333 A.H.), the *Māturīdīs* have held a middle way between the previous schools of thought, which is adopted by the *Ḥanafīs* and considered to be the most acceptable. According to them good and evil in the conduct of the *mukallaf* can indeed be determined and assessed by the human intellect. Despite the human reason comprehends the goodness and evil of acts, it does not imply that it obligates or forbids those acts simply because they are good or evil. Therefore, the human reason has no capacity to play in rulings whether it is obligation or prohibition except by the divine command in which, the knowledge of good or evil must therefore be based on divine communication.[33] The early *Māturīdīs* hold the view that reason is independent in perceiving some of the divine commands. It obligates faith in Allah and forbids unbelief for every person including a child sane in mind, whether the invitation of faith has reached him or not. As Abū Ḥanīfah is reported to have said: "No excuse is acceptable from a person for his ignorance of his Creator as he sees the indications."[34]

The Maḥkūm ʿAlayh (the subject)

The second element of the *ḥukm sharʿī* is the *maḥkūm ʿalayh* (the subject) for whose conduct the *ḥukm* is stipulated, that is *mukallaf*.

Then what/who is the *mukallaf*?

To whom the command of the *Sharīʿah* addressed is called *mukallaf* or *maḥkūm ʿalayh*. It is defined as "a person whose act is referred to by divine communication is called *mukallaf*".[35]

The *maḥkūm ʿalayh* (the subject) or the *mukallaf* (subject) is the person whose act appeals a *ḥukm*, or a *ḥukm* requires him/her to act in a prescribed manner. A *mukallaf* is a person who retains legal capacity, whether he acts directly or through given authority.

Mainly there are two conditions for the application of the command of the *Sharīʻah* to a person under legal obligation and these are intellect (*ʻaql*) and legal capacity (*ahliyyah*).

The first requirement for legal capacity is the ability to understand the communication that creates the obligation that is intellect (*ʻaql*). The power of understanding (*fahm*) is based on human intellect. However, the intellect is a hidden faculty in the body which is defined by jurists as "the intellect is a light in the body of man like the sun in the domain of earth…"[36]

As it is clearly indicated by the following verse from the *Qur'ān* and the tradition of the Prophet (ṣ) in order to fulfil the command of the Lawgiver, the intellect is a necessary faculty.

"*O you who believe! Approach not prayers with a mind befogged, until you can understand all that you say, –*"[37]

ʻAlī reported the Prophet (ṣ) as saying "there are three whose actions are not recorded: a sleeper till he awakes, a boy (minor) till he reaches his puberty, and a lunatic till he is restored to reason".[38]

Literally *ahliyyah* means absolute fitness or ability.[39] Its definition is "the ability or fitness to acquire rights and exercise them and to accept duties and perform them."[40] It is also defined by a contemporary scholar as follow: "*Ahliyyah* is a quality which the Lawgiver determines in a person and which makes him a proper subject of the command of the *Sharīʻah*".[41]

Types of ahliyyah (capacity)

The legal capacity (*ahliyyah*) is divided, according to *Ḥanafīs*, into two types: the acceptance or acquisition of rights and the performance of duties which are called *ahliyyah al-wujūb* (the capacity for acquisition of rights and obligation) and *ahliyyah al-adā'* (the capacity for execution or performance of duties).[42]

Ahliyyah al-wujūb (the capacity for acquisition of rights and obligation)

Ahliyyah al-wujūb is the ability of a human being to acquire rights and obligation, while *ahliyyah al-adā'* (the capacity for execution or performance of duties) is the capability of a human being to issue statements and perform acts to which the Lawgiver has assigned certain legal effects.[43]

The *ahliyyah al-wujūb* is defined as follows: "The capacity of obligation means fitness of man for the rights to which he is entitled, and for what he is subject to that is obligation as prescribed by the *Sharī'ah*".[44] The word obligation refers to both rights and obligations. The basis of legal capacity in here is human life. Thus, every human being is gifted with the responsibility that is technically called *dhimmah* as long as remained human.

Literally the word *dhimmah* means covenant which is illustrated in the *Qur'ān* "*They do not pay regard to ties of relationship nor those of covenant in the case of a believer; and these are they who go beyond the limits*".[45] When the human being was first created, the covenant that is the responsibility was undertaken by man alone. It is referred in the *Qur'ān* mentioning that the responsibility (*dhimmah*) is a trust (*amānah*).

> "*Surely We offered the trust to the heavens and the earth and the mountains, but they refused to be unfaithful to it and feared from it, and man has turned unfaithful to it; surely he is unjust, ignorant*".[46]

Accordingly the quality of *dhimmah* is a cause of legal capacity and intellect (*'aql*) is its conditions. Therefore, the *manāṭ* (basis) of the capacity for execution (*ahliyyah al-adā'*) is *'aql* (intellect) and *rushd* (discretion), while in *ahliyyah al-wujūb* the *manāṭ* (basis) is of being a human or natural person (*insāniyyah*).[47] *'Aql* implies the full development of the mental faculty because if, however, according to the view of the majority of the scholars, a person who has attained puberty, yet he does not possess *'aql*, the capacity for execution cannot be assigned to such a person. *Ḥanafīs*, on the view that a minor (*ṣabī*) who possesses discretion, or exhibits "mental maturity" may be assigned such a capacity, for the *khiṭāb* of *mu'āmalāt*. Therefore, even if a person whose mental faculties are not yet fully developed, can execute for purposes of some transactions. Nevertheless, there is no way in this matter in determining whether the minor has attained discretion. Although *Ḥanafī* jurists have fixed the minimum age of seven years for assigning such a capacity, the law makes it possible depends on the guardian's will and discretion.[48]

The ahliyyah al-adā' (the capacity for execution or performance of duties)

In addition to the above explanation, the *ahliyyah al-adā'* (the capacity for execution or performance of duties) is defined as follows: "the *ahliyyah al-adā'* is fitness of man for the issuing forth of acts from him in a way taken into account by the *Sharī'ah*".[49]

While a contemporary scholars *al-Zarqā* defined it "the *ahliyyah al-adā'* is fitness of a person for performance of the acts whose legal (*shar'ī*) significance depends on intelligence".[50]

This type of capacity is conditioned on maturity of the human faculties in terms of mental and physical. The capacity of execution begins once a child is possessed of understanding (*tamyīz*) the injunctions of the *Sharī'ah*. Thus a child must be the age of discretion and understanding.

The capacity of execution begins when a child reaches at the age of seven years and is possessed of understanding. A person is called minor (*ṣaghīr*) until he reaches the point of maturity of understanding, and after he has attained it is regarded as major (*bāligh*). In addition to this category, a minor also falls into two categories, namely a child possessed of understanding (*ṣabiyy mumayyiz*) and a child not possessed of understanding (*ṣabiyy ghayr mumayyiz*). Nevertheless, the age of discretion (*sinn tamyīz*) begins from the age of seven years which is based on the *ḥadīth* of the Prophet (ṣ): "Teach a child prayer when he is seven years old and strike him for it when he is ten".[51]

There are stages in legal capacity which begins with the existence of his life in mother's womb till his majority and these are:

1. Embryo, 2. Infancy, 3. Age of discretion, 4. Majority and 5. Sensibility and mature understanding (*rushd*). The stage was included by *al-Zarqā'*.[52]

The *ahliyyah al-adā'* can also be divided into three types:

a. Capacity for the *khiṭāb* of *jinā'ī* (legal capacity for criminal liability).

b. Capacity for the *khiṭāb* of *'ibādāt* (legal capacity for worshipping).

c. Capacity for the *khiṭāb* of *mu'āmalāt* (legal capacity for transections).[53]

The justification of separating the capacity for execution into different types is because a person may have the capacity for transactions, not the capacity for punishments. Therefore, it may be concluded that if all the three kinds of capacity are possessed by a person who is called a major, not the one who is lacking in possession of them which may be called a minor.[54]

Types of Ahliyyah al-Wujūb (the Capacity of Obligation)

Generally, Muslim scholars have divided legal capacity into three types and these are complete (*kāmilah*), imperfect (*qāṣirah*) and deficient (*nāqiṣah*).[55]

The complete capacity (ahliyyah kāmilah)

The complete capacity (*ahliyyah kāmilah*) for acquisition is found in a human being after his birth, which makes him eligible for the acquisition of all kinds of rights and obligations. A child bears the perfect quality of holding responsibility (*dhimmah kāmilah*) and by virtue of this quality he possesses the capacity of obligation perfectly as soon as he is born, however, an infant has only the perfect capacity of obligation till he reaches the age of seven years which is called the age of discretion (*tamyīz*).[56] Nevertheless, the execution of the capacity is established when the subject attains full mental development, and gains the ability to discriminate. The external standard of puberty is associated with this stage such as the commencement of ejaculation in a male and menstruation in a female is a sing of the attainment of puberty. In case of the absence of these signs, puberty is presumed at the age of fifteen in both males and females according to the majority of the jurists, however, according to Abū Ḥanīfah, it is at the age of eighteen for males and seventeen for females. In addition to *bulūgh* (puberty), the possession of *rushd* (discrimination in right and wrong, maturity of actions) is stipulated and attaining puberty alone is not sufficient. As it is supported by the verse *Sūrah al-Nisā'* "*Make trial of orphans until they reach the age of marriage; if then you find sound judgment in them, release their property to them; but consume it not wastefully, nor in haste against their growing up*".[57] This verse indicates that there are two conditions for capacity of *bulūgh al-nikāḥ* (the age of marriage) and *rushd.*[58]

The imperfect capacity (ahliyyah qāṣirah)

The imperfect capacity (*ahliyyah qāṣirah*) of obligation is assigned in cases where the *mānaṭ* (basis) of legal capacity is not completely developed. Such as a person may not have been born yet as unborn child or foetus, embryo (*janīn*). An embryo, in the womb of its mother before birth, has no legal capacity for obligation due to the imperfect capacity and it may not have reached complete mental development. The imperfect capacity implies that only some rights are established for the foetus because it is considered part of the mother in some respect and therefore, no obligations are imposed on it.

Nevertheless, by virtue of this imperfect capacity, the foetus acquires certain rights such as freedom from slavery, parentage, bequest and inheritance in the property of the relatives. However, the embryo is not entitled to the rights which require acceptance or rejections due to the capacity of the embryo for ownership of property is imperfect. Accordingly there are two points of view on an embryo: 1. It is part of its mother. 2. It is an independent soul. The perfect *dhimmah* (covenant of responsibility) cannot be attributed to the embryo for the exercise of rights and discharge of obligation of an embryo with part of its mother, while a defective *dhimmah* can be attributed to the independent soul who makes it fit for earning rights alone, and not obligations. Eventually, a living child in the womb cannot be fastened with liabilities, for example, if its guardian buys something on its behalf, it cannot be held liability for its price, and it cannot be realised form the property belonging to the embryo. However, if it is born dead, the legacy bequeathed in its favour will be returned to the legato and will not be distributed among its heirs.[59]

The deficient capacity (ahliyyah nāqiṣah)

The deficient capacity (*ahliyyah nāqiṣah*) is assigned in cases where the bases of capacity are present in terms of the possession of *rushd* and being a human, however an external attribute has been introduced that does not permit the recognition of the legal validity of certain acts and this capacity is attributed to women and slaves. The capacity of execution relates to two powers in man, namely the power of understanding which depends on intellect and the power of performing the acts which depends on physical fitness of body. The validity of performance of an act depends on the imperfect capacity, while its obligation depends on perfect capacity such as an idiot (*ma'tūh*).[60]

Due to the special circumstances, a woman possesses imperfect capacity. Scholars held the view that in lacking this capacity in women deny her some rights such as the rights to be the head of state, the right to be a *qāḍī* (judge), and the right to testify in cases being under *ḥudūd* and *qiṣāṣ* provision (that is duties where the right of Allah is involved), the right of divorce, as well as not having the same right of inheritance that is equal to half the share of male heirs, etc. the evidences supporting these rights are taken both from the *Qur'ān* and the *Sunnah* and the details of these issues have been discussed by many scholars.[61] In contrast to the secular laws, the right to divorce is given solely to the husband. Muslim jurists unanimously agree that this right has not been granted to wife directly. Lastly, despite the slaves do have a capacity for acquiring obligations concerning to *'ibādāt*, and for criminal offences, they do not possess the right of ownership.[62]

'Awāriḍ al-Ahliyyah (Circumstances affecting legal capacity)

The legal capacity of *mukallaf* may be destroyed or impaired by some obstacles in different circumstances. The impediments to legal capacity is called *'awāriḍ al-ahliyyah.* Linguistically *'awāriḍ* (sg. *'āriḍ*) means obstacles or impediment.

Technically, it is defined as follows: "The circumstances affecting the legal capacity are those matters which are not essential to it. They are initially accidental; that is, they are qualities or circumstances which change the commands such as journey, or destroy the capacity, for it prevents the capacity of obligation or capacity of execution from establishment, such death, sleep, and a fainting fit. In short, *'awāriḍ* are those circumstances which are incompatible with the legal capacity of man in general, and which are not necessary for him."[63]

The *'awāriḍ al-ahliyyah* is divided into two types: 1. The work of providence (*'awāriḍ samāwiyyah*) which are beyond the control of man such as lunacy (*junūn*), infancy (*ṣighār, ṣabī*), idiocy (*'uth, 'atah, 'atāhah*), forgetfulness (*nisyān*), sleep (*nawm*)), fainting fit (*ighmā'*), slavery (*riqq*), death-illness (*maraḍ al-mawt*), menstruation (*ḥayḍ*), childbed (*nifās*), and death (*mawt*). 2. The acts which are acquired by man (*'awāriḍ muktasabah*) which are under the control of man who has capacity to do or not to do them. This type of obstacles (*'awāriḍ*) is divided into two types: a) those which are occasioned by a person himself, such as ignorance (*jahl*), drunkenness (*sukr*), jest (*ḥazl*), folly (*safah*), journey (*safar*) and mistake (*khaṭa'*); b) those which are made by another man rather than the person himself, such as duress or coercion (*ikrāh*).[64]

The Maḥkūm Fīh (the act)

The *maḥkūm fīh* is the act to which the *ḥukm* is related that is the objectives of law including particularly rights and obligations. It is also called by some scholars as *maḥkūm bih*.[65] Al-Ghazālī, al-Āmidī, Ibn al-Ḥājib used *maḥkūm fīh* and Ibn al-Ḥumām (d. 861 AH) also preferred to use the same term.[66]

The *maḥkūm fīh* has been defined as "An act of man to which the address of the Lawgiver relates" (*al-fi'l alladhī ta'allaqa bihī khiṭāb al-shārī'*).[67]

Fi'l (act) has also been defined as "The word *fi'l* (act) comprehends something done by the mind and limbs of the body in general, and *'amal* (deed) applies specifically to something done by the limbs of the body".[68]

The act of *mukallaf* which is related to *maḥkūm fīh* may come in different forms when the address of the lawgiver is a *ḥukm taklīfī*. For example, a verse in the *Qur'ān* says: "*And keep up prayer and pay the poor-rate and bow down with those who bow down*".[69]

The verse contains a command which binds person (*ījāb*) to keep up prayer and pay the *zakāt*. These obligations relate to the act of *mukallaf* in the form of obligatory act (*wājib*).

Another verse in the *Qur'ān* comes in the form of recommendation (*nadb*) as saying: "*O you who believe! when you deal with each other in contracting a debt for a fixed time, then write it down;*".[70] The command here indicates recommendation (*nadb*).

A verse in the *Qur'ān* comes in the form of forbidden (*ḥarām*): *"And do not kill any one whom Allah has forbidden, except for a just cause"*.[71]

The command here indicates that killing someone unjustly is forbidden (*ḥarām*).

Another verse comes in the form of disapproval (*karāhah*): "*and do not even aim at getting anything which is bad, in order that out of it ye may give away something, when ye yourselves would not receive it except with closed eyes*".[72]

This verse indicates that giving defective things in charity is disapproval (*karāhah*) and therefore, the Lawgiver has declared such kind of act as disapproved (*makrūh*).

And another verse comes in the form of permissible (*mubāḥ*) as Allah says: "*But when the prayer is ended, then disperse abroad in the land and seek of Allah's grace*".[73]

It is interpreted that dispersing through the land for business after the Friday prayer is optional which relates to the act of *mukallaf* and it has been considered permissible (*mubāḥ*).

The *maḥkūm fīh* denotes the acts, rights and obligations of the *mukallaf* which constitute the subject-matter of a command, prohibition or permissibility. When the demand of the Lawgiver occurs in the form of a defining law (*ḥukm taklīfī*) such as fasting, *jihād*, and the payment of *zakāh*, etc., the subject-matter of the *ḥukm* is the act of the *mukallaf*. Likewise, when the demand of the Lawgiver occurs in the form of declaratory law (*ḥukm waḍʿī*), such as ablution (*wuḍū'*) being a condition of prayer, or sale which is the cause (*sabab*) of ownership, or killing which is an impediment (*māniʿ*) to inheritance, the subject-matter of *ḥukm* in all these consists of the act of the *mukallaf*. Although the *maḥkūm fīh* in the form of declaratory law (*ḥukm waḍʿī*) does not consist of the conduct of the individual, it is related to it. For example, the arrival of *Ramaḍān* which is the cause (*sabab*) of fasting is not an act of the individual, nevertheless it is related to the act of the *mukallaf* in the sense that the effect (*musabbab*) of that cause is namely the fasting.[74]

As the *maḥkūm fīh* deals with the objects of law, namely acts, rights and obligations. The acts are classified into mainly natural or perceptible (*ḥissī*) and juristic (*shar'ī*). Firstly the natural acts include acts of the body (*af'āl al-jawāriḥ*) as well as acts of the mind or mental (*af 'āl al-qalb*). The acts of the body (*af'āl al-jawāriḥ*) consist of the movement of some limbs of the human body such as utterance of words, walking, eating, etc. while the acts of the mind (*af 'āl al-qalb*) consist of believing, acknowledging, intending, wishing. Mental acts cannot be detected by a judge in a case of litigation. It can be known when one express one's acknowledgement in words or by conduct. Secondly the juristic act may be described as a totality of more than one natural act of one or more persons, such as act of faith, prayer, contract of sale, hire.[75] In addition to this acts, all voluntary acts are called *taṣarrufāt* (dispositions) which means spending one's energy or will, and *taṣarrufāt al-shar'* are act done according to the *Sharī'ah* or lawful acts.[76]

The conditions of the maḥkūm fīh

In order to constitute the subject matter of a *ḥukm*, the jurists have laid down certain conditions for the validity of legal responsibility of perform an act. Therefore, individuals must fulfil the following conditions.

1. Knowledge of the act
2. Knowledge of the source
3. The power of *mukallaf* to perform an act
4. Fulfilment of conditions stipulated by the *Sharī'ah* for legal obligations.

1. The knowledge of the act

It is a necessary condition of legal responsibility (*taklīf*) that the *mukallaf* should possess complete knowledge of the act required to be performed or not to be performed by him. The *mukallaf* should know the act itself and its dimensions, nature and qualities. According to Shawkānī, the knowledge means, in this context, understanding the nature of a command or a prohibition by the individual to the extent that he can act upon it.[77] The required knowledge of the *Sharī'ah* can be obtained simply acquiring it either directly or by asking those who have such knowledge. Similarly the ambivalent (*mujmal*) text of the *Qur'ān* concerning *ṣalāt*, *zakāh* and *ḥajj*, did not obligate anyone until these matters were explained and clarified by the Prophet (ṣ). Thus, such knowledge does not constitute the basis of either a command or a prohibition unless explained. However, when a person is in full possession of his capacities and it is possible for him to learn the required *aḥkām* (rulings), he is presumed to know his legal obligations. Thus, the *aḥkām* (rulings) is applied to him, and his ignorance of the rules of *Sharī'ah* is not excused.

2. Knowledge of the source

The demand to act or not to act must originate in an authoritative source which can command the obedience of the *mukallaf*. The *mukallaf*, therefore, should know that the obligatory character of the act he is required to perform has been laid down by Allah so that discharge may be deemed obedience to, and compliance with, the divine command. The jurists thus mentioned a rule which originates in an authoritative source referencing to the *Qur'ān* or the *Sunnah* which mean that the *ḥukm* must originate from Allah or His messenger.[78]

3. The Power of mukallaf to perform an act

In order to perform or abstain from the act, it is essential for the validity of a legal responsibility (*taklīf*) that it should be within the power of the *mukallaf* and it must be within the capacity. It is, therefore, impossible obligation beyond one's power (*taklīf bi ma lā yuṭāq* or *taklīf bi'l-muḥāl*) is not valid. An obligation which is beyond the capacity of *mukallaf* is not required as stated in the *Qur'ān* "*Allah does not impose upon any soul a duty but to the extent of its ability;*"[79] Another verse supports this reality: "*Allah does not lay on any soul a burden except to the extent to which He has granted it;*".[80] Likewise, an act may be impossible by its nature or may be beyond the capacity of the individual in view of his particular conditions make no difference such as asking a person to be awake and asleep at the same time, or asking him to do and not to do something simultaneously, similarly an act may be physically impossible, such as ordering a person to fly without the necessary means, etc.[81] Legal obligations are only operative within the limits of one's capacity, in yet another *ḥadīth* indicates this responsibility "Fulfil your duties to the extent of your capacity".[82]

Therefore, the impossible obligation has been divided into two types: 1. Impossible with reference to oneself (*mustaḥīl li-dhātih*) is that whose existence cannot be conceived of by human intellect, such as bringing two contraries (*ḍiddān*) together, such as black and white, or bringing two contradictories (*nāqiṣah*) together like existence and non-existence, as well as attainment of a thing in two spheres at the same time and in the same respect. Pronouncing an act both obligatory and forbidden at the same time and in the same respect by the Lawgiver is impossible thereof. 2. Impossible with reference to something else (*mustaqil li-ghayri*) is that whose existence can be conceived by human reason, but that is not usually practiced either by habit such as flying in the air by man without any machine, lifting a mountain, etc. According to the majority of the scholars these two types of legal responsibility (*taklīfī*) is not valid.[83]

Fulfilment of an act on behalf of another person

Fulfilment of an act on behalf of another person is also considered in the category of legal responsibility for an act which is beyond one's capacity (*taklīf bi mā lā yuṭaq*). It is, therefore, legally not valid to discharge an obligation by a person on behalf of someone else. No one may be obligated to act on behalf of another person or to stop another competent person from acting. For example, if the brother of or a relative of a person observes obligatory prayers or to pay *zakāh* on behalf of his brother or relative, or to prevent his friend from committing theft. Every *mukallaf* is responsible for fulfilling his acts by himself. This view point is expressed by the following verse in the *Qur'ān* "*and no soul earns (evil) but against itself, and no bearer of burden shall bear the burden of another*".[84] Another verse from the *Qur'ān*: "*Every man is responsible for what he earns*".[85]

On the basis of this principle vicarious responsibility in physical acts, especially in rituals (*'ibādāt*) is not lawful. But his question is disputed among the jurists. As regards prayers, all are agreed that it is not lawful to pray, whether obligatory or supererogatory, on behalf of a living or a dead person. From another perspective, there is a difference of opinion about fasting on behalf of a dead person. A group of jurists hold that it is permissible for the guardian or heirs of a dead man to fast on his behalf. They argue on the basis of a tradition reported by 'Āishah that the Prophet (ṣ) said: "If a person dies and some obligatory fasts are due to him, his legal heir or guardian (*walī*) may fast on his behalf."[86] However, the majority of the jurists take the view that it is not lawful to fast on behalf of a living or a dead person, rather some compensation, as prescribed in law, for each fast should be given. As Ibn 'Abbās is reported to have said: "One should not pray on behalf of another, and one should not fast on behalf of another. He should, instead, feed the poor a *mudd* of wheat for the fast of each day."[87]

With respect to the *ḥajj*, according to the majority of the jurists, except Imām Mālik, it is lawful to perform it on behalf of another person, whether living or dead.[88] The jurists discussed it in details within a frame work of physical and financial acts and finally concluding that the *ḥajj* is a combination of physical and financial acts. As a general rule, representation in the case of the *ḥajj*, therefore, must be unlawful. However, it is lawful as an exceptional case with a special exemption granted by the *Sharīʿah* out of divine grace and reward.[89]

Legal obligation (taklīf) with hardship (mashaqqah)

The scholars have divided the hardship (*mashaqqah*) into two types: usual hardship (*mashaqqah muʿtādah*) and unusual hardship (*mashaqqah ghayr muʿtādah*). As it has been discussed that the legal obligation (*taklīf*) should be within man's capacity, it is already known that human life is full of struggle and difficulties.

1. Usual hardship (mashaqqah muʿtādah)

The usual hardship (*mashaqqah muʿtadah*) means the hardship which a *mukallaf* can bear in performing an act of *ḥukm sharʿī* as commanded by the Lawgiver without giving unusual hardship. Logically, it is an acceptable fact that all obligations may carry bearable hardship. Nevertheless, the objectives of the legal obligations is not to give hardship but to bring benefit such as praying, fasting, paying *zakāh,* doing *jihād* (fight for the sake of Allah) etc. do not aim at tiring the body, or causing to the body by thirst or hunger, or reduce the amount of the wealth, or cause to death, rather it is aimed at submission to Allah, purification of the wealth and the soul, protection of the Muslim territories as well as spreading the religion of Islam.

2. Unusual hardship (mashaqqah ghayr muʿtādah)

The unusual hardship (*mashaqqah ghayr muʿtādah*) means a hardship which is not usually bearable by a *mukallaf* and it may cause a great burden on the *mukallaf.* It becomes an obstacle to the fulfilment of responsibilities and may cause disorder to the whole order of life. Therefore, the unbearable hardship is not intended by the commands of the *Sharīʿah.* Such as Muslims were prohibited from fasting continuously without break, praying throughout the night, living a single life without marriage etc.[90]

The Lawgiver does not aim at putting *mukallaf* under severe hardship as Allah indicates in the *Qur'ān* "*Allah desires ease for you, and He does not desire for you difficulty*".[91]

Another verse from the *Qur'ān*: "*and has not laid upon you an hardship in religion*".[92]

Ḥadīth of the Prophet (ṣ) also indicates the prohibition of severe hardship, Abū Umāmah reported the Prophet (ṣ) as saying: "I have been sent with a true and tolerant religion".[93]

The Prophet (ṣ) encouraged Muslims to perform acts which is in their capacity as reported by ʻĀ'ishah saying: "Perform the act which is within your power".[94] To follow the concessions provided by the Lawgiver is as important as following commands, if the performance of an obligation leads to hardship, special dispensations and concessions must be taken as the Prophet (ṣ) indicated this matter saying: "Allah likes that special dispensations and concessions granted by Him should be followed as He dislikes His disobedience".[95]

Imām al-Shāṭibī emphasized on the problem of hardship (*mashaqqah*) as saying "consensus of opinion (*ijmāʿ*) has been established on the non-occurrence of hardship, in respect of existence in the legal obligation (*taklīf*), and it indicates the Lawgiver's non-intention for it."[96] Which indicates that the Lawgiver has not intended hardship in them, if otherwise, that would have been self-contradictory.[97]

Types of the rights

The right is defined as "the special authority by which the law (*sharīʿah*) establishes power (over a thing) or legal obligation (to do an act)".[98]

Similarly it is defined as "an interest of an individual or society or of both together established by the Lawgiver, the Wise".[99]

Mainly, the scholars have divided the rights into two types: rights of Allah (*ḥuqūq Allah*) and rights of man (*ḥuqūq al-ʿabd*). The acts of *mukallaf*, therefore, may be either rights of Allah and rights of man or of a combination of both.

The rights of Allah (*ḥuqūq Allah*) which is the rights of which involve benefit to the community at large but not reserved exclusively for any particular individuals. These rights correspond to public rights and involve the benefits of the whole Muslim society and these are attributed to Allah not because they are of benefit to Him nor because they are His creation, in fact He is above all wants. It is certain that all rights are equal for the creation of Allah who is the creator of everything. This type of rights consist of mainly obligatory devotional acts (*ʿibādāt*) and prescribed punishment (*ḥudūd*). Fulfilling these rights actually are the benefit to the whole society not for the benefit of Allah as He is above all wants and needs. The enforcement of these rights is a duty of the state that is considered under the *Siyāsah Sharīʿah*.[100] Accordingly the rights of Allah (*ḥuqūq Allah*) is defined as follows: "By the rights of Allah is meant that which comprehends a public benefit, not peculiar to any individual. It is referred to Allah because of greatness of its significance and generality of its benefit".[101]

The rights of man (*ḥuqūq al-ʿabd*) involves private rights which comprise matters related entirely to the rights of individual men such as the rights of protection of property, enforcement of contracts etc. The rights of man is defined as follows: "By the right of man is meant that which involves a particular benefit such as the prohibition of appropriation of property of another person".[102]

The scholars have further divided these rights under four types which are as follows:

1. The acts which are purely the rights of Allah (ḥuqūq Allah al-khāliṣah)

The acts which entirely consist of the rights of Allah (*ḥuqūq Allah al-khāliṣah*) such as worshipping, acts of devotion, praying, doing *jihād* which are the main pillars of Islam and are necessary for the establishment of Islamic way of life. These acts are considered pure rights of Allah (*ḥuqūq Allah al-khāliṣah*) which are of eight types.[103]

First type: Acts of devotion which consist purely of worship (*'ibādāt maḥḍah or khāliṣah*) such as faith (*īmān*), prayer (*ṣalāt*), paying obligatory alms (*zakāt*), the pilgrimage (*ḥajj*) and struggling for the sake of Allah (*jihād*).

Second type: Acts of devotion which consist of both worship and the sense of financial liability (*'ibādah fīhā ma'nal ma'ūnah*). Such as giving charity on the occasion of the end of *Ramaḍān* (*ṣadaqah al-fiṭr*). *Ma'ūnah* literally means provisions, food, burden, trouble, and inconvenience. Technically means tax, impost or duty. This type of act is an obligatory act on a man whether in legal obligation or not. If the man is under legal obligation, the payment is paid by the guardian whom he supports and who are the under his legal guardianship, such as his minor children and servants.

Third type: Acts in which financial liability is greater than worship such as the tithe (*'ushr*) that is payable by a Muslim owner of lands on agricultural crops.

Fourth type: Acts in which it has financial liability and has a sense of punishment (*ma'ūnah fīhā ma'nal 'uqūbah*) such as the imposition of land tax (*kharāj*) which is originally levied on non-Muslims.

Fifth type: acts which consist of pure prescribed punishment (*'uqūbāt kāmilah or maḥḍah*) such as theft, adultery, drinking alcohol, slandering, etc. These are matters which purely the rights of Allah and have been instituted for public welfare. These punishments will not be inflicted by the aggrieved person but by the competent authorities.

Sixth type: Acts which consist of imperfect or minor punishment (*'uqūbah qāṣirah*) such as depriving a man, who has killed his near relative, of his right of inheritance. This type of punishment is also known as *jazā* (pl. *ajziyah*) that is retribution which denotes both meanings penalty and rewards of which is called imperfect penalty because the punishment is only confined to a financial loss. Thus physical punishment such as retaliation (*qiṣāṣ*) is not applied.

Seventh type: Cases which involve in the acts of both of worships and punishments (*baynal 'ibādah wal-'uqūbah*) such as expiations for breaking an oath, expiation (*kaffārah*) for *ẓihār* (calling one's wife mother), and expiation for accidental homicide.

Eight type: The right which exists by itself (*ḥaqq qā'im bi nafsih*). In the sense that it is exclusive right which is established in itself alone and is not necessarily imposed upon a *mukallaf* such as the right to one-fifth of the spoils of war (*ghanā'im*) acquired by waging *jihād* and the right to one-fifth of the contents of mine. These are considered public rights and therefore the spoils of war (*ghanā'im*) should obviously belong entirely to the community. However, Allah because of His grace has allowed four-fifth to go to the warriors engaged in the fighting and has reserved one-fifth for the community as Allah indicated in the *Qur'ān* "*They ask you concerning (things taken as) spoils of war. Say: (such) spoils are at the disposal of Allah and the Messenger*".[104]

2. The acts which are purely the rights of man (ḥuqūq al-'abd al-khāliṣah)

This type of acts which are purely the rights of man and also are called private rights which are aimed at protecting the individual's interests. The individual may demand them or waive them even if without any consideration made by him such as ownership of the thing sold, the right to the enforcement of contracts, the rights to compensation for loss or damage, the purchaser's right to own the object he has purchases, the right of pre-emption (*shuf'ah*), the vendor's right to own the price paid to him, etc.

3. Matters in which the rights of Allah and the rights of man are combined, but those of the former preponderate

The acts in which the rights of Allah that is the rights of the community, and the rights of individuals are combined, but of the two the former preponderate, which means the right of Allah is preferred over the rights of individual. For example, according to the *Ḥanafīs*, the right to punish a slanderer (*qādhif*), a person who falsely accuses another person of unchastity or commission of adultery, belongs to this type. Due to the attack made on the honour of one of the members of the society. The right of Allah is dominant in *qadhf* case. Thus, the victim of this offence (*maqdhūf*) cannot exempt the offender from punishment because the punishment of a false accusation of adultery (*ḥadd al-qadhf*) causes public benefit and therefore depreciation of the honour of one of the members of the community is infringed, which causes the violation of the rights of the community, that is, the rights of Allah. This punishment thus protects the right of the community. However, the *Shāfi'īs* have held the contrary view by saying that *qadhf* is an exclusive right of individual. Thus, the person who is offended is entitled to exonerate the slanderer (*qādhif*). The acts that related to protecting the human life, intellect, honour, and property fall under this type.[105]

4. Matters in which rights of Allah and rights of man are combined, but the latter preponderate

The matters in which the rights of Allah (public rights) and the rights of man (private rights) are combined but the latter preponderate which means the rights of individual is preferred over the rights of Allah. For example, retaliation (*qiṣāṣ*) which is the punishment for intentional homicide, blood-money (*diyah*) of any kind, whether for life or for serious injury, fall under this type of rights. As it is illustrated in the *Qur'ān*: "*And there is life for you in (the law of) retaliation, O men of understanding, that you may guard yourselves.*"[106] It is indicating that there is a life for retaliation to protect to society. Thus, it is considered the right of the community which is the right of Allah. Accordingly the community is entitled to punish such violations, however the right of the heirs which is individuals in retaliation is preponderant. It is because the offence causes loss and sorrow to the heirs of the person killed in the case of homicide, and it causes pain and injury to the person injured. In this case the heirs of the person murdered have the right to forgive the offender or accept blood-wit. Thus the punishment is inflicted with their consent. Similarly *diyah* is offered for erroneous killing. Although the heirs or the guardian (*walī*) of the deceased is entitled to forgive the offender or to accept a compensation from him, the state, which represents the community, is still entitled to punish the offender through a *ta'zīr* punishment (discretionary punishment imposed by a Muslim judge) even if the offender is pardoned by the heirs of the deceased.[107]

The Ḥukm (ruling)

The legal *ḥukm* (*ḥukm shar'ī*), in here, represents the conceptual part of Islamic law. The term *ḥukm* (plural *aḥkām*) linguistically means injunction, prescription, command, and *sharī'ah* values, while the term *rukn* (plural *arkān*) means elements that may be conceived as a pillar on which things is founded. It is an essential element of a thing without which it cannot stand.

Technically, *ḥukm* means a rule which may be a rule of any kind such as a rational rule for example, 3+2=5, or the rule that whole is greater than its parts, or it may be a rule perceived by the senses for example, fire burns, or it may be based on personal experiences, for example, studying regularly brings success. However, what the study of *ḥukm* concerns here is that it is the legal rules which means the *ḥukm sharʿī* and which it has been defined previously as: "A communication from Allah, the Exalted, related to the acts of the subjects through a demand or option, or through a declaration" (*Huwa khiṭābullahi taʿālā al-mutaʿalliq bi-afʿāl al-mukallafīn bil-Iqtiḍā' aw al-takhyīyr aw al-waḍʿ*).[108]

Additionally, the concept of *al-ḥukm al-sharʿī* as it has been abstracted earlier consisting of four fundamental elements (*arkān*). These elements are: the *Ḥākim* (Lawgiver), the *maḥkūm alayh* (the subject), the *maḥkūm fīh* (the act of the *mukallaf*), and the *ḥukm* (ruling). It is obvious that the true and the eternal source of the *ḥukm al-sharʿī* which the *ḥukm* originates from is Allah who is the *Ḥākim* (Lawgiver) of everything and anything in here and the hereafter. The subject for the *ḥukm* (ruling) that is ordained by the Lawgiver is the *mukallaf* who possess legal capacity. The act that is related to act of the subject by way of *taklīf* which creates obligation is of the third element of the *ḥukm sharʿī* as *maḥkūm fīh* (the act) and the *ḥukm* (ruling) which was mainly divided as *al-ḥukm al-taklīfī* (defining law) and *al-ḥukm al-waḍʿī* (declaratory law).

The Ḥukm Taklīfī (Defining Law)

The *ḥukm taklīfī* (defining law) has been defined above that it is a communication from Allah, the Exalted, related to the acts of the *mukallaf* (subjects), which consists of a demand or an option but declaration which is excluded from the definition of the *ḥukm* that is declaration (*al-waḍʿ*); it arises in the five categories of *wājīb* or *farḍ* (obligatory), *mandūb* (recommended), *makrūh* (adversity), *ḥarām* (prohibited) and *mubāḥ* (permissible). In addition, the *Ḥanafī* school deduces seven varieties from the same definition: 1. *farḍ* (obligatory) 2. *wājīb* (obligatory) 3. *mandūb* (recommended) 4. *makrūh karāhat al-taḥrīm* (strongly disapproved) 5. *makrūh karāhat al-tanzīh* (disapproval) 6. *ḥarām* (prohibited) 7. *mubāḥ* (permissible).

Individually these classifications are accepted by all the majority of the *Sunnī* schools. As we mentioned that the *Ḥanafīs* deduces seven categories from the same definition. In general, the *uṣūlī* scholars say that the *ḥukm* to be derived from the texts which is related to the subject (*mukallaf*) create an obligation, or recommendation, etc. and, it is therefore, from the perspective of the *uṣūlī* scholars, the *ḥukm* is used for the following categories: 1. Obligation (*ījāb*), 2. Recommendation (*nadb*), 3. Disapproval (*karāhah*), 4. Prohibition (*taḥrīm*), 5. Permissibility (*ibāḥah*), while the *faqīh* scholars say that the act of the subject (*mukallaf*) which is derived *ḥukm* from the text is obligatory, recommended, etc. It is from the perspective of the *faqīh*, the *ḥukm* is used for the following categories: 1. Obligatory (*wājib*), 2. Recommended (*mandūb*), 3. Reprehensible (*makrūh*), 4. Prohibited (*ḥarām*), 5. Permissible (*mubaḥ*).[109]

The *Ḥukm Taklīfī* (Defining Law)

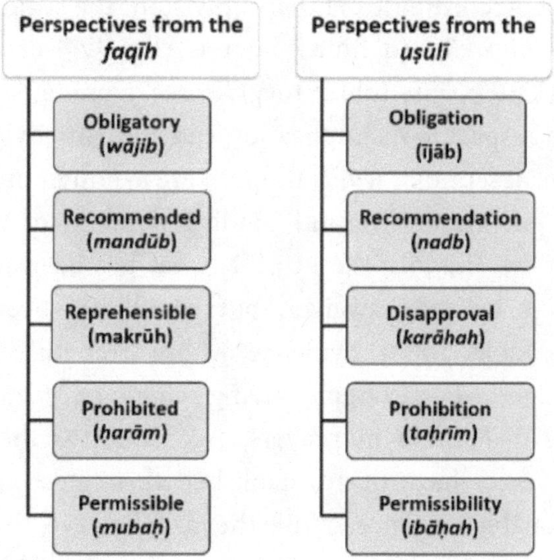

Classification of the Ḥukm Taklīfī (Defining Law)

The obligatory act (wājib)

Linguistically, the term *wājib* means an act that is compulsory to do and the performance of which is obligatory for the subject. It is necessary to do something.

Technically, it is an act whose instruction is demanded by the Lawgiver in certain and binding terms.[110] Ghazālī explains the meaning of *wājib* that "when there is a demand for the commission of an act, we conclude that there is a command (*'amr*), but when this command is accompanied by additional evidence about a consequential penalty for omission the act is obligatory *wājib*. In case we do not find such evidence, the act is recommended."[111]

Since the rule for the *wājib* is a compulsory act, it brings obligation, therefore, whoever does it will be rewarded (*thawāb*) and whoever neglects it will be punished.[112] And therefore, acting upon something *wājīb* brings reward, while omitting it brings punishment in this world and in the hereafter.

The term *wājib* has been used by the *Ḥanafī* scholars different than majority. According to *Ḥanafī's* division, the *wājīb* (obligatory) of the *ḥukm al-taklīfī* (defining law) is slightly weaker than *farḍ* (obligatory). The *wājīb* (obligatory) arises from a source that is probable with respect to its implication and authenticity. The majority of the scholars accept that *wājīb* and *farḍ* are synonymous and both of them convey an imperative and binding demand of the Lawgiver. According to the *Ḥanafīs*, the *wājib* is what has been made binding for the subject by the Lawgiver, but which has been established through a probable (*ẓannī*) evidence, whose strength is not that of a definitive evidence. For example, giving *ṣadaqah al-fitr*, praying *witr*, reciting *sūrat al-Fātiḥah* in prayers. According to the *Ḥanafīs*, all ruling of the cases have been established through a *khabar wāḥid*, which is a probable evidence. While the *farḍ*, however, has been made binding for the subject by the Lawgiver, is established through a definitive (*qaṭ'ī*) evidence which may be a verse of the *Qur'ān* or a *mutawātur* or *mashhūr* tradition such as the five daily prayers, paying *zakāt*, performing *ḥajj*, recitation of the *Qur'ān* in prayers, etc.[113]

The rule for *farḍ* is the obligation of performance and liability for punishment on omission and who denies the legal validity of *farḍ*, will be imputed with *kufr*. However, the rule for the *wājib* is the obligation of performance and liability for punishment for omission, but of a lesser severity as compared to the *farḍ*. In terms of denying the legality of a *wājib* does not bring infidelity (*kufr*). Thus, the rules for *farḍ* is different than *wājib*.[114] For example, when *farḍ* is neglected in an act required by the *sharī'ah*, the act as a whole becomes useless and void (*bāṭil*), but not the *wājib*. If one forgets to recite the *Qur'ān* in prayer, the prayer becomes void (*bāṭil*), because this is noncompliance with a definitive evidence in the *Qur'ān* requiring this recitation: "*then read what is easy of the Qur'ān*".[115] However, if one forgets to recite *sūrah al-Fātiḥah*, but does recite something else instead, it does not invalidate the prayer despite a tradition that says: "there is no prayer for one who does not recite the *Fātiḥah* of the Book".[116] It is because this tradition is a *khabar wāḥid*.[117]

The types of the obligatory act (wājib)

The obligatory act (*wājib/farḍ*), depending on who is required to perform the act, is mainly divided into two types: the personal obligation (*wājib 'aynī*) and the communal obligation (*wājib kifā'ī*). The personal obligation (*wājib 'aynī*) is that it is to be performed by each person from whom it is demanded with legal capacity for the act, such as fasting, performing *ḥajj*, prayers, paying *zakāt*, while the communal obligation (*wājib kifā'ī*) is an act whose performance is required from the whole community and not from each individual, such as *jihād*, the *hisbah* (promotion of good and prevention of evil), *janāzah* prayers, building hospitals, etc. Unlike the *'aynī*, the ruling for the *kifā'ī* is actually performed by some individuals in the community, the rest are no longer accountable for doing it, and therefore, the duty is discharged from the whole of the community.

In addition to the above explanation, the communal obligation (*wājib kifā'ī*) may become the personal obligation (*wājib 'aynī*) in exceptional situations such as the case of *jihād*. Although it is a communal obligation (*wājib kifā'ī*), it becomes personal obligation (*wājib 'aynī*) when the enemy attacks and besieges a specific country. In such situation it becomes the personal obligation of every residents to defend their country. In the same way, performing the personal reasoning (*ijtihād*) becomes personal obligation to carry out it when there is only one *mujtahid* in a specific city.[118]

Scholars have considered the obligatory act (*wājib/farḍ*) in different classifications such as classification based on the time availability for performance: *wājib muṭlaq* (absolute obligation) and *wājib muqayyad* (limited obligation). *Wājib muṭlaq* is an act whose performance is free from time limitation such as the payment of expiation (*kaffārah*) and the *nadhr* for fasting sometime in the future. It is therefore, the *mukallaf* may perform the act whenever he likes. Whereas *wājib muqayyad*, which is also called *muwaqqat*, is an obligatory act demanded by the Lawgiver from the subject for which a time period is determined that is contingent on a time limitation such as the five daily prayers, fasting during *Ramaḍān*, and *Ḥajj*, etc.

The obligatory act (*wājib/farḍ*) is also classified based on the extent or amount of the required act into *muḥaddad* (determinate) such as the amount of the *zakāt*, payment of the price (*thaman*) by the purchaser in a sale transaction, the five daily prayers, payment of rent in accordance with the terms of a tenancy agreement, enforcement of the prescribed penalties (*ḥudūd*), all which are determined by the Lawgiver; and *ghayr muḥaddad* (indeterminate) such as charity to the poor, feeding the hungry, paying a dower, (*mahr*) to one's wife, spending for the sake of Allah, all which are not determined by the Lawgiver. The rule (*ḥukm*) for this kind of *wājib*) is determined by *ijtihād* of the judge or the *imām*.[119]

Again the obligatory act (*wājib/farḍ*) is divided into *mu'ayyan* (the specified) and *mukhayyar* (the unspecified). The *mu'ayyan* (the specified) is an act which is required by the Lawgiver specifically such as fasting, prayer, payment of due wages, etc. whereas *mukhayyar* (the unspecified) is an act that is required by the Lawgiver in terms of undetermined manner such as the *kaffārah* (expiation) for breaking the oath, feeding ten needy persons, or clothing them or freeing of a slave. The *mukallaf* (subject) is free to choose one of the given alternatives.[120]

The recommended act (mandūb)

The recommended act (*mandūb*) is one of the seven categories of the defining law (*al-ḥukm al-taklīfī*). It is defined as "a demand by the Lawgiver for the commission of an act without making it binding and without assigning any blame for its omission."[121]

It refers to actions that are not required by law but are considered to be commendable. If, however, one neglects the recommended acts, no punishment would be imposed. It also denotes the following terms *mustaḥab*, *sunnah*, and *nafl*. Although, complying with the demand brings spiritual reward (*thawab*) for the *mukallaf*, no punishment is inflicted for failure to perform it. For example, creating a charitable endowment (*waqf*), giving alms to the poor, fasting on days outside *Ramaḍān*, attending the sick, etc.[122]

Sometimes, the non-binding nature of nature of the demand can be inferred from the indication of the text. For example:

> "*O you who believe! when you deal with each other in contracting a debt for a fixed time, then write it down*".[123]

Despite the word (*faktubūhu*) came in an imperative form, the demand for the documenting of the debt is inferred as recommendation from indication of the text which is non-binding. It is evidences with the continuation of the text as: "*but if one of you trusts another, then he who is trusted should deliver his trust, and let him be careful (of his duty to) Allah, his Lord*".[124] This verse indicates that the creditor may trust the debtor without writing it down.

The recommended act (*mandūb*) is conveyed in persuasive language rather than as an imperative language. For example, it comes with the *ḥadīth* of the Prophet (ṣ) as "Whoever makes an ablution for the Friday prayers, it is good, but if he takes a bath, it is better".[125]

An important point among the *Ḥanafī* scholars that once the recommended act (*mandūb*) has been commenced, it turns into an obligation and must be completed. For example, if a person commences a supererogatory fast, it must be completed since it already turned into an obligatory act according to this view. In case of failure to do so renders him liable to the duty of belated performance (*qaḍa'*). However, the *mandūb* is never turned into *wājib* and always remains as *mandūb* according to the *Shāfi'īs.*[126]

Types of the recommended act (mandūb)

As it is indicated above that the recommended act (*mandūb*) also denotes *sunnah.* Therefore, the same term is used here as *mandūb* which is divided into three types despite the scholars mainly consider it two types: *sunnah mu'akkadah* (emphatic), *sunnah ghayr mu'akkadah* (non-emphatic) and *sunnah zawā'id* (additional).

***Sunnah mu'akkadah* (emphatic)**: This type of *mandūb* is also known as *sunnah al-hudā'*. It is a recommended act that was insistently performed by the Prophet (ṣ) and the act was rarely neglected. Performing the *sunnah mu'akkadah* (emphatic) leads to spiritual reward from Almighty Allah while its neglect is simply blameworthy but not punishable. For example, the call to congregational prayers (*adhān*), attending congregational prayers (*jamā'ah*).

Scholars divided it into two different approaches: *sunnah mu'akkadah* that complements and completes a *wājib* because neglecting it may cause to some destruction in the religion and it may require legal and military action such as *adhān* and congregational prayers. Since these acts are part of the fundamental practice (*sha'ā'ir*) of Islam, neglecting them completely may cause destruction of the fundamental symbols of the religion and thus the following maxim reflects its position "an act essential for completing an obligatory act becomes an obligation in itself" (*mā lā yatimmu al-wājibu illā bihī fahuwa wājib*). The other approach is the *sunnah mu'akkadah* that does not complement or complete a *wājīb*. It is a kind of supportive acts of it such as praying two *rak'ats* before the *fajr* prayer, after *ẓuhr* prayers, *maghrib* and *'ishā'*. These acts unlike the former type, do not destroy the fundamental practices of Islam.[127]

***Sunnah* ghayr *mu'akkadah* (non-emphatic)**: This one is also called supererogatory *Sunnah* or *nafl* or *mustaḥab*. It is an act that was not performed insistently by the Prophet (ṣ) at all the time. Performing this type of *sunnah* leads to spiritual reward from Almighty Allah, unlike the former type, neglecting it is not blameworthy nor punishable such as non-obligatory charity, and supererogatory prayers preceding the obligatory prayers four *rak'ats* before *ẓuhr 'asr* and *'ishā'* prayers.[128]

***Sunnah zawā'id* (additional)**: This type of *sunnah* mainly refers to the acts and tasks, performed by the Prophet (ṣ) as a human being, such as his style of dress, type of his food and drink, his choices, his dealing with his family members, etc. Performing this type of *Sunnah* may lead to spiritual reward from Almighty Allah due to resembling his life style out of love for him, and thus, whose omission is neither abominable nor blameworthy nor punishable.[129]

The Disapproved act (makrūh)

The term *makrūh* is defined as "a demand of the Lawgiver which requires the *mukallaf* to avoid something, but not in strictly prohibitory terms."[130] *Makrūh*, unlike the *ḥaram*, does not constitute a binding law, which may be considered the opposite of *mandūb* which neglecting it may amounts to *makrūh*. According to the majority of the scholars, the perpetrator does not incur neither moral blame nor he is liable to punishment and therefore omitting something which is *makrūh* is preferable to committing it. For example a *ḥadīth* of the Prophet (ṣ), in which he discouraged any prayers at particular time, may reflect this meaning as it is narrated from him "Certainly, he – the Prophet (ṣ) – disliked prayers at midday with the exception of Friday".[131] Similarly, the term *makrūh* occurs in the *ḥadīth* of the Prophet (ṣ) about divorce with the same meaning as he said "The most hated of permissible things to Allah is divorce".[132]

The disapproved act (*makrūh*) is the lowest degree of prohibition (*taḥrim*) in *aḥkām*. Although the majority of the scholars consider it one category, *Ḥanafis* divide it into two types: *makrūh karāḥat al-taḥrīm* (strongly disapproved) which the *ḥukm taklīfī* (defining law) arises from a probable evidence expressed in binding terms which is close to prohibition. The other type is *makrūh karāḥat al-tanzīh* (disapproval) which the *ḥukm taklīfī* (defining law) is an act whose omission is demanded by the Lawgiver through a probable evidence expressed in non-binding terms. Briefly these are *makrūh taḥrīman* and *makrūḥ tanzīhan.*[133]

The first type of *makrūḥ* that is reprehensible which is closer to the category of *ḥarām*. This is what *Ḥanafis* called it as the opposite of *wājib* which is closer to *ḥarām*. The prohibition (*ḥarām*) is degreed in definitive terms but the *makrūh taḥrīmī* is not. For example, it is *makrūh taḥrīmī* for a person who is making an offer for marriage to a woman who is already promised to another man. Similarly, for a person who is making an offer for sale where the offer of another has already been made and not determined yet. As the Prophet (ṣ) forbade such kind of transections as he said: "A man should not make an offer while the offer of his brother is pending; or that he should not make a proposal of marriage while that of his brother is pending".[134] Since this *ḥadīth* is an *āḥād ḥadīth* (*khabar wāḥid*) whose authenticity is not devoid of doubt, the prohibition is thus reduced from *ḥarām* to *makrūh taḥrīmī*.

The second type of *makrūh* is *makrūh tanzīhi* that is nearer to *mubāḥ* than to *ḥarām*. Its commission is not punished but its omission is rewarded such as avoiding raw onion and garlic just before going to congregational prayers, or neglecting *ṣalāt al-nafl*, that is, supererogatory prayers preceding, for example, the *ṣalāt al-ẓuhr* (early afternoon prayers) etc. This act may be interpreted as *makrūh* rather than prohibited.[135]

The Prohibited act (ḥarām)

The prohibited act (*ḥarām*) is one of *al-ḥukm al-taklīfī* (defining law) which arises from a definitive evidence that is also known *maḥẓūr* (forbidden). It is a binding demand of the lawgiver in respect of abandoning something and committing it is punishable and omitting it is rewardable. To be considered a prohibited act (*ḥarām*), the majority of the jurists do not differentiated the evidence whether is definitive or speculative. Despite the majority opinion, *Ḥanafī* jurists the act must be based on a definitive evidence. If, however, the act is founded in speculative evidence, it constitutes a *makrūh karāhat taḥrīm* (prohibited act which is closer to prohibition) but not reached to the level of *ḥarām*. Although, the former resembles the latter in which committing both is punished and omitting them is rewarded, the later cause to *kufr* (infidelity). Since the wilful denial of the *ḥarām* leads to infidelity, the *makrūh karāhat taḥrīm* is not, due to the level of evidence that is either definitive or speculative.[136]

The binding and certain terms of *ḥarām* in which the demand is expressed are comprehended in a variety of forms which may be indicated below:

First, the binding text may clearly use the word *ḥarām* or any of its derivatives which indicate *taḥrīm* (prohibition). For example: The binding text is provided in the *Qur'ān*:

> "*Forbidden to you (for food) are: dead meat, blood, the flesh of swine*"[137];
>
> "*and Allah has allowed trading and forbidden usury*".[138]

It is also provided in the *Sunnah*: "The whole of the Muslim is sacred to his fellow Muslim, his blood, his wealth and his honor is prohibited (*ḥarām*)"[139]

Second, the term *ḥarām* may be conducted in the form of a command to avoid a certain form of behaviour. For example, Allah considered wine-drinking and gambling the works of the *Shaiṭān* which must be avoided as He said in the *Qur'ān*: "*O you who believe! Intoxicants and games of chance and (sacrificing to) stones set up and (dividing by) arrows are only an uncleanness, the Shaiṭān's work; shun it therefore that you may be successful*".[140]

Third, the term *ḥarām* is also identified by the enactment of a punishment for a certain form of behaviour, such as the *ḥudūd* penalties and devouring the property of orphans. These kind of *ḥarām* indicated in the *Qur'ān* with differently. The *ḥadd*, for example, is specifically referenced to both the quantity of punishment and the type of penalties, however, the devouring the property of orphans is indicated by an emphatic condemnation of a certain act which conducts *taḥrīm* without specifying a certain type of penalty. As Allah said in the *Qur'ān* for the former case: "*And (as for) the man who steals and the woman who steals, cut off their hands as a punishment for what they have earned, an exemplary punishment from Allah; and Allah is Mighty, Wise*"[141] and for the latter case: "*(As for) those who swallow the property of the orphans unjustly, surely they only swallow fire into their bellies and they shall enter burning fire*".[142]

Fourth, the term *ḥarām* may be carried other prohibitory terms which require the avoidance of a certain form of manner. For example, a text from the *Qur'ān* which provides this manner:

> "*And do not swallow up your property among yourselves by false means, neither seek to gain access thereby to the judges, so that you may swallow up a part of the property of men wrongfully while you know*"[143];

and

> "*do not kill the soul which Allah has forbidden except for the requirements of justice*"[144].

Fifth, the term *ḥarām* may be conducted through specific expressions such as "it is not permissible or it is unlawful" (*lā yaḥillu*) in which this term indicates for complete prohibition. For example, Allah proclaims in the *Qur'ān* "*O you who believe! It is not lawful for you that you should take women as heritage against (their) will*".[145] Similarly, the Prophet (ṣ) says in the *ḥadīth* which provides "'it is unlawful for a Muslim to take the property of another Muslim without his consent".[146]

Types of the prohibited act (ḥarām)

According to the *Ḥanafī* jurists the prohibited act is divided into two types namely *ḥarām li-dhātihi* (prohibited for an internal factor) and *ḥarām li-ghayrihi* (prohibited for an external factor).[147] **The first type** of prohibited is forbidden due to the act itself which is forbidden for its own sake for examples, theft, murder, adultery, unlawful sexual intercourse, marrying a close relative and performing prayers without an ablution, etc. while **the second type** of prohibited is forbidden because of something else which an act was not prohibited initially but became prohibited because of external factor, for example, fasting the day of *ʿid* (feast), performing prayers in stolen clothes, making an offer of betrothal to a woman who is already betrothed to another man, a sale which involves *ribā'*. Therefore, these examples are originally lawful but they became *ḥarām* due to the external factors such as fasting is initially is lawful but the Lawgiver prohibited it on the day of *ʿid* (feast). Making an offer of betrothal to a woman who is not engaged with anybody is permissible but it became prohibited when the woman is engaged. Sale is permissible in its naturel sense, however it becomes prohibited when *ribā'* (interest) involves.

The Permitted act (mubāḥ)

The permissible/ permitted act (*mubāḥ*) is one of *al-ḥukm al-taklīfī* (defining law) which the Lawgiver has granted a choice of commission or omission, without blame or praise for omission or commission that is also called *ḥalāl*. Similarly it is not a duty that is created and the subject is given a choice to perform the act or not to perform it. However it may sometimes create obligations and duties with respect to other individuals. For example, it may be said that it happens in the case of a person appointing another his agent or concluding a contract with him.

The permissible act (*mubāḥ*) is also defined as "communication from the Lawgiver concerning the conduct of the *mukallaf* which gives him the option to do or not to do something." The communication may be in terms of a clear text from the *Qur'ān* which provides "*This day (all) the good things are allowed to you; and the food of those who have been given the Book is lawful for you and your food is lawful for them*".[148] Additionally, the *Qur'ān* states "*There is no blame on you if you make an offer of betrothal or hold it in your hearts*".[149] According to this verse, the *mukallaf* will not gain a sin, blame or liability if he wishes to make an offer of betrothal for a woman. In another verse, the *Qur'ān* states "*whoever is driven to necessity, not desiring, nor exceeding the limit, no sin shall be upon him*".[150] It is obviously indicated here that if someone is compelled by necessity without desire or transgression, a sinful act becomes permissible.[151]

The permissible act (*mubāḥ*) may also be understood through the principle of the concept of *istiṣḥāb*, which states "the original rule for all things is permissibility" (*al-aṣl fī al-ashyā' al-ibāḥah*). This maxim indicates that if anything is not clearly prohibited by the *sharī'ah* is considered permissible.

Types of the permissible acts (mubāḥ)

The permissible act (*mubāḥ*) can be divided into two types. The first type of *mubāḥ* is that which does not involve any harm to the individual whether the individual acts upon it or otherwise, such as eating, walking in the fresh air, hunting etc.

The second type of *mubāḥ* is that whose commission does not harm the individual due to the necessity although it is principally forbidden such as eating the flesh of a dead carcass to save one's life, eating prohibited meat, like pork, when a life-threatening emerges. The Lawgiver has made permissible all these prohibited items on account of necessities (*ḍarūriyyāt*).[152]

The Ḥukm Waḍ'ī (Declaratory Law)

The *ḥukm al-waḍ'ī* is a communication from Allah, the Exalted, related to the acts of the *mukallaf* (subject) in a manner that is declaratory (*waḍ'ī*), in another word it is explanatory component for *al-ḥukm al-taklīfiyyah* through its fundamental tools which consist of 1. *Al-Sabab* (the cause) 2. *Al-Rukn* (the element), 3. *Al-sharṭ* (the condition) 4. *Al-māni'*(the impediment), 5. *Al-Ṣiḥḥah* (the Validity), 6. *Al-Fasād* (the Nullity), 7. *Al-Buṭlān* (the Vitiation), 8. *'Azīmah* (Strict rules), and 9. *Rukhṣah* (Concessionary rules).[153]

Simply, it can be illustrated by a verse from the *Qur'ān*, as Allah said "*The woman and the man guilty of adultery or fornication, flog each of them with a hundred stripes*".[154]

This verse indicates that the act of adultery itself as the cause of its punishment. Logically the punishment is subjected to committing the act of adultery. The defining law in this text is the ruling that the adulterer must be punished with a hundred lashes while the declaratory law is the cause (*sabab*) that is the act of adultery which the affect being the punishment. An example can be given from the *ḥadīth* of the Prophet (ṣ) as he said "there is no *nikāḥ* without two witnesses" (*lā nikāḥ illā bishāhidayn*).[155] This *ḥadīth* indicates that for a valid marriage, the presence of two witnesses is rendered a condition. In other words, without two witnesses, the *nikāḥ* (marriage) is not valid.

The difference between the two rulings, defining and declaratory, is that the demands addressed to the *mukallaf* such as prayers, fasting, *zakāh*, are normally within the capacity of the *mukallaf* within the defining ruling, while the demands addressed to the *mukallaf* are beyond the capacity of the *mukallaf* for the declaratory ruling, such as the arrival of a particular time of day which is the cause (*sabab*) of prayers is beyond the means and capacity of the worshippers.[156]

We shall now proceed to discuss each of the types of *al-ḥukm al-waḍʿī* (declaratory ruling) individually.

1. Al-Sabab (the cause)

The *sabab* literally means a way to a thing. Technically, "it is what the Lawgiver has determined to be the identifier of a legal rule so that its existence means the presence of the rule, while its absence means the absence of the rule."[157] According to the definition, the *sabab* is the indicator of a *ḥukm*. For example, unlawful sexual intercourse is a *sabab* (cause) for the obligation of implementing *ḥadd* punishment.

The *sabab* (cause) may be divided into two types with the respect to the act of the subject (*mukallaf*): A *sabab* may be an act which is within the power of the *mukallaf* and beyond the control of the *mukallaf*.

The first type is an act of the *mukallaf* and is within his power that is under the control of the *mukallaf*. For example, murder and theft in their status as the causes of retaliation (*qiṣāṣ*) and a *ḥadd* penalty respectively or formation of contracts as a cause for enforcing their performance.

The second type is not dependent on the act of the subject, nor is it within his power that is beyond the control of the *mukallaf*. For example, minority being the cause of guardianship over the person and property of a minor; the setting of the sun as a cause for the obligation of the evening prayer; the beginning of the month of *Ramaḍān* as a cause for the obligation of fasting, etc.

Nevertheless, when the *sabab* is existent, whether the *sabab* is within or beyond the control of the *mukallaf*, its result (the *musabbab*) is automatically present even if the *mukallaf* had not intended it to be. For example, if a man enters into an agreement of marriage, he is obligated to provide dower and maintenance for his wife even if he openly stipulates the opposite in their agreement. The effect of the cause comes about by virtue of the Lawgiver's decree regardless of whether the *mukallaf* intends it to be so or not, once the Lawgiver identifies something as a cause.[158] In addition to this ruling, similar acts may themselves be the subject of a *taklīfī* rule, which they would be required or prohibited or recommended and they may fall under the category of declaratory rules.[159] For example, simply a marriage act is a cause for the permissibility of marital relationship, however it becomes obligatory when there is fear of falling victim to unlawful sexual intercourse.[160]

2. Al-Rukn (the element)

Linguistically, *rukn* (pl. *arkān*) means pillar, corner, essential requirement or foundation of something and part of it. It is an integral part of an act, without it nullifies the act that depends on it. For example, the *rukūʿ* is an element (*rukn*) in prayer, without it or if it is absent, the *ṣalāt* (prayer) is nullified. Reading some verses from the *Qur'ān* is a *rukn*. If this *rukn* is absent, the prayer will be nullified.

The law or *ḥukm*, could not exist in the absence of its *rukn* (element). There will be no *ḥukm* when the whole or even a part of the *rukn* is absent, which the *ḥukm* collapses completely, it becomes null and void (*bāṭil*).

3. Al-sharṭ (the condition)

Literally *sharṭ* means an inseparable sign (*ʿalāmah lāzimah*). It has variety of usage such as *sharṭ* (pl. *shurūṭ*) means provisions in a legal document; *sharīṭah* (pl. *sharā'iṭ*) means condition; *sharaṭ* (pl. *ashrāṭ*) means sign or portent, for example it comes as the phrase *ashrāṭ al-sā'ah* (portents of the last hour).[161]

Technically, *sharṭ* means an "an evident and constant attribute whose absence necessitates the absence of the *ḥukm* but whose presence does not automatically bring about its object (*mashrūṭ*)".[162] It is a necessary condition for a *ḥukm*. The Lawgiver may affirm that a set of facts must exist or an act must take place before the cause can take effect and bring the related *ḥukm*. The existence of such a set of facts is called a *sharṭ* for the *ḥukm*. Simply it is a sign or an indication on which the existence of another thing depends, however, the existence of this sign does not necessarily mean the existence of that thing.[163] For example ablution is a condition for prayer, but the presence of ablution (*wuḍū'*) does not necessitate prayer (*ṣalāt*) and the presence of witnesses a condition for the marriage contract but the presence of witness does not necessarily mean that a marriage has taken place, yet without witness a marriage would not be valid. From other way around the presence of a valid marriage is a precondition of divorce, however, it does not mean that when there is a valid marriage, the divorce would happen.

A *sharṭ* (condition) normally complements *sabab* (the cause) for example killing is the *sabab* (the cause) of retaliation, but it requires a *sharṭ* (condition) that it is deliberate and hostile; the contract of marriage legalizes, which is a *sabab* (cause), sexual enjoyment between the spouses, but it requires a condition that two witnesses testify to the marriage. Therefore, the legal consequences of a contract are not fully materialized without the fulfilment of its necessary conditions.

Sharṭ is, therefore, divided into two types by the jurists: *sharṭ shar'ī* (legal conditions) and *sharṭ ja'alī* (condition imposed by the subject). For example, in a marriage contract a condition of two witnesses is of the *sharṭ shar'ī* (legal conditions) which is laid down by the Lawgiver and a condition of residing in a particular locality is the *sharṭ ja'alī* (condition imposed by the subject) which is stipulated by spouses.

The difference between the *rukn* (element) and *sharṭ* (condition) is that a *rukn* is always part of the act which is an internal part of it, while the *sharṭ* is external to the act. For example, bowing (*rukū'*) and prostration (*sajdah*) are each an essential requirement (*rukn*) of prayer and are internal part of it, while ablution is a *sharṭ* (condition) and is external to prayer.[164]

4. Al-Māni'(the impediment)

Literally, *māni'* means an obstacle or an impediment. It is a barrier between an injunction and the requirement of its cause.

Technically, it is an existent, evident and regular quality which signifies the denial of the injunction such as fatherhood is an impediment (*māni'*) to taking retaliation[165] which means that if a father intentionally kills his son, he will not be killed in retaliation, for he is his father. Fatherhood is an impediment to retaliation. It signifies the denial of *ḥukm* which is *qiṣāṣ* (retaliation). Therefore, the existence of an impediment (*māni'*) invalidates both *sabab* and *ḥukm*. Even if the cause is found and the condition is met, the *ḥukm* is prevented from being applied due to the impediment (*māni'*).

The presence of the impediment (*māni'*) is the absence of the *ḥukm*. For example, in the case of inheritance, killing and difference of religion are both impediment to inheritance between a legal heir and his deceased relative despite the fact that there may exist a valid relationship (*qarābah*) between them. Nevertheless, if the killing, which is impediment, is present, the inheritance which is the *ḥukm* is absent.

The impediment (*māni'*) can be divided into two types: negating the *ḥukm* and negating the *sabab* (the cause). For example, if a father kills his son, he is not liable to retaliation due to the fatherhood which impediments retaliation according to the majority of scholars, except Imām Mālik. He has held the view that the father may be retaliated against for the deliberate killing of his children. The example of the negating the *sabab* (the cause) is the indebtedness of a person who is liable to the payment of *zakāh*. If a person who is heavily indebted, this debt impediments the cause of *zakāh* such as bankruptcy case. The cause for *zakāh* is ownership, since the ownership is no longer exist with the bankruptcy, the liability to the payment of *zakāh* is nullified.[166]

5. *Al-Ṣiḥḥah (the Validity)*

Ṣiḥḥah (validity) means agreement of an act having both characteristics (agreement and disagreement) with the *Sharīʿah*. It is "legitimate by its nature and attribute" (*mā kāna mashrūʿan bi-aṣlihī wa waṣfihī*).

It is also said that validity (*ṣiḥḥah*) in rituals means extinction of compensatory performance, and validity of contract signifies the actual of its effect.[167] Such as prayer, contract of sale, and marriage. These acts are liable to agreement and disagreement with the *Sharīʿah* and sometimes they may conform to the principles of the *Sharīʿah* and sometimes may not. It means that it is conformity to the command of the Lawgiver, whether compensatory performance of the act is binding or not. Nevertheless, according to the jurists, it means the extinction of compensatory performance by doing an act again.[168]

In other words, *ṣiḥḥah* (validity) which describes and evaluates legal acts incurred by the subject (*mukallaf*). Evaluating an act according to the criteria depends on whether or not the act in question fulfils the essential requirements (*arkān*) and conditions (*shurūṭ*) that the *Sharīʿah* has laid down for it, and ensuring that there exist no obstacles to impede its proper conclusion. Such as prayer is a *sharʿī* act and is evaluated as valid (*ṣaḥiḥ*) when it fulfils all the essential requirements and conditions that the *Sharīʿah* has provided in this regard. Otherwise it becomes void (*bāṭil*).[169]

A group of scholars hold the view that it is the communication of the Lawgiver (*khiṭāb al-Shāri'*) involving demand or option which makes a thing valid (*ṣaḥīḥ*) or void (*bāṭil*). For example, "the validity (*ṣiḥḥah*) of sale means the grant of permission of the Lawgiver to the purchaser to utilize the goods, and his demand of him to pay their price to the seller and to deliver the goods by the seller to him. The meaning of voidness (*buṭlān*) of a contract of sale means the prohibition of the lawgiver from utilizing the goods by the purchaser, and his demand of him to annul the contract, thus freeing himself from the obligations resulting from the enforcement of contract."[170]

Scholars also discussed the nature of the concept of validity and invalidity. These are known as kinds of command (*ḥukm*) and are true of the acts of man and not of the commands themselves which mean that the acts may agree or disagree with the *Sharī'ah* not the commands. Similarly, the acts which do not conform to the *Sharī'ah* nor fulfil the conditions, are invalid (*bāṭil*). Although some jurists have indicated that validity and invalidity are the attributes of the command rather than acts, al-Taftāzānī clearly shown that validity and invalidity qualify act rather than command.[171]

Majority of the scholars are in agreement to the effect that acts of devotion ('*ibādāt*) can either be valid (*ṣaḥīḥ*) or void (*bāṭil*), in the sense that there is no intermediate category in between. However, according to *Ḥanafīs* there is another category between them which is vitiation (*fasād*). Therefore, *Ḥanafīs* added another category called irregular or vitiated (*fāsid*). According to them, an act can become valid if the cause of the irregularity is removed, otherwise it stays suspended. For example, a contract that is involving *ribā*. This contract remains as suspended until the offending condition is removed, once it is removed, it becomes a valid contract, otherwise it remains as vitiated (*fāsid*).[172]

6. *al-Fasād (the Nullity)*

Fasād (nullity) is the opposite of *ṣiḥḥah* (validity). As we know that

Ṣiḥḥah (validity) means that it is conformity to the command of the Lawgiver and the demand to follow the object (*al-ghāyah*). Thus, its opposite is *buṭlān* (invalidity) and *fasād* (nullity).[173] As it is mentioned above that this type is brought by the *Ḥanafī* scholars. They have distinguished an intermediate category between the valid (*ṣaḥīḥ*) and void (*bāṭil*), namely the vitiated (*fāsid*) that is defined as "It is legitimate by its nature, but not legitimate by its attribute" (*mā kāna mashrū'an bi-aṣlihī ghayri mashrū'an bi-waṣfihī*), which means that the essential elements and conditions of a contract are complete, but it is associated with a quality which is prohibited by the Lawgiver.[174]

The *Ḥanafī* scholars described the vitiated (*fāsid*) as something which is essentially lawful (*mashrū'*) but is deficient in respect of an attribute (*waṣf*) as opposed to the void (*bāṭil*) which is unlawful (*ghayr mashrū'*) on account of its deficiency in regards to both essence (*aṣl*) and attribute (*waṣf*). The *Ḥanafīs* approach to the vitiated (*fāsid*) is also grounded in the idea that the deficiency which affects the attribute but not the essence of a transaction can easily be removed and resolved. Accordingly, if the deficiency in a contract affects an essential requirement (*rukn*), the contract is null and void, and thus, it fulfils no legal actions. However, if the deficiency in a contract only affects a condition, the contract is the vitiated (*fāsid*) but not the void (*bāṭil*). A vitiated contract, although deficient in some respects, is still a contract and brings some of its legal consequences, but not all. Therefore, a vitiated contract of sale establishes the purchaser's ownership over the object of sale when he has taken possession thereof, but does not entitle the purchaser to the usufruct (*intifā'*). Similarly, a marriage contract without witness. In order to be valid (*ṣaḥīḥ*), the spouses or the *qāḍī* must either remove the deficiency or dissolve the marriage. The contract becomes suspended which is vitiated (*fāsid*) until the deficiency is removed. If it is not removed the marriage will be dissolved even if the marriage has been consummated. The wife is still entitled to the dower (*mahr*) and must observe the waiting period of *'iddah* upon dissolution of the marriage.

However, the offspring of a vitiated (*fāsid*) marriage is legitimate, but the wife is not entitled to maintenance, and no right of inheritance between the spouses can proceed from such a marriage. If the deficiency is known before the consummation of the marriage, the consummation is considered unlawful.[175]

7. al-Buṭlān (the Vitiation)

The opposite of *ṣiḥḥah* (validity) is *buṭlān* (invalidity). The acts which do not conform to the *Sharī'ah* nor fulfil the conditions, are invalid (*bāṭil*).[176] Majority of the scholars are in agreement to the effect that acts of devotion (*`ibādāt*) can either be valid (*ṣaḥīḥ*) or void (*bāṭil*). According to *Shāfi'ī* void (*bāṭil*) and vitiated (*fāsid*) are synonymous terms which denote what is invalid (*ghair ṣaḥīḥ*).[177]

The invalid contract (*'aqd bāṭil*) means a contract in which one of its essential elements is missing, or any condition which complements these essential elements is not fulfilled. Therefore, *Ḥanafīs* define it as "what is not legitimate by its nature nor by its attribute is called *bāṭil* (invalid)" (*wa mā lam yakun mashrū'an bi-aṣlihī lā bi-waṣfihī summiya bāṭilan*). For example, the sale of a young in the mother's womb, the goods which are not capable of being delivered, sale of carrion and flesh of swine, and sale of goods by a child void of understanding or by lunatic.[178]

Another jurist, Ibn Subkī, defines it as "The opposite of *ṣiḥḥah* (validity) is *buṭlān* (invalidity). It means the disagreement of an act having both characteristics with the *Sharī'ah*. In rituals it is said that it means non-extinction of compensatory performance. It is synonymous with *fasād* (voidability, irregularity)".[179]

The term *buṭlān* (invalidity) in the definition conveys two meanings: The first one is non-accruing of the effects of an act in this world; and the second one is non-accruing of the effects of an act in the hereafter. In regards to the first meaning, there is a distinction between the invalidity of rituals and invalidity of transactions. The invalidity of rituals (*buṭlān al-ʿibādāt*) means that the rituals were performed improperly, not exonerating the *mukallaf* from the discharge of his duty and not extinguishing the compensatory performance. The object of the Lawgiver is known from his commands and prohibitions. When the performance of the rituals disagrees with his commands as desired by him, they are invalid (*bāṭil*). The disagreement sometimes refers to the substance of the ritual and sometimes to its external attribute. If the performance of a ritual does not fulfil its essential elements (*arkān*) and conditions (*shurūṭ*), such as prayer without intention, purification, bowing or prostration, is invalid (*bāṭil*). This kind of invalidity refers to the defective performance of the substance of the rituals, as it disagrees with the object desired by the Lawgiver from the prayer. The examples of disagreement with the external quality of a ritual are observance of prayer in a usurped house or while wearing usurped garment, and fasting on the day of *ʿīd*. The ruling (*ḥukm*) on this issue is debatable among the scholars whether still the act of the *mukallaf* is valid or not. Some jurists hold the view that it is valid but the *mukallaf* entails sin due to the inconsistency, however it does not affect the validity of prayer, while some other group is of the view that the prayer is invalid due to the inconsistency with the intention of the Lawgiver. The first group looks at the prayer in substance and thinks that what is designed by the Lawgiver is prayer and not its attribute, while the other group looks at the inconsistency of prayer with the intention of the Lawgiver.

In addition to this, the invalidity of transactions in this world (*buṭlān al-muʿāmalāt*) means the non-accruing of benefits and non-fulfilment of rights and obligations resulting from contractual transactions, for example, the invalidity of marriage (*buṭlān*) means that the husband has no right to have sexual intercourse with his wife and therefore, he will not be responsible for her maintenance.[180]

8. 'Azīmah (Strict rules/regularity)

Literally, the word *'azm* means firm resolve (*qaṣd muwakkad*) or to make up one's mind to something (*'aqd al-qalb*). In this sense it has been used in the following verse from the *Qur'ān*: "*And certainly We gave a commandment to Adam before, but he forgot; and We did not find firmness of purpose in him*".[181]

Also for the determination of purpose and firm resolve in their right stand some Prophets have been named ulu'l-'azm: "Therefore bear up patiently as did the messengers endowed with firm resolve with patience and do not seek to hasten for them (their doom)".[182]

The word *'azīmah*, therefore, is defined as "that is binding on the servants by obligation of Allah" (*al-'azīmah 'ibāratun 'ammā lazama al-'ibād bi-īyjābullahi ta'ālā*).[183] Legally, according to the *Sharī'ah*, "*'azīmah* is a command established on the basis of a proof of the *Sharī'ah*, free from any probable impediment" (*al-'azīmatu shar'an heya al-ḥukm al-thābit bi-dalīylin shar'īyyin khālin 'an mu'ariḍin rājiḥin*).[184]

In general the word *'azā'im* (pl. *'azīmah*) which are regular commands that are applicable to all persons who are subject of law and to all ordinary situations, which consists of regular commands of the *Sharī'ah*, while the *rukhaṣ* (pl. *rukhṣah*) are the special and exceptional commands which allow to act against the regular injunctions which consists of special or exceptional commands of the *Sharī'ah*.

Technically, the word *'azīmah* is defined as "an established command, not contrary to the proof of the *Sharī'ah*, such as permission to eat and drink, or contrary to the proof of the *Sharī'ah* but not for any valid excuse, such as legal obligations".[185]

Imām al-Qarāfī defines it as "to demand the performance of an act to which a legal impediment is not well-known" (*al-'azīmatu ṭalabu al-fi'li alladhī lam yushtahar fīhi māni'un shar'iyyun*).[186] In another statement, the word *'azīmah* is briefly defined as "it is al those regular commands of the *Sharī'ah* which have been primarily promulgated" (*al-'azīmatu heya mā shuri'a min al-'aḥkām al-kulliyyah ibtidāan*).[187] The *'azīmah* applies to all those commands which have been given primarily for the good of the people who are subject of law, such as marriage, sale transactions, civil and criminal laws, prayer, *zakāh*, fasting, *ḥajj* and others. It also applies to exceptions to rules of law. Sometimes the command of the *Sharī'ah* is general. However, there are some exceptions or specific rules excluded from them such as marrying right hand possessed as it comes in the *Qur'ān*: "*Also (prohibited are) women already married, except those whom your right hands possess*".[188] It is obvious that marrying a woman who is already is married is forbidden, but exception is made by the *Qur'ān* that the female slaves are exceptional. This exception is considered an *'azīmah*.

Similarly, with a different perception, eating carrion, blood, flesh of swine, and animals slaughtered in the name of others than Allah is forbidden. But in case of compulsion and necessity one is allowed to eat them to save one's life. This exception is *'azīmah* for some jurists, while it is *rukhṣah* for some others, as it is illustrated by the following verse: "*Why should you not eat of (meats) on which Allah's name has been pronounced, when He has explained to you in detail what is forbidden to you – except under compulsion of necessity? But many do mislead (men) by their appetites unchecked by knowledge. Your Lord knows best those who transgress*".[189]

The concept of *'azīmah* comprehends the five legal categories (*aḥkām khamsah*) which applies to the following types[190]:

1. The command which does not change, such as the obligation of five daily prayers.
2. The command which is changed to what is more difficult than the original one, such as prohibitions of hunting in a state of *iḥrām* (sacredness) after its previous permission.
3. The command which is changed into ease without any valid

reason, such as permission to omit the performance of ablution to observe a second obligatory prayer, for a person whose ablution (state of purity) has not become void, after its prohibition (to say prayer without ablution).

4. The command which is changed into ease on account of some valid reason for non-existence of a cause for the original command, such as permission to abandon the steadiness, such as a single warrior from the Muslims in a battle confronting ten warriors from the infidels after its prohibition. The reason for the permission is the small number of Muslims due to the hardship involved but it does not apply to big numbers of Muslims.[191]

Nevertheless, according to al-Sarakhsī, it appears that all injunctions, whether positive or negative, are included in this category as he illustrated with the following explanation: "*ʿAzīmah* among the commands of the *Sharīʿah* is one which is promulgated by the lawgiver primarily without having its connection with an impediment (*ʿāriḍ*). This category has been named *ʿazīmah* for its being an original command extremely emphasised and strengthened, a right of Allah over us, for His our deity and we are His servants. He is the master of command. He does as He wills, and commands as He wills. We must show submission and obedience."[192]

It is a law as the Lawgiver had intended it in the first place such as prayer, *zakah*, *ḥajj*, *jihād* etc. *ʿAzīmah* is the law in its normal state, while *rukhṣah* embodies the exceptions that the Lawgiver has granted with a view to bringing facility and ease in difficult circumstances. Therefore, the law which grants a concession to travellers to break the fast during *Ramaḍān* is an exception to the norm that requires everyone to fast. The concessionary law in this case is valid only for the duration of traveling which is an exceptional reason. It becomes normal, which the *ʿazīmah* must be complied with again, when the exceptional condition is over. For example in a case where a Muslim if he is compelled to renounce his faith, he will be permitted to do so even if the regular law would require him to persist in his faith until death.[193] The permission is given due to the necessity (*ḍaruriyyāt*) to safe live of a person which is granted in the *Qur'ān*: "*Anyone who, after accepting faith in Allah, utters Unbelief, - except under compulsion, his heart remaining firm in Faith*".[194]

9. *Rukhṣah (Concessionary rules)*

Literally the word *rukhṣah* means ease and convenience. In its original meaning it is used for giving permission (*ibāḥah*) by way of facilitation providing ease, convenience and lenience.[195]

Technically, it has been defined as "*Rukhṣah* is the name of that (command) which is based on the excuses of Allah's servants. It is one permitted on account of a certain excuse which is a valid reason, despite the existence of a prohibitive cause".[196] *Rukhṣah* means a latitude given to a person under obligation in his action for an excuse, and he is unable to perform it, despite the existence of a prohibitive cause, however, permission to eat and drink by Allah is not called *rukhṣah* since they are already permitted. Despite eating carrion and drinking alcohol are prohibited, eating and drinking them in order to save one's life is called *rukhṣah*. It is therefore *'azīmah* and *rukhṣah* are interrelated in that *rukhṣah* can only exist when there is *'azīmah* in the first place. Similarly, it would also be incorrect to call the permissibility of *tayammum* (dry ablution with clean earth or sand) in the absence of water a *rukhṣah*, it is because water is not available in the first place. However, *tayammum* becomes a *rukhṣah* if it is a substitute for *wuḍū'* when the weather is extremely cold or harmful for the body.[197]

Rukhṣah is also defined as "a command which is established against a proof of the *Sharī'ah* on account of some valid reason" (*al-rukhṣah heya al-ḥukm al-thābit 'alā khilāf al-dalīyli li-'udhrin*).[198] *Al-Āmidī* defines it similarly as "*Rukhṣah* is a command which is promulgated on account of some valid reason, notwithstanding the existence of a prohibitive cause".[199]

The *rukhṣah* may happen to the following varieties:[200]

1. It may happen in the form of permitting a prohibited act on grounds of necessity (*ḍarūrah*), such as eating the flesh of a carcass, and drinking wine at the point of starvation or extreme thirst, uttering the words of unbelief with the tongue under compulsion, etc. As Allah granted permission with the following verse: "*Anyone who, after accepting faith in Allah, utters Unbelief, – except under compulsion, his heart remaining firm in Faith*".[201] This verse was revealed about 'Ammar b. Yāsir who was compelled to utter words of unbelief and blasphemy under compulsion.

2. It may happen in the form of omitting a *wājib* when conformity to that *wājib* causes hardship, such as the concession granted to the traveller to shorten quadruple prayer, or not to observe the fasting of *Ramaḍān*. It has been narrated on the authority of 'Ā'ishah who said: "Ḥamzah b. 'Amr al-Aslamī asked the Prophet (ṣ) about fasting during journey. He replied: Fast if you wish, and break if you wish."[202]

3. *Rukhṣah* may occur in the form of concessions to the Muslim *ummah* from certain rigorous laws which were imposed under previous revelations, prior to the advent of the Prophet (ṣ). Allah has released Muslim community from such burdens out of mercy. For example, *zakāh* to the extent of one-quarter of one's property, the impermissibility of prayer outside a mosque, and the illegality of taking booty (*ghanīmah*), which were imposed on people under previous religions, and eventually have been removed by the *Sharī'ah* of Islam. Allah illustrates it with the following verse: "*Our Lord! do not lay on us a burden as Thou didst lay on those before us*".[203]

4. It may occur in the area of transactions in the form of validating contracts which would normally be prohibited. For example, lease and hire (*ijārah*), advance sale (*salam*) and order for the manufacture of goods (*istiṣnā'*) are all irregular, as the object of contract therein is non-existent at the time of contract, but they have been exceptionally permitted in order to accommodate the public need for such transactions. The goods should be available at the time of contract of sale as a general rule, according to the Prophet's (ṣ) tradition. Ḥakīm b. Ḥizām reported the Prophet (ṣ) as saying "Do not sell what you do not have with you".[204]

Notes

[1] See: Elias, *ibid.*; Joseph Catafago, *ibid.*; Hans Wehr, *ibid.*

[2] Zuhaylī: *ibid*, v. 1, p. 21.

[3] Āmidī, v. 1, p. 7.

[4] Ṣadr al-Sharī'ah, *ibid.*, v.1, p. 13; Bannānī, "*Ḥāshiah*, v.1 p. 32; Nyazee, *ibid.*, p. 64.

[5] *Qur'ān* 2:183

[6] *Qur'ān* 17:32

[7] *Qur'ān* 5:1

[8] *Qur'ān* 49:11

[9] *Qur'ān* 5:2

[10] *Qur'ān* 3:97

[11] Abū Ḥāmid Muḥammad ibn Muḥammad Ghazālī (d. 505/1111), "*Al-Mustaṣfā' min 'Ilm al-Uṣūl*" (Cairo: al-Maktabah al-Tijāriyyah, 1356/1937), v. 1 p. 42; Shawkānī, "*Irshād*" p. 6; Zuhaylī, "*Uṣūl*" p. 37-43.

[12] *Qur'ān* 2:43

[13] Ṣadr al-Sharī'ah, "*Al-Tawdīḥ*" v. 1, p. 13; Isnawī, "*Sallam al-Wuṣūl*" v. 1, p. 24.

[14] Herbert Lionel Adolphus Hart, "*The Concept of Law*" p. 77-96 qf. Nyazee, *ibid.*, p. 57-58.

[15] Zuhaylī, *ibid.*, v. 1, p. 37; Khallāf, 'Abd al-Wahhāb (d. 1376/1956), "'*Ilm Uṣūl al-Fiqh*," 12th edn. (Kuwait: Dār al-Qalām, 1398/1978), see for the use of English

terminology in Nyazee, *ibid.*; Kamali, "*Principles,*" p. 321-353.

[16] *Qur'ān* 6: 57

[17] *Qur'ān* 6:62

[18] *Qur'ān* 33: 36

[19] *Qur'ān* 5:44 and 5:45

[20] Ahmad Hasan, "*Principles,*" p. 231.

[21] Ghazālī, *Mustaṣfā*, v. 1, p. 53; Abū Zahrah, *Uṣūl*, p. 54

[22] Ahmad Hasan, *Principles*, p. 232.

[23] Baḥrul 'Ulūm, 'Abd al-'Alī, *Fawātiḥ al-Raḥamūt* (Baghdād: Maktaat al-Muthammā, 1970), v. 1, p. 25.

[24] Baḥrul 'Ulūm, 'Abd al-'Alī, *Fawātiḥ al-Raḥamūt*, v. 1, p. 25-26.

[25] Al-Baṣrī, Abū al-Ḥusayn, *Kitāb al-Mu'tamad* (Damascus: al-Ma'had al-'Ilmī al-Faransī li'l Dirāsāt al-Islāmiyyah, 1964), v. 1, p. 8-9, 365-366.

[26] Ahmad Hasan, *Principles*, p. 232.

[27] Baḥrul 'Ulūm, 'Abd al-'Alī, *Fawātiḥ al-Raḥamūt*, v. 1, p. 25; Ṣadr al-Sharī'ah, *al-Tawḍīḥ* along with its commentary *al-Talwīḥ*, v. 1, p. 173.

[28] *Qur'ān* 17:15

[29] *Qur'ān* 4:165

[30] *Qur'ān* 20:134

[31] Khallaf, *'Ilm*, p. 97; Abū Zahrah, *Uṣūl*, p. 57.

[32] Al-Baṣrī, *ibid.*, v. 1, 8-9, 365-366.

[33] Abu Zahrah *Uṣūl*, p. 56; Khallaf, *'Ilm*, p. 99.

[34] Baḥrul 'Ulūm, 'Abd al-'Alī, *Fawātiḥ al-Raḥamūt*, v. 1, p. 28.

[35] Al-Taftāzānī, *Sharḥ al-Talwīḥ 'ala'l Tawḍīḥ* (Cairo: Dār al-'Ahd al-Jadīd, lil-Ṭibā'ah, 1957), v. 2, 156; Wahbah al-Zuhaylī, *Uṣūl al-Fiqh al-Islāmī* (Damascus: Dār al-Fikr, 1986), v. 1, p. 158.

[36] Al-Bazdawī, *Uṣūl al-Bazdawī*, v. 4, 1352; Al-Sarakhsi, *Uṣūl*, v. 1, 346-347.

[37] *Qur'ān* 4:43.

[38] Sunan Abū Dāwud, *Kitāb al-Ḥudūd*, Bāb fil Majnūn.

[39] Al-Sarakhsī, *Uṣūl*, v. 2, 232; Al-Ghazālī, *al-Mustaṣfā*, v.1, 53-54; Sadr al-Sharī'ah, *al-Tawḍīḥ*, v. 2, 751;

[40] 'Abd al-'Azīz al-Bukhārī, *Kashf al-Asrār 'an Uṣūl Fakhr al-Islam al-Bazdawī*, v. 4 (Beirut: Dār al-Kutub al-'Ilmiyyah, 1997), p. 335.

[41] Al-Zarqā', *al-Fiqh al-Islāmī fī Thawbihi al-Jadīd* (Damascus: Maṭba'ah Jāmi'ah Damishq, 1963), v. 2, p. 739.

[42] Al-Sarakhsī, *Uṣūl*, v. 2, p. 233; Ṣadr al-Sharī'ah, *al-Tawḍīḥ*, v. 2, p. 751.

[43] Ṣadr al-Sharī'ah, *al-Tawḍīḥ*, v. 2, p. 755.

[44] Al-Taftāzānī, *Sharḥ al-Talwīḥ 'ala'l Tawḍīḥ*, v. 2, p.161.

[45] *Qur'ān* 9:10

[46] *Qur'ān* 33:72

[47] Ṣadr al-Sharī'ah, *al-Tawḍīḥ*, v. 2, p. 751; Al-Sarakhsī, *Uṣūl*, v. 2, p. 233.

[48] Nyazee, *Islamic Jurisprudence*, p. 112.

[49] Al-Taftāzānī, *Sharḥ al-Talwīḥ 'ala'l Tawḍīḥ*, v. 2, p. 161-162.

[50] Al-Zarqā', *al-Fiqh al-Islāmī fī Thawbihi al-Jadīd* (Damascus: Maṭba'ah Jāmi'ah Damishq, 1963), v. 2, 744; Ahmad Hasan, *Principles*, p. 299.

[51] Al-Tirmidhī, Jāmi' al-Tirmidhī, *Abwāb al-Mawāqīt, Bāb mājā'a Matā Yūmaru al-Ṣabiyyu bi'l Ṣalaḥ*; Al-Sarakhsī, *Uṣūl*, v. 2, p. 343; Ahmad Hasan, *Principles*, p. 303.

[52] Wahbah al-Zuhaylī, *Uṣūl al-Fiqh al-Islāmī* (Damascus: Dār al-Fikr, 1986), v. 1, p. 165; Al-Zarqā', Muṣṭafā Aḥmad, *al-Fiqh al-Islāmī fī Thawbihi al-Jadīd*, v. 2, p. 751.

[53] Nyazee, *Islamic Jurisprudence*, p. 112

[54] *Ibid.*

[55] Sadr al-Sharī'ah, *al-Tawḍīḥ*, v. 2, p. 755; al-Bukhārī, *Kashf al-Asrār*, v. 4, p. 335.

[56] Ahmad Hasan, *Principles*, p. 302.

[57] *Qur'ān* 4:6

[58] According to the majority of the scholars, the term *rushd* signifies the handling of financial matters. A person who reached the age of this capacity is called *rashīd* who can identify avenues of profit and loss as well as act accordingly to preserve his wealth. It is the opposite of *safah* (foolishness). According the *Shāfi'ī* jurists, the *rushd* is the maturity of actions in matters of finance and of *dīn*. If a person attained both being a *bāligh* and a *rashīd*, is eligible for taking over his wealth, however, a person who attains the age of twenty-five years must be delivered his property irrespective of his attaining *rushd* according to Abū Ḥanīfah.

[59] Ahmad Hasan, *Principles*, p. 301-302.

[60] Ahmad Hasan, *Principles*, p. 304.

[61] Nyazee, *Islamic Jurisprudence*, p. 120-122.

[62] Nyazee, *ibid.*, p. 120-123.

[63] Amīr Bādshāh, *Taysīr al-Taḥrīr* (Cairo: Muṣṭafā al-Bābī al-Ḥalabī, 1350 AH), v. 2, p. 258.

[64] Ahmad Hasan, *Principles*, p. 309. See more on the details of these *'awārid* in Ahmad Hasan, *Principles*, p. 304-383.

[65] Ṣadr al-Sharī'ah, *al-Tawḍīḥ* with its commentary *al-Talwīḥ*, (Cairo: Dār al-'Ahd al-Jaḍīd li'Ṭibā 'ah, 1957), v.2, 150; al-Bayḍāwī, *Minhāj al-Wuṣūl ilā 'ilm al-Uṣūl*, with its commentary *Nihāyat al-Su'l*, (Cairo: Matba'ah al-Tawfīq al-Adabiyyah, n.d.), v. 1, p. 85,107.

[56] Ahmad Hasan, *Principles*, p. 251.

[57] Al-Taftāzānī, *al-Talwīḥ*, v. 2, 150.

[58] Al-Taftāzānī, *al-Talwīḥ*, v. 1, 15.

[59] *Qur'ān* 2:43

[70] *Qur'ān* 2:282

[71] *Qur'ān* 6:152

[72] *Qur'ān* 2:267

[73] *Qur'ān* 62:10

[74] Khallaf, *'Ilm*, p. 128; Abū Zahrah, *Uṣūl*, p. 249

[75] Ahmad Hasan, *Principles*, p. 254.

[76] 'Abdur Raḥīm, *Principles of Muhammadan Jurisprudence* (Lahore: All Pakistan legal decisions, 1958), p. 193-195; Al-Taftāzānī, *al-Talwīḥ 'ala'l Tawḍīḥ* (Cairo: Dār al-'Ahd al-Jadīd, lil-Ṭibā'ah, 1957), v. 1, 215, v. 2, 151, 161.

[77] Shawkānī, *Irshād*, p. 11.

[78] Abū Zahrah, *Uṣūl*, p. 256

[79] *Qur'ān* 2:286.

[80] *Qur'ān* 65:7

[81] Shawkānī, *Irshād*, p. 11; Khallaf, *'Ilm*, p. 128; Abū Zahrah, *Uṣūl*, 250.

[82] Muslim, *Ṣaḥīḥ Muslim*, *ḥadīth* 73

[83] Ahmad Hasan, *Principles*, p. 258.

[84] *Qur'ān* 6:164

[85] *Qur'ān* 52:21

[86] Bukhārī, *al-Jāmī al-Ṣaḥīḥ*, *Kitāb al-Ṣawm*.

[87] Ṭaḥāwī, *Mushkil al-Āthār*, (Hyderabad, Deccan: Dā'irat al-Ma'ārif al-Nu'māniyyah, 1333 AH.), v. 3, 141; Al-Bayhaqī, *al-Sunan al-Kubrā*, (Multan: Nashr al-Sunnah, n.d.), v. 4, 257.

[88] Ibn Qudāmah, *al-Muqhnī*, (Cairo: Dār al-Manār, 1368 AH), v. 2, 227-228.

[89] Ibn 'Ābidīn, *Radd al-Muḥtār* (Cairo: Musṭafā al-Bābī al-Ḥalabī, n.d.), v. 2, p. 258.

[90] *Ṣaḥīḥ al-Bukharī, Bāb al-Targhīb fī al-Nikāḥ.*

[91] *Qur'ān* 2:185

[92] *Qur'ān* 22:78

[93] *Musnad Aḥmad*, v. 5, p. 266

[94] *Ṣaḥīḥ al-Bukharī, Kitāb al-Ṣawm.*

[95] *Musnad Aḥmad*, v. 2, p. 108.

[96] Al-Shāṭibī, *al-Muwāfaqāt* v. 2, p. 122-123.

[97] Al-Shāṭibī, *ibid.*, v. 2, p. 123.

[98] Al-Zarqā', Muṣṭafā Aḥmad, *al-Fiqh al-Islāmī fī Thawbihi al-Jadīd* (Damascus, Maṭba'ah al-Ḥayāt, 1363 AH), v.3, p. 11.

[99] Muḥammad Yūsuf Mūṣā, *Al-Fiqh al-Islāmī* (Cairo: Dār al-Kitāb al-'Arabī, 1958), p. 211.

[100] Ahmad Hasan, *Principles*, p. 279

[101] Al-Taftazānī, *al-Talwiḥ 'ala'l Tawḍīḥ*, v. 2, p. 151.

[102] *Ibid.*

[103] Ahmad Hasan, *Principles*, p. 280-285; Abū Sinnah, *Naẓariyyah al-Haqq*, p.179.

[104] *Qur'ān* 8:1

[105] Kamali, *Principles*, p. 350; Ahmad Hasan, *Principles*, p. 285-286.

[106] *Qur'ān* 2:179

[107] Abū Zahrah, *Uṣūl*, p. 257; Ahmad Hasan, *Principles*, p. 286.

[108] Ṣadr al-Sharī'ah, *ibid.*, v. 1, p. 13; Bannānī, "*Ḥāshiah*, v.1 p. 32; Nyazee: *ibid.*, p. 64.

[109] Ṣadr al-Sharī'ah, *al-Tawḍīḥ*, v. 1, p. 30 and v. 2, p. 678; Nyazee, *Islamic Jurisprudence*, p. 51.

[110] Ṣadr al-Sharī'ah, *al-Tawḍīḥ*, v. 2, 680-81.

[111] Ghazālī, *al-Mustaṣfā min 'ilm al-uṣūl*, v. 1, p. 42, qf. Nyazee, *Islamic Jurisprudence*, p. 57.

[112] Ṣadr al-Sharī'ah, *al-Tawḍīḥ*, v. 2, p. 681.

[113] Ṣadr al-Sharī'ah, *al-Tawḍīḥ*, v. 2, p. 680-82.

[114] Ṣadr al-Sharī'ah, *al-Tawḍīḥ*, v. 2, p. 681.

[115] *Qur'ān* 73:20.

[116] *Ṣaḥīḥ al-Muslim*.

[117] Sarakhsī, *Kitāb al-Uṣūl*, v. 1, p. 133.

[118] Khallaf, *'Ilm*, p. 109; Qāsim, *Uṣūl*, p. 218

[119] Ghazālī, *Mustaṣfā*, v. 1, p. 47; Abū Zahrah, *Uṣūl*, p. 35; Nyazee, *Islamic Jurisprudence*, p. 63.

[120] Nyazee, *Islamic Jurisprudence*, p. 64-65.

[121] Ṣadr al-Sharī'ah, *al-Tawḍīḥ*, v. 2, p. 682.

[122] Ghazālī, *Mustaṣfā*, v. 1, p. 42; Khallaf, *'Ilm*, p. 112

[123] *Qur'ān* 2:282

[124] *Qur'ān* 2:283.

[125] Tabrīzī, *Mishkāt*, v. 1, p. 168, *ḥadīth* no. 540; Narrated by Aḥmad.

[126] Ghazālī, *Mustaṣfā*, v. 1, p. 48

[127] Nyazee, *Islamic Jurisprudence*, p. 67.

[128] Nyazee, *ibid.*

[129] Nyazee, *Islamic Jurisprudence*, p. 68; Khudarī, *Uṣūl*, p.46.

[130] Kamali, *Principles*, p. 331.

[131] *Sunan Abū Dāwud* 1083, Book 3, *ḥadīth* 1078

[132] *Sunan Ibn Mājah*, Book 10, *ḥadīth* 2096.

[133] Ṣadr al-Sharī'ah, *al-Tawḍīḥ*, v. 2, p. 685.

[134] *Al-Bukhārī* and *Muslim*, Book 18, *ḥadīth* 1778.

[135] Nyazee, *Islamic Jurisprudence*, p. 72; Kamali, *Principles*, p. 332.

[136] 'Abdur Raḥīm, *Jurisprudence*, p. 198; Qāsim, *Uṣūl*, p. 225.

[137] *Qur'ān* 5:3

[138] *Qur'ān* 2:275

[139] *Sunan Ibn Mājah* 3933, Book 36, *ḥadīth* 8.

[140] *Qur'ān* 5:90.

[141] *Qur'ān* 5:38.

[142] *Qur'ān* 4:10.

[143] *Qur'ān* 2:188.

[144] *Qur'ān* 6:151.

[145] *Qur'ān* 4:19.

[146] Bayhaqī, *al-Sunan al-Kubrā*, v. 3, p. 10.

[147] Ṣadr al-Sharī'ah, *al-Tawḍīḥ*, v. 2, p. 683.

[148] *Qur'ān* 5:5

[149] *Qur'ān* 2:235

[150] *Qur'ān* 2:173

[151] Ghazālī, *Mustaṣfā*, v. 1, 42; Khallaf, *'Ilm*, p. 115

[152] Abū 'Īd, *Mabāhith*, p. 84-88.

[153] Zuhaylī, *ibid.*, v. 1, p. 37; Kamali, "*Principles,*" p. 321-353.

[154] *Qur'ān* 24:2

[155] Abū Dāwud, *Sunan*, II, 557, *ḥadīth* no. 2079

[156] Khallaf, *'Ilm*, p. 102; Abū 'Īd, *Mabāhith*, p. 60; Kamali, *Principles*, p. 336.

[157] Al-Ghazālī, *al-Mustaṣfā*, v. 1, p. 93-94.

[158] Shawkānī, *Irshād*, p. 6; Khallaf, *'Ilm*; p. 118; Kamali, Principles, p. 337.

[159] Al-Shāṭibī, *al-Muwāfaqāt*, v. 1, p. 188.

[160] Nyazee, *Islamic Jurisprudence*, p. 75.

[161] Ahmad Hasan, "*Principles,*" p. 187.

[162] Kamali, *Principles*, p. 337.

[163] Nyazee, *Islamic Jurisprudence*, p. 75; see al-Sarakhsī, *Kitāb al-Uṣūl*, v. 2, p. 320.

[164] Nyazee, *Islamic Jurisprudence*, p. 75; Khallāf, *'Ilm*, p. 118

[165] Ibn al-Subkī, *Jam' al-Jawāmi'* along with Maḥallī's commentary, (Cairo: 1297 AH), v. 1, p. 74-75, qf. Ahmad Hasan, *Principles*, p. 193.

[166] Khallāf, *'Ilm*, p. 120

[167] Ibn Subkī, *Jam' al-Jawāmi'*, v. 1, p. 75.

[168] Ahmad Hasan, *Principles*, p. 200.

[169] Kamali, *Principles*, p. 340

[170] Al-Taaftazānī, *al-Talwiḥ 'ala'l Tawḍīḥ*, (Cairo: Dār al-'Ahd al-Jadid lil-Ṭibā'ah, 1957), v. 2, p. 123; Al-Isnawī, *Nihāyat al-Su'l*, v. 1, 29, 42-43; Ahmad Hasan, *Principles*, p. 199.

[171] Al-Isnawī, *Nihāyat al-Su'l*, v. 1, p. 43; Al-Taaftazānī, *al-Talwiḥ*, v. 2, p. 123

[172] Nyazee, *Islamic Jurisprudence*, p. 77.

[173] Ahmad Hasan, *Principles*, p. 201.

[174] Ahmad Hasan, *Principles*, p. 206.

[175] Abu Zahrah, *Uṣūl*, p. 51-52; Abu `Id, *Mabāhith*, p. 103-104; Kamali, *Principles*, p. 341

[176] Al-Isnawī, *Nihāyat al-Sū'l*, v. 1, p. 43.

[177] Al-Taaftazānī, *al-Talwiḥ*, v. 2, p. 123

[178] 'Abd al-'Azīz al-Bukharī, *Kashf al-Asrār*, v. 1, 95-97; Amīr Bādshāh, Muḥammad Amin (d. 987), *Taysīr al-Taḥrīr*, (Cairo: Muṣṭafā al-Bābī al-Ḥalabī, 1350 AH), v. 2, p. 236-237; Ahmad Hasan, *Principles*, p. 207.

[179] Ibn Subkī, *Jam' al-Jawāmi'*, v. 1, p. 80.

[180] Ahmad Hasan, *Principles*, p. 203-204.

[181] *Qur'ān* 20:115.

[182] *Qur'ān* 46:35.

[183] Al-Ghazālī, *al-Mustaṣfā*, (Cairo: Maṭba'ah Muṣṭafā Muḥammad, 1937), v. 1, p. 6.

[184] Ibn al-Laḥḥām, *al-Mukhtaṣar fī Uṣūl al-Fiqh* (Makkah: King 'Abd al-'Azīz University, 1980), p. 67.

[185] Al-Isnawī, *Nihāyat al-Sū'l*, (Cairo: Maṭba'ah al-Tawfiq al-Adabiyyah, n.d.), v. 1, p. 52.

[186] Al-Qarafī, *Sharḥ Tanqīh al-Fuṣūl* (Cairo: al-Maṭba'ah al-Khayriyyah, 1306 AH), p. 40.

[187] Ḥassān Ḥusayn Ḥāmid, *al-Ḥukm al-Shar'ī 'indal-Uṣūliyyīn*, (Cairo: Dār al-Nahḍah al-'Arabiyyah, 1972), p. 102.

[188] *Qur'ān* 4:24

[189] *Qur'ān* 6:119.

[190] Ahmad Hasan, *Principles*, p. 158-159

[191] Ahmad Hasan, *Principles*, p. 158-159

[192] Al-Sarakhsī, *Uṣūl al-Sarakhsī* (Cairo: Maṭābi' Dār al-Kitāb al-'Arabī, 1372 AH), v. 1, p. 117.

[193] Kamali, *Principles*, p. 339.

[194] *Qur'ān* 16:106

[195] Al-Sarakhsī, *Uṣūl al-Sarakhsī*, v. 1, p. 117.

[196] Al-Bazdawī, *Uṣūl al-Bazdawī*, v. 2, p. 619.

[197] Al-Ghazālī, *al-Mustaṣfā*, v. 1, p. 63.

[198] Al-Isnawī, *Nihāyat al-Sū'l*, v.1, p. 51.

[199] Al-Āmidī, *al-Iḥkām*, v. 1, p. 188.

[200] Abū Zahrah, *Uṣūl*, p. 50; Kamali, *Principles*, p. 340; Al-Sarakhsī, *Uṣūl al-Sarakhsī*, v. 1, p. 118-119; Ahmad Hasan, *Principles*, p. 163-167.

[201] *Qur'ān* 16:106

[202] Muslim, *Ṣaḥīḥ Muslim*, Kitāb al-Ṣiyām.

[203] *Qur'ān* 2:286

[204] Al-Nasāī, *Sunan*, Kitāb al-Buyū'.

CHAPTER FOUR

Methods of Deducing the Rules from the Sources

Introduction

The *Qur'ān* is an eternally valid source for Muslims. It contains general principles. Therefore it needs to be interpreted firstly by the second source, the *Sunnah*, to comprehend its indications. Methods of deducing rules mean a way to understand general rules of the sources of the *Qur'ān* and the *Sunnah* of the Prophet (ṣ) as well as the use of specific methods to deduce rulings through interpreting the language of them and thus, the language of the main sources must be clearly understood.

The sources of Islamic law, whether they are primary sources or secondary sources, are produced all in Arabic manuscript, without knowing the nature of words (*alfāẓ*), their types, and meanings, their associations with other texts and terms, is not possible to deduce thoroughly and correctly appropriated rulings. Acquiring a concrete grasp of the words of the text and their specific implications is a vital instrument to utilize these sources. In order to understand the essence of the *naṣṣ* (text), the main objectives of the Islamic law (*Maqāṣid al-Sharī'ah*) must be known well. Also indication of words (*alfāẓ*) and sentences (*'ibārāt*) to meaning might be opened to more than one possibilities. In that respect, to prefer one of the possibilities over others, the objectives of the Lawgiver must be comprehended wisely.

Somehow, there seems to be some conflicts in a case between evidences. However, in this case there might be a possibility of an evidence which might have already abrogated the other one. In this kind of conflicts (*ta'āruḍ*), to eliminate the conflict and to build consensus needs the correct understanding of the concepts of the abrogator (*nāsikh*) and the abrogated (*mansūkh*) and their relationship between them.

The scholars of the principles of Islamic jurisprudence provided space to the classification of words and their usages within the methodology of Islamic jurisprudence. Focusing on linguistic grounds of the words helps the scholars to understand the correct nature of the text (*naṣṣ*). Most of the greater part of *fiqh* is derived via interpretation and *ijtihād* which aims at the correct and mutual understanding of the words and sentences of a legal text. If the text itself clear enough to understand and its indication is obvious, the *mujtahid* does not resort to interpretation. The main role of *mujtahid* is to discover the intention of the Lawgiver. Therefore, the objective of interpretation is to determine the intention of the Lawgiver with regards to what has been left unclear as a matter of necessary deduction from the surrounding situations.[1]

Knowing the aims of the Lawgiver (*Shārī'*) should not be confined only to interpretation of text (*naṣṣ*) but also to deal with cases which are out of the scope of the text, such as introducing the secondary sources of Islamic law, *qiyās*, *istiḥsān*, or *maṣlaḥah*. In order to comprehend the methods of interpretation, the following points must be explored:

- The divisions of words (*alfāẓ*) which are based on the relationship with indications, and the types of words (*alfāẓ*) within these divisions.
- The main objectives of the Lawgiver
- Conflicts (*taāruḍ*) and consensus (*ijmā'*) between evidences as well as the concept of *nāsikh* (the abrogator) and *mansūkh*

(the abrogated).

The following points will be individually explored:

According to the *Ḥanafī* juristic scholars, in order to determine indications of the meaning of words (*alfāẓ*), could be taken into consideration to address through the following ways:

a. To which meaning a word (*lafẓ*) was formed.

b. Whether it is used on a formation or other meanings.

c. The degree of clarity and obscurity of indication of words.

d. Indication (*dalālah*) of a word whether the inferred meaning was indicated directly or indirectly.

Consequently, *Ḥanafī* scholars, from the viewpoints of clarity, scope and capacity to convey a certain meaning, divided words mainly into four types:

First Division: Based on the formation of words (*alfāẓ*) (*bi-iʿtibāri waḍʿi al-lafẓ lil-maʿnā*): 1. *ʿĀmm* (general), 2. *Khāṣṣ* (specific), 3. *Muawwal* (interpreted), 4. *Mushtarak* (equivocal, the common word). The *khāṣṣ* is subdivided into *muṭlaq* (absolute), *muqayyad* (limited), *ʿamr* (command), and *nahy* (prohibition).

Second Division: based on the usage of the words (*bi-iʿtibāri istiʿmāl al-lafẓ fīl-maʿnā*): 1. *Ḥaqīqah* (literal), 2. *Majāz* (metaphorical), 3. *Ṣāriḥ* (clear), 4. *Kināyah* (allusive).

Third Division: Based on the degree of clarity (*wuḍūḥ*) or obscurity of indication of words (*bi-iʿtibāri dalālat al-lafẓ ʿalāl-maʿnā wāḍiḥan aw ghayri wāḍiḥan*): from the view point of this words are divided into the two main categories: Clear (*wāḍiḥ*) and unclear (*ghayri wāḍiḥ*). The clear words: 1. *Ẓāhir* (manifest), 2. *Naṣṣ* (explicit), 3. *Mufassar* (unequivocal), 4. *Muḥkam* (perspicuous). The unclear words: 1. *Khafī* (obscure), 2. *Mushkil* (difficult), 3. *Mujmal* (ambivalent), 4. *Mutashābih* (intricate).

Fourth Division: Based on the rules of indications (textual indication, *dalālāt*) (*bi-i'tibāri kayfiyyat dalālat al-lafẓ 'alāl-ma'nā*): 1. *'Ibārah al-naṣṣ* (explicit meaning), 2. *Ishārah al-naṣṣ* (alluded meaning), 3. *Dalālah al-naṣṣ* (the inferred meaning), 4. *Iqtiḍā' al-naṣṣ* (the required meaning), 5. *Mafhūm al-mukhālafah* (divergent meaning).

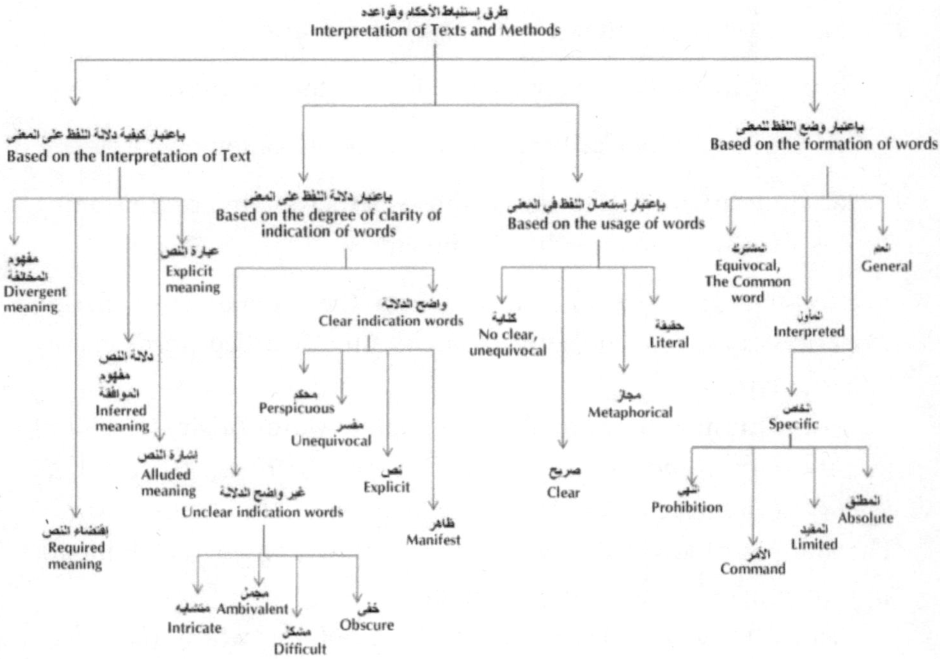

The formation of words (alfāẓ)
(bi-i'tibāri isti'māl al-lafẓ fil-ma'nā)

Introduction

In linguistic sense, it has to be remembered that every clause is a small sentence; every small sentence contains a single clause. As well as there are compound sentence, complex sentence and compound-complex sentences which contain at least two clauses. A basic structure of a sentence consists of a subject, object and a verb. Without these three main items no sentence could be clearly understood. Words bring meaning of a sentence that we wanted; herewith words are the central power of a sentence. As in every language, particularly in Arabic language, words carry general and specific meanings. Words play significant role to understand the purpose of a text, whether the text indicate general or specific could change due responsibilities otherwise. As the general meaning of words is more common in writings they remain at their first state until they are specified. As the main purpose of this study is to comprehend the meaning of the authoritative texts of Islamic law, the *Qur'ān* and the *Sunnah*, highlighting the feature of words play a significant role in textual understanding of the sources.

Certainly, in linguistic sense, mostly Arabic words are general in their origin which they may contain relevant meanings until they are specified; especially the *Qur'ān* and the *Sunnah* contain enormous meanings which needed to be interpreted. There is unanimous agreement among the Companions of the Prophet (ṣ) that the words of the *Qur'ān* and the *Sunnah* are generic, unless a reliable proof authorizes a limitation of the general indication to the specific meaning.[2] Sometimes general meaning which is explicit in the text is not intended by the Lawgiver therefore, specific subjects are excluded from the general meaning of a particular word. The clarification of the authoritative legal texts was easy for the Companions since the Prophet (ṣ) were among them; they were able to ask him directly to differentiate between the general and the specific words without any difficulty. However, the coming generations of Muslims like the followers and the followers of the followers (*tābi'ūn* and *taba' tābi'ūn*), amongst whom were many whose mother tongue was not Arabic, had no such privilege of having the Prophet (ṣ) among them, and therefore, they had difficulties differentiating between the general and the specific words. Every *mujtahids* used their personal opinion to understand the text how to deduct legal rulings which required authentic knowledge.

Islamic law, in its nature, gives emphasis on differentiating between the general (*'āmm*) and the specific (*khāṣṣ*) meaning. The text's exact meaning could not be purely comprehended otherwise. The linguistic patterns that were set by the competent Muslim scholars made these the general (*'āmm*) and the specific (*khāṣṣ*) meanings contained in the legal texts could easily be differentiated by *mujtahids* as well as by ordinary researchers. It has to be appraised the works that made by the Muslim scholars who have lucratively developed ways of distinguishing the general (*'āmm*) from the specific (*khāṣṣ*) meanings. Interestingly, they have done these significant works a thousand years ago while people were not able to even think of the forecast meaning of the legal texts. Although these specific and general meanings may be distinguishable conceptually, may not be clearly known in the grammatical forms of words. Therefore Muslim scholars set certain criteria to differentiate them. On the other hand, though the words in the text may be used generically, the intention of the Lawgiver may not be generic and might even be specific. In order to determine the meaning of words, the scope of the general provision is determined by reference to the intention of the Lawgiver (*maqāṣid al-Sharī'ah*) and the context of the provision through other proofs which may suggest their specification or restriction.

Consequently, as we have mentioned that from the view point of their formation of words (*alfāẓ*) are classified in *'āmm* (general), *khāṣṣ* (specific), *mushtarak* (equivocal, the common word), *muawwal* (interpreted). The *khāṣṣ* is subdivided into *muṭlaq* (absolute), *muqayyad* (limited, qualified), *amr* (command), and *nahy* (prohibition).

We will examine the general (*'āmm*) and the specific (*khāṣṣ*) meanings, and their effects on *'āmm* in cases of conflict as well as the level of priorities among them, however, in general sense, in the event of a conflict between linguistic meaning and common usage of the general (*'āmm*) and the specific (*khāṣṣ*) meaning, the latter has priority. We shall now explain each of these concepts individually in the following pages.

The General (al-'āmm)

Definition of the general

Linguistically the word *'āmm* refers to general, common, universal.[3] Technically, it may be defined as a word which applies to many things, not limited in number, and includes everything to which it is applicable.[4] Rāzī defined *'āmm* as 'the word that includes that to which it is applicable in one setting'.[5] According to Bayḍāwī it is "a word that includes (in its meaning) everything to which it is applicable to in one setting."[6] Besides that Anṣārī similarly defines it as "it is a word that includes what it is applicable to without any specification."[7] For example, "*As for the thief, both male and female, cut off their hands*".[8] The word 'thief' (*as-sāriq*) in the verse coined for one meaning related to theft and it includes everyone to whom the meaning of theft is applicable without specification or limitation. Therefore, it is a word that has a single meaning applied to an unlimited number of subjects without specification.

Another example, "*Lo! man is a state of loss*".[9] The word 'human being' (*al-insān*) in the verse is general and includes every human being without any limitation. All words, whether in Arabic or any other language, are basically general, and unless they are specified or qualified in some way, they retain their generality. According to the reported *ijmā'* of the Companions and the accepted norms of Arabic, the words of the *Qur'ān* and the *Sunnah* apply in their general capacity unless there is evidence to warrant a departure from the general to an alternative meaning.[10]

General Terms

There are many terms that indicate general meaning (*al-fāẓ al-'umūm*). The following most common practical examples illustrate these terms.

1. The following words every "*kullu*" (كل)[11], all "*jamī'*" (جميع),

entire "*kāffah*" (كافة) and total "'*āmmah*" (عامة)[12] are words which convey general meaning by their essence. Any of these words go with another words which include everything to which it relates as they are mentioned in the following examples: "*Lo! We have created everything by measure*"[13], the word "everything" (*kulla shay'in*) is generic which includes everything created without, exception. "*Say: Every one acts according to his manner*"[14], "*He it is Who created for you all that is in the earth*".[15] This verse means that everything on earth has been created for the benefit of human beings. "*And We have not sent you but to all the men as a bearer of good news and as a warner, but most men do not know*".[16] "All mankind" is a generic word which includes all humankind at all times.

2. When a singular or plural form of a noun is preceded by the definite article "*al*" (ال) which is not used for a definition "'*ahd*" (عهد)[17] but for inclusion and comprehension "*isti'rāq*" (إستغراف) and "*shumūl*" (شمول) or when it becomes definite by the genitive case, then these are identified as '*āmm* (عام). The following examples from the *Qur'ān* represent this reality: "*Successful indeed are the believers*".[18] and "*and Allah loves those who do good (to others)*".[19] In these verses the words "*al-mu'minūn*" (الْمُؤْمِنُونَ) and "*al-muḥsinīn*" (الْمُحْسِنِينَ) are both are preceded by the definite article "*al*" (ال) which denotes (إستغراف) and (شمول), therefore these words consist of all people who are *mu'min* and *muḥsin*.

"*The woman and the man guilty of adultery or fornication, – flog each of them with a hundred stripes*".[20] In this verse adulteress "*az-zāniyah*" (الزَّانِيَةُ) and adulterer "*az-zānī*" (الزَّانِي) are both in the singular form and they are preceded by the definite article (ال) which denotes that all adulterers male or female must suffer the prescribed punishment. "*Women who are divorced shall wait, keeping themselves apart, three (monthly) courses*".[21] The word "the divorced women" "*al-muṭallaqāt*" (الْمُطَلَّقَات) is a plural with the definite article (ال) which provides general meaning and includes all the women to whom it could apply. It is a general word "*'āmm*" (عام) which comprises all to whom this expression can apply. Herewith all it indicates that all "the divorced women" "*al-muṭallaqāt*" (الْمُطَلَّقَات)[22] who are required to observe a waiting period of three courses before they can marry again to someone else. On the other hand, the same rule applies to the singular or plural form of a noun when it is defined by the genitive.

The same rule applies when the singular or plural form of a noun is defined by the genitive as it comes in the *Qur'ān*: "*Allah enjoins you concerning your children: The male shall have the equal of the portion of two females*".[23] "*Take alms of their wealth, wherewith thou mayst purify them and mayst make them grow*".[24] In these two verses the plural 'children' "*awlād*" (أَوْلَادِ) and 'wealth' "*amwāl*" (أَمْوَال) are definite through the governed noun "*muḍāf*" (مضاف) of a genitive construction "*iḍafah*" (إضافة) – "*awlādikum*" (أَوْلَادِكُمْ) and "*amwālihim*" (أَمْوَالِهِمْ). Therefore, these are inclusive on all children and wealth without any specification or limitation.

3. Also when a word, usually a plural noun, is prefixed by a relative pronoun like "those men who" "*alladhīyna*" (الذين), "those women who" "*allatī*" (اللتي), "what" "*mā*" (ما), it becomes generic in its effect. As they are exemplified by the following verse:

   "*Those who swallow down usury cannot arise except as one whom Shaiṭān has prostrated by (his) touch does rise*".[25] The word "those" "*alladhīyna*" (الذين) includes everyone who deals in usury.

"*As for those of your women who are guilty of lewdness, call to witness four of you against them*".[26]

The Word "those women who" "*allātī*" (اللَّاتِي), includes everyone guilty of lewdness. The ruling that is indicated here is general which applies to all women who can possibly be included in its scope. It remains general unless there is evidence to specify it.[27]

"*And lawful for you are (all women) besides those, provided that you seek (them) with your property, taking (them) in marriage not committing fornication*".[28] The word "what" "*mā*" (مَا), includes all women who were not mentioned in the previous verse.

On the other hand when the plural is defined by the genitive construction[29]: "*Forbidden to you are your mothers*".[30] The word "mothers" is plural, defined by the genitive construction "your mothers" "*ummuhātikum*" (أُمَّهَاتُكُمْ). Therefore, it is generic and contains all mothers without any specification of the number.

4. Some words can be used for conditional nouns "*asmā' ash-sharṭ*" (أسماء الشرط) such as "who," "whoever" "*man*" (من), "whenever" "*aynamā*" (اينما), and "whatever" "*mā*" (ما), they have the effect of a general word.

"*It is not for a believer to kill a believer unless (it be) by mistake. He who has killed a believer by mistake must set free a believing slave, and pay the blood-money to the family of the slain, unless they remit it as a charity*".[31]

This verse indicates that anyone who kills a believer by

mistake is obliged to set free a believing slave in expiation for the offence. The following verses give similar examples too.

"*Surely those who believe, and those who are Jews, and the Christians, and the Sabians, whoever believes in Allah and the Last day and does good, they shall have their reward from their Lord, and there is no fear for them, nor shall they grieve*".[32]

"*Unto Allah belong the East and the West, and wherever you turn, there is Allah's Countenance. Lo! Allah is All-Embracing, All-Knowing*".[33]

"*Therefore whoever of you is present in the month, he shall fast therein*".[34]

The words "whoever" "*man*" (مَنْ), "whenever" "*aynamā*" (أَيْنَما) in the verses are as conditional nouns and therefore, they are generic.

5. Some others also can be used for interrogation nouns like "who, whoever" "*man*" (مَنْ)[35] and when "*matā*" (مَتَى) as in the following verses: "*Say: Have ye thought: If (all) your water were to disappear into the earth, who then could bring you gushing water?*".[36]

"*Affliction and adversity befell them, they were shaken as with earthquake, till the messenger (of Allah) and those who believed along with him said: When cometh Allah's help?*"[37]

"*Therefore whoever of you is present in the month, he shall fast therein*".[38]

This verse indicates that everyone who has reached maturity "*mukallaf*" (مكلف) is ordered to fast. Herewith, all these interrogative nouns "who, whoever" "*man*" (مَنْ) and "when" "*matā*" (مَتَى) have generic meanings.

6. Negation "*nafī*" (نفي) or indefinite words "*an-nakrah*" (النكرة) come after negation. The following *ḥadīth* is illustrated as an example for indefinite words (النكرة) which used to convey the negation. "No harm shall be inflicted or reciprocated" "*lā ḍarara walā ḍirār*" (لا ضرر ولا ضرار).[39] This *ḥadīth* negates what is applicable, because it is general in its import. Both indefinite words used in negation. When used to convey prohibition indefinite words "*an-nakrah*" (النكرة) is illustrated by the following verse of the *Qur'ān* to the Prophet (ṣ):

   "*And never (O Muḥammad) offer prayer for any one of them who dies and do not stand by his grave; surely they disbelieve in Allah and His Messenger and they shall die in transgression*".[40] The word 'one' "*aḥadin*" (أَحَدٍ) is an indefinite word "*an-nakrah*" (النكرة) and comes after negation. It is used to convey prohibition. Therefore, it is generic in its effect and the verdict "*ḥukm*" (حكم) comprehends all the non-Muslims.

   When an indefinite noun is followed by a general adjective indicates general meaning. "*A kind word with forgiveness is better than almsgiving followed by injury*".[41] The expression "a kind word" "*qawlun ma'rūf*" (قَوْلٌ مَعْرُوفٌ) provides a general meaning and includes every well-mannered word because "word" "*qawlun*" (قَوْلٌ) has been followed by the general adjective "well-mannered" "*ma'rūf*" (مَعْرُوفٌ).

Types of the general (al-'āmm) [42]

The general "*al-'āmm*" (العام) may be divided into the following types according to Muslim scholars.

1. The general (العام) which is absolutely general. The general meaning accompanied by evidence that excludes all possibility of specification of meaning which is known with certainty in

respect of the general meaning intended by the Lawgiver. It may be exemplified by the following verse:

"*And there is not a living creature in the earth but on Allah is the sustenance of it, and He knows its resting place and its depository all (things) are in a manifest book*".[43] In this verse, the prefix "there is not a living creature" "*wa mā min dābbatin*" (وَمَا مِنْ دَابَّةٍ)[44] is an expression which, according to Islamic teaching, confirms the object of divine law, which is unchangeable and therefore cannot expect any kind of specification. Therefore, "*there is not a living creature*" (وَمَا مِنْ دَابَّةٍ) applies to every kind of living creature without exception. "*And we made every living thing of water? Will they not then believe*?"[45] In this verse the prefix "every" "*kulla*" (كُلَّ) indicates the general "*al-'āmm*" (العام) which precludes any kind of specification. Therefore these are remain absolutely general which include all to which they apply without any exception.

2. The general (العام) which is meant to imply a specific "*khāṣṣ*" (خاص). Although the general meaning is not intended by the Lawgiver, it is convoyed by an evidence that a specified indication undoubtedly intends. It may include some but not absolutely all the individuals to whom it could possibly apply. The following verses are clear examples of these indications: "*And pilgrimage to the House is incumbent upon men for the sake of Allah, (upon) everyone who is able to undertake the journey to it*".[46] The indications of this verse imply that everyone who is able to undertake the journey is required to perform the duty, however children, lunatics and anyone who cannot afford it not included in the scope of this verse.

3. The general (العام) which is not accompanied by either of the foregoing two varieties of indications as to its scope. However, this indication is provided by texts which are generally

unlimited and unaccompanied by linguistic, rational or customary evidence until a reliable proof suggests otherwise. The following verse exemplifies its indication: "*And the divorced women should keep themselves in waiting for three courses*".[47] The word "divorced women" "*al-muṭallaqāt*" (الْمُطَلَّقَاتُ) in the text is apparently generic in its effect and includes all divorced women, without any specification. This type of general (العام) is explicit in respect of its generality which means that it remains general until a reliable proof specifies it. However, there is another verse which qualifies the generality of it. The waiting period "*'iddah*" (عدة) that the divorced women must observe is specified by the following verse: "*O you who believe! when you marry the believing women, then divorce them before consummating the marriage, you have in their case no period which you should reckon; so make some provision for them and send them forth a goodly sending forth*".[48] The waiting period for the women who are divorced before consummating the marriage is excluded from the general requirement of the first verse that they must observe three waiting period. Therefore, the second verse specifies the first verse.[49]

The indication of the general [50]

The indication of the general (العام) is of two types. The general which has already been specific and that which has not been specified that of it remains as the general. The scholars agreed that the indication of the general which has already been specified is speculative "*ẓannī*" (ظني) since its remaining subjects have been specified. Rationally it is obvious that when the indication is speculative, it can be any time specified by suitable proof like solitary *ḥadīth* "*khabar wāḥid*" (خبر واحد) and analogy "*qiyās*" (قياس).

The following points needed to be noted regarding the general meaning which has not already been specified in which Muslim scholars are disagree. The majority of them[51] maintain that the application of the general to all that it includes is indefinite "*ẓannī*" (ظني) so long as the general is already specified except those accompanied by evidence which excludes such a possibility since every general is supposed to be specified. As in the following verse: "*And there is not a living creature in the earth but on Allah is the sustenance of it, and He knows its resting place and its depository all (things) are in a manifest book*".[52] Here the general meaning accompanied by evidence that excludes all possibility of specification of meaning which is known with certainty in respect of the general meaning intended by the Lawgiver.

On the other hand some well-known *Ḥanafī* scholars among them Karkhī, Jaṣṣāṣ and Dabbūsī maintain that the words originally are generic in their effects that provide general meaning. With this generic sense they must continue to offer that meaning until a reliable proof designates otherwise. As the claim is exemplified by this verse "*And (as for) those of you who die and leave wives behind, they should keep themselves in waiting for four months and ten days*"[53], the indication of the words in this verse remain as general until a reliable proof suggests otherwise. Therefore this verse includes all women whose husbands have died, whether they died before consummating the marriage or after.

They discussed that Abū Ḥanīfah has clearly explored that the specific cannot remove the general but the specific may be abrogated by the general. As the general becomes definite "*qaṭʿī*" (قطعي) when its application encompasses all. This claim has been elaborated by the example of urine. Although the tradition has approved the usage of urine of animals that can be eaten[54] was abrogated by general indications in other traditions which warns Muslims were asked to stay away from it since it is considered dirty.[55]

As it has been slightly discussed above the scholars have differed in the general "*al-'āmm*" (العام) which has not been specified as to whether its indication is definitive or speculative. There are two significant points in this issue:

First: The general (العام) word, which is in the Book of Allah and the *Sunnah Mutawāterah*, which has never been specified. The disagreement among Muslim scholars is as to whether the general (العام) meaning can be specified first time by an indefinite "*ẓannī*" (ظني) proof like a solitary *ḥadīth* or an analogy.

The application of *'āmm* to all that it includes according to *Ḥanafīs* is definitive.[56] On the other hand, majority of the *'ulamā'*, including the *Shāfi'īs*, *Mālikīs* and *Ḥanbalīs*, maintain that the application of *'āmm* to all that it includes is speculative since it is open to limitation and *ta'wīl*, and therefore it is not definitive. So an indefinite (ظني) could be specified by a definite (قطعي) or could be by an equal strength like an indefinite (ظني).[57] Therefore, although *Ḥanafīs* allow this kind of specification the majority scholars do not allow it. According to the majority view, the *'āmm* of the *Qur'ān* is speculative although definitive in meaning. Therefore, the *khāṣṣ* of the *ḥadīth*, especially the weak or the solitary *ḥadīth* in which the *khāṣṣ* has definitive indication may specify a speculative indication of the *'āmm* of the *Qur'ān*.[58]

This disagreement can be illustrated with reference to the *Qur'ānic* text concerning the slaughter of animals: "*And do not eat of that on which Allah's name has not been mentioned*",[59] upon with this general ruling, there is a solitary *ḥadīth* which provides that "the believer slaughters in the name of Allah whether he pronounces the name of Allah or not."[60] According to this *ḥadīth*, the majority said that slaughter by a Muslim, even without pronouncing the name of Allah, is lawful for consumption. On the other hand for *Ḥanafīs* it is not lawful since the *'āmm* of the *Qur'ān* cannot be specified by a speculative proof like the solitary *ḥadīth* mentioned above. However, when it comes to the *mutawātir ḥadīth* or the *mashhūr ḥadīth* there is no disagreement among the scholars since these are definitive in indication.[61]

Second: In the event where *'āmm* and *khāṣṣ* indicate differently. One of them indicates abrogation of the text and the other one indicates its existence in the same event. The question arises here is that as to whether this may be considered conflict or not.

In such events, there is no conflict according to majority of scholars since the *'āmm* is speculative as a whole, whether before or after *takhṣīṣ*. Therefore the effect of *khāṣṣ* is that it remains in force, and action upon it is required because there is no contradiction between definitive and speculative. However, for the *Ḥanafīs*, the *'āmm* and the *khāṣṣ* are definitive in the first place, but when *'āmm* is partially specified, it becomes speculative in respect of the part which still remains unspecified; hence it will be treated as *ẓannī* and would be susceptible to further specification by another *ẓannī*.[62] Therefore *Ḥanafīs* accept that there is conflict between *'āmm* and *khāṣṣ* because of their indications since they are equal in the sense that both of them are definitive (قطعي). Thereupon, *takhṣīṣ* takes place when the *'āmm* and *khāṣṣ* are chronologically parallel or *khāṣṣ* comes after *'āmm*. On the other hand, if the revelation of *khāṣṣ* is determined that it comes after the *'āmm*, then the later specifies the former, and it is considered *takhṣīṣ* rather than abrogation. However, if the *khāṣṣ* and *'āmm* are chronologically parallel and the first precedes the second, as well as they are equal in terms of authenticity (*thubūt*), according to their conflict, the later in time abrogates the former. This can be explained with the following verses:

"And those who accuse free women then do not bring four witnesses, flog them, (giving) eighty stripes, and do not admit any evidence from them ever; and these it is that are the transgressors";[63] "And (as for) those who accuse their wives and have no witnesses except themselves, the evidence of one of these (should be taken) four times, bearing Allah to witness that he is most surely of the truthful ones".[64]

The indication of the first verse is *'āmm* which consists of all including husbands. The second verse is *khāṣṣ* which is limited to husband only. The second verse that contains the *khāṣṣ* ruling, even if it is mentioned immediately after the first verse in the *Qur'ān*, in terms of time, it was revealed after the first verse. The occasion of the revelation of the second verse *sūra al-Nūr* (24:6) obviously indicates its later coming. As it was narrated that Hilāl Ibn Umayyah accused his wife in the presence of the Prophet (ṣ) of committing adultery with Sharīk bin Samḥā. Then the Prophet (ṣ) said: "Provide proof or you will have *ḥadd* (punished) on your back." Hilāl said "By the One Who sent you with the truth, I am telling the truth, and Allah will send down revelation concerning my situation which will spare my back."[65] Then the following verse was revealed: "*And (as for) those who accuse their wives and have no witnesses except themselves, the evidence of one of these (should be taken) four times, bearing Allah to witness that he is most surely of the truthful ones*".[66] Thus the occasion of the revelation of this verse brought imprecation (*li'ān*). Although the revelation of this verse made the previous verse specific, the ruling remains general for other than husbands.

Conflict between 'āmm and khāṣṣ

If *khāṣṣ* is not determined whether it comes after the *'āmm* or at the same time, parallel, to the extent they differ, both are considered to be conflicting each other. The stronger one would be taken into action. However if superiority is not determined over the other, none of them would be implemented.

As it has been mentioned that *Ḥanafīs* consider that *'āmm* and *khāṣṣ* are both definitive (قطعي). Therefore a conflict between them is possible, whereas to the majority, *'āmm* is speculative (ظني) and *khāṣṣ* (قطعي) is definitive. According to this consideration the stronger one, *khāṣṣ*, prevails over the *'āmm*.

The *Ḥanafīs* uphold the view that in the event of conflict between the general and the specific in the *Qur'ān*, one must ascertain the chronological order between them. Firstly their origin must be determined for example, whether both of them are *Makkī* or *Madanī*; or one of them is *Makkī* and the other one is *Madanī* or vice versa. Secondly, whether the two came to parallel in time. If so, the *khāṣṣ* specifies the *'āmm*. However, if a different chronological order can be seen between them, then if the *khāṣṣ* is a later origin, it partially abrogates the *'amm*. However, if the *'amm* is of a later origin, it abrogates the *khāṣṣ*. This is because the *khāṣṣ* specifies the *'amm* according to *Ḥanafīs*. On the other hand if they are chronologically parallel, both of them are considered definitive and both of them are independently considered. Whereas, the majority of scholars see it differently since these two are different, *khāṣṣ* if definitive and the *'āmm* is speculative like *ẓāhir* which are speculative and both of them are open to specification and *ta'wīl* and between the *khāṣṣ* and *'āmm* there will be no conflict because when there are two rulings on the same point, one is *'āmm* and the other one is *khāṣṣ*, the latter is considered explanatory to the former one and both of them are retained.[67]

The effect of this conflict can be seen in many *fiqh* issues, however, it may be illustrated by the conflict arising in the following two *ḥadīth* regarding legal alms (*zakāt*). One of them is "Whatever is watered from the sky is subject to charity (tithe)". The second one is "there is no charity in less than five *awsāq*[68]".[69]

The *Ḥanafīs* have held that the first *ḥadīth* abrogates the second, as they consider that the first *ḥadīth* is of a later origin that the second. Although the first *ḥadīth* contains a general ruling in respect of any quantity of agricultural crops, but the second *ḥadīth* is specific on this point. Therefore, the former abrogates the latter completely because the *'āmm* is of a later origin than the *khāṣṣ*. So according to them there is no case for *takhṣīṣ* and there is no minimum quantitative limit with regard to *zakāt* on produce obtained through dry farming. On the other hand, for the majority of the scholars including the *Shāfi'īs* have held the view that the second *ḥadīth* explains and qualifies the first since the first *ḥadīth* is a general which is of a speculative indication.[70]

In general Muslim scholars may be divided on implementation of the *'āmm* into three groups.[71]

Firstly, the majority of them maintain that the external meaning of the general (العام) should be implemented unless a reliable proof suggests otherwise.

Secondly, some *Shāfi'īs* (*mutakallimūn*) and *Ash'arīs* maintain that the implementation of general words is suspended until a proof emerges to confirm the general or specific indication. These scholars who follow this opinion are named *Wāqifiyyah.*[72]

Thirdly, according to Balkhī and Jubbā'ī the general (العام) should be applied in its most specific sense which can be a generic type (*jins*) and if it is in the plural form. Although some scholars have debated this opinion, the majority of scholars are not supported by any reliable proof from the language or authoritative texts.[73] Therefore from an Islamic point of view their opinion is unacceptable since it leads to disagreement with the Prophet (ṣ) and his Companions as well as putting aside most authoritative texts.[74]

The Specific (al-khāṣṣ)

Definition of the khāṣṣ

The *khāṣṣ* (specific) is a term that denotes detailed and exact meaning connected with only one specific thing or person. For example, 'Umar, man, woman etc. besides this, even if it contains plurality, and that plurality is restricted, then the term is considered *khāṣṣ*, for example: two, three, four, a hundred, two thousand etc.

Indication of the khāṣṣ

Scholars unanimously agree that the *khāṣṣ* (specific) definitely indicates a determined meaning, so long as contrary evidence against its specificity does not exist. The specific meaning cannot define the term to anything other than what it is[75]. For example:

> *"Allah will not impose blame upon you for what is meaningless in your oaths, but He will impose blame upon you for (breaking) what you intended of oaths. Therefore, expiation is the feeding of ten needy people from the average of that which you feed your (own) families or clothing them or the freeing of a slave. But whoever cannot find (or afford it) then a fast of three days (is required)".*[76]

The words "*raqabah,*" (neck), "'*asharah,*" (ten), and "*thalāthah,*" (three) are *khāṣṣ* (specific) and denote the expiation of broken oaths, namely the freeing of a slave, the feeding of ten orphans, or fasting for three days. Indicating these with *khāṣṣ* (specific) terms excludes any possibility of their having other meanings.[77]

Again, the word "*thamānīn*" (eighty) mentioned in "And those who accuse free women then do not bring four witnesses, flog them, (giving) eighty stripes"[78], "*meah*" (hundred) in "(As for) the fornicatress and the fornicator, flog each of them, (giving) a hundred stripes" and "*unthayayn*" (two females) in "Allah enjoins you concerning your children: The male shall have the equal of the portion of two females"[79], "*niṣf*" (half) in "and if there is one, she shall have the half"[80], "*thuluth*" (third) in "but if he has no child and (only) his two parents inherit him, then his mother shall have the third"[81], "*rubu*'" (a fourth) in "but if they have a child, then you shall have a fourth of what they leave"[82], *thumun*" (the eighth) in "but if you have a child then they shall have the eighth of what you leave"[83], in the verses of inheritance, are all specific words. Indications of these words on specific meanings are definite which can be easily understood from their literal meanings without denoting any other possible meanings.

Definitive indication of the khāṣṣ

The definitive (*qaṭ'ī*) indication does not mean excluding all sort of possibilities of other meanings, but excluding only a possibility which relies on *dalīl* (evidence) so long as the definitive indication is based on a *dalīl* that excludes other possible meanings. Indeed, from a specific word, another meaning might be meant rather than its own literally given meaning. However, as long as there is no evidence denotes to that meaning, it does not effect on the definitive indication of the specific. Logically, a possibility based not on evidence and the absence of ever such possibility is the same.[84] A specific word has a literal original meaning of its own but which leaves open the possibility of an alternative interpretation. For example, the word 'lion' in the sentence 'I saw a lion' is clear enough to denote a specific meaning; on the other hand, it is possible that the speaker might have meant a brave man. However, since there is no evidence about the second meaning, it is considered as non-existent. When there be an evidence, the *khāṣṣ* accepts *ta'wīl* (interpretation) and it is departed from its own literal meaning to a possible meaning. Thus, *ḥadīth* of the Prophet (ṣ) which is concerning the legal alms (*zakāt*) of livestock, "one in every forty sheep"[85], the word "*shāt*" (sheep) is considered among the *Ḥanafīs* as the value for the sheep. The obvious text of this *ḥadīth* admittedly requires that the animal itself should be given in *zakāt*. The purpose is not the item itself but the value of it. However, it would seem in harmony with the basic purpose of the law to say that either the sheep or their equivalent monetary value may be given. For the purpose of *zakāt* is to satisfy the needs of the poor, and this could equally be done by giving them the equivalent amount of money; it is even likely that they might prefer this.[86]

Consequently it can be said that legal rules which are conveyed in specific terms are definite in application and are normally not open to *ta'wīl*. The *Ḥanafīs* have, however, been overruled by the majority on this point who say that the *khāṣṣ*, as a rule, is not amenable to *ta'wīl*. However, if there be exceptional reasons and evidences to warrant recourse to *ta'wīl*, then the *khāṣṣ* may be understood according to exceptional case and evidence which require the new meaning.[87]

Some more examples on fiqhī issues of the definitive indication of the khāṣṣ

Ḥanafī scholars took into account some *fiqhī* issues narrated from *Imāms* of their *madhhabs* in the concept of "*khāṣṣ*" and they grounded the rulings of the issues on the indications of the *khāṣṣ*. As apparent from these issues that are mainly disputed issues between the *Ḥanafīs* and other Islamic Jurists. However, the *Ḥanafī* scholars, in these issues, tried to strengthen their own *Imāms*' opinions grounding them on the ruling "definitive indication of *khāṣṣ*" that is accepted by all the Muslim jurists, while rebutting the opponents' opinions claiming that they are contradicted to this ruling. To be example to the above explanation, some explanatory examples will be given here.

The issue of qurū' (waiting for three courses)

If she is a not pregnant woman in menstruation period, how the courses (*furū'*) of a divorced woman will be calculated either on the meaning of menstruations (*hay*) or the clean periods between menstruations (*ṭuruq*)?

Muslim jurists have different opinions on this issue such as *Ḥanafīs* and *Ḥanbalī* have held the view that the meaning of menstruations (*ḥayḍ*) will be calculated, which means three completed menstruations (*ḥayḍ*) have to be consumed. The courses (*qurū'*), according to this view, will be completed by the end of the third menstruations (*ḥayḍ*). Whereas according to *Shāfi'īs* and *Mālikīs*, the clean periods between menstruations (*ṭuhr*) will be considered which means that the divorced woman's waiting period is three cleaning (*ṭuhr*) period. Therefore, according to this view, the courses (*qurū'*) only will be completed by the beginning of the third menstruations (*ḥayḍ*).[88]

The source of the ruling on this issue is referred to this verse "And the divorced women should keep themselves in waiting for three courses."[89]

Once again all the Islamic jurists are in consensus on the issue of that the word (القرء) "*al-qur'*" denotes both meaning in the dictionary menstruations (*ḥayḍ*) and clean periods between menstruations (*ṭuhr*). So it is an equivocal word which is meant to be only one of these two meanings not both meanings together. This is the point of dispute among the scholars, which of the two meanings should be meant by the Lawgiver. In this point, it has to be expressed that there is no doubt concerning the authenticity of this text, as the *Qur'ān* is authentic throughout. However its particular meaning is on the question which is open to speculation. As the courses (*qurū'*) is a homonym meaning which consists of both menstruations (*ḥayḍ*) and the clean periods between menstruations (*ṭuhr*), the scholars went different opinions, Imām Abū Ḥanīfah and Ibn Ḥanbal have adopted the meaning of menstruations (*ḥayḍ*), whereas Imām Shāfi'ī and Mālik have adopted the meaning of the clean periods between menstruations (*ṭuhr*). Consequently their respective *ijtihād* leads them to correspondingly different results.[90]

Types of the specific

As of the *ṣiyghah* (form) and the situation, *khāṣṣ* has many types. Sometimes an unrestricted word (*lafẓ*) that is absolute which may come as restricted word (*lafẓ*) that is limited. From time to time it comes on the form of *'amr* (order), or *nahy* (prohibition), or it may come also on other forms. Although there are many other forms of it, the most common four types will be considered here: a) *muṭlaq* (absolute) which is not limited nor qualified in its application; b) *muqayyad* (limited, qualified); c) *'amr* (command); and d) *nahy* (prohibition).

A) Al-Muṭlaq (the Absolute)

Linguistically *muṭlaq* refers to free, unlimited, unrestricted, general, absolute which is opposite to restricted (*muqayyad*).[91]

Technically it denotes a word which is neither qualified nor limited in its application. When it is uttered for example, a "book," a "bird" or a "man," each one is a generic noun which applies to any book, bird or man without any restrictions. Hence, in its original situation, the *muṭlaq* is unlimited and unqualified.[92]According to Āmidī, *muṭlaq* is an indefinite word (*nakirah*) used to convey the positive.[93] On the other hand, Anṣārī defines it as "an utterance that indicates an entity as it is in itself."[94] Based on these explanations *al-muṭlaq* (the absolute) can be formulated with the following definition: "*muṭlaq* is an utterance that indicates a subject or a group within a larger group (*māhiyyah*) without being specified or restricted by anything that may reduce its commonality. We may construe *muṭlaq* to include only one subject which is not specified or restricted, but not a specified or limited group. This means that *muṭlaq* excludes all words restricted by attribute, condition, place, time, etc. When *muṭlaq* is qualified it becomes *muqayyad*. For example, 'a man' is *muṭlaq* but 'a wise man' is *muqayyad*."[95]

The Value (ḥukm) of Muṭlaq

So long as a word, which denotes a *muṭlaq* indication in a *naṣṣ* (text), does not come in the form of *muqayyad*, it is taken into practice with its *muṭlaq* meaning. In other words, it is not pleasant to value it to take it as qualified (*muqayyad*) if there is no evidence which specifies it.[96] Therefore, the legal adherence to *muṭlaq* is rigorously compulsory in Islamic law, as is the implementation of its absolute meaning. However, it may not be limited until a reliable proof proposes a limitation.[97] Hence, it is not reduced its extent of indication unless a reliable proof proposes that a specified individual subject is intended. In Sum, the *muṭlaq* provides a definite indication (*qaṭʿī al-dalālah*) since it represents a form of *khāṣṣ* (specific) which is definitive (*qaṭʿī*).[98]

Examples of Muṭlaq (the Absolute)

1. The *Qur'ān* states:

> "*The month of Ramaḍān is that in which the Qur'ān was revealed, a guidance to men and clear proofs of the guidance and the distinction; therefore whoever of you is present in the month, he shall fast therein, and whoever is sick or upon a journey, then (he shall fast) a (like) number of other days;*"[99]

The word "*ayyām*" (أَيَّامٍ) "days" is absolute in the sense that it has no restriction, such as succession, either in this verse or in any other authoritative text. Therefore, it remains *muṭlaq*, whoever does not fast during *Ramaḍān* because of illness or travel must fast the same number of other days in anytime in sequence or individually.

2. The *Qur'ān* states:

> "*And (as for) those of you who die and leave wives behind, they should keep themselves in waiting for four months and ten days; then when they have fully attained their term, there is no blame on you for what they do for themselves in a lawful manner;*"[100]

The world "*azwājan*" (أَزْوَاجًا) "wives" is an absolute because it has no restriction in the sense of including those with whom the marriage was not consummated. It is not limited, either in this verse or in any other authoritative text. Therefore, it remains *muṭlaq* and includes any woman whose husband dies, whether or not the marriage was consummated.

3. The *Qur'ān* states:

> "*Allah enjoins you concerning your children: The male shall have the equal of the portion of two females; then if they are more than two females, they shall have two-thirds of what the deceased has left, and if there is one, she shall have the half; and as for his parents, each of them shall have the sixth of what he has left if he has a child, but if he has no child and (only) his two parents inherit him, then his mother shall have the third; but if he has brothers, then his*

mother shall have the sixth after (the payment of) a bequest he may have bequeathed or a debt;"[101]

The word "*waṣiyyah*" (وَصِيَّةٍ) "bequeathed" is absolute, in the sense that it does not limit the amount. According to this indication someone may give all his property as bequeath. However, this was restricted by the tradition where the Prophet (ṣ) forbade one from giving more than one third of one's entire property as bequeath in the *ḥadīth* states:

"One-third, and that is still too much. It is better to leave your heirs well-off than to leave them poor, begging people."[102]

Therefore, according to this evidence the 'bequeathed' in the verse indicates one third or less, since this ruling did not remain absolute, however it became limited.

B) Al-Muqayyad (the limited, the qualified)

Linguistically *muqayyad* refers to bound, limited, qualified, tied, restricted, confined.[103]

Technically it means that something is limited, qualified which is opposite to the absolute (*muṭlaq*), or a word which is limited its scope by evidence. Taftāzānī defined it as "what is excluded from any commonality."[104] Shawkānī defined it as "what is not widespread within its sort."[105] According to these definitions, *muqayyad* is a word that indicates a subject or non-specified group of subjects (*māhiyyah*) to which is attached what restricts their commonality e.g., 'a righteous person', 'righteous person', 'a valuable book', 'valuable books', 'a good student', 'good students', etc. Therefore, like *muṭlaq*, *muqayyad* includes only one subject or non-specified group of subjects in a multitude. But unlike *muṭlaq*, the one subject or group is limited by a restriction. These and similar words represent absolute nouns which have a restriction. Therefore, the term applies only to these restricted subjects. This means that *muqayyad* includes all restricted words limited by an attribute, condition, place, time, etc.[106]

The Value (ḥukm) of Al-Muqayyad

If a word (*lafẓ*), which denotes a *muqayyad* indication in a *naṣṣ* (text), did not come in any other *naṣṣ* (text) in the form of *muṭlaq*, it is taken into practice with its *muqayyad* meaning. So long as there is not any evidence which removes the quality of being *muqayyad*, it is not pleasant to remove the qualified (*muqayyad*) meaning.[107]As in the case of *muṭlaq*, the legal devotion to *muqayyad* is obligatory and constitutes the implementation of its restricted meaning. *Muqayyad* also provides a definite indication (*qaṭ'ī al-dalālah*) since it represents a form of *khāṣṣ* (specific) which is definitive.[108]

Examples of Muqayyad (the limited, the qualified)

1. The *Qur'ān* states:

> "*And it does not behove a believer to kill a believer except by mistake, and whoever kills a believer by mistake, he should free a believing slave, and blood-money should be paid to his people unless they remit it as alms; but if he be from a tribe hostile to you and he is a believer, the freeing of a believing slave (suffices), and if he is from a tribe between whom and you there is a covenant, the blood-money should be paid to his people along with the freeing of a believing slave; but he who cannot find (a slave) should fast for two months successively: a penance from Allah, and Allah is Knowing, Wise.*"[109]

This verse prescribes the penance for a Muslim who unjustly kills by mistake another Muslim. The word "*shahrayn*" (شَهْرَيْنِ) "two months" is restricted by "*mutatābi'ayn*" (مُتَتَابِعَيْنِ) "consecutive," since no reliable proof suggests another meaning, it continues to be qualified and the penance is for two 'consecutive' months.

2. The *Qur'ān* states:

> "*But whoever has not the means, let him fast for two months successively before they touch each other; then as for him who is not*

able, let him feed sixty needy ones; that is in order that you may have faith in Allah and His Messenger, and these are Allah's limits, and the unbelievers shall have a painful punishment."[110]

This verse prescribes the penance in cases of *ẓihār* (الظهـار). Like the previous verse it is restricted by "*mutatābi'ayn*" (مُتَتَابِعَيْنِ) "consecutive." It remains qualified because no reliable proof suggests otherwise. So the penance has to be paid according to the *muqayyad*, fasting alternately is not entertained as of the case of prescribed penance to those who are fasting in compensation to sexual relationship during the daytime in the month of *Ramaḍān*.

3. The *Qur'ān* states:

"*Forbidden to you are your mothers and your daughters and your sisters and your paternal aunts and your maternal aunts and brothers' daughters and sisters' daughters and your mothers that have suckled you and your foster-sisters and mothers of your wives and your step-daughters who are under your guardianship, (born) of your wives to whom you have gone in, but if you have not gone in to them, there is no blame on you (in marrying them), and the wives of your sons who are of your own loins and that you should have two sisters together, except what has already passed; surely Allah is Forgiving, Merciful.*"[111]

The word 'stepdaughters' has been qualified by 'are under your guardianship, (born) of your wives to whom you have gone in'. However, this restriction has been cancelled by the statement 'but if you have not gone in to them, there is no blame on you (in marrying them)'. Therefore, this *muqayyad* has not been implemented because its restriction has been nullified and it has become *muṭlaq*. So with this statement, one's stepdaughter is not forbidden to him in marrying as long as the marriage with his wife has not been consummated.

Conflict between muṭlaq and muqayyad

There are four possibilities when *muṭlaq* and *muqayyad* relate to the same issue: a) when they agree on the cause and the ruling; b) when they agree on the cause and disagree on the ruling; c) when they disagree on the cause and agree on the ruling; d) and finally when they disagree on both the cause and the ruling.

A) The muṭlaq and muqayyad agree on the cause and the ruling

Regarding the first possibility, scholars agree on that *muqayyad* prevails over *muṭlaq* and qualifies it. This conflict is illustrated by the following *Qur'ān* verses:

> *"Forbidden to you is that which dies of itself, and blood, and flesh of swine, and that on which any other name than that of Allah has been invoked, and the strangled (animal) and that beaten to death, and that killed by a fall and that killed by being smitten with the horn, and that which wild beasts have eaten, except what you slaughter, and what is sacrificed on stones set up (for idols) and that you divide by the arrows; that is a transgression. This day have those who disbelieve despaired of your religion, so fear them not, and fear Me. This day have I perfected for you your religion and completed My favour on you and chosen for you Islam as a religion; but whoever is compelled by hunger, not inclining wilfully to sin, then surely Allah is Forgiving, Merciful."*[112]

In this verse blood is forbidden for human consumption. The word "*ad-dam*" (اَلدَّمُ) "blood" is absolute but one qualified in another verse as:

> *"Say: I do not find in that which has been revealed to me anything forbidden for an eater to eat of except that it be what has died of itself, or blood poured forth, or flesh of swine – for that surely is unclean – or that which is a transgression, other than (the name of) Allah having been invoked on it; but whoever is driven to necessity, not desiring nor exceeding the limit, then surely your Lord is Forgiving, Merciful."*[113]

The word 'blood' in the second verse is restricted by the word "*masfūḥan*" (مَسْفُوحًا) "poured forth" and the restricted sense prevails over the absolute. Therefore in the both verses the causes are the same 'consumption', eating and drinking the blood harm to human body and the value (*ḥukm*) is the prohibition of the consuming of the blood.

B) The muṭlaq and muqayyad agree on the cause and disagree on the ruling

In this situation where *muṭlaq* and *muqayyad* agree on the cause which the intention to perform prayer with a need to make ritual preparation for prayer, and disagree on the ruling, however, in ablution the obligation is washing the hands with water; on the other hand in *tayammum* the obligation is rubbing the hands with a clean earth. The *muqayyad* will not qualify *muṭlaq* and everyone will treat it as it stands. This is illustrated by the verses related to *wuḍū'* and *tayammum*. The *Qur'ān* states about *wudu'*:

> *"O you who believe! when you rise up to prayer, wash your faces and your hands up to the elbows, and wipe your heads and your feet to the ankles; and if you are under an obligation to perform a total ablution, then wash (yourselves) and if you are sick or on a journey, or one of you come from the privy, or you have touched the women, and if you find no water, then perform tayammum with clean earth and rub therewith your faces and hands, Allah does not desire to put on you any difficulty, but He wishes to purify you and that He may complete His favour on you, so that you may be grateful."*[114]

In the verse, the washing of the hands is restricted to "*ilā al-marāfiq*" (إِلَى الْمَرَافِقِ) "*up to the elbows*." The same verse does not restrict rubbing the hands in *tayammum*:

"*And if you find no water, then perform tayammum with clean earth and rub therewith your faces and hands.*" Since the two verses pertain to different rulings, the first verse will not qualify the second, and thus in *tayammum* the hands should not be rubbed 'up to the elbows'. However, there is disagreement between scholars about the value (*ḥukm*) of these verses. As the Prophet (ṣ) explained the way to perform *tayammum* with this *ḥadīth*: "*Tayammum* consists of two strikings, one for face and one for hands up to elbow."[115] In terms of *tayammun*, the word "*aydīkum*" (أَيْدِيكُمْ) "hands" in the verse comes as *muṭlaq* and it is not restricted, while the word "*lil-yadayn*" (لليدين) "*ḥadd*" in the *ḥadīth* is restricted by the word "*ilā al-marāfiq*" (الى المرافقين) "up to the elbows."

Some scholars restricted the verse on *tayammum* by some traditions.[116] The value (*ḥukm*) in both the verse and the *ḥadīth*, performing *maskh* (rubbing) is obligatory (*farḍ*) and the cause of the *ḥukm* (ruling) is the same: intention to perform prayer and its preparation, and thus, in this situation, the *muqayyad* is preferred to the *muṭlaq* which extending rubbing from hand up to the elbow is obligatory. Indeed, the value (*ḥukm*) in *Ḥanafī* and *Shāfi'ī madhhab* is as such.

On the other hand, according to *Mālikīs* and *Ḥanbalīs* rubbing up to the elbows is not obligatory since the ruling that they follow is based on the *ḥadīth:* "Enough for you one strike for the face and one for the hands" does not indicate rubbing up to the elbow. Hence, *Mālikīs* and *Ḥanbalīs* limited the *muṭlaq* indication of the verse with the *ḥadīth* mentioned above.

C) The muṭlaq and muqayyad disagree on the cause and agree on the ruling

In the following scenario *muṭlaq* and *muqayyad* disagree on the cause and agree on the ruling. As an example of this scenario we may refer it to the following verse. The *Qur'ān* states:

> "*O you who believe! when you deal with each other in contracting a debt for a fixed time, then write it down; and let a scribe write it down between you with fairness; and the scribe should not refuse to write as Allah has taught him, so he should write; and let him who*

> *owes the debt dictate, and he should be careful of (his duty to) Allah, his Lord, and not diminish anything from it; but if he who owes the debt is unsound in understanding, or weak, or (if) he is not able to dictate himself, let his guardian dictate with fairness; and call in to witness from among your men two witnesses; but if there are not two men, then one man and two women from among those whom you choose to be witnesses, so that if one of the two errs, the second of the two may remind the other.*"[117]

This verse requires two witnesses in commercial transactions. The word "*rijāl*" (رِجَال) "men" is absolute because this verse does not qualify it. Another verse also deals with the subject of witness. The *Qur'ān* states:

> "*So when they have reached their prescribed time, then retain them with kindness or separate them with kindness, and call to witness two men of justice from among you, and give upright testimony for Allah. With that is admonished he who believes in Allah and the latter day; and whoever is careful of (his duty to) Allah, He will make for him an outlet.*"[118]

This verse, however, qualifies the persons with the word "*'adl*" (عدْل) "just." The ruling of these two verses is the same because both require two witnesses. The causes of these rulings are different, in the former it is commercial transactions, whereas in the latter it is the revocation of divorce. Since the qualified prevails over the absolute, the latter verse prevails over the former and the ruling is that witnesses in both commercial transactions and the revocation of divorce must be 'just'. Nevertheless, this is the opinion of *Shāfi'īs*, however, *Ḥanafī* scholars do not qualify *muṭlaq* by *muqayyad* in this situation, and according to them these verses operate as they stand.[119]

D) The muṭlaq and muqayyad disagree on both the cause and the ruling

Another possibility of conflict among *muṭlaq* and *muqayyad* is that they disagree on both the cause and the ruling. All the scholars are agree on that none of them would qualify the other one and each value (*ḥukm*) of the verse operates independently. An example of this may be seen in the verse related to ablution and theft. The *Qur'ān* states regarding ablution:

> *"O you who believe! when you rise up to prayer, wash your faces and your hands up to the elbows, and wipe your heads and your feet to the ankles; and if you are under an obligation to perform a total ablution, then wash (yourselves) and if you are sick or on a journey, or one of you come from the privy, or you have touched the women, and if you find no water, then perform tayammum with clean earth and rub therewith your faces and hands, Allah does not desire to put on you any difficulty, but He wishes to purify you and that He may complete His favour on you, so that you may be grateful."*[120]

The washing of "the hands" in this verse is restricted to "up to the elbows". On the other hand, in the verse about theft there is no such restriction. The *Qur'ān* states:

> *"And (as for) the man who steals and the woman who steals, cut off their hands as a punishment for what they have earned, an exemplary punishment from Allah; and Allah is Mighty, Wise."*[121]

Therefore, the word hand in the second verse is absolute. Due to the fact that both causes and rulings in these verses are different, the value (*ḥukm*) in the first verse is washing hands while the second it is cutting off hands as well as the cause in the first verse is the intention to perform prayer with a need to make ritual preparation for prayer while in the second one it is the crime of theft. Consequently, since there is no any relationship between these two verses, in terms of cause and value, the both qualify none of them and each verse operates as it stands according to the scholars.[122]

In relation to the qualification of *muṭlaq* by *muqayyad*, the above discussions could be summarized as follows: as stipulated by the scholars, they agreed that the *muṭlaq* are qualified by the *muqayyad* if causes and values are the same in the both verses, and the absolute and qualification do not occur in the cause but in the value (*ḥukm*) itself.

On the other hand, the scholars agreed that the *muṭlaq* are not qualified by the *muqayyad* if causes and values are different in the both verses or the causes are the same in the both verses but the values are different. In addition to that, the scholars disagreed on whether or not the *muṭlaq* are qualified by the *muqayyad* if causes and values are the same in the both verses, and the absolute and qualification occur in the cause but not in the value (*ḥukm*) itself or the values are the same in the both verses but the causes are different. Nevertheless, according to the *Ḥanafī* scholars *muqayyad* does not qualify *muṭlaq* in the above situations and each *naṣṣ* operates individually, however the majority of the scholars opine that *muṭlaq* can be qualified by *muqayyad*.[123]

In addition to that discussions, although the *muṭlaq* is unspecified and unqualified, it is differentiated that the *muṭlaq* can apply to any one of a multitude, not all, in contrast to it, the *'āmm* comprises all to which it applies.[124] In fact, the scholars have differed in vis-à-vis the *muṭlaq* and the *muqayyad*, some of them considered *muṭlaq* to be *'āmm* and the *muqayyad* is as *khāṣṣ*. For this reason, it is generalized as anything which specifies the *'āmm* can qualify the *muṭlaq*. As well as these two are complementary to *'āmm* and *khāṣṣ* which are open to *ta'wīl*.[125] In other words, the *khāṣṣ* differs from the *muqayyad* in that the later is a word which implies an unspecified individual who is totally distinguished by certain attributes and qualifications, for example, the *Qur'ān* states:

> "*And (as for) those who put away their wives by likening their backs to the backs of their mothers then would recall what they said, they should free a captive before they touch each other; to that you are admonished (to conform); and Allah is Aware of what you do.*"[126]

Therefore, the *muṭlaq* in this verse is the expiation (*kaffarah*) of futile oaths, which is "*fa-taḥrīru raqabatin*" (فَتَحْرِيرُ رَقَبَةٍ) "freeing a slave." The command in this text is not limited to any kind of slaves, whether Muslim or non-Muslim. On the other hand, in another verse, the *Qur'ān* states:

> "*And it does not behove a believer to kill a believer except by mistake, and whoever kills a believer by mistake, he should free a believing slave, and blood-money should be paid to his people unless they remit it as alms; but if he be from a tribe hostile to you and he is a believer, the freeing of a believing slave (suffices), and if he is from a tribe between whom and you there is a covenant, the blood-money should be paid to his people along with the freeing of a believing slave; but he who cannot find (a slave) should fast for two months successively: a penance from Allah, and Allah is Knowing, Wise.*"[127]

Hence, the way the expiation of erroneous killing is qualified to "*mu'minatin*" (مُؤْمِنَةٍ) "*mu'min*" therefore the compensation must be paid through "*fa-taḥrīru raqabatin mu'minatin*" (فَتَحْرِيرُ رَقَبَةٍ مُؤْمِنَةٍ) "freeing a *mu'min* slave." Consequently, the absolute term in the first verse is qualified by the word (مُؤْمِنَةٍ) "*mu'min*" which the released slave must be a *mu'min*.

The precondition for the restriction of muṭlaq by muqayyad

In addition to the above discussions, there are some certain conditions that were stipulated by scholars.[128]

1. The limitation should be in the form of attributes, where the basics of rulings are already established in both *muṭlaq* and *muqayyad*. If, for example, the limitation of the absolute establishes the fundamental ruling in the form of an increase, or an increase in the number of times, the *muqayyad* may not qualify the *muṭlaq*. As it is discussed in the verse:

   > "*O you who believe! when you rise up to prayer, wash your faces and your hands up to the elbows, and wipe your heads*

and your feet to the ankles."[129]

For *wuḍū'*, it is obligatory to wash or wipe four parts, while for *tayammum*:

"*And if you find no water, then perform tayammum with clean earth and rub therewith your faces and hands,*"[130]

the number is decreased to only two parts. Therefore, the *muqayyad* may not qualify the *muṭlaq*, since this would lead to the confirmation of a ruling which has not been mentioned, and therefore, each should be implemented independently.

2. The *muṭlaq* (absolute) should not alternate between two different limitations, which it must have only one origin which the restriction will not take place otherwise. As stated in the *Qur'ān*:

   "*And you shall have half of what your wives leave if they have no child, but if they have a child, then you shall have a fourth of what they leave after (payment of) any bequest they may have bequeathed or a debt.*"[131]

   The restriction that the inheritance between spouses should take place after regulating legacy and debts. On the other hand, inheritance has been mentioned in other places in the absolute (*muṭlaq*) form. Since the *muṭlaq* (the inheritance) mentioned in other places in reliable texts are all from the same origin, therefore, it will be qualified which the inheritance will take place after the legacy and debts are regulated.

3. The objectives of the *sharī'ah* may not be harmonized (reconciled) except by restriction since implementing their full meaning is preferred to cancelling some other meanings.

4. There should not be reliable proof which prevents the

restriction from taking place.

5. There should not be an additional meaning related to the *muqayyad* (qualified) which it may suggest that the restriction has been mentioned because of that additional meaning. If, however, such additional meaning is connected to *muqayyad*, the limitation may not be considered.[132]

C) The Command (al-amr)

Linguistically the command (*al-amr*) (الامر) refers to order, command, instruction, authority, decree etc.[133] It is evidenced in many verses of the *Qur'ān* to name a few:

> "*O you who believe! obey Allah and obey the Messenger and those in authority from among you*"[134]

and

> "*Read in the name of your Lord Who created*".[135]

Technically it is defined as a verbal demand to do something issued from a position of superiority over who is inferior.[136] According to Ibn al-Ḥājib the command (الامر) is "Requirement of an act, not abstention, from the position of superiority."[137] Naṣafī defines it as "an order to act."[138] As one of the well-known *Shāfi'ī* scholar, al-Āmidī defines it as "Amr is an order, from the position of superiority, to act."[139] Eventually it can be simply defined as it is a word or a provision of an order which implies to fulfilment of an act in the future.

Forms of the Command

The command can be expressed in a variety of forms: Regarding the following forms of the command provided there is no contrary evidence. However, *Ash'arī* scholars maintain that a command has no forms of wording. This opinion is inconsistent with Arabic language rules, the *Qur'ān* and the *Sunnah*, and therefore it is entirely rejected.[140]

1. The imperative mood of verbs demonstrated in the following verse: "*And keep up prayer and pay the poor-rate and bow down with those who bow down*".[141]

2. The jussive mood of verbs (imperfect) preceded by the command article '*li*' such as in the verse: "*therefore whoever of you is present in the month, he shall fast therein*"[142] and "*Then let them accomplish their needful acts of shaving and cleansing, and let them fulfil their vows and let them go round the Ancient House.*[143]

3. The verbs in simple passive voice demonstrated in the verses: "*O you who believe! the law of equality is prescribed to you in cases of murder*"[144] and "*O you who believe! fasting is prescribed for you, as it was prescribed for those before you, so that you may guard (against evil).*"[145]

4. The verbal imperative noun illustrated in the verse: "*O you who believe! take care of your souls; he who errs cannot hurt you when you are on the right way; to Allah is your return, of all (of you), so He will inform you of what you did*".[146] The word "*alaykum*' (عَلَيْكُمْ) is an imperative verbal noun and is regarded as a form of the command (الامر).

5. The verbal noun which is a substitute for the imperative mood of verbs, as in the verse: "*So when you meet in battle those who disbelieve, then smite the necks until when you have overcome them*"[147] The word '*ḍarb*' (ضَرْبَ) is a verbal noun which means smite, striking, hitting. In this verse, however, it acts as a substitute for the imperative mood and means 'smite'.

In addition to the above mentioned forms of command (الامر), there are other forms which may give the same indication – explicit mention of the following words: to order "*amara*" (امر), to ordain "*farada*" (فرض), to prescribe "*kataba*" (كتب), the duty upon "*ḥaqqun 'alā*" (حق على) and similar words. Included here are the provisions that indicate a moral condemnation, threats of punishment, or the expunging of someone's good deeds because of abandoned duties. A sentence that provides information by which an order is intended is illustrated in the verse: "*And the mothers should suckle their children for two whole years for him who desires to make complete the time of suckling*".[148] This information indicates that an order is intended.

The primary indication of the command (al-amr)[149]

Indication of a text (*naṣṣ*) determines the meaning. If there is a command in a text in which there is indications of it, the command should be understood according to the indications. However, if there is no such indication in the text to show the meaning of it then scholars have different point of views for understanding of the command.

First of all command in this sense differs from both supplication (*duā'*) and request (*iltimas*). Thus the former is a demand from an inferior to one who is superior, while a request is a demand among people of equal or near-equal status.

According to the majority of scholars, if, however, a form of command (الامر) is not accompanied by clues or evidences suggesting a kind of request, command implies a definite order. Nevertheless, this may change in the event of other indications being present, which might reduce a command to permissibility, recommendation, or indeed to a variety of other meanings such as a homonym (*mushtarak*) which imparts all sorts of meanings; obligation and recommendations; permission to act.

According to these views, in order to convey meaning command (الامر) must be supported by clues or circumstances. Accordingly, it may not imply obligation without additional evidence that suggests this.[150]

Therefore the following command in the *Qur'ān* indicates permissibility (ibāḥah). "*O children of Adam! attend to your embellishments at every time of prayer, and eat and drink and be not extravagant; surely He does not love the extravagant*".[151] Since eating and drinking are the necessities of human life, the command in this verse logically indicates permissibility not obligation. After performing the Friday prayers the believers are permitted to do what they have been doing before it "*And when the Prayer is finished, then may you disperse through the land, and seek of the Bounty of Allah*".[152] Although the word 'you disperse' "*fan-tashirū*" (فَانْتَشِرُوا) in an imperative form, it indicates permissibility.[153]

The absolute and the restricted order [154]

The command may also be considered an absolute order "*al-amr al-muṭlaq*" (الامر المطلق) and restricted order "*al-amr al-muqayyad*" (الامر المقيد). The absolute must include everything without which it may not be completed. For example, the order to perform prayer must include the order for ablution because the prayer will be invalid without it. This does not mean that there are no special proofs for this and similar obligations. This is when there is an absolute order. On the other hand the restricted order (الامر المقيد) is a limited one such as in the case of alms, which is restricted by the possession of a certain amount of wealth, there is no question of obligation to achieve it. This is because, by achieving it, the order, not the duty and obligation will be completed. The rule is that without which a duty may not be fulfilled is a duty, and that without which the order will not be completed is not obligatory.[155]

Variety of usages of the command [156]

The command literally implies obligation which may also imply other things, depending on the evidence (context and circumstances). It may depart from the original meaning towards other meanings. The followings are the different types of the command (الامر):

1. Recommendation (*nadb*) exemplified by the verse: "*O you who believe! when you deal with each other in contracting a debt for a fixed time, then write it down*".[157]
2. Permissibility (*ibāḥah*) as in: "*O children of Adam! attend to your embellishments at every time of prayer, and eat and drink and be not extravagant; surely He does not love the extravagant*".[158]
3. The threat as in : "*Do what you like*".[159]
4. Indebtedness as in: "*And eat of the lawful and good (things) that Allah has given you*".[160]
5. Honor and hospitality as in: "*Enter them here in peace and security*".[161]
6. Deeming powerless as in: "*And if you are in doubt as to that which We have revealed to Our servant, then produce a chapter like it and call on your witnesses besides Allah if you are truthful*".[162]
7. Equalisation as in: "*Enter into it, then bear (it) patiently, or do not bear (it) patiently, it is the same to you; you shall be requited only (for) what you did*".[163]
8. Contempt as in: "*And when the magicians came, Musa said to them: Cast down what you have to cast*".[164]
9. Consultation as in: "*And when he attained to working with him, he said: O my son! surely I have seen in a dream that I should sacrifice you; consider then what you see. He said: O my father! do what you are commanded; if Allah please, you will find me of the patient ones*"[165]. The word 'see' "*fan-ẓur*" (فَانْظُرْ) indicates consultation to his son.

10. A call for contemplation as in: "*when they begin to bear fruit, feast your eyes with the fruit and the ripeness thereof. Behold! in these things there are signs for people who believe*".[166]
11. Supplication (*duā'*), when a request comes from an inferior being (human being) to another (God), as in the verse: "*He said: My Lord! do Thou forgive me and grant me a kingdom which is not fit for (being inherited by) anyone after me*".[167]
12. Warning as in: "*O you who believe! take your precaution, then go forth in detachments or go forth in a body*".[168]
13. Insult as in: "*Taste; you forsooth are the mighty, the honorable*".[169]
14. Request when a demand comes from an equal or nearly-equal person, as when a student asks a friend: "*Give me the pen.*"[170]

The indication of command after prohibition [171]

There are some rulings in the texts which command the opposite of what has been hitherto prohibited. There may be a question in regards to the nature of a command which follows a prohibition. An example of such command in the *Sunnah* is the *ḥadīth* of the Prophet (ṣ), once he said:

"I had forbidden you from visiting the graves. Nay visit them, for it reminds you of the Hereafter."[172] Another example can be given from the *Qur'ān* in the context of the permission to hunt following its prohibition during the pilgrimage (*ḥajj*) performance as well as the permission to conduct trade following its prohibition at the time of the Friday prayers. As Allah respectively indicated in the following verses: "*O you who believe! do not violate the signs appointed by Allah nor the sacred month, nor (interfere with) the offerings, nor the sacrificial animals with garlands, nor those going to the sacred house seeking the grace and pleasure of their Lord; and when you are free from the obligations of the pilgrimage, then hunt,*"[173] and the prohibition of trade at the time of Friday prayers: "*But when the prayer is ended, then disperse abroad in the land and seek of Allah's grace*".[174]

In these situations, it may be asked whether the command convey an obligation or a mere permissibility. The majority of scholars have held the view that a command following a prohibition means permissibility not obligation.[175]

Single compliance with command (al-amr) or its repetition [176]

The command can be used in variety of types, absolute, restricted to a single act of compliance and restricted to repetition. However, a question which may arise here in connection with this matter is whether a command requires a single compliance or repetition. It is obvious that if a command is restricted, then it is implemented according to its restriction, because the qualified prevails over the absolute.

Before giving examples to repeated performance I shall give an example to single compliance which may be illustrated with the following verse: "*pilgrimage to the House is incumbent upon men for the sake of Allah, (upon) everyone who is able to undertake the journey to it*".[177] The Prophet (ṣ) was asked if it had to be performed every year, and he replied that it should be done one in a lifetime.[178] This command in the verse is a single compliance according to the *ḥadīth* of the Prophet (ṣ). On the other hand, this verse "*And (as for) the man who steals and the woman who steals, cut off their hands as a punishment for what they have earned, an exemplary punishment from Allah; and Allah is Mighty, Wise*"[179] indicates that the command implies repetition whenever theft occurs the hand must be amputated so long as all the conditions for punishment are fulfilled.

The following verse also explores the command as it is fulfilled conditionally: "*If you are in a state of ceremonial impurity, bathe your whole body.*"[180]

As the command, which indicates to take a bath, is conditional on impurity situation "*janābah*" (جنابة), that is, on sexual intercourse, then a full bath must be taken following every instance of sexual intercourse and coming of sperm due to sexual reasons. Consequently when a command is dependent on a cause or an attribute, then it must be fulfilled whenever the cause or the attribute is present.[181]

According to the majority of the scholars the question, which a command requires a single compliance or repetition, can only be determined based on indication of the text. However, in the absence of such of performance is the minimum requirement of a command. Among the indications which determine repetition is when a command is issued in conditional terms. Some scholars maintain that command (الامر) implies a single compliance, others that it implies repetition during one's lifetime.

The majority opinion and those who maintain that command implies a single act of compliance do not differ in practical terms since all of them accept that whenever a cause or an attribute occurs the repetition must be fulfilled.[182]

The indication of command on immediate (fawran) or delayed (tarākhiyan) performance [183]

Naturally, the command (الامر) itself merely consists of a demand. It is viewed above that the manner of its performance must be determined in the light of indications and related circumstances. However, a question may arise here that whether a command requires immediate "*fawran*" (فورا) or delayed "*tarākhiyan*" (تراخيا) performance.

If the command (الامر) is an absolute one, it must be performed immediately since people are generally commanded not to delay the performance of good deeds, although it may be restricted as to the time of its performance. The performance of its time may be flexible according to conditions. So it may not be strictly required. Although an absolute order may sometimes be delayed, as the Prophet (ṣ) delayed in performing the pilgrimage, the requirement to perform it as early as possible remains in effect, performing good deeds should be fulfilled at the nearest time possible due to the general requirement for the good deeds.[184] It may be illustrated with several verses: "*And hasten to forgiveness from your Lord; and a Garden, the extensiveness of which is the heavens and the earth, it is prepared for the righteous*"[185], "*therefore hasten to (do) good works*".[186] On the other hand, the time limit may be flexible. If it is flexible, like the command to perform the obligatory prayer, in that case the performance of it may be delayed until the last part of the prescribed time. However, if the command indicates no specific time, like the command to perform an expiation "*kaffārah*" (كفارة), then execution may be delayed for an indefinite period within the expected limits of one's lifetime. Nevertheless, it is advised that the immediate fulfilment of command should be performed since the time of one's death is uncertain.[187]

Who is addressed by command (al-amr)[188]

In order to know who is addressed by the command, it must be referred to the *ḥadīth* of the Prophet (ṣ) "There is no responsibility upon three persons: a sleeping person before he wakes, a youth before puberty (i.e. the legal age of maturity in Islamic law), and a lunatic before he recovers his senses".[189] According to this *ḥadīth* everyone who is outside of this circle is addressed by command. In addition to this, human being may be divided into two groups: those to whom legal or religious obligations (legal awareness) apply and those to whom they do not apply because of immaturity, or temporary or permanent loss of mental capabilities. The legal texts are not addressed to those who do not acquire legal awareness. This is a logical winding because an order is in general issued to someone who can presumably fulfill the obligation.[190]

The indication of command to its opposite

Scholars have discussed another question as to whether a command to do something implies the prohibition of its opposite. Three opinions may be discussed related to this issue. Firstly, according to the majority of the scholars a command to do something does imply the prohibition of its opposite. For example, when a person is ordered to stand up, he is in the meantime forbidden to remain sitting down; or if a person is ordered to go, he is forbidden to stay at the same place.

Secondly, the command to do something does not imply the prohibition of its opposite. For example, committing adultery is an unlawful act. It does not imply that it is obligatory to commit adultery. The cases must be determined independently with independent indications. This is the view of some scholars including al-Juwaynī, al-Ghazālī, Ibn al-Ḥājib and the *Mu'tazilah.*[191]

Thirdly, the command to do something only implies one of the opposing prohibited acts. This is the opinions of a group of the *Ḥanafī* and *Shāfi'ī* scholars.[192]

It is obvious that the command itself dictates the opposing act. Therefore, the opposition of the command would be prohibition. With the above discussion, what would be if a person who commits the opposite of a command? It may be said that the person who commits the opposite of it must be penalized. The extent of the penalizing would be determined according to the light of the surrounding circumstances, the state of mind of the individual concerned and the fundamental objectives of the Lawgiver (*maqāṣid al-Shārī'*).[193]

The Value of command (al-amr) [194]

As it is already noted that the majority of scholars have held the view that a command in general conveys an obligation unless there are indications to suggest otherwise. Therefore, command (الامر) implies a definite obligation before finding out evidences or clues which may provide other indications.

D) The Prohibition (an-nahy)

Linguistically the prohibition "*an-nahy*" (النهي) refers to ban which occurs in many verses of the *Qur'ān:*[195]

Technically it refers to the opposite of the command (الامر). Āmidī held that the prohibition (النهي) is the opposite of the command (الامر), therefore an order to act, from a position of superiority.[196] Shawkānī defines it as "The declaration that requires an abstention, from the position of superiority."[197] On the other hand Naṣafī defines it as an utterance by someone, from a position of superiority, for another not to act.[198] According to Badrān, it is a word or words which demand the avoidance of doing something addressed from a position of superiority to one who is inferior.[199]

The forms of the Prohibition (an-nahy) [200]

A prohibition may appear a variety of meanings. The form as of the prohibition (النهي) do not always imply strict prohibition. It may imply many other rulings like the command (الامر). Only the differences between the command and the prohibition is that the command (الامر) implies action and the prohibition implies abstention.[201]

The primary meaning of the prohibition (النهي)[202] is a mere reprehension "*karāhiyyah*" (كراهية). As the Prophet (ṣ) prohibited drinking from the neck of a water skin.[203] or guidance "*irshād*" (إرشاد) as exemplified in the coming verse:

> *"O you who believe! do not put questions about things which if declared to you may trouble you, and if you question about them when the Quran is being revealed, they shall be declared to you; Allah pardons this, and Allah is Forgiving, Forbearing."*[204]

or it may be in the meaning of reprimand "*ta'dīb*" (تأديب), or supplication "*du'ā'*" (دعاء) of an inferior to a superior being as in the verse:

> "*Allah does not impose upon any soul a duty but to the extent of its ability; for it is (the benefit of) what it has earned and upon it (the evil of) what it has wrought: Our Lord! do not punish us if we forget or make a mistake; Our Lord! do not lay on us a burden as Thou didst lay on those before us, Our Lord do not impose upon us that which we have not the strength to bear; and pardon us and grant us protection and have mercy on us, Thou art our Patron, so help us against the unbelieving people*".[205]

The followings are also other usages of the prohibition (النهي):

1. The imperfect preceded by the article jussive mood "lā" (لا) as in the verse: "*And do not swallow up your property among yourselves by false means, neither seek to gain access thereby to the judges, so that you may swallow up a part of the property of men wrongfully while you know.*"[206] and "*O you who believe! be not unfaithful to Allah and the Messenger, nor be unfaithful to your trusts while you know*".[207]

2. The explicit mention of a prohibition (النهي), and ban "*taḥrīm*" (تحريم), as in the following verse: "*The fornicator shall not marry any but a fornicatress or idolatress, and (as for) the fornicatress, none shall marry her but a fornicator or an idolater; and it is forbidden to the believers*".[208]

   "*Allah does not forbid you respecting those who have not made war against you on account of (your) religion, and have not driven you forth from your homes, that you show them kindness and deal with them justly; surely Allah loves the doers of justice*".[209]

3. A command that requires the avoidance of something: "*O you who believe! when the call is made for prayer on Friday, then hasten to the remembrance of Allah and leave off trading; that*

is better for you, if you know"[210] and "*That (shall be so); and whoever respects the sacred ordinances of Allah, it is better for him with his Lord; and the cattle are made lawful for you, except that which is recited to you, therefore avoid the uncleanness of the idols and avoid false words*".[211]

4. Threats against and criticism of those who do commit certain deeds: "*And they who do not call upon another god with Allah and do not slay the soul, which Allah has forbidden except in the requirements of justice, and (who) do not commit fornication and he who does this shall find a requital of sin*",[212] and "*And who is more unjust than he who forges a lie against Allah and he is invited to Islam, and Allah does not guide the unjust people*".[213]

5. Prescribing penance for certain deeds: "*And it does not behoove a believer to kill a believer except by mistake, and whoever kills a believer by mistake, he should free a believing slave, and blood-money should be paid to his people unless they remit it as alms; but if he be from a tribe hostile to you and he is a believer, the freeing of a believing slave (suffices), and if he is from a tribe between whom and you there is a covenant, the blood-money should be paid to his people along with the freeing of a believing slave; but he who cannot find (a slave) should fast for two months successively: a penance from Allah, and Allah is Knowing, Wise*".[214]

6. Prescribing a punishment "*ḥadd*" (حد) as a consequence for certain deeds: "*(As for) the fornicatress and the fornicator, flog each of them, (giving) a hundred stripes, and let not pity for them detain you in the matter of obedience to Allah, if you believe in Allah and the last day, and let a party of believers witness their chastisement*".[215]

7. Moral condemnation of certain conduct as in the verse: "*They*

ask you concerning the new moon. Say: They are times appointed for (the benefit of) men, and (for) the pilgrimage; and it is not righteousness that you should enter the houses at their backs, but righteousness is this that one should guard (against evil); and go into the houses by their doors and be careful (of your duty) to Allah, that you may be successful".[216]

8. Description of a deed as corrupt or an act of the devil: "*O you who believe! intoxicants and games of chance and (sacrificing to) stones set up and (dividing by) arrows are only an uncleanness, the Shaiṭān's work; shun it therefore that you may be successful*".[217]

9. Confirmation that Allah abhors those who falsify the Scriptures; that He will not purify "*Surely those who conceal any part of the Book that Allah has revealed and take for it a small price, they eat nothing but fire into their bellies, and Allah will not speak to them on the day of resurrection, nor will He purify them, and they shall have a painful chastisement*"[218], Allah will not speak to, or look at them, "*(As for) those who take a small price for the covenant of Allah and their own oaths – surely they shall have no portion in the hereafter, and Allah will not speak to them, nor will He look upon them on the day of resurrection nor will He purify them, and they shall have a painful chastisement*".[219]

10. In the form of information: "*The pilgrimage is (performed in) the well-known months; so whoever determines the performance of the pilgrimage therein, there shall be no intercourse nor fornication nor quarrelling amongst one another; and whatever good you do, Allah knows it; and make provision, for surely the provision is the guarding of oneself, and be careful (of your duty) to Me, O men of understanding*".[220]

The indication of the Prohibition[221]

Uṣūlī scholars are not unanimous in the prohibition (النهي) as they are not unanimous in the command (الامر). The majority of Islamic scholars maintain that the prohibition, in reality, indicates prohibition if a reliable proof does not suggest otherwise. On the other hand it may indicates reprehension "*karāhah*" (كراهة) rather than mere prohibition. For example, as of this verse: "*O you who believe! when the call is made for prayer on Friday, then hasten to the remembrance of Allah and leave off trading; that is better for you, if you know*".[222]

The prohibition indicates trading as disliked "*makrūh*" (مكروه) during the *Jum'ah* prayer. The indication, which degreases the prohibition from the degree of prohibition (تحريم) to disliking (كراهية) is based on a worry of keeping away a person from *Jum'ah* prayer due to trading. The trading itself is not prohibited in nature.

In another verse, "*Our Lord! make not our hearts to deviate after Thou hast guided us aright, and grant us from Thee mercy; surely Thou art the most liberal Giver*".[223] The Prohibition (النهي) in this verse is in the meaning of supplication (دعاء).

Therefore, in order to determine whether or not, a prohibition necessarily means actual prohibition (تحريم) or mere reprehension (كراهة), it needs more explanation. It is not always easily understood from the words of the texts "*nuṣūṣ*" (نصوص). Precise meaning of the texts (نصوص) can only be understood by virtue of clarity of their language. On the other hand as Shāṭibī pointed out that much larger portion of the texts of the *Qur'ān* cannot be determined by sole reference to the linguistic forms. Therefore the *mujtahids* must be fully equipped with the general principles and objectives of the *Sharī'ah* in order to determine the precise meaning and values of the texts of the *Qur'ān*.[224]

Essence of Prohibited may be two types

1. The prohibited acts which have never been considered by

Allah to be good or acceptable deeds: "*And go not nigh to fornication; surely it is an indecency and an evil way*"[225], and "*And serve Allah and do not associate anything with Him and be good to the parents and to the near of kin and the orphans and the needy and the neighbour of (your) kin and the alien neighbour, and the companion in a journey and the wayfarer and those whom your right hands possess; surely Allah does not love him who is proud, boastful*".[226]

The mentioned acts are prohibited because they are considered inherently bad. They are forbidden since they are naturally corrupt the society and cause problems.

2. Temporal prohibition of and act. It may be prohibited in one aspect and would be enjoined in another:

    a. Because of its attribute – e.g., prohibition for menstruation woman or a drunk person with respect to the performance of prayers;

    b. Because of a manner which necessarily accompanies it – i.e., the prohibition of fasting during the first day of Eid, because fasting prevents one from celebrating the feast day;

Because of a matter which does not accompany it – e.g., the prohibition to perform ablution with stolen water, to pray on land acquired by unlawful means, or trade after the call for Friday prayer.[227]

Immediate or repeated compliance of a prohibition [228]

The Prohibition, as it is mentioned before, indicates an order to abandon an action forever if it is not limited since scholars used it as permanent proof without limiting it. The scholars are generally in agreement that a prohibition requires both immediate and repeated compliance in order it can be observed. However, if the object of a prohibition is avoided at all times then it is not observed. The text from the *Qur'ān* concerning the property of the orphans which provides:

> *"And do not approach the property of the orphan except in the best manner until he attains his maturity".*[229]

The prohibition in this verse is one hand not limited in any way. On the other hand, the text from the *Qur'ān* concerning the believers which provides;

> *"O you who believe! when believing women come to you flying, then examine them; Allah knows best their faith; then if you find them to be believing women, do not send them back to the unbelievers".*[230]

In this verse the prohibition is conditional upon finding that they are true believers. As it is seen in this verse, if a prohibition which is limited by a condition which overrules immediate compliance, then it has to be observed within the meaning of such condition.[231]

The effect of prohibition [232]

In conclusion, the prohibition implies something to be banned and therefore if a thing is prohibited is actually illegal and invalid. According to the scholars, a prohibition (النهي) indicates illegality (تحريم) so long as there are no indications otherwise.

As we have seen that Islamic scholars explored clearly the certain linguistic and technical explanations of both the general (العام) and the specific (خاص) meanings of words in practical examples which helped us differentiate them easily.

Concept of the Specification (al-takhṣīṣ)

Linguistically *takhṣīṣ* (التخصيص) refers to particularization, specification, individualization.[233]

Technically it has several definitions since the *Ḥanafis* have a slightly different approaches to *takhṣīṣ* (التخصيص) from that of the

Shāfi'īs, their definition is also slightly different.

According to the *Shāfi'ī* school of thought Imām Ḥasan al-Baṣrī defines it as "excluding some (meanings) included by the text due to the conflict between the two."[234] In the similar way Bayḍāwī defines it as "excluding some (meanings) from the scope of the word."[235] Besides that, Ibn Ḥājib defines *takhṣīṣ* as "the limitation of the general to some of its subjects."[236] According to these definitions, *takhṣīṣ* can be simplified as the limitation of the general provision to some of its subjects.[237]

On the other hand according to *Ḥanafī* school of thought, *takhṣīṣ* is limitation of the general provision to some of its subjects by an independent and joined proof.[238] The definition excludes by the condition of "independent," attached exception (*istithnā' muttaṣil*), condition (*sharṭ*) and attribute (*ṣifah*) and extent of application (*ghāyah*), since the specification needs a kind of conflict, and these proofs do not cause conflict because they explain what a general provision does not include in its meaning.[239] However, it excludes by the condition of "joined," abrogation (*naskh*) since when a specifying proof appears after the general provision, it is abrogation, not specification. Indeed, this is the main point of disagreement between the majority and the *Ḥanafīs* when the difference between specification and abrogation is in question.[240] However, unlike the other schools of thought, *Ḥanafīs* emphasized that the qualifying poof must be independent, chronologically parallel and joined to the general.[241]

The difference between abrogation and specification

Muslim scholars brought the following conclusions about the differences between abrogation and specification.[242]

1. The specification of meaning acts upon some subjects of the general provision, while abrogation acts upon all of them.

2. Abrogation can affect any legal injunction, whether that

injunction is related to one subject or many, while specification can take place only when a number of subjects are involved.

3. Abrogation can occur after the abrogated text has already been implemented, while specification may not happen after what is specified has been implemented.

4. Abrogation cancels a ruling after it has been established, while specification explains he intention of the general proposition (i.e. that all subjects are not intended by the general, or that some of them are excluded.)

5. Specification explains 'what was intended' by the general, while abrogation explains that which was not intended by the abrogated.

6. Abrogation occurs on account of the authoritative texts, reason, evidences and other proofs.

7. The consensus (*ijmāʿ*) may be a proof for specification but not for abrogation.

8. Specification may affect only the general meanings while abrogation may affect both general and specific meanings.

9. There are several kinds of *naskh*: textual abrogation, injunction abrogation, or both, whereby *takhṣīṣ* applies only to the rulings.[243]

Specifying Proofs[244]

There is disagreement between the majority of scholars and the *Ḥanafīs* on the specifying proofs. The majority uphold the meaning that a general provision may be specified either by a dependent clause that occurs in the same text or by an independent locution that occurs in another text. They attach only one stipulation to the specifying clauses, when it is independent of the general-that it appears before the general meaning is implemented. Therefore, according to the majority, specification is the limitation of the general provision to some subjects by dependent or independent proofs, chronological or not, which appear before the general provision is implemented. If it appears after the general is implemented, it causes abrogation, not specification of meaning.[245]

The Specifying proofs according to Majority (Jumhūr)

Majority of the scholars have concluded that the specification is the limitation of the general provision to some subjects by dependent or independent proofs, chronological or not, which appear before the general provision is implemented. Therefore it may be divided into those that are independent and dependent.

1. The independent proof (المخصص المستقل)
2. The dependent proof (المخصص غير المستقل)

1. *The independent proofs (al-mukhaṣṣiṣ al-mustaqil)*

The independent "*al-mukhaṣṣiṣ al-mustaqil*" proofs which specify general provisions are not a part of the text that provides these provisions. These are of three types:

1. **Reasoning (العقل):** The first independent proof, reasoning (*'aql*) can be illustrated by the following verses. In the context of *ḥajj*, for example: "*and pilgrimage to the House is incumbent upon men for the sake of Allah, (upon) everyone who is able to undertake the journey to it*".[246] Obviously, this duty is prescribed to all of mankind since the word 'mankind' (الناس) includes all human beings. In respect of reason, however, some people, like those who are not responsible (*mukallaf*) as infants and lunatics, are excluded from the scope of this obligation as the Prophet (ṣ) said:

   "Three persons are not morally responsible: a sleeping person before waking, a youth before sexual maturity (i.e. the legal age of maturity in Islamic law), and an insane person before he becomes lucid."[247]

According to this *ḥadīth*, these three persons are not responsible (*mukallaf*) and therefore the obligations brought forward by Islamic law are not applicable to them at all. The obligation of the fast can also be given as another example, the *Qur'ān* states: "*therefore whoever of you is present in the month, he shall fast therein,*"[248] The word 'whoever' "*faman*" (فمن) is generic and includes everyone. Therefore this verse apparently includes all the believers, and however, rationally it excludes those who are not responsible (*mukallaf*).

2. **Custom and Traditions (*'urf wa 'ādah*):**[249] The usage of a general provision may be specified by custom and tradition so long as a group of people use a general provision to indicate some of its subjects. It's meaning is determined by people's custom. In other words, if a particular word which appears generic is used, however custom may include only some of its subjects, in that case, it is treated according to its customary meaning. In that respect, a *mujtahid* must consider the customs and habits of the 'linguistic' environment of the original authoritative texts in order to understand the intended meaning correctly. It is impossible to understand authoritative texts and derive rulings without having such knowledge. In regards to this point, Shāṭibī said: "It is essential for everyone who wants to study the *Qur'ān* and the *Sunnah* to know the Arabs' speech customs and practices at the time of *Qur'anic* revelation, and the explanations of Allah's Prophet (ṣ), because ignorance of these leads to ambiguities and complications, from which one cannot escape without this knowledge."[250] For example, if a Malaysian makes a business in dollars without specifying an

exact meaning of the currency, it has to be considered in the currency of Malaysian ringgit rather than currency of United States of American Dollar because by custom 'dollars' means Malaysian ringgit, not American Dollars. As an example from the *Qur'ān* the Lawgiver uses a word which provides a general provision, in linguistic sense, which has a specified meaning technical meaning, e.g. the word 'trade' in the verse: "*Those who swallow down usury cannot arise except as one whom Shaiṭān has prostrated by (his) touch does rise. That is because they say, trading is only like usury; and Allah has allowed trading and forbidden usury*".[251]

The word trade "*bay*ʿ" (بيع) is generic in Arabic, and includes all kinds of exchange of goods and other items. However, when it comes to the usage of it in technical sense in the *Qur'ān*, however, it indicates only trading in goods. Therefore the usage of a specific word in customary sense should be taken into consideration. This custom therefore does not include every kind of exchange.[252]

3. **The authoritative text (*an-naṣṣ*):** The authoritative text can be either joined to the general provision that is mentioned after it in the same text or in a separate from the text. It is illustrated with the following examples.
    a. **The first type:** For example as the *Qur'ān* states, "*Whereas Allah has permitted trade and forbidden usury*".[253] The word 'trade' "*al-bay*ʿ" (البيع) is general in the Arabic language and means exchanging goods for goods. Therefore, it is all kind of trading including usury. However, the trade was specified by an independent text in another sentence which excludes usury from the permitted transections: 'and forbidden usury' "al-ribā'" (الرِّبَا). This independent text which prohibits the usury is joined to the text which carries the general meaning.

It can be explored with another verse from the *Qur'ān* as stated above.[254] The first part of the verse is general which indicates that any subject (*mukallaf*) who is sure that the month of *Ramaḍān* has begun should fast. On the other hand, the second part specifies it and excludes from the general meaning those who are ill or travelling since it is independent and joined to the general provision in appearance.

b. **The second type:** For example, the *Qur'ān* states: [255] "*And the divorced women should keep themselves in waiting for three courses*".[256] This verse is a general verse that includes all divorced women, whether the divorce took place before consummation of the marriage or afterward. Nevertheless, another verse comes to specify it by indication that the woman which whom her husband did not consummate the marriage should not wait three menstrual period as the *Qur'ān* states:

"*O you who believe! when you marry the believing women, then divorce them before you touch them, you have in their case no term which you should reckon; so make some provision for them and send them forth a goodly sending forth*".[257]

When the later verse is taken into consideration, it can be found that it is an independent and separated text specifies the general provision of the former verse which explains that the general provision of the former verse does not include women who are divorced before having sexual intercourse with their husbands. Therefore, the former verse is specified by another verse: "*And (as for) those of your women who have despaired of menstruation, if you have a doubt, their prescribed time shall be three months, and of those too who have not had their courses;*

and (as for) the pregnant women, their prescribed time is that they deliver their burden".[258]

Therefore, pregnant women are excluded from the general provision of that verse as to whether she is divorced or her husband has died, an expectant divorcee's *'iddah* (waiting period or clean time) is until the birth of her baby.

For this matter, another example can be given to show us that how the tradition of the Prophet (ṣ) may specify the general provision of the *Qur'ān* as it states: "*Forbidden to you (for food) are: dead meat, blood, the flesh of swine*".[259] The word dead (*maytatuh*) includes all kind of animals which have not been properly slaughtered. For this point the following tradition of the Prophet (ṣ) specifies this verse and excludes from it the dead animals which live in the sea. The Prophet (ṣ) said about the dead animals which are living in the sea: "Its water is pure (for ritual ablution) and its dead is permissible (as food)".[260]

2. The dependent proofs (al-mukhaṣṣiṣ ghayr al-mustaqil)

The dependent "*al-mukhaṣṣiṣ ghayr al-mustaqil*" proofs which specify general provisions are a part of the text that contains the general provisions. According to *Shāfi'īs*, the dependent proofs cannot stand on their own and cannot be separated from the text in which they appear. Therefore, these are dependent (غير المستقل) to the text and they are joined "*muttaṣil*" (متصل). The most important dependent proofs of specification (*mukhaṣṣiṣāt*) in this type are as follows:

The first type: The exception "*istithnā'*" (إستثناء)[261] limits the general provision with a preposition like except "*illā*" (إلا), but "*faqat*" (فقط) as in the verse: "*and be not averse to writing it (whether it is) small or large, with the time of its falling due; this is more equitable in* *the sight of Allah and assures greater accuracy in testimony, and the nearest (way) that you may not entertain doubts (afterwards), except when it is ready merchandise which you give and take among yourselves from hand to hand, then there is no blame on you in not writing it down; and have witnesses when you barter with one another*".[262] The expression 'be it small or large' includes all contracts; but the exception 'except when it is ready merchandise which you give and take among yourselves from hand to hand' excludes contracts where goods are transferred from hand to hand. Therefore, the general indication 'be it small or large' has been specified, and it includes only merchandise contracts where goods are not transferred from and to hand, and these contracts have to be written down.

Scholars have different opinion on the matter[263] that when an exception comes after a few joined sentences, whether it affects all of them or only the last one. This can be exemplified by the verse: "*And those who accuse free women then do not bring four witnesses, flog them, (giving) eighty stripes, and do not admit any evidence from them ever; and these it is that are the transgressors*" and "*Except those who repent after this and act aright, for surely Allah is Forgiving, Merciful.*".[264]

The exception here follows there joined sentences. It may cause different juridical implication, depending on whether it affects all the sentences or only the last one. In responds to this the majority of the scholars maintain that the exception affects all the sentences because this is apparent, and the opposite would need to be proved. Thus, if those who accuse unjustly repent, their status will be restored, their testimony will be accepted and they will not be considered disobedient afterwards. On the other hand, Abū Ḥanīfah maintains that the exception affects the last sentence alone because this is the only certainty.[265] Consequently, such people will not be considered disobedient afterwards, but their testimony will be rejected forever.[266]

The second type: The condition "*sharṭ*" (شرط) may specify a general indication, as it is explored in the following example: "*And* *you shall have half of what your wives leave if they have no child*".[267] This verse prescribes the share of the husband in the estate of his deceased wife. When the first part of the text is taken into consideration as "*And you shall have half of what your wives leave*" it would indicate that the general indication implies that the husband should take a half in all circumstances. However, the second part of the text "if they have no child" with the condition it is naturally subjected to his wife who has no child. Therefore, this condition has specified the general provision.

The third type: The attribute "*ṣifah*" (صفة) may specify the general provision, if it is literally expressed and attached to that which is described as it is stated in the *Qur'ān*:

> "*And whoever among you has not within his power ampleness of means to marry free believing women, then (he may marry) of those whom your right hands possess from among your believing maidens*".[268]

In this text maids is specified by an adjective to include only the believing ones and exclude all others.

The fourth type: The extent of application "*ghāyah*" (غاية) which is signified by articles "*ḥattā, ilā*" (الي, حتي) that limit the extent of application, may specify general provisions. It may be illustrated with the following verse in the *Qur'ān*:

> "*And they ask you about menstruation. Say: It is a discomfort; therefore keep aloof from the women during the menstrual discharge and do not go near them until they have become clean; then when they have cleansed themselves, go in to them as Allah has commanded you*".[269]

The first part of the text '*and do not go near them*' provides a general provision indicating that it is not allowed to go near to them at all. However, the second part 'until they have become clean' specifies the time until when the general provision is applicable.

The extent of application can be illustrated by another verse in the

Qur'ān: "*O you who believe! when you rise up to prayer, wash your faces and your hands up to the elbows*".[270]

This text first prescribes the washing of the hands and faces without restriction: '*wash your faces and your hands*'. Since there is no restriction, it indicates general meaning. However, it is limited by 'up to the elbows'. With the second part of the text the limitless of the area is specified and also clarified.

The specifying proofs (al-takhṣīṣ) according to Ḥanafīs[271]

As we have mentioned earlier *Ḥanafīs* defined the specification "*al-takhṣīṣ*" (التخصيص) as limitation of the general provision to some of its subjects by an independent and chronologically joined proof.[272] According to them, the proofs of specification are of three types:

a. Reason,

b. Custom and habits,

c. An authoritative text "*an-naṣṣ*" (النص) which is independent and chronologically joined to the general.

The value of specific proof (al-khāṣṣ)

The scholars are in agreement that specific "*al-khāṣṣ*" (الخاص) of the *Qur'ān* and of the *Sunnah* are definitive. There is no conflict according to the majority of scholars since the general "*al-'āmm*" (العام) is speculative as a whole, whether before or after specification (التخصيص). Therefore the effect of specific (الخاص) is that it remains in force, and action upon it is required because there is no contradiction between definitive and speculative. However, for the *Ḥanafīs*, the general (العام) and the specific (الخاص) are definitive in the first place, but when the general is partially specified, it becomes speculative in respect of the part which still remains unspecified; hence it will be treated as speculative "*ẓannī*" (ظني) and would be susceptible to further specification by another speculative (ظني).[273] Therefore *Ḥanafīs* accept that there is conflict between the general (العام) and the specific (الخاص) because of their indications since they are equal in the sense that both of them are definitive "*qaṭ'ī*" (قطعي). Consequently, the effect of specific (الخاص) in Islamic law is that it remains in force as obligatory (الخاص) and action upon it is required which must be implemented.

The Homonym (mushtarak)

Linguistically homonym "*mushtarak*" (المشترك) is a word which denotes more than one meaning. Imām Shāfi'ī and some other scholars see that the homonym is a kind of general (عام). In fact, these two concepts are not having the same nature since the homonym inherently possesses more than one meaning, however, it is not the same for the general (العام). For example, a word "'*ayn*" (عين) in Arabic language, has many meanings such as eye, gold, spy, spring etc. In the same way, the word "*qurū'*" (قروء) in the following verse mentioned in the *Qur'ān* "*And the divorced women should keep themselves in waiting for three courses*"[274] has two meanings, namely the clean period between two menstruations "*ṭuhr*" (طهر) and menstruation "*ḥayḍ*" (حيض) period. The first meaning of the word "*qurū'*" (قروء) was taken by *Shāfi'īs*, *Mālikīs*, whereas the second meaning was taken by the *Ḥanafīs*, the *Ḥanbalīs* and the *Zaydīs*.[275]

A word "*mavlā*" (المولي) can be given as a homonym word because it donates both slave and lord. It is set for denoting for both meanings.[276]

The Causes for Homonym

There are many ways to be created of homonym words in language. These are the some of the ways for homonyms:

1. Cultural differences among Arab tribes: the plurality of meanings in a homonym may be because of the usage of

different Arab tribes. One word may be used by some for one meaning and it is used by others for different meaning.

However, the homonym "*al-mushtarak*" (المشترك) which occurs in the *Qur'ān* and the *Sunnah* denotes one meaning alone since the Lawgiver does not intended more than one meaning for a word at any given time. Exceptionally, the *Shāfi'īs* and some *Mu'tazilah* maintain that the absence of any indication in support of one of the two or more meanings of a homonym (المشترك), all may be upheld simultaneously so long as these words do not contradict one another. For example a word hand "*yad*" occurs in the *Qur'ān* "*And (as for) the man who steals and the woman who steals, cut off their hands*".[277] The word "hand" in this verse means from the tip of the fingers up to the wrist, or up to the elbow, or even up to the shoulder; on the other hand it means left or right hand. However, the scholars have agreed on the right hand up to the wrist.[278]

To give another example, the word *nakaḥa* (نَكَحَ) indicates both marriage and sexual intercourse in the context of a *prohibitory* order in the *Qur'ān* "*And marry not woman whom your fathers married, except what has already passed*".[279] The word *nakaḥa* (نَكَحَ) is a homonym. The *Ḥanafīs*, the *Ḥanbalīs*, al-Awzā'ī and others have upheld the meaning of sexual intercourse, whereas the *Shāfi'īs* and the *Mālikīs* have upheld the meaning of marriage. Therefore, the provision (*ḥukm*) of it also defers. According to the *Ḥanafīs*, a woman who has had sexual intercourse with a man is forbidden to his children and grandchildren; a mere contract of marriage, without consummation, would thus not amount to a prohibition in this case. Nevertheless, according to the *Shāfi'īs* the text under discussion only refers to the contract of marriage. Thus, a woman who has entered a contract of marriage with one's father or grandfather is unlawful for one to marry regardless as to whether the marriage had been consummated or not.[280]

2. A term may be set for a common meaning among the two different meanings. Due to the common meaning this term can be suitable to use for both meaning. In the course of time, people forget the common meaning and they accept it as a homonym term. For example, as it is mentioned in the *Qur'ān* "*And the divorced women should keep themselves in waiting for three courses*"[281] the word "*al-qurū'*" (القرء) denotes both meaning in the dictionary menstruations (*ḥayḍ*) and clean periods between menstruations (*ṭuhr*). As the courses (*qurū'*) is a homonym meaning which consists of both menstruations (*ḥayḍ*) and the clean periods between menstruations (*ṭuhr*), the scholars went different opinions, Imām Abū Ḥanīfah and Ibn Ḥanbal have adopted the meaning of menstruations (*ḥayḍ*), whereas Imām Shāfiʿī and Mālik have adopted the meaning of the clean periods between menstruations (*ṭuhr*). Consequently their respective *ijtihād* leads them to correspondingly different results.[282]
3. A term first may be put for a meaning, later the same term by a kind of relationship may be used for a different meaning through a metaphorical meaning. In the course of time this usage becomes a customary meaning. Therefore, this usage of the word can be used later both as literal meanings. Similarly, if a term has two meanings, one literal and the other juridical, later on due to the usage of the juridical meaning it prevails over the other. For example, a word *ṣalāt* (صلاة) and *ṭalāq* (طلاق), each of them possesses a literal meaning that is *ṣalāt* for 'supplication' and *ṭalāq* for 'release'. Consequently, the word *ṣalāt* would be held to refer to a particular form of worship, and *ṭalāq* would mean 'dissolution of marriage', when they are used in a juridical context.[283]

The value of the homonym (al-mushtarak)

The original principle in words is not to be homonym which was accepted by the scholars. However, if there is a possibility of having both meaning, that is homonym and not homonym, the possibility of not to be homonym one is preferable. Nevertheless, if the quality of homonym is obvious then none of the indications of the term would be preferred unless there is evidence to suggest otherwise, such as the word "*al-qurū*'" (القرء) which denotes both meaning in the dictionary menstruations (*ḥayḍ*) and clean periods between menstruations (*ṭuhr*). As the courses (*qurū*') is a homonym meaning which consists of both menstruations (*ḥayḍ*) and the clean periods between menstruations (*ṭuhr*).

As the Lawgiver does not intend to uphold more than one of the different meanings of a homonym at any given time, in order to determine which of the two or more meanings of the homonym (المشترك) is to be upheld in a particular locution, reference is usually made to the context and circumstances in which it occurs. If it is a locution that pertains to the *Sharī'ah,* then determining the precise purport of its words must also take into consideration the general principles and objectives of the *Sharī'ah.* The homonym (المشترك) is in the nature of difficult "*mushkil*" (مشكل) and it is for the *mujtahid* to determine its correct meaning by means of research and *ijtihād*; it is his duty to do so in the event where homonym constitutes the basis of a judicial order.[284]

The Allegorical Interpretation (al-ta'wīl)

As for the other sciences, Muslim scholars established substantial methods and principles for interpreting the text of Allah and the *ḥadīth* of the Prophet (ṣ). For the concept of *ta'wīl* also they have certain methods and specific conditions for scientifically acceptable interpretations or *ta'wīl.* Not all the interpretation can be acceptable as the Prophet (ṣ) warned the scholars to rely on sole opinions on the interpretation of the texts: The Prophet (ṣ) said: "He who speaks about the *Qur'ān* according to his own opinion is wrong even if he says what is right."[285]

Linguistically *ta'wīl* (التأويل) refers to interpretation, explanation, construction.[286] It is also defined as "*ta'wīl* is interpretation, reference, source and destiny."[287] It may also be defined as such "turning a verse of the *Qur'ān* from its apparent meaning to a meaning which it bears, or admits, when the latter is agreeable with the *Qur'ān* and the *Sunnah*." For instance, interpreting the following verse in the *Qur'ān*: "*He brings forth the living from the dead and He is the bringer forth of the dead from the living*"[288] as "*He (Allah) produces the bird from the egg*" is a *tafsīr*; on the other hand if it is interpreted as "*He (Allah) produces the believer from the unbeliever*" or "*the knowing from the ignorant*," is considered *ta'wīl* (التأويل). Besides these meanings, *ta'wīl* also means "explaining the meaning of that which is *mutashābih* (equivocal/ambiguous). Therefore it is needed to be interpreted for better clarification.[289]

Technically, in regards to the science of *uṣūl al-fiqh*, the meaning of *ta'wīl* became more focused and distinct from *tafsīr*. The scholars' definition of *ta'wīl* falls within the scope of "abandoning' the apparent meaning of the word for the suspected and non-preferable meaning, by way of a proof which stands in favour of the non-preferable meaning. Because *tafsīr* is an explanation of meaning by authoritative assertion, while *ta'wīl* is based on supposition and uncertainty since some of the scholars hold the view that *ta'wīl* may be produced simply based on personal opinion and vice-versa in *tafsīr*.[290] In other words, *ta'wīl* is departing from the word's essential, literal and apparent meaning towards another, possible meaning based on a proof, which suggests that it is like adopting a particular meaning from the general, as similar to specification (التخصيص). Therefore, *ta'wīl* goes beyond the literal meaning and reads hidden meanings into texts. Unlike *tafsīr*, which aims to explain authoritative texts within the limits of literal meanings.

Conditions for allegorical interpretation (al-ta'wīl)[291]

Muslim scholars have suggested some conditions for *ta'wīl* in order to avoid misinterpretation of the *Qur'ān* and the *Sunnah*. A *ta'wīl* will be accepted if the following preconditions are fulfilled, it is rejected otherwise.

1. A word (*lafẓ*) or text must be open to *ta'wīl* which accepts interpretations. For instance, according to the *Ḥanafīs* certain types of words are open to *ta'wīl* such as the manifest (*ẓāhir*) and explicit (*naṣṣ*), on the other hand to the *Shāfi'īs* the explicit (*naṣṣ*) and to the both of them, the general (*'āmm*) and the absolute (*muṭlaq*). However, the unequivocal (*mufassar*) and perspicuous (*muḥkam*) do not accept interpretation since they are obviously clear words. Thus its interpretation will be invalid and will be totally rejected.
2. A meaning that is interpreted must be a preferable meaning which is indicated either by the literal apparent meaning (*manṭūq*) or the implicit meaning (*mafhūm*). If, however, it is not consistent with the Arabic language, even with its metaphorical, customary usage or the method of the Lawgiver, is rejected naturally. Thus, so long as adopting a particular meaning from the general (*ḥaml al-'āmm 'alā al-khāṣṣ*) is acceptable if supported by a reliable proof, because the general meaning in reality assumes possible specification and restriction; adopting a metaphor (*majāz*) is acceptable if supported by a reliable proof, because the words are open to metaphorical meaning. For instance, 'transaction' (*bay'*) is transferred from its apparent meaning to a meaning of gift, because a proof suggests that this particular operation was in fact a transfer of ownership free of charge, this would be an acceptable *ta'wīl*, since the word *bay'* is open to that

interpretation. On the contrary, if a word (*lafẓ*) is not supported by a meaning that indicates such interpretation (*ta'wīl*), it will be however, rejected. In order to be acceptable, it must be consistent with its usages. For example, if someone interprets an animal like camel to a meaning of a goat or sheep is a false interpretation and it is not allowed.

3. The interpretation (*ta'wīl*) beyond the obvious import has to be supported by a correct and reliable proof such as the *Qur'ān*, the *Sunnah*, consensus of opinion (*ijmā'*), analogy (*qiyās*), or another principle of Islamic law. Thus, if there is no any reliable proof suggests other meanings, the apparent meaning of the text is implemented.
4. Lastly, a person who exercises *ijtihād* for the interpretation (*ta'wīl*) of a text must be qualified one who is a competent scholar to be able to interpret and it is consistent with the rules of the language, customary and juridical usages as well as the principles and the essence of Islamic law since no-one is allowed to talk about the *Qur'ān* without knowledge as the Prophet (ṣ) said: "He who speaks about the *Qur'ān* according to his own opinion is wrong even if he says what is right."[292]

As a conclusion, the interpretation (*ta'wil*) is accepted and it becomes a valid basis for judicial decisions and a strong rational part of personal effort (*ijtihād*) so long as it rests on proofs and principles, however, it is rejected otherwise.

Types of allegorical interpretation (al-ta'wīl)[293]

According to the scholars of *uṣūl*, the interpretation (*ta'wīl*) can be three types.

1. Close interpretation "*ta'wīl qarīb*" (قريب)
2. Far interpretation "*ta'wīl ba'īd*" (بعيد)
3. Impossible interpretation "*mustaḥīl*" (مستحيل)

1. Close interpretation "*ta'wīl qarīb*" (قريب): It is not necessary to provide a strong proof for this kind of interpretation (*ta'wīl*). A minimal proof, instead of the apparent meaning is acceptable. For example, the *Qur'ān* states:

   "O you who believe! when you get up for prayer, wash your faces, and your hands (and arms) to the elbows".[294]

   The word "to get up" "*al-qiyām*" (القيام) is interpreted to the possible meaning-namely, the 'intention' to perform prayer, not in its literal meaning (to get up). This can be comprehended by a spontaneous understanding of the verse and logically it comes to mind easily. Thus, the ablution must be taken before the prayer. Taking it after the prayer will not serve the intention of the Lawgiver since it is a preparation act for the prayer. Therefore, it is made a precondition for the prayer and without it no valid prayer can be performed.
2. Far interpretation "*ta'wīl ba'īd*" (بعيد):[295] It is necessary to provide strong proof for this kind of interpretation (*ta'wīl*) in order to be acceptable because its meaning hardly comes to the mind. It refers to an acceptance of a non-preferable meaning which is far from possible meaning. This can be illustrated in the following verse of the *Qur'ān*: "*and wipe your heads and your feet to the ankles*".[296] From this verse, scholars went on extremely different interpretation because of different reading of the verse in washing the two feet. Two readings can be extracted from it which is based on the Arabic rule that what follows the conjunction '*waw*' (و). These two readings (declensions) were transmitted (in the accusative *arjulakum* (أَرْجُلَكُمْ) and in the genitive *arjulikum* (أَرْجُلِكُمْ).[297] If the scholar "*mujtahid*" (مجتهد) relies on the genitive declension, he can interpret it in the following meanings: In the first reading it indicates that the feet should be washed, while the second reading it indicates that wiping them is enough. However, the

majority of scholars maintained that this is a far interpretation. The scholars supported their claim with various proofs from the tradition of the Prophet (ṣ) and its linguistic usage. Logically, they maintained that 'your feet' "*arjulakum*" (أَرْجُلَكُمْ) is couple with 'your hands' "*aydiyakum*" (أَيْدِيَكُمْ). As the latter is accusative, the earlier also be in the form of accusative. What is coupled to it must also be in the same form, because of the Arabic rule that what follows the conjunction '*waw*' (و) takes the same case as that to which it is followed.[298]

3. Impossible interpretation "*mustaḥīl*" (مستحيل). This kind of interpretation is an expression which is not accepted by any source of Islamic law and any methods of analysis which lead to impossibility to accept it. As Imām Ghazālī expressed, "Every interpretation which removes and eliminates a text or its part is invalid,"[299] thus, this kind of *ta'wīl* (interpretation) is not acceptable which is invalid.

Some examples on ta'wīl (allegorical interpretation)

Scholars disagreed on some kind of interpretation due to the strength of some legal proofs and their reliability such as whether it is based on the narration of one Companion only (*khabar al-wāḥid*) or analogy or should be used to restrict a general meaning to defer a particular indication (*ḥaml al-'āmm 'alā al-khāṣṣ*) or to restrict the absolute (*ḥaml al-muṭlaq 'alā al-muqayyad*). Therefore, interpretation (*ta'wīl*) may be based on the main sources[300], or any secondary sources.[301] The source may make the interpretation (*ta'wīl*) valid or invalid, for instance, the ruling on the legitimacy of using the skin of a dead animal whether it is permissible or not. The *Qur'ān* states:

> "*Forbidden to you are: dead meat, blood, the flesh of swine*".[302]

This verse apparently, in general sense, indicates that using the skin of a dead animal is forbidden under all circumstances, whether the skin is tanned or not. This understanding is originated from the general meaning of the world 'the dead' "*al-maytatu*" (الْمَيْتَةُ). However, it may be possible that the tanned skin is not meant by this general meaning because the obvious prohibition refers to 'the dead' (الْمَيْتَةُ). A tradition narrated by Ibn 'Abbās, the Prophet (ṣ) said: "When a skin is tanned it becomes clean."[303] According to this *hadith*, the skin of a dead animal is permissible. So long as the type of skin is not mentioned or restricted, it included the skin of a dead animal. In addition to that, another *ḥadīth* related to a dead sheep granted to the freed slave of Maymūnah supports the claim. The Prophet (ṣ) said: "Why have you not taken its skin, tanned it and benefited from it." They answered that it was dead. He replied: "What is forbidden is to eat it."[304] These two traditions clearly indicate that tanned skin is not under the prohibition and therefore, eating of 'the dead' (الْمَيْتَةُ) animal is forbidden. The scholars excluded leather from the general meaning of the verse since the skin is not normally eaten; it is naturally excluded from the prohibition.[305]

Another example is the *ḥadīth* of the Prophet (ṣ) on giving *zakāt*, he said "For every forty grazing sheep one is due" (فِي كُلِّ أَرْبَعِينَ شَاةً شَاةٌ).[306] *Ḥanafī* scholars have interpreted the word sheep (شَاةٌ) according to the wisdom behind it since the Lawgiver's intention has to be comprehended in every issues, the meaning of the sheep (شَاةٌ) here is its value. The wisdom behind the legislation is reason "*'illah*" (علة) for *ta'wīl* the proof on which it relies is taken. Although the apparent meaning of this *ḥadīth* is that one sheep would have to be given in every forty sheep, *Ḥanafī* scholars maintained that the monetary values of sheep may also be given instead. They relied on the practise of Mu'ādh Ibn Jabal in Yemen since the monetary values of barley and maize were collected as cloth instead, because there was a large amount of clothes available among the Yemeni population. To be given *zakāt* from cloth is easier for them. On the other hand, in order to meet the needs of the Companions in Madinah, to be taken of cloths would be more helpful.[307] Therefore, *Ḥanafīs* considered that the wisdom behind the legislation of the *zakāt* as to be given the value of the sheep may even be more beneficial to serve the need of the poor than the animal itself. Thus, either a sheep itself or value of it as money can be given.

The value of ta'wīl

In terms of personal opinion, the usage of allegorical interpretation (التأويل) seems to be sort of *ijtihād*. As it is documented that the majority of scholars maintain that *ta'wīl* can be a rigorously rational part of *ijtihād*, as long as useful it fulfils preconditions in interpreting the source of Islamic law. Although the majority accept it as a valid act in Islamic law, the *Ẓāhirī madhhab* eschews all kind of interpretations beyond the obvious meanings, to name a few, Dāvud al-Ẓāhirī and his followers[308] rejected it entirely.

They maintain that all source-texts are clear and therefore no need to interpretation beyond their obvious meanings. They do not abandon an apparent meaning unless another apparent meaning from the *Qur'ān*, the *Sunnah* or *ijmā'* suggests otherwise, because language is created by Allah as a way of conveying meaning. With that reason they even rejected analogy (*qiyās*).[309] Consequently, the meaning determined through proper *ta'wīl* is an acceptable ruling therefore it is obligatory to adhere it. However, it is not an obsolete determination on the ruling since it is based on an opinion which might consist of error and right.

Based on the usage of the words (bi-i'tibāri isti'māl al-lafẓ fil-ma'nā)

Introduction

The usage of words takes part in the authentic text especially in the

Qur'ān differently. The effort to understand these words helps to comprehend the intention of the Lawgiver. The different usage of the words indicates the beauty and artistic values of the text. A word may be used in its literal "*al-ḥaqīqah*" (الحقيقة) sense, which is, for its primary meaning, or it may be used in metaphorical "*al-majāz*" (مجاز) sense, that is secondary meaning. The primary meaning of a word is taken in its literal sense so long as it is not used in a metaphorical meaning. When its metaphorical meaning is used, its primary meaning is transferred to a secondary meaning.[310] Hermeneutically, knowing the indication of a world suggests understanding the connotative meaning of a word. The allusive "*al-kināyah*" (كناية) meaning of a word cannot be comprehended easily without recourse to primary and secondary meaning of a word. In regards to this, the literal and the metaphorical meanings have a great deal of connections.[311]

In sum, the words, from the view point of the usage "*al-isti'māl*" (الإستعمال), are classified into four types: 1. The literal (*al-ḥaqīqah*) (الحقيقة); 2. The metaphorical (*al-majāz*) (المجاز); 3. The clear (*al-ṣarīḥ*) (الصريح); 4. The allusive (*al-kināyah*) (الكناية).

We shall now briefly explain them in the following pages.

1. The literal (al-ḥaqīqah)

Linguistically, the literal (الحقيقة) means the exact or primary meaning of a word. It is a word which is used in its either dictionary meaning (الحقيقة اللغوية), such as 'lion' for that animal, 'woman' for the female gender of the human being, 'sun' for that substance etc; or *shar'ī* literal (الحقيقة الشرعية), such as prayer (الصلاة), pilgrimage (الحج), marriage (الزواج), *zakāt* (الزكاة) etc.; or customary literal (الحقيقة العرفية), such as car (السيارة), animal (الدابة).[312]

Every type of literal words occurs in the *Qur'ān*, and each of them conveys their respective meanings. For instance, in the *Qur'ān* "*kill not your children on a plea of want*"[313] the statement "لَا تَقْتُلُوا" carries its literal meaning. Thus as it is mentioned above, the literal may be used, according to the context where it occurs, into three types:

a. Dictionary Literal (*al-ḥaqīqah al-lughawīyah*)

b. Juridical Literal (*al-ḥaqīqah al-shar'īyah*)

c. Customary Literal (*al-ḥaqīqah al-'urfīyah*),

a. **Dictionary Literal (*al-ḥaqīqah al-lughawīyah*)** is a word which is used in its dictionary meaning that is the exact or primary meaning of a word such as 'lion' for that animal, and 'man' for the male gender of the human being, 'sun' (الشمس), 'moon' (القمر), 'star' (النجم) for that substances etc. These words were given to the known meanings. Thus, if they are used in these meanings they are called literal used in dictionary meaning.

b. **Juridical Literal (*al-ḥaqīqah al-shar'īyah*)** is defined as a word which is used for a juridical meaning that the Lawgiver has given it in the first place such as prayer (الصلاة) which literally means 'supplication', however it is, in its well-established juridical sense, a particular form of worship; the word *zakāt* (الزكاة) literally means 'purification', however, in its juridical sense, it denotes a particular form of charity in Islam;[314] pilgrimage (الحج), marriage (الزواج), etc

c. **Customary Literal (*al-ḥaqīqah al-'urfīyah*)** is a word which is used in its customary sense. It occurs in the two varieties of general and specific. If a word is used in its customary sense and it is absolutely common among the people, then the word is called 'customary literal general' such as the word (الدابة), in Arabic language, indicates 'all living beings that walk on the face of the earth', however, it has been assigned a different meaning by general custom that is 'an animal walking on four legs'. On the other hand, if the customary literal is used for a meaning that is common to a particular profession or group, the customary literal is called specific custom such as the grammatical sense of Arabic language, a word in nominative case (حالة الرفع) and accusative case (حالة النصب), prepositions (حروف الجر), passive voice (المجهول) have each acquired a technical meaning that is common among grammarians and experts in the language.

2. The Metaphorical (al-majāz)

The metaphorical (المجاز) is a form of speech in which a word or phrase is applied to something or action to which it is not literally applicable due to a connection (علاقة) or a context (قرينة) that its meaning is transferred to other meaning. It is an implied meaning rather than a literal meaning. Thus, the metaphorical usage of a word, term or a speech consists of a transfer from the literal to a connected meaning. For example, if a person says in his will "I bequeath my property to my offspring." Primarily, the word 'offspring' (اولاد) means sons and daughter, not grandchildren. In that respect, for applying it to grandchildren is a secondary usage of it and therefore it is metaphorically used which is not original meaning of its usage.[315]

The metaphorical (المجاز) usage also occurs commonly in the *Qur'ān*. For example, Allah says in the *Qur'ān* "*He (Allah) sends down for you sustenance from heaven*"[316] which means Allah sends rain which causes the production of food. Another example is that the *Qur'ān* recites "*Allah is the light of the heavens and the earth*"[317]; "*whenever they kindle a fire for war Allah extinguished it*"[318]. The statements "the light of the heavens"; "extinguished," which are both used in the sense of metaphorical meaning.[319]

Value of the literal and the metaphorical

If a word is simultaneously used in both literal and metaphorical sense, the literal one will prevail because "It is a fundamental principle that words shall be construed literally."[320] Words are used in their literal sense in normal situations. However, if there is a connection or context which prevents to understand its literal meaning then its metaphorical meaning will be applied, "When the literal meaning cannot be applied, the metaphorical sense may be used."[321] Therefore, these two concept are connected each other. As the two, literal and metaphorical occur in the *Qur'ān* they convey their respective meanings. In a position where a word convey both a literal and a metaphorical meaning simultaneously however, if the later is dominant, it is most likely to prevail over the former. For example, the word *ṭalāq* (طلق) literally means 'release' or 'removal of restriction', be it from the tie of marriage, slavery, or ownership, etc. However, when it comes in the *Qur'ān* "*And when you divorce women and they reach their prescribed time*",[322] in which the juridical meaning has become totally dominant which is 'divorce', unless there is any other evidence to suggest otherwise, the dominant meaning is most likely to prevail.[323]

3. The Clear (al-ṣarīḥ)

The Clear (الصريح) is a form of a word or statement in which it is such that it clearly discloses the speaker's intention clearly either of literal or metaphorical usages. For example for the usage of literal "I have sold" (بعت); and for the metaphorical "Ask at the town" (وَاسْأَلِ الْقَرْيَةَ) can be given. In the both examples in which the meanings are obviously clear. Intentions of the speakers in such situations are not considered since the meanings have clear indications, for instance, in a sales contract in which one of the parties says 'I sold it' and the other one says 'I bought it', theirs intentions are not considered since usage of the words are clear and have clear indications, therefore, without seeking their intention the sale contract is concluded.[324] In another example, if a person says 'I swear Allah I will not eat from this tree' (والله لا آكل من هذه الشجرة). Although this sentence is a metaphorical meaning, its indication is very clear according to the customary usage. Thus, the oath is converted from the literal meaning to metaphorical meaning that is 'the fruit of the tree' (ثمرها).[325]

Value of the clear (al-ṣarīḥ)

The value (حكم) of the clear is proven without recourse to intention. It will be the same value, whether the speaker intents the clear meaning or not, the clear meaning is taken into the consideration. Intentions of the speaker in such situations are not considered since the meanings have clear indications, for instance, the word of divorce (طلق) since it is set by the Lawgiver for a specific purpose, the intention of the speaker is not important. So long as it is uttered, the clear meaning of divorce (طلق) will take action, if the condition of the validity of divorce is fulfilled.[326]

4. The Allusive (al-kināyah)

Literally, it is a word that you speak something and you mean something else. Technically, it is a form of speech in which the intended meaning is hidden according to its use; it is not understood except via context "*qarīnah*" (قرينة) whether the word is literal or metaphorical. The speech does not clearly disclose the intention of its speaker and it may combine the both meaning of the literal and the metaphorical. For example, supposing that a man addresses his wife and tells her 'start counting' (اعتدي) or 'you are forbidden to me' (انتِ حرام لي), or 'join your relatives (الحقي بأهلك). These phrases are called allusive (الكناية) from divorce (الطلاق).[327] Another example, when a person wishes to disclose in his friend in front of others, he might say "I met your friend and spoke to him about the matter that you know." The sentence does not give a clear meaning about the speaker's intention. The structure is a combination of the literal and the allusive in which all the words used to convey their literal senses. Thus, it may imply something since it does not disclose the speaker's purpose clearly.[328]

Value of the allusive (al-kināyah)

The value (حكم) will not take place unless there is evidence to show that the speech comes with intention. Therefore, even if a husband tells his wife(s) 'start counting' (اعتدي) or 'you are forbidden to me' (انتِ حرام لي), or 'join your relatives (الحقي بأهلك), no divorce will take place unless there is evidence or indication to show that the husband intended a divorce. Regarding the phrase 'start counting' (اعتدي), it literally means taking a record of numbers, in order to be taken account it must be used in the meaning of counting the days of the waiting period of divorce (طلق).[329]

Conclusion

Suffice it to point out here that the interpretation of the words which is based on the usage of words (إستعمال) has been divided into four types, the literal (الحقيقة) which was of three types, dictionary literal (الحقيقة اللغوية), juridical literal (الحقيقة الشرعية) and customary literal (الحقيقة العرفية); the metaphorical (المجاز); the clear (الصريح) and allusive (الكناية). Nevertheless, it has to be emphasied here that legal matters which require certainty, for instance offences entailing a capital punishments (الحدود), cannot be established by language which is not plan, "Capital punishments are removed by doubt" (الحدود تدرأ بالشبهات).[330] As it is indicated in *Majallah* "The judge must abstain from any act during the trial likely to arouse suspicion or cause misunderstanding, such as receiving one of the parties alone in his house, or retiring with one of them with his hand or his eye or his head, or speaking to one of them secretly or in a language not understood by the other."[331] If a person admits to such crime in an allusive word, he is not liable to punishment.[332]

Interpretation of the text based on the degree of clarity and ambiguity of indication of words (bi-i'tibāri dalālat al-lafẓ 'alāl-ma'nā wāḍiḥan aw ghayri wāḍiḥan)

Introduction

The words, from the view point of the degree of clarity or obscurity of indication, are divided into the two main categories: Clarity of indication "*wāḍiḥ ad-dalālah*" (واضح الدلالة) and obscurity of indication "*ghayr wāḍiḥ ad-dalālah*" (غير واضح الدلالة). A clear word conveys an idea which is intelligible without recourse to any interpretation (*ta'wīl*), and therefore, a ruling (*ḥukm*) which is derived from a clear word constitutes the basis of obligation. It is a self- sufficient text which needs no recourse to extraneous evidence. The clear words: 1. The manifest "*al-ẓāhir*" (الظاهر), 2. The explicit "*al-naṣṣ*" (النص), 3. The unequivocal, explained "*al-mufassar*" (المفسر), 4. The perspicuous/firm "*al-muḥkam*" (المحكم). These four types are arranged in a ranking which starts with the least clear to the highest in respect of clarity which means the manifest (الظاهر) is the least clear and the perspicuous/firm (المحكم) is the highest clear.

Shāfi'ī scholars, on the other hand, have different approach to clear (*wāḍiḥ*) words from that of the *Ḥanafīs*. They divided clear words into two categories only: the manifest (الظاهر) and the explicit (النص). As it is indicated above that *Ḥanafīs* divided clear words (واضح) into four categories which may suggest that their division is clearer and more detailed.

On the other hand the words, from the viewpoint of the degree of ambiguity in their meaning, are classified into four types which begin with the least ambiguous and ends by the most ambiguous in the range. An unclear word does not convey an idea which is not intelligible without recourse to interpretation. It conveys ambiguity and incompleteness, due to the ambiguity, it requires clarification and it cannot constitute the basis of action. It can only be completed through external evidences since the text itself is lacking and failing to convey a complete meaning without recourse to external evidence. The unclear words (غير واضح): 1. The obscure "*al-khafī*" (الخفي), 2. The difficult "*al-mushkil*" (المشكل), 3. The ambivalent "*al-mujmal*" (المجمل), 4. The intricate "*al-mutashābih*" (المتشابه).

We shall now explain each of these concepts individually in the following pages.

Ḥanafī and Shāfi'ī Approaches to Clear (wāḍiḥ) Words

The Manifest (al-ẓāhir)

Linguistically the manifest "*al-ẓāhir*" (الظاهر) refers to plan, manifest, apparent, evident. It is derived from a word 'to appear' "*ẓahara*" (ظهر) which indicates to become clear and evident after being concealed.[333] It is a word which has a clear meaning and yet it is open to interpretation (*ta'wīl*) since the meaning that it conveys is not in harmony with the context in which it occurs. For instance, if a speaker says "I saw a lion," the word 'lion' is a clear word to understand its meaning, however, the speaker might have meant a brave man instead. Therefore, it is open to interpretation since the meaning that it conveys a clear meaning is not in harmony with the context in which it occurs.[334]

Technically, the *Ḥanafī* scholars have provided various definitions for the manifest (الظاهر). Imām Sarakhsī (d. 490/1096) defines it "What can be understood by pure hearing without thinking. It precedes the mind because it reflects the meaning by which it is employed."[335] He excludes from his definition the use of 'reason' and analysis in the definition of *ẓāhir*.[336] Dabbūsī (d. 430/1039) defines it as "whatever becomes apparent to a listener by his hearing only."[337] Bazdawī's (d. 482/1089) definition is "It is a name for any speech the aim of which became apparent to a listener by its wording"[338] in which he concentrates on the 'wording' (*bi-sīghatih*) as the defining element. According Ibn al-Humām (d. 861/1457) the manifest (الظاهر) shows its linguistic meaning automatically,[339] while Naṣafī (d. 710/1310) sees it as the name for speech whose aim is apparent to a listener by its wording.[340]

The above definitions show that *Ḥanafī* scholars appear to have the similar opinion on the concept of the manifest (الظاهر), while, *Shāfi'īs*, however, it provides alternative meanings, such as a word that is given as a name to many subjects or a word with a shared meaning (*lafẓ mushtarak*). Ghazālī maintained that *ẓāhir* is open to interpretation, stating that given meaning for *ẓāhir* which is more likely to be understood, however, the understanding is unspecified.[341] In addition to this, it may also be specified and fixed meaning which excludes another meaning that is *mubayyan* or *naṣṣ*. Whatever meaning it has, if none of the meaning has priority over the others, the expression is named as *mujmal*, and nevertheless, if one takes priority then it became *ẓāhir*.[342] Al-Āmidī highlights that *ẓāhir* indicates its meaning according to the literal or customary meaning while supposing other less expected meanings.[343] While Taftāzānī stating on *ẓāhir* as: "What signifies its meaning clearly"[344], Al-Anṣārī defined that *ẓāhir* is what signifies an indefinite meaning.[345]

The concept can be explored by the following examples:

First example: The Lawgiver states in the *Qur'ān*: "*Those who swallow down usury cannot arise except as one whom Shaiṭān has prostrated by (his) touch does rise. That is because they say, trading is only like usury; and Allah has allowed trading and forbidden usury.*"

The manifest (ظاهر) meaning of this verse indicates with the word 'allowed' "*ḥalla*" (حَلَّ) that trading is permissible and with the word 'forbidden' "*wa-ḥarrama*" (وَحَرَّمَ) that usury is prohibited. However, this is not the principle theme of the verse that was revealed for. The purpose for which this verse was revealed is to deny what some people claimed that trading and usury are alike.[346] It was revealed to show the extreme differences between these two trading and usury with the manifest meaning "Allah has allowed trading and forbidden usury" in which these two concepts are differentiated clearly without recourse to any kind of evidences internally or external (*qarīnah*).

Second example: Allah states in the *Qur'ān*: "*And if you fear that you cannot act equitably towards orphans, then marry such women as seem good to you, two and three and four; but if you fear that you will not do justice (between them), then (marry) only one or what your right hands possess*".[347]

This verse apparently explains without recourse to any external evidence that legitimate marriage is permissible. This meaning is the manifest (الظاهر) because its meaning is clear. However, this verse was not revealed for this purpose. The principal themes of this verse are polygamy is permissible and it is limited to the maximum number of four wives and it is also prohibited to men marrying more than one woman if they fear that they cannot act equitably towards orphans and the limited number of four wives justly.[348]

Third example: Allah states in the *Qur'ān*: "*O Prophet! When you do divorce women, divorce them at their prescribed periods, and count (accurately), their prescribed periods*".[349] This verse was revealed in order to explain the period during which wives may be legally divorced. Thus the manifest (الظاهر) meaning of this verse is the prescribed period of a legally divorced woman that is after the completion of the menstruation period.[350] On the other hand, this verse indicates another instruction for Muslims that the number of divorce should not be more than once in one time which was deduced from the apparent meaning that is not the principle theme of the verse. Thus it is the manifest (الظاهر).[351]

The value of manifest (al-ẓāhir)

The value of the manifest (الظاهر) is that obedience to the ruling (*ḥukm*) of the manifest (الظاهر) is strictly obligatory (*wājib*) unless there is any other evidence to suggest otherwise and therefore its obvious indications must be followed in legal reasoning because it signifies definite indication. According to the basic rules of interpretation which require that the obvious meaning of words should be applied and followed unless there is a reliable proof[352] that suggests an alternative meaning for abandoning the obvious meaning. The manifest (الظاهر) is open to interpretation (*ta'wīl*) that means it may be specified when it is general; it may be restricted and qualified when it is absolute; it may be abandoned in favour of a metaphorical meaning and it is also susceptible to abrogation which could only be possible during the time of the revelation.[353] Despite the clear meaning of the manifest (الظاهر) it is open to interpretation since it is not the principle theme of the text.

The Explicit (al-naṣṣ)

Linguistically explicit "*naṣṣ*" (نص) refers to explicit, declared, manifest; a religious legal term; text of a manuscript; the author's original text. In addition to that it refers primarily to the text of the *Qur'ān* and the *ḥadīth*.[354]

Technically, it is defined by *Ḥanafī* scholars almost the same definition such as Naṣafi (d. 710/1310) defines it as "*Naṣṣ* is that which is clearer than *ẓāhir* by virtue of the meaning of speech, not the text itself.[355] According to Dabbūsī (d. 430/1039) it is defined "It clarifies *ẓāhir* further when compared with it."[356] On the other hand, Bazdawī's (d. 482/1089) emphasises the meaning given by the speaker: "Nass is that which is clearer than *ẓāhir* because of the meaning conveyed by the speaker, not by the text itself."[357] As similar to that Sarakhsī defines the explicit (النص) from the perspective of the speaker's evidence. "It is what becomes more explicit through the evidence (*qarīnah*) given by the speaker."[358]

In addition to the technical meaning the explicit "*al-naṣṣ*" (النص) has a more general meaning which has been generally used by the scholars. In the terminology of *fiqh*, it indicates a definitive text of the ruling of the *Qur'ān* and the *Sunnah*. Therefore, when a ruling or injunction is referred to the *Qur'ān* and the *Sunnah*, it is said that this or that ruling is a *naṣṣ* (نص). However as the explicit (النص), opposed to the manifest (ظاهر), is a word or words that convey a clear meaning of the text, and it represents the principal theme of the text in which it occurs.[359]

The *Shāfi'īs'* approaches to *wāḍiḥ* is obvious that they are less clear on this matter than the *Ḥanafis*, since the *Shāfi'ī* scholars did not draw much distinction between *ẓāhir* and *naṣṣ*. As if they used two names for the same concept they have considered them within the linguistic meaning. They defined *naṣṣ* as a word the intended legal ruling of which is known individually, or by the assistance of any other factor.[360] They are the founder of the *mutakallimūn* school in *uṣūl al-fiqh*. Imām Shāfi'ī as the founder of the *madhhab* explained *naṣṣ* in his book al-*Risālah* as that which is in definite and indefinite meaning. He said: "The sum-total of what Allah has declared to His creatures in His Book, by which He invited them to worship Him in accordance with His prior decision, includes various categories. One of these is what He has declared to His creatures by '*naṣṣ*' (in the *Qur'ān*), such as the aggregate of duties (*jumal farā'id*) owed to Him: That they shall perform the prayer, pay the alms tax, perform the pilgrimage and observe the fast. And that He has forbidden disgraceful acts – both visible and hidden – and in the textual (prohibition of) adultery, (the drinking of) wine, eating (the flesh of) dead things and of blood and pork; and He has made clear to them how to perform the duty of (the major) ablution and other matters stated precisely in the *naṣṣ* (of the *Qur'ān*)."[361] *Shāfi'ī* uses the term *naṣṣ* to refer to rulings to which either the *Qur'ān* or a *ḥadīth* refers.[362] Later, the majority of *mutakallimūn*[363] distinguished between *ẓāhir* and *naṣṣ*, but they disagreed in their approach to it, although the majority of them consider *ẓāhir* and *naṣṣ* opposed to *mujmal*. They also sometimes speak about *naṣṣ* as *mubayyan* or as a category of *mubayyan*. Baṣrī consider *naṣṣ* a provision which is not open to any other meaning.[364] Similar to Shīrāzī, he upholds the view that *naṣṣ* is every expression which provides a ruling by its explicit meaning, in a way which leads to no other possibilities,[365] such as the following verses indicate: "*Muḥammad is the Messenger of Allah*"[366]; "*And go not nigh to fornication; surely it is an indecency and an evil way*".[367]

Ghazālī also goes with the similar point of view in regards to the *naṣṣ*, despite the fact that he emphasises that *ẓāhir* may be called *naṣṣ*, he mentioned that although scholars have different approaches on *naṣṣ* he prefers that *naṣṣ* is a provision (a meaning) that is not open to different meanings like numbers and name of animals such as horse which indicates neither donkey nor camel. Thus it may exclude other potential meanings.[368] Ibn Qudāmah also followed the view of Ghazālī with the opinion as: "The meaning taken only from the provision which is not susceptible to any other possibility"[369], which was explained by the following verse "*these (make) ten (days) complete*".[370] The number 'ten days' mentioned in the text is *naṣṣ* since the meaning of the number is unchangeable as well as it is not open to interpretation (*ta'wīl*). Shawkānī obviously defined it as "What leaves no room for interpretation beyond the obvious sense (*ta'wīl*),[371] and Ansārī went for the similar meaning for: "What provides a definite meaning." [372] Qarāfī also, almost went with the similar opinions that it provides definitive meaning and is not open to another definite meaning, as in the case of numbers. [373] Despite the fact that, it may give another meaning but still remains definitive, which was explained by this example that the plural (*siyagh al-jumū'*) which indicates the smallest definite amount of plural,[374] and may include more than that, such as the word *ikhwāh* (brothers) in the following, verse: "*but if he has brothers, then his mother shall have the sixth*"[375] the word 'brothers' is in the plural sense, but it could indicate any number larger than two.

Besides the disagreement on the definition of *naṣṣ* between *Ḥanafī* and *Shāfiʿī* scholars, there are disagreement over the matter between the *mutakallimūn* themselves. This may occur in the *Qur'ān* and the *ḥadīth* rarely[376] such as "*Say: He, Allah, is One*"[377] and "*Muḥammad is the Messenger of Allah, and those with him are firm of heart against the unbelievers, compassionate among themselves*",[378] as well as in the *ḥadīth*, the Prophet (ṣ) said, "*O Unays go to this woman. If she admits adultery stone her.*"[379] However some other scholars maintain that there can be given more cases for *naṣṣ*. Nevertheless, despite the fact that *Shāfiʿī* scholars go with different opinion on *naṣṣ*, they are common with the opinion that it is not open to interpretation (*ta'wil*). However it may be concluded that *ẓāhir* in the *Shāfiʿī madhhab* represents only one of the *Ḥanafī* categories of *naṣṣ*, since the schools accept that different explanations can be possible.[380]

The concept of the explicit (النص) can be explored by the following examples based on *Ḥanafī* approaches:

First example: The *Qur'ān* states: "*That is because they say, trading is only like usury; and Allah has allowed trading and forbidden usury*".[381]

This verse is the explicit (النص) as it clarifies that trade and usury are not alike in respect of lawfulness and prohibition since trading is lawful and the usury is prohibited. These two different concepts cannot be the same. This is what it clearly means and therefore, it was revealed for that purpose "*sabab an-nuzūl*" (سبب النزول) in response to those people who claimed that trade and usury are alike.[382]

Second example: Allah states in the *Qur'ān*: "*And the divorced women should keep themselves in waiting for three courses*".[383] The explicit meaning of the verse is to explore the period (العدة) that the divorced women should wait for before remarrying. It is not allowed her remarry unless the period is fulfilled.[384] This meaning represents its principal theme since it was revealed for this purpose; therefore it is the explicit (النص).[385]

Third example: The Lawgiver states in the *Qur'ān*: "*And if you fear that you cannot act equitably towards orphans, then marry such women as seem good to you, two and three and four; but if you fear that you will not do justice (between them), then (marry) only one or what your right hands possess; this is more proper, that you may not deviate from the right course*".[386]

Although this verse contains the manifest (ظاهر) meaning which relates to legalising the marriage of women, it is not the main purpose of the verse. This verse also provides the following clear meanings: the number of wives and prohibition against more than one wife if there is a fear that justice will not be achieved among the wives. The main purpose of the verse is these clear meanings. Thus these meanings are the explicit (النص). It is obvious that the lawfulness of marriage was known from the practice of the Prophet (ṣ) and even before this verse was revealed. However, the limitation on the number of wives was unknown since at the time of ignorance (*jāhiliyyah*) and in early Islam, men could marry any number of free women. A maxim of *fiqh* indicates: "Establishing [a new meaning] has preference over the confirmation [of an existing meaning]."[387]

Differences between the manifest and the explicit

The difference between the manifest (الظاهر) and the explicit (النص) depends mainly on their relationship with the context in which they occur. Although these two concepts both denote clear meanings, the former does not constitute the dominant theme of the text whereas the latter does and it increases the lucidity of the text. The explicit (النص) is the purpose of the revelation (سبب النزول) and its indication represents the principal theme of the text, however not the manifest (الظاهر). Hence, strict adherence to the explicit (النص) is an obligation to the subjects until a reliable proof indicates otherwise.[388]

Although these two words convey clear meanings, both of them are open to interpretation (*ta'wīl*), however, only the difference between them is their relationship with the context in which they occur. The manifest (الظاهر), as it is indicated, does not constitute the dominant theme of the text whereas the explicit (النص) does.[389]

The value of explicit (al-naṣṣ)

The value of explicit (النص) is like the *ḥukm* (ruling) of the value of the manifest (الظاهر) that is, its obedience to the ruling (*ḥukm*) of the manifest (الظاهر) is strictly obligatory (*wājib*) unless there is any other evidence to suggest otherwise and therefore its obvious indications must be followed in legal reasoning because it signifies definite indication. However, the possibility of interpretation of the explicit (النص) is less likely to the manifest (الظاهر).[390] For the *Shāfi'ī* school of thought also adherence to *naṣṣ* is obligatory and its meaning must be applied due to the same reason that the majority of the *Shāfi'ī* schools went the ruling that it is not open interpretation (*ta'wīl*).

The unequivocal, explained (al-mufassar)

Linguistically the explained "*al-mufassar*" (المفسر) refers to something which is expounded, explained, interpreted and disclosed. Technically, from the *uṣūl al-fiqh* point of view, it refers to a text from the *Qur'ān* or the *Sunnah* that is explained by a meaning included within the text or recourse to other sources.[391]

Bazdawī defined it as "(a text) that is clearer than *naṣṣ* due to a meaning included in the text or taken from other sources, so that was ambiguous (*mujmal*), but supplemented by a definite explanation (*bayān qaṭ'ī*) that closes the possibility of *ta'wīl*; or is taken to be *lafẓ 'āmm* (a general word) supplemented by certain explanations that excludes the possibility of *takhṣīṣ*."[392] Similarly, Sarakhsī defines it as "a name given to the unconcealed whose aim is revealed in a way that leaves no possibility for *ta'wīl*."[393] Finally Naṣafī defines it as "*Mufassar* is (a text) that is clearer than *naṣṣ* in a way that leaves no possibility for *ta'wīl* and *takhṣīṣ*."[394]

Simply the concept of *mufassar* is a word or a text whose meaning is completely clear and it is harmony with the context in which it occurs. Due to the high level of clarity in the meaning of *mufassar*, there is no need for recourse to *ta'wīl*. However the *mufassar* may still be open to abrogation which might have taken place during the lifetime of the Prophet (ṣ) similarly to *ẓāhir* and *naṣṣ*, however a *mufassar* is unquestionably clearer, because it is not open to the possibilities of *ta'wīl* and *takhṣīṣ*. Thus, the focal point of the *mufassar* is that the text explains itself. The *mufassar* is of two types: The first one is a text which is self-explained, or *mufassar bidhātih*. The other one is when the ambiguity in one text is clarified and explained by another source that is known as *mufassar bighayrih*.[395]

Examples of the explained (al-mufassar)

First example: Allah states in the *Qur'ān*:

> "*Allah enjoins you concerning your children: The male shall have the equal of the portion of two females; then if they are more than two females, they shall have two-thirds of what the deceased has left, and if there is one, she shall have the half; and as for his parents, each of them shall have the sixth of what he has left if he has a child, but if he has no child and (only) his two parents inherit him, then his mother shall have the third; but if he has brothers, then his mother shall have the sixth after (the payment of) a bequest he may have bequeathed or a debt; your parents and your children, you know not which of them is the nearer to you in usefulness; this is an ordinance from Allah: Surely Allah is Knowing, Wise*".[396]

This verse prescribes specific shares for the legal heirs. The proportions in the verse are explained (المفسر) in nature since their values are unchangeable. Thus, there is no possibility for an interpretation beyond the obvious meaning, and every legal heir is prescribed to his or her exact share of inheritance.

Second example: Allah states in the *Qur'ān*:

> "*And those who accuse free women then do not bring four witnesses, flog them, (giving) eighty stripes, and do not admit any evidence from them ever; and these it is that are the transgressors*".[397]

The word 'eighty' (*thamānīn*) is number, and it does not assume greater or lesser value than what is stated. Thus, numbers are always counted as explained (المفسر). The verse clearly means that the slanderers should be flogged with eighty stripes which indicate definitive (*qaṭ'ī*) meaning which is not open to *ta'wīl* or *takhṣīṣ*.

Third example: Allah states in the *Qur'ān* that the following verses are all at the first stage are ambivalent:

> "*And keep up prayer and pay the poor-rate and bow down with those who bow down*",[398]

> "*O you who believe! fasting is prescribed for you, as it was prescribed for those before you, so that you may guard (against evil)*",[399]

> "*In it are clear signs, the standing place of Ibrahim, and whoever enters it shall be secure, and pilgrimage to the House is incumbent upon men for the sake of Allah, (upon) everyone who is able to undertake the journey to it; and whoever disbelieves, then surely Allah is Self-sufficient, above any need of the worlds*",[400] "*and Allah has allowed trading and forbidden usury.*"

The words *ṣalāt*, *zakāt*, *ṣiyām*, *ḥajj* and usury (*ribā'*) at the first stage are ambivalent (*mujmal*). Upon closer examination of the respected texts, we find that the Lawgiver used these words not for their linguistic meaning but for special meanings, which are sometimes almost entirely different from their literal and original meanings. These words may indicated more than one meaning. Thus, the verses in which they appear in the text are ambiguous at the first stage. Hence the Prophet (ṣ) explained the necessary explanation in the form of both verbal and technical, practical instructions. In this way the text which was initially ambivalent (*mujmal*), later on became explained (المفسر). As the Prophet (ṣ), said about the prayer "Pray as you see me pray."[401] He talked about *zakāt*,[402] explained the rules for *ṣiyām*.[403] He performed the pilgrimage and eventually said: "Take from me your rituals [holy rites]."[404] And warned strongly the *ummah* about the usury.[405] With the explanation of the intended meaning by the Prophet (ṣ), the ambivalent provisions (*mujmalah*) became explained (المفسر).

The value of the explained (al-mufassar)

The value of the explained (المفسر) is that acting upon it is obligatory according to the explained meaning. As Bukhārī emphasized saying that "there is no disagreement among the scholars in this case."[406] As it is mentioned that the clear meaning of an explained is not open to interpretation. Thus the obvious meaning of a text must be followed unless another reliable proof abrogates it. So long as it is clear that abrogation was possible during the life of the Prophet (ṣ). After his demise the entire *Qur'ān* became the perspicuous/firm (المحكم) in the sense that it was no longer open to abrogation and the explained (المفسر) became equivalent to the perspicuous/the firm (المحكم).

The perspicuous/firm (al-muḥkam)

Linguistically the perspicuous/firm "*al-muḥkam*" (المحكم) refers to perspicuous, exact, precise, accurate, firm; a verse of the *Qur'ān* whose meaning is secured from change, alternation, specification, and interpretation beyond the obvious import, and abrogation as the Lawgiver indicates in the *Qur'ān*:

> "*He it is Who has revealed the Book to you; some of its verses are*

decisive, they are the basis of the Book, and others are allegorical; then as for those in whose hearts there is perversity they follow the part of it which is allegorical, seeking to mislead and seeking to give it (their own) interpretation, but none knows its interpretation except Allah, and those who are firmly rooted in knowledge say: We believe in it, it is all from our Lord; and none do mind except those having understanding".[407]

In the technical sense of *uṣūl al-fiqh*, the term refers to an entirely clear text, of either the *Qur'ān* or the *Sunnah*, which is not open to interpretation (*ta'wīl*) or specification (*takhṣīṣ*) or abrogation (*naskh*).[408]

Technically it is a words and sentences whose meaning is clear beyond doubt and are not open to *ta'wīl* and abrogation as well as have character of being continuity and invariability that are called the perspicuous/firm (المحكم). Al-Bazdawī defined it in the following terms: "If the *mufassar* is strengthened, and its purpose is beyond doubt, then it is called *muḥkam.*[409] Naṣafī provides the following definition: "It is an expression, the objective of which is beyond doubt and which excludes the possibility of abrogation (*naskh* and change *tabdīl.*"[410] Al-Sarakhsī defined it in the following terms: "what went beyond and exceeded in its clarity and explicitness."[411]

The above definitions conclude that the *Ḥanafī madhhab* considers it within a meaning which hastens to one's mind that it is beyond doubt that no possibility for interpretation beyond the obvious meaning or for abrogation. This was applicable even both during the life of the Prophet (ṣ) and after his demise from this world.

Like the explained (المفسر), some scholars divided the perspicuous/the firm (المحكم) into two types:[412] a) the perspicuous/the firm by itself "*muḥkam bi-dhātih*" (محكم بذاته) and b) the perspicuous/the firm because of other factor "*muḥkam bi-ghayrih*" (محكم بغيره). If the firmness of the text comes from within the text itself, in other words, if abrogation (*naskh*) of a text is impossible because of the meaning of the text itself, such a text is said to be intrinsically and by itself *muḥkam*. This is especially obvious when the text is not open to a different meaning, like the verses about the Oneness of Allah the existence of the Creator, His attributes, etc. On the other hand, the second type of the perspicuous/the firm (المحكم) could be because of the absence of an abrogating text not from within the text itself but because of another factor. Thus it is called the perspicuous/the firm because of other factor (محكم بغيره) and it includes the manifest (الظاهر), the explicit (النص), the unequivocal/the explained (المفسر) and the perspicuous/firm (المحكم).[413]

Examples of the perspicuous/firm (al-muḥkam)

First type of example: It is related to the *aḥkām* in which the impossibility of abrogation that is indicated within the text itself. Such as an undisputable legal rulings based on undisputed authoritative text that is illustrated by matters relating to the religion (*dīn*) and these are foundation of the religion[414]. Thus these are neither changed and altered, nor limited to time to time since these are not open to any changes. Such as the Oneness of Allah:

> *"Say: He, Allah, is One"*[415]; *His attributes "Allah is He besides Whom there is no god, the Ever-living, the Self-subsisting by Whom all subsist; slumber does not overtake Him nor sleep; whatever is in the heavens and whatever is in the earth is His; who is he that can intercede with Him but by His permission? He knows what is before them and what is behind them, and they cannot comprehend anything out of His knowledge except what He pleases, His knowledge extends over the heavens and the earth, and the preservation of them both tires Him not, and He is the Most High, the Great.*[416]

The belief in His angels, His books, His prophets:

> *"The messenger believes in what has been revealed to him from his Lord, and (so do) the believers; they all believe in Allah and His*

> *angels and His books and His messengers; We make no difference between any of His messengers; and they say: We hear and obey, our Lord! Thy forgiveness (do we crave), and to Thee is the eventual course*"[417];
>
> The Last Day "*It is not righteousness that you turn your faces towards the East and the West, but righteousness is this that one should believe in Allah and the last day and the angels and the Book and the prophets...*"[418] etc.

The *aḥkām* which are related to the news and information about what happened in the past and what will happen in the future. Allah states in the *Qur'ān* "*Alif Lām Mīm. The Romans are vanquished; In a near land, and they, after being vanquished, shall overcome; Within a few years. Allah's is the command before and after; and on that day the believers shall rejoice*".[419]

The legal *aḥkām* that characterise a basis for unchangeable ethical principles under any circumstances such as justice "*O you who believe! Be upright for Allah, bearers of witness with justice, and let not hatred of a people incite you not to act equitably; act equitably, that is nearer to piety, and be careful of (your duty to) Allah; surely Allah is Aware of what you do*".[420]

Ethical values "*And your Lord has commanded that you shall not serve (any) but Him, and goodness to your parents. If either or both of them reach old age with you, say not to them (so much as) "Ugh" nor chide them, and speak to them a generous word*".[421]

Fulfilment of promises or covenant "*And draw not near to the property of the orphan except in a goodly way till he attains his maturity and fulfill the promise; surely (every) promise shall be questioned about.*"[422] etc.

The second type of Examples: The perspicuous/firm (المحكم) occurs when the given meaning comprehended from the external reason or another factor and it is followed by the declaration of continuity which precludes the possibility of abrogation (*naskh*). As Allah stated in the *Qur'ān* "*O you who believe! do not enter the houses of the Prophet unless permission is given to you for a meal, not waiting for its cooking being finished – but when you are invited, enter, and when you have taken the food, then disperse – not seeking to listen to talk; surely this gives the Prophet trouble, but he forbears from you, and Allah does not forbear from the truth And when you ask of them any goods, ask of them from behind a curtain; this is purer for your hearts and (for) their hearts; and it does not behove you that you should give trouble to the Messenger of Allah, nor that you should marry his wives after him ever; surely this is grievous in the sight of Allah*".[423]

It is understood from the verse that marrying the Prophet's widows is prohibited however, the continuity of the prohibition is highlighted by the words 'ever after him' (مِنْ بَعْدِهِ أَبَدًا). This verse indicates that the prohibition of the *ḥukm* is a clear declaration of continuity which makes it *muḥkam* that there is no way for abrogation (*naskh*).

Another example, as Allah stated in the *Qur'ān* "*And those who accuse free women then do not bring four witnesses, flog them, (giving) eighty stripes, and do not admit any evidence from them ever after; and these it is that are the transgressors*".[424]

The ruling (*ḥukm*) that is taken from this verse is that the testimony of someone who accuses an decent person without producing four witnesses to support his allegation must be rejected and the punishment must also be applied to accuser. The continuity nature of the verse with this words 'ever after' "*abadan*" (أَبَدًا) makes it *muḥkam* which obviously means longevity and it excludes the possibility of abrogation.

In addition to the examples brought from the *Qur'ān*, the *Sunnah* also provides the similar perspicuous/firm (المحكم) meanings. The Prophet (ṣ) said "*O people, I had permitted you to contract temporary marriage with women, but Allah has forbidden it [now] until the Day of Resurrection. So he who has any [women with this type of marriage contract] he should release her, and take nothing back.*"[425] The first stage of prohibition in this *ḥadīth* is the prohibition of temporary marriage (*mut'ah*), whereas the continuity is firmed by the Prophet's words 'until the Day of Resurrection'. Thus the *ḥukm* of the prohibition of temporary marriage (*mut'ah*) continues and it became eternal. This continuity make it *muḥkam* since it precludes the possibility of abrogation.

Another example is given in this context that the Prophet (ṣ) said regarding fighting for the sake of Allah (*jihād*), "*Jihād* is under way from the time when Allah sent me, until the last [members] of my ummah fight the Antichrist (*Dajjāl*)."[426] The first stage of ruling in this *ḥadīth* is that the *jihād* had begun by the beginning of the Revelation, whereas the continuity is the Prophet's words "until the last person of my *ummah* fight Antichrists." The Antichrist will appear shortly before the Last day according to Muslim belief. Thus the ruling is valid forever and since the *ḥukm* became *muḥkam*, it is not open to *ta'wīl* and *takhṣīṣ*, therefore, it precludes any ambiguity or possibility for interpretation beyond the obvious meaning. Consequently this *ḥukm* is not open to abrogation, neither in the time of Revelation nor after the Prophet's (ṣ) departure from this world.[427] Thus, the ruling of *jihād* (holy struggle) remains valid until the day of resurrection.

The value of the perspicuous/firm (al-muḥkam)

After all the explanations and the examples, it is clear that the *muḥkam* is not open to abrogation that may be indicated in the text itself or it may be because of the absence of an abrogating text. Therefore, the perspicuous/firm (المحكم) should be strictly obligatory due to the impossibility of interpretation (*ta'wīl*), specification (*takhṣīṣ*) or abrogation (*naskh*).[428]

Conflict (ta'āruḍ) within the Clarity of Indication

The categories of the clarity of indication (واضح الدلالة) in the *Ḥanafī* School are not at the same level of clarity. The clearest one among them is the *muḥkam*, followed by *mufassar*, *naṣṣ*, and lastly is *ẓāhir*. The inequality between these categories becomes apparent and substantial in the event of a conflict. Sarakhsī emphasised that there is unanimous agreement among Muslim Scholars that the contradiction in authoritative texts (*Qur'ān* and the *Sunnah*) are apparent due to real contradiction is only when texts are at the same level, presented at the same time. However, this kind of contradictions never happens, although it may exist in the mind of the *mujtahid* due to a lack of knowledge of when the text was brought, of an understanding of the same text, etc.[429] As it was explained that discrepancy between the two words can only happen in respect of clarity and ambiguity; however, there should not be any discrepancy in respect of certainty and uncertainty. All categories should be *qaṭ'ī al-thubūt*, otherwise there would be no proper disagreement because the indefinite (*ẓannī*) cannot oppose the definite (*qaṭ'ī*). Finally, among these clear words, the clearer one has priority over the other.

Conflict between the manifest and the explicit

As the characteristics of the manifest (الظاهر) and the explicit (النص) were identified above that the manifest (الظاهر) is suitably apparent and the deduced legal ruling of it is not the main objective for the presence of the text and does not represent its principal theme. The possibility of interpretation beyond the obvious meaning, specification (*takhṣīṣ*) and abrogation (*naskh*) still exists on one hand. The characteristic of the explicit (النص), on the other hand, are that it is also suitably clear. However, the inferred legal ruling of *naṣṣ* is the main objective for the presence of the text and represents its main theme of the text. Nevertheless, the possibility of interpretation beyond the obvious meaning, specification (*takhṣīṣ*) and abrogation (*naskh*) still exists.

Although both are the same, in the case of *naṣṣ* it is less possible than in the case of *ẓāhir* since *naṣṣ* represents the principal theme of the text, not the *ẓāhir*. Therefore, if a conflict occurs between the two, the *naṣṣ* will prevail over the other.

For example: The *Qur'ān* states: "*And all married women except those whom your right hands possess (this is) Allah's ordinance to you, and lawful for you are (all women) besides those, provided that you seek (them) with your property, taking (them) in marriage not committing fornication. Then as to those whom you profit by, give them their dowries as appointed; and there is no blame on you about what you mutually agree after what is appointed; surely Allah is Knowing, Wise*".[430]

This verse has manifest meaning which permits any number of women to be taken in marriage. Following the previous verse (*Qur'ān* 4:23) that was mentioned the forbidden women to marry. Apart from these mentioned women, "*all others are lawful.*" Thus, according to the manifest meaning of this verse a man may marry more than four wives at the same time. It is obvious that this verse is not *naṣṣ* because it was not revealed for the purpose of explaining the particular meaning, which means, it does not represent the principal theme of the text.

If the following verse is considered, the principle theme of the text may appear. As the Lawgiver indicates in the *Qur'ān*: "*And if you fear that you cannot act equitably towards orphans, then marry such women as seem good to you, two and three and four; but if you fear that you will not do justice (between them), then (marry) only one or what your right hands possess; this is more proper, that you may not deviate from the right course*".[431]

There is an obvious conflict between this verse and the previous verse on the number of wives to be taken for marriage. Despite the former verse does not limit the number, the later verse limits it to four. The principle theme of the text, which is *naṣṣ*, in the later is the number of the wives. Thus it prevails over the *ẓāhir* which is not the principle theme of the text. Finally, the legal ruling that is obtained from the text is the number of women which is permitted to have them is maximum of four at the same time. It can be concluded that in the case of conflict, it has to be identified whether its indication is the manifest (الظاهر) or the explicit (النص).

Conflict between the explicit and the explained

In addition to the general characteristics of the explicit (النص)[432], the explained (المفسر) is also clear word, represent the principles theme of the text and the possibilities of specification (*takhṣīṣ*) and interpretation (*ta'wīl*) do not exist in the explained (المفسر). Nevertheless it is open to abrogation only during the life time of the Prophet (ṣ). Despite the both words have the same qualities, the explained (المفسر) is clearer than the explicit (النص) since the former is not open to specification (*takhṣīṣ*) and interpretation (*ta'wīl*), but the later. Thus in the case of conflict, the explained (المفسر) would prevail over the explicit (النص) simply because of its extra quality.

It will be better understood with the following example. If a person states "I have married a woman for a month" which refers to a temporary marriage, not a legal marriage because legal marriage is not open to the limited duration. Within the statement, "the marriage" is interpreted by a statement "for a month." The statement of "I have married to a woman" is the explicit (النص) which clearly indicates to a marriage, however, "for a month" made it explained and indicates to that of a limited time period that is temporary (*mut'ah*). Since the temporary is an illegal marriage according to the majority of scholars. The explained (المفسر) prevails over the explicit (النص). Thus his statement is taken as not a legal marriage but a temporary (*mut'ah*) marriage.[433]

Conflict between the explained and the perspicuous/firm

In addition to the previous explanations, the perspicuous/firm (المحكم) is the clearest one among the four words. The inferred legal ruling of the perspicuous/firm (المحكم) is the main objective for the presence of the text and represents the principal theme of the text. However, it is not open neither to *ta'wīl* nor to *takhṣīṣ* and nor to abrogation in which it is applicable both during the lifetime of the Prophet (ṣ) and after him.

Although the both have the similar characteristics, they are not common in the case of abrogation. The perspicuous/firm (المحكم) is not open to abrogation neither at the time of the Prophet (ṣ) nor after his demise, in contrast to the explained (المفسر) which is susceptible and open to abrogation during the lifetime of the Prophet (ṣ). Therefore, the perspicuous/firm (المحكم) has priority of the explained (المفسر) when the two words conflict.[434] In reality, the perspicuous/firm (المحكم) is nothing other than the explained (المفسر) with only one different character that it is not open to abrogation.

To prove this, it is evidenced in the *Qur'ān* about the person who was punished for having unjustly accused a free woman: "And those who accuse free women then do not bring four witnesses, flog them, (giving) eighty stripes, and do not admit any evidence from them ever; and these it is that are the transgressors".[435]

This verse is the perspicuous/firm (المحكم) due to the existence of the word "forever" which carries the meaning of continuity and thus prevents all possibility of abrogation.

In addition to the above verse, another one comes immediately after that: "*Unless they repent thereafter and mend (their conduct); for Allah is Oft-Forgiving, Most Merciful*".[436] This verse, accordingly, is considered the explained (المفسر). Thus, even if the person, who accused a free woman, has repented for accusing a free woman and has been punished for slandering (*qadhf*) is not accepted. Although this issue has been widely debated by *Ḥanafīs* and *Shāfi'īs*, because of the priority of the perspicuous/firm (المحكم) over the explained (المفسر), the status of the accuser will not be changed, that is the slanderer (*qādhif*), may never be admitted as a witness even if he repents.

The conflict continues between these two since giving the perspicuous/firm (المحكم) preference over the explained (المفسر) may not be good enough here, the reason why Muslim scholars do not depend on entirely on this proof in their argumentation, and avail themselves of other proofs, is because with the demise of the Prophet (ṣ) the *mufassar* immediately becomes the same as the *muḥkam* due to the sole difference between the two concept, that is the *mufassar* may be abrogated during the lifetime of the Prophet (ṣ).[437]

Conflict between the explicit and the perspicuous/firm

It will be comprehended better with the following example that the perspicuous/firm (المحكم) due to its characteristics will prevail over the explicit (النص) since *muḥkam* is more powerful. It is known that the *muḥkam* is not open to interpretation (*ta'wīl*), specification (*takhṣīṣ*) or abrogation (*naskh*).[438] Despite the fact that the *naṣṣ* is clear and the text represents its main theme, it is still open to specification (*takhṣīṣ*) and abrogation (*naskh*). Therefore, when they conflict, *muḥkam* takes precedence, as illustrated in the following example:

The *Qur'ān* states: "*and lawful for you are (all women) besides those*".[439] This indicates a clear meaning that it permits any number of women to be taken in marriage. The legal ruling deduced from this verse addresses also the Prophet (ṣ) whose wives could also remarry after his demise. However, in other verse the *Qur'ān* states: "*and it does not behove you that you should give trouble to the Messenger of Allah, nor that you should marry his wives after him ever; surely this is grievous in the sight of Allah*".[440]

This verse is *muḥkam* with respect to the prohibition of marrying any of the Prophet's (ṣ) wives even after his demise. It is *muḥkam* because the word 'ever after' indicates impossibility of interpretation (*ta'wīl*), or abrogation (*naskh*) due to the perspicuous/firm (المحكم) that it prevails over the explicit (النص).

Ḥanafī and Shāfi'ī Approach to the Unclear Words

Introduction

At the beginning of this chapter, the words, from the view point of the degree of clarity or obscurity of indication, were divided into the two main categories: Clarity of indication (واضح الدلالة) and obscurity of indication (غير واضح الدلالة).

From the viewpoint of the obscurity of indication (غير واضح الدلالة) or the degree of ambiguity in their meaning, the words are classified into four types which begin with the least ambiguous and ends by the most ambiguous in the range. An unclear word does not convey an idea which is not intelligible without recourse to interpretation. It conveys ambiguity and incompleteness, due to the ambiguity, it requires clarification and it cannot constitute the basis of action. It can only be completed through external evidences since the text itself is lacking and failing to convey a complete meaning without recourse to external evidence.

Differently, Taftāzānī (d. 1390) divided the unclear words into two groups. In the first group the obscurity is due to the expression itself which includes the difficult "*al-mushkil*" (المشكل), the ambivalent "*al-mujmal*" (المجمل) and the intricate "*al-mutashābih*" (المتشابه). The second group of obscurity is because of an incidental reason which includes the obscure "*al-khafī*" (الخفي) alone. The ambiguity of the first group can be removed by legal reasoning (*ijtihād*). If legal reasoning is sufficient for this duty, the unclear "*ghayr wāḍiḥ aw mubham*" (غير واضح او مبهم) is called the difficult (المشكل), however, if it is not insufficient, but needs support from an authoritative text, it is called the ambivalent (المجمل). If, however, neither of the legal reasoning nor the authoritative text is sufficient, then it is called the intricate

(المتشابه).[441] From one hand *Ḥanafī* scholars, in general, divided the unclear words (غير واضح او مبهم) in four types, on the other hand, *Shāfi'ī* scholars classified it into two types: the ambivalent (المجمل) and the intricate (المتشابه). Despite the fact that they disagree among themselves, many of them consider the intricate a category of ambivalent, while some others consider it a part of ambivalent. Nevertheless, these unclear words (غير واضح او مبهم) are considered from wider perspective as the obscure (الخفي), the difficult (المشكل), the ambivalent (المجمل) and the intricate (المتشابه).

We shall now explain each of these unclear words individually in the following pages.

The obscure (al-khafī)

Linguistically obscure "*khafī*" (خفي) refers to hidden, covert, talent, unperceived or barely perceived, unknown, invisible.[442]

Technically, *Ḥanafī* scholars first provided different yet similar definitions of the obscure "*al-khafī*" (الخفي). Naṣafī defined the obscure (الخفي) as "An expression whose meaning is obscured due to an external matter rather than the language mood itself, which means that it could be grasped as a result of research only."[443] Bazdawī went for the similar definition which is: "As expression whose meaning is dubious not due to the language mood but due to an external factor in which the meaning can only be grasped if analysed."[444] Additionally, Dabbūsī expressed it as: "An expression whose meaning is obscured not by the language itself but because of an external factor, this would cause the meaning to be less understandable, unless analysed."[445]

According to the *Ḥanafī* school of thought, it may be concluded that *khafī* has a basic manifest meaning (*ẓāhir*), however such manifest meaning is disrupted by an external factor which causes ambiguity and vagueness due to its applicability to more than one cases in which one of them can be clear and the others can be obscure.

Nevertheless, the ambiguity may be eliminated only through exercising the *ijtihād* by referring to authoritative texts in order to achieve the objectives of the *Sharī'ah.*[446]

First example for the obscure (al-khafi)

The *Qur'ān* states: "*And (as for) the man who steals and the woman who steals, cut off their hands as a punishment for what they have earned, an exemplary punishment from Allah; and Allah is Mighty, Wise*".[447]

The word thief "*as-sāriqu*" (السَّارِقُ) has a manifest meaning when applied to a person who secretly takes from others personal goods which are kept in their normal keeping place according to the Muslim jurists (*fuqahā*).[448] At the same time the word thief (السَّارِقُ) can also be known as pickpocket (*ṭarrār*), grave robber (*nabash*), etc. due to this reason it becomes obscure since it is not known which type of thief is it. According to scholars the punishment for each type of the stealing is different. Therefore it has to be clarified to be applied the cutting off of his right hand when the thief fulfils the necessary conditions and stipulations or what punishment should be then applied to the alike stealing?

The meaning of theft is well known. The basic elements of theft, however, are present in many other illegal activities. People may seize the possessions of others (*māl al-ghayr*) illegitimately in various ways. These people are called by names other than thief, and their misdeeds may not count as theft. Should they then receive the same verdict as the thief, or should the verdict be different?

How the pickpocket (الطرار) and the grave robber (النباش) [449] will be differentiated? Although all of these actions have the similar characteristics of a thief, they may not be still called a thief. Will then the same punishment be prescribed as the thief mentioned in the verse?

To compare between pickpocket and the thief, *Ḥanafī* jurists found that all elements of theft are existing in the action of the pickpocket. Its skill and proficiency in stealing, danger, crime, offence is more evident in the deed of the pickpocket than in theft itself because the protected good is stolen from the pocket by a person who has skill and proficiency. After giving a careful thought the ambiguity is removed by bringing the similarities between the ordinary stealing. Therefore, the *Ḥanafī* jurists were with an agreement that the pickpocketing is also be classified as a thief and receive the same punishment.[450] Nevertheless, from one hand, Abū Ḥanīfah asserted that if it is pickpocketed from inside the pocket, *ḥadd* (punishment) should be applied, but if it is stolen from outside, *ḥadd* should be avoided which was based on this *ḥadīth* "*avoid implementing ḥadd punishments in the cases of doubt*" (ادرؤوا الحدود بالشبهات)[451], on the other hand Abū Yūsuf maintained that *ḥadd* applies in both cases.[452]

Unlike the pickpocketing, the grave robber (النباش) has different ruling. The majority of *Ḥanafī* jurists[453] uphold the view that the grave robber should not receive the same capital punishment (*ḥadd*) applied to the thief. It is explained by saying that the grave robber (النباش) is not at the same conditions and stipulations since the property of a dead person, in the graveyard, is not under protection. What the grave robber (النباش) steals something from a graveyard is not considered stolen goods due to the nature of that was not preserved in an adequately safe place. Thus, the ownership of a person's belongings is legally incomplete. Since there is a doubt, *ḥadd* punishment is avoided.[454]

Second example for the obscure

The similar circumstances is applied to the *ḥadīth* of the Prophet (ṣ) about "killer" as he said: "*The killer shall not inherit.*" (لقاتل لا يرث).[455] The act of killing is not clear enough since it includes also unintentional killing. What about killing which caused by negligence, killing by a mad person, lawful killing, justifiable killing, etc.? Due to the varieties of ways in which a person is killing is obscure that is uncertain. Thus the uncertainty of killing, accordingly, must be clarified first. This obscurity caused disagreement among the scholars. Such as *Mālikīs* uphold the view that killing by unintentional or an error is not included in this *ḥadīth*, while *Ḥanafīs* consider it in order to safeguard lives.[456]

In conclusion, the ambiguities with these authoritative texts in relation to their possible applications of pickpocket and grave robber have different names and attributes due to this differences the rulings must be different. It is the same which applies to the killing that needs to be clarified to remove the obscurity which can be removed by exercising *ijtihād* to determine whether or not these acts include the characteristics of killing and theft, etc. This has an important bearing on the verdict attached to that action, and on whether it should be classified as a theft or not. If in the deed all the elements stipulated by *Sharīʿah* are found, the person should receive the same verdict; if not the verdict should be different.[457]

The value of the obscure

It should be comprehended first that the intended meaning of the obscure (الخفي) is true even if it occurs as obscure. The scholars should give every effort to determine the intended meaning until the ambiguity is removed.[458] Nevertheless, a careful approach is necessary to remove the ambiguity and it should not be implemented before serious research and proper exercise of *ijtihād* is made. It is obvious that *ḥadd* (punishment) should not be applied in the case of doubt as the Prophet (ṣ) emphasized with this *ḥadīth* "*avoid implementing ḥadd punishments in the cases of doubt*" (ادرؤوا الحدود بالشبهات)[459]. In his legal reasoning the competent scholar (*mujtahid*) should depend on the aims and objectives of Islamic law and try to find the wisdom behind it.

The difficult (al-mushkil)

Linguistically difficult "*mushkil*" (مشكل) refers to problematic, complex, hard to solve, difficult, intricate, and equivocal.[460]

Technically the difficult (المشكل) has various definitions provided by *Ḥanafī* scholars. Naṣafī defined it as an expression that "involves various equal meanings."[461] Dabbūsī defined it as an expression that "has a meaning which is ambiguous to understand for the listener. The ambiguity is caused by the subtlety of that meaning or the metaphor, not by the deceptive action of the originator."[462] Sarakhsī indicated that the difficult (المشكل) is a name for an expression whose intended meaning cannot be identified because it has a determined meaning. It may be clarified only by a proof that can emphasize it among other meanings.[463] According to the above definitions, it may be briefly defined as it is a self-obscured expression. Thus its obscurity occurs because of its variety of meanings.[464] It signifies a word which is inherently ambiguous, and whose ambiguity can only be removed by means of research and *ijtihād*.[465] The intended meaning of *mushkil* cannot be known without recourse to external evidence to differentiate it from others. Although the difficult (المشكل)[466] and the obscure (الخفي) are unclear words, the difficult is more ambiguous that the obscure. Therefore, to discover the difficult (المشكل) needs more effort than the obscure (الخفي).

First example of the difficult (al-mushkil)

An expression is mentioned in the *Qur'ān* regarding family relationship, as the Lawgiver states: "*Your wives are a tilth for you, so go into your tilth when (or how) you like, and do good beforehand for yourselves, and be careful (of your duty) to Allah, and know that you will meet Him, and give good news to the believers*".[467]

The word "when (or how)" "*annā*" (أَنَّىٰ) is a homonym (*lafẓ mushtarak*).[468] It is a difficult (مشكل) when it forms part of an expression, because it could mean different things. For example, in the verse: "*He said: O Maryam! whence comes this to you?*".[469] Here the word "whence (or how)" (أَنَّىٰ), also mentioned in the *Qur'ān* twenty eight times, is used to mean '*from were*'. The word (أَنَّىٰ) is also used to mean 'how', as in the verse: "*He said: My Lord! when shall there be a son (born) to me, and old age has already come upon me, and my wife is barren?*".[470] All these verses in which the word (أَنَّىٰ) is mentioned indicate that the (أَنَّىٰ) is a homonym which can be interpreted in variety of meanings and therefore the word (أَنَّىٰ) in the first verse can be interpreted differently.[471]

According to Ibn 'Abbās, the word (أَنَّىٰ) means "how" (كيف) as he mentions, "*He approaches her however he likes, in any manner, as long as it is not from the rear, or during her menstrual period*" which means 'any position you like'. Eventually it may be concluded by the opinion of the majority of Muslim jurists[472] as "have sexual relations with your wives in any manner, in any position, and at any time, as long as it is through the vagina and not the rear."[473]

As it is expressed in the *Qur'ān* that women are called 'tilth' "Your wives are a tilth for you" (نِسَآؤُكُمْ حَرْثٌ لَّكُمْ). They are the place for you to cultivate for your generation. Thus it is described as a place of cultivation since the vagina is the only place to cultivate of seed. The 'seed' can be planted only in a woman's uterus since it is a fertile place, not the rear. Thus the rear is not allowed. The actual place of the intercourse is indicated by another verse in the *Qur'ān* "*And they ask you about menstruation. Say: It is a discomfort; therefore keep aloof from the women during the menstrual discharge and do not go near them until they have become clean; then when they have cleansed themselves, go in to them as Allah has commanded you; surely Allah loves those who turn much (to Him), and He loves those who purify themselves*".[474]

In addition to this explanation from the *Qur'ān*, Ibn al-'Arabī said: 'I asked al-Imām al-Qāḍī al-Tūsī about this question and he answered: "The sexual act from the rear with the wife is forbidden under any circumstances. Allah has forbidden vaginal penetration during the period of menstruation because of the temporary dirtiness that accompanies it. Therefore it is all the more fitting that the sexual act from the rear is forbidden because of the inevitable dirtiness."[475]

After careful examination, the ambiguity in the word (أَنَّى) is removed and thus it can be concluded that the word (أَنَّى) generalizes ways to ejaculate from the vagina by 'how' and 'when', and not 'where', but not the places in which not from the rear.

Second example of the difficult

Another example can be given for this context is as the *Qur'ān* states: "*And the divorced women should keep themselves in waiting for three courses*".[476] The word courses (قُرُوءٍ) is a homonym which means both cleanliness and menstruation. Some scholars including Imām Shāfi'ī exercised *ijtihād* and concluded that the word (قُرُوءٍ), in this verse, means cleanliness (طهر). Others including Imām Abū Ḥanīfah have said that it means menstruation (حيض).[477] Whichever of these distinct meanings is agreed, the legal ruling will differ accordingly since the two meanings are used in Arabic language for the word (قُرُوءٍ), there is no definite indication unless recourse to research and *ijtihād*. Thus following a certain school of *madhhab* becomes necessary for ordinary people (*muqallid*).

The value of the difficult

In conclusion, Muslim jurists believe that the intended meaning of difficult (مشكل) after careful examination and using the method of *ijtihād* is correct, even if the preferred meaning remains obscure. So long as the *mujtahid* made an effort to find out the intended meaning and finally discovered it then the obscurity is considered removed. A significant point to discover the intended meaning is whether it has taken the process through analysis, scrutiny, and careful examination or not. If so, then it may be implemented because the difficult (مشكل) is removed and it becomes clear.[478]

The ambivalent (al-mujmal)

Linguistically ambivalent "*mujmal*" (مجمل) refers to summarized, outlined, abridged, condensed, epitomized, concise, indecisive, brief, short; a word, phrase, or speech which includes or implies a number of unexplained things requiring elaboration.[479]

Technically it has various definition, such as *Ḥanafī* scholars provided several definitions for the ambivalent "*al-mujmal*" (المجمل). Dabbūsī (d. 1039) defined it as an expression "whose meaning cannot essentially be understood due to unfamiliar language or metaphorical semantics."[480] Bazdawī (d. 1089) maintained that *mujmal* as an expression which "carries various concise meanings, and the intended meaning becomes so ambiguous that it cannot be comprehended from the same expression but is rather arrived at by referring to the explanation, research and thinking"[481] Sarakhsī (d. 1096) explained that *mujmal* is a word whose purpose cannot be understood without an explanation from the speaker, due to metaphorical semantics or its unusual syntax.[482] Later on Naṣafī (d. 1310) offered an identical definition to that of Bazdawī's, but excluded the word *ta'ammul* (thinking or contemplation).[483]

Shāfi'ī scholars (*mutakallimūn*) also provided several definitions for *mujmal* such as Ghazālī defined it as: "It is an expression which alternates between two or more meanings, none of which have precedence over the others.[484] Although Qarāfī (d. 1285) is not a *Shāfi'ī* scholar, as Mālikī, he defined it similarly: "It is an expression which alternates between two or more meanings."[485] Rāzī (d. 1209) divided the ambivalent into three types and defined it as "*mujmal* occurs when an expression accepts many possible meanings, none of which is preferred over the others.[486] Āmidī (d. 1233) also brought a similar definitions that of Rāzī.[487] To sum up, their definition almost similar to each other that of it cannot be understood from its words but needs to be explained by another expression.[488] Although some *Shāfi'ī* scholars yet to discuss its existence in the authoritative text, most of them confirm that they recognize it in their *madhhabs*. However most of them did not differentiate between *mujmal* and *mutashābih*.[489]

It may concluded that *mujmal*, in the *Ḥanafī madhhab*, is an expression the intended meaning of which is inherently hidden and unclear. Therefore, without an explanation from the originator, whether the ambiguity is due to the special meaning intended by the Lawgiver, or due to homonymous meanings, or the unusual usage of the word, is difficult to comprehend. Unless, the ambiguity is removed by referring back to the explanation of the Lawgiver either from the *Qur'ān* and the *Sunnah*.

Types of the ambivalent (al-mujmal)

In respect of causes to ambivalence, the ambivalent (المجمل) may be divided into three categories:

First type of the ambivalent (al-mujmal)

It is an ambivalent which occurs through the use of the word in a particular legal context, no in its apparent literal meaning, in this manner conveying a technical or juridical concept intended by the Lawgiver, that is known as "*naql shar'ī*" in which it is the most common used type of the *mujmal*.

Islam came with a new system of live which consist of new principles, terms and way of worshiping. Thus many words, perhaps, redressed by new attributes and meanings in order reflect the purpose of the Lawgiver, such as the word prayer (*ṣalāt*), alms tax (*zakāt*), pilgrimage (*ḥajj*) which had certain literal meanings which were later on enhanced and renamed accommodating with the intended meanings. The literal meanings of the words need to be clarified by the authentic texts in order to remove ambiguity caused by the literal meanings in order to reflect the purpose of the Lawgiver. In this matter, the second source of Islamic law, the *Sunnah*, may play a significant role in removing the ambiguity. An interesting point, as we remember from the concept of *mufassar*, when a *mujmal* is explained it becomes *mufassar*, however, if the explanation is insufficient to remove the ambiguity, it may remain as *mushkil*. Thus the ambiguity can only be removed by a proper method of *ijtihād*.

For example, in regards to prayers, it is an obligatory act of worship upon every responsible Muslim. As the Lawgiver mentions in the *Qur'ān*: "*And keep up prayer and pay the poor-rate and bow down with those who bow down*".[490] Literally the word prayer (*ṣalāt*) means call, invocation, supplication (*duā'*). [491] However, these meanings are not the intended meaning of the word. It is defined by the jurists as a special acts and sayings: "Special acts and sayings (utterance) opened by *takbīr* (*Allahu Akbar*) and concluded (ended) by *taslīm* (*assalāmu 'alaykum*)."[492] Therefore, the literal meaning of prayer (*ṣalāt*) is transferred into a new meaning and became a definition for the word (*ṣalāt*) as a ritual which linguistically refers to supplication.[493] In addition to this new definition, there is no single verse to explain its details, the forms, parts, number of prayers, their times, conditions etc. since the Lawgiver requests from the subjects to perform it perfectly, it has to be done accordingly. However the details of it was explained practically and verbally by the *Sunnah* of the Prophet (ṣ) and he said "Indeed, I have done this that you may copy me and learn my prayer,"[494] and "Pray as you see my pray".[495] It is obvious now that through the *Sunnah*, the ambiguity of the prayers was removed and it became unequivocal/explained (المفسر).

The life of the Prophet (ṣ) is a practical explanation of the *Qur'ān*, therefore, many verses, including worship, dealings (business), crime, war and peace, international relations, related to the commandment of Allah are ambivalent (مجمل) which need to be explained. As Shāṭibī indicates the significance of referring the *Sunnah* by saying that the *mujtahid* must refer to the *Sunnah* when exercising *ijtihād*.[496] The *Qur'ān* as the first source of Islamic law may not explained everything in details in order to be clarified or explained by the *Sunnah* as the second source of Islamic law.[497]

Second type of the ambivalent (al-mujmal)

It is an ambivalent which is caused by a competition of equal meanings (homonyms) with no possibility of preference to any one among them, and without any indication of which one might be the correct one. For example, in regards to a word *mawlā* (pl. *mawālī*) which indicates two meanings, a master and a slave therefore it is called homonym which includes both meanings. If a person who makes a will to the effect that property should be given to this *mawālī*. If the testator dies before explaining whom he meant by his will, whether to frees (the master) or to freed (his freed slave), otherwise, the will be invalid.[498] In order to make it clear, it needs further explanation since *mawlā* (pl. *mawālī*) is a homonym and includes both the one who frees (the master) and the one freed (his freed slave). Therefore, in order the will not to be invalid the *mujtahid* should remove the ambiguity. If, however, the statement remains unclear, the beneficiary became unknown due to the fact that one meaning does not have preference over the other.[499]

Third type of the ambivalent (al-mujmal)

It is an also an ambivalent which is caused by the oddity of a totally unfamiliar or unusual word which is inherently vague. For example, in regards to characteristics and the nature of man, Allah states in the *Qur'ān*: "*Surely man is created of a hasty temperament*".[500] The word "hasty" (هَلُوعًا) is, an unusual word, a person who shows extreme impatience and anxiety when he receives something good. It meant with this word is extremely impatient. However, this type of usage is an unusual and unfamiliar. Nevertheless, in order to know it, it has to be explained by the *Shārī'*. Therefore, Allah made an explanation with the continuation of the verse "*Being greatly grieved when evil afflicts him, And niggardly when good befalls him*".[501] In order to support this explanation, Aḥmad ibn Yaḥyā was asked regarding the meaning of the word "hasty" (هَلُوعًا) and he answered "Allah explained it, and no explanation can be clearer than that. It is a human being who, touched by evil, becomes frightened; and who, on gaining something good, becomes miserly and tries to keep everything to himself."[502] At the beginning the word "hasty" (هَلُوعًا) was ambiguous due to the unfamiliar nature of it and thus, the ambiguity is removed by the following verses.

Finally, one may think that the ambivalent (المجمل) and the difficult (المشكل) seems to be the same and however ambiguity occurs in the used expression which is not an external matter. However, the explanation required in the case of the ambivalent (المجمل) can only be provided by the speaker, whereas, in the case of the difficult (المشكل) the explanation is attainable through analysis and *ijtihād*. Therefore, the ambivalent (المجمل) is more ambiguous than the difficult (المشكل).

The value of the ambivalent

According to *Ḥanafī* scholars, it is impermissible to act upon the ruling of the ambivalent (المجمل) unless it is explained by the originator's explanation (البيان). The intended meaning of the Lawgiver must be appeared even if we do not know it either by the originator or by way of explanation, if it was not explained then it will turn into the difficult (المشكل) to refer it to method of *ijtihād*.[503] Since nothing is left ambiguous, the competent scholars are required to investigate and make research from respected sources to determine intended meaning of the originator.

The Intricate (al-mutashābih)

Linguistically intricate "*mutashābih*" (متشابه) refers to similar, alike, akin, analogous, parallel, comparable, identical, and intricate. It is mentioned in the *Qur'ān* which refers to the verses that are ambiguous that is unintelligible some verses to the mind of people and it refers to the specific letters of openings of some chapters.[504]

Technically, the most ambiguous category of unclear in the *Ḥanafī madhhab* is the intricate (المتشابه). Sarakhsī described it as "the name for (an expression) for which there is no hope of understanding the meaning."[505] The other *Ḥanafī* scholars also maintained the similar definitions to that of Sarakhsī.[506] In fact it is a total mystery for us, nobody could know it except the Lawgiver alone, or except those people who have high level of understanding in knowledge. However, these intricate words still remain mystery.

Despite the *Ḥanafīs'* definition of the intricate, *Shāfi'ī* scholars, as we mentioned above, did not differentiate between the two, *mujmal* and *mutashābih*. However, they attribute four special features to *mutashābih* as *Shīrāzī* perceived: "The both unclear words, *mujmal* and *mutashābih* have the same definition and they are in fact one. The meaning of *mutashābih* is known by Allah alone. It includes, maxims, parables, the narratives, wisdom, the lawful and unlawful. *Mutashābih* contains also the individual letters at the beginning of some chapters.[507] In the contrary Ibn Ḥazm does not recognize *mutashābih* in the commandments (*awāmir* and *nawāhī*). According to him, the only category of ambiguity (*mubham*) is *mujmal* and thus anyone who makes such a claim is ignorant.[508]

However some scholar like Sha'bān said that after investigation and analysis lead us to believe that intricate (متشابه) in this sense does not exist neither in the *Qur'ān* nor in the *Sunnah* to clarify practical legal rulings. Thus, the intricate can be found within the texts which are not related to the *uṣūl al-fiqh* rulings.[509] Apart from this, they may be found relate to the field of *tawḥīd* and *'ilm al-kalām*, in some verses which refer to Allah and ascribe certain attributes to Him as well as pertaining to individual (abbreviated) letters (*muqaṭṭa'āt*) such as "الم-□-م-يس" which are found at the beginning of some *Qur'anic* chapters, as Allah (swt says in the *Qur'ān*: "*Surely those who swear allegiance to you do but swear allegiance to Allah; the hand of Allah is above their hands* ".[510]

Making similarity between Allah and His creatures with some attributes such as hand (يد), face (وجه) etc. should not be taken as their literal meaning of the verses since the *Qur'ān* openly rejects such similarity "*nothing like a likeness of Him; and He is the Hearing, the Seeing*".[511]

The exact indication of the text is not known, except by Allah, other interpretation may only be assumptions. The meanings of the individual (abbreviated) letters (*muqaṭṭa'āt*) are not known which remains hypothesis unless their meanings revealed to the Prophet (ṣ). In regards to these letters, a narration was given from Abū Bakr as-Ṣiddīq said: "Allah has placed His mystery in every book, and His mystery in the *Qur'ān* are these letters."[512] Therefore, these letters or other attributes should not be tried to be interpreted in any way. Despite the fact that the attributed words like hand (يد), face (وجه) etc. yet to be interpreted beyond their literal meanings would rather be in suitable metaphorical meanings. Allah mentioned the word the intricate (المتشابه) in the *Qur'ān*: "*He it is Who has revealed the Book to you; some of its verses are decisive, they are the basis of the Book, and others are allegorical; then as for those in whose hearts there is perversity they follow the part of it which is allegorical, seeking to mislead and seeking to give it (their own) interpretation. but none knows its interpretation except Allah, and those who are firmly rooted in knowledge say: We believe in it, it is all from our Lord; and none do mind except those having understanding*".[513]

This verse made the scholars to think differently. In the one hand, the first group who predicted that these intricate words can only be known to Allah made the full stop after the word "Allah" (ٱللَّهُ), in the other hand, those who made the full stop after the word "knowledge" (ٱلْعِلْمِ), interpreted that those are firmly grounded in knowledge also know the meaning of the intricate words. Although there are different opinions based on their *ijtihād* interpretations on this issue, the intricate meanings, in real sense, be known only by the Lawgiver Himself.[514] As the Prophet (ṣ) warned to those who are attempting to interpret the text of the *Qur'ān* based on their personal opinion, interpreting a text is a serious matter, "*He who speaks his own view of the Qur'ān is wrong even if what he says is right*".[515]

The value of the intricate (al-mutashābih)

The author also goes with the scholars of principles of Islamic jurisprudence (*uṣūl al-fiqh*) that they did mention the disagreement on the possibility of understanding the intricate verses. As the explanations of it and the examples provided within the technical approach the meaning of the intricate is known by the Lawgiver alone although there are different opinions. Since the scholars did not provide any certain examples related to jurisprudence (*fiqh*), because of the fact that it is not a matter of *uṣūl-al-fiqh* rather it is believed that it is for those of *'ilm al-kalām* and *tawḥīd*.

Conclusion

It is clearly explored above that clarity of indication (واضح الدلالة) which conveys an idea which is intelligible without recourse to any interpretation (*ta'wīl*), and therefore, a ruling (*ḥukm*) which is derived from a clear word constitute the basis of obligation. It is a self-sufficient text which needs no recourse to extraneous evidence. These are the manifest (الظاهر), the explicit (النص), the unequivocal, explained (المفسر), and the perspicuous/firm (المحكم). These four types are arranged in a ranking which starts with the least clear to the highest in respect of clarity which means the manifest (الظاهر) is the least clear and the perspicuous/firm (المحكم) is the highest clear. The *Ḥanafī* scholars have provided various definitions for each one of the concepts, while the *Shāfiʿī* scholars have different approach to clear (*wāḍiḥ*) words from that of the *Ḥanafīs*. They divided clear words into two categories only: the manifest (الظاهر) and the explicit (النص).

The unclear words (غير واضح او مبهم) in *Ḥanafī madhhab* is more comprehensive than *Shāfiʿī madhhab* in which their classifications are included. In other words *Shāfiʿī* scholars did not differentiate between the two, the ambivalent (المجمل) and the intricate (المتشابه) which were considered two in one that of *mujmal* is considered within the category of *mutashābih*, and therefore, most of the *Shāfiʿī* scholars consider *mujmal* and *mutashābih* the same. Nevertheless, all scholars agree that every unclear or ambiguous authoritative text which contains commandments is clarified by other source either from the *Qur'ān* or the *Sunnah*.

The level of obscurity is increased from less ambiguity to more ambiguity like the obscure (الخفي), the difficult (المشكل), the ambivalent (المجمل) and the intricate (المتشابه). The last one, on the one hand, is the most ambiguous and the first one is the less ambiguous on the other hand. Such as the *khafī* is the less ambiguous since it is the lowest level in ambiguity. The obscurity in *khafī* can be easily removed by exercising *ijtihād*

The less obscure category of *mubham* is *khafī*. In *khafī*, the apparent meaning has been disrupted by an external factor which can easily be eliminated by exercising *ijtihād*. However, the intended meaning is not discovered without external evidence and the obscurity may not be easily removed from the *mushkil* unless recourse to research a proper *ijtihād*. The *mujmal* became clear through a direct explanation by the text unless it remains ambiguous, because it is naturally ambiguous, once the ambiguity is removed it turns into *mufassar*.

As it has been seen that the *Ḥanafī* approach to unclear words

(غير واضح او مبهم) seems to be more precise and easy to comprehend. Removing the obscurity was the focal point in *Ḥanafī* division and anything that can help remove the ambiguity is essential to discover the intended meaning of the text.

Rules of Interpretation based on the Textual Implication (Dalālāt) (bi-i'tibāri kayfiyyat dalālat al-lafẓ 'alāl-ma'nā)

Introduction

Interpretation of the text, from the view point of the rules of indications or textual implications (*dalālāt*), is considered differently among the schools of thoughts especially among the *Ḥanafīs* and *Shāfi'īs*. In general the textual implications (*dalālāt*) will be divided into basically five categories and these are: 1. Explicit meaning "*'ibārah an-naṣṣ*" (عبارة النص), 2. Alluded meaning "*ishārah an-naṣṣ*" (إشارة النص), 3. Inferred meaning "*dalālah an-naṣṣ/Mafhūm al-muwafaqah*" (دلالة النص مفهوم الموافقة), 4. Required meaning "*iqtiḍā'an-naṣṣ*" (إقتضاء النص), 5. Divergent meaning "*mafhūm al-mukhālafah*" (مفهوم المخالفة). Despite a different approach that the both schools of thought, they have many common characteristics. *Shāfi'īs*, which is different from the *Ḥanafīs*' classification, divided it into mainly two types: the pronounced meaning (*dalālah al-manṭūq*) and the implied meaning (*dalālah al-mafhūm*).

In contrast to the *Ḥanafīs*, who classified textual indication as being of four types, the *Shāfi'ī* school of thought[516] divided it into two: pronounced meaning "*dalālah al-manṭūq*" (دلالة المنطوق) and implied meaning "*dalālah al-mafhūm*" (دلالة المفهوم). Both these indications are derived from the text and its words. The first one is consisted of two types: frank "*manṭūq ṣarīḥ*" (منطوق صريح) and not frank "*manṭūq ghayri ṣarīḥ*" (منطوق غير صريح). The not-frank consists of three types: required meaning "*dalālah al-iqtiḍā'*" (دلالة الإقتضاء), gestured meaning "*dalālah al-īmā'*" (دلالة الإيماء) and alluded meaning "*dalālah al-ishārah*" (دلالة الإشارة). The second one is consisted of agreed meaning "*mafhūm al-muwāfaqah*" (مفهوم الموافقة), which corresponds to the inferred meaning (دلالة النص) of the *Ḥanafīs*,[517] and the divergent meaning (مفهوم المخالفة), which is rejected by the *Ḥanafīs*. As it will be seen that the differences betweenthe two madhhab is only the divergent meaning (مفهوم المخالفة). It seems to be that the difference is based on a technical sense which the way the concepts are considered. Thus, more or less their approaches to the textual implication is very similar.

From the *Shāfi'ī* approach the pronounced meaning (*dalālah al-manṭūq*) linguistically refers to pronounced, uttered, said, text, wording.[518] Technical it is defined by several *Shāfi'ī* scholars who have offered similar definitions. For example Āmidī defined it as "what is undoubtedly understood with certainty from the word's indication."[519] Ījī offered *manṭūq* as "what has been understood with certainty from the text's words."[520] Ibn al-Subkī and Shawkānī also provided similar to this definition "that which the text indicates by its words."[521] These definitions seem to be that very much similar to the explicit meaning of the *Ḥanafī* division.

To the *Shāfi'ī* approach, if the *manṭūq* is not open to *ta'wīl* then it is considered *naṣṣ*, if otherwise, it is considered as *ẓāhir*. For them the *manṭūq* was divided into two types: frank (منطوق صريح) and not frank (منطوق غير صريح). It is when the text's necessary indication on a ruling intended by the speaker or not intended by the speaker that is indicated by the wording itself. Among the not-frank division, *dalālah al-iqtiḍā'* reflects the correctness of the text in one's mind and its rational and legal validity (*'aql* and *shar'*) that depend on its presumption. While the *dalālah al-īmā'* reflects the correctness of the text in the mind that its validity does not depend on its presumption and the *dalālah al-ishārah* is when the text's necessary indication on a ruling is not intended by the speaker.[522]

The second type of textual implications of the *Shāfiʿī* approach is the implied meaning (دلالة المفهوم) that is the implicit meaning reached by way of inference, and is not indicated by the word's apparent indication. It is accepted by the majority of Muslim scholars as a method of interpretation of the texts, except Ibn Ḥazm, the only one, who entirely rejected, claiming that it is a kind of analogy (*qiyās*) which is rejected entirely in the *Ẓāhirī* school of thought.[523] Despite the fact that, the founder of *Ẓāhirī* School, Dāwūd al-Ẓāhirī, who rejected analogy in general, recognized some kinds of the implied meaning (دلالة المفهوم) such as the clear analogy (*qiyās jalī*), if not, it is known as *mafhūm al-muwāfaqah*.[524]

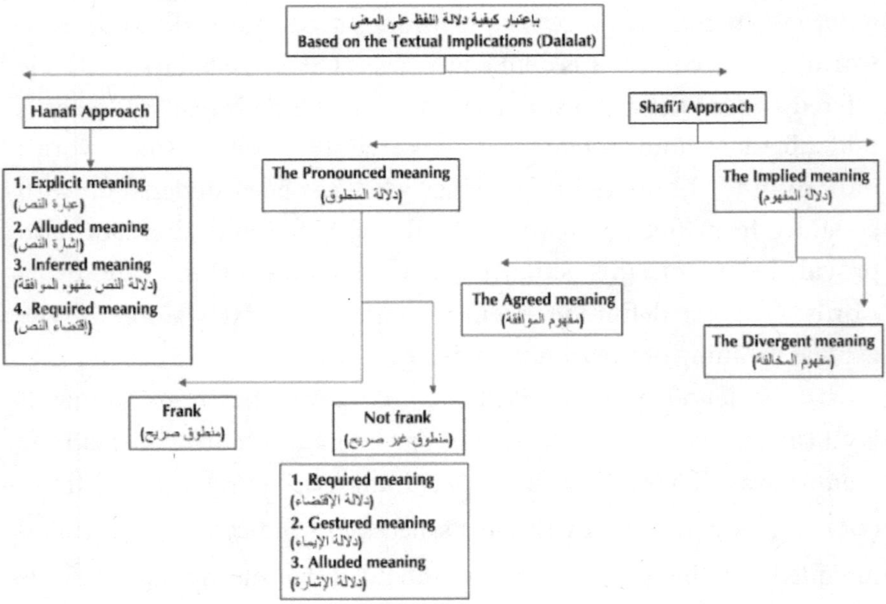

It has to be indicated that from the beginning of the journey towards to textual implication of the text of the *Qur'ān* and the *Sunnah*, deriving legal rulings from the main sources would be very difficult without a clear understanding and implication which reflect from the texts. Studying *uṣūl al-fiqh* in relation to the textual implication is so essential to understand the intention of the Lawgiver. Since the rulings derived from the text not always clearly indicated the methods of interpretation of the text will help the mujtahid to uncover the hidden meanings just like a treasure which is hidden under the earth can be disclosed by excavation through research and hardworking and sensitive excavation in order not to damage the underground historic monuments and treasures.

Ḥanafīs arrive at the textual implication through the following way either of explicit meaning, a meaning indicated by signs and allusion, a meaning derived from the logical and juridical purport of the text or logical and necessary meaning without which the text would remain incomplete and fail to achieve its purpose. Therefore, from this understanding they divides it into four types a) Explicit meaning (عبارة النص), b) Alluded meaning (إشارة النص), c) Inferred meaning (دلالة النص), d) Required meaning (إقتضاء النص).[525]

These categorisation are also divided into mainly two types from the view point of indication of the text. From one hand it is based on the indication of the words which is whether intended or not by the speaker. If it is directly indicated which indication represents the principle or subsidiary theme of the text is called the explicit meaning (عبارة النص), while it is not directly indicated or the intention of the speaker is not directly given is called the alluded meaning (إشارة النص). On the other hand, it is not derived from the text itself but based on logical or legal understanding from the text. If it is linguistically understood then it is called the inferred meaning (دلالة النص), if however, it is understood legally and logically, without which the text would be incomplete and fail to achieve its purpose that is based on the *Sharī'ah* then it is called the required meaning (إقتضاء النص). Lastly, according to *Ḥanafī* jurists the last one which indicates the opposite meaning of the text that is called divergent meaning (مفهوم المخالفة) is not considered a valid interpretation.

In a nutshell, the lowest level of indication is the required meaning (إقتضاء النص) and the inferred meaning (دلالة النص) is the next, followed by the alluded meaning (إشارة النص) and the last as well as the highest level of indication is the explicit meaning or immediate meaning (عبارة النص). If however, any conflict arises among these levels, the highest one would prevail over the lowest due to their levels of clarity of indication.

Besides the *Ḥanafīs'* main division of the four types of the textual implication, they considered them also differently as they are a) Indication with the text (دال بالعبارة); b) Indication with the alluding (دال بالاشارة); c) Indication with the indicating (دال بالدلالة); d) Indication with the requiring (دال بالاقتضاء).[526] Nevertheless, general types of textual implications from *Ḥanafī* and *Shāfiʿī* perspectives will be discussed in details at the following pages.

The Explicit Meaning ('ibārah al-naṣṣ)

Linguistically the explicit or immediate meaning "*'ibārah al-naṣṣ*" (عبارة النص) refers to declared, manifest meaning of the text. It also refers to an author's original text and it is whatever the speaker articulates as well as it is a written passage.[527] *Naṣṣ* also refers to the text of the *Qur'ān* or *ḥadīth* which is presented as justification for a legal ruling.[528]

Technically, it is defined by the juristic scholars as follows: Bazdawī defined, "The argumentation by the explicit meaning (*'ibārah al-naṣṣ*) is acting according to the apparent meaning that the speech is stated for."[529] Sarakhsī stated, "The established ruling according to the explicit meaning is that ruling which agrees with the context of the statement. This ruling is normally understood as the subject of that text even without thinking."[530] It is an immediate meaning of the words that is intended to provide such ruling no matter whether it represents the principal theme and purpose of the text or a subsidiary theme or themes. It is also a meaning which comes to the mind without further consideration even if more than one meaning appears in the mind of *mujtahid* can be considered within this definition even if it represents the principal theme and purpose of the text or a subsidiary theme which are derived apparently from the text.[531] The explicit meaning (*'ibārah al-naṣṣ*) which corresponds to the frank (منطوق صريح) of the *Shāfi'ī* school of thought since it linguistically states and plainly pronounces the ruling.

First example of the explicit meaning ('ibārah al-naṣṣ)

In regards to the prohibition of usury (*ribā*) and the permissibility of trade, the *Qur'ān* states: "*Those who swallow down usury cannot arise except as one whom Shaiṭān has prostrated by (his) touch does rise. That is because they say, trading is only like usury; and Allah has allowed trading and forbidden usury*".[532]

According to this verse, two meanings are distinguishable and both denote a ruling. One is the permissibility of trading and prohibition of usury. The other one is the differences of the two rulings of that one denotes that trading is permissible and the other one denotes that usury is prohibited. It is obvious that these two rulings are different from the point of view that the former is subsidiary, while the latter is the principle theme and purpose of the text, because the verse was not revealed for the purpose of explaining the rules of the both, however it was revealed for the purpose of denying the claim of similarity between trade and usury.[533] Although the both rulings are derived from the same verse, one reflects the principle theme of the text and the other is not. Despite the fact that no extra effort is needed or *ijtihād* to achieve these meanings, the apparent meanings are deduced from the apparent meaning of the text obviously. Thus every authoritative text relating to legal rulings which convey an apparent meaning is an example of *'ibārah al-naṣṣ*, because the Lawgiver has delivered these expressions in order to convey meanings and rulings obviously. Since this verse linguistically states that trading is allowed and usury forbidden and plainly pronounced the ruling is considered *manṭūq ṣarīḥ* for *Shāfi'ī* school of thought.

Second example of the explicit meaning

In regards to a ruling on marriage the *Qur'ān* states: "*And if you fear that you cannot act equitably towards orphans, then marry such women as seem good to you, two and three and four; but if you fear that you will not do justice (between them), then (marry) only one or what your right hands possess; this is more proper, that you may not deviate from the right course*".[534]

This verse may provide a few obvious meanings as follow: The legality of marriage, limiting polygamy to a maximum of four wives, remaining monogamous for someone who fears that polygamy may lead to injustice, and the requirement that orphaned girls must be accorded fair treatment, a meaning which is indicated in the first part of the text.

All of these rulings are clearly indicated by the actual words and sentences of the text. However, all these meanings and rulings are not the whole principle theme and purpose of the text. Rather the first and the last are subsidiary and incidental (secondary) whereas the second and the third represent the explicit themes and meanings of the text, which are the reason for its revelation[535] and eventually it is called the explicit meaning (عبارة النص). Thus, this verse came down as a warning against injustice to women. Men were not to take more than four wives, and if they fear that they may commit an injustice then only one. Basically, limiting polygamy to the maximum of four is the explicit meaning which takes absolute priority over all the implied and secondary meanings by this verse.

In terms of its indication, majority of *Ḥanafīs* retain that the indication of *'ibārah al-naṣṣ* is definite (*qaṭ'ī*) as long as there is no a reliable proof exist.[536] In addition to that according to *Ḥanafīs* the definite meaning (*qaṭ'ī al-dalālah*) has wider importance than its apparent linguistic meaning.[537]

The value of the explicit meaning

The implementation of the explicit meaning (عبارة النص) as well as its legal adherence should be strict obligation (واجب).[538]

The Alluded Meaning (ishārah al-naṣṣ)

Linguistically alluded "*ishārah*" (إشارة) refers to gesture, sign, symbol, signal, indication, allusion, and hint. In Arabic rhetoric the word has acquired the technical meaning of 'allusion'.[539] The word text (*naṣṣ*) in the science of principles of Islamic law (اصول الفقه) refers to either the text of the *Qur'ān* or the *ḥadīth*. Therefore, the concept of the alluded meaning (إشارة النص) has to deal with a text from the *Qur'ān* and the *ḥadīth*.

Technically, the alluded meaning "*ishārah al-naṣṣ*" (إشارة النص) was considered by the *Ḥanafī* scholars in different definitions. Such as Dabbūsī defined it as "That which is established by allusion is neither required nor conveyed by the speech context. However, *ishārah al-naṣṣ* is indicated specifically by the apparent (meaning) without increasing or decreasing its meaning."[540] Bazdawī explained it with this definition "It is that which has been composed through language, although it is not in the subject matter of the context or the text. Moreover, it is not apparent in all aspects."[541] Similarly Sarakhsī maintained it with the following expression: "What is established by allusion is not the purpose of the text. It can, however, be understood by considering the meaning of the word without increasing or decreasing that meaning."[542] It is known that the alluded meaning does not represent the principal theme of the text and yet expresses a necessary implication. Nevertheless, it may be easily detectable in the text, or a serious investigation and *ijtihād* may be needed to explore the alluded meaning.

The alluded meaning (إشارة النص) which corresponds to the alluded meaning (دلالة الإشارة) of the *Shāfiʿīs*. The meaning that is indicated by the text even if its correctness and validity, rationally and legally, do not depend on the presumption of that meaning which, presumably, was not intended by the speaker. In other words, it is a necessary meaning which is not intended by the speaker.

First example of the alluded meaning

The *Qur'ān* states in regards to the duty of a father towards his wives and children: "*And the mothers should suckle their children for two whole years for him who desires to make complete the time of suckling; and their maintenance and their clothing must be – borne by the father according to usage*".[543]

In order to bring out alluded meaning of the text, explicit meaning of the text first should be provided. The explicit meaning of the text is that the maintenance of mothers and their children is the fathers' duty. The pronoun 'his' (لَهُ) clearly explores that no one else but 'the father' bears this obligation, and such ruling is understood from the explicit meaning of the text since the explicit meaning is apparent from the text and thus the reason for which this text was revealed it is called the explicit meaning (عبارة النص).[544] Besides this apparent meaning, there may be some more meaning or rulings derived through further analysis or by the use of *ijtihād* as in the following rulings: first, the child's descent is solely attributable to the father and the identity of him is determined with reference to the father. Second, the child follows the tribe of the father, no matter what tribe the mother belongs to. Third, the duty of the child solely belongs to the father since the child is considered him.[545] Fourth, the father may take what he needs from the wealth of his children without permission and without any obligation to return it. As this ruling was derived from the narration in which the Prophet (ṣ) was asked by one of the Companions: "O Messenger of Allah, I have wealth and children and my father wants to take from my wealth." The Prophet (ṣ) replied, "You and your property belong to your father"[546] This ruling is derived from *ishārah al-naṣṣ.*"Another ruling is that the father may not be punished with a prescribed had punishment against his child, if he commits a crime such as the father would not receive capital punishment if he killed his child, yet he will not be punished in the case of slanderous accusation of fornication against his own child.[547] Although the above rulings, which are derived by the alluded meaning (إشارة النص), are the inevitable consequences of that attribution by way of the alluded meaning (إشارة النص), these meanings do not represent the principal or subsidiary theme or purpose of the text. It is the fact the all these rulings are the natural consequences of the reality that a child's descent is solely attributable to the father.

Second example of the alluded meaning

In regards to be kind towards his parents the *Qur'ān* states: "*And We have enjoined on man doing of good to his parents; with trouble did his mother bear him and with trouble did she bring him forth; and the bearing of him and the weaning of him was thirty months*".[548]

The context of the verse obviously indicate the favour, grace and kindness of parents towards their children through the explicit meaning (عبارة النص). The verse also clearly indicate that children are commanded to be kind to their parents due to their kindness to them since the mother who bears her child with hardship and brings them forward with difficulties. However, at the same time, this verse indicates by alluded meaning (إشارة النص) that the bearing of a child takes at least six months, since another verse states that weaning is for two years: "*And We have enjoined man in respect of his parents, his mother bore him in weakness upon weakness; and his weaning is in two years – be thankful to Me and to your parents, for unto Me is the final destination*".[549]

The explicit meaning of the text was the reason for which this text was revealed and which however, the textual allusion of this verse which are derived through further analysis of the signs detectable within the text in which if both the bearing and the weaning are thirty months and the weaning alone is two years in the other verse, then logically a new ruling which may be extracted that the bearing takes six months that is the alluded meaning (*ishārah al-naṣṣ*) which was remained hidden for the majority of the Companions until a further analysis is needed for the discovery which happened to ʻAli Ibn Abū Ṭālib.[550]

The value of the alluded meaning

The legal obedience on the alluded meaning (إشارة النص) is strictly obligatory (وجوب). The effect of the alluded meaning (*ishārah al-naṣṣ*) is that it conveys a definitive ruling (*ḥukm qaṭʻī*) on its own and that is similar to that of the explicit meaning (عبارة النص) since they indicate obligation, no need of confirmatory evidence, unless there is reliable evidence suggesting otherwise.[551] However, the *ishārah al-naṣṣ* alternates between definite (*qaṭʻī*) and indefinite (*ẓannī*), depending on the circumstances and position of the expression which may be either real or metaphorical, if not, it is definite. This opinion is upheld by Sarakhsī, Bazdawī and Bukhārī.[552] *Ḥanafī* scholars, with the opinion of Sarakhsī, have agreed that if *ishārah al-naṣṣ* supposes another meaning based on a reliable proof, its indication would be indefinite (*ẓannī al-dalālah*); otherwise it has a definite meaning (*qaṭʻī al-dalālah*) which means ʻthe non-existence of a possibility based on a proof and that the general meaning when limited becomes indefinite (*ẓannī al-dalālah*).[553] Supposing that if a conflict occurs between these two, *ʻibārah* and *ishārah*, due to their level of indication, *ʻibārah* would prevail over the *ishārah* since, it is obvious that the majority of scholars maintain that *ʻibārah al-naṣṣ* indicates a definite meaning, while *ishārah al-naṣṣ* may indicate either definite or indefinite meanings depending on the circumstances and position of the expression which may be either real or metaphorical. Even if the both indicate a definite meaning, *'ibārah al-naṣṣ* has priority over the *ishārah al-naṣṣ* due to the fact that the meaning intended by the speaker is stronger than that which is not intended by the speaker. Eventually, in the event of a conflict between the two, the *'ibārah al-naṣṣ* would be preferred over the *ishārah al-naṣṣ*.

The inferred meaning (mafhūm al-muwāfaqah/dalālah al-naṣṣ)

Linguistically *dalālah* (دلالة) refers to sign, indication, denotation, notion; word signification or indication of meaning and these may be divided into three types: complete correspondence (*muṭābaqāh*); partial inclusion (*taḍammun*) and a necessary idea attached to the meaning in the mind (*iltizām*).[554]

Technically, Bazdawī expressed his definition while referring to its meaning as "What the inferred meaning establishes is obtained by the linguistic meaning of the text, and not by legal reasoning or deduction."[555] Similarly, Sarakhsī offered the following definition: "What the inferred meaning establishes it does so linguistically by the composition's meaning not by rational deduction."[556] Precisely, Bukhārī provided a definition with this fashion: "*Dalālah al-naṣṣ* is understanding the unpronounced from the pronounced by the context and purpose of speech."[557] These are the definitions provided by the *Ḥanafī* scholars about the inferred meaning (دلالة النص).

Considering the above definitions, a ruling based on *dalālah al-naṣṣ* may be established linguistically, not based on scholarly deduction or legal reasoning *ijtihād*. It may also be concluded that *dalālah al-naṣṣ* is the indication of the text that the ruling is valid for another case, because both of these cases have a common effective cause (*'illah*).[558] It is very obvious that anyone who understands the language would understand it without recourse to *ijtihād* or further investigation. The inferred meaning (*dalālah al-naṣṣ*) is derived from identification with the effective cause of the ruling (*'illah al-ḥukm*) that is common to both the explicit meaning (*'ibārah al-naṣṣ*) and the meaning derived through inference (*dalālah al-naṣṣ*), in contrast to the explicit meaning (*'ibārah al-naṣṣ*) and the alluded meaning (*ishārah al-naṣṣ*), which are both indicated through words and signs in the text. In other words, the ruling that was deduced from the explicit meaning (*'ibārah al-naṣṣ*), may also be valid for another case which has not been mentioned that is named as the inferred meaning (دلالة النص) due to the same cause is used for the both.[559]

In *Shāfi'ī* approach of the textual implication, the gestured meaning (دلالة الإيماء) may also correspond to the inferred meaning (دلالة النص). The gestured meaning (دلالة الإيماء) is a necessary meaning intended by the speaker when correctness of the text and its rational and legal validity do not depend on the presumption. It is explored by the *Shāfi'ī* scholars with the following verse: "*And (as for) the man who steals and the woman who steals, cut off their hands as a punishment for what they have earned, an exemplary punishment from Allah; and Allah is Mighty, Wise*".[560]

The ruling announced in this verse includes an intended explanation and justification that the speaker offers for the ruling. It clearly affirms that theft was the reason for the introduction of this ruling. The actual meaning of the text is established by simple linguistic meaning.

Some other scholars have used this indication for the meaning of the purpose of statement and objective as "*fahwā al-khitāb*" (فحوى الخطاب) or "*dalālah al-dalālah*" (دلالة الدلالة). It is clear that the ruling in the case of *dalālah al-naṣṣ* is taken from the meaning of the text and not from its words. In the *Shāfi'ī* school of thought, it is termed "*mafhūm al-muwāfaqah*" (مفهوم الموافقة) because the indication of the words, in the instance pronounced, corresponds to its indication in the instance which has not been manifested. Therefore *'ibārah al-naṣṣ* and *dalālah al-naṣṣ* agree with each other when the same effective cause for a ruling is a matter of case.[561]

The agreed meaning (مفهوم الموافقة) of the *Shāfiʿī* school of thought which corresponds to the inferred meaning (دلالة النص) since these two implicitly indicate and agree with the meaning of the text which indicates the ruling. Linguistically the agreed meaning (*mafhūm al-muwāfaqah*) is consisted of two words: *mafhūm* (مفهوم) and *muwāfaqah* (الموافقة).[562] The former refers to understood, known implied, implicit, tacit, notion, connotation; the meaning, or sense in which the word is understood,[563] and the later refers to correspondence, agreement, conformity, coincidence, compatibility, consistence, accordance, harmony.[564]

Technically, it is defined by Āmidī with two similar definitions: "Where the ruling of the unpronounced agrees with the ruling of the pronounced."[565] The other one is: "It is the implicit indication which agrees with the pronounced indication."[566] Shawkānī maintained with a similar statement of Āmidī: "Where the unpronounced agrees with the pronounced."[567] These *Shāfiʿī* definitions reminds the definitions of the *Ḥanafīs*. Therefore *mafhūm al-muwāfaqah* is also share a common effective cause (*ʿillah*) with the indication of the certain meaning (ruling) of the text and the pronounced meaning (ruling) within another text. Thus, the implicit indication takes the ruling of the pronounced. The understanding of that effective cause is so simple which it does not need any legal reasoning (*ijtihād*). For example, the *Qur'ān* states, in the verse (17:23) which will be explained later, about the prohibition of offensive behaviour in any way to parents. The agreed meaning (*mafhūm al-muwāfaqah*) indicates that other forms of offensive behaviour, like cursing, beating etc., are also forbidden because the effective cause for the prohibition applies to them equally or with even more reason. According to the *Shāfiʿī* methodology, if however, another form of offensive behaviour that is mentioned in the text as "*ʿuff*" is equal with another words, it would be termed *laḥn al-khitāb* (parallel meaning), if it is more offensive than the original word such as beating and cursing, it would be termed *fahwā al-khitāb* (superior meaning) that is the prohibition of something in small amounts indicates its prohibition in greater amounts. It is, vice versa, inferred from the *ḥadīth* of the Prophet (ṣ) "If a large amount of anything causes intoxication, a small amount of it is prohibited."[568] However, some scholars of *uṣūl al-fiqh* disagreed about the consideration of the two types of *mafhūm* as *laḥn al-khitāb* (parallel meaning) and *fahwā al-khitāb* (superior meaning).[569] Nevertheless, both *Ḥanafīs* and *Shāfi'īs* consider that the effective cause of the pronounced is equivalent to that of the unpronounced.[570]

The indication of mafhūm al-muwāfaqah resembles that of later Ḥanafī scholars who considered dalālah al-naṣṣ with definite and indefinite. Thus Shāfi'ī scholars divided mafhūm al-muwāfaqah into two types: definite (*qaṭ'ī*) and indefinite (*ẓannī*).[571]

The above explanations may be better comprehended by considering the below examples that of *Ḥanafī* and *Shāfi'ī* scholars illustrated similar discussions.

First example of the inferred meaning (dalālah al-naṣṣ)

The *Qur'ān* states: "*And your Lord has commanded that you shall not serve (any) but Him, and goodness to your parents. If either or both of them reach old age with you, say not to them (so much as) "Uff" nor chide them, and speak to them a generous word; And make yourself submissively gentle to them with compassion, and say: O my Lord! have compassion on them, as they brought me up (when I was) little*".[572]

The statement in the text "say not to them (so much as) "*uff*" (فَلَا تَقُل لَّهُمَا أُفٍّ) obviously indicates forbidding utterance to the slightest respect to parents. Firstly, it is explicitly understood from the text that any kind of disrespect towards parents is forbidden. It requires a duty upon children to treat his parents gently with high respect and honour. From the language perspective, the effective cause for the prohibition against uttering the slightest word of disrespect to parents is the avoidance of offending them, and any kind of respect should be extended towards them. Secondly, even if such an utterance a slight word of disrespect to parents is forbidden, other forms of offensive behaviour like beating, cursing must be forbidden and this behaviour is implicit in the text that is the inferred meaning (*dalālah al-naṣṣ*). The effective cause for the prohibition applies to both equally, slight words and any other forms of offensive behaviour. Without recourse to legal reasoning and research, any forms of abuse words and acts which offend the parents are forbidden. This ruling can be understood by anyone who understand the language even if these offensive words are not mentioned in the text.[573]

Second example of the inferred meaning

The *Qur'ān* states: "*(As for) those who swallow the property of the orphans unjustly, surely they only swallow fire into their bellies and they shall enter burning fire*".[574]

This verse also explicitly indicate that the unjustified 'swallowing' or eating up of the property of orphans is forbidden (*ḥarām*). It is forbidden (*ḥarām*) for facilitators, guardians anyone who looks after them, for using it for their own personal achievement. The effective cause of this prohibition (unjustified swallowing) may be understood by anyone who knows the language. The clear effective cause may be extended to other situations where the effective cause for protecting orphans' property by fear of Allah from its ruin, waste, and misuse by way of the inferred meaning (*dalālah al-naṣṣ*). For example, since it is not your own property, the fear prevents you from financial mismanagement that involves no personal benefit and yet causes the loss and destruction of orphans' property when it is involved in business. Despite the fact that, the financial mismanagement, carelessness, and destruction were not indicated in the verse, by way of the inferred meaning (*dalālah al-naṣṣ*) these indications are equally forbidden due to the same affective cause.

Third example of the inferred meaning

The *Qur'ān* states: "*And the divorced women should keep themselves in waiting for three courses; and it is not lawful for them that they should conceal what Allah has created in their wombs, if they believe in Allah and the last day; and their husbands have a better right to take them back in the meanwhile if they wish for reconciliation; and they have rights similar to those against them in a just manner, and the men are a degree above them, and Allah is Mighty, Wise*".[575]

Indication of the text from the first part as of a period of waiting before remarriage is obligatory for a divorced women is explicit meaning (*'ibārah al-naṣṣ*) which is clearly understood from the text. In addition to that, one may easily detect from the viewpoint of the Arabic language, the effective cause for this ruling is establishing whether the woman carries a child from her former husband or not. From this perception, paternity will not be confused when she wants to remarry. However, this effective cause, perhaps may become ineffective by technological advancement.[576] Nevertheless, this effective cause occurs in every kind of separation between husband and wife, whether the divorce is by *khul* (a request from the wife for divorce)[577] or the death of the husband. The inferred meaning (*dalālah al-naṣṣ*) of the text here is that in all cases women have to wait the prescribed period, like the divorced wife mentioned in the verse similar to the explicit meaning (*'ibārah al-naṣṣ*) which share the same effective cause with the inferred meaning (*dalālah al-naṣṣ*).

Fourth example of the inferred meaning

The *Qur'ān* states: "*So, he who has done an atom's weight of good shall see it. And he who has done an atom's weight of evil shall see it*".[578] The pronounced apparent meaning (*mafhūm al-muwāfaqah*) is clear and the reader can understand the meaning of the text easily, that people will also see the good they did which is greater than an atom's weight, just as those who do evil will see more than an atom's weight interchangeably. In addition, the Prophet (ṣ) states, "*He who steals a staff (walking stick) from his brother must return it.*"[579] The meaning of the ḥadīth can also be easily understood by way of the pronounced apparent meaning (*mafhūm al-muwāfaqah*). Thus, any stolen good that is more valuable should also be returned.

The value of the inferred meaning

Since the effective of the inferred meaning (*dalālah al-naṣṣ*) relates to the effect of the textual allusion (*ishārah al-naṣṣ*), and the adherence to dalālah al-naṣṣ should be obligatory which means that both indicate the definite (*qaṭ'ī*) meaning if there is no proof which suggests otherwise. For the *Shāfi'ī* scholars, the adherence to *mafhūm al-muwāfaqah* (مفهوم الموافقة) is strictly obligatory as of the same as the inferred meaning (*dalālah al-naṣṣ*). There is unanimous agreement between Muslim scholars that *mafhūm al-muwāfaqah* is a *ḥujjah* (legal proof) that must be obeyed.[580]

Nevertheless, still there is some little conflict which may occur due to the conceptual difference as well as similarity of the effective cause with the concept of *qiyās*.[581] From *Ḥanafī* scholars Bazdawī and Sarakhsī[582] explained the difference between *dalālah al-naṣṣ* and *qiyās*, but they did not consider if the indications of *dalālah al-naṣṣ* is definite (*qaṭ'ī*) or indefinite (*ẓannī*). Sarakhsī explained that understanding the effective cause in the case of *dalālah al-naṣṣ* is common with both what is pronounced (*manṭūq*) and what is not unpronounced (*maskūt 'anh*) which entirely depends entirely on knowledge of the language. However, in analogy, discovering the common effective cause in an original case (*maqīs 'alayh*) and in a subsidiary (a new) case (*maqīs*) requires certain specialized abilities from the *mujtahid*. Therefore, the effective cause, in the case of *dalālah al-naṣṣ*, can be understood by scholars who possess legal knowledge (*fuqahā'*) and others with a knowledge of the language only, while in the case of analogy the effective cause can be understood only by scholars with legal knowledge. In other words the difference relies on the type of knowledge whether it is from language or from legal. In addition to the above consideration, some later *Ḥanafī* scholars,[583] focused on the indication of *dalālah al-naṣṣ* whether it is definite (*qaṭī'*) or indefinite (*ẓannī*) approaches.

If, however, any conflict occurs among the inferred meaning (دلالة النص) and the alluded meaning (إشارة النص), the later would prevail over the former. Although the inferred meaning and the textual allusion seems to be at the same level of strength and value, because both have a definite indication if a reliable proof does not suggest otherwise since the indication of the both is derived from the understandable meaning of the text, which its spirit and notion by relying on linguistic knowledge, rather than on legal reasoning and deduction as opposed to the methodology of analogical deduction (*qiyās*). Despite the fact that the both have the equality of the effective cause, the textual allusion (إشارة النص) has priority in the event of conflict with the inferred meaning.[584]

The Required Meaning (iqtiḍā' al-naṣṣ)

Linguistically *iqtiḍā'* (إقتضاء) refers to need, necessity, exigency, requirement, request, demand, such as *iqtiḍā' al-dayn* (he required the debt) etc.[585]

Technically, the required meaning is an indication on which the text itself is silent and seems to be a missing word in the text and yet which must be interpreted by which it must fit the proper objective of the text. It is unlike the previous three kinds of indications, the required meaning "*iqtiḍā' al-naṣṣ*" (إقتضاء النص) is not indicated by the text or its meaning, nevertheless, a meaning which is suitable with the text or valid in *Sharī'ah*, by way of requirement that is presumed to explain the missing meaning for its objective.

Hanafi scholars like Dabbūsī defined *iqtiḍā' al-naṣṣ* as "an addition to the text without which the meaning of the text cannot be fulfilled."[586] Further Sarakhsī defined it as "an addition to that which is laid down in the text."[587] They differ on the issue of whether or not *iqtiḍā' al-naṣṣ* includes absent and concealed words (*mahdhūf* and *muḍmar*). Nevertheless, they did not make any distinction between *iqtiḍā' al-naṣṣ* and *muhdhūf.*

Dabbūsī, for example, included *mahdhūf* by making that which has to be presumed as one division as he provided an example that he did not differentiate between *iqtiḍā' al-naṣṣ* and *mahdhūf* with this verse "*And inquire in the town in which we were and the caravan with which we proceeded, and most surely we are truthful*".[588]

According to him the enquiry "And inquire in the town" is directed to the people in town, not the town itself since the aim of the enquiry is to be achieved through the people. Thus, the presumed word or the object would be "the people" in order to make the speech reasonable.[589]

Similarly, Sarakhsī considered that *iqtiḍā' al-naṣṣ* indicated a meaning upon which depended the truthfulness of speech or its validity in the *Sharī'ah*. Thus, he excluded the absent and the concealed and maintained that those who included them in *iqtiḍā' al-naṣṣ* did so by mistake because what is absent is different from what is required (*muqtaḍā*).[590]

However, later *Ḥanafī* scholars distinguished between *iqtiḍā' al-naṣṣ* and *mahdhūf*, maintaining that the meaning which must be presumed in order to make the text reasonable and valid in *Sharī'ah* is called *muqtaḍā*, and the meaning which must be presumed in order to make the text truthful and correct in the mind is said to be absent (*mahdhūf*) or concealed (*muḍmar*). In spite of the fact that the two groups of scholars. The majority do not acknowledge the distinction, while the second group of scholars, restrict *iqtiḍā' al-naṣṣ* to what has to be presumed in order to make speech accurate and valid for *Sharī'ah*, not language or mind.[591] Thus, the majority's opinion which is not distinguished between *iqtiḍā' al-naṣṣ* and *mahdhūf* that depend the correctness of that text and its validity in the *Sharī'ah* and mind (*'aql*) is preferable. In addition to the *Ḥanafī's* consideration of the *iqtiḍā' al-naṣṣ* which corresponds to the *dalālah al-iqtiḍā'* of *Shāfi'ī* consideration. *Dalālah al-iqtiḍā'* reflects the correctness of the text in one's mind and its rational and legal validity (*'aql* and *shar'*) depend on the presumption of a meaning, in other words, it is a necessary meaning that is intended by the speaker.

Examples of the required meaning

The following examples come with some missing words which are need to be presumed. The *Qur'ān* states: "*Forbidden to you are your mothers and your daughters and*".[592]

This verse explains the prohibited degree of relations in marriage. However, it does not mention explicitly the word 'marriage'. Thus, this word is required in order to make the verse sounds the truth. With that reason, the missing word "marriage" has to be read into the text to complete the meaning.

Similarly, the *Qur'ān* states in regards to the prohibited items for consuming: "*Forbidden to you is that which dies of itself, and blood, and flesh of swine, and...*"[593]Although this verse does not mention the word "for consumption," this must be presumed in order to complete the meaning of the text, otherwise, it cause confusion since the aim of prohibition is not mentioned in the text such as for eating, touching, smelling, looking etc.

The value of the required meaning

The *iqtiḍā' al-naṣṣ* is a definite meaning in which the ruling based on it has the same value as that based on the explicit, alluded or inferred meanings so long as no proof suggests otherwise. The obedience to *iqtiḍā' al-naṣṣ* should be a strict obligation (*wājib*).[594] Therefore, the effect of the required meaning is similar to that of the three previously mentioned meanings. Sarakhsī discussed these four indications in his work.[595]

The Divergent Meaning (mafhūm al-mukhālafah)

The divergent meaning "*mafhūm al-mukhālafah*" (مفهوم المخالفة) is the only major difference between the *Ḥanafīs* and the *Shāfiʿī* schools of thought, the former rejected it,[596] while the latter accepted it under certain conditions.[597] In fact the rejection of the *Ḥanafīs* is based only when authoritative texts and their implications are in question.[598] However, as we mentioned that it seems to be that the difference is based on a technical sense which the way the concepts are considered. Thus, more or less their approaches to the textual implication is very similar.

Linguistically, this concept is composed of two words: *mafhūm* and *al-mukhālafah*. *Mafhūm* refers to understood, implied, known, tacit; notion, connotation; the meaning, or sense, in which a word is understood,[599] and *mukhālafah* refers to opposite, divergent, varying, different; inconsistent, incompatible, contradictory.[600]

Technically, the divergent meaning (مفهوم المخالفة) is defined by Āmidī, it is an implicit indication which is opposite to the pronounced indication.[601] Similarly Qarāfi defined it as follows: "Establishing for an unpronounced a ruling opposite to the pronounced."[602]

As it is mentioned above that *Ḥanafīs* do not recognize the divergent meaning (مفهوم المخالفة) and its implications if it is based on authoritative texts, because it leads to distortion.[603] They brought the following example to justify their claim, for instance, the *Qur'ān* states: "*Surely the number of months with Allah is twelve months in Allah's ordinance since the day when He created the heavens and the earth, of these four being sacred; that is the right reckoning; therefore be not unjust to yourselves regarding them, and fight the polytheists all together as they fight you all together; and know that Allah is with those who guard (against evil)*".[604]

According to explicit meaning this text indicates that four months are sacred, and during these months injustice should be avoided.

Therefore, the divergent meaning indicates that injustice is allowed in the rest of the year. However, it obviously contradicts the purpose of this verse, since oppression (*ẓulm*) or injustice is always forbidden, whenever it happens regardless of the time and the month.

Types of the divergent meaning

Despite *Ḥanafīs* rejected the divergent meaning (مفهوم المخالفة), the *Shāfi'īs* and the *Mālikīs* validated the application of it to the *nuṣūṣ*. They have conditioned further restrictions which consist of specifying exactly what forms of linguistic expressions are amenable to this method of textual implication. Therefore, the *Shāfi'īs* have divided it into four types for the sake of introducing greater accuracy into the practice of it, stating that the divergent meaning (مفهوم المخالفة) is an acceptable method of textual implication if it corresponds to the set condition.[605] The divergent meaning (مفهوم المخالفة) thus may appear in the following types according to the *Shāfi'ī* school of thought.[606]

First: Implication of the Attribute (mafhūm al-ṣifah)

The "*mafhūm al-ṣifah*" is an implication of the word that is limited by an attribute or quality, suggesting that an opposite ruling is established in the case of the silent or unpronounced only when that quality is existing. The following example may explain it. The *Qur'ān* states: "*O you who believe! if an evil-doer comes to you with a report, look carefully into it, lest you harm a people in ignorance, then be sorry for what you have done*".[607]

According to this text, the explicit meaning that is pronounced meaning indicates that if the reporters of the news is an evil person it must be carefully investigated, however, by the way of the divergent meaning if the reporter is not an evil person, the news must not be investigated or verified. The reporter of the news is attributed by a word "*fāsiq*" (evil person). Thus the reporter is qualified with that attribute which is conditioned by its existing.

Another example, in regards to the prohibited degrees of relations in marriage. The *Qur'ān* states: "*and the wives of your sons who are of your own loins and*".[608]

The explicit or pronounced meaning of the text indicates the wives of one's own son in marriage is prohibited. The one's own son is qualified in the text by the statement "*of your own loins.*" Therefore, it is concluded from this qualification that the wife of a son by fosterage (*raḍā'a*), which is a child who has suckled the breast of one's wife, or an adopted son, is not prohibited by way of the divergent meaning (مفهوم المخالفة).

Second: Implication of the Condition (mafhūm al-sharṭ)

The "*mafhūm al-sharṭ*" happens when the ruling of a text is depending on a condition, then the ruling obtains only in the existence of that condition, otherwise it lapses. The key point is that the indication of the word depends on a condition, if, however, opposite ruling may happen in the case of the unpronounced when that condition is not occurred. An example can be given about the entitlement to maintenance of divorced women who are observing their waiting period (*'iddah*). The *Qur'ān* states: "*Lodge them where you lodge according to your means, and do not injure them in order that you may straiten them; and if they are pregnant, spend on them until they lay down their burden; then if they suckle for you, give them their recompense and,*".[609]

According to the pronounced meaning of the text that a man should provide maintenance for the divorced wife if she is pregnant. The condition here is pregnancy and the ruling (*ḥukm*) is given only when this condition is existing. Therefore, by way of the divergent meaning (مفهوم المخالفة) that maintenance is not required from the husband if the divorced wife is not pregnant.

In the same way, the *Qur'ān* provides another example in regards to fasting in conditional way which is stated: "*therefore whoever of you is present in the month, he shall fast therein, and whoever is sick or upon a journey, then (he shall fast) a (like) number of other days*".[610]

As this text obviously provides a concession in regard to fasting that is conveyed in conditional terms. The pronounce meaning indicates that if someone is on a state of journey or ill, fasting is not required. The condition here is travelling or being sick. Therefore, by way of the divergent meaning (مفهوم المخالفة), if, however someone is neither ill nor travelling, the condition that of travelling and sickness is not present, the concession to break the fast does not apply.

Third: Implication of the Extent (mafhūm al-ghāyah)

Implication of the extent "*mafhūm al-ghāyah*" (مفهوم الغاية) is an indication of a text with a ruling when the text itself separate the extent or scope of the operation of its ruling. An opposite ruling may be established beyond this extend. It is conditioned by an extent which limits, however, it lapses when the limits is exceeded. This implication is explained by the following text: "*And they ask you about menstruation. Say: It is a discomfort; therefore keep aloof from the women during the menstrual discharge and do not go near them until they have become clean; then when they have cleansed themselves, go in to them as Allah has commanded you; surely Allah loves those who turn much (to Him), and He loves those who purify themselves*".[611]

The text indicates that the pronounce meaning is that the husband should avoid sexual relations with his wife during the menstrual period. The text concludes by way of the implication of the extent (مفهوم الغاية) that the prohibition is limited by this extent (*ghāyah*) "*until they have become clean.*" However, the divergent meaning indicates that beyond this extent the prohibition is no longer valid.

Another example *Qur'ān* provides, in the same way, that the time of fasting on time is illustrated with the following verse: "*and eat and drink until the whiteness of the day becomes distinct from the blackness of the night at dawn, then complete the fast till night*".[612]

This text indicates that one may eat and drink until whiteness of the day becomes distinct from the blackness of the night at dawn, however, by way of the implication of the extent (مفهوم الغاية) that eating and drinking is not allowed when whiteness appears in the horizon.

Fourth: Implication of the Stated Number (mafhūm al-'adad)

This type of indication of the text provides a ruling restricted by a specific number. In the absence of that implication of the stated number "*mafhūm al-'adad*" (مفهوم العدد), an opposite ruling may be established. Thus, the stated number must be carefully observed. This type of ruling is explored by the following verse from the *Qur'ān*: "*And those who accuse free women then do not bring four witnesses, flog them, (giving) eighty stripes, and do not admit any evidence from them ever; and these it is that are the transgressors*".[613]

This verse clearly stated a specific number, which is eighty strikes, on the punishment for slanderous accusation. However, according to the divergent meaning (مفهوم المخالفة) the stated number of strikes is not allowed either to increase or decrease.

Another example is about the punishment of adultery that is clearly stated by a verse in the *Qur'ān* "*(As for) the fornicatress and the fornicator, flog each of them, (giving) a hundred stripes, and let not pity for them detain you in the matter of obedience to Allah, if you believe in Allah and the last day, and let a party of believers witness their chastisement*".[614]

This verse also clearly indicates that the punishment of adultery is to be one hundred lashes. However, by way of the divergent meaning (مفهوم المخالفة) the stipulated number of the lashes is not permissible both to increase and decrease.

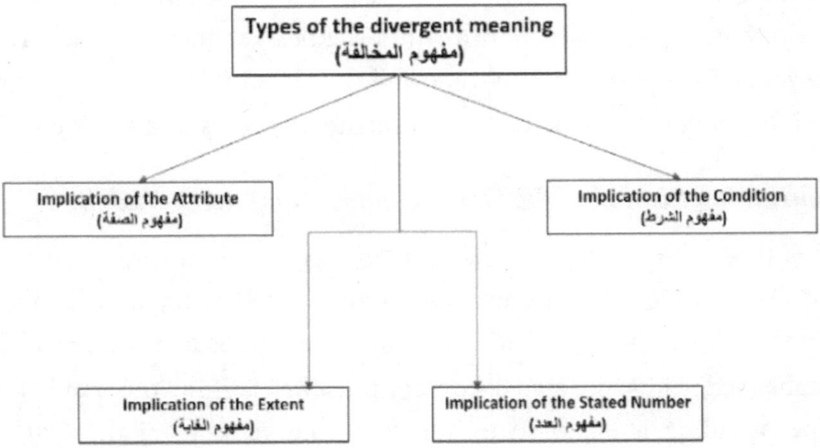

Conditions of the divergent meaning

Although *Shāfiʿī* school of thought recognized the divergent meaning (مفهوم المخالفة), they did not use it unconditionally, yet they formulate certain conditions to be valid for its application.[615] If the following conditions are fulfilled, the usage of it becomes acceptable as a way of deducing legal rulings. The following six conditions are essentials:

First: The divergent meaning (مفهوم المخالفة) does not go against the practices of custom of the Muslim society. This may be illustrated by the following verse that the *Qur'ān* states: "*and your step-daughters who are in your guardianship, (born) of your wives to whom you have gone in*".[616]

The text provides concerning the prohibited degrees of relationship in marriage. The text is clear on the point that marriage to a step-daughter who is under the guardianship of her stepfather is forbidden. Eventually the step-daughter in the text is restricted by the point that she lives in the house of her mother's husband. By way of the divergent meaning (مفهوم المخالفة), this verse might be taken to indicate that a step-daughter who does not live in the house of her mother's husband may be lawfully married. The restriction in the text for the step-daughter is not for a meaning to derive a ruling by the divergent meaning (مفهوم المخالفة) since it is a common practice that customary situation in this case would be that the step-daughter lives with her mother and eventually with her stepfather, which is why the *Qur'ān* refers to this restriction, not because of legalizing marriage with the step-daughter who did not live with her mother's husband (stepfather) in the same house. Finally, even if a step-daughter who lives under someone else's guardianship is not allowed. Therefore, the probable ruling may be derived by way of divergent meaning that the step-daughter under someone else's guardianship is allowed to marry her stepfather is not acceptable because of the common practice of the Muslim society and it is even rare and infrequent.

Second: The divergent meaning (مفهوم المخالفة) does not exceed the scope of the pronounced meaning. This may be illustrated by the following verse which concerns the attitude of children towards their parents that the *Qur'ān* states: "*And your Lord has commanded that you shall not serve (any) but Him, and goodness to your parents. If either or both of them reach old age with you, say not to them "uff" (in disrespect) nor chide them, and speak to them a generous word*".[617]

The statement in the text "say not to them "*uff*" (in disrespect)" is explicit on the point that uttering such word towards the parents is forbidden. Therefore, this verse prohibits "saying *uff*" to one's parents may not be given a divergent meaning so as to make physical abuse such as hitting, punching, etc. of them permissible. However, the divergent meaning that imply greater abuse than a word of "*uff*" (disrespect) exceeds the scope of the pronounced meaning and is therefore any kind of exciding meaning is not acceptable.

Third: The divergent meaning should oppose another textual ruling. This may also be illustrated by the following verse which refers to the requirement of retaliation: "*O you who believe! retaliation is prescribed for you in the matter of the slain, the free for the free, and the slave for the slave, and the female for the female*".[618]

This text explicitly indicates that prescribed punishment of retaliation is the free for the free, and the slave for the slave, and the female for the female. Therefore, by way of the divergent meaning (مفهوم المخالفة) a man is not retaliated against for murdering a woman. However, this conclusion would violate the explicit meaning of another verse "life for life" (أَنَّ النَّفْسَ بِالنَّفْسِ)[619] which requires retaliation for all intentional homicides without discrimination. Consequently, the ruling derived by way of the divergent meaning (مفهوم المخالفة) that is a man is not retaliated against for murdering a woman is not acceptable simply because it opposes to another verse which explicitly indicates for it.

Fourth: The divergent meaning (مفهوم المخالفة) does not depart from the particular state of affairs, that is, from the reality which the text is known to have imagined. It may be explored by the text in the *Qur'ān* about the relations between Muslims and non-Muslims. The *Qur'ān* states: "*Let not the believers take the unbelievers for friends rather than believers; and whoever does this, he shall have nothing of (the guardianship of) Allah, but you should guard yourselves against them, guarding carefully; and Allah makes you cautious of (retribution from) Himself; and to Allah is the eventual coming*".[620]

This verse explicitly indicate that having friendship with the non-Muslims is forbidden and whoever does it, apparently will not get any help from Allah. By the divergent meaning, it prohibits also ordinary relationship such as friendship and neighborship in the school, in the town, in the apartment, etc. However, this is not the real purpose of the text. In fact this verse was revealed in reference to a particular state of affairs, such as concerning a group of believers who exclusively befriended the unbelievers besides the believers and fully attached with them besides Muslims yet his friendship would harm the believers and such relationship is forbidden. Therefore, this text should not be taken out of context by recourse to the divergent meaning

(مفهوم المخالفة) to the enactment of a general principle.

Fifth: The divergent meaning (مفهوم المخالفة) should not be prowling the use the text by the restriction given in the text for unpronounced meaning. This may be illustrated by the verse about usury in the *Qur'ān*: "*O you who believe! Do not devour usury, making it double and multiplied, and be careful of (your duty to) Allah, that you may be successful*".[621]

This verse apparently indicate that the doubled and multiplied usury is prohibited. According to the divergent meaning, this verse suggests that taking usury which is not doubled and multiplied is lawful. However, the so-called divergent ruling is not acceptable since the restriction "*doubled and multiplied*" (أَضْعَافًا مُضَاعَفَةً) were not mentioned only for the sake of disliking for it and establishing deterrence from such trading as existed at that time, and which was leading to the loss of all the property of those who were indebted,[622] and yet it is to show the severeness and destructiveness of it. The following evidence from the *Qur'ān* supports this claim: "*But if you do (it) not, then be apprised of war from Allah and His Messenger; and if you repent, then you shall have your capital; neither shall you make (the debtor) suffer loss, nor shall you be made to suffer loss*".[623]

It is obvious with this verse that not only doubled and multiplied usury is forbidden but also all kind of usury is forbidden, similar to the intoxication which is based on the *ḥadīth* of the Prophet (ṣ) "Whatever intoxicates in large quantities and a little of it is prohibited" (مَا أَسْكَرَ كَثِيرُهُ فَقَلِيلُهُ حَرَامٌ).[624] Therefore, the restriction in the given text has no other use of the meaning except to establish the ruling opposite to the unpronounced which means the restriction that is mentioned is not for the opposite meaning but for the emphasis on it.

Sixth: The restriction provided in the text should be independent. This condition may be illustrated by the verse related to retreat (*i'tikāf*) in the mosques. The *Qur'ān* states: "*and do not engage in* *sexual relations with (your wives) while you are in i'tikāf in the mosques"*.[625]

The verse explicitly indicate that having sexual relationship with spouse is prohibited in the mosque. One may understand from the restriction "in the mosques" (فِي الْمَسَاجِدِ) by the divergent meaning that retreating (*i'tiqāf*) in other places does not prohibit sexual relations. However, this restriction does not justify the divergent meaning, because the phrase "in the mosques" is mentioned parenthetically and therefore, the restriction should be considered independently.

The value of the divergent meaning

The indication of the divergent meaning (مفهوم المخالفة) would be indefinite (*ẓannī al-dalālah*) which implies disagreement among scholars. The purpose of the *Ḥanafīs* that they have imposed on the divergent meaning is because there are many injunctions in the *Qur'ān* and *Sunnah* whose meaning will be distorted if they were to be given divergent interpretation. In addition to that *Shāfi'īs* also restricted the use of it by putting certain conditions in order to prevent it from misuse it. Therefore, *Ḥanafīs* restricted it not to be applied to a revealed text, namely the *Qur'ān* and the *Sunnah* as method of interpretation to control its potential misusages. The divergent meaning (مفهوم المخالفة) may be a useful method of interpretation and legal reasoning if it would not be distorting the intention of the Lawgiver.

Conclusion

From the view point of the rules of indications or textual implications (*dalālāt*) while exercising the interpretation of the text that is explored that it is considered differently among the school of thoughts especially among the *Ḥanafīs* and *Shāfi'īs*. In general the textual implications (*dalālāt*) is mainly considered with five categories and these are: 1. Explicit meaning (عبارة النص), 2. Alluded meaning (إشارة النص),

3. Inferred meaning (دلالة النص مفهوم الموافقة), 4. Required meaning (إقتضاء النص), 5. Divergent meaning (مفهوم المخالفة). Despite a different approach that it has been seen above that the both schools of thought, they have many common characteristics. *Shāfiʿīs*, which is different from the *Ḥanafīs*' classification, divided it into mainly two types: the pronounced meaning (*dalālah al-manṭūq*) and the implied meaning (*dalālah al-mafhūm*). The first one is consisted of two types: frank (*ṣarīḥ*) and not frank (*ghayr ṣarīḥ*). *Ghayr al-ṣarīḥ* consists of three types: required meaning (*dalālat al-iqtiḍāʾ*), gestured meaning (*dalālah al-īmāʾ*) and alluded meaning (*dalālah al-ishārah*). The second one is consisted of agreed meaning (*mafhūm al-muwāfaqah*), which corresponds to the inferred meaning (*dalālah al-naṣṣ*) of the *Ḥanafīs*, and the divergent meaning (*mafhūm al-mukhālafah*), which is rejected by the *Ḥanafīs*. As it has been seen that the differences between the two madhhab is only the divergent meaning (*mafhūm al-mukhālafah*). It is now clear that the difference is based on a technical sense which the way the concepts are considered. Thus, more or less their approaches to the textual implication is very similar.

Nevertheless, the meaning directly taken from the text is the intended meaning indicated by its actual words, while the meaning indirectly taken from the text is a necessary indication of the meaning of its text in such a way that they cannot be separated. It is considered an indication by way of acquiescence. Besides this, the meaning derived from its *dalālah* is a meaning indicated by its spirit and rational reason, while the meaning derived from its *iqtiḍāʾ* is a necessary meaning required by the text to fulfil the objective and validity in the *Sharīʿah* and mind. The *Ḥanafīs* termed the indication of the text which is not understood from the text's words but can be understood from the meaning which was provided by the text's words as the inferred meaning (*dalālah al-naṣṣ*) or may be termed as the indication of the indication (*dalālah al-dalālah* or *fahwā al-khitāb*) or agreed meaning (*mafhūm al-muwāfaqah*). This is the indication of the text that is what the text means (*mafhūm*) however, it is not what has been explicitly mentioned and pronounced (*manṭūq*).

In a nutshell, as it is clearly indicated that the lowest level of indication is the required meaning (إقتضاء النص) and the inferred meaning (دلالة النص) is the next, followed by the alluded meaning (إشارة النص) and the last as well as the highest level of indication is the explicit meaning or immediate meaning (عبارة النص). If, however, any conflict arises among these indications the stronger prevails over the weaker one. In other words, the highest level of indication would prevail over the lowest due to their levels of clarity of indication.

Notes

[1] 'Abdur Raḥīm, "*Principles of Muḥammadan Jurisprudence*," (London: Luzac and Co., 1911), p. 78.

[2] Badrān, *Uṣūl al-Fiqh al-Islāmī*, p. 375

[3] *Al-Mu'jam al-Waṣīt*, 2: 629; Ba'labakī, *al-Mawrid*, p. 745.

[4] Ghazālī, *Mustaṣfā*, v. 2, p. 12; Abdur Raḥīm, *Jurisprudence*, p. 79

[5] Rāzī, *al-Maḥṣūl*, v. 1:2: 513.

[6] Asfaḥānī, *Sharḥ al-Minhāj*, v. 1, p. 351.

[7] Anṣārī, *Ghāyat al-Wuṣūl*, p. 69.

[8] *Qur'ān* 5:38

[9] *Qur'ān* 103:2

[10] Khallāf, *'Ilm*, p. 178; Badrān, *Uṣūl*, p. 375 qf. Kamali, "*Principles*," p. 104

[11] The generic meaning of (كل) is individual, single, solitary – i.e. it includes all related subjects but in individual form, one after another. This word, moreover, is considered the most general one in linguistic term. See in Shawkānī, *Irshād al-Fuḥūl*, p. 110.

[12] The generic meaning of all (جميع), entire (كافة) and total (عامة) is that of a group – i.e. it includes everything that relates to a group.

[13] *Qur'ān* 54:49

[14] *Qur'ān* 52:21

[15] *Qur'ān* 2:29

[16] *Qur'ān* 34:28

[17] For example, "The man come" (جاء الرجل) if the person is known (معهود) to them.

[18]*Qur'ān* 23:1

[19]*Qur'ān* 5:93

[20] *Qur'ān* 24:2

[21] *Qur'ān* 2:228

[22]Khallaf, *'Ilm*, p. 182; Badrān, *Uṣūl*, p. 371.

[23] *Qur'ān* 4:11

[24] *Qur'ān* 9:103

[25] *Qur'ān* 2:275

[26] *Qur'ān* 4:15

[27] This verse has been specified by another verse "*As for those who accuse their wives but have no witnesses except themselves; let the testimony of one of them be four testimonies, (swearing) by Allah that he is of those who speak the truth;*" *Qur'ān* 24: 6, which made an exception for the husband who is allowed to prove a charge of adultery against his wife by taking four solemn oaths instead of four witness. However, the wife may rebut such by taking the same oaths for herself. Herewith, the first verse (4:15) has then been qualified as long as it relates to a married couple.

[28] *Qur'ān* 4:24

[29] Scholars disagree about whatever the indefinite plural is generic in effect. Most maintain that the indefinite plural is not generic. See the discussion about the verse: *Qur'ān* 21:22, in *Qurtubi, al-Jāmī' li Aḥkām al-Qur'ān*, v. 2, p. 279.

[30] *Qur'ān* 4:23

[31] *Qur'ān* 4:92

[32] *Qur'ān* 2:62

[33] *Qur'ān* 2:115

[34] *Qur'ān* 2:185

[35]Who (مَنْ) was used as a conditional (شرطية) but can also be used as interrogative (إستفهامية), relative pronoun (إسم موصول), and substantive (موصول). In the former two cases it is definitely the general meaning, while in the latter it is general and specific. The specific meaning may be illustrated by the following verse: "*Of them there are some who (pretend to) listen to you*" *Qur'ān* 6:25; "*And among*

them are some who look at you" *Qur'ān* 10:43. In these two verses, who (man) refers to some of the hypocrites, though not all them. These are why translators have translated them as 'some who'.

[36] *Qur'ān* 67:30

[37] *Qur'ān* 2:214

[38] Qur'ān 2:185

[39] Ibn Mājah, *Sunan*, II: 784 no. 2340.

[40] *Qur'ān* 9:84

[41] *Qur'ān* 2:263

[42] Shāfi'ī, *Risālah*, p. 96-108; Shawkānī, *Irshād al-Fuḥūl*, p. 140-141; Khallāf, *Uṣūl al-Fiqh*, p. 219; Bardīsī, *Uṣūl al-Fiqh*, p. 404.

[43] *Qur'ān* 11:6.

[44] Living creature (دَابَّةٍ) is any moving living creature on earth including man.

[45] *Qur'ān* 21:30

[46] *Qur'ān* 3:97

[47] *Qur'ān* 2:228

[48] *Qur'ān* 33:49

[49]Badrān, *Uṣūl*, p. 386-387; Khallāf, *'Ilm*, p. 185.

[50] Sarakhsī, *Uṣūl, al-Sarakhsī*, v. 1, p. 134; Bukhārī, *Kashf al-Asrār*, v. 1, p. 291; Shāṭibī, *al-Muwāfaqāt*, v. 3, p. 164-165; Ibn Qudāmah, *Rawḍāt al-Nāẓir*, v. 2, p. 166; Taftāzānī, *Sharḥ al-Talwīh 'alā al-Tawḍīḥ*, v. 1, p. 39-40.

[51] Sarakhsī, *Uṣūl, al-Sarakhsī*, v. 1, p. 144; Bukhārī, *Kashf al-Asrār*, v. 1, p. 294; Taftāzānī, *Sharḥ al-Talwīh 'alā al-Tawḍīḥ*, v. 1, p. 39-40; Sha'bān, *Uṣūl al-Fiqh al-Islāmī*, p. 274.

[52] *Qur'ān* 11:6

[53] *Qur'ān* 2:234

[54]Bukhari, *Jāmi' al-Ṣaḥīḥ*, 7:13 (76:6).

[55] Ibn Mājah, *Sunan*, I: 125, no: 347, 348, 349.

[56] Shāṭibī, *al-Muwāfaqāt*, v. 3, p. 153; Abū Zahrah, *Uṣūl*, p.124; 'Abdur Raḥīm, *Jurisprudence*, p. 82.

[57] Abū Zahrah, *Uṣūl*, p.125; Badrān, *Uṣūl*, p.381.

[58]Abū Zahrah, *Uṣūl*, p.125; Badrān, *Uṣūl*, p.381

[59] *Qur'ān* 6:121

[60] Bayhaqī, *Al-Sunan al-Kubrā*, v. 7, p. 240; Badrān, *Uṣūl*, p. 383

[61] Shawkānī, *Irshād*, p. 157; Abū Zahrah, *Uṣūl*, p.125

[62]Khallāf, *'Ilm*, p. 183; Abū Zahrah, *Uṣūl*, p. 129

[63] *Qur'ān* 24:4

[64] *Qur'ān* 24:6

[65] *Sunan Ibn Mājah*, Book 10, *ḥadīth* no. 2145.

[66] *Qur'ān* 24:6

[67]Kamali, *ibid.*, p. 112; Abū Zahrah, *Uṣūl*, p. 131; Badrān,*Uṣūl*, p. 383.

[68] *Awsāq*: a *wasaq* (sing. of *awsāq*) is a quantitative measure equivalent to about ten kilograms. Kamali, *ibid.*, 113.

[69] Al-Tabrīzī, *Mishkāt*, I, 563-65, *ḥadīth* nos. 1794 & 1797; Abū Zahrah, *Uṣūl*, p. 131

[70] Abū Zahrah, *Uṣūl*, p. 132

[71] Sarakhsī, *Uṣūl al-Sarakhsī*, v. 1, p. 132; Bukhārī, *Kashf al-Asrār*, v. 1, p. 298; Taftāzānī, *Sharḥ al-Talwīh 'ala al-Tawḍīḥ*, v. 1, p. 138. Bazdawī and Sarakhsī, divided them into two groups and they mentioned the second and the third groups together calling them as *Wāqifiyyah*, see more in Sukrija Husejn Ramic, "*Language and the Interpretation of Islamic Law*," (Cambridge: The Islamic Text Society, 2003), p. 144-146.

[72] Sarakhsī claims that this group emerged in the fourth century AH. Sarakhsī, *Uṣūl, al-Sarakhsī*, v. 1, p. 132.

[73] Ghazālī, *al-Mustaṣfā*, v. 1, p. 225-233; Ibn Ḥazm, *al-Iḥkām fi Uṣūl al-Aḥkām*, v. 3, p. 109-117; 'Īji, *Mukhtaṣar al-Muntahā*, v. 2, p. 102; Shawkānī, *Irshād al-Fuḥūl*, p. 116.

[74]Sukrija Husejn Ramic, *ibid.*, p. 145.

[75]Zakī al-Dīn Sha'bān, "*Islam Hukuk İlminin Esasları*," tr. İbrahim Kafi Dönmez (Ankara: Türkiye Diyanet Vakfı, 1990), p. 265.

[76]*Qur'ān* 5: 89.

[77]Sha'bān, *ibid.*, p. 266

[78]*Qur'ān* 24:4

[79]*Qur'ān* 4:11

[80]*Qur'ān* 4:11

[81]*Qur'ān* 4:11

[82]*Qur'ān* 4:12

[83]*Qur'ān* 4:12

[84]See: *Al-Tawdīḥ Sharḥ al-Tanqīḥ*, v. 3, p. 129.

[85]Abū Dāwud, *Sunan*, II, 410, *ḥadīth* no. 1567

[86] Khallāf, *'Ilm*, p. 165; Āmidī, *'Iḥkām*, v. 3, p. 57 considers this to be a *ta'wīl* which is far-fetched. See in Kamali, p. 93.

[87] Zakī al-Dīn Sha'bān, *ibid.*, p. 267; Kamali, *ibid.*, p. 105.

[88] Zakī al-Dīn Sha'bān, *ibid.*, p. 267.

[89]*Qur'ān* 2:228

[90] Kassāb, *Adwā'*, p. 29; Badrān, *Uṣūl*, p. 473. See in Kamali, *ibid.*, p. 368.

[91] *Al-Mu'jam al-Wasīṭ*, II, 564.

[92] Khallāf, *'Ilm*, p. 192; Badrān, *Uṣūl*, p. 351, 371

[93] Āmidī, *al-Iḥkām fī Uṣūl al-Aḥkām*, v. 3, p. 5.

[94] Anṣārī, *Ghāyat al-Wuṣūl*, p. 82.

[95] Sukrija Husejn Ramic, *ibid.*, p. 174.

[96] Zakī al-Dīn Sha'bān, *ibid.*, p. 270.

[97] 'Uthaymīn, *al-Uṣūl min 'Ilm al-Uṣūl*, p. 58.

[98] Sukrija Husejn Ramic, *ibid.*, p. 176.

[99] *Qur'ān* 2:185.

[100] *Qur'ān* 2: 234.

[101] *Qur'ān* 4:11.

[102] Muslim, *Waṣiyyah*, 5. 7.8.

[103]*Al-Mu'jam al-Wasīṭ*, II, 769; Wehr, *Arabic English Dictionary*, p. 804.

[104] Taftāzānī, *Sharḥ al-Talwīḥ 'alā al-Tawḍīḥ*, v. 1, p. 63.

[105]Shawkānī, *Irshād al-Fuḥūl*, p. 144.

[106] Sukrija Husejn Ramic, *ibid.*, p. 176.

[107] Zakī al-Dīn Sha'bān, *ibid.*, p. 271.

[108] Sukrija Husejn Ramic, *ibid.*, p. 176.

[109] *Qur'ān* 4:92.

[110] *Qur'ān* 58:4.

[111] *Qur'ān* 4:23.

[112] *Qur'ān* 5:3

[113] *Qur'ān* 6:145

[114] *Qur'ān* 5:6

[115] Tirmdhī, *Ṭahārat*, 110, without the word (ضربتان)

[116] Ibn Rushd, *Bidāyat al-Mujtahid*, v. 1, p. 68-70.

[117] *Qur'ān* 2:282

[118] *Qur'ān* 65:2

[119] Sukrija Husejn Ramic, *ibid.*, p. 178.

[120] *Qur'ān* 5:6.

[121] *Qur'ān* 5:38.

[122] Zakī al-Dīn Sha'bān, *ibid.*, p. 276; Sukrija Husejn Ramic, *ibid.*, p. 178.

[123] Zakī al-Dīn Sha'bān, *ibid.*, p. 278-279.

[124] Khallaf, *'Ilm*, p. 192; Badrān, *Uṣūl*, p.351, 371

[125] Anṣarī, *Ghāyat al-Wuṣūl*, p. 84

[126] *Qur'ān* 58:3

[127] *Qur'ān* 4:92.

[128] Shawkānī, *Irshād al-Fuḥūl*, p. 146-147; Sukrija Husejn Ramic, *ibid.*, p. 178-179.

[129] *Qur'ān* 5:6

[130] *Qur'ān* 5:6

[131] *Qur'ān* 4:12

[132] Sukrija Husejn Ramic, *ibid.*, p. 178-179.

[133] *Al-Mu'jam al-Wasīṭ*, I, 26; Wehr, *Arabic English Dictionary*, p. 26.

[134] *Qur'ān* 4:59

[135] *Qur'ān* 96:1

[136] Badrān, *Uṣūl*, p. 360

[137] Ījī, *Sharḥ Mukhtaṣar al-Muntasā*, v. 2, p. 365.

[138] Naṣafī, *Kashf al-Asrār*, v. 1, p. 44.

[139] Āmidī, *al-Iḥkām fī Uṣūl al-Aḥkām*, v. 2, p. 365.

[140] Sālim, *Tashīl al-Wuṣūl ilā Fahm 'ilm al-Uṣūl*, p. 23, see in Sukrija Husejn Ramic, *ibid.*, p.179.

[141] *Qur'ān* 2:43

[142] *Qur'ān* 2:185

[143] *Qur'ān* 22: 29

[144] *Qur'ān* 2: 178

[145] *Qur'ān* 2: 183

[146] *Qur'ān* 5: 105

[147] *Qur'ān* 47: 4

[148] *Qur'ān* 2: 233

[149] Shīrāzī, *al-Lumma'*, p. 13; Asfaḥānī, *Sharḥ al-Minhāj*, v. 1, p. 314-324; Anṣārī, *Ghāyat al-Wuṣūl*, p. 64; Shawkānī, *Irshād al-Fuḥūl*, p. 83; Kawrānī, *Sharḥ Mukhtaṣar al-Manār fī Uṣūl al-Fiqh*, p. 28; Badrān, *Uṣūl al-Fiqh*, p. 360.

[150] Shīrāzī, *al-Lumma'*, p. 13; Anṣārī, *Ghāyat al-Wuṣūl*, p. 64; Shawkānī, *Irshād al-Fuḥūl*, p. 83.

[151] *Qur'ān* 7:31

[152] *Qur'ān* 62:10

[153] Shāṭibī, *al-Muwāfaqāt*, v. 3, p. 88

[154] Shīrāzī, *al-Lumma'*, p. 12.

[155] Sukrija Husejn Ramic, *ibid.*, p. 187.

[156] Shīrāzī, *al-Lumma'*, p. 12; Asfaḥānī, *Sharḥ al-Minhāj*, v. 1, p. 309-312; Anṣārī, *Ghāyat al-Wuṣūl*, p. 64; Shawkānī, *Irshād al-Fuḥūl*, p. 85-86.

[157] *Qur'ān* 2:282

[158] *Qur'ān* 7:31

[159] *Qur'ān* 41:40

[160] *Qur'ān* 5:88

[161] *Qur'ān* 15:46

[162] *Qur'ān* 2:23

[163] *Qur'ān* 52:16

[164] *Qur'ān* 10:80

[165] *Qur'ān* 37:102

[166] *Qur'ān* 6:99

[167] *Qur'ān* 38:35

[168] *Qur'ān* 4:71

[169] *Qur'ān* 44:49

[170] Sukrija Husejn Ramic, *ibid.*, p. 181.

[171] Shīrāzī, *al-Lumma'*, p. 13-14; Asfaḥānī, *Sharḥ al-Minhāj*, v. 1, p. 327-329; Anṣārī, *Ghāyat al-Wuṣūl*, p. 65.

[172] Ghazālī, *Mustaṣfā* v. 1, p. 83; Āmidī, *Iḥkām*, v. 4, p. 211; Tabrīzī, *Mishkāt*, v. 1, p. 554, *ḥadīth* no.1796.

[173] *Qur'ān* 5:2

[174] *Qur'ān* 62:10

[175] Badrān, *Uṣūl*, p. 363; Hitu, *Wajīz*, p.141

[176] Shīrāzī, *al-Lumma'*, p. 14-15; Asfaḥānī, *Sharḥ al-Minhāj*, v. 1, p. 329-335; Anṣārī, *Ghāyat al-Wuṣūl*, p. 65; Shawkānī, *Irshād al-Fuḥūl*, p. 86.

[177] *Qur'ān* 3:97

[178] Ibn Kathīr, *Tafsīr al-Qur'ān al-'Azīm*, v. 1, p. 512.

[179] *Qur'ān* 5:38

[180] *Qur'ān* 5:6

[181] Kamali, "*Principles*," p. 142

[182] Sukrija Husejn Ramic, *ibid*., p. 188.

[183] Shīrāzī, *al-Lumma'*, p. 15-17; Asfaḥānī, *Sharḥ al-Minhāj*, v. 1, p. 337-342; Anṣārī, *Ghāyat al-Wuṣūl*, p. 65; Shawkānī, *Irshād al-Fuḥūl*, p. 88-89.

[184] Sukrija Husejn Ramic, *ibid*., p. 188.

[185] *Qur'ān* 3:133

[186] *Qur'ān* 2:148

[187] Shawkānī, *Irshād*, p.99-100; Badrān, *Uṣūl*, p. 365-366; Kamali, *ibid*., 142.

[188] Shīrāzī, *al-Lumma'*, p. 20-23; Kawrānī, *Sharḥ Mukhtaṣar al-Manār fī Uṣūl al-Fiqh*, p. 42; 'Uthaymin, *al-Uṣūl min 'Ilm al-Uṣūl*, p. 39.

[189] Tirmidhī, *al-Jāmi' al-Ṣaḥīḥ*, no: 1423, iv, 24; Nasāī, *Sunan*, no: 3432, iv, 146.

[190] Sukrija Husejn Ramic, *ibid*., p. 182.

[191] Shawkānī, *Irshād al-Fuḥūl*, p.101-102

[192] *Ibid.*

[193] Kamali, "*Principles*," p. 143.

[194] Anṣārī, *Ghāyat al-Wuṣūl*, p. 65.

[195] *Al-Mu'jam al-Wasīṭ* , II, 960; Wehr, *Arabic-English Dictionary*, p. 1005.

[196] Āmidī, *al-Iḥkām fī Uṣūl al-Aḥkām*, v.2, p. 406.

[197] Shawkānī, *Irshād al-Fuḥūl*, p. 96.

[198] Naṣafī, *Kashf al-Asrār*, v. 1, p. 140.

[199] Badrān, *Uṣūl*, p. 366

[200] Sālim, *Tashīl al-Wuṣūl ilā 'Ilm al-Uṣūl*, p. 28.

[201] Anṣārī, *Ghāyat al-Wuṣūl*, p. 67.

[202] Shīrāzī, *al-Lumma'*, p. 24-25; Anṣārī, *Ghāyat al-Wuṣūl*, p. 67; 'Uthaymīn, *al-*

Uṣūl min 'Ilm al-Uṣūl, p. 37-39.

[203] Nawawī, *Riyāḍ al-Ṣāliḥīn*, p. 269.

[204] *Qur'ān* 5:101

[205] *Qur'ān* 2:286

[206] *Qur'ān* 2:188

[207] *Qur'ān* 8:27

[208] *Qur'ān* 24:3

[209] *Qur'ān* 60:8-9

[210] *Qur'ān* 62:9

[211] *Qur'ān* 22:30

[212] *Qur'ān* 25:68

[213] *Qur'ān* 61:7

[214] *Qur'ān* 4:92

[215] *Qur'ān* 24:2

[216] *Qur'ān* 2:189

[217] *Qur'ān* 5:90

[218] *Qur'ān* 2:174

[219] *Qur'ān* 3:77

[220] *Qur'ān* 2: 197

[221] Shīrāzī, *al-Lumma'*, p. 25; Aṣfahānī, *Sharḥ al-Minhāj*, v. 1, p. 343, 345-347; Anṣārī, *Ghāyat al-Wuṣūl*, p. 68; Shawkānī, *Irshād al-Fuḥūl*, p. 96-98; Kawrānī, *Sharḥ Mukhtaṣar al-Manār fī Uṣūl al-Fiqh*, p. 44; 'Uthaymīn, *al-Uṣūl min 'Ilm al-Uṣūl*, p. 36.

[222] *Qur'ān* 62:9

[223] *Qur'ān* 3:8

[224] Shāṭibī, *al-Muwāfaqāt*, v. 3, p. 90

[225] *Qur'ān* 17:32

[226] *Qur'ān* 4:36

[227] Sukrija Husejn Ramic, *ibid.*, p. 189.

[228] Aṣfahānī, *Sharḥ al-Minhāj*, v. 1, p. 343-344; Anṣārī, *Ghāyat al-Wuṣūl*, p. 67;

[229] *Qur'ān* 6:152

[230] *Qur'ān* 60:10

[231] Badrān, *Uṣūl*, p.370 see in Kamali, *ibid.*, p. 145

[232] 'Uthaymīn, *al-Uṣūl min 'Ilm al-Uṣūl*, p. 36.

[233] Ibn Manẓūr, *Lisān al-'Arab al-Muḥīṭ*, I, 841-842; Ba'labakī, *al-Mawrid*, p. 294.

[234] Baṣrī, *al-Mu'tamad*, v. 1, p. 252.

[235] Aṣfahānī, *Sharḥ al-Minhāj*, v. 1, p. 361,

[236] Ījī, *Mukhtaṣar al-Muntahā*, v. 1, p. 129.

[237] Anṣārī, *Ghāyat al-Wuṣūl*, p. 67; Fattuḥī, *Sharḥ Kawkab al-Munīr*, p. 387.

[238] Bukhārī, *Kashf al-Asrār*, v. 1, p. 37; Bādshaḥ, Taysīr al-Taḥrīr, v. 1, p. 271; Mayḥāwī, *Sharḥ Nur al-Anwār*, v. 1, p. 169.

[239] Sukrija Husejn Ramic, *ibid.*, p. 170.

[240] *Ibid.*

[241] Sukrija Husejn Ramic, *ibid.*, p. 160.

[242] Baṣrī, *al-Mu'tamad*, v. 1, p. 251-252; Shawkānī, *Irshād al-Fuḥūl*, p. 125-126.

[243] Sukrija Husejn Ramic, *ibid.*, p. 161.

[244] Sha'bān, *Uṣūl al-Fiqh*, p. 270-273.

[245] Sukrija Husejn Ramic, *ibid.*, p. 170.

[246] *Qur'ān* 3:97

[247] Tirmidhī, *al-Jāmi' al-Ṣaḥīḥ*, 4:24, no. 1423; Nasā'ī, *Sunan*, 6:156, no. 3432.

[248] *Qur'ān* 2:185

[249] There is a disagreement about whether or not practical customs and habits specify general provisions. *Ḥanafīs* and most *Mālikīs* maintain that they do specify general provisions (Ibn Amīr al-Ḥajj, *al-Taqrīr wa al-Taḥbīr*, v. 1, p. 282; Isnawī, *Nihāyat al-Sūl Sharḥ Minhāj al-Wuṣūl*, v. 2, p. 269.

[250] Shāṭibī, *al-Muwāfaqāt*, v. 3, p. 151.

[251] *Qur'ān* 2:275

[252] When it is used in technical term may carry a different meaning that linguistic meaning in the science of *uṣūl al-fiqh* that is called *naql* (move, transfer). See Ramic, *ibid.*, p. 171

[253] *Qur'ān* 2:275.

[254] *Qur'ān* 2:185

[255] Ibn Kathīr, *Tafsīr al-Qur'ān al-'Aẓīm*, v. 2, p. 363-264, v. 3, p. 657-658, v. 4, p. 489-491.

[256] *Qur'ān* 2:228.

[257] *Qur'ān* 33:49

[258] *Qur'ān* 65:4

[259] *Qur'ān* 5:3

[260] Narrated by Abū Dāwud, Tirmidhī, Ibn Mājah and others from Abū Hurayrah. See Asqalānī, "*Bulūgh al-Marām*," p. 9.

[261] Scholars do not unanimously agree on the disconnectedness of the exception (*istithnā' munqatī'*) specifies the general indication. See Sālim, *Tashīl al Wuṣūl ilā Fahm 'Ilm al-Uṣūl*, p. 37

[262] *Qur'ān* 2:282

[263] Ibn Kathīr, *Tafsīr al-Qur'ān al 'Azīm*, v. 3, p. 354-355; Sālim, *Tashīl al-Wuṣūl ilā Fahm 'ilm al-Uṣūl*, p. 38.

[264] *Qur'ān* 24:4-5

[265] See the details in Sukrija Husejn Ramic, *ibid.*, p. 171.

[266] Sukrija Husejn Ramic, *ibid.*, p. 163.

[267] *Qur'ān* 4:12

[268] *Qur'ān* 4:25

[269] *Qur'ān* 2:222

[270] *Qur'ān* 5:6

[271] Taftāẓānī, *Sharḥ al-Talwīḥ, 'ala al-Tawḍīḥ*, v. 1, p. 42-43; Bukhārī, *Kashf al-Asrār*, v. 1, p. 306; Mayhawī, *Sharḥ Nūr al-Anwār*, v. 1, p. 169.

[272] Bukhāri, *Kashf al-Asrār*, v. 1, p. 37; Bādshāh, *Taysīr al-Taḥrīr*, v. 1, p. 271; Mayhawī, *Sharḥ Nūr al-Anwār*, v. 1, p. 169.

[273] Khallāf, *'Ilm*, p. 183; Abū Zahrah, *Uṣūl*, p. 129

[274] *Qur'ān* 2:228

[275] Abū Zahrah, *Uṣūl*, p. 132; Zakī al-Dīn Sha'bān, *ibid.*, p. 267.

[276] Zakī al-Dīn Sha'bān, *ibid.*, p. 307.

[277] *Qur'ān* 5:38

[278] Khallāf, *'Ilm*, p. 180

[279] *Qur'ān* 4:22

[280] Badrān, *Bayān*, p. 103-104; see Kamali, *ibid.*, p. 116.

[281] *Qur'ān* 2:228

[282] Kassāb, *Adwā'*, p. 29; Badrān, *Uṣūl*, p. 473. See in Kamali, *ibid.*, p. 368.

[283] Kamali, *ibid.*, p. 117.

[284] Abū Zahrah, *Uṣūl*, p.133; Khallāf, *'Ilm*, p.179; see Kamali, *ibid.*, p. 117.

[285] Tirmidhī, *al-Jāmī‘ al-Ṣaḥīḥ*, v:183, no:2950; Abū Dāwud, *Sunan*, iii:320, no:3652.

[286] Ba‘labakī, *al-Mawrid*, p. 265.

[287] Muthannā, *Majāz al-Qur'ān*, v. 1, p. 87. Ṭabarī gave the same linguistic definition (*Jāmī‘ al-Bayān ‘an Ta'wīl Āyah al-Qur'ān*, v. 6, p. 204).

[288] *Qur'ān* 6:95

[289] *Al-Mu‘jam al-Wasīṭ*, v. 1, p. 33; Lane, Arabic-English Lexicon, i:1257, ii:239; El, i:412, i:1039.

[290] Taftāzānī, *Sharḥ al-Talwīḥ, ‘ala al-Tawḍīḥ*, v. 1, p. 125; see in Sukrija Husejn Ramic, *ibid.*, p. 163.

[291] Āmidī, *al-Iḥkām fi Uṣūl al-Aḥkām*, v. 3, p. 50; Shawkānī, *Irshād al-Fuḥūl*, p.156; Sha‘bān, *Uṣūl al-Fiqh al-Islāmī*, p. 288-289.

[292] Tirmidhī, *al-Jāmī‘ al-Ṣaḥīḥ* v. 5, p. 183, no:2950; Abū Dāwud, *Sunan*, iii:320, no:3652.

[293] Ghazālī, *al-Mustaṣfā*, p. 196; Shawkānī, *Irshād al-Fuḥūl*, p. 156

[294] *Qur'ān* 5:6

[295] Ghazālī, *al-Mustaṣfā*, p. 197-202; Āmidī, *al-Iḥkām fi Uṣūl al-Aḥkām*, v. 3, p. 51-60

[296] *Qur'ān* 5:6

[297] Ibn Kathīr, *Tafsīr al-Qur'ān al-‘Azīm*, v. 2, p. 36-40.

[298] Qabash, *al-Kāmil fi al-Naḥw wa al-Ṣarf*, p. 190.

[299] Ghazālī, *al-Mustaṣfā*, p. 198.

[300] Such as *Qur'ān, Sunnah, Ijmā‘, Qiyās*

[301] Such as *istisḥāb, istiḥsān, ‘urf, istiṣlāḥ* etc.

[302] *Qur'ān* 5:3

[303] Muslim, *Ṣaḥīḥ Muslim*, I:227 (no. 366)

[304] Bukhāri, *al-Jāmī‘ al-Ṣaḥīḥ*, vi:231 (72:30)

[305] Kāsānī, *Badā'i‘ al-Sanā'ī*, I:85. There are other views on this question. Ibn Rushd, *Bidāyat al-Mujtahid*, v. 1, p. 78-79; Ibn Qudāmah, *al-Mughnī*, v. 1, p. 66.

[306] Bukhāri, *al-Jāmī‘ al-Ṣaḥīḥ*, II:124 (24:38). (See: ‘Asqalānī, *Bulūgh al-Marām*, p. 168); Tirmidhī, *zakāt*, 4.

[307] Zakī al-Dīn Sha‘bān, *ibid.*, p. 323.

[308] One of the most famous followers of Dāwud was Ibn Ḥazm who received the *Ẓāhirī madhhab* and himself became the leader of this *madhhab*. The followers

of the *madhhab* accept only the *ijmā'* of the Companions of the Prophet (ṣ). Khudarī, *Tārīkh al-Tashrī' al-Islāmī*, pp.267-268; Madkūr, *Tārīkh al-Tashrī' al-Islāmī wa Maṣādiruh*, pp. 194-195.

[309] Ibn Ḥazm , *al-Aḥkām fī Uṣūl al-Aḥkām*, v. 3, p. 41

[310] 'Abdur Raḥīm, *Jurisprudence*, p. 93; Badrān, *Uṣūl*, p. 394

[311] See for details Shawkānī, *Irshād*, p. 23-24.

[312] Zakī al-Dīn Sha'bān, *ibid.*, p. 310.

[313] *Qur'ān* 6:151

[314] Badrān, *Uṣūl*, p.394; Hitu, *Wajīz*, p. 112

[315] Badrān, *Uṣūl*, p. 395; Hitu, *Wajīz*, p.115

[316] *Qur'ān* 40:13

[317] *Qur'ān* 24:35

[318] *Qur'ān* 5:64

[319] Ghazālī, *Mustaṣfā*, p. 67-78.

[320] *Al-Majallah Al-Aḥkām Al-'Adliyyah* (*The Ottoman Courts Manual (Ḥanafī)*), maxim: 12

[321] *Ibid.*, maxim: 61

[322] *Qur'ān* 2:231

[323] Hitu, *Wajīz*, p. 115

[324] Zakī al-Dīn Sha'bān, *ibid.*, p. 312.

[325] 'Abdul Karīm Zaydān, "*al-Wajīz fī Uṣūl al-Fiqh*," (Beirut: Muassasah ar-Risālah, 2009), p. 266.

[326] *Ibid.*

[327] *Ibid.*

[328] Kamali, *ibid.*, p. 118

[329] Badrān, *Uṣūl*, p. 398; 'Abdul Karīm Zaydān, "*al-Wajīz*," p. 267.

[330] Ibn Nujaym, *Al-Ashbāh Wa Al-Nazā'ir*, (Beirut: Dār al-Kutub al-'Imiyyah, 1999), p. 127

[331] *Al-Majallah Al-Aḥkām*, maxim: 1798.

[332] 'Abdur Raḥīm, *Jurisprudence*, p. 98.

[333] M.L. 'A, *Al-Mu'jam al-Wasīṭ*, II:578; Lane, *Arabic-English Lexicon*, II:1926-30; Ba'labakī, *al-Mawrid*, p. 736.

[334] Kamali, p. 89; Khallāf, *'Ilm*, p.161; Badrān, *Uṣūl*, p. 403; Abū Zahrah, *Uṣūl*, p.

93.

[335] Sarakhsī, *Uṣūl al-Sarakhsī*, v. 1, p. 164.

[336] Sukrija Husejn Ramic, *Ibid.*, p. 69.

[337] Dabbūsī, *al-Asrār fī al-Uṣūl wa al-Furūʿ fī Taqwīm Adillat al-Sharʿ*, v. 1, p. 260.

[338] Bukharī, *Kashf al-Asrār*, v. 1, p. 46.

[339] Ibn Amīr al-Ḥajj, "*al-Taqrīr wa al-Takhbīr*," v. 1, p. 146; Bādshāh, "*Taysīr al-Taḥrīr*," v. 1, p. 136.

[340] Naṣafī, *Kashf al-Asrār*, v. 1, p. 295. It is clear that there is no need for analysis to understand its meaning, and no textual or external evidence (*qarīnah*) was added to the text. The listener, however, has to be fluent in the language (*min ahl al-lisān*). see in Mayhawī, *Sharḥ Nūr al-Anwār*, 205-206).

[341] Ghazālī, *al-Mustaṣfā*, p.196

[342] Ghazālī, *al-Mustaṣfā*, p.187

[343] Āmidī, *al-Iḥkām fī Uṣūl al-Aḥkām*, v. 3, p. 48-49

[344] Taftāzānī, *Ḥāshiyat al-Taftāzānī*, v. 2, p. 168. According to this definition, *ẓāhir* is part of *naṣṣ*.

[345] Anṣārī, *Ghāyat al-Wuṣūl*, p. 83

[346] Ibn Kathīr, *Tafsīr al-Qur'ān al-ʻAẓīm*, v. 1, p. 437.

[347] *Qur'ān* 4:3

[348] This verse in fact was revealed to protect the rights of orphans. In a situation in which a man who is the caretaker of a female orphan and who fears that he might not give her a dowry that is suitable for her status, he should marry other women, who are plenty as Allah has not restricted him. Al-Bukhārī recorded that "'A'ishah said, "*A man was taking care of a female orphan and he married her, although he did not desire to marry her. That girl's money was mixed with his, and he was keeping her portion from her. Afterwards, this Ayah was revealed about his case.*" Also, it was narrated that 'Urwah b. al-Zabayr, who asked 'A'ishah regarding this verse: "*if you fear that you shall not be able to deal justly with the orphans.*" She said, "*O my nephew! This is about the orphan girl who lives with her guardian and shares his property. Her wealth and beauty may tempt him to marry her without giving her an adequate dowry which might have been given by another suitor. So, such guardians were forbidden to marry such orphan girls unless they treated them justly and gave them the most suitable dowry; otherwise they were ordered to marry woman besides them.*" 'A'ishah further said, "*After*

that verse, the people again asked the Messenger of Allah (about marriage with orphan girls), so Allah revealed the Ayah." See in Bukhārī, *al-Jāmī' al-Ṣaḥīḥ*, v:177, 65:4:1

[349] *Qur'ān* 65:1.

[350] An incident was narrated by 'Abdullah b. 'Umar that he divorced his wife while she was menstruating. 'Umar b. Al-Khaṭṭāb asked the Prophet about this matter. The Prophet (ṣ) replied. "*Command (your son) to take her back and keep her until she is clean and then wait until her next period when she will be clean again. If he wishes to stay with her, he may; if he wishes to divorce her he may do so before the marriage is consummated. This is the prescribed period which Allah has fixed for the women meant to be divorced.*" see in Bukhārī, *al-Jāmī' al-Ṣaḥīḥ*, vi:163, 68:1.

[351] Sukrija, *ibid.*, p. 70.

[352] Ibn Nujaym, *al-Ashbāh wa al-Naẓā'ir*, p. 145; Lubnānī, *Sharḥ al-Majallah*, p.24.

[353] Kamali, *ibid.*, p. 92

[354] M.L. 'A, *Al-Mu'jam al-Wasīṭ*, II:296; Lane, *Arabic-English Lexicon*, II: 2797-99; Ba'labakī, *al-Mawrid*, p. 1173.

[355] Naṣafī, *Kashf al-Asrār*, v. 1, p. 206.

[356] Dabbūsī, *al-Asrār fī al-Uṣūl wa al-Furū' fī Taqwīm Adillat al-Shar'*, v. 1, p. 260.

[357] Bazdawī, *Uṣūl al-Bazdawī*, v. 1, p. 46.

[358] Sarakhsī, *Uṣūl al-Sarakhsī*, v. 1, p. 164.

[359] Kamali, *ibid.*, p. 93.

[360] Baṣrī, *al-Mu'tamad*, v. 1, p. 319; Ghazālī, *al-Mustaṣfā*, p.196.

[361] Shāfi'ī, *al-Risālah*, p. 67-68. Also, Baṣrī, *al-Mu'tamad*, v. 1, p. 319.

[362] Shāfi'ī, *al-Risālah*, p. 81

[363] Baṣrī, *al-Mu'tamad*, v. 1, p. 39; Ghazālī, *al-Mustaṣfā*, p.187, 196; Rāzī, *al-Maḥṣūl*, v. 1, p. 316; Shawkānī, *Irshād al-Fuḥūl*, p.156.

[364] Baṣrī, *al-Mu'tamad*, v. 1, p. 319.

[365] Shīrāzī, *al-Lumma'*, p. 48.

[366] *Qur'ān* 48:29

[367] *Qur'ān* 17:32

[368] Ghazālī, *al-Mustaṣfā*, p.196.

[369] Ibn Qudāmah, *Rawḍat al-Nāẓir*, v. 2, p. 27-28.

[370] *Qur'ān* 2:196

[371] Shawkānī, *Irshād al-Fuḥūl*, p.156.

[372] Anṣārī, *Ghāyat al-Wuṣūl*, p. 83.

[373] Qarafi, *Sharḥ Tanqīḥ al-Fuṣūl*, p. 36-37.

[374] Although two is dual, the majority of scholars see it as a plural based on the *ḥadīth*: "Two and more than that are a core" (Rāzī, *al-Maḥṣūl*, v. 1, 2, p. 605)

[375] *Qur'ān* 4:11

[376] Qarafi, *Sharḥ Tanqīḥ al-Fuṣūl*, p. 36; Ibn al-Ḥājib, *Sharḥ al-'Aḍūd ma'a Mukhtaṣar al-Muntahā*, v. 2, p. 168; Anṣārī, *Ghāyat al-Wuṣūl*, p. 83; Shawkānī, *Irshād al-Fuḥūl*, p.156.

[377] *Qur'ān* 112:1

[378] *Qur'ān* 48:29

[379] Bukhārī, *al-Jāmī' al-Ṣaḥīḥ*, VIII:24-25, no. 86:30

[380] Sukrija Husejn Ramic, *ibid.*, p. 103.

[381] *Qur'ān* 2:275

[382] Ibn Kathīr, *Tafsīr al-Qur'ān al-'Aẓīm*, v. 1, p. 363-364.

[383] *Qur'ān* 2:228.

[384] One may note that there are some exceptions. Some divorcees are not included in this legal ruling and their waiting period is shorted. (Ibn Kathīr, *Tafsīr al-Qur'ān al-'Aẓīm*, v. 1, p. 363)

[385] Ibn Kathīr, *Tafsīr al-Qur'ān al-'Aẓīm*, v. 1, p. 363-364

[386] *Qur'ān* 4:3

[387] Isnawī, *al-Tamhīd*, p.167; Suyūṭī, *al-Ashbāh wa al-Naẓā'ir*, p.135; Ibn Nujaym, *al-Ashbāh wa al-Naẓā'ir*, p. 149.

[388] Bazdawī, *Uṣūl al-Bazdawī*, v. 1, p. 48; Naṣafi, *Kashf al-Asrār*, v. 1, p. 207.

[389] Kamali, *ibid.*, p. 93.

[390] Naṣafi, *Kashf al-Asrār*, v. 1, p. 207; Bazdawī, *Uṣūl al-Bazdawī*, v. 1, p. 48; Sha'bān, *Uṣūl al-Fiqh al-Islāmī*, p. 315.

[391] M.L. 'A, *Al-Mu'jam al-Wasīṭ*, II:688; Lane, Arabic-English Lexicon, II:2397; Ba'labakī, *al-Mawrid*, p. 1083.

[392] Bukhārī, Kashf al-Asrār, v. 1, p. 49.

[393] Sarakhsī, *Uṣūl al-Sarakhsī*, v. 1, p. 165.

[394] Naṣafi, *Kashf al-Asrār*, v. p. 208.

[395] Abū Zahrah, *Uṣūl*, p. 96; Badrān, *Uṣūl*, p. 404-405.

[396] *Qur'ān* 4:11

[397] *Qur'ān* 24:4

[398] *Qur'ān* 2:43

[399] *Qur'ān* 2:183

[400] *Qur'ān* 3:97

[401] Bukhārī, *al-Jāmī' al-Ṣaḥīḥ*, I:155 (10:18)

[402] Bukhārī, *al-Jāmī' al-Ṣaḥīḥ*, II:123-124 (24:35); Muslim, Ṣaḥīḥ Muslim, II:673

[403] Bukhārī, *al-Jāmī' al-Ṣaḥīḥ*, II:225-251 (30); Muslim, Ṣaḥīḥ Muslim, II:758:783.

[404] Nawawī, *Sharḥ Ṣaḥīḥ Muslim*, ix: 45; 'Asqalānī, *Fatḥ al-Bārī*, v. 3, p. 264; Shawkānī, *Nayl al-Awṭār*, v. 5, p. 70; Bayhaqī, *al-Sunan al-Kubrā*, v. 5, p. 130.

[405] Bukhārī, *ḥadīth* 8.840; *Sunan of Abu-Dāwud*, *ḥadīth* 3327; Tirmidhī, *ḥadīth* 2826.

[406] Bukhārī, *Kashf al-Asrār*, v. 1, p. 50

[407] *Qur'ān* 3:7

[408] M.L. 'A, *Al-Mu'jam al-Wasīṭ*, I:190; Lane, Arabic-English Lexicon, I:618; Ba'labakī, *al-Mawrid*, p. 993.

[409] Bukhārī, *Kashf al-Asrār*, v. 1, p. 51.

[410] Naṣafī, *Kashf al-Asrār*, v. 1, p. 209.

[411] He means *mufassar*, Sarakhsī, *Uṣūl al-Sarakhsī*, v. 1, p. 165.

[412] Bukhārī, *Kashf al-Asrār*, v. 1, p. 51.

[413] Sukrija Husejn Ramic, *ibid.*, p. 82, these are all had become the perspicuous/the firm (المحكم) in the sense that they may not be abrogated due to the absence of an abrogating text and because such a text may not appear after the demise of the Prophet's (ṣ).

[414] Ibn Abī al-'Izz, *Sharḥ al-'Aqīdah al-Taḥawiyyah*, v. 2, p. 511-513.

[415] *Qur'ān* 112:1

[416] *Qur'ān* 2:255 also see 42:11; 29:62.

[417] *Qur'ān* 2:285

[418] *Qur'ān* 2:177.

[419] *Qur'ān* 30:1-4

[420] *Qur'ān* 5:8.

[421] *Qur'ān* 17:23.

[422] *Qur'ān* 13:20; *Qur'ān* 17:34.

[423] *Qur'ān* 33:53

[424] *Qur'ān* 24:4

[425] Muslim, *Ṣaḥīḥ Muslim*, II:1025 no. 1406

[426] Abū Dāwud, *Sunan*, III:18 no.2532

[427] Sarakhsī, *Uṣūl al-Sarakhsī*, v. 1, p. 165; Mayhawī, *Sharḥ Nūr al-Anwār 'ala al-Manār*, v. 1, p. 209-210; Bukhārī, *Kashf al-Asrār*, v. 1, p. 151.

[428] Naṣafī, *Kashf al-Asrār*, v. 1, p. 209.

[429] Sarakhsī, *Uṣūl al-Sarakhsī*, v. 2, p. 12

[430] *Qur'ān* 4:24

[431] *Qur'ān* 4:3.

[432] See the characteristics of the explicit (النص).

[433] Naṣafī, *Kashf al-Asrār*, v. 1, p. 212; Mayhawī, *Sharḥ Nūr al-Anwār 'ala al-Manār*, v. 1, p. 212-213.

[434] Mayhawī, *ibid.*, v. 1, p. 213-214.

[435] *Qur'ān* 24:4

[436] *Qur'ān* 24:5

[437] Ibn Kathīr, *Tafsīr al-Qur'ān al-'Aẓīm*, v. 3, p. 354-355; Qurṭubī, *al-Jāmī' li Aḥkām al-Qur'ān*, v. 12, p. 180-181.

[438] Naṣafī, *Kashf al-Asrār*, v. 1, p. 209.

[439] *Qur'ān* 4:24

[440] *Qur'ān* 33:53

[441] Taftāzānī, *Sharḥ al-Talwīh 'alā al-Tawḍīḥ*, v. 1, p. 126.

[442] Lane, *Arabic-English Lexicon*, I: 776; Ba'labakī, *al-Mawrid*, p. 157.

[443] Naṣafī, *Kashf al-Asrār*, v. 1, p. 214.

[444] Bazdawī, *Uṣūl al-Bazdawī*, v. 1, p. 52

[445] Dabbūsī, *al-Asrār fī al-Uṣūl wa al-Furū' fī Taqwīm Adillat al-Shar'*, v. p. 263.

[446] Sukrija Husejn Ramic, *ibid.*, p. 107.

[447] *Qur'ān* 5:38

[448] Marghinānī, *al-Hidāyah*, v. 2, p. 118; Ibn Rushd, *Bidāyat al-Mujtahid*, v. 2, p. 445; Ibn Qudāmah, *al-Mughnī*, v. 8, p. 240.

[449] *Ṭarr* is taking goods from someone who is in a wakeful state, and who consciously protects and guards his goods, but is in a state of ignorance

(Kawrānī, *Sharḥ Mukhtaṣar al-Manār*, p. 54)

450 Naṣafī, *Kashf al-Asrār*, v. 1, p. 215; Sarakhsī, *Uṣūl al-Sarakhsī*, v. 1, p. 167; Bukhārī, *al-Tawḍīḥ fī Ḥall Ghawāmiḍ al-Tanqīḥ*, v. 1, p. 126; Kawrānī, *ibid.*, p. 54.

451 Tabrīzī, *Mishkāt*, v. 2, p. 1061, *ḥadīth* No 3570; Abū Yūsuf, *Kitāb al Kharāj*, p. 152; Ibn Qayyīm, *I'lām*, v. 1, p. 209.]

452 Ṭaḥāwī, *Mukhtaṣar al-Ṭaḥāwī*, p. 271; Naṣafī, *Kashf al-Asrār*, v. 1, p. 216; Sarakhsī, *Uṣūl al-Sarakhsī*, v. 1, p. 167; Bādshāh, *Taysīr al-Taḥrīr*, v. 1, p. 157. It is worth mentioning here that the punishment fixed by *ḥad* (capital punishment) cannot be established by analogy (*qiyās*), because the *ḥudūd* are prevented by doubts and *qiyās* consist of doubt.

453 Ṭaḥāwī, *Mukhtasar al-Ṭaḥāwī*, p. 273; Marghinānī, *al-Hidāyah*, v. 2, p. 121.

454 Naṣafī, *Kashf al-Asrār*, v. 1, p. 215; Sarakhsī, *Uṣūl al-Sarakhsī*, v. 1, p. 167; Bukhārī, *Al-Tawḍīḥ fī Ḥall Ghawāmiḍ al-Tanqīḥ*, v. 1, p. 126; Kawrānī, *Sharḥ Mukhtaṣar al-Manār*, p. 54.

455 *Sunan Ibn Mājah* Chapter no: 24, *ḥadīth* no: 2645; Dārimī, *Sunan*, II:385.

456 Badrān, *Uṣūl*, p. 411.

457 The conditions for theft punishment according to the *Sharī'ah*: 1. The good is taken away secretly; 2. It is taken away with criminal purpose; 3. The stolen item is legally possessed by the person from whom it is stolen; 4. The stolen item had been taken from the ownership of its real possessor; 5. The stolen item should already have come into the ownership of the thief; 6. The stolen item should reach the value of *niṣāb*. If these conditions are found in any kind of action, it would be considered as theft. However, if any is missing, the *ḥadd* punishment will not be implemented. See in Doi, A.R.I. "*Sharī'ah: the Islamic Law*," (Lagos: Ṭāḥā, 1984), 254-261.

458 Sarakhsī, *Uṣūl al-Sarakhsī*, v. 1, p. 168

459 Ṭabrīzī, *Mishkāt*, v. 2, p. 1061, *ḥadīth* No 3570; Abū Yūsuf, *Kitāb al-Kharāj*, p. 152; Ibn Qayyīm, *I'lām*, v. 1, p. 209.

460 Lane, *Arabic-English Lexicon*, II:1588; Ba'labakī, *al-Mawrid*, p. 1049.

461 That is, an equivocal expression in its meanings. Naṣafī, *Kashf al-Asrār*, I:216

462 Dabbūsī, *al-Asrār fī al-Uṣūl wa al-Furū' fī Taqwīm Adillat al-Shar'*, v. 1, p. 264.

463 Sarakhsī, *Uṣūl al-Sarakhsī*, v. 1, p. 168

464 Sukrija Husejn Ramic, *ibid.*, p. 112

[465] Kamali, *Principles of Islamic Jurisprudence*, p. 100.

[466] Although *mushkil* and *mujmal* are very close to each other, they are not the same. See in Sarakhsī, *Uṣūl al-Sarakhsī*, v. 1, p. 168.

[467] *Qur'ān* 2:223

[468] The word *annā* could have three different meaning: where, how and when. See in Bādshāh, *Taysīr al-Taḥrīr*, v. 1, p. 158-159.

[469] *Qur'ān* 3:37

[470] *Qur'ān* 3:40

[471] Ṭabarī, *Jāmī' al-Bayān an Ta'wīl aya al-Qur'ān*, v. 4, p. 398-416; Ibn Kathīr, *Tafsīr al-Qur'ān al-'Aẓīm*, v. 1, p. 351-358

[472] Ibn al-'Arabī, *Aḥkām al-Qur'ān*, v. 1, p. 174; Qurṭubī, *al-Jāmī' li Aḥkām al-Qur'ān*, v. 3, p. 91-94.

[473] Qurṭubī, *ibid.*, v. 3, p. 91-94; Ibn Kathīr, *Tafsīr al-Qur'ān al-'Aẓīm*, v. 1, p. 351-358.

[474] *Qur'ān* 2:222

[475] Ibn al-'Arabī, *Aḥkām al-Qur'ān*, v. 1, p. 174.

[476] *Qur'ān* 2:228

[477] Ibn Kathīr, *Tafsīr al-Qur'ān al-'Aẓīm*, v. 2, p. 89.

[478] Naṣafī, *Kashf al-Asrār*, v. 1, p. 216; Sarakhsī, *Uṣūl al-Sarakhsī*, v. 1, p. 168.

[479] Lane, *ibid.*, I:461; Ba'labakī, *al-Mawrid*, p. 981.

[480] Dabbūsī, *al-Asrār fī al-Uṣūl wa al-Furū' fī Taqwīm Adillat al-Shar'*, v. 1, p. 265.

[481] Bukhārī, *Kashf al-Asrār*, v. 1, p. 54.

[482] Sarakhsī, *Uṣūl al-Sarakhsī*, v. 1, p. 168.

[483] Naṣafī, *Kashf al-Asrār*, v. 1, p. 218.

[484] Ghazālī, *al-Mustaṣfā*, p. 187.

[485] Qarafī, *Sharḥ Tanqīḥ al-Fuṣūl*, p. 275-277.

[486] Rāzī, *al-Maḥṣūl*, v. 1, p. 3, 233-234.

[487] Āmidī, "*al-Iḥkām fī Uṣūl al-Aḥkām*," v. 3, p. 10

[488] Shīrāzī, *al-Lumma'*, p. 49.

[489] Shawkānī, *Irshād al-Fuḥūl*, p. 148.

[490] *Qur'ān* 2:43.

[491] Ibn Qudāmah, *al-Mughnī*, v. 1, p. 369.

[492] Qal'ajī, *Mu'jam Lughat al-Fuqahā'*, p. 275.

[493] Ibn Athīr, al-Nihāyah fī Gharīb *al-ḥadīth*, v. 1, p. 273.

[494] Abū Dāwud, *Sunan*, I:283-284 no. 1080.

[495] Bukhārī, *al-Jāmi' al-Ṣaḥīḥ*, v. 1, p. 155, (10:18).

[496] Shāṭibī, *al-Muwāfaqāt*, v. 3, p. 218.

[497] Simply, if the explanation is fully detailed, the text becomes an interpreted text (*mufassar*) which does not need neither further clarification nor *ijtihād*. However, if the explanation is insufficient, the text becomes problematic (*mushkil*), and thus, further research and *ijtihād* are necessary for clarification.

[498] This opinion is narrated from Abū Ḥanīfah (*ẓāhir al-riwāyah*). Ibn Amīr al-Ḥajj, *Tafsīr wa al-Taḥbīr*, v. 1, p. 159.

[499] See more examples in Bukhārī, *Kashf al-Asrār*, v. 1, p. 52-53.

[500] *Qur'ān* 70:19

[501] *Qur'ān* 70:20-21

[502] Bukhārī, *Kashf al-Asrār*, v. 1, p. 50; Ibn Kathīr, *Tafsīr al-Qur'ān al-'Aẓīm*, v. 4, p. 542.

[503] Sarakhsī, *Uṣūl al-Sarakhsī*, v. 1, p. 168; Naṣafī, *Kashf al-Asrār*, v. 1, p. 219.

[504] *Al-Mu'jam al-Wasīṭ*, I:471; Lane, *ibid.*, II:1499; Ba'labakī, *al-Mawrid*, p. 958.

[505] Sarakhsī, *Uṣūl al-Sarakhsī*, v. 1, p. 169.

[506] See Bukhārī, *Kashf al-Asrār*, v. 1, p. 55; Naṣafī, *Kashf al-Asrār*, v. 1, p. 221

[507] Shīrāzī, *al-Lumma'*, p.52

[508] Ibn Ḥazm, *al-Iḥkām fī Uṣūl al-Aḥkām*, v. 1, p. 42, v. 4, p. 123.

[509] Sa'bān, *Uṣūl al-Fiqh al-Islāmī*, p.331.

[510] *Qur'ān* 48:10; and others, *Qur'ān* 11:37; *Qur'ān* 58:7.

[511] *Qur'ān* 42:11

[512] Naṣafī, *Kashf al-Asrār*, v. 1, p. 223.

[513] *Qur'ān* 3:7

[514] Ibn Kathīr, *Tafsīr al-Qur'ān al-'Aẓīm*, v. 1, p. 460-464.

[515] Tirmidhī, *al-Jāmi' al-Ṣaḥīḥ*, v:183, no. 2950; Abū Dāwud, *Sunan*, III: 320, no. 3652.

[516] Āmidī, *al-Iḥkām fī Uṣūl al-Aḥkām*, v. 3, p. 63; Ījī, *Mukhtaṣar al-Muntahā*, v. 2, p. 171; Ibn Amīr al-Ḥajj, *al-Taqrīr wa al-Taḥbīr*, v. 1, p. 111; Shawkānī, *Irshād al-Fuḥūl*, p.156.

[517] According to Abū Zahra, the division of *Ḥanafī* on *dalālah* may be classified

under *dalālat al-manṭūq*. See in Abū Zahrah, *Uṣūl al-Fiqh*, p. 116. In addition to him it would be better if it is classified as of that some divisions are derived from *mafhūm*, just as the inferred meaning (*dalālat al-naṣṣ*) and *mafhūm* are derived from *manṭūq*, see in Ramic, p. 41.

[518] *Al-Mu'jam al-Wasīṭ*, v. 2, p. 931; Ba'labakī, *al-Mawrid*, p.1124.

[519] Āmidī, *al-Iḥkām fī Uṣūl al-Aḥkām*, v. 3, p. 63

[520] Ījī, *Mukhtaṣar al-Muntahā*, v. 2, p. 171.

[521] Shawkānī, *Irshād al-Fuḥūl*, p.156; Ibn Amīr al-Ḥajj, *al-Taqrīr wa al-Taḥbīr*, v. 1, p. 111

[522] Ījī, *Mukhtaṣar al-Muntahā*, v. 2, p. 171; Anṣārī, *Ghāyat al-Wuṣūl*, p. 36; Ibn Amīr al-Ḥajj, *al-Taqrīr wa al-Taḥbīr*, v. 1, p. 111, Shawkānī, *Irshād al-Fuḥūl*, p.156.

[523] Ibn Ḥazm, *al-Iḥkḥm fī Uṣūl al-Aḥkām*, v. 7, p. 2-4, 53-59.

[524] Ibn 'Abd al-Barr, *Jāmī' Bayān al-'Ilm wa Faḍlih*, v. 2, p. 55-69; Āmidī, *al-Iḥkām fī Uṣūl al-Aḥkām*, v. 4, p. 272-286; Ibn Qayyīm al-Jawziyyah, *I'lām al-Muwaqqi'īn*, v. 1, p. 197; Shawkānī, *Nayl al-Awṭār*, v. 4, p. 129; despite the fact that Āmidī claims that Dāwud al-Ẓāhirī did not consider it as a proof (*ḥujjah*) see in Āmidī, *al-Iḥkām fī Uṣūl al-Aḥkām*, v. 3, p. 64-65.

[525] Bukhārī, *Kashf al-Asrār*, v. 1, p. 28; Sarakhsī, *Uṣūl al-Sarakhsī*, v. 1, p. 236; Taftāzānī, *Sharḥ al-Talwīḥ 'alā al-Tawḍīḥ*, v. 1, p. 130.

[526] Sha'bān, *Uṣūl al-Fiqh al-Islāmī*, p. 333

[527] *Fīruzabādī, al-Qāmūs al-Muḥīṭ*, v. 2, p. 83; *Al-Mu'jam al-Wasīṭ*, II:580; Lane, *Arabic-English Lexicon*, II:1938; Ba'labakī, *al-Mawrid*, p. 747.

[528] Lane, *ibid.*, II:2797-9; II:1938; Ba'labakī, *al-Mawrid*, p. 1173.

[529] Bukhārī, *Kashf al-Asrār*, v. 1, p. 68

[530] Sarakhsī, *Uṣūl al-Sarakhsī*, v. 1, p. 236, see in Sukrija Husejn Ramic, *ibid.*, p. 6.

[531] Kamali, *Principles*, p. 125

[532] *Qur'ān* 2:275

[533] Ibn Kathīr, *Tafsīr al-Qur'ān al-'Aẓīm*, v. 1, p. 437

[534] *Qur'ān* 4:3

[535] Bukhārī, *al-Jāmī' al-Ṣaḥīḥ*, v:177 (65:1); Ṭabarī, *Jāmī' al-Bayān 'an Tafsīr Āyat al-Qur'ān*, VII:536; Qurṭubī, *al-Jāmī' li-Aḥkām al-Qur'ān*, v:11-12; Ibn Kathīr, *Tafsīr al-Qur'ān al-'Aẓīm*, v. 1, p. 597-600.

[536] Sarakhsī, *Uṣūl al-Sarakhsī*, v. 1, p. 236-237; Bukhārī, Kashf al-Asrār, v. 1, p.

70.

[537] Taftāzānī, *Sharḥ al-Talwīḥ 'alā al-Tawḍīḥ*, v. 1, p. 35-36, 130-131

[538] Khallāf, *'Ilm Uṣūl al-Fiqh*, p. 143.

[539] *Al-Mu'jam al-Wasīṭ*, I:499; Lane, *ibid.*, II:1616; Ba'labakī, *al-Mawrid*, p. 110.

[540] Dabbūsī, *al-Asrār fī al-Uṣūl wa al-Furū' fī Taqwīm Adillat al-Shar'*, v. 1, p. 292.

[541] Bukhārī, *Kashf al-Asrār*, v. 1, p. 68, v. 2, p. 210.

[542] Sarakhsī, *Uṣūl al-Sarakhsī*, v. 1, p. 236.

[543] *Qur'ān* 2:233

[544] Ṭabarī, *Jāmi' al-Bayān 'an Tafsīr Āyat al-Qur'ān*, v. 5, p. 43.

[545] Bukhārī, *Kashf al-Asrār*, v. 1, p. 71; Sarakhsī, *Uṣūl al-Sarakhsī*, v. 1, p. 237

[546] Ajlounī, *Kashf al-Khafā' wa Muzīl al-Ilbās*, v. 1, p. 307; Ibn Mājah, *Sunan Ibn Mājah*, II:769 no:2291; Ṭaḥāwī, *Mushkil al-Athār*, v. 2, p. 230.

[547] See more on this matter: Jaṣṣāṣ, *Aḥkām al-Qur'ān*, v. 1, p. 168-169

[548] *Qur'ān* 46:15

[549] *Qur'ān* 31:14

[550] The incident happened at the reign of Caliph 'Uthmān. It is narrated that a man was married and his wife gave birth after six months. He went to 'Uthman and informed him of this incident. 'Uthmān ordered that the woman be stoned. When 'Ali heard it he asked him: "*Do you read the Qur'ān? Did you not read Allah's words…*" 'Ali recited these two verses and explained the ruling that the shortest time for gestation is six months. See in Ibn Kathīr, *Tafsīr al-Qur'ān al-'Aẓīm*, v. 4, p. 200-201; Zamakhsharī, *al-Kashshāf*, v. 3, p. 520; Sarakhsī, *Uṣūl*, v. 1, p. 237.

[551] Kawrānī, *Sharḥ Mukhtaṣar al-Manār*, p. 64

[552] Sarakhsī, *Uṣūl al-Sarakhsī*, v. 1, p. 236-237; Bukhārī, *Kashf al-Asrār*, v. 1, p. 70

[553] Taftāzānī, *Sharḥ al-Talwīḥ 'alā al-Tawḍīḥ*, v. 1, p. 35-36, 130-131.

[554] *Al-Mu'jam al-Wasīṭ*, I:294; Lane, *ibid.*, I:901; Ba'labakī, *al-Mawrid*, p.458.

[555] Bukhārī, *Kashf al-Asrār*, v. 1, p. 73.

[556] Sarakhsī, *Uṣūl al-Sarakhsī*, v. 1, p. 241.

[557] Bukhārī, *Kashf al-Asrār*, v. 1, p. 73.

[558] Bukhārī, *Kashf al-Asrār*, v. 1, p. 73; Taftāzānī, *Sharḥ al-Talwīḥ 'alā al-Tawḍīḥ*, v. 1, p. 133

[559] Ramic, *ibid.*, p. 18-19

[560] *Qur'ān* 5:38

[561] Bukhārī, *Kashf al-Asrār*, v. 1, p. 73; Taftāzānī, *Sharḥ al-Talwīḥ 'alā al-Tawḍīḥ*, v. 1, p. 133; Sha'bān, *Uṣūl*, p. 339; Ramic, *ibid.*, p. 27.

[562] In Arabic language, this construction is known as genitive construction (*iḍafah*), where the first word is the adjunct or governed word (*muḍāf*) and second is the governing noun of the genitive construction (*muḍāf ilayh*).

[563] M.L.A. *Al-Mu'jam al-Wasīṭ*, II:704; Lane, *ibid.*, II:2454; Ba'labakī, *al-Mawrid*, p. 1084-1085.

[564] M.L.A. *ibid.*, II:1046; Ba'labakī, *ibid.*, pp. 1136.

[565] Āmidī, *al-Iḥkām fī Uṣūl al-Aḥkām*, v. 3, p. 466.

[566] Āmidī, *ibid.*, v. 3, p. 63.

[567] Shawkānī, *Irshād al-Fuḥūl*, p. 156.

[568] *Sunan Abū Dāwud*, Book 26, Number 3673.

[569] Anṣārī, *Ghāyat al-Wuṣūl*, 37; Ibn Amīr al-Ḥajj, *al-Taqrīr wa al-Taḥbīr*, v. 1, p. 112; Shawkānī, *Irshād al-Fuḥūl*, p. 156.

[570] Ramic, *ibid.*, p. 51

[571] Ījī, *Mukhtaṣar al-Muntahā*, v. 2, p. 173, see more on the indication: Ramic, *ibid.*, p. 51-54.

[572] *Qur'ān* 17:23-24

[573] Some scholars, such as Shāfi'ī, may consider it as clear analogy (*qiyās jalī*) rather than an inferred meaning (*dalālat al-naṣṣ*) with this statement: "This is (the kind of knowledge) of which nobody is allowed to be ignorant or indefinite (as to its certainty)" (Shāfi'ī, *al-Risālah*, p. 289). In the contrary, the majority of scholars do not agree with this opinion indicating that the inferred meaning is different from analogy because the effective cause (*'illah*) in the case of the inferred meaning is established by language only. It can be understood by anyone who understands the language. However, the originating of the effective cause in analogy requires a proper *ijtihād* and can be understood only by competent scholars. Thus, the simple knowledge of the language is not enough when analogy (*qiyās*) is applied. See in Sha'bān, *Uṣūl al-Fiqh al-Islāmī*, p. 340

[574] *Qur'ān* 4:10

[575] *Qur'ān* 2:228

[576] Ramic observes the following explanation on this matter: "Islamic scholars normally mention only this effective cause for the waiting period. One may

observe that in this case other reasons may be regarded as the effective cause for the legislation of the waiting period – for example, the need for rest and relief from the stress which normally accompanies separation; physical, emotional and mental preparation for a new life; resolving important matters before a divorcee can remarry; etc. if detection of pregnancy is the only effective cause, one may argue that nowadays there are medical techniques by which pregnancy or lack therefore can be accurately detected. The length of the *'iddah* ruling is therefore questionable. However, to my knowledge no Muslim scholar seems to have discussed this matter. This may be because they are of the opinion that there are other reasons which count as effective causes of the ruling." Ramic, *ibid.*, p. 27.

[577] "Khul' is a request of the wife for divorce from her husband, whereby she may receive divorce in return for monetary compensation for her husband by the consent of the husband." Ramic, *ibid.*, p. 27.

[578] *Qur'ān* 99:7-8

[579] Tirmidhī, *Sunan*, IV:402, no. 2160.

[580] Āmidī, *al-Iḥkām fī Uṣūl al-Aḥkām*, v. 3, p. 64.

[581] Naṣafī, *Kashf al-Asrār*, v. 1, p. 385

[582] Bukhārī, *Kashf al-Asrār*, v. 1, p. 73-74; Sarakhsī, *Uṣūl al-Sarakhsī*, v. 1, p. 241.

[583] Such as 'Abd al-'Azīz al-Bukhārī and Kamāl b. al-Humām, Bukhārī, *Kashf al-Asrār*, v. 1, p. 73; Ibn Amīr al-Ḥajj, *al-Taqrīr wa al-Taḥbīr*, v. 1, p. 113-115)

[584] Naṣafī, *Kashf al-Asrār*, v. 1, p. 385-386.

[585] *Al-Mu'jam al-Wasīṭ*, II:743; Ba'labakī, *al-Mawrid*, p.147.

[586] Dabbūsī, *al-Asrār fī al-Uṣūl wa al-Furū' fī Taqwīm Adillat al-Shar'*, v. 1, p. 305.

[587] Sarakhsī, *Uṣūl al-Sarakhsī*, v. 1, p. 248

[588] *Qur'ān* 12:82

[589] Dabbūsī, *ibid.*, v. 1, p. 305-306.

[590] Sarakhsī, *Uṣūl al-Sarakhsī*, v. 1, p. 251-252.

[591] See the discussion on this matter in Sarakhsī, *Uṣūl al-Sarakhsī*, v. 1, p. 248-254; Naṣafī, *Kashf al-Asrār*, v. 1, p. 293-398; Bukhārī, *Kashf al-Asrār*, v. 1, p. 75-78, v. 2, p. 237-252; Taftāzānī, *Sharḥ al-Talwīḥ 'alā al-Tawḍīḥ*, v. 1, p. 137-140; Ibn 'Abd al-Shakūr, *Fawātiḥ al-Raḥamūt*, v. 2, p. 412.

[592] *Qur'ān* 4:23

[593] *Qur'ān* 5:3

[594] Isnawī, *al-Tamhīd*, p. 242.

[595] Sarakhsī, *Uṣūl al-Sarakhsī*, v. 1, p. 236.

[596] Bukhārī, *Kashf al-Asrār*, II:253.

[597] Ghazālī, *al-Mustaṣfā*, p. 264; Qarāfī, *Sharḥ Tanqīḥ al-Fuṣūl*, p. 270; Āmidī, *al-Iḥkām fī Uṣūl al-Aḥkām*, v. 3, p. 67.

[598] Ibn Amīr al-Ḥajj, *al-Taqrīr wa al-Taḥbīr*, v. 1, p. 177

[599] M.L.'A. *Al-Mu'jam al-Wasīṭ*, II:704; Lane, *ibid.*, II:2454; Ba'labakī, *al-Mawrid*, pp. 1084-1085.

[600] M.L.'A. *Al-Mu'jam al-Wasīṭ*, II:251; Wehr, Arabic-English Dictionary, p. 258.

[601] Āmidī, *al-Iḥkām fī Uṣūl al-Aḥkām*, v. 3, p. 67

[602] Qarāfī, *Sharḥ Tanqīḥ al-Fuṣūl*, p. 55.

[603] Ibn Amīr al-Ḥajj, *al-Taqrīr wa al-Taḥbīr*, v. 1, p. 177

[604] *Qur'ān* 9:36

[605] Kamali, *Principles*, p. 136.

[606] Āmidī, *al-Iḥkām fī Uṣūl al-Aḥkām*, v. 3, p. 67-69; Qarāfī, *Sharḥ Tanqīḥ al-Fuṣūl*, p. 55-61

[607] *Qur'ān* 49:6

[608] *Qur'ān* 4:23.

[609] *Qur'ān* 65:6

[610] *Qur'ān* 2:185

[611] *Qur'ān* 2:222

[612] *Qur'ān* 2:187

[613] *Qur'ān* 24:4

[614] *Qur'ān* 24:2

[615] Ījī, *Mukhtaṣar al-Muntahā*, v. 3, p. 173; Tilmisānī, *Miftāḥ al-Wuṣūl*, p. 66; Shawkānī, *Irshād al-Fuḥūl*, 179.

[616] *Qur'ān* 4:23

[617] *Qur'ān* 17:13

[618] *Qur'ān* 2:178

[619] *Qur'ān* 5:45

[620] *Qur'ān* 3:28.

[621] *Qur'ān* 3:130

[622] Ibn Kathīr, *Tafsīr al-Qur'ān al-'Aẓīm*, v. 1, p. 536.

[623] *Qur'ān* 2:279; Ibn Kathīr, *ibid.*, v. 1, p. 442.

[624] Tirmidhī, *ḥadīth* no: 1865.

[625] *Qur'ān* 2:187

CHAPTER FIVE

Concept of *Ijtihād*

Introduction

The institution of *ijtihād* is the most important mechanism of Islamic law to use both divine and rational sources to bring solutions to the problems of the Muslim *Ummah*. Besides the fundamental sources of Islamic law, the *Qur'ān* and the *Sunnah*, it uses the intellect (*'aql*) to arrive at solutions. In other words, it is a continues instrument of interpreting the divine messages under different circumstances of the time and situations which accommodate itself to the changing conditions of the Muslim *Ummah* (community) in order to attain justice, happiness, fairness, truth, and easy. It is a way to understand the essential objectives of the Lawgiver using personal effort with the support of recognized sources of Islamic law.

Following the demise of the Prophet (ṣ) and eventually end of the revelation, Islamic law was developed with abundant effort by those who had the authority, competent knowledge and expertise, despite the rapid changes in political, social, and economic life. The jurists' contributions greatly developed Islamic law's ability to manoeuvre and to be flexible in finding solutions for the problems of the Muslim Community. With enormous contribution of the *mujtahids* (competent scholars) Islamic law as a source of jurisprudence is considered as a law made by jurists.[1]

Therefore, the concept of *ijtihād* is one of the most important key words of the *Sharīʿah*, and its goal is defined as comprehending the purpose of the *Qur'ān* and the *Sunnah*. The main purpose of law is to maintain the continuity of answering people's needs. A legal system that answers the questions of its era while offering solutions for future generations can be realized only by constantly renewing itself. In this sense, *ijtihād* has very important functions in keeping the law alive, which is one of the *Sharīʿah's* main dynamics.[2]

The *Qur'ān* indicates that the use of *ijtihād* is a religious duty and encourages Muslims to avoid disagreements amongst themselves. When they differ, the *Qur'ān* refers them to the Messenger of Allah or the one who is in authority amongst Muslims (*ʿulul ʿamr*): "*O you who have believed, obey Allah and obey the Messenger and those in authority among you. If you differ in anything amongst yourselves, refer it to Allah and His Messenger. If you believe in Allah and in the Last Day. That is better and more suitable for final determination.*"[3] Referring the disagreements to Allah and His Messenger is an effort made to find solutions according to *naṣṣ*; this is an example of *ijtihād*[4] and an encouragement to Muslims to perform *ijtihād* in the future.

The *Sunnah* of the Prophet (ṣ) encourages the use of *ijtihād*.[5] "When a judge exercises *ijtihād* and gives a right judgment, he will have two rewards, but if he errs in his judgment, he will still have earned one reward."[6] Another example of this concept is the case of the *ḥadīth* of Muʿādh.[7] Shāfiʿī *(d.* 204/819*)* believes that the rulings inferred by *ijtihād* have a divine character: "The rulings which are inferred by *qiyās* are considered to have a divine quality."[8] "The rulings of many cases where there are no direct indications in the Book or the *Sunnah* have to be deduced by means of *qiyās* (analogy) and interpretations of the *naṣṣ*."[9] Juwaynī *(d.* 478/1085*)* says that, "When there is no direct trace within the *naṣṣ*, nine out of ten rulings and legal opinions (*fatwā'*) are deduced by way of personal opinions (*ra'y*) and inferences."[10]

Shahristānī *(d.* 548/1153*)* believes that performing *ijtihād* is an obligatory duty: "Definitely we know that either *ʿibādāt* (worshiping) or *taṣarrufāt* (transactions) are numerous and cannot be calculated. We also have to realise that every single matter has not been revealed in the *naṣṣ* (*text*), for it would not be practical. Therefore in respect of the unlimited matters, performing *ijtihād* is an obligatory duty."[11]

Ibn Ṣiddīq indicated that a *mujtahīd* has two ways to obtain the objectives of the lawgiver in the *naṣṣ*. These are as follows:

a. Linguistically investigating *naṣṣ*: While doing this investigation, the general principles become a part of an activity and if the general principles and particular principles are not in harmony then the general principles are preferred.

b. Investigating *naṣṣ* in the context of the objectives of the *sharī'ah*.[12] As it is known that the main sources of *sharī'ah* are first divided into two parts: the *Qur'ān* and the *Sunnah*. The concept of *ijtihād* is the main method of making new rulings in Islamic law relying on the two main sources which are indicated in the *Qur'ān* in *sūrah al-Nisā'* (4:59).

The Definition of Ijtihād

Linguistically the word *ijtihād* is derived from two words: *juhd* (exertion of effort or energy) and *jahd* (the forbearance of hardship, namely, striving and self-exertion in any activity that entails a measure of hardship). Therefore, it would be suitable to use *jahada* (جهد) for one who carries a heavy load, but not if he/she carries a trivial weight. The *ijtihād* is, then, the expenditure of effort to arrive at the correct judgment, whether physical (e.g., walking or working) or intellectual (e.g., inferring a ruling or a juristic and linguistic theory).[13]

Technically, the juristic meaning of *ijtihād* has several definitions according to the *uṣūlī* scholars. Some define it as the jurist's action and activity to reach a solution. Al-Ghazālī (d. 505/1111) defines it as the "total expenditure of effort made by a jurist for the purpose of obtaining the religious rulings."[14] Similarly the *ijtihād* is defined as "it is the effort made by the *mujtahid* in seeking knowledge of the *aḥkām* (rules) of the *sharīʿah* through interpretation."[15]

Al-Āmidī (d. 631/1233) considers it to be the expenditure of one's total effort in search of *ẓann* (probability), to the extent that the jurist feels obliged to exert himself/herself further in proving that the ruling is correct. His definition implies that it is not enough just to exert effort; rather, the jurist should feel that he/she has spared no effort to pursue the issue further: "*Ijtihād* is the application of the jurist using all of his faculties, either in inferring the *Sharīʿah's* practical rules from the sources or in implementing such rules and applying them to a particular issue."[16]

From this point of view that *ijtihād* essentially consists of an inference (*istinbāṭ*) that extents to a probability (*ẓann*). Thus it excludes the extraction of a ruling from a clear text as well as a ruling obtained from a learned person by simply asking about the relevant matter without recourse to the legal exercise of a competent scholar. In other words, if a knowledgeable person who gives a ruling on *Sharīʿah*, but not able to exercise his judgement in the inference of the rulings (*aḥkām*) from the sources is not considered mujtahid rather he is named *muftī*. Exercising the *ijtihād* is confined to only a jurist (*faqīh*) who is eligible doing it. As any other sciences, the qualifications for exercising *ijtihād* is one of the conditions, it is inevitable that the *mujtahid* cannot be among ordinary knowledgeable people who can infer rulings, rather among the *mujtahids* who must be a jurist (*faqīh*).[17] *Mujtahid* who exercises his abilities to give his personal opinion freely recourse to the main source of the *Sharīʿah*, and therefore, *ijtihād* is the formulation of an opinion in related to the legal rulings (*ḥukm sharʿī*).[18] The *Sharīʿah's* definitive rulings that are known by necessity are therefore excluded from *ijtihād*, such as the Five Pillars of Islam, rulings related to the *ʿaqīdah* (creed), and realizing the attributes of Allah, all of which are determined by explicit textual statements. There is only one correct view in regards to these matters, and anyone who differs is wrong.[19]

Al-Qarāfī (d. 684/1285) defines *ijtihād* "the expenditure of total effort while considering a case which is condemned by religion."[20] Al-Isnawī (d. 772/1370) explains it as "the expenditure of effort to arrive at and realize the rulings of the *Sharī'ah*, whether definitive (*qaṭ'ī*) or probable (*ẓannī*)."[21] Kamāl Ibn al-Humām (d. 861/1457) describes it as the expenditure of efforts by the *faqīh* (jurisprudent) to arrive at a juristic ruling, such ruling being either rational (*'aqlī*) or transmitted (*naqlī*), definitive (*qaṭ'ī*) or speculative (*ẓannī*).[22] Ibn Ḥazm (d. 456/1064) differs and interprets it as "investigating the rules of Allah solely in the *Qur'ān* and in the *Sunnah*."[23] Fazlur Rahman (d. 1988) defines it technically as "the effort to understand the meaning of a relevant text or precedent in the past, containing a rule, and to alter that rule by extending, restricting or otherwise modifying it in such a manner that a new situation can be subsumed by a new solution."[24] Abū Zahrah defines the *ijtihād* as the application by a jurist of all his capacities either in implementing the rules and applying them to particular issues, or in inferring such rules of *Sharī'ah* from their sources.[25]

The Validity of Ijtihād

There are plenty of evidences from the *Qur'ān* and the *Sunnah* that validate the *ijtihād* as a recognized way for deriving rulings. The *Qur'ān* states: "*Verily, in these things are verses (e.g., proof, evidences, lessons, signs) for people who reflect*"[26]; "*Verily, in these things are verses for the people who understand*".[27]; and "*Surely, We have sent down to you (O Muḥammad) the book (this Qur'ān) in truth that you might judge between people by that which Allah has shown you*".[28] Taking these verses into the consideration that the statements, 'people who reflect', 'the people who understand', 'judge between people', are all indicating on the use of personal effort which support the use of *ijtihād* by analogical deduction.[29]

In addition to the previous verses, the following verses obviously indicate its validity: "*And consult them in their affairs; so when you have decided, then place your trust in Allah; surely Allah loves those who trust*"[30]; and "... *who (conduct) their affairs by mutual consultation*".[31]

Besides the evidences from the *Qur'ān*, there are many *ḥadīth* validate the concept of *ijtihād* that the following *ḥadīth* which was narrated by 'Amr ibn al-'Āṣ (d. 65/684) who heard that the Prophet (ṣ) said: "If a jurist exerts efforts and arrives at a correct ruling, he will be rewarded twice. If he arrives at an erroneous ruling, he will be rewarded once."[32] According to Mu'adh ibn Jabal's (d. 18/640) famous *ḥadīth*: The Prophet (ṣ) asked: "How will you judge when the occasion of deciding a case arises?" He replied: "I shall judge in accordance with Allah's book." The Prophet asked: "(What will you do) if you do not find guidance in Allah's book?" He replied: "(I will act) in accordance with the *Sunnah* of the Messenger of Allah." The Prophet (ṣ) asked: "(What will you do) if you do not find guidance in the *Sunnah* of the Apostle of Allah and in Allah's book?" He replied: "I shall do my best to form an opinion and spare no pains." The Apostle of Allah then patted him on the chest and said: "Praise be to Allah who helped the messenger of the Apostle of Allah to find a thing which pleases the Apostle of Allah."[33]

Sa'īd Ibn al-Musayyab narrated a *ḥadīth* and said: "I asked the Messenger of Allah. O! Messenger of Allah what shall we do when we face a problem, which has no answer in the *Qur'ān* and the *Sunnah*?" The Apostle of Allah said: "Your scholars (*'ulama'*) come together, or worshippers come together from among the believers, and make consultation among yourselves; do not judge on the basis of only one opinion."[34]

As we can see, the Prophet (ṣ) encouraged the Companions to perform *ijtihād* during his life time. The encouragement of people to perform *ijtihād* gave them the ability to find answers to their problems, and to open doors that would never be closed[35]. When 'Umar ibn Khaṭṭāb appointed Shurayḥ as a judge to Kūfah, he said to him: "First of all look into the *Qur'ān* as though it was revealed to you without asking anyone, then rule with it. If you cannot find what you are looking for in the *Qur'ān* then follow the Prophet's *Sunnah*. If you cannot find the right guidance in the *Sunnah* then perform *ijtihād* by *ra'y* with your personal opinion and consult the people of righteousness (virtuousness, justness) and honesty."[36]

According to Muḥammad al-Dasūqī, all jurists are to use *ijtihād* that is valid and unanimously accepted. Undertaking it is a key to the ongoing development of Islamic law and opens a gate to *fiqh* that will develop the law when dealing with new issues. He further says that its use is a kind of revelation of Islamic *fiqh*.[37]

Personal Opinion (Ra'y)

The word *ra'y* is derived from the verb *ra'a* (to see something or somebody), which was used later on as a verbal noun. It may also denote a dream or a vision, a view, that which is known by the heart but cannot be seen with the eyes (i.e., an opinion),[38] or *i'tiqād* (faith, belief), *ẓann* (assumption), *'ilm* (knowledge, science), *'aql* (reason, intellect, mentality), *tadbīr* (precaution), and *iṣābah* (target).[39] Ibn al-Qayyīm (d. 751/1350) points out that one aspect of *ra'y* is "after considering a subject and making a judgment from the heart, a search through the evidence and inferences, both of which have their own considerations, is made to implement the truth, reality."[40] Rāghib al-Isfahānī (d. 502/1109) defines *ru'yah* as "to perceive an object which is seen." This perception is divided into the following parts: (1) the five senses and that which replaces the senses in a similar activity; (2) *wahm* (illusion, false impression) and *taḥayyul* (imagination), (3) *tafakkur* (contemplation), and (4) *'aql* (intellectual faculty) and *idrāk* (perception).[41]

Studying *ra'y* from the historical perspective shows that there have been different views as to its first use. The majority of scholars state that its use began during the Prophet's (ṣ) lifetime. An alternative point of view with regard to the ruling being based on *ra'y* suggests that *ra'y* was used only after the Prophet's (ṣ) death, when the Companions were faced with issues that had not been detailed in the *Qur'ān* and the *Sunnah*. This view is disputed by such scholars as Ibn Khaldūn (d. 808/1405) and Ibn Ḥazm. Ibn Khaldūn writes: "The rulings had been taught either during the time of the Prophet (ṣ) through revelation, which was sent to the Prophet (ṣ), or his direct speeches and attitudes; therefore, it was unnecessary to apply intellectual reasoning or *qiyās*."[42] Ibn Ḥazm says: "The claim that *ra'y* appeared at the time of the Companions had nothing to do with the Companions' actions, contrary to the report that the Companions used *ra'y*; the validity of such reports and narrations is uncertain."[43] According to these scholars, the sources of Islamic law at the time of the Prophet (ṣ) were confined to the *Qur'ān* and the *Sunnah*. *Ijmā'* took shape after the time of the Companions, and *qiyās* (analogy) was used when a ruling did not have a *naṣṣ* (textual) reference in the main sources of guidance.[44]

The Relationship between ijtihād and ra'y

The *uṣūlī* scholars have called the practice of inference to reach a ruling *ijtihād*, *qiyās*, or *ra'y*.[45] There are different views on whether *ra'y* is a kind of *ijtihād* or *qiyās*. For example, al-Shāfi'ī (d. 204/819) says that *ra'y* is not based on a validated source of the *Sharī'ah*, but that it is only a making of inferences that depends purely on intellectual reasoning and inclination. Therefore, he criticizes scholars who used it in their *ijtihād*. He also considers *ra'y* and *qiyās* to be opposed to one another.[46] Al-Ghazālī sees *ra'y* and *qiyās* as synonyms: "*Ra'y* consists of comparing and representing any ruling to itself."[47] Some jurists, particularly Shāfi'ī scholars, opine that *ra'y* is synonymous with *qiyās*. Taking into account the practice of the Companions and the Successors, some scholars view it as a kind of comprehensive method of *ijtihād* consisting of *qiyās*, *istiḥsān*, *al-*

maṣāliḥ al-mursalah (consideration of the public interest), and *sadd al-dharā'i'* (blocking the means).[48] Al-Sarakhsī (d. 483/1090) believes that *ra'y* is more extensive than *qiyās*. For example, he interprets "*Then take admonition, O you with eyes (to see)*"[49] by saying that *i'tibar* (admonition) means practicing *ra'y* in place of that which has no *naṣṣ* and *qiyās*."[50] 'Abd al-Wahhāb Khallāf (d. 1956), who defines it as "analogizing and thinking in order to reach the right ruling in a field where no *naṣṣ* is available by the *Sharī'ah* provided for the purpose of inference," says that *ra'y* is more comprehensive than *qiyās*.[51] Al-Shawkānī (d. 1250/1834) points out that *ra'y* could have been applied to explaining and interpreting the *naṣṣ*: "*Ijtihād* by *ra'y* can be the way of inference from the *Qur'ān* and the *Sunnah*. It was originally permitted in the *Sharī'ah* for the consideration of benefit and in cases of necessity."[52] Fatḥī Dirīnī believes that confining *ijtihād* to *ra'y* on issues that have no *naṣṣ* is incorrect, for he says that the Companions' interpretations should also be included in the circle of *ijtihād* by *ra'y*. For example, when Abū Bakr was questioned on *kalālah* (a matter dealing with inheritance),[53] he replied: "I will express my point of view on this issue. If it is correct and rightly done, then it is from Allah; if I fall into error, then it is from me and from Satan."[54] Accordingly, we can see that *ra'y* has virtually the same meaning as *ijtihād*. The Companions applied *ijtihād* by *ra'y* according to their perception of the Prophet's action.[55] However, it is clear that *ijtihād* is more comprehensive than *ra'y*. At the time of the Companions and the Successors, the constituent parts of *ra'y* were clear and extensive, as opposed to the *naṣṣ*, which was not obviously clarified and defined. Following that period, some jurists continued to use *ra'y*, in the meaning of *ijtihād*, in a wider range. At the same time, the majority of jurists confined the use of inference to issues on which no *naṣṣ* was available to reach a right and just ruling. In addition to *qiyās*, they also used *istiḥsān*, *al-maṣāliḥ al-mursalah*, *sadd al-dharā'i'*, and *'urf* that agreed with the *Sharī'ah's* general aim and spirit. Hence, the field of *ra'y* is narrow when compared to that of *ijtihād*. However, it is more comprehensive than *qiyās* and, consequently, is called *ijtihād* by *ra'y*.[56]

Ijtihād by ra'y at the time of the Prophet (ṣ)

Muslim scholars disagree on whether the Prophet (ṣ) performed *ijtihād* by *ra'y* on such issues as daily maintenance, the rules related to war and peace or attack and defence, or solving disputes or juridical and political issues.[57] According to Ibn al-Humām, some *Ḥanafī* jurists confined his *ijtihād* by *ra'y* to *qiyās* in situations where there was no revelation.[58] At this time, many rulings and legislations were determined by *waḥy* (revelation). Problems were solved either by revelation or by the Prophet (ṣ) through inspiration. Even in situations where there was no revelation, the Prophet (ṣ) used his knowledge-based experience and *ra'y* to perform *ijtihād*. He is reported to have said: "When I do not receive a revelation, I adjudicate among you on the basis of my opinion."[59] If he made a mistake, it was corrected through subsequent revelations.[60] Revelation enabled the Prophet (ṣ) to give general rules of guidance for social issues during his time and for future generations, thereby ensuring that Muslims could carry out their affairs.[61] However, according to the *Ash'arīs*, the *Mu'tazilah*, Ibn Ḥazm al-Ẓāhirī, and some *Ḥanbalī* and *Shāfi'ī* scholars, the *Qur'ān* provides clear evidence that every utterance of the Prophet (ṣ) partakes of *waḥy*: "*He says nothing of his own desire; it is nothing other than revelation sent down to him*".[62] In other words, all of his rulings consist of divine revelations and are not considered *ijtihād*.[63] Another view is that we cannot judge his situation due to the evidence's conflicting nature. This view is attributed to al-Shāfi'ī and upheld by al-Baqillānī (d. 403/1013) and al-Ghazālī. Al-Shawkānī, however, rejects the idea that the *Qur'ān* gives us clear indications that *ijtihād* was permissible for the Prophet (ṣ) and that he could make mistakes.[64] On the other hand, the scholars who support this view say that any errors that the Prophet (ṣ) might have made were rectified either by him or through a subsequent revelation.[65] For example, the *Qur'ān* rebuked him for one of his mistakes: "*It is not fitting for a Prophet that he should have prisoners (of war) until he has thoroughly subdued the earth*".[66] This verse was revealed concerning the reported seventy captives taken during the Battle of *Badr*. The Prophet (ṣ) first asked Abū Bakr what should be done with them. Abū Bakr suggested that they should be ransomed, whereas 'Umar ibn al-Khaṭṭāb opined that they should be executed. The Prophet approved of Abū Bakr's view, but then the verse disapproving of such an action was revealed. Elsewhere, Allah asks the Prophet (ṣ): "*Allah granted you pardon, but why did you permit them to do so before it became clear to you who was telling the truth?*"[67] This verse shows that the Prophet (ṣ) pardoned those who did not participate in the Battle of *Tabuk*. These verses indicate that the Prophet (ṣ) had, on some occasions, acted on his own *ijtihād*, for if he had followed a divine command, there would have been no cause for a reprimand or the granting of divine pardon for his mistakes. Several narrations document the use of *ijtihād* by *ra'y*. For example, when the Prophet (ṣ) the people of *Madinah* fertilizing palm trees, he forbade it. But when he heard that the trees had become barren, he said: "I'm a human being. If I order you to do something in the name of your religion, then conform to it. However, if I order something that depends on my personal *ra'y*, I am only a human being."[68] In another narration, a woman from Juhayna asked him: "My mother vowed to make a pilgrimage, but she died before she could fulfil the vow. Can I do it in her name?" The Prophet (ṣ) replied: "Yes, fulfil the pilgrimage instead of her. If your mother had a debt, would you not pay it? Pay your debts (fulfil your promises), because Allah fulfils promises too."[69] Here, the Prophet (ṣ) compares two similar things, showing that to fulfil a promise made to Allah is the same as fulfilling a promise made to a human being. This type of analogy is called *awlā'*.[70] Another example of *qiyās* is as follows. A nomad tried to reject his ancestors by telling the Prophet: "My wife gave birth to a black baby." The Prophet asked: "Do you have grey camels among your red ones?" When the nomad said that he did, the Prophet asked: "Where did they come from?" The nomad said: "They presumably look like their ancestors." The Prophet then told him: "Your child presumably also looks like his ancestors."[71] The Prophet (ṣ) preserved most of the pre-Islamic Arabic customs, although a few were changed, such as trade, pawn, rent, *salam* (contract of purchase of goods with pre-payment), marriage, equality between husband and wife, and murder.[72] When the Prophet came to *Madinah*, he saw that its people were making *salam* agreements for one or two years. To emphasize this, he said: "Anyone who makes *salam* agreements should do this according to specific measurements and for determined periods."[73] This practice, which was common among the Arabs, was practiced freely after a few amendments.[74] Thus, the Prophet (ṣ) applied and practiced *ijtihād* by *ra'y* and trained the Companions to follow his example. His instruction was practical rather than theoretical. The Prophet's practice of *ijtihād* by *ra'y* provided the example for *qiyās*, *istiḥsān*, *maṣlaḥah*, *sadd al-dharā'ī'* and *'urf*.

The Companions' Use of ijtihād by ra'y

There is evidence that the Companions performed *ijtihād* by *ra'y* both in the Prophet's (ṣ) presence and absence[75] concerning such matters as the *adhān* (the call to prayer), *ghusl* (ritual ablution of the whole body), and postponing the prayer. The Prophet included rulings pertaining to law within the range of *ijtihād*.[76] During the time of revelation and as long as there were no explanations or prohibitions from Allah, the Companions considered *ijtihād* permissible.[77] When an issue arose and no relevant verses could be found in the *Qur'ān*, the Prophet (ṣ) performed *ijtihād* by *ra'y*. He also authorized the Companions to use the same method under the same circumstances.[78]

For example, Muʿadh ibn Jabal, ʿAmr ibn al-ʿĀṣ, and ʿUqbah ibn ʿĀmir (d. 58/677) performed *ijtihād* in his presence.[79] Muʿadh ibn Jabal's *ḥadīth*, "I shall spare no pains to do my best to form an opinion,"[80] has already been mentioned. Other examples are as follows: During the Battle of *Dhāt Thalāsī*, ʿAmr ibn al-ʿĀṣ led a group of soldiers. While fighting, he entered the state of *junūb* (requiring a ritual ablution of the entire body). Afraid that such an ablution made during the severe cold might kill him, he made *tayammum* (using clean sand or soil when water is unavailable) and led the prayer, saying: "Allah says in the *Qur'ān*: 'Do not kill yourselves.'" When he returned, he told the Prophet what he had done, and the Prophet (ṣ) approved of it.[81] Due to his fear, ʿAmr applied a practice that was permissible when there was no water or when the person was too ill to use it. I agree that ʿAmr used a form of *istiḥsān* by taking ease as the basis of his decision, in accordance with the *Sharīʿah's* spirit but contrary to the general rule. When he was a *qāḍī* (judge) in Yemen, ʿAli used *ijtihād* by ra'y when deciding which of the three men who had had sexual intercourse with the same woman over a certain period of time was the father. He asked them to draw straws, saying that whoever drew the shortest straw would have the child acknowledged as his and would pay two *diyah* (monetary compensation) to the other two. When the Prophet (ṣ) learned of this, he acknowledged the correctness of ʿAli's action.[82] Muḥammad ibn Ḥasan al-Hajawī (d. 1956), considers this ruling a form of *istiḥsān*.[83] If this or any similar issues arose today, modern technology would be the vehicle used to confirm paternity. Thus, using technology can be a method of *istiḥsān* based on *maṣlaḥah*. During the Prophet's lifetime, both he and the Companions, with his permission, used *ijtihād* in light of the *Sharīʿah*. Accordingly, personal judgment and human contributions were integrated into the life of Islamic law. This integration is not regarded as strange, for the law's cornerstone, the *maqāṣid al-sharīʿah* (the objectives of the Islamic law), has to be taken into consideration when performing *ijtihād*.

Types of ijtihād

Ijtihād is mainly divided into two types: independent *ijtihād* which aims at deducing the law from the evidence in the sources; and limited *ijtihād* which is concerned mainly with the elaboration and implementation of the law within the confines of a particular schools of thought.

It is necessary to know that the use of *ijtihād* to derive *sharī'ah* rulings is crucial for everyday life. Today's Muslims actually need two types of *ijtihād*: the first is to understand its nature by preferring and choosing *ijtihād* to select the main objectives of the *sharī'ah* rules. The most basic of *sharī'ah* rules is to accommodate the benefit of people and the most suitable opinions for modern life's circumstances. These rules have been handed down from former jurists. The second type is the derivation of new rulings in law using legal methods such as *qiyās*, *istiḥsān*, *maṣlaḥah*, *istiṣlāḥ*, *'urf*, and so on, where the jurists' performance of *ijtihād* has room for manoeuvre, according to Qaradāwī.[84]

Al-Ghazālī (d. 505/1111) was the first to divide *ijtihād* into two main categories and after him this was developed into more divisions. There was no any attempt to classify it into categories before al-Ghazālī. The ranks of the competent scholars (*mujtahidūn*) reached seven ranks by the sixteenth century although it was considered two ranks only from the twelfth century onwards.[85]

An interesting method is suggested by Fazlur Rahman, to make *ijtihād*, since the *Qur'ān* is our guidance, the *Qur'ān's* general principles, values, long term purposes must be determined and systemized; it is important that these principles and purposes are to be formulated and conveyed into the present time. According to him, the general principles, values, long term purposes could become applicable for recent issues pertaining to humankind; in other words, determined principles and purposes should be rationally integrated into present circumstances.[86] In his model, the principle of *ijtihād* would be performed as a 'double movement': "the process of interpretation proposed here consist of double movements, from the present situation to the *Qur'ān* times, and then back to the present."[87] First, travelling to the time of the revelation of the *naṣṣ*; verses must be investigated, the wisdom behind them discovered, and the purpose of the revelation considered along with their historical circumstances. It is necessary to discover and comprehend the *Qur'ān*'s purpose in its entirety and its detailed response to particular circumstances. Generalizing the individual responses sets the precedent for future ethical and social structures. Secondly, returning to the present and pertaining the general systemized principles to issues. This requires from us that the present circumstances be analysed in detail with its various constitutive components. Historians, sociologists, moralists, should co-operate in the *ijtihād* of the double movement.[88] If people do not consult the *Qur'ān* and give credence to its fixed ideas, the double movement process would be the sole hope for an ideal technique for a successful interpretation.[89]

As for *ijtihād* based on the *maqāṣid*, Muḥammad Tahir Ibn 'Āshūr (d. 1973) says that it has five main divisions.[90]

a. Comprehending the commands of the *sharī'ah* and its *naṣṣ*, which must be in the context of linguistic meanings and *shar'ī* (legal) meanings.

b. Cases which are contradictory to *naṣṣ* must be examined with a view to *naskh* (abrogation), *takhṣīṣ* (specifying the general), and *rājiḥ* (preference).

c. To perform analogy based on the effective cause, which is obtained from the rulings.

ḍ. Creating a rule in an area where there is no availability of *naṣṣ* (text) and analogy.

e. The *ta'abbudī* (worship) rulings would be accepted as they are.

In performing *ijtihād* the jurist is to consider these five divisions; a jurist needs to know the objectives of the *sharī'ah* (*maqāṣid al-sharī'ah*).

Ijtihād with regard to the amount of effort exerted by the *mujtahid* is divided into two types:

a. Full or Complete *ijtihād*: The *mujtahid* exerts all efforts possible in searching and investigating until he feels that he is incapable of further efforts. This is what Mu'ādh Ibn Jabal indicated in the *ḥadīth* stated above "I shall spare no pains to do my best to form an opinion."[91]

b. Imperfect (Incomplete) *ijtihād:* when there is a lack of effort in searching and investigating. This type of *ijtihād* is not considered as *shar'ī ijtihād.*[92]

Ghazālī (d. 505/111) was the first to divide *ijtihād* into two categories in general[93]:

1. Absolute *(muṭlaq) ijtihād*: This is where the *mujtahid* is unrestricted by the rules of a particular *madhhab*. This level of *ijtihād* is for those who have fulfilled all the requirements of *ijtihād*, and also deduced the *aḥkām* from the evidence in the sources.

2. Limited *(muqayyad) ijtihād*: This is where the *mujtahid* expounds the law within the confines of a particular school while adhering to the principles laid down by their *imāms.*[94]

Ijtihād is also divided into the general and the specific:

1. General ('āmm) *ijtihād*: deals with all sections of Islamic fiqh.

2. Specific, individual *(khāṣṣ) ijtihād*: deals with a particular section of *fiqh* or evidence such as *ijmā'* and *qiyās.*[95]

Further classifications are individual and collective as follows:

1. Individual *ijtihād:* is when a person fulfils the conditions or requirements of a *mujtahid* without any contribution or participation by another *mujtahid.* Alternatively, it is an *ijtihād* performed by several *mujtahids* on an issue in which there is no evidence of agreement on an opinion. The above type of *ijtihād* is that which the *ḥadīth* of Mu'ādh Ibn Jabal has indicated.

2. Collective *(jamā'ī) ijtihād*: This is the *ijtihād* where consultations take place amongst scholars and jurists regarding current issues of importance to the general public. This type of *ijtihād* has been proven by the textual statement of the *Qur'ān* and the *Sunnah* as well as the works of the Companions and their Successors.[96]

Besides the above consideration, the *mujtahids* can also be classified and graded based on their knowledge and ability to infer rulings which were explored by Kamali[97] on the concept of *ijtihād*:

First Grade: Full *Mujtahid* (*mujtahid fi'l-shar'*) who fulfils all the requirements of *ijtihād.* The full *mujtahid* deduce the *aḥkām* from the evidences in the sources of Islamic law and by doing so, he is not restricted by the rules of a particular *madhhab* and they provide original and independent thought rulings to name but a few among the Companions and the succeeding generation, Sa'īd Ibn al-Musayyab and Ibrāhīm al-Nakhā'ī, the leading *Sunnī Imāms* of the four schools, Abū Ḥanīfah, Shāfi'ī, Mālikī and Ḥanbalī, the leading *Shī'ah Imāms* Muḥammad al-Bāqir and his son Ja'far al-Ṣādiq, etc. are well-known independent *mujtahids.* The well-known colleagues of Abū Ḥanīfa, Abū Yūsuf and al-Shaybānī are also regarded as full *mujtahid* by Abū Zahrah. Many secondary sources such as analogy, *istiḥsān* (juristic preference), *maṣlaḥah mursalah* etc. were formulated and established as the secondary sources of the *Sharī'ah.*[98]

Second Grade: *Mujtahids* within the *Madhhab* (School of thought) who explained the *aḥkām* (rulings) within the borders of a particular school while observing the principles and methods formulated by the leading *Imām* of a specific school, such as Zufar b. al-Hudhayl, Ḥasan b. Ziyād from the *Ḥanafī* school; Ismā'īl b. Yaḥyā al-Muzanī, 'Uthman Taqī al-Dīn b. al-Ṣalāḥ and Jalāl al-Dīn al-Suyūṭī from the *Shāfi'ī*; Ibn 'Abd al-Barr and Abū Bakr b. al-'Arabī from the *Mālikī*; and Ibn Taymiyyah his student Ibn Qayyīm al-Jawziyyah from the *Ḥanbalī* school. From the perspective of freedom of thought, these scholars may have different opinions from their leading *Imāms* whose opinions may be contradicted.

Third Grade: The *Aṣḥāb al-Masā'il* (*Mujtahids* on Particular Issues): this type of jurists who are competent to interpret and to exercise *ijtihād* on certain aspects of the law in precise matters which were not explored by the jurists from the first and the second level. The main duties of such jurists are to explain the law on new points which were not obviously settled by the other jurists. Nevertheless, they do not contradict to the leading jurists and they follow the general established principles of their own *madhhab*. Among the prominent scholars who are mentioned within this category as follow: Abū al-Ḥasan al-Karkhī and Abū Ja'far al-Ṭaḥawī in the *Ḥanafī* school, Abū al-Faḍl al-Marwazī and Abū Isḥāq al-Shīrāzī in the *Shāfi'ī*, Abū Bakr al-Abḥarī in the *Mālikī* and 'Amr b. Ḥusayn al-Khiraqī in the *Ḥanbalī* schools. The three ranks that were mentioned above are classified as *mujtahids* but the remaining ranks are considered as followers (*muqallidūn*).[99]

Fourth Grade: The *Aṣḥāb al-Takhrīj* (Jurists who resolvers of ambiguity) who do not infer the law (*aḥkām*) but are well knowledgeable about the doctrine and are able to designate a preferable one in cases of ambiguity and among different rulings when it comes to interpretation of the texts.[100]

Fifth Grade: The *Aṣḥāb al-Tarjīḥ* (Jurists of Assessment) who are competent to make comparisons and distinguish the rulings from the correct (*ṣaḥīḥ*) and the preferred (*rājiḥ*, *arjaḥ*) and the agreed upon (*muftā bihā*) views from the weak ones by weighing and analysing the strengths of differing verdicts in the *madhhab*. Among the scholars to name but a few are 'Alā' al-Dīn al-Kāsānī and Burḥān al-Dīn al-Marghinānī of the *Ḥanafī* school, Muḥyi al-Dīn al-Nawawī of the *Shāfi'ī*, Ibn Rushd al-Qurtubī of the *Māliki* and Muwaffaq al-Dīn ibn Qudamah of the *Ḥanbalī* schools.[101]

Sixth Grade: The *Aṣḥāb al-Taṣḥīḥ* (Jurists of Correction) who have authority to determine whether a particular type of the law is strong or weak or differentiate between the manifest (*ẓāhir*) and the obscure (*khafī*) views of the schools. Thus the jurists only quote the correct rulings and ignore the rests which have no substantial basis. Mostly textbook writers are considered within this category.[102]

Seventh Grade: The *Muqallidūn* (imitators) who are knowledgeable scholars who know the law and rulings, do not interest in deducing new rules or they may have no ability to deduce new rulings. Such scholars are of the later ages and contemporary jurists who became famous for their knowledge since they may not distinguish between the weak and the strong, right and left, but get together whatever they find in terms of rulings.[103]

Despite the fact that, from one hand, the majority of scholars have held the view that once a person has fulfilled the necessary conditions of *ijtihād* he is considered as qualified to practice it in all areas of the *Sharī'ah*. *Ijtihād* is indivisible and it is said that a person is a *mujtahid* in the area of matrimonial law and an imitator (*muqallid*) in regard to devotional matters (*'ibādāt*) or vice-versa is not reasonable since *ijtihād* and *taqlīd* cannot be combined in one and the same person. Thus, intellectual ability and competence of a *mujtahid* cannot be divided into sections or divisions.[104]

On the other hand, some *Mālikī*, *Ḥanbalī* and *Ẓāhirī* scholars have held the view that *ijtihād*, however, is divisible and the idea was supported by many prominent scholars including Abū al-Ḥusayn al-

Baṣrī, al-Ghazālī, Ibn al-Humām, Ibn Taymiyyah, his disciple Ibn al-Qayyīm and al-Shawkānī.[105] Kamali comments on this matter saying that in modern times, in view of the sheer bulk of information and the more speed of its growth, specialisation in any major area of knowledge would seem to hold the key to originality and creative *ijtihād*. In regards to this realities, he suggest that the divisibility of *ijtihād* seems to be in greater harmony with the conditions of research in modern times, as well as the classification of *mujtahids* into various ranks should be considered thus the idea that *ijtihād* is divisible as *mujtahids* in a particular school or on particular issues.[106]

Conditions of the Ijtihād

The aims of the conditions are to ensure the ability of a person to perform *ijtihād*. The earliest complete account of the qualifications of a *mujtahid* was given in Abū al-Ḥusayn al-Baṣrī's *(d.* 436/1044*)* "*Al-Mu'tamad fī Uṣūl al-Fiqh.*" Shīrāzī (d. 467/1083), Ghazālī (d. 505/1111) and Āmidī (d. 632/1234) later accepted the broad outline of Baṣrī's exposition, with minor changes. This does not mean that the requirements of *ijtihād* received no attention from the *'ulamā'* who came before Baṣrī'.[107]

Besides the essential condition that the *mujtahid* must be a Muslim and a competent person of sound mind who is able to use his intellectual competence to form an independent judgment, the first condition is "to perceive the *maqāṣid* (objectives) of the Lawgiver. The second condition, in the same context, is to have the ability to infer rules based on awareness of the *maqāṣid*."[108] *Uṣūlī* scholars for many centuries prepared extensive lists of the abilities jurists must possess to enable them to perform *ijtihād*. Some increased and others decreased the conditions. An outstanding scholar, Shāṭibī, ignored these lists[109] and reduced the conditions of *ijtihād* to one comprehensive point: the precise comprehension of the *maqāṣid* and in the light of this comprehension the ability to deduce rules from the sources.[110]

Ibn al-Subkī *(d.* 771/1370*)* mentions the conditions of *ijtihād* in his book "*Jam' al-Jawāmī'*."[111] In the explanation of "*Minhāj*," Ibn al-Subkī stated that one of the conditions of *ijtihād* is "to know the objectives of the Lawgiver before specializing in that field."[112] Ṣuyūtī *(d.* 911/1505*)* quotes from "*Al-Tanqīḥ*" of Amīnuddīn b. Muḥammad Tabrīzī (d. 621/1224) the following statement: "Knowledge of providing evidence of rulings is obtained by investigating every single word of the main sources (the *Qur'ān* and the *Sunnah*) in the context of the *maqāṣid*."[113]

Shāṭibī believes that there are some who think that they are competent in the concept of *ijtihād* but who are unable to perceive the objectives of the Lawgiver. Their self-belief in their ability to arrive at a just ruling undermines Islamic law. Shāṭibī says: "the incorrect use of partial ruling destroys the general principles. Without realizing their lack of knowledge in understanding the *maqāṣid al-sharī'ah* questions are never asked, and the ruling is established with the first thought that comes to mind, with no further investigation deemed necessary…"[114]

If a ruling relating to people's needs is adequate and the *muftī* does not possess the ability to comprehend Allah's purposes the ruling may cause problems and therefore it is necessary for the *muftī* to understand the *maqāṣid al-sharī'ah* .[115] It must be kept in mind that a person who fails to meet one or more of the requirements of *ijtihād* is disqualified and may not exercise the method of performing *ijtihād*. The essential requirements are as follow:

Firstly, the *mujtahid* must possess the knowledge of the objectives (*maqāṣid*) of the *Sharī'ah*, and the essential seven[116] values namely, religion, life, intellect, lineage, property, honour and state are the recognised objectives of the Lawgiver. According to Al-Shāṭibī, this point is the foregoing requirements of *ijtihād*. For him there are two main points, one of which is the ability to comprehend the objectives of the *Sharī'ah*, while the other is the knowledge of the sources and the methods of deduction. The first of these is essential, and the second serves as an instrument of achieving the first.[117] In connection with these values, the *mujtahid* must know the types of the objectives (*maqāṣid*) of the *Sharī'ah* as the essentials (*ḍarūriyyāt*), the complementary (*ḥājiyyāt*) and the embellishments (*taḥsīniyyāt*) as well as the general maxims of *fiqh* (*qawā'id al-fiqhiyyah*).[118]

Secondly, the person who perform *ijtihād* must have knowledge of Arabic to the extent that enables the scholar to enjoy a correct understanding of the *Qur'ān* and the *Sunnah* in order to deduce the *aḥkām* from them.[119]

Thirdly, the *mujtahid* must also be knowledgeable about the occasions of its revelation (*asbāb al-nuzūl*) and the incidences of abrogation therein in the *Qur'ān* and the *Sunnah* as well as be knowledgeable whether the verses are the *makkī* and the *madinese* nature. More importantly, he must have a full understanding of the legal contents, or the *āyāt al-aḥkām* which are consisted of around five hundred verses and the related commentaries (*tafāsīr*) with special reference to the *Sunnah* and the views of the Companions.[120]

Fourthly, the *mujtahid* must have a satisfactory knowledge of the *Sunnah* related to *aḥkām* and the subject of his *ijtihād*.

Fifthly, he must also know the incidences of abrogation in the *Sunnah*, the general and the specific, (*'āmm* and *khāṣṣ*), the absolute and the qualified (*muṭlaq* and *muqayyad*), and the reliability or otherwise of the narrators of *ḥadīth*, in general to know the method of interpretation of the text, everything related to the *aḥādīth aḥkām* in the famous books of *Sunan Abī Dāwūd*, *Sunan al-Bayḥaqī*, or the *Musnad of Ibn Ḥanbal* etc. and the *Sunnah* in details.[121]

Sixthly, the *mujtahid* must also possess the knowledge of the substance of the *furū'* works, and the points on which there is an *ijmā'* of the Companions, the Successors, and the leading *Imāms* and *mujtahidūn*. He must also be aware of the opposing views, as it is said, "the most learned of people is also one who is most knowledgeable of the differences among people." [122]

Seventhly, the *mujtahid* must give a special emphasis on the knowledge of *qiyās*, he would be able to recourse to analogical deduction in order to discover the ruling for exceptional cases, capable of distinguishing strength and weakness in reasoning and evidence, and thus he must have a knowledge of logic (*manṭiq*).[123]

Eight and finally, the *mujtahid* must be just (*'ādil*) and sincere Muslim who abstains from committing sins as well as who is seeking the interest of the public rather than his own interest.[124]

Is the door of ijtihād closed?

It has been a curial question among the Muslim and non-Muslim scholars who deal with the Islamic law and sciences. The conditions of *ijtihād* stated above are the criteria for anyone who wants to qualify in practicing *ijtihād*, irrespective of the era in which the person may live. In later centuries, restrictions were imposed on *ijtihād* which, by the end of the third century, led to the allegation that the Gate of *ijtihād* was closed. The closure of the gate of *ijtihād* arose in order to prevent those who were incapable of practicing *ijtihād* – yet who claimed to do so – from bringing the concept into disrepute. To those who are capable, the doors to the gate of *ijtihād* remained opened.[125]

Furthermore, recent western scholars, in particular Wael Hallaq, and W. Montgomery Watt, have also assumed that the door of *ijtihād* is still open and the term "The closing of the door of *ijtihād*" is a myth.[126] In reality, the door of *ijtihād* was never completely closed, as properly qualified scholars must have the right to perform *ijtihād* continuously. *Ijtihād* is not confined to the four schools of law and can be performed by all capable scholars. Consequently, the gate of *ijtihād*, in my personal opinion, is still and must remain open.

Dihlawī (1703/1762) strongly criticizes those who claimed that the door of *ijtihād* was closed. He calls them: "The simpletons of our time" who are, "totally averse to *ijtihād*. Like she-camels, in the nose of which a piece of wood is put to guide them, they do not know where they are going." *Ijtihād* is actually a *farḍ kifāyah* (a collective duty, the fulfilment of which by a sufficient number of individuals excuses the other individuals from fulfilling it) for every epoch since "every age has its own countless specific problems, and cognisance of the divine decisions with respect to them is essential"[127]. He continues: "The occupant of this office is qualified to exercise *ijtihād* whenever an affair arises for which he does not find an unequivocal judgement of the founder (*imām*) of the *madhhab*; he has the right to elicit judgements in the same manner and by preceding analogously the verdicts of the *imām*."[128]

The Muslim scholars are not in agreement whether the gate of *ijtihād* is discontinued or continued. Some claim that the independent *ijtihād* is discontinued, and others say that it is never been closed. Kamal al-Dīn Ibn al-Humām from the *Ḥanafi* school of thought he claims that it is not closed although his *madhhab* with the view that independent *ijtihād* has discontinued, contrary to the other three *madhhabs*, the *Ḥanbalīs* who maintain that *ijtihād* in all of its forms remains open.[129] Despite the view of the many scholars including al-'Āmidī, Ibn al-Ḥājib, Ibn al-Humām, Ibn al-Subkī, and Zakarīya al-Anṣārī that qualified *mujtahids* are extinct, the *Ḥanbalīs* have opposite view point that *ijtihād* is an obligatory duty of the Muslim *Ummah* supporting it with the *ḥadīth* of the Prophet (ṣ) "My community shall never agree on an error."[130] With the following *ḥadīth* "A group of people from my *Ummah* will continue to fight in defence of truth and remain successful until the Day of Judgment."[131] It is interpreted that defending the truth is not achieved without knowledge, and accordingly exercising *ijtihād* becomes an obligatory duty and therefore the gate of *ijtihād* may never be closed. Since Allah, the Almighty, has opened the gate of performing *ijtihād*, closing it is unacceptable. Abū Zahrah totally rejects the idea of closing the gate of *ijtihād* and it must remain open till the day of Resurrection.[132]

Areas where ijtihād is applicable

The scope of *ijtihād* is varies in which it can be applied to everywhere related to the legal matters except issues where *sharīʿah* is not concerned. In other words, *ijtihād* is dealt with the practical rules of *sharīʿah* that usually regulate the manner of the *mukallaf* (the subject). However, the scope of *ijtihād* precludes from the customary (*ʿurfī*) issues, purely intellectual (*ʿaqlī*) matters, or something that is not related to the inference of a legal matter (*ḥukm sharʿī*) as well as matters related to sense (*ḥissī*). The prohibition of murder, theft, and adultery etc. are exceptional since these are obvious realities of the *sharīʿah* which are determined in the explicit statements of the texts as well as the existence of a Creator, createdness of the universe, the obligatory status of the pillars of the faith, the sending of prophets and so forth, are exceptional since these are related to the faith which are not from the scope of the *ijtihād*.[133]

In addition to the above explanation on the scope of *ijtihād*, the decisive rules of *sharīʿah* deal with positive and definitive knowledge, all are excluded from the scope of *ijtihād*. Since the *qatʿī* of the *Qur'ān* and the *Sunnah* is basically not open to interpretation, the scope is only confined to the probable (*ẓannī*) proofs.[134] Nevertheless, despite the fact that, *ijtihād* is confined to the speculative proofs, some definitive sources such as specific (*khāṣṣ*) and *ʿāmm* of the *Qur'ān* may sometimes need interpretation.

Ijtihād and Istiḥsān

Since the definition of *ijtihād* is clearly elaborated many scholars, among the *Ḥanafī* jurists the definitions of *istiḥsān* were given by Karkhī, Sarakhsī, Jaṣṣāṣ, Bazdawī, Nasafī, and Ibn Humām; jurists from the other schools remained flexible.[135]

The concept of *istiḥsān* is a developed form of *ra'y*. One could extend the fundamental basis of *isthṣān* to the time of the Prophet (ṣ), given his advice to Muʿadh (d. 18). This actually advocates a defining role for the community, teaching the people how to use their own discretion and understanding; in this context, if the Prophet (ṣ) had not persuaded Mu'adh to use his own judgment after considering the main sources, the development of Islamic law would not have been successful, and would have remained stagnant. The Prophet's (ṣ) question "What will you do if you do not find guidance in the *Sunnah* of the Apostle of Allah and in Allah's Book?"[136] and Mu'adh's response, "I shall do my best to form an opinion and spare no pains"[137] which contains the key to the evolution and dynamism of Islamic law.

From the *ḥadīth* of Mu'adh, it can be concluded that the Prophet (ṣ) approved *ijtihād* because Mu'ādh was far from the Prophet (ṣ) and thus had less access to revelation than companions who were at the Prophet's (ṣ) side. This *ḥadīth* clearly does not support the argument that when the revelation was still in progress, nothing else should be followed, under any circumstances. And after the death of the Prophet (ṣ), the community was in need of some sort of *ijtihād* supported by a *dalīl;* and *istiḥsān* falls within this category of *ijtihād.*[138]

Ḥanafī scholars see *istiḥsān* as a valid source of *sharī'ah* and a basis for the formulation of legal rulings. They also see most criticism of *istiḥsān* as the product of misunderstanding, and the imputation to Abū Ḥanīfah this is because of ulterior motives. However, it is difficult to believe that he would have abandoned a ruling that had been established on true *sharī'* foundations for his personal preference.[139]

One definition which generally gives the meaning of *istiḥsān* as understood by the jurists of *uṣūl* (principles), and also reflects the definition adopted by the *Ḥanafī* jurists, who consider it accurate and comprehensive, is that of Abū al-Ḥasan al-Karkhī (d. 340/952). He defines *istiḥsān* as follows: "*istiḥsān* is when one takes a decision on a certain case different from that on which similar cases have been decided on the basis of its precedents, for a reason which is stronger than the one found in similar cases and which requires departure from those cases."[140] This definition has been espoused and accepted by many jurists such as Ṭūfī (d. 716/1317), Shīrāzī (d. 476/1083), Ghazālī (d. 505/1111), and the contemporary jurist Abū Zahrah (d. 1974). It contains all types of *istiḥsān* in general.[141] Abū Zahrah (d. 1974) comments on the definition, saying that "This definition is the clearest one in which the true nature of *istiḥsān* is expressed by the *Ḥanafī* jurists, highlighting its aspects, its principle and its essence. The basis of *istiḥsān* is, instead of conforming to one rule, to find a solution with a ruling on the evidence that is presented; this evidence could be against the general principle but in keeping with the aim of the *sharīʿah*. In respect of the new solution regarding the problem, the evidence is stronger than the analogy."[142] Another contemporary scholar ʿAbd al-Wahhāb Khallāf, considers Karkhī's definition as "the best," saying that "in my view the definition is the definition of Karkhī from *Ḥanafīs,* Ibn Rushd (d. 595) from among the *Mālikīs* and Ṭūfī (d. 716) from among the *Ḥanbalīs.*"[143] The clearest and most comprehensive definition of *istiḥsān* that the researcher has found is that of Khallāf: "In the view of the jurists the technical definition of *istiḥsān* is the authorization to depart from an established ruling to a different ruling when legal evidence is presented. The legal evidence which is presented is known as the authority of *istiḥsān.*"[144]

To summarise, *istiḥsān* is evidence which is preferred over an accepted established ruling after ensuring that this evidence does not contravene the Islamic legal ruling. In fact, Khallāf's definition is not a new one; the only difference is its expression, and thus the meanings of the two definitions are similar. According to Karkhī, "departure" must be based on particular evidence which warrants a move from an established ruing to a different ruling on a similar case. The purpose of the stronger reason or evidence requires the departure; the jurist (*mujtahid*) departs from the established ruling because of the stronger reason. A strong statement, which was narrated that Imām Mālik (d. 179 AH) said, "*Istiḥsān* represents nine-tenths of human knowledge"[145] may give the value of *istiḥsān* to understand the connection of it with *ijtihād*.

As Abū Ḥanīfah is considered the father of *istiḥsān*, his method of performing *ijtihād* at the same time *istiḥsān* help us know the connection with it. The area in which Abū Ḥanīfah lived attracted many scholars and developed into a thriving intellectual milieu.[146] Abū Ḥanīfah's father's occupation as a trader enabled him to associate with those who took an active part in the social and economic activities of their society.[147] Abū Ḥanīfah stood against the government[148] was a staunch supporter of *ahl al-bayt* (the household of the Prophet (ṣ)) and used *qiyās* and *istiḥsān* when asked for guidance in various situations. He had a powerful understanding of *qiyās*, and in the words of Imām Shāfi'ī, was described in terms of great respect: "Many scholars could be considered the heirs of Abū Ḥanīfah in their use of *qiyās* and *istiḥsān*."[149]

The failure of Abū Ḥanīfah to leave any written manuscripts explaining the concept or procedure of *istiḥsān*, or the conditions of its validity, is a source of conflict amongst the jurists, for the lack of written material has led him to be accused of judging cases without depending on any textual evidences. When he made the following statement: "*qiyās* is such and such but we apply *istiḥsān*"[150], he was criticized by many scholars such as Ibn Ḥazm (d. 456/1064)[151] and especially Imām Shāfi'ī, who said "Whoever approves of juristic preference is making himself the Lawmaker."[152]

However, it is not entirely true to say that there is no trace of any reports regarding Abū Ḥanīfah's techniques; in fact he left writings giving indications as to his methods of performing *ijtihād* and his use of the principle of *istiḥsān*. He expressed this method as follows: "I read Allah's book to obtain guidance. If I am unable to find any guidance in the *Qur'ān* then I resort to the Tradition (*Sunnah*) of the Prophet (ṣ) and the true reports (*ḥadīth*) which have been transmitted from generation to generation by trustworthy narrators. If neither the *Qur'ān* nor the *Sunnah* yields any guidance, I then refer to the opinions of the Companions. Consequently, when I make my personal decision then I do not ask others' opinions. However, if a matter has been considered by Ibrāhīm al-Nakhā'ī (d. 96), Shā'bī (d. 103), Ḥasan (d. 110), Muḥammad b. Shirīn (d. 110), Sa'īd Ibn al-Musayyab (d. 94) *et al.* I also act on their *ijtihād.*"[153]

Abū Ḥanīfah also seriously considers the issue of abrogated *ḥadīth.* Accordingly, his way of recourse to the Tradition was to research intensively a Tradition and to see whether it had been narrated through trustworthy narrators from the Prophet (ṣ) through the Companions; if it had, he would then apply it in his judgments.[154] In addition to his authority in *ḥadīth* and *fiqh,* he was also aware of the customs (*'urf*) and traditions of the people, and how previous *ijtihāds* had been incorporated and practiced.[155] He was also a master in *qiyās.* Abū Ḥanīfah explained his methods when applying *qiyās* as follows: "We make *qiyās* from one matter to another based on the *Qur'ān* or the *Sunnah* or *ijmā'* (consensus) of the Muslim Community. We consider seriously our *ijtihāds* and whether they adhere to certain principles or not."[156] He points out that *qiyās* would not be applied to every case without a reason, saying: "*Qiyās* cannot be applied to everything."[157] The application of *qiyās* is a great responsibility because it may cause unexpected results and bad solutions. In this respect he says "To urinate in a mosque is better than some kinds of *qiyās.*"[158]

Abū Yūsuf (d. 182) made a statement regarding his master's method of performing *ijtihād,* saying, "In any case which is presented to Abū Ḥanīfah, his first requirement is information as to whether there are any Traditions (*athar*) regarding this matter. When we show him what there is, he then applies his knowledge after examining the case and ensuring that it is according to procedure. If two opinions are given and the information is stronger in the Tradition then the stronger opinion is chosen to resolve the issue. However if the two opinions are similar, he judges the case on his own personal opinion (*ra'y*). Thirdly, if any Traditions do not exist relating to this issue, he refers it to *qiyās*. Whenever *qiyās* yields an unacceptable result, he eventually abandons it in favour of *istiḥsān*.[159]

Abū Zahrah summarizes Abū Ḥanīfah's method of performing *ijtihād* similarly: "He performs *ijtihād* when he cannot find any guidance in the *Qur'ān*, in the *Sunnah* or within the *qawl al-Ṣaḥābah* (the saying of the Companions). To ensure a competent judgment, he assesses a case on opinion and investigates it using different aspects of deduction. Sometimes he goes with *qiyās* and occasionally makes *istiḥsān*. He considers people's benefit and obeys the principle which states that "No harm shall be inflicted or reciprocated in Islam"[160]. If he decides to use *qiyās* when its results conflict with the custom of the people, he then applies *istiḥsān*. Whatever he chooses to perform, whether *qiyās* or *istiḥsān*, the customs of the people are taken into consideration.[161]

Abū Ḥanīfa's connection with trade life gave him an intensively absorbed knowledge on how to deal with the common practices and needs of the people, and the newly-occurring problems of daily life. This knowledge gave him the flexibility to depart from the unexpected results of analogy and arrive at rulings that might benefit the people, through the principle of *istiḥsān*.[162]

According to Shaybānī, "Abū Ḥanīfah was discussing *qiyās* with his friends who always debated with him fiercely in order to arrive at the truth. When Abū Ḥanīfah said, "I am making *istiḥsān*," nobody could fault him because he had judged so many cases on the grounds of the principle of *istiḥsān*. Eventually everyone abandoned their previous opinions and followed him."[163]

The reason for Abū Ḥanīfah's success is that he automatically recognizes the effective causes (*'illah*), distinguishes between the explicit and implicit, and applies the ruling that is consonant with the people's benefit, thereby obtaining justice and equity.[164] His use of the principle of *istiḥsān* was performed proficiently without contradicting the main principle of religion and the soul of the *sharī'ah*. Ibn

Shubrumah extols Abū Ḥanīfah's supremacy in the application of *istiḥsān* by saying, "If someone is allowed to present just one opinion in Allah's religion, it can only be Abū Ḥanīfah's saying, "I approve *istiḥsān*."[165] In addition to this, Abū Ḥanīfah was reported to have said about the validation of this principle "*istiḥsān* is a principle that is necessary for the production of legal rulings in the religion."[166]

Abū Ḥanīfah and his disciples were highly respectful of the Traditions, and used them in their *ijtihād;* even if it was a *ḥadīth ḍaīf* (weak tradition) they would prefer it over *qiyās.* Ibn Ḥazm has affirmed that Abū Ḥanīfah and his disciples were united concerning the effectiveness of a weak *ḥadīth* against *qiyās,* considering it to be on a higher level.[167] Yaḥyā b. Ādam (d. 203/818) comments on Abū Ḥanīfah's method of departing from *qiyās* due to a *ḥadīth ṣaḥīḥ* (authentic tradition): "Whoever says that Abū Ḥanīfah approves *qiyās* over *athar* (*ḥadīth*), is making an unfair accusation. Abū Ḥanīfah's practices and his disciples' writings are full of examples of his departing from *qiyās* and applying the rule of *athar* (*ḥadīth*).[168]

The criteria of personal judgment in *istiḥsān* indicates a direct relationship between *istiḥsān* and *ijtihād by ra'y* which is a personal judgment. It is viewed that *istiḥsān* is a product of *ijtihād*. In fact, Abū Ḥanīfah performed *ijtihād* from his personal opinions (conforming to the *Qur'ān* and the *Sunnah*) by saying, "*Qiyās* rules this, but we "*nastaḥsinū*" (prefer) that, or we proved this by *istiḥsān* contrary to *qiyās*, or the *qiyās* of this is so and so and the *ijtihād* of this is so and so, and the *ijtihād* we take".[169]

The Value (ḥukm) of Ijtihād

Ijtihād is a very demanding requirement in modern day life, and therefore it is sometimes an individual duty (*farḍ 'aynī*) and sometimes a collective duty (*farḍ kifāyah*) for Muslims.[170] If the requirement of *ijtihād* is ignored then the whole Muslim community will be considered sinful. The scholars unanimously agree that *ijtihād* is included in the scope of the following verses: "*So keep your duty to Allah and fear Him as much as you can*"[171] and "*Then take admonition, O you with eyes (to see)*"[172]. Qarāfi expresses his anxiety, saying "Allah save us if there is not an available competent *mujtahid*."[173]

Muslim scholars are in agreement that *ijtihād* is the collective obligation (*farḍ kifāyah*) of all qualified jurists, in other words the practice of *ijtihād* is a religious duty. Since it is a religious duty, at least one *mujtahid* should perform *ijtihād* to be free from the obligation otherwise all the Muslim scholars would be accountable, the religious duty remains unfulfilled. Practicing *ijtihād*, therefore, can be categorized differently such as a personal obligation (*wājib* or *farḍ 'ayn*) and collective obligation (*farḍ kifāyah*). On one hand, if a matter is addressed to two *mujtahids*, or to two judges, and one of them exercises it to formulate a reasonable solution, the other is forgiven of this duty. In addition to this responsibility, performing *ijtihād* becomes a personal obligation (*wājib* or *farḍ 'ayn*) of the qualified *mujtahid* in critical matters in which the justice or the truth may be lost if practising *ijtihād* is not immediately performed. For a competent *mujtahid*, who is capable of performing it, to take already given rulings, to follow another *mujtahid* that is imitation (*taqlīd*) is forbidden. It is allowed for layman (*'ammī*) who is not capable of performing *ijtihād*. In any case, seeking knowledge is encouraged by Allah, the *Qur'ān* states: "*Then ask those who have knowledge (ahl al-dhikr) if you yourselves do not know*".[174] Nevertheless asking and seeking guidance is requested from those who have not ability and knowledge, not from those who have already knowledge to derive the correct respond from the sources. It has to be differentiated between the *mujtahid* and the layman. Accordingly the statement in the verse "those who have knowledge" (أَهْلَ الذِّكْرِ) refers to the scholars (*'ulamā'*) who have capacity to deduce or investigate the solution regardless as to whether they actually know the correct ruling of an issue or not.[175]

However, the preferred view is that he must avoid *taqlīd*, even of one who might be more learned than him. Only an *'ammī* (layman) who is capable of *ijtihād* is allowed to follow the opinion of others.[176] On the other hand, if there are other available *mujtahids* who can perform it or there is no critical or urgent matter to be solved, the religious duty remains as a collective duty (*farḍ kifāyah*), in which the responsibility is shared. The collective duty can also be considered as recommended (*mandūb*) *ijtihād* since it is not an obligatory duty and there is no specific matters have been referred to him (*mujtahid*). However, performing *ijtihād* may become forbidden (*ḥarām*) if a deduced ruling by the way of *ijtihād* contradicts to the main principles of the *Sharī'ah*. It is therefore, there should be no ruling contradicts to the *Qur'ān*, the *Sunnah* and a definite consensus (*ijmā'*).[177]

The source of Islamic law during the first period was the *Qur'ān* and the *Sunnah*. The growth of Muslim society engendered different social issues and problems, which meant that the established law based on the *Qur'ān* and the *Sunnah* needed to be reconsidered, expanded, and reinterpreted to give adequate answers to new issues. As a result, Islamic law made improvements according to the circumstances of the era. This practice is ongoing. The independent reconsidering and interpretation of the law was known as *ijtihād*. *Ra'y* was the main element of *ijtihād* and became widespread, gradually paving the way for the development of *qiyās* and *istiḥsān*.[178] For many years, it was believed that only those with an outstanding intellectual ability could be involved in the process of rational rule-making. As many other verses Allah with this verse "*Do they not then earnestly seek to understand the Qur'ān, or are their hearts locked up by them?*"[179] strongly encourages people to contemplate every single verse and then apply their intellect and personal opinion to the new legal issues. The Prophet (ṣ) is a good example of this practice, for he always considered the Companions' opinions regarding those issues on which the *naṣṣ* was silent. The problems faced by the Muslim community were solved easily and effectively during the Prophet's lifetime, as he was the supreme authority to comment on the verses and explain them to the people. Following his death, the problems increased and became more complex. The Companions had the *Qur'ān* and the *Sunnah* to guide them concerning the new issues that emerged from the Muslim community's increasingly complex social life. They also used their own opinion to decide which verses or *aḥadīth* could be applied to a particular case. Thus, they employed their own opinion in order to understand the verses correctly and then apply them to new situations, and to devise solutions for the more problematic cases in the absence of any clear verses.

Concept of Taqlīd

Uṣūl al-Fiqh as a principle of Islamic law passed through significant periods to develop its principles as an independent science. Although some authors tend to write separately the historical development of jurisprudence from the *uṣūl al-fiqh* itself, together with all complete the science independently. However, the process passed various stages to reach the maturation period namely the era of the Prophet (ṣ), the period of the Companions, the early schools of law in the *Hijāz* and Iraq, the emergence of the school of thoughts (*madhāhib*), the period of imitation (*taqlīd*), and the call for a return to *ijtihād* and finally the period of *ijtihād* and *taqlīd* together. Though, it is indicated earlier that *ijtihād* is indivisible, and if a person is a *mujtahid* in the field of specific law, he cannot combine both *ijtihād* and *taqlīd*, however it is vice-versa in different field.[180] Nevertheless, as an institution these two institutions supported each other to solve problems of the Muslim community, former developed it and the later preserved it from evil attacks aiming to destroy the religion among the society.

In a sense that the so-called closure of the gate of *ijtihād* at around the beginning of the 10th century did not affect the development of *uṣūl al-fiqh* since it deals with the principles but the *fiqh* due to the nature of it which it is outcome of the *uṣūl al-fiqh*. More importantly, the period of imitation (*taqlīd*) which followed have added value to the role and distinction of *uṣūl al-fiqh* in the sense that the imitators (*muqallidūn*) observed, and relied on, the principles of the *uṣūl al-fiqh* as a measure of validity for their opinions.[181] Even more, it protected the Muslim community from radicalism, social corruption and serialized (*tafriqā*) thinking. In other words the institution of imitation (*taqlīd*) played enormous role making religion alive in the community and sustained it till present.

Definition of imitation (taqlīd)

Linguistically, *taqlīd* means simulation or imitation. Imitation (*taqlīd*) is derived from *qalādah* (neckless) which is an ornament tied around the neck[182] or it is the strap that holds the sheath of the sword and is usually swung around the shoulders. It is also used for the meaning of a piece of wood is hung from the neck of an animal in which it prevents the animal from running astray, because it strikes it on the knees when it attempts to run.[183]

Technically, as a term of *uṣūl al-fiqh*, imitation (*taqlīd*) means taking someone else's opinion without knowing the evidence and of a person whose opinion is not *hujjah* (proof or lawful authority). It is defined by Ibn al-Ḥajj as "acting upon the word of another without *ḥujjah*".[184] In general understanding it means following the opinion of the schools of thought (*madhāhib*) in matters of conduct such as a followers of *Ḥanafī madhhab* follows the opinion of the *Ḥanafī school*, while a followers of *Shāfi'ī madhhab* follows the opinion of the *Shāfi'ī* school.

The purpose of *taqlīd* is to rely on a methodology for the *faqīh* for discovering and applying the law in the light of the already settled law while the *ijtihād* is, as stated earlier, a legislative function, because it lays down the law for the first time.

The Ruling (ḥukm) of imitation (taqlīd)

In referring to the definition of Ibn al-Ḥajj "acting upon the word of another without *ḥujjah*" scholars understood in two different meaning.

The first meaning is that to mean the following of the opinion of another without knowledge or authority for such opinion.[185] In this type of *taqlīd*, a person should follow the ruling of jurist without question and he does not need to ask just about the basis for his opinion whether it has been derived from the *Qur'ān*, the *Sunnah* or *ijmā'* or some other sources. Although most of the contemporary scholars accept this meaning, the earlier jurists have different understanding about it.

As Nyazee explains that according to the earlier jurists, the word *ḥujjah* means permission given by the *sharī'ah. Taqlīd*, on the other hand, means following the opinion of another when the *sharī'ah* has not given permission to do so. This type of understanding about *taqlīd* makes it unlawful since following the opinion of another without permission of the *sharī'ah* is an unlawful act which is obviously rejected. Therefore, such opinion of a jurist is not considered as *taqlīd* since it contradicts to the *sharī'ah*. Muslim jurists took it differently saying that following the opinion of a qualified jurist is permitted by the *sharī'ah* is not considered *taqlīd*.[186] Following the philosophical explanation of *taqlīd* we may briefly conclude that there are acceptable *taqlīd* that is permissible and not acceptable *taqlīd* that is prohibited.

To remember, the founder of schools of thought have two main functions. Firstly, the *Imām* of the school lays down the principles (*uṣūl*) of interpretation and secondly, he implements these principles to determine the issues of the law (*furū'*). Abū Ḥanīfah is one of the schools of thought, who laid down the principles of interpretation for the *Ḥanafī* School and he used these principles to originate the detailed rulings (*aḥkām*) of the practical law, just like the founders of other schools of thought did. As it is mentioned earlier, this type of jurists are called the *mujtahid muṭlaq* or the absolute jurist. Therefore, such jurists are not allowed to do *taqlīd* since they are completely independent and they are called *mujtahid muṭlaq* insofar as they do not involve in any type of *taqlīd*.

Similar to the first type of jurists, there are jurist who are well qualified to undertake the responsibility of *ijtihād*. However, these kind of jurists who follow the principles of interpretation determined by their teacher. Simply they use these rules of interpretation to derive the practical law, and their opinions in this area may differ from those of their teacher. Nevertheless, these jurist are still following the opinion of their teacher about the principles of interpretation and thus they perform the method of *taqlīd*. Due to the teacher-student relationship, this type of *taqlīd* is called *taqlīd fī al-uṣūl* or *taqlīd* in the principles of interpretation in a particular school. The jurists who perform the *taqlīd fī al-uṣūl* is called *mujtahid fī al-madhhab* or the *mujtahid* who is independent within the school.

Apart from the types of jurists, above, there are also jurists in the school who are well qualified, however they have not been granted the status of *mujtahid fī al-madhhab*. These jurists perform only one type of *taqlīd*, and this is called *taqlīd fī al-furū‘* or following the decisions of the jurists of the higher grade.[187] These jurists follow the opinions or decisions of the school determined by the *mujtahid muṭlaq* and the *mujtahid fī al-madhhab*.

Following the clear explanation of the type of *taqlīd* of jurist, a question may arise at this stage as to which opinion of the jurists of the school do they follow, since there may be several opinions on a single issue, such as Abū Yūsuf may differ on the same issue from Muḥammad al-Shaibānī or from Zufar. The question may be settled by explanation given by Ibn ‘Abidīn, since there will always be a single preferred opinion within the same school of thought (*madhhab*).

Ibn ‘Abidīn states on this matter as follows: "The preferred opinion of the school is to be followed, and the opinion not preferred is to be treated as non-existent (*al-marjūḥ kal-'adam*). It is as if the preferred opinion has abrogated the other opinion."[188] Since we have documented treasure of great experiences, there will be no confusion about which opinion of the school is to be followed. The respond of Ibn 'Abidīn also sets aside the objection raised by some people that there are so many opinions in Islamic law that one does not know which opinion to follow. However, the schools bring uniformity into their law through this method,[189] thus the followers need to know which *madhhab* to follow first. We may conclude that *taqlīd* is not allowed for the *mujtahid* but is allowed for those who cannot reach the level of *ijtihād*.

In principle, studying basic knowledge about Islam with its *'ibādāt*, *i'tiqād* and *mu'āmalāt* is an obligatory duty (*farḍ 'ayn*) for each individual in order to obey Allah and His Messenger rightly. Since the right obedience requires right knowledge, a person must obtain knowledge of prohibitions, commands, permissible, reprehensible acts from the *Qur'ān*, the *Sunnah* or the reliable sources, as well as studying the high objectives of the *sharī'ah* fundamental principles of Islamic law, etc. as Allah indicated in the *Qur'ān*: "*And obey Allah and the Messenger, that you may be shown mercy*"[190]; "*But no! by your Lord! they do not believe (in reality) until they make you a judge of that which has become a matter of disagreement among them, and then do not find any straitness in their hearts as to what you have decided and submit with entire submission.*"[191]; "*and whatever the Messenger gives you, accept it, and from whatever he forbids you, keep back, and be careful of (your duty to) Allah; surely Allah is severe in retribution (evil)*"[192].

Nevertheless, only studying the *Qur'ān* and the *Sunnah* or knowing the basic principles are not enough to identify or determine rulings (*aḥkām*). Thus, following this method and determining the rulings for the conducts of the liable person requires a broad knowledge and the ability of performing *ijtihād*. Yet if a person who is able to perform *ijtihād* cannot determine the rulings (*aḥkām*) regarding their conduct through *ijtihād*, he can apply to the *mujtahid* who is higher level than him or expert on the issue. As Allah states in the *Qur'ān*: "*And We did not send before you any but men to whom We sent revelation, so if you (o people) do not know, then ask the people of expert knowledge*".[193]

Therefore, performing *taqlīd* should be permissible for the layman in legal matters. Not everybody can be a *mujtahid*, even at the time of the Companions some of them were expert in performing *ijtihād* and some of them were not. There are many examples can be given in this matter that 'Umar Ibn al-Khaṭṭāb though, he is able to perform *ijtihād*, most of the time he used to refer legal matters to 'Ali Ibn Abī Ṭālib. So individuals can ask any capable scholar about the rulings related to their conducts or they can even learn them through referring their rulings and reading their legal books. Allah does not impose difficulties on people more than their capacity. It is almost impossible for everyone to perform the duty of *ijtihād*. Thus it is up to the *mujtahids* to derive rulings from the sources. As Allah states in the *Qur'ān* "*Allah does not impose upon any soul a duty but to the extent of its ability*".[194]

Those who have reached to the level of *ijtihād* can perform the duty on behalf of the Muslims since to be able to perform *ijtihād* requires particular, high level of knowledge and time to obtain them, not everybody can do this duty. Therefore, it is preferable Muslims to follow rulings given by certain *mujtahids*.

Concept of Talfiq

Literally *talfiq* means picking things up from different places or sewing two things together to produce a complete article or cloth,[195] and joining, patching up, combining to things together. It is derived from the word "*laffaqa*" (لفق) For example, it is said: "*laffaqa al-thawb*" (someone combines two pieces of garment and sew them together).[196]

Technically *talfīq* may be defined as the constructing of an opinion by using bits and pieces from different schools of law (*madhhab*).[197] It becomes necessary, in some cases to recourse to "patch up" legal rules by a procedure properly termed *talfīq* which is a combination of the view or particular elements from the views of different schools and jurists.[198]

In relation to the technical sense, that is, *uṣūl al-fiqh*, the *talfīq* submits a kind of selection between different opinions of the jurists in order to attain the best opinion. However, it is necessary to highlight that the selection of opinions from different schools of law must be on a certain issue in order to be accepted, otherwise it is rejected. If, for example, the selection of the opinions of different schools of law in different issues such as following an opinion of the *Ḥanafīs* in prayer, and the opinion of the *Shāfiʿīs* in fasting. This kind of practices are not named as *talfīq* since these are taken from different issues. Similarly, mixing opinions of different schools of law in one matter is not accepted. For example, if a person while taking an ablution followed the ruling of *Shāfiʿīs* in some part and followed *Ḥanafīs* in other part which the opinions of the both schools are different in these parts. Such as sufficing to sweep only a small part of the hair and having contact with a woman after the ablution. The ablution is invalidated according to the both schools of law because *Ḥanafīs* on this matter say that it is necessary to wipe at least one fourth of the hair to be valid and *Shāfiʿīs* say on this matter that the ablution is nullified once he got contact with a woman. Similarly, in the case of marriage, it would not be permissible to follow *Ḥanafī* ruling related to governing consent, while following *Shāfiʿīs* ruling on the dowry.[199]

It is, therefore, the jurists developed in practice the meaning of *talfīq* which involves the act of combining together two or more opinions of different schools of law (*madhhab*) in a certain issue. Zuhaylī defines it as "to construct a mode of practice that no jurists acknowledge it."[200]

Historically, there is no issue of *talfīq* emerged during the life time of the Prophet (ṣ) since the source of law was the revelation and the Prophet (ṣ) himself was alive. Yet the Prophet (ṣ) encouraged the Companions to exercise *ijtihād*, and this was obviously evident from the story of the Muʿadh ibn Jabal when he was sent to Yemen and such practices continued during the period of *Tābiʿīn* and *Tabaʿī Tābiʿīn*. However, the term *talfīq* was only emerged among the jurists after the formation of the schools of law namely, *Ḥahafī*, *Shāfiʿī*, *Mālikī* and *Ḥanbalī*. It can be said that the emergence of *talfīq* was concurrent with the *taqlīd* and may be the result of the practice of it. In addition to that the legality of *talfīq* had only be discussed long after the foundation of the *Sunnī* schools of law. Thus, the response of the jurists was found in the works of the jurists of around thirteen century and beyond.[201] Nevertheless, some other claimed that it was commonly practiced by the Muslims prior to the formation of the different schools of law. It is currently practiced as the best means of solving issues arrised in the contemporary Muslim life.[202]

Despite the fact that, the application of *talfīq* remained as controversial amongst the scholars, it has been confirmed by many scholars from several of the four *Sunnī* schools of law. Some scholars, in one hand, claimed that it is permissible as long as the motive in picking and choosing between the rules of different jurists must not to satisfy every whim and fancy desire of a person.[203] On the other hand, some other scholars claimed that it is invalid and illegal to practice it for everyone especially after the formation of the four *Sunnī* schools of law (*madhhab*).[204]

Talfīq, takhayyur and tarjiḥ

Besides the concept of *talfīq*, a similar concept, *takhayyur*, is used similarly. The term *takhayyur* literally means to select, to prefer or to choose one among several things.[205] Technically, it denotes a process of selection and preference of one among the available rulings or opinions in a certain school of law or among the existing schools of law (*madhhabs*).[206]

Similar to *talfīq*, the concept of *takhayyur* was not known to classical Muslim jurists, and had not been used by jurists in any their works. Despite the same historical sense, the concept of *talfīq* was narrower that the concept of *takhayyur* as it is known in contemporary practices. Every *talfīq* practices may involve in *takhayyur* but not vice-versa which means that *talfīq* involves only if the selection of opinions of jurists from various schools is made in one matter, but it is not considered *talfīq* if it is involved in more than one issue. Therefore using these two concept interchangeably is not real usage of them.[207]

It is claimed that mostly the concept of *talfīq* is found in the modern literature of Islamic law, especially among the so-called "reformers."[208] For them it is allowed to adopt different legal opinions from different jurists or schools of law without any hesitation.[209]

An orientalist Wael Hallaq considers *talfīq* (amalgamation) and *takhayyur* kind of an interpretive approach which sometimes known as neo-*ijtihād* and emphasised that adoption of a principle which indicates any ruling that does not contradict the principle of *Sharīʿah* may be reckoned lawful.[210] The concept of *talfīq*, somehow, is resembled to the concept of *tarjīḥ*. It is said that there are some similarities between them, firstly, both are formulated on the comparative study of different schools of law and the different *ijtihād* of the various recognized jurists. Secondly, the rules selected through *talfīq* are caused by mutually contradictory interpretations of the textual sources.[211] Thirdly, the role of *talfīq* is merely to choose between already existing rules of the four schools of law which is also applicable to *tarjīḥ*.[212] Despite the fact that the concept of *tarjīḥ* is more comprehensive than *talfīq* for it concerns the methodological aspects of Islamic legal theory in deducing the rulings, which means *talfīq* is simply a process of selection and combination of the various legal opinions while *tarjīḥ* is more progressive involving many potential discussions in the whole *uṣūl al-fiqh*.[213]

The usage of *talfīq* can be acceptable if necessity (*ḍarūrah*) or needs (*ḥājah*) occur.[214] Scholars emphasized on the point that if *takhayyur* that involves *talfīq* does not lead to *tatabbu' rukhaṣ*, that is running after the easiest opinion of every school of law, is accepted. This opinion maintained some jurists such as al-Ghazālī, Ibn Ḥazm, the *Ḥanbalīs*, Ibn 'Abd al-Barr and prevailing opinion of the *Mālikīs*.[215]

Concept of Legal Loopholes (ḥīlaī shar'īyyah)

Ḥiyal (plural of *ḥīlah*) is a legal device for evading the incidence of the strict law. It may also be referred to legal fictions or legal loopholes. It is defined as "a means to accomplish an end, a stratagem, artifice, maneuver, and expedient."[216]

The concept of legal loopholes (*ḥila-i shar'īyyah*)[217] is one of the developments originated from the principle in order to be an aid to the removal of legal obstacles. The main point of the legal loophole is to reach a solution when stagnation has occurred about particular issue. As Shāṭibī says, "As Allah rendered some things prohibited or permitted without giving any reason such as fasting or the payment of interest. Allah also gave reasons why He prohibited or permitted some issues such as making *zakāh* (tax) obligatory or benefiting from usurped commodities prohibited. If one can find an acceptable reason to make what is obligatory, non-obligatory, and to make the prohibited look permissible that is called a loophole."[218] Therefore, it is considered as one of the important methods in Islamic law for removing legal obstacles.

Muslim jurists have devised it from second century of Islam in order to co-ordinate actual practice with ideal theory. The use of *ḥiyal* or legal fictions devices by which the interested parties might achieve by perfectly legal means. Due to the economic conditions of the time the usage of earliest *ḥiyal* were simply evasions of irksome prohibitions by merchants, then Muslim scholars began to formulate it according to legal manner.[219] Yet it is also claimed that the *ḥiyal* was one of the formal devices, used by early jurists which has proved invaluable to the modern jurists, is the restriction of the competence of *qāḍīs* by political power.[220] Literatures of *ḥiyal* indicate that the term seems to have originated with the *Ḥanafīs* especially with Abū Yūsuf and al-Shaybānī composing essays. Despite the other schools opposed to the concept,[221] later on they began accepting it with dividing into different types such as *maḥẓūr*, *makrūh*, and *mubāḥ*, Al-Qazwīnī from a *Shāfi'ī* jurist is one of them. The *Ḥanbalīs* accepted a number of *ḥiyal* to be legal[222] and al-Shāṭibī, from *Mālikī* school, also distinguished the permitted one from the prohibited one on the basis of the *maqāṣid al-sharī'ah.*[223]

Scholars consider *ḥīlah* into two types, those that are permissible and those whose permissibility has been in dispute. The first type is aimed to attain preventing an injury or easing situation due to necessity such as the contract of *bay' al-wafā'* (redemption sale). As the *Ḥanafī* school did not approve long-lease contracts for orchards. Despite the fact, a certain custom of Muslim territories used it and thus due to the custom of the people, it is referred to a legal loopholes whereby the long-lease contract permitted through selling the orchards and the vendor retained the right to redeem it. The second type of legal loopholes is aimed to change well-established *shar'ī* rules into other different rules through an action which is explicitly correct but implicitly invalid. Such as applying it to legalize interest or compensation on a loan. For example, the legal loopholes is applied to make payment of compensation or interest on the loan is for the borrower to sell to the lender the goods at a price below its value, or to buy from the lender the goods at a price higher than its actual value, or to present to the lender in the cover of a gift a sum equivalent to the interest on the loan etc.[224] Nevertheless, the following statement has been attributed to Abū Ḥanīfah saying that "It is prohibited to intend to suspend rules overtly but the suspension of such rules implicitly is not prohibited." Accordingly, this type of loopholes has been used by the *Ḥanafīs* and some *Shāfiʿīs.*[225] Ibn al-Qayyīm emphasised on the types of the legal loopholes and draw a distinction between permissible and impermissible legal loopholes through giving lengthy explanations.[226]

Nyazee states that the concept of *ḥiyal* was erroneously designated as legal fictions by Western scholars to show that the Islamic law consider the *Sharīʿah* is fixed and immutable which the idea was a split in the Islamic legal system, and the *fuqahā'and* their works became increasingly isolated from the actual administration of justice.[227] Schacht emphasises that the concept of *ḥiyal* was one of the casuistical methods which brought by Muslim jurists to bridge the gap between theory and practice.[228] Goldziher also pointed out that the existence of casuistry was through *ḥiyal* and he considered *ḥiyal* as "tricks" which emerged from the soul destroying pedantry of the jurists that were an outrage to the moral and spiritual order but he considers it as an integral part of *fiqh.*[229] This concept is, however, considered that it has close relationship with the concept of *shurūṭ* (conveyances) within the *ḥiyal* literature. Schacht, for example, considered *ḥiyal* as precautionary devices indicating as saying "the concept of "precaution" dominates the literature of *ḥiyal* and *shurūṭ.*"[230] It may be related to unintentional divorce cases in order to avoid clashing with it due to carelessness. For example, if a man wants to threaten his wife with divorce, but he does not actually want to divorce his wife as saying "I will divorce you if you do this." Nevertheless, it takes effect according to *Ḥanafīs* if the wife adventurous enough to commit that act of the condition and eventually she will be considered as divorced.[231] As it is seen with such example that *ḥiyal* and *shurūṭ* (conveyances) are merely procedural matters warning people to be careful in making contracts and framing legal statements which may result unwanted consequences.

The Maqāṣid al-Sharī'ah (the Higher Objectives of Islamic law)

Introduction

Whatever the world contents inside and outside has been created for a purpose, nothing is left for idle and created for purposeless, as Allah states in the *Qur'ān*: "*Did you think that We had created you in play (without any purpose), and that you would not be brought back to Us?*"[232]

Linguistically, *maqāṣid* is derived from a word *qaṣada* (قصد) and the term '*maqṣad*' (*maqāṣid*) refers to a purpose, intent, objective, principle, end, goal,[233] *Maqāṣid* of the Islamic law are the objectives/purposes behind Islamic rulings (*aḥkām*).[234]

Technically, *maqāṣid* is defined by many traditional and contemporary scholars. The concept of *maqāṣid al-sharī'ah,* as it has been recently called *falsafah al-tashrī'* can be defined as the purpose of the rule maker for normative regulations and the benefits anticipated from these.[235]

Thus, in general, Tunisian scholar Muḥammad al-Ṭāhir ibn Āshūr (d. 1973) defines *maqāṣid al-sharī'ah* in the following terms: "The general objective[s] of Islamic Law are the meanings and wise purposes on the part of the Lawgiver which can be discerned in most or all of the situations to which the Law applies such that they can be seen not to apply exclusively to a particular type of ruling. Included here are the occasions for the Law's establishment, its overall aim, and the meanings can be discerned throughout the Law. It likewise includes objectives which are not observable in all types of rulings, although they are observable in many of them."[236] He also elaborates upon it with details concerning its specific and general objectives.

This concept could also be considered together with the principle of *maṣāliḥ al-mursalah.*[237] Thus the concept should be approached from two viewpoints: that of the *maqāṣid* and the *maṣāliḥ al-mursalah*. Etymologically speaking, *maṣlaḥah* means benefit/beneficial, appropriate/suitable, convenient, and so on. It is the opposite of *mafsadah* (evil), according to *Lisān al-'Arab*. The author of *Al-Mu'jam al-Wasīṭ* defines *maṣlaḥah* as removing evil. An infinitive noun of the root (*ṣ-l-ḥ*), its plural form is *maṣāliḥ* and it is synonymous with *istiṣlāḥ*, of which *mafsadah* is its precise antonym. The verb *ṣaluḥa* means something that has become beneficial or suitable. When one *aṣlaḥa* something, one removes the evil; when something is *iṣṭalaḥa*, it has become ready to expel the evil existing inside it.[238] *Mursalah*, on the other hand, means unrestricted. According to *Lisān al-'Arab*, the verb *arsala* means that one has removed or ignored the restriction.[239]

In technical terms, Shāṭibī defined *maṣlaḥah mursalah* as follows: "I mean by *maṣlaḥah* that which concerns the subsistence of human life, the completion of man's livelihood, and the acquisition of what his emotional and intellectual qualities requires of him, in an absolute sense"[240] In more precisely technical terms, it is "a consideration which is proper and harmonious (*waṣf munāsib mulā'im*) with the objectives of the Lawgiver; it secures a benefit or prevent a harm; and the *Qur'ān* or the *Sunnah* provides no indication as to its validity or otherwise."[241]

Obviously, the concept of *maṣlaḥah* has a very close relationship with *maqāṣid al-sharī'ah*. Even more, it is used interchangeably with *maqāṣid* and is briefly maximized as obtaining *maṣlaḥah* (benefit) and preventing *mafsadah* (evil). The first significant work in this regard was done by Ghazālī (d. 505/1111), for according to him his master al-Juwaynī held that the direct relation between the two could be realized "in a real sense the *maṣlaḥah* consists of obtaining *manfa'ah* (benefit) and preventing *maḍarrāt* (evils). However, we do not use that meaning ... by the term *maṣlaḥah*, we mean, to protect the objectives of the *sharī'ah* (*maṣlaḥah al-sharī'ah*) which consist of five essential values, namely religion, life, intellect, lineage, and property."[242]

Al-Qarāfī (d. 1285 ah/1868) linked maṣlaḥah and *maqāṣid* by a fundamental principles stating that "A purpose (*maqāṣid*) is not valid unless it leads to the fulfilment of some good (*maṣlaḥah*) or the avoidance of some mischief (*mafsadah*)."243

Maṣlaḥah is a proper basis for legislation in the absence of an explicit ruling within the *Qur'ān* and the *Sunnah*, as well as within *ijmā'* and *qiyās*. If this is the case, then the *mujtahid* can resort to it to protect humanity's benefit and prevent corruption on Earth[244] for, as Shāṭibī (d. 790/1388) indicated, "in the religious context the aim of obtaining the benefits (*jalb al-ṣalāḥ*) and avoiding evils (*daf' al-fasād*) are to provide the needs of this world for the sake of the hereafter and not providing personal desires or avoiding personal hatreds. Religion prevents people from following their desires and guides them to be a servant of Allah."[245] It is, however, required that no *maṣlaḥah* contradict the *sharī'ah*'s spirit and general principles.

The *sharī'ah*'s ultimate objectives are to protect the seven values: life, religion, intellect, lineage, property, honour and state. Some contemporary scholars have considered "eliminating corruption", which enables rulers to use their discretionary powers to penalize evildoers, as one of the values of the *Sharī'ah*, however, rather it can be considered under the value of state. This is essential if the government seriously wants to achieve *falāḥ* (welfare) and prevent *fasād* (destruction) according to the legal maxim of "*jalb al-maṣāliḥ wa dar' al-mafāsid.*"

As the Ultimate Creator, Allah, sets standards for every creation and specific standards for governing that is the *sharī'ah* which determines all other activities, whether they are *sharī'ah*-compliant or not,[246] as well as make sure that they not separated from such good values as *akhlāq* (good manners), defined in the *Qur'ān* as honesty and integrity (*Qur'ān* 16:92), the administration of justice (*Qur'ān* 4:58 and 42; 6:153; 42:15), loyalty (*Qur'ān* 4:59), personal responsibility (*Qur'ān* 6:164), and cooperation (*Qur'ān* 5:2; 76:24).[247] In order to achieve *siyāsah sharī'ah*, the following values should also be considered: faith (*īmān*) to hold sovereignty to Allah and His Messenger (*ṣ*), accountability and trust (*amānah*), moral values (*akhlāq*), consultation (*shūra*), and an office that prevents and forbids wrongdoing (*ḥisbah*).[248]

The Maqāṣid al-Sharī'ah

In addition, the *maqāṣid al-sharī'ah, maqāṣid al-Shārī'* (the higher objectives of the Lawgiver), and *maqāṣid al-shar'īyyah* (legal objectives) are all used interchangeably in the field of *maqāṣid.*[249] Recently, it has also been called *falsafah al-tashrī'*, for it can be understood as the rule-maker's purpose as regards normative regulations.[250] After reviewing several terms employed to describe this concept, Shāṭibī points out[251] that the purpose of the *sharī'ah* is to promote the people's welfare and prevent corruption and hardship, as the *Qur'ān* clearly states: "*We have not sent you but as a mercy for all creatures*" (*Qur'ān* 21:107) and "*Allah never intends to impose hardship on people*" (*Qur'ān* 22:78) Allah also informs humanity that He "*does not want to place you in difficulty, but He wants to purify you*" (*Qur'ān* 5:6).

There is no doubt that all the divine rulings that govern the affairs of this world and the universe have purposes, and that these are the purposes that *Shārī'* (Lawgiver) wishes us to accomplish. It is supported by the belief that the *Shārī'* did not create anything without purpose: "*We created not the heavens and the earth and all that is between them for a (mere) play*"[252], "*Did you think that We had created you in play (without any purpose), and that you would not be brought back to Us?*"[253]

Understanding the purposes of the *sharī'ah* is an indispensable qualification for a *mujtahid* in order to perform *ijtihād*. Imām Mālik (d. 179/795) regards *istiḥsān* as a purpose-centred method interpretation; in his estimation, "*Istiḥsān* represents nine-tenth of human knowledge."[254]

Ibn 'Āshūr opines that "Realizing *maqāṣid al-sharī'ah* rescues people from narrow mindedness and literalism. The *maqāṣid al-sharī'ah* leads to undiscovered horizons through eternal principles, and the essence and true meaning of Islam. To discover the true spirit of *maqāṣid al-sharī'ah* is to distinguish the earthly from the divine, the temporary from the permanent, the alterable from the inalterable and the particular from the general. If man does this the light of Islam will shine again upon the people and peace and wellbeing will be brought to our stressful world."[255]

In general, scholars have divided the *maqāṣid al-sharī'ah* into three categories: *ḍarūriyyāt* (the essentials), *ḥājiyyāt* (the complementaries), and *taḥsīniyyāt* (the desirable, the luxurious or the embellishments). However, Ibn 'Āshūr divides the *maṣlaḥah* into *al-maṣlaḥah al-āmmah*, which benefits everyone or at least to the majority of the community, and *al-maṣlaḥah al-khāṣṣah*, which refers to individual consideration of the benefits for people.[256] The social order is considered in three groups; however, in terms of the entire community, it is divided into *kullī* (whole) and *juz'ī* (partial). Nevertheless, in terms of the people's situations it consists of *qaṭ'ī* (definite), *ẓannī* (speculative), and *wahmī* (superstitious).[257]

The *ḍarūriyyāt* are seven in number: religion, life, intellect, lineage, property, honour and state. They are considered essential because any neglect of them would cause a total social disruption and anarchy. Ibn al-Ḥājib (d. 646/1249), al-Qarāfī, al-Ghazālī, and Ibrāhim al-Shāṭibī (d. 790/1388) considered these values, the second last of which was added by al-Qarāfī, as protecting the honour of each Muslim which is attributed to al-Ṭūfī.[258] As I mentioned earlier, in my perception, the *darūriyyāt* are now seven in number. These are considered essential because neglecting them would cause total social disruption and anarchy. Therefore, not only must they be upheld, but they must also be protected from any real or unexpected threat. According to al-Ghazālī, destroying even one of them is *ḥarām*.[259] These values can be protected either by maintaining the essentials or removing the disruption.[260] In general, the *sharī'ah* seeks to protect and promote these essentials in order to, for example, protect Islam. In that context, *jihād* for the sake of Allah has been confirmed as an obligatory act. To protect life, Allah prescribed *qiṣāṣ* (retaliation); to protect the intellect, alcohol is forbidden; to preserve one's lineage, adultery is prohibited; to protect one's property, theft is prohibited. In fact, all threats to the social order are punishable offenses. Honour is vital to protecting the dignity of Muslims, who were created in the best manner and are Allah's representatives on Earth. Therefore, *jihād* protects their life, for without honour life would be incomplete and surely even be worse. How can a humiliated or enslaved Muslim represent the law of Allah on Earth? Therefore, honour is just as essential as the other five values. More importantly, protecting the seventh value (the state) becomes an indispensable value in terms of guaranteeing the other six values. Now on, these values are illustrated briefly on the following pages.

1. The Protection of religion (al-dīn)

This value is the most important value that must be protected by the Muslims individually and collectively. Individually it may be achieved through the fulfilments of the various *'ibādāt*, such as performing five prayers, fasting, paying *zakāt* and performing *ḥajj*. Performing all these *'ibādāt* increase the faith of the subject and keeps him in the circle of the religion since these acts protect him from commiting sins. The *Qur'ān* indicates this fact "*surely prayer keeps (one) away from indecency and evil*".[261]

In a wider sense, the protection of the religion involves in defending the Muslim territories from the enemies of Islam when it is attacked. The protection can be achieved by various ways such as in physical fighting, writings, speeches, intelligence services, technological advancements in defend industries, etc. Allah emphasises this matter in the *Qur'ān* "*and fight the polytheists all together as they fight you all together*".[262]

In order to protect the religion of Islam, it is necessary to all Muslims individually and collectively revitalizing the act of *jihād* for the sake of Allah. It is an obligatory act for Muslims which is emphasised in the *Qur'ān* "*And fight in the way of Allah with those who fight with you, and do not exceed the limits*".[263]

The religion of Allah can be protected by preventing evil as mentioned in a ḥadīth of the Prophet (ṣ): "If any one of you sees something objectionable (evil), he should change it with his hand if he can change it with his hand. But if he cannot (do so), he should do it with his tongue, and if he cannot (do so with) his tongue he should do it in his heart, that being the weakest form of faith".[264]

2. The Protection of life (al-nafs)

The protection of life (*al-nafs*) is essential since the Almighty Allah created man in the best manner, the life of him must be protected. Especially protection of the life of a Muslim, irrespective of his race, wealth, language, status, is equally important and obligatory to each and every individual, society and government level. In that respect the Lawgiver has ordained not killing anyone except for just reason to protect the life of individual which save the society from chaos and enmity. The Lawgiver emphasised it in the *Qur'ān*:

> "*And do not kill any one whom Allah has forbidden, except for a just cause, and whoever is slain unjustly, We have indeed given to his heir authority, so let him not exceed the just limits in slaying; surely he is aided.*"[265]

The *ḥadīth* of the Prophet (ṣ) strengthen the protection of life as he said: "When two Muslims are engaged in a combat against each other with their swords and one is killed, both are doomed to Hell." I said, "O Messenger of Allah! As to the one who kills, it is understandable, but why the slain one?" He (ṣ) replied: "He was eager to kill his opponent".[266]

In that respect the Lawgiver has ordained the retaliation (*al-qiṣāṣ*) to protect the life of individual. If a person kills an innocent person the death penalty is applied to the killer. The enactment of the death penalty save the society from chaos and enmity. The enmity is removed from the society through the application of the death penalty (*al-qiṣāṣ*) as the Lawgiver stresses in the *Qur'ān*:

> "*O you who believe! Retaliation is prescribed for you in the matter of the slain, the free for the free, and the slave for the slave, and the female for the female*".[267]

In this sense, it may seem to be that it is contradictory to the concept of protection of life, however the protection of life is actualized here through applying the death penalty in order to save the rest of the society, like making an operation in the body of a person to remove diseases to save the rest of the body. It is indicated in the following verse of the *Qur'ān*: "*And there is life for you in (the law of) retaliation, O men of understanding, that you may guard yourselves*".[268]

3. *The Protection of intellect (al-'aql)*

The intellect (*al-'aql*) is a great gift from Allah to human being to differentiate good from evil, to realize greateness of Allah as well as to understand his insignificancy in front of Him. This is one of the human capacities that differentiates man from animal and to make him the subject of responsibility (*taklīf*), he then is addressed by the command of Allah. The Prophet (ṣ) emphasised the role of intellect in *taklīf* as saying: "*There is no responsibility upon three persons: a sleeping person before he wakes, a youth before puberty (i.e. the legal age of maturity in Islamic law), and a lunatic before he recovers his senses*".[269]

The intellect is essential to understand the command of the Lawgiver, therefore, it must be protected from anything that might harm the ability and functioning of the intellect. This includes any kind of consumption of intoxicated drinks or similar substances that may disable the functions of the intellect. The *Qur'ān* prohibits drinking alcohol with the following verse:

> *"O you who believe! intoxicants and games of chance and (sacrificing to) stones set up and (dividing by) arrows are only an uncleanness, the Shaiṭān's work; shun it therefore that you may be successful".*[270]

The Lawgiver prohibits the consumption of intoxicated drinks with this verse. Despite this verse specifies a specific drink, it can be extended to similar substances by virtue of the principle of analogy (*qiyās*) finding the same cause (*'illah*).

4. The Protection of lineage (al-'irḍ)

One of the essentials is also the Protection of lineage (*al-'irḍ*) which is confused by many scholars with the concept of the protection of honour (*al-sharaf*) due to the usage of the terms in cultures differently. Despite the similarities of the two values of lineage (*al-'irḍ*) and honour (*al-sharaf*), in fact they are different. The former is a physical value, while the later is a spiritual value. Therefore, the lineage indicates generation, progeny, family relationship, origination, ancestry which means a lineal descent from an ancestor.

Islam is a comprehensive religion contains everything related to human being both in this world and the hereafter. It also regulates the relationship between men and women in order to protect their lineage that is generation not mixing their progeny unless by legal ways ordained by the *sharī'ah*. The relationship is regulated by meeting the couples with marriage contract which protects them from evil acts. The *Qur'ān* strongly warns people from such evil acts as saying: "*And go not nigh to fornication; surely it is an indecency and an evil way*".[271]

The Prophet (ṣ) is reported to have said in this matter:

> "O young men, those among you who can support a wife should marry, for it restrains eyes (from casting evil glances) and

> preserves one from immorality; but he who cannot afford it should observe fast for it is a means of controlling the sexual desire."[272]

In order to protect the society from illegal relationship, the Lawgiver imposed severe punishments as stoning to death for married people and hundreds stripes for unmarried people who commits adultery. The stoning to death is imposed by the *ḥadīth* of the Prophet (ṣ):

> "It is not permissible to spill the blood of a Muslim except in three [instances]: the married person who commits adultery, a life for a life, and the one who forsakes his religion and separates from the community,[273]

while applying the hundreds stripes is imposed by the *Qur'ān*: "The woman and the man guilty of adultery or fornication, – flog each of them with a hundred stripes".[274]

Alternatively Allah has permitted polygamy to prevent the people from commiting adultery as the *Qur'ān* indicates this permissibility: "*then marry such women as seem good to you, two and three and four*".[275]

5. The Protection of property (al-māl)

Attaining wealth or property is one of the necessities of man in this world. Therefore, it has to be protected. The *sharī'ah* has prohibited transgressing and attaining the property of others without legitimate reasons and proper agreement or contract. There are many ways of gaining the property of others illegally such as taking usury (*ribā*), cheating in transections, stealing the property of others etc. The Lawgiver prohibits such illegal gainings which emphasised in the *Qur'ān*: "*And do not swallow up your property among yourselves by false means, neither seek to gain access thereby to the judges, so that you may swallow up a part of the property of men wrongfully while you know*",[276] and the following verse: "*And their taking usury though indeed they were forbidden it and their devouring the property of people falsely, and We have prepared for the unbelievers from among them a painful chastisement*".[277]

In order to protect the property of people, as the Lawgiver has warned people with a painful chastisement in the hereafter, it is imposed severe punishments in this world for those who gain illegal property of others as the *Qur'ān* indicates it: "*And (as for) the man who steals and the woman who steals, cut off their hands as a punishment for what they have earned, an exemplary punishment from Allah; and Allah is Mighty, Wise*".[278]

6. *The Protection of honour (al-sharaf)*

The protection of honour (*al-sharaf*), which has been neglected especially for around one century after collapse of the Muslim leadership (caliphate), is as significant as the others. If however, destruction of this value, such as physical or intellectual slavery, humiliation, etc. would cause total destruction to the rest of the values. The rest of the values will not be protected if the honour of men is humiliated or destructed. It is because Islam is very concerned about the honour of a person and highlights the importance of protecting it. The protection of honour (*al-sharaf*) includes protecting individual rights and privacy.

The *Qur'ān* emphasises the importance of protecting the honour of a person in the following verse: "*And those who accuse free women then do not bring four witnesses, flog them, (giving) eighty stripes, and do not admit any evidence from them ever; and these it is that are the transgressors*".[279]

In fact, providing four witnesses is almost impossible in one case and for a legal action each allegation must be substantiated by concrete evidences. Otherwise, a punishment will be imposed for accuser because of the false accusation (*al-qazf*), and the accuser will face three consequences, punished with eighty flogs, be considered *fāsiqūn* (transgressors, liars) and rejected his testimony forever. It is therefore, concealing the sin is better than disclosing it even if the accusation is accurate. The Lawgiver made it impossible with requesting four witnesses to protect the honour of Muslim.

After all, the *Qur'ān* indicates that Allah's curse is upon those who commit such accusation crimes. "*Surely those who accuse chaste believing women, unaware (of the evil), are cursed in this world and the hereafter, and they shall have a grievous chastisement*".[280]

In an affirmative sense, the *sharī'ah* encourages the protection of human life and offers alternatives to all prohibited acts: non-alcoholic drinks to alcohol, education to illiteracy, polygamy to adultery, work and trade to theft, and so on. Protecting one's honour becomes a vital element for the dignity of Muslims, who were created in the best manner and are Allah's (swt) representatives on Earth as caliph (*khalīfah*).

7. The Protection of State (al-Dawlah):

The Protection of State (*al-Dawlah*) is the most essential one among these values because it's the one which provides security for the previous values.

The religion of Islam's most important objectives are mainly to ensure the protection of benefit (*maṣlaḥah*) of man and prevent evil (*mafsadah*) from him for both this world and the hereafter. As it has been mentioned earlier, Allah revealed His commands and prohibitions for protecting each of the six values and the last one that is state provides security for the other values. The other six values will be in danger if the state is jeopardized. In other words, the religion of Allah cannot be well established without a state. As history shows that the essential values (i.e., the *maqāṣid al-sharī'ah*) were destroyed whenever a Muslim state collapsed. It's evidenced that the situation of Muslims in Iraq, Syria, Libya, East Turkistan (Xinjiang) and, most recently in Myanmar's Arakan state, were in danger. But in addition to protecting these essential values, the state is also required to preserve the Muslims' economic and financial activities. Therefore, the author of this book strongly emphasises that establishing a state or a government, in a general sense, is a vital necessity for communities to protect and sustain the essential values as well as to regulate the peoples' affairs in terms of social, economic, cultural, psychological and religious values that create unity against internal and external threats.

Establishing and preserving an Islamic state can be inferred from the following verses: "*Surely Allah commands you to make over trusts to their owners and that when you judge between people you judge with justice. Surely Allah admonishes you with what is excellent. Surely Allah is Seeing, Hearing. O you who believe! Obey Allah, the Messenger and those in authority from among you. If you quarrel about anything, refer it to Allah and the Messenger, if you believe in Allah and the Last Day. This is better and very good in the end.*"[281] These verses indicate that establishing a just society and obeying Allah, the Messenger and those Muslims placed in authority are natural duties, the outcome of the concept of siyāsah sharī'ah.[282]

In addition to the Prophet's (ṣ) practical life, his sayings affirm the exigency of establishing a legitimate government: "When three persons set out on a journey, they should appoint one of them as their leader."[283]

It has been narrated on Abu Hurairah's authority that the Prophet (ṣ) emphasised this point: "Whoever defected from obedience (to the leader) and separated from the main body of the Muslim – and then died in that state – would die the death of one belonging to the days of *Jāhiliyyah*."[284] Another narration on Abu Hurairah's authority is that the Messenger of Allah (ṣ) said: "It is obligatory for you to listen to the ruler and obey him in adversity and prosperity, in pleasure and displeasure, and even when another person is given (rather undue) preference over you."[285]

Likewise, Allah says "*And hold fast to the covenant of Allah all together and be not disunited.*"[286] *For the sake of "enjoining what is good and forbidding what is evil*", Allah ordains that a group of people, like an institution, organization or a state, be established to undertake this holy task, as indicated by "*From among you there should be a party who invites to good, enjoins what is right and forbids the wrong. These are the ones who will be successful.*"[287]

In this context, Ibn Taymīyyah stresses the state's indispensable nature: "It should be noted that regulating the people's affairs is one of the most important requirements (*wājibāt*) of the religion (*al-dīn*)."[288] Ibn Taymīyyah continues emphasizing its importance as saying: "Sixty years of an unjust *imām* (ruler) are better than one night without a *sulṭān.*"[289] Clearly, from the experience of many contemporary Muslims, any type of authority is better than anarchy and chaos. This opinion is supported by Al-Ghazālī and Ibn Jamā'ah, who opine that any effort to overthrow rulers, even a tyrannical *sulṭān*, is liable to create chaos and lawlessness.[290] Therefore, removing an established but unjust ruler may cause serious disaster and chaos to society without substitute of a just ruler.

The message of Allah must be conveyed to others, thus, to convey Allah's message, Muslim leadership is an inescapable duty for the whole *Ummah* - and this leadership is only possible under a state. Allah enjoins the believers to promote good and prevent evil "*From among you there should be a party who invites to good, enjoins what is right and forbids the wrong. These are the ones who will be successful.*"[291] Al-Mawārdī (d. 450/1058) mentions the ten essential duties of a Muslim leader in his "*Kitāb al-Aḥkām al-Sulṭāniyyah*"[292], none of which has ever been achieved without establishing an Islamic state. This leader's first duty is to protect the religion of Allah in its original form, the second one is to establish justice, and the third one is to protect the territory of Islam and so on.[293] For those reasons, the value of state must be protected because the religion of Allah and its essential values cannot be well established and preserved without a state authority.

The *ḥājiyyāt* are not completely independent within themselves. For example, neglecting this *maṣlaḥah* might cause hardship to the community, but not to cause its collapse. However, the *sharīʿah* still seeks to protect and promote these essential values at the secondary stage. Shāṭibī defines *ḥājiyyāt* as that which is needed for *tawassī* (widening) and *rafʿul ḥaraj* (avoiding hardship). If they were ignored people would face harm and difficulty, but not as much as if the essentials were neglected.[294] In the context of *ʿibādāt*, the concessions (*rukhaṣ*) granted to the sick and travellers in terms of suspending the fast and shortening the prayers (*ṣalāt*) are designed to prevent hardship. This is the objective of all such concessions; however, they are not considered essential because the affected people could survive without them. In the area of criminal law, the prophetic *ḥadīth* of "suspend the prescribed penalties (*ḥudūd*) in all cases of doubt (ادرؤوا الحدود بالشبهات)" can be seen as providing a complementary *maṣlaḥah*, because the burden of proof for crimes with prescribed penalties (*ḥudūd*) is very severe.[295] In the area of *muʿāmalāt*, the *sharīʿah's* allowance of certain contracts (e.g., the sale of a *salam* contract [deferred delivery] and *ijārah* [lease and hire]) is not absolutely essential to maintain normal life. Thus they are classified as *ḥājiyyāt* (complementary).

The third type, *taḥsīniyyāt* or *kamāliyyāt* (luxurious, embellishments), complete the first two types by representing the interests and awareness of the *mukallaf* (subject) in all areas and at all levels. Shāṭibī indicated that they may be summarized as part of the moral constitution of *ʿibādāt* (e.g., eliminating that which is dirty and considering all types of cleanness), customary matters (e.g., good conduct in eating and avoiding wastefulness in consumption), transactions (e.g., preventing others from selling that which is impure) and *jināyāt* (i.e., criminal offences, among them killing women, children, and religious people during *jihād*).[296] Therefore *sadd al-ḍarā'i'* is considered as a type of *taḥsīniyyāt.* The *sharī'ah* encourages gentleness (*rifq*), good manners and conduct (*ḥusn al-khulq*), fair dealing (*iḥsān*), as well as being a devoted person (*'ābid*) in terms of performing the supererogatory prayers, voluntary fasting, generosity to the poor and those in need in regard to all kind of customary matters, interpersonal relations, family matters, religious duties, and so on. The purpose behind performing all of these acts in the best possible manner is to improve one's self and quality in all areas related to human behaviour. Therefore, this third type of *maqāṣid* is vital for gaining Allah's blessings.

Kamali explores this notion by saying that "the *taḥsīniyyāt* are a very important category, as they are all-pervasive and relate to all the other *maṣāliḥ*. One can perform the obligatory *ṣalāt*, for example, in different ways. It may vary from performing it with full and proper concentration, giving each of its parts their due attention, to performing it with haste and thoughtlessness. The difference between the two ends of the spectrum is that at one end the *ṣalāt* is espoused with the attainment of both the essential and the desirable, and at the other end, it can at best be seen as discharging a duty. One can extend this analysis to the implementation of almost all the *aḥkām* of the *sharī'ah*, and indeed, to almost every area of human conduct."[297] Moreover, the Prophet (ṣ) said that "Allah is beautiful and He loves beauty"[298] and "The best amongst you are those who have the best manners and character."[299] Thus conducting oneself in the best possible manner reflects His blessings. The *taḥsīniyyāt* cause our deeds to be accepted or rejected, for the Lawgiver is not in not need of our deeds.

Regulators of the Maqāṣid al-Sharī'ah

Scholars formulated certain regulations to protect the *maqāṣid* from misuse, and thus some strict and indisputable conditions have been implemented to make it a valid source of the *sharī'ah.* One of the foremost of these is that the *maqāṣid* must be attached to the Lawgiver's objectives. Ghazālī remarked that "interpreting the *maṣlaḥah* as protecting the *maqāṣid al-sharī'ah* [means that] nobody would oppose obeying the *maṣlaḥah* unless they could produce positive evidence"[300]and "We occasionally consider *maṣlaḥah* and rulings when indications interchangeably reflected one another."[301]

The following conditions were laid out in an attempt to ensure that the *maqāṣid* could not be established arbitrarily based on what the authorities would like to see in terms of legislation. The *maṣlaḥah,* (1) must not conflict with a principle or value sustained by the *naṣṣ* (text) or *ijmā'* which must not contradict a definitive indication or evidence[302]; (2) must be genuine (*ḥaqīqīyyah*) as opposed to inaccurate (*wahmīyyah*), which is an improper ground for legislation. For example, recording marriages in the courts and issuing marriage certificates, as well as recording contracts in the registry department, prevents *shahādāt al-zūr* (false testimony) and stabilizes the *mu'āmalāt*[303]; and 3) must be *kullī* to secure its benefits and prevent harm as a whole, and not just to a particular person or a group of people.[304]

Imām Mālik (d. 179/795) added two more conditions: (1) The *maṣlaḥah* must be *ma'qūlah* (rational) and adequate to the people of comprehend and (2) must prevent or eradicate hardship, as proclaimed in the *Qur'ān* 5:6: "*Allah never intends to impose hardship upon people.*"[305] Yet al-Ghazālī maintained that *maṣlaḥah* must be *ḍarūriyyāt* in order to be valid.[306]

In short, the law's main purpose is to obtain benefit (*jalb al-ṣalāḥ*) and avoid evil (*daf' al-fasād*). *Maṣlaḥah* or *maqāṣid* are obtained by improving humanity's situation and removing evil, because humanity is Allah's vicegerent and holder of His truth. Therefore, a peaceful humanity would manage to create a peaceful world.[307] If evaluating the *maṣlaḥah* and *mafsadah* were left to humanity, the Lawgiver's objectives would face the danger of being ignored. In that sense, Shāṭibī says that "in the religious context the aim of obtaining the benefits (*jalb al-ṣalāḥ*) and avoiding evils (*daf' al-fasād*) are to provide the needs of this world for the sake of the hereafter and not providing personal desires or avoiding personal hatreds. Religion prevents people from following their desires and guides them to be a servant of Allah."[308] Allah states this clearly: "*And if the truth had been in accordance with their desires, verily, the heavens and the earth, and whosever therein would have been corrupted*" (Q. 23:71).[309]

A Historical Approach to the Maqāṣid

In terms of the *sharī'ah* approach, when the *uṣūl al-fiqh* (principles of Islamic jurisprudence) were being formulated, the concept of *maqāṣid al-sharī'ah* was implicitly considered within its scope. But due to its nature, it was located within the philosophy of law and its objectives rather than the formulation of the principles of the text.[310] This might be because the *maqāṣid* were already embedded within *uṣūl al-fiqh* and thus there was no need to consider them explicitly, for *ijtihād* was widely used to investigate the Lawgiver's purpose for the texts.

The *maqāṣid* emerged with Ḥakīm al-Tirmidhī (d. 255/869), the first person in the written literature to introduce it through the principle of *istiqrā'* (induction). Although he may not have been a jurisprudent (*faqīh*) or a scholar of the principles of jurisprudence (*uṣūli*), he was known as both a Ṣūfī and a philosopher.[311] He was followed by Imām Abū Manṣūr al-Māturīdī (d. 333/944).[312] In addition, it should be noted that Juwaynī (d. 478/1085) was the first one actually attempted to evaluate the *maqāṣid* and *maṣlaḥah.*[313] He focused on the *maqāṣid,* for "whoever is unable to realize the purposes and wisdoms behind the orders and prohibitions of *Shārī'* cannot be considered wise."[314] He led their organization into five categories to make them easily understandable and was among the first jurists to refer to some of the five *ḍarūriyyāt.*[315]

Juwaynī's student al-Ghazālī, another exemplary personality who expounded on the *maqāṣid*, divided rulings into the main categories of *mu'allal* (justifiable) and *ghayri mu'allal* (unjustifiable). He categorized his tutor's categorization into three main divisions, namely, *ḍarūriyyāt*, *ḥājiyyāt*, and *taḥsīniyyāt*. He also brought the concept of *takmīlāt* into the field.[316]

Other significant jurists who discussed *maqāṣid al-sharī'ah* were Fakhr al-Dīn al-Rāzī (d. 606/1209), Sayf al-Dīn al-Āmidī (d. 631/1233), Ibn al-Ḥājib, and 'Izz b. 'Abd al-Salām (d. 660/1262).[317] Shihāb al-Dīn al-Qarāfī, and Najm al-Dīn al-Ṭūfī (d. 716/1316) are also very well-known names, as their opinions on *maṣlaḥah* were outside the traditional frame.[318] According to al-Ṭūfī, given that the Lawgiver's primary purpose is "obtaining *maṣlaḥah* and removing evil," this principle must be applied to *'ādāt* (customs) and *mu'āmalāt* even when the *naṣṣ* and *ijmā'* contradict them.[319] Of course there is no objection when the latter two accommodate the *maṣlaḥah*; but when they contradict them, priority should be given to the *maṣlaḥah* that can be applied by restricting (*takhṣīṣ*) the *naṣṣ* and *ijmā'* or in the form of a declaration (*bayān*). As such, it would never imply nullifying or having either or both of them excluded from the process. Giving more priority to the *Sunnah* due to its explanatory nature, rather than to the *Qur'ān*, is a good example here.[320]

Later on, Ibn Taymiyyah, Ibn al-Qayyīm, and al-Shāṭibī reassessed the concept of *maqāṣid* by formulating a new and systemized method. Dihlawī (d. 1176/1762) reassessed the *maṣlaḥah* and reform via passionate arguments that "whoever does not understand the purposes of *shar'ī* rulings and whoever insists that these rulings do not include any *maṣlaḥah* has not benefited from knowledge or wisdom. This person should shed tears for his own situation rather expect praise..."[321] Ṭāhir ibn 'Āshūr's *Maqāṣid al-Sharī'ah al-Islāmiyyah* is a great contribution to this field,[322] as is Aḥmad al-Raysūni's *Imām al-Shāṭibī's Theory of the Higher Objectives and Intents of Islamic Law.*[323]

Shāṭibī made a great effort to ensure that the door was open for everyone to understand the wisdom and subtlety of Islamic law.[324]

Muḥammad Fāḍil b. ʻĀshūr comments on his *Muwāfaqāt* by declaring "with this book, Shāṭibī actually constructed a pyramid erected to the sky in terms of Islamic culture and he succeeded in something that his ancestors simply did not bother to deal with, and he discovered evidences and methods which guaranteed the everlasting permanence and purity of the religion. Those who made an effort to uncover the subtlety of the religion became key personalities. The importance of Shāṭibī's work has found more resonance during the re-awakening of the Islamic world from its long sleep, when religious rulings contradicted the requirements of contemporary life, especially in current and previous centuries. In this context, Shāṭibī's *Muwāfaqāt* is a real saviour."[325] Thus he deserves to be called "the father" of the *maqāṣid.*

The contemporary scholar ʻAllāl Fāsī emphasizes the importance of the *maqāṣid al-sharīʻah* for *ijtihād,* given his view that they are "an eternal source for the fields related to legislation and jurisdiction and it is not outside of the Islamic law; rather it is a source which is at the very heart of Islamic law. It is also not a complicated concept like the 'law of nature' which is not certifiable in terms of its purpose and borders…when it is necessary, the *maqāṣid* may even be effective for a matter resolved by *naṣṣ.*"[326]

According to Ibn Rushd, *sharʻī* sources are a matter for juristic thought seen from the angle of *Ḥanafī istiḥsān* and *Mālikī istiṣḥāb*, which complement each other. It is important not to accept one and deny the other purely on sectarian grounds, for either one can be used to reach a solution as long as they do not contradict general principles. *Istiḥsān* considers *maṣlaḥah* and justice when delivering a ruling, and jurists supposedly have a better awareness of the Lawgiver's purposes when a ruling's superficial meaning(s) is likely to induce injustice and is authorised and qualified to make such rulings more just, fair, and specific. However, this should never be done by an arbitrarily determined *maṣlaḥah.* Even though the *sharīʻah* provides direct information regarding all rulings, when their superficial meanings are contradictory they must be interpreted according to the *naṣṣ*.[327]

Ibn 'Āshūr recommends using *ijtihād* to resolve issues when the *naṣṣ* and *qiyās* are silent, for "jurists' need of *maqāṣid* is obvious for such situations, because they have the responsibility to maintain continuity of the rulings given by Islam for generations and eras after the Prophet (ṣ)."[328] Moreover, scholars have established standards and principles to set the criteria for determining the Lawgiver's purposes, orders, and prohibitions.[329] The concept of means (*wasā'il*) related to the *maqāṣid al-sharī'ah* are the main instruments for achieving the *maqāṣid*.[330] Purposes and means must be assessed together, for the means depend on the ends: "Once the purpose is dismissed, then there is no means to pay attention,"[331] as *al-Majallah al-Aḥkām* proclaims, for "if the principle fails, the accessory also fails."[332]

The fundamental issue is to first determine the Lawgiver's purposes. For Māturīdī, an unalterable monotheistic religion is just like rainwater falling from the sky, for it takes a shape only when it hits the ground and assumes the shape of a river, a muddy pool, or a flood. Different social structures and cultures require different laws to accommodate their needs. The essence of the *Sharī'ah* revealed to the prophets is always the same, because it was revealed from the same source. It has two aspects: the divine, which looks to revelation (*waḥy*) and the *Sunnah* (tradition) and thus cannot be altered (however, their interpretation can change according to different situations and conditions) and the human, which represents the accumulated rulings given by jurists after interpreting the sources in accordance with reason and the needs of the age. Evolution is possible at any time, for it is based to new occurrences and situations.

To sum up, the purpose of the *Sharī'ah* is to maintain the social structure and secure the *maṣlaḥah* in order to prevent evil.[333] Therefore, one of the Prophets' (ṣ) main duties is to make an effort to establish and maintain justice, as Allah proclaims: "*And Moses said to his brother Aaron, replace me among my people, act in the Right Way and follow not the way of the mufsidūn (mischief-makers)*" (*Qur'ān* 7:142 and 85; *Qur'ān* 24:55.[334]

Notes

[1] This subject was partially published in Saim Kayadibi, *Ijtihād by ray; the main source of inspiration behind istiḥsān* (juristic preference, *American Journal of Islamic Social Sciences*, Herndon, USA, 24:1 winter (2007), 73-95.

[2] Joseph Schacht, *An Introduction to Islamic Law* (Oxford: Clarendon Press, 1964), 212; Sawa Pasha, *Islam Hukuku Nazariyatı*, tr. Baha Arıkan (Ankara: 1965), 2:354.

[3] *Qur'ān* 4:59.

[4] Shāfi'ī, "*Al-Risālah,*" 368.

[5] Shāfi'ī, "*Al-Ūmm,*" v. 7, p. 272.

[6] Abū Dāwūd, "*Sunan*" iii, 1013, *ḥadīth* no: 3567; Bukhārī "*Saḥīḥ,*" 8/157.

[7] Abū Dāwūd, iii, 1019 *ḥadīth* no:3585.

[8] Shafi'ī, "*Al-Risālah,*" p. 81, 368.

[9] *Ibid*: 368; Shafi'ī "*Al-Ūmm,*" v. 3, p. 85, 278.

[10] Sayyid 'Afifi, "*Uṣūl al-Tashrī',*" v. 9, p. 344.

[11] Shahristānī, Abū al-Fatḥ Muḥammad b. 'Abd al-Karīm b. Abū Bakr (d. 548/1153), "*Al-Milal wa al-Niḥal,*" edt. Muḥammad Sayyid Kaylānī, (Cairo: 1976), v. 1, p. 348.

[12] 'Abd al-Ḥay Ibn al-Ṣiddīq, "*Naqdu Maqāl fī Masāilah min 'Ilm al-Ḥadīth wa al-Fiqh wa Uṣūlih wa Tafḍīlih Baghḍ al-Mazāhib*" (Maghrib: 1988), p. 100.

[13] Ibn Manzur, *Lisān*, "*Juhidah*" part 2, p. 133-34.

[14] Al-Ghazālī, *Al-Muṣtasfā*, v. 2, p. 350.

[15] Nyazee, *Islamic Jurisprudence*, p. 263

[16] Al-Āmidi, *Al-Iḥkām*, v. 3, p. 204.

[17] Shawkānī, *Irshād*, p. 250

[18] Shawkānī, *Irshād*, p. 250; Zuhayr, *Uṣūl*, v. 4, p. 223-25; Badrān, *Uṣūl*, p. 471.

[19] Al-Āmidī, *Al-Iḥkām*, v. 3, p. 204.

[20] Al-Qarafī, *Sharḥ*, p. 189.

[21] Al-Isnawī, *Nihāyat*, v. 2, p. 232.

[22] Ibn al-Humām, *Al-Taḥrīr fī al-Uṣūl*, v. 3, p. 291.

[23] Ibn Ḥazm, *Al-Iḥkām*, 41:977, 1155; and *Ibṭāl al-Qiyās*, 42.

[24] Fazlur Rahman, *Islam and Modernity* (Chicago: University of Chicago Press, 1984), 8.

[25] Abū Zahrah, *Uṣūl*, p. 301

[26] *Qur'ān* 13:3

[27] *Qur'ān* 13:4

[28] *Qur'ān* 4:105

[29] Al-Amidi, *Al-Ihkam*, v. 3, p. 140.

[30] *Qur'ān* 3:159

[31] *Qur'ān* 42:38

[32] Abū Dāwud, *Sunan*, iii:1013, *ḥadīth* no. 3567; Al-Bukhārī, *al-Ṣaḥīḥ*, viii:157.

[33] Abū Dāwud, *Sunan*, iii:3585, 1019; Ibn 'Abd al-Barr, *Jāmi' Bayān al-'Ilm*, ed. Muḥammad 'Abd al-Qādir 'Aṭā (Beirut: Mu'assasat Kutub al-Saqafiyyah, 1997), 2:275-76.

[34] Tabarānī, Sulaymān b. Aḥmad (d. 360/971), "*Al-Mu'jam al-Saghīr wa al-Mū'jam al-Awsāt*" (Beirut: M. Shakūr Maḥmūd al-Ḥajj Amīr, 1985), Narated by Tabarānī in al-Awṣat. See in "*Mujmā' al-Zawā'id*," v.1, p. 178.

[35] This is my view but also it is still a controversial subject. A more detailed discussion on the "gate of *ijtihād*" appears in the final chapter of this work.

[36] Ibn Taymīyyah, "*Al-Fatāwā al-Kubrā*," *Dār al-Kutub al-'Ilmiyyah*, 19/200-201; Ibn al-Qayyīm "*I'lām*," v. 1, p. 171.

[37] Muḥammad Dasūqī, *Al-Ijtihād wa al-Taqlīd fī al-Sharī'ah al-Islāmiyah* (Doha: Dār al-Thaqāfah, n.d.), 39.

[38] Ibn Manzur, *Lisān al-'Arab* (Cairo: Taba`ah Bulaq, n.d.), 14:291, 295, 297, 299; Ibn al-Qayyīm, *I'lām al-Muwaqqi'īn min Rabb al-'Alamīn*, ed. 'Abd al-Raḥmān al-Wakīl (Cairo: n.d.), 1:113.

[39] Ibn Manzur, *ibid.*, 14:300, 301

[40] Ibn al-Qayyīm, *I'lām*, v. 1, p. 113.

[41] Al-Rāghib al-Isfaḥānī, *Mufradāt fī Gharīb al-Qur'ān*, ed. Muḥammad Ḥusayin Kaylānī (Beirut: Dār al-Ma'rifah, n.d.), 208, 209.

[42] Ibn Khaldūn, *Muqaddimah*, ed. 'Ali 'Abd al-Waḥīd Wāfī (Cairo: Naḥḍat al-Miṣr, n.d.), v. 3, p. 1061-62.

[43] Ibn Ḥazm, *Mulakhkhaṣ Ibṭāl al-Qiyās wa al-Ra'y wa al-Istiḥsān wa al-Taqlīd*

wa al-Ta'līl, ed. Sa'īd al-Afghānī (Damascus: Matba'ah al-Jāmi'at al-Dimashq, 1960), p. 4.

[44] Bashīr Idrīs Jum'ah, *Al-Ra'y wa Atharuh fī al-Fiqh al-Islāmī* (Cairo: n.d.), p. 24.

[45] *Ibid.*, 10.

[46] Shāfi 'ī, *Jimā' al-'Ilm*, ed. Muḥammad Aḥmad 'Abd al-'Azīz (Beirut: Dār al-Kutub al-'Ilmiyyah, n.d.), p. 51-52.

[47] Al-Ghazzālī, *Al-Mustaṣfā*, v. 2, p. 255.

[48] 'Abd al-Wahhāb Khallāf, *Maṣādir al-Tashrī' al-Islāmī fī mā-lā Naṣṣah fīh* (Kuwait: Dār al-Qalam li al-Nashr wa al-Tawzī', 1993), p. 8; Muḥammad Muṣṭafā Shalabī, *Al-Madkhal fī al-Ta'rīf al-Fiqh al-Islāmī* (Beirut: Dār an-Naḥḍat al-'Arabiyyah, 1985), p. 108; Muḥammad Abū Zahrah, *Tārīkh Madhāhib al-Islāmiyah* (Beirut: Dār al-Fikr al-'Arabī, n.d.), p. 244.

[49] *Qur'ān* 59:2

[50] Al-Sarakhī, *Uṣūl*, v. 2, p. 106.

[51] Khallāf, *Maṣādir*, 7.

[52] Al-Shawkānī, *Irshād*, p. 202.

[53] *Kalālah* are those who inherit from a person who dies leaving neither ascendants nor descendants.

[54] Ibn al-Qayyīm, *I'lām*, v. 1, p. 122; Fatḥī Dīrīnī, *Al-Manāhij al-Uṣūliyyah fī al-Ijtihād bi al-Ra'y fī al-Tashrī' al-Islamī* (Damascus: al-Sharikāt al-Muttaḥidah, 1985), p. 12-14.

[55] Al-Āmidī, *Iḥkām*, v. 4, p. 398-99; Ibn al-Qayyīm, *I'lām*, v. 1, p. 257-61; 'Ali Ibn Muḥammad al-Bazdawī al-Ḥanafī, *Uṣūl al-Bazdawī* on the margin of 'Abd al-'Azīz al-Bukhārī, *Khashf al-Asrār* (Istanbul: 1308 AH), v. 3, p. 205; reprint: Beirut: Dār al-Kitāb al-'Arabī 1394/1974.

[56] Muḥammad Sallām Madkūr, *Al-Ijtihād fī al-Tashrī' al-Islāmī* (Cairo: Dār al-Naḥḍat al-'Arabiyyah, 1984), p. 40-41. For more information, see Bashīr Idrīs Jum'ah, *Al-Ra'y wa Atharuh fī al-Fiqh al-Islāmī*, p. 16-18.

[57] Al-Bukhārī, *Kashf*, v. 3, p. 205-06; Ibn Ḥazm, *Al-Iḥkām*, v. 5, p. 127-28.

[58] Ibn Humām, *Taḥrīr*, v. 4, p. 183; Ibn 'Abd al-Shakūr, *Musallam*, v. 2, p. 366.

[59] Abū Dāwud, *Sunan*, iii:1017, *ḥadīth* no. 3578; al-Sayyid 'Abd al-Laṭīf Kassāb, *Adwā'*, 58.

[60] Khallāf, *Khulāsat al-Tārīkh al-Tashrī' al-Islāmī* (Istanbul: al-Maktabat al-Islāmiyyah, 1984), 284; Hayreddin Karaman, *Yeni gelişmeler karşısında İslam*

Hukuku (İstanbul: İz Yayıncılık,1998), p. 56.

[61] Karaman, *Yeni gelişmeler*, p. 56; Zaydān, *Al-Madkhal*, p. 110.

[62] *Qur'ān* 53:3-4

[63] Al-Shawkānī, *Irshād*, 255.

[64] Al-Ghazālī, *Mustaṣfā*, v. 2, p. 104; al-Shawkānī, *Irshād*, p. 256.

[65] Kassāb, *Adwā'*, p. 61.

[66] *Qur'ān* 8:67

[67] *Qur'ān* 9:43

[68] Muslim, *Al-Jāmī' al-Ṣaḥīḥ*, (Istanbul: 1981), 140.

[69] Al-Bukhārī, "*Waṣāyā*," 19; Muslim, "*Nadhr*," 1.

[70] Ibn al-Qayyim, *I'lām*, v. 1, p. 258.

[71] Muslim, "*Li'an*," 18.

[72] Sha'bān, *Islam Hukuk İlminin Esasları*, p. 176-77.

[73] Al-Bukhari, "*Salam*," 1, 2; Muslim, "*Musāqāt*," 25; *Tirmīdhī*, "*Buyū'*," 70; Abū Dāwud, "*Buyū'*," 57; Nasāī, "*Buyū'*," 63.

[74] 'Abd al-'Azīz Khayyāt, *Naẓariyāt al-'Urf* (Amman: Maktabat al-Aqṣā', 997), p. 116-17.

[75] Al-Ghazālī, *Mustaṣfā*, v. 2, p. 354; al-Āmidī, *Al-Iḥkām*, v. 4, p. 407; Bādishāh, *Taysīr*, v. 4, p. 193.

[76] Al-Sarakhsī, *Uṣūl*, v. 2, p. 93-94, 130-31; al-Shawkānī, *Irshād*, p. 257.

[77] Ibn al-Qayyīm, *I'lām*, v. 1, p. 281-82.

[78] Muḥammad Ḥamidullah, "Al-Ijtihād fī 'Aṣr al-Ṣaḥābah," *Majallah al-Kulliyah al-Dirāsah al-Islāmiyah wa al-'Arabiyah*, 3, no. 4 (1984): 23.

[79] Bādishāh, *Taysīr*, v. 4, p. 195; al-Āmidī, *Al-Iḥkām*, v. 4, p. 408; al-Ghazālī, *Al-Mustaṣfā*, v. 2, p. 355; al-Shawkānī, *Irshād*, p. 257.

[80] Narrated from al-Tirmīdhī, al-Dārimī, *Sunan*; Abū Dāwud, 3:1019, *ḥadīth* no. 3585.

[81] Al-Bukhārī, "*Tayammum*," no. 7; Abū Dāwud, "*Ṭaharah*," no. 124.

[82] Aḥmad, *Musnad*, 4:373, 374; Abū Dāwud, "*Ṭalaq*," 32; Ibn Mājah, "*Aḥkām*," no. 20.

[83] Muḥammad ibn Ḥassān Hajawī, *Al-Fiqh al-Sami fi Tarikh al-Fiqh al-Islami* (Cairo: Dār al-Turāth, 1396), v. 1, p. 94.

[84] Yūsuf al-Qaradāwī, "*Islam Hukuku Evrensellik Süreklilik*," translated by Yusuf Işıcık, Ahmet Yaman, (Istanbul: Marifet Yayınları, 1999), p: 12.

[85] Wael B. Hallaq, "*The Gate of Ijtihād: A study in Islamic Legal History,*" PhD dissertation, University of Washington, p. 18.

[86] Fazlur Rahman, "*Islam and Modernity,*" the University of Chicago, 1984, p. 13.

[87] *Ibid:* p. 5.

[88] Fazlur Rahman, "*Islam ve Çağdaşlık*" p. 73-76, 95; Hayreddin Karaman, "*Modernist Proje ve İjtihād,*" in (*Maqāṣıd ve İjtihād*, Ahmed Yaman), p. 433.

[89] Fazlur Rahman, "*Islami Çağdaşlaşma,*" in *Islamic research magazine*, p. 318.

[90] Ibn 'Āshūr, "*Maqāṣid,*" p. 27-28.

[91] Abū Dāwūd, "*sunan,*" iii, 1019 *ḥadīth* no:3585

[92] Ghazāli, "*Al-Mustaṣfā,*" v. 2, p. 350.

[93] Wael B. Hallaq, "*The Gate of Ijtihād: A study in Islamic Legal History,*" PhD dissertation, University of Washington, p. 18.

[94] Ibn al-Qayyīm, "*I'lām,*" v. 4, p. 212.

[95] Ibn Taymīyyah, "*Al-Musawwadah,*" p. 356.

[96] Qaradāwī, "*Al-Ijtihād fī Sharī'ah al-Islāmiah,*" Kuwait, 1989, p. 182.

[97] Kamali, "*Principles,*" p. 386-389.

[98] Abū Zahrah, *Uṣūl*, p. 310; Kassāb, *Adwā'*, p. 38; 'Abdur Raḥīm, *Jurisprudence*, p. 182-83

[99] Abū Zahrah, *Uṣūl*, p. 314; Kassāb, *Adwā'*, p. 40; Aghnides, Muhammedan Theories, p. 95.

[100] *Ibid.*, ; Aghnides, *Muhammedan Theories*, p. 96

[101] *Ibid.*

[102] *Ibid.*

[103] Abū Zahrah, *Uṣūl*, p. 316

[104] Shawkānī, *Irshād*, p. 254, Abū Zahrah, *Uṣūl*, p. 318; Badrān, *Uṣūl*, p. 486

[105] Shawkānī, *Irshād*. p. 255; Abū Zahrah, *Uṣūl*, p. 318; Badrān, *Uṣūl*, p. 486; Ghazālī, *Mustaṣfā*, v. 2, p. 103.

[106] Kamali, "*Principles,*" p. 379.

[107] Hallaq, "*The Gate,*" p. 14-17.

[108] Shāṭibī, "*Al-Muwāfaqāt,*" v. 4 p. 105-106.

[109] For more about conditions of *al-Ijtihād* see: Shāṭibī, "*Al-Muwāfaqāt,*" v. 4, p. 60, 105-106, 111, 114, 162, 170; Bannānī, "*Jam' al-Jawāmī',*" v. 2, p. 832; Isnawī, "*Al-Minhāj,*" v. 3, p. 175, 200; Ghazālī, "*Al-Mustaṣfā,*" v. 2, p. 54, 101,102;

Shawkānī, "*Irshād*," p. 250-252; Abū Zahrah, "*Uṣūl*," p. 302-307; Karadāwī, "*Al-Ijtihād*," p. 47; Badrān, "*Uṣūl*," p. 208; Qarafī, "*Kitāb Anwār al-Burūq fī Anwār al-Furūq*" (Beirut: Dār al-Mā'rifah, nd.), v. 1, p. 78; Qurtūbī, "*Al-Jāmī' li Aḥkām al-Qur'ān*" (Beirut: Dār al-Iḥyā' al-Turās al-'Arabi, 1967), part 11, p. 310-311; Zuhayr, Muḥammad Abū al-Nūr, "*Mudhakkarāt fī al-Uṣūl al-Fiqh*" (Cairo: Dār al-Ta'līf, Kullīyyāt al-Sharī'ah, al-Azhar, nd.), v. 4, p. 226.

110 Aḥmad Raysūnī, "*Nazariyyāt al-Maqāṣid 'inda al-Imām al-Shāṭibī*," the IIIT, Maryland USA, 1995, p. 353; Wael B. Hallaq, "*The Origins and Evolution of Islamic Law*," p. 146, Cambridge University Press, 2005.

111 Ibn al-Subkī, "*Jam' al-Jawāmī'*," v. 2, p. 383.

112 Subkī and Ibn al-Subkī, "*Al-Ibhāj fī Sharḥ al-Minhāj*" (Beirut: 1984), v. 3, p. 206.

113 Raysūnī, *ibid*, p. 355.

114 Shāṭibī, "*Al-Muwāfaqāt*," v. 4 p. 174-175.

115 Orhan Çeker, "*Ifta ve Bir Fetva Defteri Örneği*" (Konya: Damla offset, 2000).

116 The sevent one which is "state" that I included it to the values of *maqāṣid al-sharī'ah* and the details of it is under the theme of the values of *maqāṣid al-sharī'ah* in this chapter.

117 Shāṭibī, "*Al-Muwāfaqāt*," v. 4, p. 56; Abū Zahrah, *Uṣūl*, p. 307

118 Shawkānī, *Irshād*, p. 252; Abū Zahrah, *Uṣūl*, p. 307; Badrān, *Uṣūl*, p. 208

119 Abū Zahrah, *Uṣūl*, p. 302; Ghazālī, *Mustaṣfā*, v. 2, p. 102; Shāṭibī, "*Al-Muwāfaqāt*," v. 4, p. 60

120 Ghazālī, *Mustaṣfā*, v. 2, p. 101; Shawkānī, *Irshād*, p. 250-51; Abū Zahrah, *Uṣūl*, p. 304; Zuhayr, *Uṣūl*, v. 4, p. 226.

121 Shawkānī, *Irshād*, p. 251; Abū Zahrah, *Uṣūl*, p. 304. According to a view attributed to Aḥmad ibn Ḥanbal, the *aḥadīth al-aḥkām* are likely to number in the region of one thousand and two hundreds. Ghazālī, *Mustaṣfā*, v. 2, p. 101; *Shawkānī, Irshād*, p. 251.

122 Shawkānī, *Irshād*, p. 251; Ghazālī, *Muṣtaṣfā*, v. 2, p. 101; Abū Zahrah, *Uṣūl*, p. 305

123 Ghazālī, *Muṣtaṣfā*, v. 2, p. 54; Shawkānī, *Irshād*, p. 252; Abū Zahrah, *Uṣūl*, p. 306 and 308-309; Ghazālī, *Muṣtaṣfā*, v. 2, p. 103.

124 Ghazālī, *Muṣtaṣfā*, v. 2, p. 101; Shawkānī, *Irshād*, p. 252. See more on *ijtihād*, Kamali, *Principles*, p. 366-392.

125 Sha'bān, "*Uṣūl*," p. 332-333.

126 Wael B. Hallaq, "*Was the Gate of Ijtihad Closed?*" in *International Journal of*

Middle East Studies. xvi, 1, 1984, 3-41; Montgomery Watt, "*The closing of the door of ijtihād*" in Oriehtakia hispanica, sive studia F M Pareja octogenaria dictata edenda curavit J M Barral, Leiden 1974, I, 675-8.

[127] Dihlawī, "*Al-Muṣaffā'*," Delhi, v. 1, p. 11. Quoted from Baljon, "*Religion and thought of Shah Walī Allāh Dihlawī,*" p. 167.

[128] Dihlawī, "*Iqd*" quoted from Baljon, "*Religion and thought of Shah Walī Allāh Dihlawī,*" p. 167.

[129] Abū Zahrah, *Uṣūl*, p. 311

[130] Muslim, *Ṣaḥīḥ*, p. 290, *ḥadīth* no. 1095; Shawkānī, *Irshād*, p. 253; Ghazālī, *Mustaṣfā*, v. 1, p. 111

[131] Ṣaḥīḥ Muslim, the Book on Government (*Kitāb Al-Imāra*), *ḥadīth* no: 4718

[132] Abū Zahrah, *Uṣūl*, p. 318

[133] Zuhayr, *Uṣūl*, v. 4, p. 225; Shawkānī, *Irshād*, p. 252; Badrān, *Uṣūl*, p. 471; Aghnides, Muhammedan Theories, p. 91.

[134] Khallāf, *'Ilm*, p. 35, Abū Zahrah, *Uṣūl*, p. 711; *Shaltūt*, *Al-Islām*, p. 498; Shawkānī, *Irshād*, p. 250; Badrān, *Uṣūl*, p. 471.

[135] See more on the concept of *istiḥsān*, Saim Kayadibi, *Istiḥsān The Doctrine of Juristic Preference in Islamic Law,* (Kuala Lumpur: Islamic Book Trust, 2010)

[136] Abū Dāwud, "*Sunan,*" iii, 1019 *ḥadīth* no: 3585.

[137] *Ibid.*

[138] 'Abd al-Ḥāfiẓ, "*Al-Istiḥsān,*" p. 142.

[139] Bukhārī, "*Kashf,*" v. 4, p. 3.

[140] Bukhārī, "*Kashf,*" part 4, p. 3.

[141] Ghazālī, "*Mustaṣfā,*" v. 1, p. 283; Juwaynī, "*Talkhīṣ,*" v. 3, p. 311,313.

[142] Abū Zahrah, "*Uṣūl,*" p. 251.

[143] Khallāf, "*Maṣāder,*" p. 71.

[144] *Ibid.*

[145] Abū Zahrah, "*Uṣūl,*" p. 207; Shāṭibī, "*Al-I'tiṣām,*" v. 2, p. 137.

[146] *Kūfa* was one of the biggest cities of *Irāq*, consisting of various tribes and communities, and was a center of the ancient civilizations. Before *Islam*, schools were established there for the teaching of Greek philosophy. It was also later the base for *Shī'ah*, *Mu'tazilah*, *Khawārij* and *mujtahid* 'Successors' such as: Alqamah b. Qays (d. 62), Masrūq b. al-Ajdā' (d. 63), al-Aswad b. Yazīd (d. 75), Shuraykh b. al-Ḥārith (d. 78), who spread the teaching of the Companions, 'Ali

Ibn Abī Ṭālib (d. 40), Ibn Mas'ūd (d. 32), Ibn 'Umar (d. 73), Ibn 'Abbās (d. 68), of the Prophet (ṣ). See: Abū Zahrah, "*Abū Ḥanīfah,*" p. 30, 31.

[147] Abū Ḥanīfah's father was a silk trader. Abū Ḥanīfah grew up in a wealthy family and took over the business from his father. Shā'bī (d. 110) one day advised him to attend a scholarly gathering, which he did. The rest is history. See: Makkī, "*Manāqib,*" v. 2, p. 106.

[148] Abū Ḥanīfah lived 52 years of his life in the period of Umayyad dynasty, and the remaining 18 years under the Abbāsīd dynasty. He lived under the rule of the despot governor Hajjāj b. Yūsuf Thaqafī and was witness to the murders of various members of the *ahl al-bayt.* He was also imprisoned. Later on, he understood that the Abbāsid dynasty was a continuation of the same tyrannical system; he took a stand against them, which caused him to be persecuted. See: Abū Zahrah, "*Abū Ḥanīfah,*" p. 19, 104, 107, 108. See also: Khatīb Baghdādī, "*Tārīkhi Baghdād,*" v. 13, p. 239.

[149] Saymarī Ḥusain b. 'Ali (d. 436/1045), "*Akhbār Abū Ḥanīfah wa Aṣḥābuh*" (Beirut: 1985), p. 26.

[150] Bazdawī,"*Kashf,*" p. 1125.

[151] Ibn Ḥazm, "*Al-Iḥkām,*" v. 2, p. 195-196; Chejne, "*Ibn Ḥazm,*" p. 122.

[152] 'Alwānī, "*The Ethics,*" p. 75; Ansārī, "*Ghāyat al-Wusūl,*" p.139.

[153] Makkī, "*Manāqib,*" v. 1, p. 80; Saymarī, "*Akhbār,*" p. 24; Baghdādī, "*Tārīkh,*" v. 13, p. 368.

[154] Muḥammad Qāsim 'Abduh Ḥārithī, "*Makānāt al-Imām Abū Ḥanīfah bayn al-Muḥaddithīyn,*" p. 23, PhD dissertation, at the University of Islamic studies, Pakistan, p. 23.

[155] Makkī, "*Manāqib,*" v.1, p. 80.

[156] Makkī, "*Manāqib,*" v. 1, p. 74.

[157] *Ibid.*

[158] Saymarī, "*Akhbār,*" p. 27; Makkī, "*Manāqib,*" v. 1, p. 81.

[159] Makki, "*Manāqib,*" v. 1, p. 85

[160] Ibn Mājah, "*Sunan,*" ii, 784, *ḥadīth* no: 2340; Shāṭibī, "*Muwāfaqāt,*" v. 3, p. 17; Khudarī, "*Tārīkh,*" p. 199.

[161] Abū Zahrah, "*Abū Ḥanīfah,*" p. 342, also see: Uzunpostalcı,"*Ebu Hanife,*" DIA, X, 136.

[162] Abū Zahraḥ, "*Abū Ḥanīfah,*" p. 75.

[163] Saymarī, "*Akhbār,*" p. 25; Makkī, "*Manāqib,*" v. 1, p. 81.

[164] Abū Zahrah, "*Abū Ḥanifah*," p. 330, 332, 334; Uzunpostacı, *ibid.*, 136.

[165] Makkī, "*Manāqib*," v. 1, p. 84.

[166] Māwardi, "*Adab al-Qādi*," p. 649-650.

[167] Haytamī, "*Al-Ḥayat al-Ḥisān*," p. 42, 106.

[168] Jaṣṣāṣ, "*Fuṣūl*," v. 4, p. 116-117; Makkī, "*Manāqib*," v. 1 p. 83; also for more examples, see: Sarakhsī, "*Al-Mabsūṭ*," v. 1, p. 53, 169, v. 13, p. 122, v. 17, p. 63-64.

[169] Muḥammad Muṣṭafā Shalabī, "*Uṣūl al-Fiqh al-Islāmī*" (Beirut: 1986), p. 258.

[170] Hayreddin Karaman, "*Islam Hukukunda İctihād*," MUIFV, İstanbul, 1996, p. 29. For further details on *ijtihād* see: Maudūdī, Abū al-'Alā' "*Islamic Law and Constitution*," Islamic publications ltd Lahore, translated by Khurshid Aḥmad, 1960, p. 79-96.

[171] *Qur'ān* 64:16.

[172] *Qur'ān* 59:2

[173] Qarafī, "*Tanqīḥ*," 4th chapter of *ijmā'*, quoted from Ibn Āshūr, "*Maqāsid al-Sharī'ah*," p. 197-198.

[174] *Qur'ān* 16:43

[175] Āmidī, *Iḥkām*, v. 4, p. 206; Kassāb, *Adwā'*, p. 121.

[176] Āmidī, *Iḥkām*, v. 4, p. 204; Ghazālī, *Mustaṣfā*, v. 2, p. 121

[177] Khudari, *Uṣūl*, p. 368; Shawkānī, *Irshād*, p. 235; Zuhayr, *Uṣūl*, v. 4, p. 227.

[178] Ḥasan, *The Early*, p. 115.

[179] *Qur'ān* 47:24

[180] Shawkānī, *Irshād*, p. 254, Abū Zahrah, *Uṣūl*, p. 318; Badrān, *Uṣūl*, p. 486

[181] Badran, *Uṣūl*, p. 14

[182] Shawkānī, *Irshād*, p. 246.

[183] Nyazee, *Islamic Jurisprudence*, p. 329.

[184] Ibn Ḥajj, *al-Taqrīr wa al-Takhbīr* (Bulaq: 1316 AH), v. 4, p. 340.

[185] 'Abdur Raḥīm, *Muhammadan Jurisprudence*, p. 171

[186] Nyazee, *Islamic Jurisprudence*, p. 330.

[187] Either the mujtahid *muṭlaq* (the absolute jurist) or *mujtahid fi al-madhhab* (the mujtahid who is independent within the school).

[188] Ibn 'Abidīn, *Rasā'il Ibn 'Abidīn*, (Lahore: 1976), p. 49.

[189] Nyazee, *Islamic Jurisprudence*, p. 333-334.

[190] *Qur'ān* 3:132

[191] *Qur'ān* 4:65.

[192] *Qur'ān* 59: 7.

[193] *Qur'ān* 21:7

[194] *Qur'ān* 2:286

[195] Al-Rāzī, Muḥammad b. 'Ali Bakr b. 'Abd al-Qādir, *Mukhtār al-Siḥāḥ*, ed. Maḥmūd Khaṭīr (Beirut: Dār al-Fikr, nd.), p. 601, qf. Daud Bakar, "*Conflict of Law and the Methodology of Tarjīḥ: A Study in Islamic Legal Theory*," unpublished PhD thesis, (Scotland: University of St Andrews, 1993), p. 122.

[196] Ibn al-Manzur, *Lisān al-'Arab*, v. 10, p. 330-331; Lane, *Arabic-English Lexicon*, v.2, p. 3011

[197] Nyazee, Imran Ahsan Khan, *Theories of Islamic Law: The Methodology of ljtihād* (Pakistan: The International Institute of Islamic Thought, 1994), p. 125

[198] Ahmad bin Mohamed Ibrahim, "*Source and Development of Muslim law*," (Singapore: Malayan Law Journal ltd., 1965), 95.

[199] Kerr, Malcolm H, *Islamic Reform: The Political and Legal Theories of Muhammad 'Abduh and Rashid Rida* (Cambridge and California University Press, 1966), p. 216.

[200] Wahbah Zuhayli, *Uṣūl al-Fiqh al-Islāmī* (Damascus: Dār al-Fikr, 1986), v. 1, p. 1142

[201] Al-Ghanzi, Sa'd, al-Talfiq fi al-Fatwa, *Journal of Shari'ah and Islamic Studies*, v. 14, issue 38, August 1999, p. 272; Aznan Hasan, The Concept of Tahayyur and its Application in Islamic Banking and Finance: an Appraisal, Paper Presented at *the 2nd International Law and Commerce Conference*, Victoria Law Schooi, Victoria University, Melbourne, 8-9 December, 2003, p. 7.

[202] Quadri, Syed Moinuddīn, Traditions of Taqlīd and Talfiq, *Islamic Culture*, vol. 57 (January and April) 1983, pp. 39-61 and 123-145. p. 123.

[203] Anderson, J. N. D., Recent Developments in Shari'a Law, *Moslem World*, vol. 40, 1950, pp. 224-256, p. 250; Daud Bakar, "*Conflict of Law*, p. 124.

[204] See Shah Wali Allah, *al-Inṣāf*, as cited in Quadri, "*Traditions of taqlīd and talfiq*," in IC, v. 57, no. 1.1983. p. 39.

[205] Ibn al-Manzur , *Lisan al-'Arab*, Dār al-Ṣadr, Beirut n. d., v. 4, p. 266, Lane, Edward, *Arabic English Lexicon*, Islamic Texts society Trust, Cambridge, 1984, v. 1, p. 829

[206] Coulson, Noel J., *A History of Islamic Law*, Edinburgh University Press, 1978, p. 185.

[207] Nyazee, *Theories of Islamic Law: The Methodology of Ijtihād*, p. 125

[208] Kerr, *Islamic Reform*. p. 216-217; see also Esposito, John L. *Muslim Family Law in Egypt and Pakistan: A Critical Analysis of Legal Reform, its Sources and Methodological Problems*, Ph. D dissertation, Temple University. 1974 and Muslim Family Law Reform: Towards an Islamic Methodology, *Islamic Studies*, v. 15, no. 1,1976, p. 19-51; Layish, Aharon, The Contribution of the Modernists to the Secularization of Islamic Law, *Middle Eastern Studies*, v. 14,1978, p. 263-277, p. 263.

[209] Ibn Taymiyyah, *Majmū' al-Fatāwā*, collected and arranged by 'Abd al-Raḥmān b. Muḥammad b. Qāsim al-'Aṣimī al-Najdī al-Ḥanbalī, Riad, 1962, v. 2, p. 387; Schacht, Joseph, *An Introduction to Islamic Law*, Oxford University Press, 1964, p. 68, for details see Nyazee, "The scope of taqlīd in Islamic law," in *IS*, v. 22, 1983, p. 24-26.

[210] Hallaq B. Wael, *An Introduction to Islamic law*, (UK: Cambridge University Press, 2009), 115-117

[211] Anderson, "*Recent Development*," p. 255

[212] Kerr, *Islamic Reform*, p. 217; Muslim, 'Abdul Ghafūr, Islamization of Laws in Pakistan: Problems and Prospects, *Islamic Studies*, vol. 26. no. 3, 1987, pp. 256-276, p. 77.

[213] Daud Bakar, "Conflict of Law," p. 127.

[214] Al-Bani, Muḥammad Sa'īd *'Umdat al-Tahqiq fi al-Taqlīd wa al-Talfiq*, (Dimishq: al-Maktab al-Islāmī, 1981), p. 22.

[215] Al-Ghanzi, *al-Talfiq fī al-Fatwa*, p. 283.

[216] Feisal Abdul Rauf, *Islam a Sacred Law*, (Vermont: Qiblah Books, 1998), p. 88

[217] For the *ḥila-i shar'iyyah*, see: Abu Zahrah, "*Abū Ḥanīfah*," p. 446-468; Baktrī, "*Zarūret*," p. 153-164; Ibn al-Qayyim, "*Ighāsat al-Lahfān*," p. 183-285; *ibid*., v. 3, p. 107-417; Karaman,"*İslam Hukuk Tarihi*," p. 77-78; Shāṭibī, "*Muwāfaqāt*," v. 2, p. 380-390.

[218] Shāṭibī, "*Muwāfaqāt*," v. 2, p. 378-380. see more about legal loopholes: Saffet Köse "*İslam Hukukunda Kanuna Karşı Hile*" (Istanbul: Birleşik Yayıncılık, 1996).

[219] Ahmad bin Mohamed Ibrahim, "*Source and Development of Muslim law*," (Singapore: Malayan Law Journal ltd., 1965), 34.

[220] *Ibid*., 95.

[221] Schacht, *An Introduction*, p. 81.

[222] *Ibid.*, p. 81.

[223] Shāṭibī, *al-Muwāfaqāt*, v. 2, p. 378-91, v. 4, p. 201.

[224] Feisal Abdul Rauf, *Islam a Sacred Law*, (Vermont: Qiblah Books, 1998), p. 89.

[225] Ibn al-Qayyīm, I'lām, v. 3, p. 247.

[226] Ibn al-Qayyīm, I'lām, v. 3, p. 119-352 and v. 4, p. 1-40.

[227] Imran Ahsan Khan Nyazee, "*Theories of Islamic Law, the Methodology of Ijtihād*," (Kuala Lumpur: IBT, 2002), 109.

[228] Joseph Schacht, *An Introduction to Islamic Law*, (Oxford: Clarendon Press, 1964), p. 205, 210.

[229] Ignaz Goldziher, *Introduction to Islamic Law and Theology*, trans A. & R. Hamori, (Princeton, NJ: Princeton University Press, 1981), p. 62-65.

[230] Schacht, *An Introduction*, p. 210.

[231] Nyazee, *Theories*, p. 304.

[232] *Qur'ān* 23:105.

[233] Moḥammad al-Ṭāhir ibn Āshūr, *Treatise on Maqāṣid al-Sharī'ah al-Islāmiyyah*, trans. Muḥammad el-Ṭāhir el-Mesawī (London, Washington: International Institute of Islamic Thought (IIIT), 2006), p. 2.

[234] Ibn Āshūr, *Maqāṣid al-Sharī'ah al-Islāmiyyah*, p. 183.

[235] Raysūnī, "*Nazarīyyāt al-Maqāṣid*," p. 17; Yaman, "*Maqāṣid ve ictihād*," p. 7.

[236] Muḥammad al-Ṭāhir ibn 'Āshūr, "*Maqāṣid al-Sharī'ah al-Islāmīyyah*" (Tunis: 1946), qf. Aḥmad al-Raysūnī, "*Imām al-Shāṭibī's Theory of the Higher Objectives and Intents of Islamic Law*," *ibid.*, p. xxii.

[237] This information was partially published in Saim Kayadibi, An Approach to the Position of Islamic Law with the Consideration of the Reform through the Aiding Factors, *Journal of Islamic Law Studies (IHAD)*, 12, (2008), p. 155-182.

[238] Abdurraḥman Haçkalı, "Islam Hukuk Tarihinde Maṣlaḥat Tanımları ve Bunların Analizi," *İslami Araştırmalar Magazine*, v. 13, no. 1, 2000, p. 47-61.

[239] Ibn Manẓūr, Jamāluddīn Muḥammad ibn Mukarram al-Anṣārī (d. 711/1311), "*Lisān Al-'Arab*" (Cairo: Ṭaba'ah Bulāq, nd.)

[240] Al-Shāṭibī "*al-Muwāfaqāt*," v. 2, p. 25.

[241] Badrān, Abū al-'Aynāyn Badrān, "*Uṣūl al-Fiqh al-Islāmi*" (Alexandria: Mu'assasah Shabāb al-Jāmiah, 1404/1984), p. 210.

[242] Ghazālī, "*al-Muṣtaṣfā*," p. 174-179.

[243] Shihāb al-Dīn al-Qarāfi, *al-Dhakhirah* (Beirut: Dar al-'Arab, 1994), v. 5, p.

478; Jasser Auda, *Maqāṣid al-Sharī'ah as Philosophy of Islamic Law A Systems Approach*, (London: The International Institute of Islamic Thought, 2007), p. 2

[244] Kamali, "*Principles,*" p. 268.

[245] Shāṭibī, "*al-Muwāfaqāt,*" v. 2, p. 29-30.

[246] See the rules and guidelines related to governance in the *Qur'an* 4:58-59, 5:2, 21:105, 22:40-41, 24:55, and 57:25.

[247] Sharifah Hayaati Syed Ismail al-Qudsy and Asmak Ab Rahman, "Effective Governance in the Era of Caliphate 'Umar Ibn Al-Khaṭṭāb," *European Journal of Social Sciences*, v. 18, no. 4 (2011), p. 618.

[248] Sharifah Hayaati Syed Ismail al-Qudsy and Asmak Ab Rahman, *ibid.*, p. 619.

[249] Aḥmad al-Raysūnī, "*Imām al-Shāṭibī's Theory of the Higher Objectives and Intents of Islamic Law*" (Selangor: Islamic Book Trust, 2006), p. xxi.

[250] Raysūnī, "*Naẓarīyyāt al-Maqāṣid,*" p. 17; Yaman, "*Maqāṣid ve Ictihād,*" p. 7.

[251] Al-Shāṭibī "*al-Muwāfaqāt,*" v. 2, p. 3.

[252] *Qur'ān* 21:16.

[253] *Qur'ān* 23:105.

[254] Shāṭibī, "*Muwāfaqāt,*" v. 4, p. 208.

[255] 'Āshūr, "*Maqāṣid,*" p. introduction (Hayreddin Karaman), translated by Mehmet Erdoğan-Vecdi Akyüz, (İstanbul: Rağbet, 1999).

[256] Ibn Āshūr, Muḥammad Ṭāhir (d. 1973), "*Maqāsid al-Sharī'ah al-Islāmīyyah*" (İslam Hukuk Felsefesi, Gaye Problemi), tr. Vecdi Akyüz and Mehmet Erdoğan (İstanbul: Rağbet, 1999), p. 123,

[257] Ibn Āshūr, *ibid.*, p. 138.

[258] Ibn Āshūr, *ibid.*, p. 139.

[259] Ghazālī, "*al-Muṣtaṣfā,,*" v. 1, p. 288.

[260] Shāṭibī "*al-Muwāfaqāt,,*" v. 2, p. 8.

[261] *Qur'ān* 29:45

[262] *Qur'ān* 9:36

[263] *Qur'ān* 2:190

[264] *Sunan Abū Dāwud, ḥadīth ṣaḥīḥ*, no: 4340.

[265] Qur'ān 17:33

[266] Al-Bukhārī and Muslim, *Book 1, ḥadīth* 9.

[267] *Qur'ān* 2:178

[268] *Qur'ān* 2:179

[269] Tirmidhī, *al-Jāmi' al-Ṣaḥīḥ*, no: 1423, iv, 24; Nasāī, *Sunan*, no: 3432, iv, 146.

[270] *Qur'ān* 5:90

[271] *Qur'ān* 17:32

[272] Ṣaḥīḥ Muslim, 1400.

[273] Al-Bukhārī and Muslim, 40 *ḥadīth* Nawawī, 14

[274] *Qur'ān* 24:2

[275] *Qur'ān* 4:3

[276] *Qur'ān* 2:188

[277] *Qur'ān* 4:161

[278] *Qur'ān* 5:38

[279] *Qur'ān* 24:4

[280] *Qur'ān* 24:23

[281] *Qur'ān* 4:58-59

[282] Saim Kayadibi, (2015), The Theory of Syarī'ah Oriented Public Policy. *Ahkam*, XV (2). pp. 171-180.

[283] Abū Dāwūd, Book 8, *ḥadīth* no: 960.

[284] Ṣaḥīḥ Muslim, Book 20, *ḥadīth* no: 4557.

[285] Ṣaḥīḥ Muslim, *ḥadīth* no: 4524.

[286] *Qur'ān* 3:103

[287] *Qur'ān* 3:104

[288] Ibn Taymīyyah, *Al-Siyāsah al-Shar'īyyah* (Cairo: Dār al-Fikr, n.d.), p. 150-151.

[289] Ibn Taymīyyah, *ibid.*, p. 185.

[290] Erwin I. J. Rosenthal, Political Thought in Medieval Islam (Cambridge: Cambridge University Press, 1962), p. 200, qf. Abdul Azim Islahi, *Economic Concepts of Ibn Taimīyah*, (Leicester: The Islamic Foundation, 1988), p. 174.

[291] *Qur'ān* 3:104 and see more about *Qur'ān* 9:71.

[292] Abūl Ḥasan al-Mawārdī al Shāfi'ī (450/1058), "*Kitāb al-Aḥkām al-Sulṭāniyyah*," (Cairo: Dar al-Hadith, 2006), p. 40-41; Al-Mawārdī, "*The Ordinances of Government*," translated by Asadullah Yate, (London: Ta-Ha publishers, nd.), p. 27-28.

[293] Al-Mawārdī, *Al-Aḥkām*, p. 40-41; Al-Mawārdī, *The Ordinances*, p. 27-28.

[294] *Ibid.*, v. 2, p. 10-11.

[295] Kamali, "*Al-Maqāṣid al-Sharī'ah* (The Objectives of Islamic Law)," p. 2

[296] Shāṭibī "*al-Muwāfaqāt*," v. 2, p. 327.

[297] Kamali, "*Al-Maqāṣid al-Sharī'ah* (The Objectives of Islamic Law)," p. 3

[298] Muslim, *Ṣaḥīḥ Muslim*, Book 1, *ḥadīth* No. 164.

[299] *Ṣaḥīḥ Bukhārī*, v. 4, Book 56, Number 759.

[300] Ghazālī, *ibid.*, v. 1, p. 311.

[301] Ghazālī, "*Al-Mankhūl min Ta'līqāt Al-Uṣūl,*" 2nd ed. (Damascus: Dār Al-Fikr Al-'Arabī), p. 355.

[302] Aṭṭār, Ḥasan bin Muḥammad bin Maḥmūd (d. 1250/1835), "*Ḥāshiyah 'alā Sharḥ Jalāl al-Maḥallī 'alā Jam'u Al-Jawāmi'*" (Egypt: Maṭba'ah 'Ilmīyyah, 1316 A.H.), part 2, p. 339,

[303] Zuhailī, "*Uṣūl,*" part 2, p. 799.

[304] Khallāf "*'Ilm*" p. 87; Badrān "*Uṣūl,*" p. 214.

[305] Shāṭibī, "*al-I'tisām,*" part 2, p. 307-314.

[306] Ghazāli, "*al-Mustaṣfā,*" part 1, p. 141.

[307] Ibn 'Āshūr, "*Maqāṣid,*" p. 121.

[308] Shāṭibī, "*al-Muwāfaqāt,*" v. 2, p. 29-30.

[309] *Qur'ān* 23:71

[310] Kamali, "*Al-Maqāṣid al-Sharī'ah* (The Objectives of Islamic Law)," p. 3

[311] Raysūnī, "*Nazariyyāt al-Maqāṣid,*" p. 26.

[312] *Ibid.*, p. 29.

[313] *Ibid.*; For more about historical approach, see Saim Kayadibi, An Approach to the Position of Islamic Law with the Consideration of the Reform through the Aiding Factors, *Journal of Islamic Law Studies (IHAD)*, 12, (2008), 155-182.

[314] Juwaynī, "*Al-Talkhiṣ,*" v. 1, p. 206.

[315] Juwayni, "*Al-Burḥān,*" v. 2, p. 747.

[316] Ghazālī, "*Al-Mustaṣfā,*" v. 1, p. 286.

[317] Masood, "*Islamic Legal Philosopy,*" p. 157.

[318] Koca, Ferhat, "İslam Hukukunda Maslahat'ı Mursalah ve Necmeddin el-Ṭūfi'nin bu Konudaki Görüşlerinin Değerlendirilmesi," *ILAM Research Magazine*, v. 1, no. 1, p. 93-122, (January-June) İstanbul, 1996.

[319] Masood, *ibid.*, p. 165.

[320] Tūfi, "*Al-Ta'yīn,,*" p. 238.

[321] Dihlawī, "*Ḥujjat Alāh al-Bālīghah,*" v. 1, p. 29.

[322] Ibn 'Āshūr, "*Maqāṣid al-Sharīat al-Islāmiyyah*" (Tunis: n.p., 1366 A.H.).

[323] See Aḥmad al-Raysūnī, "*Imām al-Shāṭibī's Theory of the Higher Objectives and*

Intents of Islamic Law" (Selangor: Islamic Book Trust, 2006).

[324] Raysūnī, "*Nazariyyāt*," p. 351.

[325] Muḥammad F. Ibn 'Āshūr, "*Ā'lam al-Fikr al-Islāmī' fī Tārikh al-Maghrīb al-'Arabī*," p. 76, qf Raysūnī, "*Nazariyyāt*" p. 352-353.

[326] 'Allāl Fāsī, "*Maqāṣid*," p. 51-52.

[327] Ibn Rushd, "*Bidāyat al-Mujtahid*," v. 1, p. 136, 137, v. 2, p. 154, 246.

[328] Ibn 'Āshūr, "*Maqāṣid*," p. 15-16.

[329] For this criterion and principles, see Būṭī, "*Ḍawābiṭ*," p. 115-118; Ḥādimī, "*Al-Ijtihād*" p. 23-24; Ghazālī, "*Al-Mustaṣfā*," p. 179.

[330] Ibn 'Abd al-Salām "*Qawā'id*," v. 1, p. 104; Qarafī, "*Furūq*," v. 2, p. 23; Ibn 'Āshūr, "*Maqāṣid*," p. 207.

[331] Qarafī, "*Furūq*," v. 2, p. 33.

[332] *Al-Majallah al-Aḥkām*: clause: 50.

[333] Ibn 'Āshūr, "*Maqāṣid*," p. 119.

[334] *Qur'ān* 7:142; 7:85; 24:55.

CHAPTER SIX

The Abrogation

Introduction

The science of *naskh* (abrogation) is as important as the other Islamic science, even more. There are substantial narrations indicating that it is essential to know in order to guide people to the right direction. Lack of having knowledge of the chronological order of the revelations, scholars may not be able to identify which rulings were abolished and which ones were still in action. It is logical that the latter rulings should be followed by the people then the earlier rulings, similar to the current laws of a country. For the importance of studying the knowledge of *naskh* (abrogation), scholars have quoted a number of reports attributed to prominent early Muslims. 'Ali bin Abi Ṭālib (40/661), the cousin of the Prophet (ṣ) and the fourth caliph after him, once asked a scholar whether he had knowledge of the *nāsikh* (abrogating ruling) and the *mansūkh* (abrogated ruling), when the answered was "no," he told him that he was seriously deceiving and misleading others.[1] A narration from Dārimī (255/869) stating that one should consider giving rulings to people only if he has distinguished "the abrogating verses from the abrogated ones in the *Qur'ān*" or is a ruler who needs to enact laws.[2] 'Ali bin Abī Ṭālib once again questioned a man in the mosque, who was giving a talk, whether he knew the science of the abrogating and abrogated rulings to which the man answered in the negative way, then 'Ali told him to leave the mosque and to not preach in it again.[3] Aḥmad al-Naḥḥās (338/949) says that Ibn 'Abbās (68/687) is said to have interpreted the verse from the *Qur'ān* "*and anyone who is given wisdom has been given much good*"[4] as referring mainly to the science of *naskh*.[5] Jalāl al-Dīn al-Suyuṭī (d. 911 AH.) emphasises on the importance of knowing this science with the following quotation "no one should try to interpret the Book of Allah before learning its abrogating and abrogated verses."[6]

The knowledge of abrogation reflects the Lawgiver's authority Who can replace any ruling with any other ruling anytime He likes since He is the one Who supreme power over all. As Allah states in the *Qur'ān*: "*Whatever communications We abrogate or cause to be forgotten, We bring one better than it or like it. Do you not know that Allah has power over all things?*"[7]

Immediately after this verse Allah challenges the people by saying "Do you not know that Allah's is the kingdom of the heavens and the earth, and that besides Allah you have no guardian or helper?"[8]

Definition of naskh

Linguistically, *naskh* has two different meanings. The first, which is shared by the related term *intisākh*, is copying a book from a source. The second meaning is replacing a practice with another. For example, "a verse that introduces a particular commandment that is later made easier so that verse is abrogated (*tunsakh*) by another."[9] The replacing verse is known as *nāsikh*, which is the active participle of *naskh*, whereas the replaced verse is referred to with the passive participle *mansūkh*.[10] Besides these meanings, *nasakh* also means "obliteration," such as in *nasakhat al-rīḥ athar al-mashy* (the wind obliterated the footprint). Similar to above mentioned meaning, it means transcription or transfer (*al-naql wa al-tahwīl*) of something from one state to another while its essence remains unchanged. The word *naskh* is used in the *Qur'ān* which states "*This is Our book that speaks against you with justice; surely We wrote what you did*".[11]

In addition to these meaning, the following expressions are used in Arabic language *tanāsukh al-mawārīth* (the transfer of inheritance from persons to persons) and *tanāsukh al-arwāḥ* (reincarnation). In regards to the usage of the word, Abū Bakr al-Baqillānī and al-Ghazālī, have held that "*naskh*" is a homonym and applies equally to either of its two meanings, literal (*haqīqī*) and metaphorical (*majāzī*). However, according to the majority of the scholars, *naskh* for the meaning of obliteration (*al-raf' wa al-izālah*) is the primary, and transcription/transfer is the secondary, that is scholars have used it mainly for the meaning of annulment of a divine rulings by a later divine ruling or abrogation.[12]

Technically, *naskh* is defined as the abrogation of annulment of a divine ruling by a later divine ruling.[13] Similarly, it is the suspension or replacement of one *Sharī'ah* ruling by another ruling provided that the second one is of a later origin.[14]

According to Imām Shāfi'ī, *naskh* is a form of explanation (*bayān*) which does not entail a total rejection of the original ruling which he maintained the view that, in his famous book *al-Risālah*, *naskh* is not a form of annulment (*ilghā'*), it is, however, rather a suspension or termination of one ruling by another.[15] In contrast to his opinion, the majority of scholars do not accept the view that *naskh* is a form of *bayān*. However, it is the fact that *naskh* terminates and puts an end to a ruling differentiates it from *bayān*, it cannot be explained when a ruling is terminated.[16]

Naskh is explanatory in the sense that it tells us of the termination of a particular ruling, the manner and the time of its termination, whether the whole of a ruling or only a part of it is terminated, and of course, the new ruling which is to take its place.

Historical approach on naskh

It is discussed that the concept of *naskh* (abrogation) began to occur at the *Madinah* period as a result of the changes that the Muslim community encountered following the migration of the Prophet (ṣ) and the Companions. At the *Makkah* period, at the early stage of the advent of Islam, the revelation focused mostly on winning the hearths of the people via warning them with hell and glad-tiding them with paradise, faith, oneness of Allah etc. Thus, *mut'ah* (temporary marriage) was initially permitted but was subsequently prohibited when the Prophet (ṣ) migrated to *Madinah* and even the number of daily prayers which was initially fixed at two but was later increased to five.[17]

Naskh among the sources of Islamic law

The *naṣṣ* of the *Qur'ān* or a *mutawātir ḥadīth* (recurrent tradition) cannot be abrogated by a weaker *ḥadīth*, by *ijmā'* or by *qiyās* because they are not of equal authority to the *naṣṣ* of the *Qur'ān*. The *Qur'ān* and the *Sunnah* may be abrogated by themselves or by one another only according to the majority (*jumhūr*) view. Similarly, one *mutawātir ḥadīth* may abrogate another one since they are in the same strength. The textual ruling of the *Qur'ān* may be abrogated either by another text from the *Qur'ān* which is similar in strength or by a *mutawātir ḥadīth*, even if it is by a *mashhūr ḥadīth* (well-known) according to the *Ḥanafīs*, so long as, is later origin. According to the preferred (*rājiḥ*) view, neither the *Qur'ān* nor the *mutawātir ḥadīth* may be abrogated by a solitary *ḥadīth*. However, according to Imām Shāfi'ī, the *Sunnah*, whether as *mutawātir* or *āḥād*, may not abrogate the *Qur'ān*.[18]

And therefore, it is obvious that *ijmā'*, *qiyās* and *ijtihād*, being weaker in comparison to the *nuṣūṣ* according to the general principle, therefore, they cannot abrogate the rules of divine revelations.[19] In spite of the fact that here are some scholars from *Ḥanafī* and *Mu'tazilī* have held the view that *ijmā'* can abrogate a ruling of the *Qur'ān* or the *Sunnah*. They claimed that it was due to *ijmā'* that 'Umar bin al-*Khaṭṭāb* stopped the share of the *mu'allafah al-qulūb* in the *zakāh*,[20] although the *Qur'ān* assigned them a share in *zakāh* in *sūrah al-Tawbah "Alms are only for the poor and the needy, and the officials (appointed) over them, and those whose hearts are made to incline (to truth) and the (ransoming of) captives and those in debts and in the way of Allah and the wayfarer; an ordinance from Allah; and Allah is knowing, Wise"*.[21] Nevertheless, it is something that it was stopped actually because the *mujtahidūn* of the time reached a unanimous agreement to this reality. Despite the differences in opinions, *ijmā'* cannot abrogate nor can be abrogated itself. According to the general ruling, a later *ijmā'* may abrogate an existing *ijmā'* which might be founded in considerations of public interest, or *maṣlaḥah mursalah.* [22]

When it comes to the concept of *qiyās*, for example, it is normally based on a textual ruling and is bound to remain valid for as long as the original text remains valid. *Qiyās* cannot either abrogate, nor can itself be abrogated. Therefore, *qiyās* has no place in the theory of *naskh* since *qiyās* is weaker than the *naṣṣ* and *ijmā'*, it cannot be an abrogator. It is obvious that *naskh* applies to binding proofs, which *qiyās* is not one of them. Thus it has nothing to do with *naskh.* Logically, *ijtihād* of *mujtahids* do not abrogate each other since the *mujtahid* deserves a reward for his effort even if his *ijtihād* is incorrect. Thus two *qiyās* (analogies) which can coexist are considered as two *ijtihādī* opinions of *mujtahids* which do not necessarily abrogate one another.[23]

Differences between naskh and takhṣīṣ

The differences between abrogation (*naskh*) and specification (*takhṣīṣ*) can easily be detectable when both concept are clearly highlighted. In general the both concept resemble one another in some way qualifying or specifying the subject matter. Specification (*takhṣīṣ*) was defined briefly as limitation of the general provision to some of its subjects by an independent and joined proof,[24] while the abrogation (*naskh*) is the suspension or replacement of one *Sharī'ah* ruling by another ruling provided that the second one is of a later origin.[25] Although the both resembling one another, they differ from one another in principle. These two rulings are genuinely in conflict and that they could not coexist. *Takhṣīṣ* can occur in respect of a general ruling only whereas *naskh* can occur in respect of either a general or a specific ruling.[26]

The differences between abrogation and specification has been summarised by the Muslim scholars.[27]

1. The specification of meaning acts upon some subjects of the general provision, while abrogation acts upon all of them.

2. Abrogation can affect any legal injunction, whether that injunction is related to one subject or many, while specification can take place only when a number of subjects are involved.

3. Abrogation can occur after the abrogated text has already been implemented, while specification may not happen after what is specified has been implemented.

4. Abrogation cancels a ruling after it has been established, while specification explains the intention of the general proposition (i.e. that all subjects are not intended by the general, or that some of them are excluded.)

5. Specification explains 'what was intended' by the general, while abrogation explains that which was not intended by the abrogated.

6. Abrogation occurs on account of the authoritative texts, reason, evidences and other proofs.

7. The consensus (*ijmā'*) may be a proof for specification but not for abrogation.

8. Specification may affect only the general meanings while abrogation may affect both general and specific meanings.

9. There are several kinds of *naskh*: textual abrogation, injunction abrogation, or both, whereby *takhṣīṣ* applies only to the rulings.[28]

Subject matter of the naskh

The concept of *naskh* is not applicable to the certain subjects, namely the perspicuous (*muḥkamāt*) texts of the *Qur'ān* and *ḥadīth*, provisions pertaining to the attributes of Allah, belief in the principles of the faith, belief in the hereafter and the doctrine of *tawhīd* (oneness of Allah). Similarly, the subject matter of the *Sharī'ah* of Islam itself since it is the last of the revealed laws which can never be abrogated in its entirety.[29] Besides this, the texts of the *Qur'ān* and the *Sunnah* which relate the occurrence of certain events in the past are also not open to abrogation such as the story of the nation of Samood or 'Ad etc. which is mentioned in the *Qur'ān* "*Then as to Samood, they were destroyed by an excessively severe punishment. And as to Ad, they were destroyed by a roaring, violent blast*".[30]

The scholars are also in agreement that rational matters and moral facts, namely the virtue of doing justice or being good to one's parents, and vices such as telling lies are not open to abrogation and cannot be replaced by their opposites. For example, good cannot be turned into evil and immoral cannot be turned into a moral simply by the application of abrogation (*naskh*).[31]

The time of the naskh

The application of *naskh* to the *Qur'ān* and the *Sunnah* is confined to the life time of the Prophet (ṣ) alone. Which means, there will be no abrogation after the demise of the Prophet (ṣ) because the revelation stopped with the demise of the Prophet (ṣ). Nevertheless, *naskh* (abrogation) applies almost exclusively to the *Qur'ān* and the *Sunnah* as well as to the *ijmā'* and *qiyās*. As it is obvious that due to the different instances when some of the rulings of the *Qur'ān* and the

Sunnah were either totally or partially revoked by subsequent rulings because of the change of circumstances in the life of the community and the fact that the revelation of the *Qur'ān* extend over a period of twenty-three years. The scholars are unanimous on the occurrence of *naskh* in the *Sunnah*, but not the *Qur'ān*. There are some disagreement both in principle as well as on the number of instances in which *naskh* (abrogation) is said to have occurred.[32]

Type of the naskh

In general, *naskh* is divided into two types, explicit (*ṣarīḥ*) and implicit (*ḍimnī*). In the case of explicit abrogation, the abrogating text (*nāsikh*) clearly nullifies one ruling and substitutes another in its place. For example of explicit abrogation in the *Qur'ān* is the passage about the change in the direction of the *qiblah* from Jerusalem to the *Ka'bah*. Allah said in the *Qur'ān*: "*(O Muḥammad), indeed We see the turning of your face to heaven, so We shall surely turn you to a qiblah which you shall like; turn then your face towards the Sacred Mosque, and wherever you are, turn your face towards it, and those who have been given the Book most surely know that it is the truth from their Lord; and Allah is not at all heedless of what they do*".[33]

It is obvious that the direction of the *qiblah* is clear before and after the new ruling.

An example of explicit abrogation in the *Sunnah* is the *ḥadīth* of the Prophet (ṣ) as he said "I had forbidden you from visiting the graves. Nay, visit them, for they remind you of the hereafter".[34]

Another example, the Prophet (ṣ) is reported to have said "I had forbidden you from storing away the sacrificial meat because of the large crowds. You may now store it as you wish".[35]

The two of the *ḥadīth* of the Prophet (ṣ) indicate that the early orders were not permitted neither visiting the graves nor storing away the sacrificial meat during the *'īd* festival (*'īd al-Adḥā*). However, later this restriction was removed as the circumstances had changed. In both *ḥadīth* we see that the texts obviously explain the nature of the two rulings before and after abrogation.

In the case of implicit abrogation, in a situation where the Lawgiver introduces a ruling which seems to be in conflict with a previous ruling and the two cannot be reconciled, while it remains somewhat doubtful whether the two rulings present a genuine case for abrogation. Thus it does not clarify all the relevant details. The following two verses may highlight this type of abrogation. As Allah permitted bequests to one's parents and relatives in *sūrah al-Baqarah* "*Bequest is prescribed for you when death approaches one of you, if he leaves behind wealth for parents and near relatives, according to usage, a duty (obligatory) upon those who guard (against evil)*".[36]

This verse indicates that if death approaches anyone, it is obligatory on him to make bequest (الْوَصِيَّةُ) to relatives. However, the following verse in *sūrah al-Nisā'* "*Allah enjoins you concerning your children: The male shall have the equal of the portion of two females; then if they are more than two females, they shall have two-thirds of what the deceased has left, and if there is one, she shall have the half; and as for his parents, each of them shall have the sixth of what he has left if he has a child...*".[37]

The above verse which entitled the legal heirs to specific shares in inheritance. When these two verses are taken into consideration, they are not completely opposed to one another, yet they may be both used in certain cases.[38] Nevertheless, the later abrogates the earlier as the majority of scholars have held that the ruling of making bequest to relatives has been abrogated by the new rules of inheritance which is supported by a *ḥadīth* of the Prophet (ṣ) which is reported to have said "Allah has assigned a portion to all who are entitled. Hence there shall be no bequest to legal heirs."[39] It is because of that making bequest to legal heirs is seen as a principal source of such interference is completely prohibited.[40]

The implicit abrogation is considered further in two sub-division namely total abrogation (*naskh kullī*) and partial abrogation (*naskh juzī*).

In the case of the total abrogation (*naskh kullī*), the whole of a particular *naṣṣ* is abrogated by another one and the ruling of the new one is enacted to replace it as a new ruling. This type of abrogation may be illustrated by *sūrah al-Baqarah* (*Qur'ān* 2:240) "*And those of you who die and leave wives behind, (make) a bequest in favour of their wives of maintenance for a year without turning (them) out, then if they themselves go away, there is no blame on you for what they do of lawful deeds by themselves, and Allah is Mighty, Wise*".

Concerning the waiting period (*'iddah*) of widows, which was initially prescribed to be one year but was subsequently changed to four months and ten days by the *sūrah al-Baqarah* (*Qur'ān* 2:234) "*And (as for) those of you who die and leave wives behind, they should keep themselves in waiting for four months and ten days; then when they have fully attained their term, there is no blame on you for what they do for themselves in a lawful manner; and Allah is aware of what you do*".

These two verse, as if, contradict to each other since the provision concerning the waiting period of widows in the first *āyah* has been totally replaced by the new ruling in the second. Although the both of these rulings are exclusively concerned with the same subject, namely, the widows, only one of them must be observed. Therefore, the latter abrogates the former. This may be similar to that of an implicit *naskh*, however, the difference is the certainty of conflict because there is no reference to either maintenance or residence in the second *āyah* which may introduce an element of doubt concerning the maintenance and the *'iddah*.[41]

Partial abrogation (*naskh juz'ī*) is a form of *naskh* in which some part of the text is abrogated while the other part of it remains to be operative. As it may be explained in the following verse of the *Qur'ān* regarding *qadhf* (slanderous accusation). Allah says in *sūrah al-Nūr* "*And those who accuse free women [of adultery] and then do not bring four witnesses, flog them, (giving) eighty stripes, and do not admit any evidence from them ever; and these it is that are the transgressors"*.[42]

This verse indicates that anyone be it a spouse or otherwise, who accuses chaste women of adultery (*zinā*) must produce four witnesses for proof, otherwise, will be punished. However, another verse in the same *sūrah* "*And (as for) those who accuse their wives and have no witnesses except themselves, the evidence of one of these (should be taken) four times, bearing Allah to witness that he is most surely of the truthful ones*".[43]

The verse which indicates that if the accuser happens to be a spouse who cannot provide four witnesses and yet insists on pursuing the charge of adultery (*zinā*), he may take four solemn oaths to take the place of four witnesses. Thus the second verse abrogates the ruling of the first text. The following verse (*Qur'ān* 24:7 and 8) lay down ruling which the husband invokes the curse of Allah upon himself if he tells a lie "*And the fifth (time) that the curse of Allah be on him if he is one of the liars*", and "*And it shall avert the chastisement from her if she testify four times, bearing Allah to witness that he is most surely one of the liars*". According to these verses, her punishment is partially revoked by the verse of imprecation (*li'ān*) which make their marriage null and void.[44]

Once again the abrogation (*naskh*) has been classified into three types. Briefly it is better to highlight here that the text of the *Qur'ān* has two distinctive features, namely: these are the words of the text, and the ruling (*ḥukm*) that is legal inference. Despite its ruling is abrogated, reading and reciting the words of the *Qur'ān* is still valid, which has spiritual value. Since the words are still regarded as part of the *Qur'ān*, reciting it within the prayer (*ṣalāt*) is permissible because only the ruling (*ḥukm*) of it abrogated not the text of the *Qur'ān*.

The first type is abrogation of the ruling (*naskh al-ḥukm*). It is an abrogation that the ruling alone is abrogated while the words of the text are remained. Such as the examples that are given previously in the context of general *naskh* in the *Qur'ān* fall into this category, namely the words of the text in the *Qur'ān* concerning bequests to relatives (*al-Baqarah* 2:180) and the one concerning the waiting period (*'iddah*) of widows (*al-Baqarah*, 2: 240) are still a part of the *Qur'ān* and we still recite them but not apply the law that they carry despite the fact that these have been both abrogated.

The second type is *naskh al-tilāwah* (or *naskh al-qirā'ah*) which means abrogation of the words of the text while the ruling is retained. For example, a report attributed to *'Umar bin al-Khaṭṭāb* that there was a passage which is a part of the *Qur'ān* despite the passage in question does not appear in the ordinary text. The reported version of this text is "When a married man or a married woman commits adultery (*zinā*), their punishment shall be stoning as a retribution ordained by Allah".

Accordingly *'Umar bin al-Khaṭṭāb* is quoted to have added: "Had it not been for fear of people saying that 'Umar made an addition to the *Qur'ān*, I would have added this to the text of the *Qur'ān*."[45] Although the ruling conveyed by the passage in question still represents authoritative law.

The third type is *naskh al-ḥukm wa al-tilāwah*, which means abrogation of both the words and the ruling. This type is rare and the examples of it is not supported by definite proof. Although the scholars are generally in agreement on the occurrence of abrogation in the last two forms, minority of *Mu'tazilī* scholars are exceptional.[46]

Due to the disagreement among the scholars and perception of them on the abrogation of the *Qur'ān* and the *Sunnah*, once again it is considered into four types:

Firstly, abrogation of the *Qur'ān* by the *Qur'ān*, which has already been illustrated earlier while the case was explored by the explicit abrogation in the *Qur'ān* about the change of the direction of the *qiblah* from Jerusalem to the *Ka'bah* as Allah said in the *Qur'ān* in *sūrah al-Baqarah* (*Qur'ān* 2:144); in the case of bequests that was permitted in *sūrah al-Baqarah Qur'ān* 2:180 and *Qur'ān* 4:11; concerning the waiting period (*'iddah*) of widows in *sūrah al-Baqarah* (*Qur'ān* 2:240) and the *sūrah al-Baqarah* (*Qur'ān* 2:234); regarding the *qadhf* (slanderous accusation) in the *Qur'ān sūrah al-Noor* (*Qur'ān* 24:4-6 and 7-8).

Secondly, abrogation of the *Sunnah* by the *Sunnah*, which has also been illustrated above by the two *aḥādīth* which we quoted under the title of explicit abrogation in regards to the prohibition of visiting the graves and storing away the sacrificial meat during the *'īd* festival (*'īd al-Aḍḥā*).

Thirdly, abrogation of the *Qur'ān* by the *Sunnah* which may be illustrated by the case of permitted bequests to one's parents and relatives in *sūrah al-Baqarah* "*Bequest is prescribed for you when death approaches one of you, if he leaves behind wealth for parents and near relatives, according to usage, a duty (obligatory) upon those who guard (against evil)*".[47]

This verse has been abrogated by the ḥadīth which provides that "Allah had given to everyone his due, therefore there shall be no bequest to an heir".[48]

Since then, according to the general agreement that the *Qur'ān* itself does not abrogate the *āyah* of bequest which remains little doubt that it has been abrogated by the *Sunnah.*[49]

Fourthly, abrogation of the *Sunnah* by the *Qur'ān* which may be illustrated by the case of changing the initial ruling of the Prophet (ṣ) on the practice of the *qiblah* towards the direction of Jerusalem (*Quds*) which was later revoked by the *Qur'ān* in *sūrah al-Baqarah* (*Qur'ān* 2:144) ordering the Muslims to turn their faces toward the *Ka'bah*, the holy mosque of the Muslims.[50]

In regards to the last divisions of the abrogation, Imām Shāfi'ī and the majority of the *Mu'tazilah*, and Aḥmad bin Ḥanbal who have validated the first two divisions of abrogation, but negated the validity of the last two saying that abrogation of the *Qur'ān* by the *Sunnah* and vice versa is not valid and therefore, Imām Shāfi'ī explored his view by providing a number of verses from the *Qur'ān* in *sūrah al-Naḥl* (*Qur'ān* 16:101)[51] and in *sūrah al-Baqarah* (*Qur'ān* 2:106)[52] indicated that the *Qur'ān* can only be abrogated by the *Qur'ān* itself.[53]

According to Imām Shāfi'ī the abrogation (*naskh*) in the *Qur'ān* is a completely internal phenomenon, and there is no evidence in the *Qur'ān* to suggest otherwise, which means the *Qur'ān* precludes the possibility of it being abrogated by the *Sunnah*.

Conditions of abrogation (naskh)

The Muslim scholars have structured certain conditions for the realization of abrogation (*naskh*), therefore no abrogation can happen unless the following conditions are fulfilled.

First, it is necessary that the abrogating (*nāsikh*) text must be a later origin than the potential abrogated (*mansūkh*) text.

Second, that the two texts, which may be considered under the concept of *naskh*, must be openly in conflict and there is no way can they be reconciled with one another.

Third, that the two texts must be equal strength in regard to meaning (*dalālah*) and authenticity (*thubūt*).

Fourth, that the verse of the *Qur'ān* or the text of the *Sunnah* must not be excluded the possibility of abrogation. For example a text from the *Qur'ān*[54] regarding a person who is convicted of slanderous accusation (*qadhf*) that he/she may never be admitted as witnesses. Another example from the *Sunnah* is the *ḥadīth* which decrees that "*jihād* shall remain valid till the day of resurrection," obviously excludes the possibility of abrogating the permanent validity of *jihād*, because the duty of *jihād* is an obligatory until the day of judgement for all who is eligible.[55]

Fifth, that the two text must be differentiated from whether specification (*takhṣīṣ*), or qualification (*taqyīd*) rather than abrogation. It has to be clarified that the issue is not related to the condition (*sharṭ*), qualification (*waṣf*) or exception (*istithnā'*) of the specification (*takhṣīṣ*) since the two subjects, abrogation (*naskh*) and specification (*takhṣīṣ*) are not the same.

Lastly, that the subject matter must be open to the possibility of abrogation, such as the principles of belief, the attributes of Allah, rational truths and moral virtues etc. are not open to abrogation and thus cannot any such matters be considered.[56]

Conclusion

The *naskh* was, in general, applied to the definite rulings of the divine revelation by the *Qur'ān* and the *Sunnah* which ultimately ended with the demise of the Prophet (ṣ) and therefore, no more *naskh* can be applied afterwards.

The abrogating (*al-nāsikh*) and the abrogated (*al-mansūkh*) portions of the text is determined by the chronological order in the revelation of the relevant verses which is based on the general principle that the later abrogates the former. Thus studying the knowledge of the verses historically as the *Makkī* and *Madanī* is essential in which these knowledge facilitate a better understanding of the features of the text either from the *Qur'ān* or the *Sunnah.*

Ta'āruḍ al-Adillah (Conflict of Evidences)

Introduction

The concept of conflict of evidences is as essential as other tools of the principles of Islamic law to comprehend the ways that the rulings are derived from the sources. It explores circumstances in which the conflict occurs and accordingly it grands priorities among the proofs, evidences, and sources. For example, conflict (*ta'āruḍ*) arises only when two evidences are in equal strength. Therefore, no conflict could arise between unequal two evidences. It is because the stronger of the two evidences would naturally prevail over the weaker one.

Linguistically, the word *ta'āruḍ* is derived from an Arabic word *'urḍ* which means a side, a course and a direction. For example, if a word prevents the meaning of another, then it is articulated as *muta'āriḍ kalām* in Arabic.[57] Technically, scholars have defined it as a conflict of evidences. For example, if two evidences of equal strength require the opposite of each other, then conflict occurs.[58] Basically, *ta'āruḍ* means conflict. It is sometimes used in the terminology of *uṣūl al-fiqh* more than one terms such as *tanāqud*, *ta'ādul*, etc. The *ta'āruḍ* (conflict) happens whenever what is implied by one piece of evidence is opposed by another for one reason or another.[59] It occurs when two pieces of evidences of equal strength require two contrary rulings to be applied to the same case at the same time.[60] If any contradiction of evidences happen in the science of *uṣūl al-fiqh*, the *ta'āruḍ* term is used as a common practice. Similarly the phrase '*ta'āruḍ al-bayyināt* (conflict of pieces of evidences) means that one piece of the evidence opposes the other which makes both pieces inapplicable[61] which concurrently application of the two evidences become impossible. Besides the above explanation, there are different definitions of *ta'āruḍ*, however, the literal meaning of it remains appropriate to a common and central point of it.

Place of the Conflict of Evidences:

Some scholars tend to confine *ta'āruḍ* to the conflict that arises only between two speculative evidences (*amārah*) instead of between two definitive (*qaṭ'ī*) evidences (*dalīl*).[62] *Ḥanafīs*, however, on the view that *ta'āruḍ* comes to exist when one of the two *dalīl* or *ḥujjah* of equal strength contradicts what is inferred by the other in cases such as an opposition between permissibility and prohibition on the one hand and between affirmation (*ithbāt*) and negation (*nafī*) on the other hand at the same time.[63] If, however, each of the two evidences are not equal strength, no conflict (*ta'āruḍ*) would arise because the stronger one would naturally prevails over the weaker one. Therefore, there is no conflict would arise between a definitive (*qaṭ'ī*) and a speculative (*ẓannī*) evidence, nor could there be a conflict between the *naṣṣ* and *ijmā'*, nor between *ijmā'* and *qiyās* since these evidences are not equal strength, some of them stronger than the others. Eventually, a conflict may be encountered between two pieces of evidences of equal strength such as between the two texts of the *Qur'ān* or between two rulings of *ḥadīth*, or between a *Qur'anic* ayah and a *mutawātir ḥadīth* (recurrent tradition), or between two non-*mutawātir ḥadīth*, or between two rulings of analogy (*qiyās*). In addition to these qualities, the strength of two conflicting evidences is determined by reference to the evidence itself or to the additional factors which might provide the balance in favour of the one over the other because of the extraneous factor such as the quality of the narrator. If, for example, one of the two solitary (*āḥād*) *ḥadīth* is narrated by a *faqīh* (jurist) is considered stronger than the one which is narrated by non-*faqīh*.[64]

The essential point that should be highlighted here is that the evidences are contradicting each other, cannot be reconciled, the subject matter of one cannot be distinguished from the other, and nor can they be so distinguished in respect of the time of their application. However, the case of drinking alcohol does not fall into the case of *ta'āruḍ al-adillah* since the ruling of drinking wine has passed three different stage of rulings in the *Qur'ān*, one after the other. Thus, no conflict can arise among them because they are not revealed simultaneously. Additionally, once again there will be no conflict, if clearly conflicting rules are applied to the same issue under a different set of circumstances.[65]

The method to be followed in resolving conflicts:

The first attempt should be a method to find reconciliation between the two conflicting texts. In order to reconcile removing the conflict among them, the scholars must know the objectives of the Lawgiver. It has to be highlighted here that, indeed, there is no any real conflict among the divine laws since these laws were revealed by Allah for a purpose. Thus all the principles of Islamic law and the methods to derive rulings from the sources are to discover the wisdom behind them, that is, the objectives of the laws.

Mujtahids of the *Ummah* have great responsibility to find ways to solve problems. The conflicting evidences should be identified for interpretation as to limit and qualify the absolute terms of the other one. The interpretation methods, in the foregoing chapters, must be observed carefully. Thus it must be determined whether the verses are general (*'āmm*) or specific (*khāṣṣ*) etc. For example in the event where one of the two conflicting rulings is general (*'āmm*) and the other one is specific (*khāṣṣ*), they can be reconciled by preferring the latter over the former through a procedure which is known as *takhṣīṣ al-'āmm* (specifying a part of the general). If the first attempt at reconciliation fails, the next step in resolving a conflict which is to give preference to one over the other is applied. Such as specific (*khāṣṣ*) one is preferred over general (*'āmm*) one or the literal is preferred to the metaphorical, the clear (*ṣarīḥ*) to the implicit (*kināyah*), the explicit meaning (*'ibārah al-naṣṣ*) to the allusive meaning (*ishārah al-naṣṣ*), and the latter is preferred to the inferred meaning of the text (*dalālah al-naṣṣ*). In terms of clarity of indication of the words, the greater clarity words are to be preferred to those which are less clear, such as the *muḥkam* (perspicuous) is preferred to the *mufassar* (unequivocal), the latter to the *naṣṣ* (explicit) and the *naṣṣ* to the *ẓāhir* (manifest). Similarly, unclear words, the *khafī* (obscure) takes priority over the *mushkil* (difficult), the latter over the *mujmal* (ambivalent) and the *mujmal* over the *mutashābih* (intricate) etc. Thus the rules of interpretation must be taken into consideration.

At least, if there is no any way for reconciliation then the *mujtahid* should provide his effort and discretion to prefer one over the other one. The concept of abrogation that is the final method may be applied if the effort given by the *mujtahid* is not appropriated in his situation. Nevertheless, if the final method does not also solve the problem of the conflict, then the matter should be suspended for future investigation.[66]

Resolving conflicts among the nuṣūṣ (texts):

Based on the foregoing explanation, scholars have identified the way of resolving conflicts among the *nuṣūṣ* (texts). Indeed, it may be illustrated with the precise duration of the waiting (*'iddah*) period of widows. For example, when the following two verses taken into consideration, it seems to be that here is a conflict between them. According to the verse in *sūrah al-Baqarah* "*And (as for) those of you who die and leave wives behind, they should keep themselves in waiting for four months and ten days; then when they have fully attained their term, there is no blame on you for what they do for themselves in a lawful manner; and Allah is aware of what you do*".[67]

The widow must observe a waiting (*'iddah*) of four months and ten days following the death of her husband. This verse consists of a general ruling which applies to every widow regardless as to whether she is pregnant at the time her husband dies or not in one hand. However, another verse which indicates that there is a different ruling concerning the waiting (*'iddah*) of pregnant women in the *sūrah al-Ṭalāq* "*Such of your women as have passed the age of monthly courses, for them the prescribed period, if ye have any doubts, is three months, and for those who have no courses (it is the same): for those who carry (life within their wombs), their period is until they deliver their burdens: and for those who fear Allah, He will make their path easy*".[68]

This verse also carries a general ruling to the effect that the waiting period (*'iddah*) of pregnant women continues until the delivery of the child. However, she should still wait for four months and ten days according to the first ruling. Therefore, the two texts thus appear to be in conflict regarding the *'iddah* of a pregnant widow. The conflict here seems to be no genuine and can be easily reconciled which can also be both implemented under different circumstances. Thus, the conflict would accordingly not arise and there would be no case for abrogation. The prescribed *'iddah* of widows in the first verse is to be four months and ten days, while the second enacted the *'iddah* of pregnant women is until the termination of pregnancy. The two verses could be reconciled according to the longer period, which means if the pregnant widow delivers her child before the expiry of four months and ten days following the death of her husband, then she should wait until this period expires. However, if she waits four months and ten days and she has still not delivered the child, then her waiting period (*'iddah*) should continue until the birth of the child. As it is clear that the apparent conflict between the two verses is removed by recourse to specification (*takhṣīṣ*) which means the second verse specifies the first verse.[69]

In order to reconcile two evidences, the evidences should be identified in terms of their situation whether they are general (*'āmm*) or specific (*khāṣṣ*) etc. For example in the event where one of the two conflicting rulings is general (*'āmm*) and the other one is specific (*khāṣṣ*), they can be reconciled by preferring the latter over the former through a procedure which is known as *takhṣīṣ al-'āmm* (specifying a part of the general).

In terms of conflicting evidences among the *aḥādīth*, it is clear that the *mutawātir* (successive narration) is preferred to the *mashūr* (famous narration) and the *mashhūr* takes priority over the solitary *ḥadīth* (*āḥād ḥadīth*), as well as a *ḥadīth* narrated by a jurists (*faqīh*) is preferred over a *ḥadīth* narrated by a non-jurists, a narration by a person who is known to be retentive of memory is preferred over those which are transmitted by persons whose retentiveness is unclear. Similarly, a *ḥadīth* that is transmitted by leading Companions are given preference to those transmitted by Companions who are less well known for their prominence and continuity of contact with the Prophet (ṣ). The report of a narrator who is directly involved in an incident is preferable to other reports. Such as the report of Maymūnah who is the wife of the Prophet (ṣ) is preferred to the narration of Ibn 'Abbās.[70] The *ḥadīth* which is reported by Maymūnah to the effect that the Prophet (ṣ) married her while both of them were not in the state of *iḥrām*, in contrary to the report of Ibn *'Abbās* that the Prophet (ṣ) married her while he was in the sacred state of *iḥrām*.[71]

Additionally, the school of *Mālikīs* prefer a *ḥadīth* that is in agreement with the practice of the people of *Madinah* over one which is not, while the school of *Ḥanafīs* consider the action of the transmitter upon his own narration to be a supportive factor which adds to the strength of a *ḥadīth*. A *ḥadīth* which is supported by a more reliable chain of narration is preferred to a *ḥadīth* which is weak in its proof of authenticity. The scholars of *ḥadīth* (*Muhaddithīn*) are in agreement that a *ḥadīth* which is reported by all the six scholars of *ḥadīth*, namely al-Bukhārī, Muslim, al-Tirmīdhī, al-Nasā'ī, Ibn Mājah and Abū Dāwud, take priority over that which might have been reported only by some and not all of these authorities. Additionally, al-Bukhārī is preferred to Muslim if there is any conflict occurs between them. Similarly, these two scholars are preferred to the rest of the scholars if any conflict occurs among them.[72]

Additionally, if there are two conflicting rules of equal strength on the same issue, one indicates prohibition and the other one permissibility, the former will take priority over the latter because prohibition has priority over permissibility. Despite the fact that *mujtahid* may depart from this rule to another rule which brings ease based on the maxim that hardship begets ease.[73]

In a situation where the solution cannot be found, and reconciliation is not successful between two rulings of the *Qur'ān*, there is still a way for solution. In this case, *Mujtahid* may depart from both and determine the matter with reference to the *Sunnah* which the process continues towards descending order such as towards to *fatwā* of the Companions, and *qiyās*. If, however, still the *mujtahid* fails to find a solution among any of the descending categories of proofs, he may recourse to the general norms of *Sharī'ah* which may be applicable to the case. In spite of the deadlock, *mujtahid* must give his highest effort to find alternative solutions. The effort of the *mujtahid* may be demonstrated in the case of recitation of the portion of the *Qur'ān* in congregational prayers. A conflict arose in this matter whether whether in a congregational prayers, the congregation member (*muqtaḍī*), is required to recite the *sūra al-Fātiḥah* following the recitation of the *imām*, or whether he should keep on silent. As Allah indicates in *sūrah al-A'rāf* "*And when the Qur'ān is recited, then listen to it and remain silent, that mercy may be shown to you*".[74]

As well as in sūrah al-Muzammil "therefore recite what is easy of the *Qur'ān*".[75]

These two verses seem to be conflicting each other since the first one appears to be that the congregation member (*muqtaḍī*) should remain silent whereas the second one indicates that everyone, both the *imām* and the *muqtaḍī*, is ordered to recite what is easy for them. These two verses appear to be in conflict with regard to the position of the *muqtaḍī*, although neither of the two texts make a particular reference to *ṣalāt*. No an additional evidence could be found from the *Qur'ān* to enable the preference of one to the other. The case remained unreconciled. Thus it is suspended on both and the case is determined with reference to the *Sunnah*. According to the practice of the Prophet (ṣ), he instructed the congregation member (*muqtaḍī*) not to recite the *Qur'ān* behind the *imām*. It is, therefore, reported that on one occasion when the Prophet (ṣ) led the *ṣalāt*, he asked the members of the congregation whether they recited the *Qur'ān* with him, and having heard their answers, he instructed them not to recite the *Qur'ān* behind the *imām*. Despite the fact that the leaders of the schools of thought such as Abū Ḥanīfah, Mālik, Ibn Ḥanbal, and al-Shāfi'ī went on different opinions. Although the *Ḥanafī* jurists have held the view that it is not necessary for the congregation member (*muqtaḍī*) to recite the *Qur'ān* behind the *imām* neither he recites the *Qur'ān* aloud nor quietly, *al-Shāfi'īs*, on the other hand, have held that it is necessary for the congregation member (*muqtaḍi*) to recite *al-Fātiḥah* behind the *imām* when he recites quietly but not when he recites the *Qur'ān* aloud.[76]

Resolving conflicts through recourse to the Companions and the ijmāʿ

At the outset of resolving conflicts through recourse to the *ijmāʿ*, it has to be emphasised that no matter of conflict between the two texts, either *Qur'ān* or the *Sunnah* and *ijmāʿ* can be accepted due to the obvious reason that no *ijmāʿ* can be determined which is contrary to the *Qur'ān* and the *Sunnah*. A preference is not given over the any sources other than the texts in a situation where a conflict arises between two *qiyās* (analogies) or other sources of Islamic law and no reconciliation can happen. It is however finally suspended. An alternative course of action such as abrogation is also irrelevant to *ijmāʿ* and it is not possible to apply abrogation in cases of conflict between speculative evidences here since the scope of abrogation is confined to the definitive rulings of the *Qur'ān* and *Sunnah* alone.[77]

This type of conflict can be highlighted by an example which an apparent conflict between the two reports regarding the way that the Prophet (ṣ) performed the *ṣalāt al-kusūf* (prayer offered on the occasion of a solar eclipse). According to one of the reports that the Prophet (ṣ) offered the two *rakʿat* (units) which contained three bowing, and three prostrations, while another report indicates that the Prophet (ṣ) offered two *rakʿat* of *ṣalāt* which each of them is consisting of two bowings (*rukūʿ*) and two prostration, (*sajdah*). However, there is yet another report the Prophet (ṣ) offered *ṣalāt* (prayer) which each of the two units contained four bowings and four prostrations.[78] These reports apparently indicate that there is a conflict among them. Therefore, the conflicting contents of these reports have to be removed either through reconciliation or abrogation or preference over the other one. However, it can neither be reconciled nor be abrogated and nor be given preference one over the other. For this reason, all the action must be suspended and the conflict can be removed by determining it by analogy (*qiyās*) on the ground that if an issue cannot be determined by reference to the

Sunnah, nor be solved by the rulings (*fatāwā*) of the Companions. As in the case of *ṣalāt al-kusūf* which has variety of *ṣalāt*, the normal rules of *ṣalāt* can be applied to it. Knowing that all obligatory *ṣalāt*, which contains one bowing and two prostrations, may also be extended to *ṣalāt al-kusūf* by way of analogy.[79]

Resolving conflicts among the qiyās (analogy)

The resolving conflicts among the sources may be extended to the analogical reasoning (*qiyās*). In the event where a conflict may arise between two analogies, the stronger one would be preferred over the weaker one based on the effective cause (*'illah*) such as the *qiyās* whose effective cause (*'illah*) is stated in an explicit text is to be preferred to the one whose *'illah* has been derived through inference (*istinbāṭ*) because the explicit text naturally is preferred over the implicit or one which is derived via inference. Likewise, an analogy whose effective cause is founded in an allusive text (*ishārah al-naṣṣ*) is preferred to analogy whose effective cause is simply a reasonable attribute which may be derived through inference and *ijtihād*. However, if the effective cause (*'illah*) is explicitly stated in the text or the result of an analogy is maintained by consensus (*ijmā'*) then no conflict would arise in this situation.[80]

Differently, in an event where a conflict arise between two analogies which both of them are founded on an inferred effective cause, the *mujtahid* may give his own opinion even if two different *mujtahids* have different conclusions with regard to the identification of an effective cause due to the types of effective cause which involves a measure of speculative reasoning and *ijtihād*. Therefore, the opinions of scholars and their conclusion may be different because of different effective cause such as the *'illah* of compulsory guardianship (*wilāyah al-ijbār*) in the marriage of a minor girl. Imām Shāfi'ī considers the *'illah* to be her virginity whereas Imām Abū Ḥanīfah considers the *'illah* of the guardian's power of *ijbār* in marriage to be the minority of the ward. The ruling of the scholars on this matter may be different due to the different effective cause that they may assume. In such situation, it is for the *mujtahid* to choose the one that seems good to him even if there is no basis for such preference other than his own personal opinion and therefore, none of the two conflicting analogies can be preferred to another one.[81]

In conclusion, since the scholars of Islam, *mujtahids* of the *Ummah*, have upheld the responsibility of solving problems of the *Ummah*, they must find ways to solve them. Problems may occur due to the conflicting evidences, for this reason, firstly the conflicting evidences should be identified for interpretation as to limit and qualify or prefer one to other by acceptable reasons. The interpretation methods, therefore, must be carefully comprehended to determine the situation of the verses. To remove the conflicts or to find a way for reconciliation between the two conflicting sources, scholars must also know the objectives of the Lawgiver (*maqāṣid al-sharī'ah*). As it is mentioned above if there is no any way for reconciliation then the *mujtahid* should provide his effort and discretion to prefer one over the other one. The concept of abrogation and requirements for suspension should also be taken into consideration.

However, in a case where none of the foregoing methods can be applied in order to determine the ruling of the issue, then the *mujtahid* may base his own decision on the original norms of the *Sharī'ah* based on the basic objectives of the Lawgiver.

Notes

[1] Abū 'Ubaid al-Qāṣim b. Sallām, *Al-Nāsikh wal-Mansūkh fī al-Qur'ān al-'Azīz wamā fihi min al-Farā'id wal-Sunan*, edited by Muḥammad al-Muḍaifar, (Riyadh: Maktabat al-Rushd, 1990), p. 4, qf. Louay Fatoohi, *Abrogation in the Qur'ān and Islamic Law, A Critical Study of the Concept of Naskh and its Impact*, (Selangor: IBT, 2013), p. 2.

[2] 'Abd Allah al-Dārimī, *Musnad al-Dārimī*, edited by Ḥusain al-Dārānī, (Riyadh:

Dār al-Maghnī lil-Nashr wal-Tawzī', 2000), I, no. 178, p. 272-273.

[3] Aḥmad b. Muḥammad al-Naḥḥās, *Al-Nāsikh wal-Mansūkh fī Kitāb Allah 'Azza wa-Jall wa-Ikhtilāf al-'Ulāma' fī dhālik*, edited by Sulaiman al-Lahim, (Beirut: Mu'assasat al-Risālah, 1991), v. 2, p. 410.

[4] *Qur'ān* 2:269

[5] al-Naḥḥās, *ibid.*, v. 2, p. 411.

[6] Jalāl al-Dīn al-Suyūṭī, *Al-Itqān fī 'Ulūm al-Qur'ān*, edited by Markaz al-Dirāsat al-Islāmiyyah, (Madinah: Mujamma' al-Malik Fahad li-Ṭibā'at al-Muṣḥaf al-Sharīf, 2005), v. 4, p. 1435.

[7] *Qur'ān* 2:106

[8] *Qur'ān* 2:107

[9] Al-Khalīl b. Aḥmad al-Farāḥidī, *Kitāb al-'Ain*, edited by 'Abd al-Ḥamīd Hindāwī, (Beirut: Dār al-Kutub al-'Ilmiyyah, 2003), v. 4, p. 215

[10] Louay Fatoohi, *Abrogation in the Qur'ān and Islamic Law, A Critical Study of the Concept of Naskh and its Impact*, (Selangor: IBT, 2013), p. 17.

[11] *Qur'ān* 45:29.

[12] Kamali, *Principles*, p. 149; Louay Fatoohi, *Abrogation*, p. 18; Āmidī, *Aḥkām*, v. 3, p. 102; Hitu, *Wajīz*, p. 241; Ghazālī, *Mustaṣfā*, v. 1, p. 69.

[13] Louay Fatoohi, *ibid.*, p. 36.

[14] Badrān, *Uṣūl*, p. 442

[15] Shāfi'ī, *Risālah*, p. 103, Abū Zahrah, *Uṣūl*, p. 148

[16] Kamali, *Principles*, p. 152.

[17] Shāṭibī, *al-Muwāfaqāt*, v.3, p. 63; Badrān, *Uṣūl*, p. 447.

[18] Shāfi'ī, *Risālah*, p. 54; Āmidī, *Iḥkām*, v. 3, p. 146 onward.

[19] Khallāf, *'Ilm*, p. 228

[20] Tāj, *Siyāsah*, p.14

[21] *Qur'ān* 9:60

[22] Badrān, *Uṣūl*, p. 458-459.

[23] Āmidī, *Iḥkām*, v. 3, p. 163; Badrān, *Uṣūl*, p. 459

[24] Bukhārī, *Kashf al-Asrār*, v. 1, p. 37; Bādshāh, *Taysīr al-Taḥrīr*, v. 1, p. 271; Mayhawī, *Sharḥ Nūr al-Anwār*, v. 1, p. 169.

[25] Badrān, *Uṣūl*, p. 442

[26] Ghazālī, *Mustaṣfā*, v. 1, p. 71; Badrān, *Uṣūl*, p. 452

[27] Baṣrī, *al-Mu'tamad*, v. 1, p. 251-252; Shawkānī, *Irshād al-Fuḥūl*, p. 125-126.

[28] Sukrija Husejn Ramic, *ibid.*, p. 161.

[29] Ghazālī, *Mustaṣfā*, v. 1, p. 72

[30] *Qur'ān* 69:5-6

[31] Badrān, *Uṣūl*, p. 454; Hitu, *Wajīz*, p. 244.

[32] Kamali, *Principles*, p. 150; Khallāf, *'Ilm*, p. 222; Abū Zahrah, *Uṣūl*, p. 148

[33] *Qur'ān* 2:144

[34] Tirmidhī, *Janāiz* 60; *Ṭabrīzī, Mishkāt*, v.1, p. 552, *ḥadīth* no. 1762; Muslim, *Ṣaḥīḥ*, p. 340

[35] Ghazālī, *Mustaṣfā*, v. 1, p. 83. Āmidī, *Iḥkām*, v. 3, p. 181.

[36] *Qur'ān* 2:180

[37] *Qur'ān* 4:11

[38] Shāfi'ī, *Risālah*, p. 69

[39] Abū Dāwud, *Sunan*, II, 808, *ḥadīth* no. 2864

[40] Shāfi'ī, *Risālah*, p. 69; Khallāf, *'Ilm*, p. 224; Kamali, *Principles*, p. 155

[41] Kamali, *Principles*, p. 156

[42] *Qur'ān* 24:4

[43] *Qur'ān* 24:6

[44] Shāfi'ī, *Risālah*, p. 72; Khallāf, *'Ilm*, p. 227

[45] Ghazālī, *Mustaṣfā*, v. 1, p. 80; Āmidī, *Iḥkām*, v. 3, p. 141.

[46] Āmidī, *Iḥkām*, v. 3, p. 141

[47] *Qur'ān* 2:180

[48] Tirmidhī, Book of inheritance, 6:258 no: 2203, *ḥadīth ṣaḥīḥ*

[49] Hitu, *Wajīz*, p. 252. See also Qadrī, *Islamic Jurisprudence*, p. 230; Kamali, *Principles*, p. 156

[50] Hitu, *Wajīz*, p. 252; Qadrī, *Islamic Jurisprudence*, p. 230.

[51] *Qur'ān* in *sūrah al-Naḥl* (16:101) "And when We substitute one ayah in place of another ayah [*āyatun makāna āyatin*], and Allah knows best what He reveals".

[52] *Qur'ān* in *sūrah al-Baqarah* (2:106) "None of our revelations do We abrogate [*mā nansakh min āyatin*] or cause to be forgotten unless We substitute for them something better or similar".

[53] Shāfi'ī, *Risālah*, p. 54; Āmidī, *Iḥkām*, v. 3, p. 153-156

[54] *Qur'ān* 24:4

[55] Dāwud, *Sunan*, II, 702, *ḥadīth* no. 2526; Abū Zahrah, *Uṣūl*, p. 150

[56] Hitu, *Wajīz*, p. 244; Khallāf, *'Ilm*, p. 223.

[57] Shawkānī, *Irshād*, p. 241.

[58] Sarakhsī, *Uṣūl*, v. 2, p. 12

[59] Ibn Qudāmah al-Magdisī, Muwaffaq al-Dīn 'Abdallah b. Aḥmad, *Rawḍah an-Nāẓir wa Jannat al-Manāẓir fī Uṣūl, al-Figh 'ala Madhhab al-Imām Aḥmad b. Ḥanbal*, (Beirut: Dār al-Nadwah al-Jadīdah, n. d.), p. 208; Sarakhsī, *Uṣūl*, v. 2, p. 12

[60] *Ibid.*

[61] Ma'ṣumī, Ṣaghīr Ḥasan, Imām Taḥawī's Ikhtilāf al-Fuqahā', *Islamic Studies*, vol. 8, 1969, p. 199; Ma'ṣumī, Disagreement of the *Ṣaḥāba* and Early Jurists, *Hamdard Islamicus*, v. 3, 1979, p. 15-42.

[62] Isnawī, *Nihāyat al-Sūl fī Sharḥ Minhāj al-Wuṣūl fī 'Ilm al-Uṣūl*, 1st ed., Dār al-Kutub al-'Ilmiyyah, Beirut, 1984), v. 3, p. 211; Ghazālī, *al-Mustaṣfā*, v. 2, p. 393; Shawkānī, *Irshād*, p. 273.

[63] Sarakhsī, *Uṣūl*, v. 2, p. 12; *Kashf*, v. 3, p. 77; *al-Taqrīr*, v. 3, p. 2; see in Mohd. Daud Bakar, "*Conflict*," p. 51,

[64] Badrān, *Uṣūl*, p. 461; Khuḍarī, *Uṣūl*, p. 359; Kamali, *Principles*, p. 356.

[65] Kamali, *Principles*, p. 357

[66] Khallāf, *'Ilm*, p. 229; Khuḍarī, *Uṣūl*, p. 359

[67] *Qur'ān* 2:234

[68] *Qur'ān* 65:4

[69] Abū Zahrah, *Uṣūl*, p. 245; Badrān, *Uṣūl*, p. 467; Khallāf, *'Ilm*, p. 231

[70] A Narration from Ibn 'Abbās "The Prophet (ṣ)

got married while he was in the state of *iḥrām*. *Ṣaḥīḥ al-Bukhārī*, v. 7, Book 62, no. 49, and A Narration from Maymūnah that Yazīd ibn al-'Āṣam reported from Maymūna daughter of al-Ḥārith narrated to me that Allah's Messenger (pubh) married her and he was not in the state of *iḥrām*. And she (Maymūnah) was my mother's sister and that of Ibn 'Abbās. *Ṣaḥīḥ Muslim*, Book 008, no. 3285.

[71] Abū Dāwud, *Sunan*, II, 486-87, *ḥadīth*, no. 1839 and 1840; Ghazālī, *al-Mustaṣfā*, v. 2, p. 128; Khuḍarī, *Uṣūl*, p. 367.

[72] Abū Zahrah, *Uṣūl*, p. 246; Kamali, *Principles*, p. 361-362.

[73] Khallāf, *'Ilm*, p. 232; Badrān, *Uṣūl*, p. 470; Khuḍarī, *Uṣūl*, p. 367.

[74] *Qur'ān* 7:204.

[75] *Qur'ān* 73:20.

[76] Abū Dāwud, *Sunan*, II, 211, *ḥadīth* no. 825; Badrān, *Uṣūl*, p. 468-69; Khuḍarī, *Uṣūl*, p. 359.

[77] Kamali, *Principle*, p. 357.

[78] Abū Dāwud, *Sunan*, I, 304, *ḥadīth* no: 1173-7

[79] Badrān, *Uṣūl*, p. 469.

[80] Khallāf, *'Ilm*, p. 232; Badrān, *Uṣūl*, p. 470.

[81] Abū Zahrah, *Uṣūl*, p. 247-48; Khuḍarī, *Uṣūl*, p. 360.

Glossary

Adillah (pl. of *dalīl*): proofs, evidences, indication

Adillah al-sharī'ah: proofs of Islamic law

Adā': execution or performance

Af'āl: acts

af 'āl al-qalb: acts of the mind or mental

Af'āl al-jawāriḥ: acts of the body

Āḥād: solitary tradition, report by a single person or by odd individuals.

Aḥadīth (pl. of *ḥadīth*): narratives, reports, deeds, sayings, traditions of the Prophet Muḥammad (ṣ)

Aḥkām (pl. of *ḥukm*): rules, laws, practical rules and ordinances

Aḥkām al-'amaliyyah: rulings related to the sayings and doings of the individuals and his relationships with others.

Aḥkām al-i'tiqādiyyah: rulings related to beliefs. Creed, convictional, which is belief in the existence of God, His oneness, His qualities, the truth of the mission of the Prophet (ṣ), belief in the Day of Judgment etc.

Aḥkām al-khuluqiyyah: rulings related to moral and ethics

Aḥkām al-shar'iyyah: The knowledge of the legal rules

Ahl al-Kitāb: literally the People of the Book; non-Muslims who believe in the holy scriptures, Christians and Jews.

Ahl al-qadar: the beliefs of *ahl al-qadar* deals with the basic tenets of Islam like faith, unity of Allah, His attributes, the life hereafter, prophecy, etc.

Ahl al-Sunnah: those who follow the *Sunnah* correctly

Ahliyyah: legal capacity

Ahliyyah al-adā': the capacity for execution or performance of duties

Ahliyyah al-wujūb: the capacity for acquisition of rights and obligation

Ahliyyah nāqiṣah: the deficient capacity

Ahliyyah qāṣirah: the imperfect capacity

Akhlāq: moral values

Alfāẓ: words

Amānah: trust

Amārah: signs or allusions, probable, speculative evidences.

'Āmm (*'āmmah*): general

'Amr (pl. *awāmir*): command, affair, matter.

'Aqā'id: the tenets of faith

'Aql: reason, intellect, rationality.

'Aqliyyah: rational, intellectual

Arkān: (sg. *rukn*) means element, pillar, corner, essential requirement or foundation of something and part of it. It is an integral part of an act, without it nullifies the act that depends on it. For example, the *rukū'* is an element (*rukn*) in prayer, without it or if it is absent, the *ṣalāt* (prayer) is nullified.

Asās: foundation

Aṣḥāb al-Masā'il: Mujtahids on Particular Issues

Aṣḥāb al-Takhrīj: Jurists who resolvers of ambiguity

Aṣḥāb al-Tarjīḥ: Jurists of Assessment

Ashbāh wa al-Naẓā'ir: Legal maxims have been collected and compiled in works known as *al-Ashbāh wa al-Naẓā'ir* authored by *Jalāl al-Dīn al-Suyūṭī*.

Ash'arīs: the school of 'ilm al-kalām named after *al-Ash'arī*.

Aṣl (pl. *uṣūl*): literally root, essence, base; that upon which something else is constructed; technically, the sources of law or the principles of jurisprudence and original case in the concept of analogy.

'Atah: idiocy

'Awāriḍ: obstacles

'Awāriḍ al-Ahliyyah: Circumstances affecting legal capacity

'Awāriḍ muktasabah: The obstacles related to the acts which are acquired by man, under the control of man, who has capacity to do or not to do them.

'Awāriḍ samāwiyyah: The obstacles related to the work of providence which are beyond the control of man such as lunacy (*junūn*), infancy (*ṣighar*, *ṣabiy*), idiocy (*'uth*, *'atah*, *'atāhah*), etc.

'Azīmah: strict rules, regularity law which remains in its original rigour due to the absence of mitigating factors.

'Azm: firm resolve

Bāligh: major

Bāṭil: void

Bay' al-ṭa'ātī: give-and-take sale

Bay' al-wafā': redemption sale

Burhān: proof, evidence

Buṭlān: vitiation

Buyū' al-ajal: deferred sales

Ḍaīf: weak

Dalālah (pl. *dalālāt*): meaning, implication of words.

Dalālāt al-alfāẓ: verbal indications.

Dalālah al-īmā': gesture, meaning of a given text which is borne out by the text's gesture.

Dalālah al-iqtiḍā': required meanings of a given text; a technical term which normally refers to a meaning of the text necessarily presumed.

Dalālah al-mafhūm: implied meaning of a given text.

Dalālah al-manṭūq: pronounced meaning of a given text.

Dalālah al-naṣṣ: inferred or implied meaning of a given text.

Dalīl (sg. of *dalīl*): indication, proof, evidence

Dalīl ijmālī: general evidence

Dalīl qaṭ'ī: definite proof

Dalīl tafṣīlī: specific evidence

Ḍarūrī: necessity

Ḍarūriyyāt: necessities

Dhimmah: the responsibility

Diyah: monetary compensation

Fahm: understanding

Faḥwā al-khiṭāb: superior meaning.

Falāḥ: welfare

Falsafah al-tashrī': philosophy of the legal rulings

Faqīh (pl. *fuqāhā'*): jurist, one who is authority in *fiqh*

Far': literally a branch or sub-division, and a new case in the context of analogy.

Farḍ: obligatory, obligation.

Fasād: nullity

Fāsid: vitiated, corrupt, void, deficient,

Fatwā': legal opinions

Fi'lī: physically

Fiqh: literally understanding, the science of Islamic law and its jurisprudence

Fiqh al-Akbar: It is a book attributed to Abū Ḥanīfah (d. 150) against the beliefs of *ahl al-qadar* deals with the basic tenets of Islam like faith, unity of Allah, His attributes, the life hereafter, prophecy, etc.

Fiṭrī: natural

Fuqahā' (sg. *Faqīh*): jurists, legal scholars, those who are learned in *fiqh*.

Furū' (pl. *far'*): subsidiary legal rules, branches or subsidiaries.

Ghanā'im: spoils of war

Ghanīmah: booty

Ghāyah: extent of application

Ghayri wāḍiḥ: unclear

Ghayri ṣarīḥ: unclear, latent, ambiguous, equivocal.

Ghusl: ritual ablution of the whole body

Ḥadd (pl. *ḥudūd*): literally limit; prescribed punishment.

Ḥadd al-qadhf: the punishment of false accusation of adultery

Ḥadīth Āḥād: solitary tradition

Ḥadith Mashhūr: well known tradition

Ḥadīth mursal: discontinued tradition

Ḥadīth Mutawātir: continuously recurrent.

Ḥadīth muttaṣil: continuous tradition

Ḥadīth qudsī: It is what has been transmitted to us as isolated reports from the Prophet (ṣ) with its chain (*isnād*) going back to his Lord.

Ḥājiyyāt: complementary

Ḥajj: pilgrimage, it is an obligation for Muslim who is financially eligible to visit the holy Ka'ba once-in-a lifetime.

Ḥākim: Lawgiver

Ḥanafī: Sunni school of law which developed in *Kūfa* in *Iraq* named after Abū Ḥanīfah.

Ḥanbalī: Sunni school of law named after Aḥmad ibn Ḥanbal.

Ḥaqīqah: literal

Ḥaqīqī: which means true, genuine, authentic and real

Haqīqīyyah: genuine

Ḥaqq: the right cause, right of somebody or something.

Ḥarām: prohibited

Ḥarām li-dhātihi: prohibited for an internal factor.

Ḥarām li-ghayrihi: prohibited for an external factor

Ḥasan: good

Ḥayḍ: menstruation

Ḥazl: jest

Ḥikmah: philosophy or wisdom

Ḥīlah: (sg. of *ḥiyal*) is a legal device for evading the incidence of the strict law. It may also be referred to legal fictions or legal loopholes.

Ḥīlaī shar'īyyah: legal loopholes

Hisbah: promotion of good and prevention of evil

Ḥiss: intuition.

Ḥissiyyah: law of sense perception

Ḥudūd (sg. *ḥadd*): literally: limit, technically: prescribed punishment.

Ḥujjah: legal proof or evidence.

Ḥukm (pl. *aḥkām*): ruling, law, value, as in *ḥukm shar'ī* or the injunction of the *Sharī'ah*.

Ḥukm al-taklīfī: defining law, law which defines rights and obligations.

Ḥukm al-waḍ'ī: declaratory law, law which regulates the proper implementation of the defining law.

Ḥukm shar'ī: legal rulings

Ḥuqūq al-'abd: rights of man

Ḥuqūq al-'abd al-khāliṣah: the acts which are purely the rights of man

Ḥuqūq Allah: rights of Allah

Ḥuqūq Allah al-khāliṣah: the acts which are purely the rights of Allah.

Ḥusn: good

Ibāḥah: permissibility, allowance.

I'jāz: inimitability

I'tiqād: faith, belief

'Ibādāt: worshiping

'Ibārah al-naṣṣ: explicit meaning of a given text.

'Ibārāt: sentences

Ibṭāl al-Istiḥsān: Invalidating Juristic Preference

'Iddah: the waiting period following dissolution of marriage by death or divorce.

Ighmā': fainting fit

Ījāb: obligation

Ijārah: lease and hire

Ijmā': consensus, one of the unanimously accepted sources of Islamic law.

Ijmā' ṣarīḥ: explicit *ijmā'*

Ijmā' sukūtī: tacitly approved *ijmā'*

Ijtihād: literally: exertion, and technically it is defined as the expenditure of efforts by the *faqīh* to arrive at a juristic ruling, such ruling being either rational (*'aqlī*) or transmitted (*naqlī*), definitive (*qat'ī*)or speculative (*ẓannī).*

Ijtihād al-taqdīrī: which allows jurists all to give rulings and on which there is no cause for disagreement amongst the scholars.

Ikhtilāf: juristic disagreement.

Ikrāh: forcing someone to do or say something against his will, coercion or duress.

Ilhām: inspiration

'Illah: cause and reason, effective cause of a particular ruling in analogy.

'Ilm: knowledge

Iltimas: request

Iltizām: a necessary idea attached to a meaning in the mind.

Indhār: warning, legal notice.

'Iqāb: punishment

Iqtiḍā': demand

Iqtiḍā' al-naṣṣ: the required meaning of a given text.

Irshād: guidance.

Iṣābah: target

Ishārah al-naṣṣ: the allusive or alluded meaning that can be detected in a given text.

'Iṣmah: infallibility, immunity from making errors. It is one of the characteristics of the prophets.

Isti'ārah badī'ah: rhetoric metaphor.

Istighrāq: inclusion by one concept of many others.

'Itāb: blame

Isti'māl: usage

Isti'rāq: inclusion and comprehension

Istidlāl: inference

Istiḥsān: to deem something, good, juristic preference

Istaḥsana: approved as the better judgment

Isṭilāḥ: convention.

Istinbāṭ: inference, deducing a somewhat hidden meaning from a given text.

Istinbāṭ al-aḥkām: juridical deduction, deduction of legal rulings.

Istiqrā': induction

Istiqrā' tāmm: complete induction

Istiqrā' nāqiṣ: incomplete induction

Istiṣḥāb: it is presuming continuation of the *status quo ante* or presumption of continuity.

Istiṣlāḥ: consideration of public interest

Istiṣwāb: discretion

Istiṣnā': This is the giving of an order to a laborer or artisan to make a definite article with agreement to pay a definite price for that article when made.

Istithnā': exception

I'tibār: a calling for contemplation, admonition, something consequential.

Jahl: ignorance

Jāhiliyyah: ignorance; a term used to refer to the period before the advent of the Prophet and the final revelation.

Janīn: foetus, embryo

Jarḥ wa-ta'dīl: the criteria by which to appraise narrators of ḥadīth.

Jihād: literally striving, fighting for the sake of Allah, self-exertion and struggle for the sake of establishing truth and justice.

Jins: kind, type.

Judhr: root

Juhd: exertion of effort or energy

Jumhūr: the majority of the scholars, or dominant majority.

Junub (*janābah*): a state requiring a ritual ablution of the whole body after sexual intercourse or contact.

Junūn: lunacy

Kāffah: entire

Kaffarah (pl. *kaffārāt*): expiation, penance.

Kalālah: a matter dealing with inheritance. It is a person who inherit from a person who dies leaving neither ascendants nor descendants.

Kalām: literally means speech, it is used as abbreviation for *'ilm al-kalām*, that is theology.

Kamāl: perfection

Kamāliyyāt: luxurious, embellishments

Kāmilah: complete

Karāhah (karāhiyyah): disapproval, abhorrence, abomination.

Karāhat al-taḥrīm: strongly disapproved

Karāhat al-tanzīh: weakly disapproval

Khabar wāḥid: a solitary tradition narrated by a limited number of narrators.

Khafī: latent, hidden, obscure; which also refers to category of unclear words.

Kharāj: the imposition of land tax

Khāṣṣ: specific, a word or a text which conveys a specific meaning.

Khilāf al-aṣl: opposite to the basic, original and approved status.

Khul': release or redemption, a form of divorce by mutual agreement, a dissolution of the marriage bond by an utterance of this word or its derivatives and for which the wife pays the dowry or any agreed amount to her husband.

Khiṭāb: communication

Khiṭāb of *'ibādāt*: legal capacity for worshipping

Khiṭāb of *jinā'ī*: legal capacity for criminal liability

Khiṭāb of *mu'āmalāt*: legal capacity for transections

Kināyah: allusive

Kullī: whole

Kulliyyah: general

Laḥn al-khiṭāb: parallel meaning.

Li'ān: literally imprecation, cursing, a form of irrevocable dissolution of marriage whereby the husband/wife affirms four times under oath that his wife/her husband committed adultery and invokes the curse of God on himself/herself should he/she be telling a lie. Both say it interchangeably and it is also called *mulā'anah*.

Lughawiyyah: linguistic rules

Madhhab (pl. *madhāhib*): classical juridical/ theological schools of legal thought.

Ma'tūh: idiot

Maḍarrāt: evils

Mafhūm: notion, concept, implicit meaning, implication.

Mafhūm al-'adad: implication of the stated number.

Mafhūm al-ghāyah: Implication of the extent.

Mafhūm al-mukhālafah: Implication of the divergent meaning. An interpretation which diverges from the obvious meaning of a given text.

Mafhūm al-muwāfaqah: Implication of the agreed meaning.

Mafhūm al-sharṭ: Implication of the Condition.

Mafhūm al-ṣifah: Implication of the Attribute

Mafqūd: a missing person

Mafsadah: evil

Maḥḍ: pure

Maḥdhūf: omitted.

Maḥkūm ʿalayh: the subject

Maḥkūm fīh: the act

Maḥr: also called *ṣadāq*, dowry, sum of money or other property payable by the husband to the wife for the fulfilment of marriage contract.

Maḥẓūr: forbidden

Majāz: metaphorical

Majallah: Ottoman court manual

Makrūh: discouraged, adversity, blameworthy, reprehensible.

Mālikī: a Sunni school of law named after Mālik bin Anas.

Manāṭ al-ḥukm: effective cause.

Mandūb: commendable, praiseworthy.

Manfaʿah: benefit

Mānīʿ: impediment

Mansūkh: abrogated, repealed.

Manṭūq: pronounced.

Maqīs: subsidiary new case in the concept of analogy.

Maqīs 'alayh: original cause in analogy.

Maqāṣid (pl. of *maqṣūd*): objective and goals.

Maqāṣid al-sharī'ah: objective of the *Sharī'ah*

Maqbūl ḥadīth: acceptable tradition

Maqdhūf : the victim of false accusation of adultery offence (*maqdhūf*)

Maraḍ al-mawt: death-illness

Mardūd ḥadīth: rejected tradition

Marfū':

Marjūḥ: non-preferable opinion.

Mashaqqah: hardship

Mashhūr: a well-known tradition of the Prophet (ṣ).

Mashrūṭ: stipulated.

Maskūṭ 'anh: not mentioned, concealed unpronounced rulings.

Maṣlaḥah: benefit, interest

Maṣlaḥah mursalah: consideration of public interest

Ma'ṣūm: infallible, immune from making errors (normally) refers to the Prophets.

Mawḍū' (pl. of *mawḍū'āt*): fabricated, forged.

Mawlā (pl. *mawālī*): a homonym that means both the freer (the master) and the freed (slave).

Mayyitah: dead animal, or cattle which is not slaughtered according to the requirements of Islamic law.

Mu'ayyan: specified, determined and explained words.

Mu'ḍal: It is a *ḥadīth* where two or more narrators missing from one or more places in the chain.

Mu'awwal: Interpreted beyond the obvious meaning of the text.

Mubaḥ: permissible

Mubham: ambiguous, and unclear words.

Muḍmar: concealed, implicit words in a given text.

Mufassar: explained, clarified, which refers to a category of explained and clarified words.

Muḥaddithūn: the scholars of *ḥadīth*

Muḥarabah: highway robbery.

Muḥkam: perspicuous, a word or a text conveying a firm and unequivocal meaning which refers to a word or text is susceptible neither to *ta'wīl* nor abrogation.

Mujmal: ambivalent, ambiguous, referring to a category of unclear words. Technically it refers to a category of unclear words.

Mujtahid: competent jurist who exercises *ijtihād.*

Mukallaf: subject, a competent person who is in full possession of his faculties.

Mukhayyar: unspecified

Mukhaṣṣiṣ (pl. *mukhaṣṣiṣāt*): articles which offer specification, proofs of specification.

Mukhtaṣar: abridgement, summary.

Muktasabah: obtained

Munqaṭi': discontinued

Muqallid: imitator/follower

Muqaṭṭa'āt: individual, abbreviated letters in the *Qur'ān.*

Muqayyad: limited, dependent, confined, qualified words.

Muqtaḍā: required indication of a given text without which the meaning of the text would be incomplete.

Muqtarin: joined and associated.

Murshid: guide, conductor

Musāwāt: equals, equality

Mushkil: difficult, it also refers to a category of unclear words.

Mushtarak: equivocal, common word, homonym, a word or phrase imparting more than one meaning.

Musnad: a *ḥadīth* with a continuous chain of transmitters.

Mustaqil: independent

Muṭābaqah: complete correspondence.

Mutawāṭi': a specified personal meaning.

Mut'ah: literally pleasure, maintenance; temporary marriage recognized only by the *Shī'ah* school, and it is considered illegal by the Sunnis.

Mutakallimīn: scholars of *kalām*, theologians of *uṣūl al-fiqh*.

Mutashābih (pl. *mutashābihāt*): intricate, equivocal, ambiguous, unintelligible, referring to a word or a text whose meaning is totally unclear, beyond human comprehension.

Mutawātir: literally means continuously recurrent. In the present context, it means a report by an indefinite number of people related in such a way as to preclude the possibility of their agreement to perpetuate a lie.

Muṭlaq: absolute, unqualified; which refers to a word that is not specified or qualified.

Nabīdh: fermented dates

Nadb: recommendation

Nafl: supererogatory worship.

Najāsah: impurity, uncleanness, dirt.

Nahy: prohibition

Nakirah: indefinite noun, unknown person.

Nāqiṣah: deficient

Naqlī: transmitted, e.g. in transmitted proofs which are to be distinguished from rational proofs.

Nasab: lineage and stock.

Naskh: abrogation, repeal, cancellation.

Nāsikh: the abrogator, as opposed to the *mansūkh* (abrogated)

Naṣṣ: text, a clear injunction, an explicit textual ruling, which also refers to the clear words.

Naẓarī: theoretical

An-Naẓariyyah al-Fiqhiyyah: theories of fiqh, maxims of fiqh.

Nifās: childbed; women's menstruated period after giving birth.

Nikāḥ: marriage contract.

Niṣāb: wealth up to a determined minimum values.

Nisyān: forgetfulness

Niyyah: intention.

Nuṣūṣ (pl. of *naṣṣ*): clear textual rulings.

Qā'idah: principles

Qabīḥ: evil

Qadhf: slanderous accusation of illicit sexual relations.

Qādhif: slanderer, slanderous accuser.

Qāḍī: judge

Qalbī: which takes place in the heart

Qarīnah: evidence, context or circumstantial evidence.

Qāṣirah: imperfect

Qaṣr: limitation, shortening.

Qaṭʿī: definitive, decisive, free of speculative content.

Qaṭʿī al-dalālah: the definite meaning or indication.

Qawāʿid: principle

Qawāʿid al-fiqhiyyah: maxims of *fiqh;* rules extracted from Islamic law by the *fuqahā'* to form a general rule or maxim.

Qawl al-ṣaḥābī: the sayings of a companion of the Prophet (ṣ)

Qawlī: relating to speech.

Qinṭār: measuring unit.

Qiṣāṣ: just retaliation

Qiyās: analogy; the process of forming Islamic jurisprudence through logical deduction based on the original sources of Islamic law.

Qiyās al-adnā: analogy of the inferior

Qiyās al-awlā: analogy of the superior

Qiyās al-musāwāt: analogy of equals

Qiyās jalīy: obvious analogy

Qiyās khafī: latent, hidden analogy.

Qubḥ: evil

Rajm: stoning to death.

Ra'y: Opinion

Ra'y bāṭil : invalid; null, and void

Ra'y mashkūk: doubtful, uncertain

Ra'y ṣaḥīḥ: valid, authentic

Riwāyah: transmitted *ḥadīth*

Rujḥān: preference, preferability

Ribā': usury, interest

Riqq: slavery

Rujḥān: preference, preferability

Riwāyah: narration, transmission of *ḥadīth*.

Rukhṣah: exemptions, concession or concessionary law, which is modified due to the presence of mitigating factors.

Rukn: pillar, essential ingredient.

Sabab (pl. *asbāb*): reason, cause, means of obtaining something.

Ṣabī: minor

Sadd: blocking

Sadd al-dharā'i': blocking the means

Salam : contract of purchase of goods with pre-payment, forward sale, prepaid sale

Salām: conclusion of prayer

Ṣalāt: prayer

Safah: folly

Safar: journey

Safih: mentally defective

Ṣaghīr: minor

Ṣaḥabah (sg. *ṣaḥābī*): Companions of the Prophet (ṣ).

Ṣaḥīḥ: valid, authentic tradition.

Ṣaḥīḥ ḥadīth: authentic.

Salaf: the first generation of Muslims.

Salam: contract of purchase of goods with pre-payment

Ṣalāt al-kusūf: prayer offered on the occasion of a solar eclipse

Sanad: basis, proof, authority.

Ṣāriḥ: clear, plain, unambiguous.

Shādh: irregular

Shāfi'ī: a Sunni school of law named after Muḥammad b. Idrīs al-Shāfi'ī.

Shāhid: witness

Shahādāt al-zūr: false testimony

Shahwah: passion

Sharī'ah: Islamic law, the divine law of Islam.

Shar' man qablanā: revealed laws preceding to the *sharī'ah* of Islam

Sharṭ (pl. *shurūṭ*): condition.

Shirk: worshipping somebody or something other than Allah, or associating somebody or something with Him; polytheism, idolatry.

Shuf'ah: the right of preemption

Shūrā: consultation.

Ṣifah: attribute

Ṣiḥḥah: Validity

Siyāsah Sharī'ah: Sharī'ah Oriented Public Policy

Sukr: drunkenness

Sunnah: It is the second unanimously accepted sources of Islamic law; traditions attributed to the Prophet (ṣ).

Sunnah ghayr *mu'akkadah*: non-emphatic tradition

Sunnah mu'akkadah: emphatic tradition

Sunnah Zawā'id: additional tradition

Ta'āruḍ: conflicts

Ta'āruḍ al-adillah: Conflict of Evidences

Taba'ī Tābi'īn: Successors of the Successors

Tābi'īn: Successors; next generation of Muslims after the Companions.

Tadbīr: precaution

Taḥlīl: an intervening marriage contract for the sole purpose of legalising remarriage between a divorced couples.

Taḥrif: distortion

Taḥrīm: prohibition, or rendering something into *ḥarām*.

Ta'diyah: transferability.

Takhṣīṣ: specifying the general provision.

Talāq bā'in: divorce to be absolute

Talāq raj'ī: revocable

Talazzuz: deriving pleasure

Ta'līl: ratiocination, search for the effective cause of a ruling.

Ta'wīl: allegorical interpretation

Ta'zīr: deterrence, discretionary penalty determined by the *qāḍī* (judge)

Taḥsīniyyāt: embellishments

Takhayyur: select, to prefer or to choose one among several things

Takhrīj: a method of resolving ambiguity

Takhṣīṣ: specification, specifying the general

Takhyīr: choice

Taklīf: liability, obligation

Ṭalab: request

Ṭalāq: divorce initiated by the husband

Talfīq: Literally it means picking things up from different places or sewing two things together to produce a complete article or cloth, and joining, patching up, combining to things together. Technically it may be defined as the constructing of an opinion by using bits and pieces from different schools of law (*madhhab*).

Tamyīz: a child is possessed of understanding

Tanāsukh al-arwāḥ: reincarnation

Tanāsukh al-mawārīth: the transfer of inheritance from persons to persons

Taqiyyah: concealment of one's views to escape persecution.

Taqlīd: imitation, following the views and opinion of others.

Targhīb: invitation, attraction

Tarhīb: intimidation, threatening.

Taṣarrufāt: dispositions

Tashahhud: To say while sitting in the prayer: "There is no god but Allah and Muḥammad (ṣ) is the messenger of Allah."

Tashrīʿ: legislation.

Taswiyah: equalisation between two things.

Taṭhīr: purification.

Ta'wīl: allegorical interpretation which is beyond the obvious sense of a given text.

Tawātur: continuous testimony, continuous recurrence; It is perfect plurality of narrators which continue from one generation to another.

Tawbah: repentance

Tawḥīd: the belief in the oneness of Allah.

Tayammum: ablution with clean sand, earth in the event no water may be found.

Taʿzīr: deterrence; non-fixed punishment, discretionary penalty determined by a judge (*qāḍī*).

ʿUdūl: the departure

ʿUlamā' (sg. *ʿālim*): scholars

ʿŪlū al-ʿamr: person in authority and in charge of community affairs.

ʿUmum al-balwā: general calamity

Ummah: the whole Muslim community

ʿUrfʿ: custom

ʿUrf 'āmm: general custom

ʿUrf khāṣṣ: specific custom

ʿUrf qawlī: verbal customs and habits prevalent in society.

ʿUshr: the tithe

Uṣūl al-fiqh: principles of Islamic jurisprudence

Uṣūlīyyūn (sg. *Uṣūlī*): juristic scholars

Waḍ'ī: declaration

Wāḍiḥ: Clear, lucid, plain, obvious, technically it refers to clear words.

Wahmī: superstitious

Wahmīyyah: inaccurate

Waḥy: divine revelation

Waḥy bāṭin: un-recited or internal revelation

Waḥy matlū: recited or manifest revelation

Wājīb: obligatory, strict obligation which Muslims must observe; often synonymous with *farḍ* in *Ḥanafīs.*

Wājib 'aynī: personal obligation

Wājib kifā'ī: a communal obligation of the entire community.

Wājib muqayyad: limited obligation

Wājib muṭlaq: absolute obligation

Walī: legal heir or guardian

Waqf: charitable endowment

Wasā'il: means

Waṣf (pl. of *awṣāf*): attribute, quality, adjective.

Wujūb: necessity, obligation, rendering something obligatory.

Wuḍū': ablution with clean water.

Wuḍūḥ: clarity

Yanqadihu: embedded

Ẓāhir: manifest, apparent; technically it refers to the apparent meaning of a text.

Ẓāhirī: a school of Islamic law. The followers rely exclusively on the literal meaning of authoritative texts.

Zakāt: legal alms; a religious obligation on Muslims to pay annually a predetermined percentage of the value of their assets.

Zakāt al-fiṭr: a religious obligation on Muslims to pay at the end of Ramaḍān.

Ẓann: speculation, doubt, conjecture.

Ẓannī: speculative, indefinite, and doubtful; the legal value attached to the results of juristic reasoning.

Ẓannī al-dalālah: indefinite indication.

Ẓihār: calling one's wife mother as saying 'you are to me like the back of my mother'.

Zinā: adultery, fornication.

Ẓulm: oppression, injustice.

Bibliography

'Abd al-Ḥāfiẓ, Madīḥah 'Alī, "*Al-Istiḥsān wa Atharuh fī-Bināi al-Fiqh al-Islāmī,*" unpublished PhD dissertation, Faculty of Arabic and Islamic Studies, Al-Azhar University, Egypt, 1984.

Abdur Rahim, "*The Principles of Muḥammadan Jurisprudence,*" (London: Luzac and Co., 1911).

Abū Dāwud, Sulaymān bin al-Ash'ās. (d. 275/888) "*Sunan,*" tr. Ahmad Hasan (Lahore: sh. Muḥammad Ashraf, 1984)

Abū 'Iyd, Ḥasan Muḥammad Salīm. "*Al-Imām al-Shāfi'ī wa Atharuhu fī Uṣūl al-Fiqh,*" unpublished PhD dissertation at Faculty of *Sharī'ah* and Qānūn Al-Azhar University, Egypt, 1976.

Abū 'Īd, 'Abd Jalīl, *Mabāhith fī Uṣūl al-Fiqh* (Dār al-Furqān, 1987).

Abū Sunnah, Aḥmad Fahmī, "*Al-'Urf wa al-'Adah fi-Ra'y al-Fuqahā,*" Cairo, 1947.

Abū Yūsuf, Yāqūp Ibrāhim (d. 182), "*Kitāb al-Kharāj,*" Dār al-Ma'rifah, Beirut, 1970.

Abū Zahrah, Muḥammad (d. 1395/1974), "*Uṣūl al-Fiqh*" (Cairo: Dār al-Fikr al-'Arabi, 1958)

- "*Abū Ḥanīfah*" Translated into Turkish by: Osman Keskioğlu, 3rd ed., Ankara, Diyanet Yayınları, 1999.

- *Tārīkh Madhāhib al-Islāmiyah* (Beirut: Dār al-Fiqr al-ʻArabī, n.d.)

Aghnides, Nicolas P. "*Muḥammadan Theories of Finance*," New York, Longmans Green &Co. 1916, reprint, Lahore: Premier Book House, 1957.

Ajlounī, Ismāʻil b. Muḥammad. "*Kashf al-Khafa'*," Cairo, n.d.

Akgündüz, Ahmed. "*Introduction to Islamic Law*," (Istanbul: Pasifik Ofset, 2010),

ʻAlwānī, Ṭāhā Jābir, "*The Ethics of Disagreement in Islam*," the International Institute of Islamic Thought, VA, USA, 1993.

Āmidī, ʻAli bin Abī ʻAli Muḥammad bin Sālim Al-Thaʻlabī, Sayf al-Dīn. (d. 631/1233), "*Al-Iḥkām fī Uṣūl al-Aḥkām*," ed. ʻAbd al-Razzāq ʻAfīfī, 2nd ed. (Beirut: Maktabah al-Islāmi, 1402/1982),

Amīr Bādshāh, Muḥammad Amin (d. 987), *Taysīr al-Taḥrīr*, (Cairo: Muṣṭafā al-Bābī al-Ḥalabī, 1350 AH)

Anderson, J. N. D., Recent Developments in Shari'a Law, *Moslem World*, vol. 40, 1950, pp. 224-256,

Anees Ibrahīm, "*Al-Muʻjam al-Wasīṭ*" (Cairo: Dār al-Maʻārif, 1973)

Anṣārī, Abū Zakarīyyah Shaikh al-Islam "*Ghāyāt al-Wuṣūl sharḥ lub al-Uṣūl*" (Cairo: Muṣṭafā bāb al-Ḥalabī wa awlāduh, 1360/1941)

Asfaḥānī, Shams al-Dīn Maḥmūd, *Sharḥ al-Minhāj* (Riyadh: Maktabah al-Rushd, 1410 AH).

Asqalānī, Aḥmad b. Ḥajar, "*Bulūgh al-Marām*" (Kuwait: Revival of Islamic Heritage Society, 1994)

Auda, Jasser. *Maqāṣid al-Sharīʻah as Philosophy of Islamic Law A Systems Approach*, (London: The International Institute of Islamic Thought, 2007).

Atar, Fahrettin. "*Fıkıh Uṣulü*" (İstanbul: MÜİFY, 1996)

Aṭṭār, Ḥasan bin Muḥammad bin Maḥmūd. (d. 1250/1835), "*Ḥāshiyah 'Alā Sharḥ Jalāl al-Maḥallī 'Alā Jam' al-Jawāmi*'" (Egypt: Maṭba'ah 'Ilmīyyah, 1316 AH)

Azami, Muhammad Mustafa. *Studies in Ḥadīth Methodology and Literature* (Indianapolis: American Trust Publication, 1977)

- "*Al-Mustashriq Schacht wa al-Sunnah al-Nabawīyyah*" (Riyad: 1985)

Azharī. Abū Manṣūr Muḥammad b. Aḥmad. (d. 370/980), "*Tahdhib Al-Lughah*" (Cairo: al-Dār al-Misriyyah, 1966)

Ba'labakī, *al-Mawrid*, 4th ed. (Beirut: Dār al-'Ilm līl-Malāyīyn, 1992)

Badrān, Abū al-'Aynāyn Badrān, "*Uṣūl al-Fiqh al-Islāmī*" (Alexandria: Mu'assasah Shabāb al-Jāmi'ah, 1404/1984),

Bakar, Daud. "*Conflict of Law and the Methodology of Tarjīḥ: A Study in Islamic Legal Theory*," unpublished PhD thesis, (Scotland: University of St Andrews, 1993)

Baktrī, Muṣṭafā. "*İslam Hukukunda Zaruret*," Ankara, 1986.

Baljon, J M S. "*Religion and thought of Shah Wali Allah Dihlawi*," Leiden: E. J. Brill, Netherlands, 1986.

Bani, Muḥammad Sa'īd *'Umdat al-Tahqiq fī al-Taqlīd wa al-Talfīq*, (Dimishq: al-Maktab al-Islāmī, 1981)

Bannānī, 'Abd al-Raḥmān bin Jād Allah al-Bannānī, al-Maghribī (d. 1198/1784), "*Ḥāshiah 'alā Sharḥ Jalāl al-Dīn al-Maḥallī 'alā Jam' al-Jawāmī' li Ibn Subkī*" (Cairo: Muṣṭafa Bābī al-Ḥalabī, 1937)

Bashīr Idrīs Jum'ah, *Al-Ra'y wa Atharuh fī al-Fiqh al-Islāmī* (Cairo: n.d.)

Baṣrī, Abī al-Ḥusayn Muḥammad b. 'Ali b. al-Ṭayyib al-Basrī al-Mu'razilī (d. 436/1044), "*Al-Mu'tamad fī 'Uṣūl al-Fiqh*," edt. Shaykh Khalīl al-Mays (Beirut: 1983).

Bazdawī, 'Ali bin Muḥammad bin 'Abd al-Karīm Abū al-Ḥasan Fakhr al-Islam al-Ḥanafī. (482/1089), "*Uṣūl Al-Bazdawī on the margin of 'Abd al-'Azīz al-Bukhārī Khashf al-Asrār*" (Istanbul: 1308 AH), reprint, Beirut Dār al-Kitāb al-Arabi 1394/1974.

- *Minhāj al-Wuṣūl ilā 'ilm al-Uṣūl*, with its commentary *Nihāyat al-Su'l*, (Cairo: Matba'ah al-Tawfīq al-Adabiyyah, n.d.)

Bayḍāwī, Naṣr al-Dīn 'Abd Allah bin 'Umar bin Muḥammad bin 'Ali Al-Shīyrazī. (d. 685/1286), "*Al-Ibhāj fī Sharh Al-Minhāj 'alā' Minhāj al-Wuṣūl ilā 'Ilm al-Uṣūl*," Beirut.

Bukhārī. 'Abd al-'Azīz bin Aḥmad bin Muḥammad, 'Alā al-Dīn. (d. 730/1329), "*Sharḥ Kashf al-Asrār 'Alā Uṣūl al-Bazdawī*" (Beirut: Dār al Kutūb al-'Arabi, 1394)

- *Kashf al-Asrār 'an Uṣūl Fakhr al-Islam al-Bazdawī*, (Beirut: Dār al-Kutub al-'Ilmiyyah, 1997)

Bukhārī, Abū 'Abd Allah Muḥammad b. Ismā'īl (d. 256/69), "*al-Jāmī' al-Ṣaḥīḥ*" (Istanbul: 1981).

Būtī, Ramaḍān, "*Ḍawābiṭ al-Maṣlaḥah fī al-Sharī'ah al-Islāmiyyah*" (Muassasah al-Risālah, 1982).

- "*Ḍawābiṭ al-Maṣlaḥah fī al-Sharī'ah al-Islāmiyyah*" (Beirut: 1986).

Baṣrī, Abū al-Ḥusayn, *Kitāb al-Mu'tamad* (Damascus: al-Ma'had al-'Ilmī al-Faransī li'l Dirāsāt al-Islāmiyyah, 1964)

Bardīsī, Muḥammad Zakariyyā. *Uṣūl al-Fiqh*, 2nd ed. (Cairo: Maṭba'at Dār al-Ta 'līf, 1381 AH)

Bedir, Murteza. "Fikih to Law: Secularization Through Curriculum," in *Islamic Law and Society* 11, 3, Leiden, 2004, p. 378-401.

Catafago, Joseph. "*English and Arabic Dictionary*" (London, 1958)

Chejne, A.G. "*Ibn Ḥazm*" (Chicago: Kazi Publications inc. 1982).

Coulson, Noel J., *A History of Islamic Law*, Edinburgh University Press, 1978

Çeker, Orhan. "*Ifta ve Bir Fetva Defteri Örneği*" (Konya: Damla offset, 2000).

Dabbūsī, Abū Zayd 'Abd Allah, 'Ubayd Allah b. 'Umar bin 'Iysā (d. 430/1039), "*Taqwīm al-Adillah al-Shar', al-Asrār fī al-Uṣūl wa al-Furū'*" (original paper) Suleymaniye, Laleli 690.

- "*Kitāb Ta'sīs al-Naẓar*," edt. Muṣṭafa Muḥammad al-Qubbānī, Beirut.
- *al-Asrār fī al-Uṣūl wa al-Furū' fī Taqwīm Adillat al-Shar'*, PhD thesis submitted by Maḥmūd Tawfīq al-'Awāṭilī al-Rughā'ī at Al-Azhar University, Cairo.

Dārānī, 'Abd Allah al-Dārimī, *Musnad al-Dārimī*, edited by Ḥusain. (Riyadh: Dār al-Maghnī lil-Nashr wal-Tawzī', 2000), I, no. 178, p. 272-273.

Dasūqī, Muḥammad. *Al-Ijtihād wa al-Taqlīd fī al-Sharī'ah al-Islāmiyah* (Doha: Dār al-Thaqāfah, n.d.)

Dihlawī, Shaḥ Walī Allah. (d. 1176/1776), "*Ḥujjah Allah al-Bālighah*" (Delhi: 1954)

- "*Tafhīmati Ilāhiyyah*," Dabhel 1936.

Dīrīnī, Fatḥī. *Al-Manāhij al-Uṣūliyyah fī al-Ijtihād bi al-Ra'y fī al-Tashrī' al-Islamī* (Damascus: al-Sharikāt al-Muttaḥidah, 1985),

Doi, 'Abd al-Raḥmān I. "*Sharī'ah the Islamic Law*" (London: Ta Ha Publishers, 1997).

- "*Sharī'ah: the Islamic Law*," (Lagos: Ṭāḥā, 1984)

Elias A. Elias, "*Elias Modern Dictionary*," 5th edition (Cairo: 1950)

Esposito, John L. *Muslim Family Law in Egypt and Pakistan: A*

Critical Analysis of Legal Reform, its Sources and Methodological Problems, Ph. D dissertation, Temple University. 1974

- Muslim Family Law Reform: Towards an Islamic Methodology, *Islamic Studies*, v. 15, no. 1,1976, p. 19-51

Farāḥidī, Khalīl b. Aḥmad. *Kitāb al-'Ain*, edited by 'Abd al-Ḥamīd Hindāwī, (Beirut: Dār al-Kutub al-'Ilmiyyah, 2003).

Fāsī, Allāl. "*Maqāṣid al-Sharī'ah al-Islāmīyah wa-Maqārimuhā*" (al-Maghrib: Matba'ah al-Risālah, 1979)

Fatoohi, Louay. *Abrogation in the Qur'ān and Islamic Law, A Critical Study of the Concept of Naskh and its Impact*, (Selangor: IBT, 2013).

Fīruzabādī, Muḥammad ibn Ya'qūb al-Fīruzabādī al-Shīrāzī (d. 817/1414), "*Al-Qāmūs al-Muḥīṭ*" (Beirut: Muassasat al-Risālah, 1986).

Ghanzi, Sa'd, al-Talfiq fi al-Fatwa, *Journal of Shari'ah and Islamic Studies*, v. 14, issue 38, August 1999.

Ghazālī, Abū Ḥāmid Muḥammad ibn Muḥammad. (d. 505/1111), "*Al-Mustaṣfā' min 'Ilm al-Uṣūl*" (Cairo: al-Maktabah al-Tijāriyyah, 1356/1937)

- "*Al-Mankhūl min Ta'līqāt Al-Uṣūl*," 2nd ed. (Damascus: Dār Al-Fikr Al-'Arabī)

Goldziher, Ignaz. *Introduction to Islamic Law and Theology*, trans A. & R. Hamori, (Princeton, NJ: Princeton University Press, 1981)

Haçkalı, Abdurrahman. "Islam Hukuk Tarihinde Maṣlaḥat Tanımları ve Bunların Analizi," *İslami Araṣtırmalar Magazine*, v. 13, no. 1, 2000, p. 47-61.

Hajawī, Muḥammad ibn Ḥassān. *Al-Fiqh al-Sami fi Tarikh al-Fiqh al-Islami* (Cairo: Dār al-Turāth, 1396)

Ḥakīm, Muḥammad b. 'Abd Allah (d. 405/1015), "*Al-Mustadrak 'ala al-Ṣaḥīḥayn*," edited by Muṣṭafā 'Abd al-Qadīr 'Aṭā (Beirut: 1990).

Hallaq, Wael B. *An Introduction to Islamic law*, (UK: Cambridge University Press, 2009),

- "*The Gate of Ijtihād: A study in Islamic Legal History*," PhD dissertation, University of Washington, p. 18.
- "Was the Gate of Ijtihad Closed?" in *International Journal of Middle East Studies*. xvi, 1, 1984, 3-41.
- "*The Origins and Evolution of Islamic Law*" (Cambridge: Cambridge University Press, 2005).

Ḥāmid, Ḥassān Ḥusayn. *al-Ḥukm al-Shar'ī 'indal-Uṣūliyyīn*, (Cairo: Dār al-Nahḍah al-'Arabiyyah, 1972)

Ḥamidullah, Muḥammad. "Al-Ijtihād fī 'Aṣr al-Ṣaḥābah," *Majallah al-Kulliyah al-Dirāsah al-Islāmiyah wa al-'Arabiyah*, 3, no. 4 (1984)

- "*İslam Peygamberi*" (Istanbul: 1980)

Hans Wehr "*A Dictionary of Modern Written Arabic*," edited by J. Milton Cowan, 4th edition (Germany: 1979).

Ḥārithī, Muḥammad Qāsim 'Abduh. "*Makānāt al-Imām Abū Ḥanīfah bayn al-Muḥaddithīyn*," p. 23, PhD dissertation, at the University of Islamic Studies, Pakistan.

Hart, Herbert Lionel Adolphus. "*The Concept of Law*" (Oxford: 1961).

Hasan, Ahmad. "*The Early Development of Islamic Jurisprudence*," (Islamabad: Islamic Research Institute, 1994).

- *Principles of Islamic Jurisprudence, The Command of the Sharī'ah and Juridical Norm* (Islamabad: Islamic Research Institute, 1993)
- "*Analogical Reasoning in Islamic Jurisprudence*" (Islamabad: Islamic research Institute, 1986)
- "*The Doctrine of Ijmā' in Islam*" (Islamabad: Islamic Research Institute, 1992)

Hasan, Aznan. The Concept of Tahayyur and its Application in Islamic Banking and Finance: an Appraisal, Paper Presented at *the 2nd International Law and Commerce Conference*, Victoria Law Schooi, Victoria University, Melbourne, 8-9 December, 2003.

Ḥaydarī, 'Alī Taqīy, "*Uṣūl al-Istinbāt*" (Baghdat: Matba'ah al-Rābitah, 1959)

Hitu, Muḥammad Ḥasan. "*al-Wajīz fī Uṣūl al-Tashrī' al-Islāmī*" 2nd ed., (Beirut: Mu'assasah al-Risālah, 1984)

Ḥusaynī, Hāshim Maghrūf. "*Mabadi' al-'Āmmah li al-Fiqh al-Jaghfarī*" (Baghdat: Dār al-Nashr li al-Jam'īyyīyn Maktabah al-Naḥḍah, nd.)

Husraw, Mollah. Muḥammad bin Firāmūz (885/1480), "*Mir'āt al-Uṣūl Sharḥ Mirkāt al-Wusūl*" (Istanbul: Matba'ah al-Amīrah, 1309)

Ibn 'Ābidīn, *Radd al-Muḥtār* (Cairo: Musṭafā al-Bābī al-Ḥalabī, n.d.)

Ibn 'Abd al-Barr, Abū 'Umar Yūsuf (d: 463/1071), "*Jāmī' Bayān al-'Ilm wa Faḍlih*" edt. Muḥammad 'Abd al-Qadīr 'Aṭā, (Beirut: Muassasah al-Kutub al-Saqafiyyah, 1997).

Ibn al-'Arabī, Muḥammad ibn 'Abd Allah. *Aḥkām al-Qur'ān* (Beirut: Dār al-Kutub al-'Ilmīyah, 2008).

Ibn Athīr, Majd al-Dīn Muḥammad, *al-Nihāyah fī Gharīb al-Ḥadīth wal-Āthar* (Cairo: Matba'ah al-'Uthmāniyyah, 1311 AH).

Ibn Abī al-'Izz 'Alī. *Sharḥ al-'Aqīdah al-Ṭaḥāwīyyah*, (Beirut: Mu'assasat al-Risālah, nd.)

Ibn 'Abd al-Shakūr, Muḥib Allah al-Baḥarī al-Hindīy (d. 1119/1707) "*Musallam al-Thubūt ma'a Fawātiḥ al-Raḥamūt fī Uṣūl al-Fiqh*" (Cairo: 1906)

Ibn 'Abd al-Salām, 'Izz al-Dīn 'Abd al-'Azīz (d. 660/1262), "*Qawāid al-Aḥkām fī Maṣāliḥ al-An'ām,*" Cairo.

Ibn Amīr al-Ḥajj Muḥammad bin Muḥammad Shams ad-Dīn (d. 879), "*Al-Taqrīr wa al-Takhbīr 'alā Taḥrīr al-Kamāl ibn al-Humām fī 'ilm al-Uṣūl*" (Cairo: Matbaah al-Amīriyyah Bulāq, 1316)

Ibn Āshūr, Moḥammad al-Ṭāhir. (d. 1973), *Treatise on Maqāṣid al-Sharī'ah al-Islāmiyyah*, trans. Muḥammad el-Ṭāhir el-Mesawī (London, Washington: International Institute of Islamic Thought (IIIT), 2006)

- "*Maqāsid al-Sharī'ah al-Islāmīyyah*" (İslam Hukuk Felsefesi, Gaye Problemi), tr. Vecdi Akyüz and Mehmet Erdoğan (İstanbul: Rağbet, 1999).

Ibn Fares, Aḥmad. (d. 395/1004), "*Mu'ājam Maqāyīs al-Lughah*" (Beirut: Dār Iḥyā' al-Turāth al-'Arabi)

Ibn Ḥājib, 'Uthmān b. 'Amr b. Abū-Bakr b. Yūnus Abū 'Amr Jamāl al-Dīn. (d. 646/1249), "*Mukhtaṣar Muntahā' al-Sūl wa al-'Āmal* " (Constantinople: al-Maktabah al-Islāmiyyah, 1310)

Ibn Humām, Kamāl al-Dīn, Muḥammad bin 'Abd al-Waḥīd bin 'Abd al-Ḥamīd bin Mas'ūd al-Ḥanafī (d. 861/1457), "*Fatḥ al-Qadīr*" (Cairo: Maṭba'ah al-Amīrīyyah Bulāq, 1316).

- "*Al-Taysīr Sharḥ Al-Tahrīr fī 'Uṣūl al-Fiqh*" (Cairo: al-Amīyrīyyah Bulāq, 1317).
- "*Sharḥ Fatḥ al-Qadīr*" (Beirut: Dār al-Fiqr, nd).

Ibn Ḥazm, Abū Muḥammad 'Alī al-Andalūsī al-Ẓāhirī. (d. 456/1064), "*Al-Iḥkām fī Uṣūl al-Aḥkām*" (Beirut: Dār al-Kutup al-'Ilmīyyahm nd.)

- *Mulakhkhaṣ Ibṭāl al-Qiyās wa al-Ra'y wa al-Istiḥsān wa al-Taqlīd wa al-Ta'līl*, ed. Sa'īd al-Afghānī (Damascus: Matba'ah al-Jāmi'at al-Dimashq, 1960)

Ibn Kathīr, 'Imād al-Dīn. *Tafsīr al-Qur'ān al-'Azīm, al-'Azīm* (Kuwait: Revival of Islamic Heritage Society, 1994).

Ibn Khaldūn 'Abd al-Raḥmān bin Muḥammad (d. 808/1405), "*Muqaddimah,*" edt 'Ali ,Abd al-Wāḥīd Wāfī (Cairo: Naḥḍat al-Miṣr, n.d.)

Ibn al-Laḥḥām, 'Alī ibn Muḥammad. (d 803 AH) *al-Mukhtaṣar fī Uṣūl al-Fiqh* (Makkah: King 'Abd al-'Azīz University, 1980)

Ibn Mājah Abū 'Abd Allah Muḥammad (d. 273/886), "*Sunan*" (Istanbul: 1981).

Ibn Nujaym, Zayn al-'Abid al-Dīn b. Ibrāhīm al-Shāhir (d. 970/1562), "*Fatḥ al-Ghaffār al-Maghrūf bi-Mishqāt al-Anwār fī Uṣūl al-Fiqh*" (Cairo: Matba'ah Muṣṭafā Ḥalabī, 1936).

- "*Al-Ashbāh wa al-Naẓāir,*" (Beirut: Dār al-Kutub al-'Ilmiyyah, 1985).

Ibn al-Qayyīm Muḥammad b. Abū Bakr b. Ayūb b. Sa'd Shams al-Dīn Dimishqī (d. 751/1350), "*I'lām al-Muwaqqi'īn min Rabb al-'Ālamīn,*" edt. 'Abd al-Raḥmān al-Wakīl, Cairo.

- "*Ighāsat al-Lahfān min Masāyidi al-Shaiṭān,*" ed: Majdī Fathī al-Sayyīd, Cairo, 1310.
- "*Al-Ṭurūq al Ḥukmiyyah fi al-Siyāsah al-Shar'iyyah*" (Cairo: 1317).

Ibn Qudāmah al-Magdisī, Muwaffaq al-Dīn 'Abdallah b. Aḥmad. (d. 620 AH) *Rawḍah an-Nāẓir wa Jannat al-Manāẓir fī Uṣūl, al-Figh 'ala Madhhab al-Imām Aḥmad b. Ḥanbal,* (Beirut: Dār al-Nadwah al-Jadīdah, n. d.)

- *al-Muqhnī*, (Cairo: Dār al-Manār, 1368 AH),

Ibn Rushd, Abū Walīd Muḥammad b. Aḥmad b. Muḥammad, al-Qurtubī al-Mālikī (d. 520/1126), "*Bidāyat al-Mujtahid wa Nihayat al-Muqtaṣid*" (Beirut: Dār al-Ma'rifah, nd.)

Ibn Sa'd, Muḥammad. (d. 230/844), "*Al-Ṭabaqāt al-Kubrā*" (Beirut: 1957)

Ibn al-Subkī, *Jam‘ al-Jawāmi‘* along with Maḥallī's commentary, (Cairo: 1297 AH)

Ibn Taymiyyah, Taqīy al-Dīn Abū al-‘Abbās Aḥmad b. ‘Abd al-Ḥalīm. (d. 728/1328), "*Al-Musawwadah fī Uṣūl al-Fiqh*" (Cairo: Al-Maṭba‘ah al-Madani, 1964)

- *Majmū‘ al-Fatāwā*, collected and arranged by ‘Abd al-Raḥmān b. Muḥammad b. Qāsim al-‘Aṣimī al-Najdī al-Ḥanbalī, Riad, 1962

- "*Al-Fatāwā al-Kubrā*" (*Dār al-Kutub al-‘Ilmiyyah*)

Ibrahim, Ahmad bin Mohamed. "*Source and Development of Muslim law*," (Singapore: Malayan Law Journal ltd., 1965)

Isfaḥānī, Rāghib. *Mufradāt fī Gharīb al-Qur'ān*, ed. Muḥammad Ḥusayin Kaylānī (Beirut: Dār al-Ma‘rifah, n.d.)

Isnawī, Jamāl al-Dīn ‘Abd al-Raḥīm al-Ḥusayn Shāfi‘ī. (d. 772/1370), "*Nihāyāt al-Sūl fī Sharḥ al-Minhāj al-Uṣūl*," (Beirut: 1982)

- *Nihāyat al-Sūl fī Sharḥ Minhāj al-Wuṣūl fī ‘Ilm al-Uṣūl*, 1st edition, Dār al-Kutub al-‘Ilmiyyah, Beirut, 1984)

Izmirlī, Ismā‘īl Hakkı. (d. 1946), "*‘Ilm al-Khilāf*" (Istanbul: 1330)

Jaṣṣāṣ, Abū Bakr Aḥmad b. ‘Alī al-Rāzī. (d. 370/981), "*Al-Fuṣūl fī al-Uṣūl*," edt. Ājil Jasīm al-Nashmī, (Kuwait: Wazārāh al-Awkāf wa al-Shu‘ūn al-Islāmiyyah, 1988)

Kamali, Muhammad Hashim. "*Principles of Islamic Jurisprudence*" (Cambridge: Islamic Text Society, 1997)

- "*Al-Maqāṣid al-Sharī‘ah* (The Objectives of Islamic Law)"

Karaman, Hayreddin, *Yeni gelişmeler karşısında İslam Hukuku* (İstanbul: İz Yayıncılık, 1998)

- "*Islam Hukukunda İctihād*" (İstanbul: MUIFV, 1996)

- "*İslam Hukuk Tarihi*" (İstanbul: İz Yayıncılık, 1999)

Karamastī, Yūsuf b. Ḥusayn (d. 906/1500), "*Al-Wajīz fī Uṣūl al-Fiqh,*" edited by al-Sayyid 'Abd al-Laṭīf Kassāb (Cairo: Dār al-Hady, 1984).

Kasānī, Abū Bakr 'Alā al-Dīn b. Mas'ūd (d. 587/1191), "*Badāi' al-Sanāi' fī Tartīb al-Sharā'*" (Beirut: Dār al-Kutub al-'Arabi, 1982).

Kassab, al-Sayyid 'Abd al-Laṭīf, "*Adwā' Ḥawl Qadiyyah al-Ijtihād fī al-Sharī'ah al-Islāmiyah*" (Cairo: Dār al-Tawfīq, 1404/1984).

Kawrānī, Ṭāhā b. Aḥmad. *Sharḥ Mukhtaṣar al-Manār fī Uṣūl al-Fiqh*, edt. Sha'bān Muḥammad Ismā'īl (Dār al-Salām, 1988)

Kayadibi, Saim. *Istiḥsān the Doctrine of Juristic Preference in Islamic Law* (Selangor: IBT, 2010).

- *Ijtihād by ray; the main source of inspiration behind istiḥsān* (juristic preference, *American Journal of Islamic Social Sciences*, Herndon, USA, 24:1 winter (2007), 73-95.
- An Approach to the Position of Islamic Law with the Consideration of the Reform through the Aiding Factors, *Journal of Islamic Law Studies (IHAD)*, 12, (2008), 155-182.
- Lectures in the theory of law and the principles of Islamic law (Muḥādarāt fī Naẓariyyah al-Ḥukm wa Maṣādir al-Tashrī'), (Kuala Lumpur: 2011)

Kerr, Malcolm H, *Islamic Reform: The Political and Legal Theories of Muhammad 'Abduh and Rashid Rida* (Cambridge and California University Press, 1966).

Khallāf, 'Abd al-Wahhāb (d. 1376/1956), "*'Ilm Uṣūl al-Fiqh,*" 12th edn. (Kuwait: Dār al-Qalām, 1398/1978)

Khallāf, 'Abd al-Wahhāb. *Maṣādir al-Tashrī' al-Islāmī fī mā-lā Naṣṣah fīh* (Kuwait: Dār al-Qalam li al-Nashr wa al-Tawzī', 1993)

Khallāf, *Khulāsat al-Tārīkh al-Tashrī' al-Islāmī* (Istanbul: al-Maktabat al-Islāmiyyah, 1984)

Khayyāt, 'Abd al-'Azīz. *Naẓariyāt al-'Urf* (Amman: Maktabat al-Aqṣā', 997)

Khuḍarī, Muḥammad (d. 1927), "*Tārīkh Tashrī' al-Islāmi,*" translated into Turkish: Haydar Hatipoğlu (İstanbul: Kahraman yayınları, 1974)

- "*Tārīkh Tashrī' al-Islāmi*" (Beirut: Dār al-Kutub al-'Ilmīyyah, 1985)
- "*Uṣūl al-Fıqh,*" 7th ed. (Cairo: Dār al-Fikr, 1401/1981).

Koca, Ferhat, "İslam Hukukunda Maslahat'ı Mursalah ve Necmeddin el-Ṭūfī'nin bu Konudaki Görüşlerinin Değerlendirilmesi," *ILAM Research Magazine*, v. 1, no. 1, p. 93-122, (January–June) İstanbul, 1996.

Köse, Saffet. "*İslam Hukukunda Kanuna Karşı Hile*" (Istanbul: Birleşik Yayıncılık, 1996).

Laknawī, 'Abd al-'Ali Muḥammad bin Nizām al-Dīn Anṣārī, Baḥr al-'Ulūm, Abū al-'Abbās, Ḥanafī (d. 1180/1767), "*Fawātiḥ al-Raḥamūt sharḥ Musallam al-Subūt fī Uṣūl al-Fiqh*" (Cairo: Matba'ah al-Amīriyyah Bulāq, 1906)

- *Fawātiḥ al-Raḥamūt* (Baghdād: Maktaat al-Muthammā, 1970)

Laldin, Mohamad Akram. "*Islamic Law an Introduction,*" (Kuala Lumpur: Research Centre of iium, 2006),

Layish, Aharon, The Contribution of the Modernists to the Secularization of Islamic Law, *Middle Eastern Studies*, v. 14, 1978, p. 263-277

Lubnānī, Sālim Rustem Baz. "*Sharḥ al-Majallah,*" 3rd ed. (Beirut: Dār Iḥyā'al-Turāth al-'Arabī, 1986).

Madkūr, Muḥammad Salām. *Al-Ijtihād fī al-Tashrī' al-Islāmī* (Cairo: Dār al-Naḥḍat al-'Arabiyyah, 1984)

- *Tārīkh al-Tashrī‘ al-Islāmī wa Maṣādiruh*, 2nd ed. (Cairo: 1955)

Maghribī, ‘Abd al-Raḥmān bin Jād Allah al-Bannānī. (d. 1198/1784), "*Ḥāshiah ‘alā Sharḥ Jalāl al-Dīn al-Maḥallī ‘alā Jam‘ al-Jawāmī‘ li Ibn Subkī*" (Cairo: 1937)

Maḥillāwī, Muḥammad ‘Abd al-Raḥmān ‘Aid, Al-Ḥanafī al-Qāḍī bil-Maḥkamah al-‘Ulyā’ al-Shar‘iyyah, "*Tashīl al-Wuṣūl ilā ‘Ilm al-Uṣūl*" (Cairo: Bāb Al-Ḥalabī Publishers, 1341 AH).

Mahmassānī, Subkī Rajab. *Falsafah al-Tashrī‘, fī al-Islam: The Philosophy of Jurisprudence in Islam*, trans. Farhat J. Ziadeh (Leiden: E. J. Brill, 1961).

Majallah Al-Aḥkām Al-‘Adliyyah (The Ottoman Courts Manual (Ḥanafī),

Majmā‘ al-Fiqh al-Islāmī, "*Karārāt wa al-Tawsīyyāt*" (Kuwait, 1988).

Marghinānī, Burhan al-Dīn ‘Alī b. Abī Bakr al-Ḥanafī (d. 593), "*Al-Hidayah Sharḥ Bidāyat al-Mubtadī*" (Istanbul: 1327).

Makkī, Muwaffaq b. Aḥmad (d. 568/1172), "*Manāqib Abī Ḥanīfah*" (Beirut: 1981).

Maqdisī, Abū Muḥammad Muwaffiq al-Dīn, ‘Abd Allah bin Aḥmad bin Muḥammad bin Qudāmah. (d. 620/1223): "*Rawḍah al-Nāẓir wa Jannat al-Manāẓir*" (Cairo: Matba‘ah al-Salafīyyah, 1342)

Masood M. Khālid, "*Islamic Legal Philosophy*" (Delhi: International Islamic Publishers, 1989).

- "*Islam Ḥukuk Teorisi,*" translated by Muḥarrem Kılıç (İstanbul: 1977).

Ma‘ṣumī, Ṣaghīr Ḥasan. Imām Taḥawī's Ikhtilāf al-Fuqahā’, *Islamic Studies*, vol. 8, 1969, p. 199

- Disagreement of the *Ṣaḥāba* and Early Jurists, *Hamdard*

Islamicus, v. 3, 1979, p. 15-42.

Maudūdī, Abū al-'Alā' (d. 1979) "*Islamic Law and Constitution,*" Islamic publications ltd Lahore, translated by Khurshid Aḥmad, 1960

- Maudūdī, Abū al-'Alā, "*Towards Understanding of Islam,*" trans by Khurshid Aḥmad (Lahore: Islamic publications ltd, 1960).

Māwardī, 'Alī b. Muḥammad b. Ḥabīb Abū al-Ḥasan al-Māwardī al-Baṣrī al-Shāfi'ī (d. 450/1058), "*Adab al-Qāḍī,*" edt. By Muḥyi Hilāl al-Sarhan (Baghdad: Matba'at al-Irshad, 1971).

Mayḥāwī, Mulla Jiyūn b. Abī Sa'īd. *Sharḥ Nur al-Anwār 'alā al-Manār,* printed on the margin of *Kashf al-Asrār Sharḥ al-Muṣannif 'alā al-Manār,* (Mecca: Dār al-Bāz, 1986)

Muqrī, 'Ālim Aḥmad b. Muḥammad b. 'Alī al-Fayyūmī. (d. 770), "*Misbāḥ al-Munīr fī Gharīb al-Sharkh al-Kabīr li al-Rāfī',*" edt. Abd al-'Aẓīm al-Shannāwī, (Cairo: Dār al-Ma'ārif, nd.)

Mūṣā, Muḥammad Yūsuf. *Al-Fiqh al-Islāmī* (Cairo: Dār al-Kitāb al-'Arabī, 1958)

Muslim, 'Abdul Ghafūr, Islamization of Laws in Pakistan: Problems and Prospects, *Islamic Studies*, vol. 26. no. 3, 1987, pp. 256-276.

Muthannā, Abū 'Ubaydah. *Majāz al-Qur'ān*, 1374.

Naḥḥās, Aḥmad b. Muḥammad. *Al-Nāsikh wal-Mansūkh fī Kitāb Allah 'Azza wa-Jall wa-Ikhtilāf al-'Ulāma' fī dhālik,* edited by Sulaiman al-Lahim, (Beirut: Mu'assasat al-Risālah, 1991).

Nasafī,'Abd Allah bin Aḥmad bin Maḥmùd Ḥafiz al-Din Ab Al-Baraqât Al-Ḥanafī (d. 710/1310) "*Madārik al-Tanzīl wa Haqāik al-Ta'wīl*" (Beirut: nd.)

- *Kashf al-Asrār fī Sharḥ al-Muṣannaf 'alā al-Manār fī al-Uṣūl*" 2 vols, (Cairo: al-Maṭba'ah al-Kubrā al-Amīrīyyah, 1316).

Nyazee, Imran Ahsan Khan "*Islamic Jurisprudence*," (Kuala Lumpur: The Other Press, 2003)

- *Theories of Islamic Law* (Delhi: 1996),
- *Theories of Islamic Law: The Methodology of Ijtihād* (Pakistan: The International Institute of Islamic Thought, 1994)

Okur, Kaşif Hamdi. "*Maqāṣid ve İctihād*," in *Islamic Legal Philosophy Researches* (Konya: Yediveren, 2002), p. 275.

Pasha, Sawa. *Islam Hukuku Nazariyatı*, tr. Baha Arıkan (Ankara: 1965)

Qabash, Aḥmad. *al-Kāmil fī al-Naḥw wa al-Ṣarf*, 6th ed. (Dār al-Rashīd, 1986).

Qal'ajī, Muḥammad Rawwās. *Mu'jam Lughat al-Fuqahā'* (Beirut: Dār l-Nafā'is, 1985).

Qaradāwī, Yūsuf. "*İslam Hukuku Evrensellik Sυreklilik*," tr. By Yusuf Işıcık and Ahmet Yaman (Istanbul: Marifet

- "*Khaṣā'is al-Āmmah li al-Islam*"(Beirut: 1985).
- "*Al-Ijtihād fī Sharī'ah al-Islāmiah*" (Kuwait: 1989)

Qarafī, Shihāb al-Dīn Aḥmad bin Idrīs bin 'Abd al-Raḥmān, Abū 'Abbās al-Sanhājī al-Mālikī. (d. 684/1285), "*Sharḥ Tanqīḥ al-Fuṣūl fī Ikhtisār al-Mahṣūl fī al-Uṣūl*," edt. Tāhā 'Abd al-Raūf Sa'd, (Cairo: Maktabah al-Azharīyyah, nd.)

- "*Sharḥ Tanqīh al-Fuṣūl*" (Cairo: al-Maṭba'ah al-Khayriyyah, 1306 AH)
- "*Kitāb Anwār al-Burūq fī Anwār al-Furūq*" (Beirut: Dār al-Mā'rifah, nd.)
- "*al-Dhakhirah*" (Beirut: Dar al-'Arab, 1994),

Quadri, Syed Moinuddīn, Traditions of Taqlīd and Talfīq, *Islamic*

Culture, vol. 57 (January and April) 1983, pp. 39-61 and 123-145.

Qurtubī, Abū 'Abd Allah Muḥammad b. Aḥmad (d. 760/1359), "*Al-Jāmī' li Aḥkām al-Qur'ān*" (Beirut: Dār al-Iḥyā' al-Turās al-'Arabi, 1967).

- "*Al-Jāmī' li Aḥkām al-Qur'ān*" (Cairo: Dār al-Kutub al-Maṣriyyah, 1939)

Rahim, Abdur. *The Principles of Muhammadan Jurisprudence* (Lahore: All Pakistan legal decisions, 1958)

Rahman, Fazlur. *Islam and Modernity* (Chicago: University of Chicago Press, 1984)

- "*Islam*" (London: 1966)

Ramic, Sukrija Husejn. "*Language and the Interpretation of Islamic Law*," (Cambridge: The Islamic Text Society, 2003).

Rauf, Feisal Abdul. *Islam a Sacred Law*, (Vermont: Qiblah Books, 1998)

Raysūnī, Aḥmad. "*Nazariyyāt al-Maqāṣid 'inda al-Imām al-Shāṭibī*" (Maryland USA: the IIIT, 1995).

- "*Imām al-Shāṭibī's Theory of the Higher Objectives and Intents of Islamic Law*" (Selangor: Islamic Book Trust, 2006).

Rāzī, Fakhr al-Dīn Muḥammad b. 'Umar b. al-Ḥusayn Abū 'Abd Allah. (d. 606/1210), "Mafātīḥ al-Ghayb: Al-Mushtahar bi-al-Tafsīr al-Kabīr" (Cairo: al-Matba'ah al-Āmirah al-Sharafīyah, 1324-1327)

- "*Al-Maḥṣūl fī 'Ilm al-Uṣūl al-Fiqh*" (Beirut: 1988).

Rāzī, Muḥammad b. Abī Bakr (d. 660), "*Mukhtār al-Ṣiḥaḥ*" (Beirut: Dār al-Ma'rifah, nd.)

- "*Mukhtār al-Siḥāḥ*," edt. Maḥmūd Khaṭīr (Beirut: Dār al-Fikr, nd.)

Ṣadr al-Sharī'ah, 'Ubayd Allah Ibn Mas'ūd bin Tāj al-Sharī'ah al-Ḥanafī. (d. 747/1346), "*Al-Tawdīḥ fī Ḥall Jawāmid al-Tanqīḥ*" (Karachi: 1979)

- "*Al-Tawdīḥ fī Ḥall Jawāmid al-Tanqīḥ*" (Cairo: Maṭba'ah Muḥammad 'Alī Ṣabīh, nd.)

Sālim, 'Atiyyah Muḥammad. (et al.) *Tashīl al Wuṣūl ilā Fahm 'Ilm al-Uṣūl* (Cairo: Dār al-Imām Aḥmad, 2011).

Sallām, Abū 'Ubaid al-Qāṣim b. *Al-Nāsikh wal-Mansūkh fī al-Qur'ān al-'Azīz wamā fīhi min al-Farā'id wal-Sunan*, edited by Muḥammad al-Muḍaifar, (Riyadh: Maktabat al-Rushd, 1990)

Sarakhsī, Muḥammad bin Aḥmad bin Sahl Abū Bakr Shams al-Aimmah al-Ḥanafī (d. 483/1090), "*Uṣūl al-Sarakhsī*," edt. Abū al-Wafā' al-Afghānī, (Beirut: Dār al-Fikr, 1991).

- "*Uṣūl al-Sarakhsī*" (Cairo: Maṭābi' Dār al-Kitāb al-'Arabī, 1372 AH)

- "*Kitāb al-Mabsūṭ*" (Beirut: nd).

Saymarī, Ḥusain b. 'Ali. (d. 436/1045), "*Akhbār Abū Ḥanīfah wa Aṣḥābuh*" (Beirut: 1985)

Schacht, Joseph. *An Introduction to Islamic Law*, (Oxford: Clarendon Press, 1964)

Sha'bān, Muḥammad Isma'īl. "*Uṣūl al-Fiqh al-Muyassar*" (Cairo: Kitāb al-Jāmī' Tawfīqiyyah, 1994).

Sha'bān, Zakī al-Dīn. "*Islam Hukuk İlminin Esasları*," tr. İbrahim Kafi Dönmez (Ankara: Türkiye Diyanet Vakfı, 1990)

- "*Manhaj al-Qur'ān fī Bayān al-Aḥkām*," in ed., Muḥammad Tawfiq 'Uwayḍah, *Al-Fiqh al-Islamī Asās al-Tashrī'* (Cairo: Maṭābi' al-Ahrām, 1971)

- "*Uṣūl al-Fiqh al-Islāmī*" (Cairo: University Book House, 1964-

65).

Shafi'ī, Imām Abī 'Abd Allah Muḥammad bin Idrīs. (d. 204/819), "*Al-Risālah,*" edt. Muḥammad Sayyīd Kīlāni, 2nd ed., (Cairo: Muṣṭafā al-Bābi al-Ḥalabī, 1983).

- "*Jimā' al-'Ilm,*" edt. Muḥammad Aḥmad 'Abd al-'Azīz (Beirut: Dār al-Kutub al-'Ilmiyyah, n.d.)
- Shāfi'ī, "*Al-Ūmm*" (Beirut: 1983).

Shahristānī, Abū al-Fatḥ Muḥammad b. 'Abd al-Karīm b. Abū Bakr (d. 548/1153), "*Al-Milal wa al-Niḥal,*" edt. Muḥammad Sayyid Kaylānī, (Cairo: 1976)

Shalabī, Muḥammad Muṣṭafā. "*Uṣūl al-Fiqh al-Islāmī*" (Beirut: 1986).

- "*Ta'līl al-Aḥkām 'Arḍ wa Taḥlīl li-Ṭarīqat al-Ta'līl wa Taṭawwurātihā fī 'Uṣūr al-Ijtihād wa al-Taqlīd*" (Cairo: 1947).
- "*Al-Madkhal fī al-Ta'rīf al-Fiqh al-Islāmī*" (Beirut: Dār an-Naḥḍat al-'Arabiyyah, 1985)

Shaltūt, Maḥmūt. "*Al-Islam 'Aqīdah wa Sharī'ah*" (Kuwait: Maktabi Dār al-Qalam, 1966)

Shāṭibī, Abū Isḥāq Ibrāhīm bin Mūsa al-Ghirnāṭī. (d. 790/1388), "*Al Muwāfaqāt fi-Uṣūl al-Sharī'ah,*" edt. 'Abd-Allah Diraz (Beirut: Dār al-Ma'rifah)

- "*Al-Muwāfaqāt fi-Uṣūl al-Sharī'ah,*" translated into Turkish "*İslami İlimler Metodolojisi*" by Mehmet Erdoğan (İstanbul: İz yayıncılık, 1999).
- "*Al-I'tiṣām*" (Beirut: nd.)

Shāshī, Isḥāq bin Ibrāhīm Abū Ya'qūp al-Khorasānī. (d. 325/937), "*Uṣūl al-Shāshī with 'Umdah al-Ḥawāshī*" (Delhi: 1303),

Shawkānī, Abū 'Ali Badr al-Dīn Muḥammad bin 'Ali. (d. 1250/1834), "*Irshād al-Fuḥul ilā Taḥqīq al-Ḥaq min 'Ilm al-Uṣūl*" (Cairo: 1937),

Shīrāzī, Abū Ishāq Ibrahīm b. Ali b. Yūsuf al-Fayrūzabādī (d. 476/1083), "*Sharḥ al-Luma*," edt. 'Abd al-Majīd Turkī (Beirut: nd).

- "*Al-Tabaṣṣurah fī Uṣūl al-Fiqh*," edt. Muḥammad Ḥusain Hītū (Dār al-Fiqr, nd).

Sibā'ī, Muṣṭafa Ḥusnī. *Al-Sunnah wa Makānatuhā fil-Tashrī' al-Islāmī*, 3rd ed. (Beirut, np, 1982)

Ṣiddīq, 'Abd al-Ḥay Ibn. "*Naqdu Maqāl fī Masāilah min 'Ilm al-Ḥadīth wa al-Fiqh wa Uṣūlih wa Tafḍīlih Baghḍ al-Mazāhib*" (Maghrib: 1988)

Subkī, 'Abd al-Wahhāb bin 'Alī bin 'Abd al-Kāfī Tājj al-Dīn al-Subkī (d. 771/1370), "*Jam' al-Sharḥ al-Jalāl al-Maḥallī 'Alā' Jam' al-Jawāmī*'" (Cairo: Maktabah al-Tijārīyyah, nd.)

Suyūtī, Jalāl al-Dīn 'Abd al-Raḥmān bin abī Bakr bin Muḥammad bin Sābiq al-Din al-Khudayrī. (d. 911/1505), "*Muftāh al-Jannah fī al-Ihtijāj bi al-Sunnah*" (Beirut: 1987)

- "*Al-Itqān fī 'Ulūm al-Qur'ān*," edt. Markaz al-Dirāsat al-Islāmiyyah, (Madinah: Mujamma' al-Malik Fahad li-Ṭibā'at al-Muṣḥaf al-Sharīf, 2005)

Syed Ismail, Sharifah Hayaati. (et. al) "Effective Governance in the Era of Caliphate 'Umar Ibn Al-Khaṭṭāb," *European Journal of Social Sciences*, v. 18, no. 4 (2011).

Tabarānī, Sulaymān b. Aḥmad (d. 360/971), "*Al-Mu'jam al-Saghīr wa al-Mū'jam al-Awsāt*" (Beirut: M. Shakūr Maḥmūd al-Ḥajj Amīr, 1985)

Tabarī, Abū Ja'far Muḥammad b. Jarīr. (d. 310/922), "*Jāmi' al-Bayān Ta'wīl al-Qur'ān*" (Bulāq: 1329),

Tabrizi, Muḥammad b. 'Abd Allah al-Khatib, "*Mishkāt al-Masābih*," edt. Muḥammad al-Dīn al-Albānī. 2nd ed (Beirut: al-Maktaba al-Islāmī, 1399/1979).

Taḥwānī, Muḥammad ʻAli bin ʻAli. *Kashf ʻIṣṭilāḥāt al-Funūn* (Beirut: Dār Ṣadr, 1961)

Taftazānī, Masʻūd bin ʻUmar bin ʻAbd Allah Saʻd al-Dīn (d. 793/1390), " *Al-Talwīḥ ʻalā Al-Tawḍīḥ*" on the margin of ʻUbayd Allah bin Masʻūd Ṣadr al-Sharīʻah" (Cairo: ʻĪsā al-Bābi al-Ḥalabī 1327/1957)

- *Sharḥ al-Talwīḥ ʻala'l Tawḍīḥ* (Cairo: Dār al-ʻAhd al-Jadīd, lil-Ṭibāʻah, 1957)

Ṭaḥāwī, Abū Jaʻfar Aḥmad b. Muḥammad (d. 321/933) *Mushkil al-Āthār*, (Hyderabad, Deccan: Dā'irat al-Maʻārif al-Nuʻmāniyyah, 1333 AH.)

- "*Sharḥ Maʻānīʻ al-Āthār*," published by Muḥammad Zuhrī al-Najjār and M. Sayyid Jād al-Ḥaq, (Beirut: 1399).

Tilmisānī, Muḥammad bin Aḥmad bin ʻAlī al-Idrīsi, al-Sharīf al-Mālikī. (d. 771/1370), "*Muftāḥ al-Wuṣūl Ilā Binā' al-Furūʻ ʻalā al-Uṣūl*," Jāmiʻah al-Azhar, Kullīyah al-Sharīʻah reg.no: 72 Cairo.

Ṭūfi Najm al-Dīn Sulaymān bin Abū al-Qawey bin ʻAbd al-Karīm Abū al-ʻAbbās Ḥanbalī (d. 716/1316), "*Sharḥ'u Mukhtasar al-Rawḍah*," edt. ʻAbd Allah b. ʻAbd al-Muḥsin al-Turkī, (Muassasah al-Risālah, 1409).

- "*Risālah fi al-Maṣlaḥah al-Mursalah*" (Beirut: 1324/1906).

ʻUthaymīn, Muḥammad b. Ṣaliḥ. *al-Uṣūl min ʻIlm al-Uṣūl* (5 Pillars Publishing, 2013).

Uzunpostalcı, Mustafa. "*Ebu Hanife, Hayatı ve İslam Fıkhındaki Yeri*," Institute of Social Science at University of Selçuk, 1986.

- "*Ebu Hanife*," DIA (Diyanet İslam Ansiklopedisi), X, 136.

Yaman Aḥmet, "*Maqāṣid ve İjtihād, İslām Hukuk Felsefesi Araştırmaları*" (Konya: Hüner, 2002).

Watt, Montgomery. "*The closing of the door of ijtihād*" in Oriehtakia hispanica, sive studia F M Pareja octogenaria dictata edenda curavit J M Barral, Leiden 1974, I, 675-8.

Zamakhsharī, Jār Allah Maḥmūd bin 'Umar (d. 538/1144), "*Al-Kashshāf al-Ḥaqā'iq Ghawāmiḍ al-Tanẓī wa 'Uyūn al-Aqāwīl fī Wujūh al-Ta'wīl*" (Beirut: Dār al-Kitāb al-'Arabi, 1366),

Zanjānī, Maḥmūd bin Aḥmad bin Maḥmūd Abū al-Manāqib Sha'b al-Dīn, min al-Shāfi'ī. (d. 656/1258), "*Takhrīj al-Furū' 'Alā al-Uṣūl,*" edt. Muḥammad Adīb Ṣālīḥ (Dimishq: Muassasah al-Risālah, 1962)

Zarqā', Muṣṭafā Aḥmad. *Al-Madkhal al-Fiqhī al-'Āmm*, 9th ed. (Damascus: Dār al-Fikr, 1968)

- *al-Fiqh al-Islāmī fī Thawbihi al-Jadīd* (Damascus: Maṭba'ah Jāmi'ah Damishq, 1963)
- "*Çağdaş Yaklaşımla İslām Hukuku,*" tr: by Servet Armağan, Timaş, İstanbul, 1993.

Zaydān, 'Abdul Karīm. *Al-Madkhal li Dirāsat al-Sharī'ah al-Islāmiyyah* (Baghdād: Mu'assasah al-Risālah and Maktabah al-Quds, 1976)

- "*al-Wajīz fī Uṣūl al-Fiqh,*" (Beirut: Muassasah ar-Risālah, 2009)

Zuhaylī, Wahbah. "*Uṣul al-Fiqh al-Islāmi*" (Beirut: Dār al-Fikr al-Mu'āsir, 1406/1986)

Zuhayr, Muḥammad Abū al-Nūr, "*Mudhakkarāt fī al-Uṣūl al-Fiqh*" (Cairo: Dār al-Ta'līf, Kullīyyāt al-Sharī'ah, al-Azhar, nd.)

Index

www.ingramcontent.com/pod-product-compliance
Lightning Source LLC
LaVergne TN
LVHW100132061126
851857LV00010B/58
* 9 7 8 9 6 7 0 5 2 6 3 3 1 *